European Union and its Neighbours in a Globalized World

Volume 26

The series publishes monographs and edited volumes in the field of European and international law and policy. A special focus is put on the European neighbourhood policy, current problems in European and international law and policy as well as the role of the European Union as a global actor. The series supports the publishing and distribution of research results of cross-border research consortia. Besides renowned scientists the series is also open for publication projects of young academics. The series emphasizes the interplay of the European Union and its neighbouring countries as well as the important role of the European Union as a key player in the international context of law, economics and politics.

Kristina Koldinská • Grega Strban
Attila Kun • Marcin Wujczyk
Editors

Labour Law and Social Security Law in Central and Eastern Europe

20 Years of EU Membership

Springer

Editors
Kristina Koldinská
Faculty of Law
Department of Labour Law and Social
Security Law
Charles University
Prague, Czech Republic

Grega Strban
Faculty of Law
University of Ljubljana
Ljubljana, Slovenia

University of Johannesburg
Johannesburg, South Africa

Attila Kun
Faculty of Law, Department of Labour Law
and Social Security
Károli Gáspár University of the Reformed
Church in Hungary
Budapest, Hungary

Faculty of Public Governance and
International Studies, Department of Human
Resources
Ludovika University of Public Service
Budapest, Hungary

Marcin Wujczyk
Department of Labour Law and
Social Policy
Jagiellonian University
Kraków, Poland

ISSN 2524-8928 ISSN 2524-8936 (electronic)
European Union and its Neighbours in a Globalized World
ISBN 978-3-032-04495-2 ISBN 978-3-032-04496-9 (eBook)
https://doi.org/10.1007/978-3-032-04496-9

This Springer imprint is published by the registered company Springer Nature Switzerland AG
The registered company address is: Gewerbestrasse 11, 6330 Cham, Switzerland

Preface

Membership in the European Union has profoundly influenced the development of labour and social security laws in the countries that joined the EU in 2004. Key areas such as anti-discrimination law, working time regulations, rules on posting workers, and work–life balance have undergone significant transformations. EU accession has also reshaped the functioning of social security regulations. Fundamental aspects of employee–employer relations, including collective bargaining and occupational health and safety, have seen notable changes as well.

This book presents an in-depth comparative analysis of the legal and social policy challenges emerging from EU accession in Central and Eastern European countries. It aims to enhance comparative understanding of the impact on labour and social security laws resulting from participation in the EU. The book not only clarifies the main characteristics and current dynamics of social law regulations in an ever-evolving Europe but also provides invaluable insights into potential methods for addressing these challenges through improved labour regulations.

The labour and social security laws of the countries that joined the European Union in 2004 have undergone significant transformation. As part of the European integration process, these member states were required to align their national legislation with EU directives and regulations. In the realm of labour and social security, the EU establishes standards for minimum working conditions, fair wages, worker health and safety protections, and equal treatment in the workplace.

EU integration has substantially standardized and improved labour and social welfare laws in Central and Eastern European countries, enhancing worker protections, improving working conditions, and promoting equality and social justice. However, several challenges persist. Not all EU standards have been fully implemented into national laws, and those that have been adopted often lack effective enforcement mechanisms. Emerging trends, such as the operational challenges faced by trade unions, also warrant attention.

This book offers a comprehensive comparative analysis of the legal and social policy challenges posed by EU accession in various Central and Eastern European countries with diverse social models and the emerging gig economy workforce. It aims to deepen the comparative understanding of risks to the European social model, addressing both the theoretical foundations and practical implementation of EU labour and welfare law at the national level.

Prague, Czech Republic
Ljubljana, Slovenia
Budapest, Hungary
Kraków, Poland

Kristina Koldinská
Grega Strban
Attila Kun
Marcin Wujczyk

Contents

Impact of EU Regulations on Labour and Social Law of Central and Eastern European Countries

EU-Enlargement 2004: The Founding and the Accession Member States' View on EU Social Law

Eberhard Eichenhofer and Kristina Koldinská

1 Introduction

EC-enlargement materialized as the late outcome of an originally mere political vision, even more—a utopian idea. Since the very beginning European law upheld the aspiration that its rules will become relevant one day and in the very far future for the entire continent.[1] Hence, the institutions of European integration offered all states in Europe the right to accede.

For decades this vision seemed vague, idealistic, and far away from the then existing world. When in fall 1989 the split of Europe ended the unforeseen and abrupt accession to the EC turned out as new prospect for the CEE states. After a while it matured to a more and more realistic aim. The pathways to EC-membership unveiled, however, as hard and cumbersome, as it imposed the future Member States to undertake a series of political, economic, and cultural changes and to implement and effectuate beforehand. These reforms were accompanied by profound social reorganizations with unpredictable and harmful consequences. The states must

[1] In the preamble of the Rome Treaty (1957) the founding Member States declared to be determined "to preserve and deepen peace and freedom by bundling their economic forces combined with the request to other peoples in Europe, to confess themselves to the same high goal and to join these aspirations."

E. Eichenhofer
Berlin, Germany
e-mail: eichenhoferberlin@t-online.de

K. Koldinská (✉)
Faculty of Law, Department of Labour Law and Social Security Law, Charles University, Prague, Czech Republic
e-mail: koldinsk@prf.cuni.cz

K. Koldinská et al. (eds.), *Labour Law and Social Security Law in Central and Eastern Europe*, European Union and its Neighbours in a Globalized World 26,
https://doi.org/10.1007/978-3-032-04496-9_1

undergo already in advance of accession a profound process of transformation, which created new social disruptions and economic imbalances.

The old EC-Member States regarded accession of the CEE states as an incident without any impact on their own economy and society; they envisaged it not emphatically, but strategically as a mere expansion of EC law, the old Member States were familiar to, as it existed for them even beforehand. If due to accession this law should become relevant for new Member States, it would simply widen its territorial space! So, within the accession process the roles of both old and new Member States were distributed clearly, drastically, and explicitly: The new ones were expected by the old ones, if joining the club to comply vigorously with the pre-existing rules and to observe them meticulously.

The old Member States perceived accession as a lesson, which they must teach to the new Member States. But the real accession process did not comply with this image: It was not that one-sided, but driven by unprecedented experiences, which demanded common efforts from all involved Member States. This did not comply with the original expectations.

2 EU: Enlargement—An Old Idea Becomes True

2.1 United Europe: A Vision Against A Dreadful Reality

The idea of EU-enlargement has deep traces. It was rooted in the long history of Europe and ripened to plans to unite Europe politically, after the European idea in World War II was defeated. Europe had been constructed as a series of international organizations as legal entities on their own with the common aim of an ever-closer union between the forming states.[2]

This ambition stood in sharp contrast with the real order after World War II. It divided and separated the continent in two “eastern” and “western” halves, which should and did follow opposite roads in economics, society, politics, and culture. The split of the continent led, therefore, into a deep antagonism, frozen during the long decades of the” Cold War.”

The separation in and of Europe was epitomized by the “Iron Curtain” and seemed to remain endless. The monstrous assembly of barbed wire, watch towers, and walls was supervised by hundreds of thousands of armed forces. It demanded an enormous investment in both money as manpower and it had just one goal and outcome: It separated physically and mentally men and women in Europe from one another.

[2] Judt (2006), Briggs (1961), p. 221; Eichenhofer (2007).

In the 1960ies the former French President Charles De Gaulle imagined a "Europe from the Atlantic to the Ural."[3] This goal should replace the then existing split world in Europe, under which it suffered in those years severely. De Gaulle's vision addressed the divided continent as a deplorable reality, which should be supposed and imagined to be overcome one day. During and under the impression of the Cold War this utopian prospect underlined and emphasized that Europe is more than Western Europe.

In the 1950ies the European Community of Coal and Steel (ECCS) and the European Community (EEC) this law as supranational legal communities under European law, with own legislative, administrative and judicial bodies and competences. Already in the formative statues of the united Europe the promise was given and enshrined, to be open for accession for each European country, which follows their rules.

2.2 *Detention in Europe*

In the 1970ies the East and West states resumed new contacts, as the old ties had been scattered in the Cold War. At the Helsinki Conference on Security and Cooperation in Europe of 1975 the governments' leaders of East and West accepted that the factual post-World War II territorial status is acknowledged as a reality in Europe and agreed that this status should never be altered or reversed violently by military forces.[4]

In addition, they proclaimed their intention to a peaceful cooperation among one another in the very near future. The conference created the Organization for Security and Co-operation in Europe (OSCE) as the first European organization of East and West states. This conference did not formally proclaim that Europe should become a joint continent; but the conclusions made, and the compromises found opened the door for reducing tensions in Europe. It emerged as a joint vision to overcome the division of Europe by taking the reality of a divided continent as a given fact and at the same time as basis for further co-operation.

Was this assumption not driven by too many dialectic thoughts? In the detention process, which started in the mid 1970ies and was rolled out step by step, the internationally acknowledged human rights played a leading, even more: a decisive role. In the conclusions of the Helsinki conference, they were accepted as the common basis of the incumbent development for cooperation in Europe and assumed a central role as a model for the joint future in Europe.

On this basis detention by co-operation could and did gain ground. The East-West contacts, which in the Cold War era had been drastically reduced, were

[3] Ernst Weidenfeld, Europa vom Atlantik zum Ural, in ders., De Gaulle, Deutschland und Europa, Opladen 1991, p. 71.

[4] Helsinki Final Accords (1975).

re-established by new ones. They ripened later and led to increases of economic exchanges and joint initiatives in science and culture and got, finally, momentum also in their political relations.

The more the Iron Curtain became open doors and the more mutual links in Europe were established- above all among the ordinary citizens, the more corrosive it got and the more anachronistic the harsh existing border regime became. The longer the co-operation pursued and the deeper the personal links between people from the West and the East became, the less the postwar border regime could be justified. So, the question arose whether the Iron Curtain could be upheld in the future at all!

2.3 End of the Iron Curtain

In springtime 1989, at the Hungarian Austrian border by the ministers of foreign affairs of both states lifted the Iron Curtain by a symbolic act of cutting the existing barbed wire, which had got in the decades of its existence a rusty surface and needed more and more cost-intensive repairs. Within a few weeks and without any massive previous indications, the entire Eastern bloc collapsed.

Whereas in the decades of European divide the imminent collapse of communism was widely and commonly predicted in the rhetoric of Western governments, the sudden implosion of the socialist states in fall 1989 succeeded in an unforeseen manner. The Western leaders were as puzzled as the Eastern leaders! The citizens were likewise surprised by the emergence of unexpected new opportunities! Nobody at either side disposed of a masterplan, but each one was likewise surprised in the light of the swift and noiseless end of communism—which happened without violence.

The collapse of the Eastern bloc coincided with the implosion of the Soviet Union. The enormous multinational state and its postwar empire formed by the neighbor states lost its political sphere of influence, which it had acquired in the sequence and as the practical outcome of World War II. In 1990 also Yugoslavia had been dissolved and was replaced by new states, which afterwards came into existence.

3 EU: Accession—A Process of Profound Transformation

3.1 Post 1989 Prospects for the CEE States

For the CEE states arose the question about their political, cultural, economic and social destiny in the nearer and the farer future. The Baltic States expressed by by their declarations of independence the determination to reconquer their lost national status of self-government. This decision raised immediate questions as to their relations to the Western and central European neighbors. For all other CEE states the question arose what should replace the post-wartime military alliances and economic structures of their societies?

1993 both NATO and EC offered the CEE states the option for membership. This meant: They were invited to join the club and accept its rules! 1993 the EC outlined the road to EC- accession in the Copenhagen Criteria.[5] The acceding states were exposed to take over the political, economic and social achievements of the EC, adapt them in their institutions and incorporate them into their laws. The details were figured out in bilateral agreements which the acceding countries concluded with the EC.[6]

3.2 Accession Means Transformation

These arrangements envisaged deep transformations of the former socialist states. They were required to alter profoundly their political, economic, cultural and social structures, which were erected in line with the ones once established in the Soviet Union. The transformation countries succeeded by the end of a decade. The adoption of EU standards by the CEE states can be compared to the unification of Germany, which likewise imposed to the East German society to implement institutions formed under West German law.

Immediately after the end of Soviet or Yugoslav rule the CEE states transformed their political, economic and social order. This transformation was accompanied by a lot of profound economic, cultural and social changes. Traditional industries and enterprises have disappeared; workplaces of many people got lost. New industries came into existence with new international supply changes and products.

Many workers left the transforming CEE states; they moved to the old Member States; there they carried out low qualified jobs, for what they received a low salary. For many citizens of the former socialist societies economic tough years began, which exposed them to profound changes of their entire lives.

3.3 Accession a New Beginning and the End of Waiting

Taking this in mind, the EC-enlargement in May 2004 was not only the start of a new phase of European history, but for the people of the countries involved also the end of a very long and demanding period of social and cultural reorientation. A new

[5] European Council in Copenhagen, June 22 and 23, 1993, DOC 93/3.

[6] On this legal basis also the mobility of workers in advance and after the accession was ruled on a bilateral basis.

political, legal and social system matured with new conflicts, disappointments and backlashes. The new Member States witnessed with the date of accession not only the starting point for their full EC- membership, it ended at the same time a transitory period, in which EC law to be incorporated into the legislation paved the way of development for the new Member States.

4 Accession: A Piecemeal Procedure

4.1 Accession a Multi-Step Process

It became obvious to the new Member States with the day of accession that further steps should be taken until the membership matures to a fully-fledged status. On May 1st, 2004, the new Member States were directly bound by the entire EC-legislation; at the same time, they took an active part in the making of new EC law within the legislative bodies of the EC they adhered to since this date.

For labour and social security this meant that all regulations and directives of the EC were to be applied and respected. The imposition of an elaborated part of EC labour and social security law implied a whole bundle of legislative and administrative changes. The achievements under the EC legislation materialized in a series of new legislative rules, the creation of new legal standards, the erection of new legal institutions, and the implementation of new administrations. So, the accession states had to take over many institutions and implement in their own law and administration, which had been created beforehand in the old Member States. As to the wide scope of laws on health and safety at the workplace,[7] working time, protection in cases of economic crises[8] and equal treatment at the workplace under various aspects,[9] the impact on the law of the new Member States was remarkable. Many organizational and technical changes accompanied the implementation. The status of women in labour underwent profound changes (References to further articles in the book) and the organization of health and safety at the workplace was exposed to substantial new orientations as to the technical standards but also the leading goals and targets of decent workplace policy.

The specific EC-provisions on atypical, albeit precarious work– part-time, seasonal, and fixed-term contract work[10]—became immediately relevant and applica-

[7] Reg. (EEC) Nr. 3820/85; Directive 89/656/EEC of 30.12.1989, O.J. L 393/18 (Framework on health and safety at the workplace).

[8] Directive 89/391//EEC O.J. of 29.6.1989 L 183/1.

[9] Directive 75/129 O.J. of 17.2.1975 L48 /29 (Mass layoffs); Directive 77/187 O.J. of 14.21977 L 61/26 (Transfer of Undertakings); Directive 80/987 O.J. of 20.10.1980 L283/23 (Protection of wages in employers 'insolvency).

[10] Directive 97/81/EC O.J. of 20.10.1998 L 14 /9 (part time work); Directive 1999/70/EC O.J. of 28.6.1999, L 175/43(fixed term contract); Directive 2008/104/EC O.J. L 327/2008 (Temporary Work).

ble. In social security the EC-law on coordination had a direct effect on social administrations.[11]

A multilateral system of administrative support and cooperation had to be established to guarantee social security rights based on a work history spent in various Member States, it brings about transnational rights, which implies a transnational social security cooperation and mindset.[12] The vision of the social model in Europe got a more and more outspoken profile and became a reality in both the old and new Member States.[13]

4.2 Freedom of Movement Postponed

Accession did not immediately to the full enjoyment of all fundamental freedoms established in EC law. As substantial parts of the fundamental freedoms are essential parts of EC law, the freedoms of goods, services, capital and persons[14] had been guaranteed by accession. But as to the freedom of persons a decisive restriction was established: The accession rules provided for freedom of movement for workers of the new Member States that this right should be suspended for up to 7 years. The suspension of the freedom of movement followed the roads taken in previous enlargement process, above all those with Greece, Spain, and Portugal.

In the light of the fundamental freedoms of EC law the transitory introduction of freedom of movement was problematic as the fundamental freedoms of EC law were suspended temporarily to the citizens of the new Member States. Such a restriction can be only justified by strong arguments in favour of the General Interest of the EC. What was the protective aim of these provisions?

The answer unveils a protectionist stand of the old member States' side. Workers and employers of the old Member States should not be confronted with the harsh consequences immediately, which could be induced by a sudden influx of workers from the new Member States. In the light of the strong wage differences between West and East—the sudden opening of the labour markets of the old Member States was conceived as detrimental to the competition and the wages. So, the workers of the New Member States had to pay a price in favour of the economy and the workers of the old Member States.

The transitional period for free movement to a lengthy period of up to 7 years could be prolonged. So, a core component of the Single Market i.e. the Single Labour Market had been phased in years after the accession happened. The decision to open the Labour Market was taken by each Member State.

---

[11] Fuchs and Cornelissen (2015).

[12] Eichenhofer (2025).

[13] Gold (2005).

[14] Barnard (2022).

Whereas the United Kingdom open its economy swiftly and so laid quite early after accession a fundament for the transborder activities of the famous and legendary "Polish Plumber", the neighbour countries to the accession states—Germany and Austria—took the utmost possible option to refrain workers from the new Member States if they want to become permanently active on the German and Austrian labour markets. The decisions were inspired by the fear of "social dumping."

4.3 Posted Work Gained Momentum

The limitation of the freedom of movement in the initial phase after accession did not substantially impede growing economic exchange between the new and old Member States. But the increase took place in different legal formations. As the freedom of services was safeguarded from the very beginning, the employers of the new Member States offered transborder services by utilizing their personnel hired under the labour law of the state of their establishment.[15]

So, the limitations in the freedom of movement were compensated by the export of services, which was made possible by the posting of workers. Posting gave the employers of the new Member States the chance to take advantage of the lower levels of wages, taxes and social security contributions of the new Member States compared to the old ones. Above all in the work-intensive, low-skilled services—e.g. construction work, housekeeping, care and transportation the companies established in the new Member States could get a broad access to work to be done in the old Member States.

Companies based in the old Member States saw themselves as exposed to unfair competition, due to the territorial widening of the Single market to the CEE states. So, the topic of posting workers became after the accession of the CEE states a new EC—law issue, dealt with in the context of the transborder delivery of services.

The outcome was a change in labour law. Due to the Posted Workers Directive EC law provisions on transborder conditions in the context of posted work provided for taking more and more the working conditions of the place, where the word should be physically done, as the relevant legislative dimension. So, EC law provided for more favourable rules of the law of the country, where the work is temporarily to be executed, should determine also the labour statute of posted workers. This regulatory tendency culminated in a provision, that also the wages of the posted workers should be determined by the collective agreements or minimum wage statutes of the country, where posted workers do carry out their work.

[15] Posted Workers' Directives 96/71/EC, O.J. of 21.1.1997 L18/1; revised by Directive 2018/957/EU, O.J. Of 28.6.2018 L 173/16.

The entire debate came to a summarizing end in the judgment before the ECJ[16] in the Case "EU-Parliament and EU-Council versus Hungary. "In this judgment the Court held, that European legislation which intends to establish labour and socially supportive standards for the Single Market is in line with the principles of the Internal Market, and that the Member States are not entitled under European law to improve their competitiveness by lowering of their national social and labour standards.

4.4 Social Policy Becomes an Issue in the EU Currency Union

A last example for the understanding of accession as a piecemeal procedure with differentiated phases to go through becomes visible under the European Currency Union perspective. The Currency Union was established by the Maastricht Treaty and encompassed the Euro as the common currency of the united Europe. In 1999 the joint currency issued by the European Central Bank became a reality. All EC member States are supposed to join the currency union, but some of them abstain by conviction, or because of lacking abilities.

After the 2008-2010 Greek, banks, debts and Euro crisis the Member States were submitted by virtue of their membership in the Euro currency-union to a strict control by the commission on whether they spend public expenditures in a fair and sustainable manner. With this expanded task of the EU also the social expenditures of the Member States were exposed to European control.

4.5 Migration Became a European Topic

The united Europe witnessed the consequences of international refugee movements and migration from outside the EU. The Member States became aware, that the international community is not only a space for unrestricted economic cooperation and exchange, but it imposes to all participating states also commitments to respect, protect and fulfil human rights established in a variety of international declarations, conventions and treaties. After the collapse of the Iron Curtain many refugees tried to enter the EC. The breakdown of Yugoslavia in 1994 unleashed the migration of tens of thousands of Bosnian citizens to Central Europe. The Member States agreed on their protection within the EC for the time of civil war. In the Maastricht Treaty the EU committed to foster human rights and humanitarian law.[17] In Article 2 of the TEU this commitment to human rights is explicitly stated. In this context the EC

---

[16] ECJ of December 8th, 2020 C-620/18, ECLI:EU:C:2020:1001.

[17] Wouters and Ovádek (2021).

started to develop a migration policy, which outlined common standards of humanitarian protection for refugees.[18]

The Geneva 1951 Convention on the rights of refugees[19] is neither self-executing, nor dispose international organisations of an independent executive. Therefore, they cannot act without the support of their members states, which do form them.

Guarantees of international human rights depend on the support of each state to bring about their efficacy. Insofar, states take part in the global task to assist refugees and asylum seekers. The Geneva Refugee Convention 1951 "remains quite 'state-centric', in the sense that it represents undertakings and obligations, agreed between the parties, to respect, protect, or accord certain rights and benefits".[20]

In the first decades, migration was conceived as a matter external to European law. After primary legislation underwent a deep revision by the Maastricht and the Amsterdam Treaty provides that the EU is endowed with a wide range of legal competencies to regulate the status of third- country-nationals.

This new field of activities touched the instruments on how to safeguard freedom of movement; in 1990 it was expanded, stabilized and made effective by the Schengen system.[21] This system transformed the EU into an Area of Freedom, Security and Justice. Most Member States agreed on abandoning the previous border controls; they were replaced by the European Border Regime. It allows individuals to cross the intra—EU border without any personal control. Since then, external migration became a specific and explicit issue of and for EU law. Under such system one Member States' "third country nationals become those of the whole unified territory".[22]

The legislative achievements brought about general rules, dealing with visa,[23] the status of third-country nationals[24] as residents in the Member States and the returning of nationals of third states lacking a right of residence.[25] Demands on the protection of the human right of private and family life, the right on family unification was enacted.[26] Access to employment for researchers[27] and highly qualified personnel

---

[18] Directives (EC) 2001/55 (of July 20, 2001, O.J. of 7.8.2001 L 212, p.12 -Minimum Standards of Protection); 2004/83 (of April 29,2004 O.J. of 30.9.2001, L 304, p.12 Asylum Seekers);2005/85 (of December 1st, 2005, O.J. of 13.12.2005, L 3226, p. 13 – Withdrawal of the Status of an Asylum Seeker.

[19] Refugee Convention Geneva 28th July 1951, in force 1954,189 UNTS 150.

[20] Goodwin-Gill and Mc Adam (2011), p. 54 et sequ.

[21] Clayton et al. (2014), pp. 145–150.

[22] Guild (2001), p. 90.

[23] Community Code on visas (Reg. (EC) Nr. 810/2009 of 15.9.2009, O.J. L 243/1).

[24] Directive 2003/109, O.J. of 23.1.2004 L 16/44.

[25] Directive 2008/115/EC, O.J. of 24.12.2008 L 348/98.

[26] Directive 2003/86/EC, O.J. L 2003 of 3.10.2003 L.251/12.

[27] Directive 2016/81/ EU, O.J. of 11.5.2016 L 132/21 (Researcher).

(Blue-Card—Directive)[28] were cornerstones of the EU migration policy. The Member States had to make these rights effective.

5 Impacts of Accession to the Old Member States

5.1 New Modes of Decision-Making and New Geographic Orientations

By enlargement the EC had to integrate the new Member States as partners in the joint decision-making process in the EC. Society had to cope with new EU—citizens which witnessed for decades the working and living conditions of a socialist society, which gave them a meagre, but existing form of social protection. The new EU citizens expected from the membership of their countries in the EC that these social achievements would be conserved and improved, and not be jeopardized nor demolished.

On the political level the old Member States were bound to find a compromise with the representatives of the new Member States. Due to their substantial number the new Member States played an important role in the decision-making process in the EC. It became more complex and the requirements for a consensus became more complicated and demanding. The administration and integration of an increased number of Member States became more ponderous and time-consuming.

The experiences, demands and perceptions of the new Member States altered the topics of European importance and concern. The eastern enlargement of the EC altered the geographical horizon. As Central and Eastern European States joined the EC, also their eastern neighbour states entered in the political horizon of the EC.

With the accession of Slovenia, the question arose on whether other post Yugoslavian states should have a prospect to join the EC. With the Eastern enlargement of the EC the Western Balkan became a neighbouring region. The same is true for other post-soviet territories, Russia included. Eastern enlargement led the EC more to the East as before. As the EC established its rules in the Central and Eastern part of Europe this region increased its influence on EC politics considerably.

[28] Directive 2009/50/EC, O.J. of 18.6.2009 L 155/17 (highly qualified personnel) "Blue Card".

5.2 EU Labour Law and Social Security Gained Ground

The EC enlargement gave rise to a debate on fair labour and social protection standards in the enlarged Single Market.[29] In the first phase after accession, when the differences in wages and social protection were still drastically high, the debate started on whether these differences should be taken as a competitive momentum for the new Member States, which could improve their economic position in the enlarged Single Market, or whether the differences in labour and social standards could erode the sociopolitical basis within the EC.

The more the new Member States could cope with the demands of the Single Market and were enabled by it to increase prosperity and competitiveness of their economies, the more the potential to further steps towards a growing adjustment of EC and EU social standards grew.

An expression of the joint social upwards strategy of the EU is epitomized in the European Pillar of Social Rights. It translated the economic progress achieved by and since accession of the CEE states into a comprehensive restatement of all the social policy achievements by the European integration, combined with the prospects for further development.

The European Pillar of Social Rights enacted as a Recommendation 2017 identified 20 social rights in relation to the free and fair access to the labour market, fair labour standards and a well-developed system of social protection. The European Pillar translated the idea of Social Europe, which stands for the European Social Model to combine the economic freedoms of the market with solid labour and social protection laws.

With recent directives on standards for minimum wages, widening the protection of collective labour agreements, minimum standards for minimum income protection systems and a strategy for an improved standard for long-term care the social dimension of the EU became broader, deeper and sharper.

5.3 EU and Social Human Rights

In accordance with the European Pillar on Social Rights the EU and its legal system strengthened the human rights' basis of labour and social security law. This outcome is the fruit of the recent EU legislation—which by the Lisbon Treaty put an emphasis on human rights as the conceptual basis of EU law, which is epitomized also in the European Charter of Human Rights as an integral part of the EU-primary legislation.

[29] Which were likewise relevant in the international world: ILO, Social Security for social justice and a fair globalization, International Labour Conference 100th session Geneva 2011; ILO Declaration on Social Justice for a Fair Globalization (2008).

This development had been also brought about by the ECJ—case law and its interpretation of the EU labour and social security law. There are the well-established requirements to safeguard equal treatment in work, social protection and supply of goods and services, which made the EU societies becoming more inclusive, and attentive to all sorts of discrimination.

There are the European fundamental rights, which encompass the fundamental social rights to work, education, health care, social security and social assistance, and the rights to decent work in accordance with one's family commitments and a fair remuneration—which become more and more visible as the backbones of European labour and social security law. And there are, finally, the fundamental freedoms of EU law. They do not only facilitate economic exchanges within the Single market without any hindrances, but they build the backbone of a transnational legal order, which is to be elaborated under the EU law and further necessary steps of legislation.

For the new Member States accession meant in substance to become part of the transnational legal order which matured within the EU since its start in the late 1950ies.

6 Impacts of Accession to the New Member States

Accession to the EU undoubtedly meant a huge opportunity for the new Member States to develop a democratic welfare state. It is true that until now the socialist states belonging to the sphere of political and economic influence of the USSR have provided their inhabitants with a relatively strong degree of social protection, and at first glance these states could be described as "welfare state". However, this impression did not entirely correspond to reality, and the social protection of the population functioned more externally, a bit like the proverbial "Potemkin village". The pensions were low[30] compared with the working population and the health care was not as advanced as in Western countries.

The mandatory implementation of EU law meant for the new Member States the opportunity to complete the social reforms already begun after 1989 and, with the contribution of obligations arising from EU law, to set up new social protection instruments that would help to effectively address social events that affect the inhabitants of Europe today differently and often more intensively than in the 1990s.

For the new member states, EU membership meant "going west", even in terms of social systems. At the same time, however, it also meant not always an equal position in the creation of some legislation. Let's just mention, for example, the adoption of the new basic coordination regulation, which was adopted on 30. April 2004, i.e. on the eve of the accession of new Member States to the EU. The new

[30] Andrews, Emily S. / Mansoara, Rachid, The financing of pension systems in Central and Eastern Europe: an overview of major trends and their determinants (1990–1993), World Bank Technical Paper WTB 33; Fultz and Ruck (2000).

members thus did not get a chance to influence the wording of the coordination regulation, which was then reflected in the relatively long and complicated negotiations on the implementing regulation,[31] which was adopted only in 2009 and came into effect on 1 May 2010, so the basic regulation could not be used until then.

The changes brought about by EU accession to mainly post-socialist new Member States can be characterized in four points.

1. Freedom—especially freedom of movement and migration as such
2. Equality in access to social rights
3. Social protection
4. Labour protection and collective rights

The law of socialist countries knew guarantees of these aspects and was proud of them. However, in social reality social rights did not find real fulfillment in socialist countries: The declared and protected high level of social protection often remained only "on paper".[32] That is why the EU membership was a unique opportunity for the post-socialist countries, hence, at the end of the day, for the whole of Europe.

6.1 Freedom: Especially Freedom of Movement and Migration as Such

Freedom, not only political freedom, but also freedom of movement, was a main goal of revolutionary movements in the post-communist countries at the turn of the 1980s and 1990s. The communist countries declared that true freedom, especially for the working class, is life under the communist system. In reality, however, entire nations were confined within the borders of their states, people could not travel abroad, let alone work or study there. Many people from the then communist bloc paid with their lives for their desire for freedom when they were killed while trying to illegally cross the border to the West.[33] However, the freedoms gained also brought responsibility and new challenges.

At the beginning of the 90s, the borders with the West were opened, but work in one of the old Member States still represented many obstacles for citizens of post-communist countries, due to residence rules and conditions for entering the labour market. Therefore, with the accession of new Member States to the EU the real freedom of movement came, firstly, as a prospect, later as matter of right! Free

[31] Regulation (EC) No 987/2009 of the European Parliament and of the Council of 16 September 2009 laying down the procedure for implementing Regulation (EC) No 883/2004 on the coordination of social security systems.

[32] Tomková (2009). In: Bobek, Molek, Šimíček, (eds) (2009), pp. 670–723; Havelková (2017).

[33] Some estimate that around 250 people were killed while trying to cross the border of East Germany. Others estimate that actually 400 people died trying to cross borders. The number of people killed trying to cross borders of Czechoslovakia is around 250 between the years of 1948 and 1989. Mašková and Ripka (2015), p. 58.

access to the labour market in the old Member States represented a great opportunity for the whole of Europe.

However, this opportunity was used with some embarrassment on both sides—fears of the inhabitants of the old member states that people from the new states would distort the labour market and lower social welfare standards, and a certain disappointment and feeling of rejection on the part of the inhabitants of the new countries.[34]

The responsibility of the old Member States to open the borders to workers stemming from the new Member States was a political challenge for many of them. The transitional rules that allowed individual Member States to restrict free residence of persons, caused an unprecedented restriction of this freedom, which was then limited only once, with the onset of the Covid-19 pandemic.[35]

The free movement of people has also meant new opportunities for contact between countries that were still culturally and historically distant. The presence of people from the new Member States in the labour market in the old Member States has meant opportunities for mutual enrichment in many areas. At the same time, it should be emphasized that the introduction of freedom of movement did not represent a very dramatic increase in migration "from east to west", as many feared.[36]

The fact that citizens from the new countries began to enjoy the freedom of movement of persons and began to work in the old Member States, not always being treated in the same way as their own citizens, led, among other things, the EU to adopt a directive aimed at ensuring that equality and decent working conditions are respected for those who have benefited from the free movement of persons.[37]

By this piece of law, the equality of all EU citizens has been underlined once again, this time as regards equality irrespective of citizenship in access to

[34] Even if most EU citizens believed that granting EU membership to new countries was 'historically and geographically natural and, therefore, justified' (Eurobarometer 61, Spring 2004), situation soon started to change and mutate into what has come to be known as 'enlargement fatigue', a lack of enthusiasm and/or confidence in the overall enlargement project, as stated by Österreichische Gesellschaft für Europapolitik - https://www.oegfe.at/policy-briefs/from-eu-enlargement-fatigue-to-enlargement-enthusiasm/?lang=en.

[35] European Court of Auditors. Free movement in the EU during the COVID-19 pandemic: Limited scrutiny of internal border controls, and uncoordinated actions by Member States together with the replies of the Commission and the European Centre for Disease Prevention and Control (ECDC). Speacial Report 13/2022. avaialable on https://www.eca.europa.eu/Lists/ECADocuments/SR22_13/SR_free-movement-phase-I_EN.pdf.

[36] Since the 2004 enlargement, about 1.8 per cent of the EU-8 population has moved to the EU-15, raising the host country population by 0.3 per cent. Of this, approximately 75 per cent can be attributed to the enlargement process itself. Since 2007, about 4.1 per cent of the EU-2 population has moved to the EU-15, raising the host country population by a further 0.3 per cent. Of this, just over 50 percent can be attributed to the enlargement process itself. Holland et al. (2011).

[37] Directive 2014/54/EU of the European Parliament and of the Council of 16 April 2014 on measures facilitating the exercise of rights conferred on workers in the context of freedom of movement for workers. A study on its impact on workers in EU. Cfr. What has Happened with Directive 2014/54 on Strengthening the Rights of EU Workers? Minderhoud, P.E. 2019, Part of book or chapter of book (Minderhoud, Mantu, Zwaan, (ed.), pp. 163–173.

employment. While the free movement of workers had to be, in certain way, understood better by the old Member States, which had to face a new reality in the EU (actually, the EU did never have to face such a "big" enlargement), the equality principle and ban of discrimination, as enrooted in EU law, was quite a challenge for post-socialist countries.

6.2 Equal Access to Social Rights

Many socialist countries have emphasized equality as part of their propaganda. After all, one of the foundations of communist ideology was egalitarianism, i.e. the effort to erase (even natural) social differences between members of society. As a result, however, at the end of communism in Eastern Europe, the population of these countries was about the same poor and had the same lack of access to quality social protection, including health care of good quality, or to even sufficiently high social benefits.

In addition, it should be noted that e.g. women's employment in socialist countries reached a higher level than in the West, but this did not lead to equality between men and women in the labour market, as was shown particularly by the development in post-socialist countries in the 1990s. In fact, women were often those, who were discriminated in access to employment and career. Moreover, in years when the gender-pay-gap widened and women remained the main informal caregivers, childcare and modern elderly care services became less and less accessible.

The implementation of the set of anti-discrimination directives meant one of the biggest changes for the new Member States, and even though egalitarianism was declared in these countries, the anti-discrimination directives acted (and still do) as a foreign and sometimes undesirable element. In fact, in new Member States, people in general do not accept the concept of anti-discrimination and see it as something too progressive and dangerous for "traditional values". On the other hand, views on discrimination as such are similar in new as well as old Member States.[38] This is evidenced, for example, in some infringement procedures, where the new Member States are more frequent than the old ones. For instance, since 2014, the Commission has launched several infringement proceedings (against the Czech Republic (2014), Slovakia (2015, 2023) and Hungary (2016)) for failure to correctly implement the Racial Equality Directive (2000/43/EC). Discrimination against and segregation of Roma children in schools persists, even though a significant amount of EU funding has been provided to address the situation in recent years.[39]

Following the accession of new Member States to the EU, some equal treatment directives have been adopted with great difficulty. A prime example is the Commission's proposal in 2008 to adopt a directive that would prohibit

[38] See e.g. https://europa.eu/eurobarometer/surveys/detail/2972.

[39] https://www.europarl.europa.eu/doceo/document/O-9-2023-000039_EN.html.

discrimination in areas other than employment and occupation.[40] This proposal has not yet been adopted and negotiations on it or its other form are apparently frozen.

In the context of equality issues, it is also necessary to realize that the EU has become more ethnically diverse with the accession of new Member States to the EU. The countries of Central and Eastern Europe have contributed to the diversity of the EU with their large Roma minority.[41] However, this has not always been accepted by the old Member States, and the problems of discrimination against Roma in the new EU countries have also persisted. After all, the new countries undoubtedly have more problems with implementing Directive 200/43/EU than the older countries—at least as far as the application of this directive to the Roma ethnic area is concerned. However, it is only in recent years that the Commission has begun to actively enforce compliance with this bill.[42]

6.3 More Social Protection

In the area of social protection, there has been a major change in the new Member States in the form of the need for national administrations to manage and administer a relatively demanding and complex system of social security coordination. Some countries have already prepared for these tasks in preparation for EU membership by concluding bilateral agreements with existing EU Member States, on the implementation of which they have learned to apply coordination rules in future, after they will join the EU.

After accession the new Member States have been fully involved in the negotiations of the Administrative Commission, which provides common interpretations of some of the disputed provisions and is a space for resolving possible discrepancies between Member States, or between Member States and the Commission regarding the interpretation and implementation of coordination rules.

---

[40] Proposal for a Council Directive of Commission of 2 July 2008 on implementing the principle of equal treatment between persons irrespective of religion or belief, disability, age or sexual orientation COM/2008/0426.

[41] Although no official data is available, it is estimated that between 10 and 12 million Roma live in Europe, constituting its largest ethnic minority. It is spread throughout the European continent but is highly concentrated in Central and Eastern Europe, in particular Romania (est. 2 million persons), Bulgaria (est. 700,000), Hungary (est. 500,000), Slovakia (est. 450,000) the Czech Republic (est. 300,000); as well as in the Iberian peninsula (circa 700,000 Roma in Spain, and another 55,000 in Portugal). – data available at https://www.gitanos.org/la_comunidad_gitana/roma_community_europe.html.en.

[42] Pending case of non application of the Racial Equality Directive - discrimination of Roma children in education by the Czech Republic from 25 September 2014, pending case of non application of the Racial Equality Directive - discrimination of Roma children in education by Slovakia from 29 April 2015, pending case of Non-conformity with Directive 2000/43/EC on Racial Equality - Discrimination of Roma children in education by Hungary from 26 May 2016.

In the area of social protection, some directives have also been adopted over the last twenty years, which were also influenced by the fact that the EU has been enlarged to include countries with a different level of social security than in the old Member States. Some employers have therefore started to take advantage of this situation and have taken full advantage of the opportunities offered by the coordination rules.

Patients have also begun to take advantage of cross-border healthcare much more, which brings benefits for all involved. For instance, the Czech healthcare system is able to provide health care, including medical procedures, in a comparable quality to German healthcare facilities, but at a lower cost. In fact, German patients often go to the Czech Republic for health care, while Czech providers are happy to provide this predatory care and German insurance companies are happy to pay for it, because it is cheaper than if they paid for the same health care to a German medical facility.

For some situations, the procedure of prior authorization by healthcare insurance company for a planned health care abroad, enrooted in coordination regulations, seemed to be not flexible enough. Thanks to after 2004 enlargement increasing demand on cross-border health care, the Cross-Border Healthcare Directive was adopted in 2014, which, among other things, meant a breakthrough in the hitherto established principles in the sense that even planned health care that was not approved in advance by the health insurance company is obliged to be reimbursed by the relevant health insurance company.

6.4 Labour Protection and Collective Rights

Socialist countries were proud that they provide very intensive protection to their employees and that overall labour law protection is at a high level. Trade unions played an important role in these countries, but it was not possible to speak of a real social dialogue, if only because the state was essentially the only employer.

In the 1990s, there were significant changes in this area, it was necessary to set up social dialogue in a new and modern way, but this was usually not entirely successful.

In the new Member States, for example, the regulation of works councils and European works councils did not find much understanding.[43]

[43] For workers' representatives, the consultation process shows deficiencies in practice despite the improvement of the legal framework and the insertion of definitions in the EWC agreements. Among the main reasons they cited was a lack of joint understanding regarding consultation or the absence of consultation. ETUI (2016), *Survey conducted among EWC coordinators*. p. 98. [online] [2. 11. 2024]. Available at: https://www.etui.org/sites/default/files/2020-06/09_ETUI_Survey_UK_print%20and%20web_0.pdf. With limited rights to information and little influence, European Work Councils have been criticized for beingineffective, on account of unclear definitions, non-dissuasive sanctions and ineffective access to justice. Pape (2024).

On the contrary, the opportunities offered by temporary agency work across the whole EU have begun to be widely used in the new Member States. Posting of workers, as currently regulated, is often abused for dumping practices, as has already been mentioned above. This also often leads to disagreements between the old and new Member States, and it can also mean hostility between the population of one state towards one of the new Member States. Moreover, some authors have recently shown that in some sectors posting might provide space for severe exploitation.[44]

The issue of working time, which is regulated by the Working Time Directive, has also been the subject of debate in the new Member States, as the tendencies towards a gradual reduction in the working week and the protection of the maximum weekly working time limit do not correspond to economic trends in the new countries. The protection of working time and holiday protection is thus one of the important benefits of the EU for the new Member States.

The question remains how the new Member States will react to the completely newly adopted directives—like directive on transparent and predictable working conditions, directive on platform work or the directive on the balanced representation of women in companies listed on stock exchanges.[45]

Even though the Member States which joined the EU in 2004 did not have such a smooth entry into the EU as others, during the previous enlargements of the European Communities, and even though it is an indisputable fact that the new member states could not influence the existing form of EU law in any way and simply had to accept the acquis communautaire as it had already been created, EU membership represented a huge opportunity for the new Member States, especially in the social area.

Countries whose economic and social situation was not very good, thanks to the basic outlines of the European social model reflected in binding EU legal norms, very quickly, over the course of twenty years, reached the top of the world, and today, together with other European countries, they represent a model and a longed-for goal for the rest of the world. The EU has therefore apparently given more to the new member states than it has taken. This statement is true even though the implementation of EU law and the creation of new regulations do not always go as smoothly as the parties involved would probably like.

[44] Robin-Olivier (2022).

[45] Directive (EU) 2019/1152 of the European Parliament and of the Council of 20 June 2019 on transparent and predictable working conditions in the European Union, Directive (EU) 2024/2831 of the European Parliament and of the Council of 23 October 2024 on improving working conditions in platform work, Directive (EU) 2022/2381 of the European Parliament and of the Council of 23 November 2022 on improving the gender balance among directors of listed companies and related measures.

7 Enlargement: A Successful Step Towards a United Europe!

7.1 *Europe Regained Its Lost Centre*

EC enlargement overcame the Post-World-War II European divide. This gave the continent its historic and geographic centre back. During the Cold War its geographic centre was located at the peripheries of "West" and "East" and, hence, at the margins of the former separated Europe of the past.

The enlargement led the EC back to its geographical and historic centre, as the enlarged united Europe located the continent in its midst. This healed also the wounds caused in and by Worl War II, which broke out at the centre of Europe and ended in the catastrophe of a for decades divided continent.

The EC and EU at large moved more to the East; and this process was—unintentionally—deepened by Brexit, when with the United Kingdom an important Member State got lost at the Western part. So, the Eastern enlargement of the EC underlined the continental character of the project of legal, social, cultural and economic unity in Europe.

7.2 *EU-Law Became More Relevant*

As enlargement widened the territorial scope of application of EU law to new countries, customers, workers, citizens and social welfare and social security recipients, Eu law became more relevant for the living conditions of a growing number of persons and territories in Europe. The economic, cultural, political and social impact of EU law grew, and the global influence of the EU in the world increased.

7.3 *Enlargement Strengthened the Social Profile of the EU*

Seen from historical distance the expansion of EU law driven by the enlargement did also deepen European integration. In the last 20 years labour law and social security law became a stronger and integral part of EU law. This law was inspired by the international human rights' development.[46] This development echoes the visions of the Post War period, that human rights -above alle economic freedoms and social guarantees—a transnational legal order should be erected, which will foster prosperity in solidarity.

---

[46] Alston (2005), p. 1; Arendt (2007), pp. 3–14; Glendon (2000), Hunt (2007).

Official Documents and Directives

European Council in Copenhagen, June 22–23, 1993, DOC 93/3.
Helsinki Final Accords (1975).
Refugee Convention, Geneva, July 28, 1951, in force 1954, 189 UNTS 150.
Directive 2014/54/EU on workers' rights.
Directive (EU) 2019/1152 on transparent and predictable working conditions.
Directive (EU) 2024/2831 on improving working conditions in platform work.
Directive (EU) 2022/2381 on improving gender balance among directors.

References

Alston P (2005) Labour rights as human rights. Oxford University Press, Oxford, p 1
Arendt H (2007) The origins of totalitarianism
Barnard C (2022) The substantive law of the EU. The four freedoms. Oxford University Press, Oxford
Briggs A (1961) The welfare state in historical perspective. Archives européennes de sociologie 2:221
Clayton G, Sawyer C, Toner H, Fifth W, Wray H (eds) (2014) Immigration and asylum law, 6th edn. Oxford University Press, pp 145–150
Eichenhofer E (2007) Geschichte des Sozialstaats in Europa. Verlag C.H. Beck, München
Eichenhofer E (2025) Sozialrecht der EU, 9th edn. Nomos-Verlag
Fuchs M, Cornelissen R (2015) EU-social security law. Nomos, Baden-Baden
Fultz E, Ruck M (eds) (2000) Pension reform in Central and Eastern Europe: an update on the restructuring of national pensions schemes in selected countries. International Labour Office, Geneva
Glendon MA (2000) A world made new. Eleanor Roosevelt and the universal declaration of human rights. Random House, New York
Gold M (ed) (2005) The social dimension. Employment in the European Community. Macmillan, Basingstoke
Goodwin-Gill S, Mc Adam J (2011) The refugee in international law, 3rd edn. Oxford University Press, p 54. et sequ
Guild E (2001) In: Guild E, Harlow C (eds) Implementing Amsterdam: immigration and asylum law in the EC. Hart, Oxford
Hunt L (2007) Inventing human rights – a history. W.W. Norton & Co, New York/London, p 21
Judt T (2006) Postwar: a history of Europe Since 1945. Penguin Books
Mašková T, Ripka V (2015) Železná opona v Československu: Usmrcení na československých státních hranicích v letech 1948–1989. Ústav pro studium totalitních režimů, Prague, p 58. ISBN 978-80-87912-31-7
Pape M (2024) Revision of the European Works Councils Directive. BRIEFING EU Legislation in Progress, p 1
Robin-Olivier S (2022) Posting of workers in the European Union: an exploitative labour system. Eur Law Open 1(3):679–689
Wouters J, Ovádek M (2021) The European Union and human rights. Oxford University Press, Oxford

Online Sources

ETUI (2016) Survey among EWC coordinators. Available at: https://www.etui.org
Eurobarometer 61, Spring 2004
Europarl EU Document O-9-2023-000039_EN
Holland D et al (2011) Labour mobility within the EU. NIESR, London. Available at: https://www.niesr.ac.uk
Österreichische Gesellschaft für Europapolitik. Available at: https://www.oegfe.at

The Transformative Journey of CEE Countries to the EU

Cristina Mihes

1 Introduction

The landscape of labour law and industrial relations arena has undergone significant reshaping in most CEE countries since the outset of their journey towards integration into the European Union. Following or inspired by new international visions on economic governance for sustainable growth, all CEE countries have carried out labour policy changes, which have been translated into overhauling labour law reforms.

These reforms unfolded in two distinct phases: the preparation for accession to the EU and the integration of the European acquis.

In the first phase, all governments strived to transpose into domestic legislations the EU Treaties and directives during a long, sinuous and sometime painful process of "Europeanization" of domestic regulations, legislative legacies of communist regimes, and socialist industrial relations systems.[1] During the preparation phase, the impact of the EU acquis has been very strong in areas such as equality, health and safety, labour migration, business restructuring and working conditions, including regulation of new forms of employment (fixed term contract, temporary agency work, part-time work), working time, and soft collective rights: information and consultation, and workplace cooperation.[2]

[1] Czarzasty (2024).

[2] An exemplificative list: Council Directive 2000/43 /EC implementing the principle of equal treatment between persons irrespective of racial or ethnic origin; Directive 2006/54/EC on the implementation of the principle of equal opportunities and equal treatment of men and women in matters of employment and occupation; Directive 89/39/EEC on Occupational Safety and Health (Frame

C. Mihes (✉)
ILO, Geneva, Switzerland

K. Koldinská et al. (eds.), *Labour Law and Social Security Law in Central and Eastern Europe*, European Union and its Neighbours in a Globalized World 26,
https://doi.org/10.1007/978-3-032-04496-9_2

After accession, however, significant setbacks in the regulation and realization of some fundamental labour rights could be noted across Central and Eastern Europe. The most remarkable example is that of collective bargaining, which will be addressed below.

2 Contradictory Signals from the EU

Under Article 151 TFEU, the promotion of dialogue between management and labour is recognized as a common objective of the EU and the Member States. In the aftermath of the 2008 economic and financial crisis, social dialogue came however under increased pressure, as it was weakened by decentralization, a decline in bargaining coverage and state intervention in wage policy.

At the European Union level, the six-pack of initiatives and the Euro Plus Pact[3] came into force in 2011. To foster competitiveness, the Pact called for Member States to "review the wage setting arrangements and, when necessary, the degree of centralization in the bargaining process, and the indexation mechanisms, while maintaining the autonomy of the social partners in the collective bargaining process."[4] While acknowledging that wages are fixed through collective bargaining without government intervention in most States, according to the European Commission "reforms of labour markets should also contribute to making wage setting processes more efficient."[5] Decentralized collective bargaining was described as "employment-friendly," and recommendations have been issued encouraging governments to "decrease the bargaining coverage (e.g., by revising the modalities and conditions for the extension of collective agreements to non-signatory parties) or to decentralize the bargaining system (e.g., by introducing/extending the possibility to derogate from higher level agreements or to negotiate firm-level agreements)."[6]

The Juncker Commission took measures to counter this decline, announcing a 'new start for social dialogue' at a high-level conference in March 2015 and a quadripartite agreement, signed in June 2016 by the social partners, the Commission and the presidency of the Council of the European Union. The 2017 European Pillar of

Directive); Council Directive 1999/70/EC concerning the framework agreement on fixed-term contract concluded by ETUC, UNICE and CEEP; Directive 2008/104/EC on temporary agency work; Directive 2003/88/EC on certain aspects of the organization of working time; Directive 2002/14/EC establishing a general framework for informing and consulting employees in the European Community.

[3] The Euro Plus Pact was signed by the Eurozone Member States (including Slovakia and Slovenia), plus Bulgaria, Denmark, Latvia, Lithuania, Poland and Romania. In the meantime, Latvia and Lithuania have become members of the Euro area.

[4] European Council (2011), Presidency Conclusions, Brussels, 24–25 March.

[5] European Commission (2010).

[6] European Commission (2012).

Social Rights (EPSR) also establishes respect for the autonomy and the right to collective action of the social partners, and recognizes their right to be involved in designing and implementing employment and social policies, including through collective agreements. The first von der Leyen Commission has repeatedly reaffirmed a commitment to social dialogue in communications, such as those on the European Green Deal and on a Strong Social Europe for Just Transitions, in the Annual Sustainable Growth Strategy/Survey and the (draf) Country-Specific Recommendations, and in the objectives for the Recovery and Resilience Facility. The Commission published a report (the Nahles report) on strengthening social dialogue in February 2021, which fed into the action plan implementing the EPSR presented in March 2021. In May 2021, the Porto Social Commitment (signed by the Commission, Parliament and European social partners) and the European Council Porto Declaration both underlined the key role of social dialogue.

In line with the action plan implementing the EPSR, the Council of the European Union adopted the recommendation of 12 June 2023 on strengthening social dialogue in the European Union. The Recommendation seeks to support Member States in promoting social dialogue and collective bargaining at national level, by addressing three main elements: consultation of social partners on the design and implementation of economic, employment and social policies; encouraging social partners to negotiate and conclude collective agreements, while respecting their autonomy and the right to collective action.

3 The Impact on Collective Bargaining Regulation and Industrial Relations Systems in CEE

In 2011–2012, major labour law reforms took place across CEE.[7] Generally, the policy objectives of the reforming governments prioritized adjusting both the individual and collective labour relationships to the current dynamics of the labour market, aiming to boost economic growth. Without exception, increasing the flexibility of labour regulations has been seen as the way to reach that goal. In most countries, labour law reforms have also aimed to curb widespread undeclared work. In some cases, compliance with the European Social Charter (revised), the Universal Declaration of Human Rights, the International Covenant on Economic, Social and Cultural Rights, and the ILO conventions and recommendations was also mentioned as a goal of reforms.

Many existing norms, especially in relation to hiring and firing and labour redundancies, were considered too rigid to promote the recovery of the national economy, especially in times of crisis or post-crisis. Centralized wage-fixing mechanisms set out in collective agreements have been challenged, along with the genuine

[7] Chivu et al. (2013), Vaughan-Whitehead (2013), Gyulavari and Kartias (2012), pp. 167–188 (Xullo-Decembro, 2012) ISSN 1132-9947.

representativeness of *erga omnes* binding agreements concluded at the national and sectorial levels. In the view of some national legislators, labour law reform was the stand-alone policy tool to fix dysfunctions in the labour market. Legal changes accelerated the existing erosion of collective bargaining, whose traditional normative complementary role to lawmaking has been significantly diminished.

Across CEE, the uncoordinated decentralization of collective bargaining to the company level and a shift towards emphasizing enterprise performance, competitiveness, and productivity could be noted. In many cases, this has happened at the expense of solidarity-oriented social policy goals such as equity, inclusiveness, and the protection of vulnerable workers.

Financial assistance memoranda, such as those signed by several EU Member States[8] with the "troika" (the EU, the ECB and the IMF) or the "Stand-by Arrangements" signed by Hungary and Lithuania with the IMF, added another layer of stringent labour policy requirements. Austerity measure packages were devised to reduce fiscal deficits by downsizing public expenditure, freezing or cutting public sector pay, and capping pensions and social benefits. The implementation of these measures implied a drastic remodeling of wage-fixing mechanisms in general, and in the public sector in particular. When those mechanisms were laid down in collective agreements at the national or sectorial levels, it sometimes led to dismantling existing collective bargaining infrastructures or unilaterally abolishing the collective agreements in force.

The impact of 2011–2012 labour law reforms on national industrial relations systems has been dramatic in some cases. Across the sub-region, the industrial relations systems are statutory in nature, laid down in labour legislations enacted after the collapse of the communist regimes. By requiring higher representativeness thresholds for collective bargaining or abolishing bargaining at the national and sectorial levels, some labour law reforms disempowered trade unions and employers' organizations in labour policymaking. Even where industrial relations frameworks were less severely impacted, the effectiveness of tripartite social dialogue and the collective bargaining processes has decreased.[9]

4 New Rules of the Game: Who Is Representative for Collective Bargaining

Representativeness is critical for establishing the legitimacy of the social dialogue actors, and for ensuring their capability to commit to their constituencies and to further enforce those commitments. Since collective agreements have increasingly become an important source of legally enforceable rights, the teams negotiating on behalf of a certain group of workers or employers need to be backed by their group

[8] Greece, Ireland, Latvia, Portugal, Spain, and Romania.

[9] Mihes (2020).

and empowered by the law to conclude the collective agreements that bind their members. Moreover, representativeness is also important because of the series of privileges that accompany this status, such as the right to sign a collective agreement, the right to participate in tripartite or bipartite bodies, and the right to nominate delegates to the International Labour Conference and other international forums.

The representativeness of the social partners for collective bargaining, and how to determine such representativeness, remains one of the long-standing debatable key issues for industrial relations in the sub-region.[10]

For trade unions, the more traditional organizations that generally succeeded the trade unions of the former communist regimes have increasingly been challenged by newly-emerging trade unions. These new trade unions often refer to themselves as "free" or "independent," and claim representativeness status and the rights associated with it. Competition is particularly fierce in the public sector, with a much smaller trade union presence in the private sector. A tendency towards confrontation rather than cooperation on common negotiation platforms has deepened the fragmentation of the union movement at the national and sectorial levels in most of the CEE countries.

With a brief history dating back to the early 1990s, employers' organizations in the sub-region have remained stable in their mission, vision and programmes. They usually represent a mix of state managers, private employers and business associations, and act mainly as lobbyists to the government rather than trade unions' counterparts in social dialogue. Employers face significant organizational gaps, mainly at the sectorial level, and are increasingly confronted with strong competition from national or international chambers of commerce and foreign investor associations who claim their presence in the national policy dialogue.

Often, however, the "top-to-bottom" structures of some of the social partner organizations continue to raise legitimacy questions. In addition, the coordination between national, sectorial, and enterprise representativeness remains unclear or blurred. In fact, the multiplicity of competing actors and the lack of a voluntary mutual recognition by the social partners have required governments to set out certain rules for determining representativeness status.

International labour standards do not require the establishment of representativeness criteria, as both voluntary and statutory systems are acceptable in the view of the ILO's supervisory bodies. However, they require that certain legal and practical safeguards of independence and objectivity are observed for compulsory determination, such as the establishment of objective, pre-determined, and clear criteria that have been consulted by the concerned parties and certified by an independent body.

The EU also sees the establishment of representativeness criteria as crucial to upholding the principles of democracy in national industrial relations systems.[11] EU norms leave up to the member states the establishment of representativeness criteria at national, sectorial and company level. Art. 28 of the EU Charter of Fundamental

[10] Ibidem; Kahancova and Martiskova (2011).

[11] European Court of Justice (1996).

Rights stipulates that "workers and employers, or their respective organisations, have, in accordance with Union law and national laws and practices, the right to negotiate and conclude collective agreements at the appropriate levels and, in cases of conflicts of interest, to take collective action to defend their interests, including strike action".

The 2012 Law on Social Dialogue in Romania raised the threshold for a trade union to engage in collective bargaining at the company level from 30 per cent to 50 per cent plus one. Furthermore, for registering a collective agreement at the sectorial level, the members of signatory employers' organizations had to employ at least 50 per cent plus one of the total workforce at the sectorial level. The collective agreement at national level was abolished.

For a decade, until the adoption of the new law on social dialogue in 2022, the coverage of collective bargaining plummeted from 100% to around 20 per cent,[12] whereas only one sectorial collective agreement has been registered (pre-university education), without provisions concerning wages.

The principle of autonomy of the parties in collective bargaining is reflected in their freedom to choose the level of negotiation, the negotiation agenda, its conclusion, and the duration of the concluded collective agreement. In some EU Member States, decentralization of collective bargaining to the company level has been a legislative policy goal, which was implemented through labour law reforms. In Hungary, the law regulates collective bargaining at the sectorial and company levels, but the practice of sectorial social dialogue remains weak. In Croatia, Poland and Slovakia, collective bargaining is legally permitted at all levels, but in practice has mainly taken place at the company level.[13]

The principle of favourability is one of the guiding principles in the implementation of collective agreements according to the ILO's supervisory bodies,[14] and it has been upheld by most national labour legislation in the sub-region. While the "pyramid" of labour protection (labour law, collective agreements, and employment contracts, with the latter offering the highest protection) has been generally maintained, it has become possible in some CEE countries to deviate in practice through labour law reform. The majority of CEE labour codes stipulate that the negotiated labour standards shall at least be at the level of the statutory standards (Bulgaria) or above them (Romania, and Slovakia). In Poland, the trade union and the employer may conclude an agreement at the company level that deviates from the provisions of the

[12] Chivu et al. (2013).

[13] CEELex database, www.CEELex, ILO.

[14] In its 2012 Observation on the application of the Right to Organize and Collective Bargaining Convention, 1949 (No. 98) in Greece, the ILO Committee of Experts on the Application of Conventions and Recommendations (CEACR) stated that amendments introduced to the collective bargaining system in Greece that abrogated the principle of favourability that had previously applied were incompatible with Convention No. 98. The CEACR made specific reference to para. 3 (1) of ILO Recommendation No. 91.

labour law[15] with exception of the Labour Code, if it is justified by the company's financial situation. The social partners can negotiate *in peius* and conclude an agreement suspending the provisions of a: (a) typical collective labour agreement; (b) the provisions of other autonomous sources of labour law, i.e., atypical collective agreements, internal regulations issued by the employer, and statutes. Furthermore, an employer that is not covered by a collective agreement and employs less than 20 people may modify individual employment contracts through an agreement with the elected workers' representatives that provides for less favourable working conditions than stipulated in the employment contracts, to the extent and for the period set out in the agreement. The 2012 Labour Code of Hungary also allows, in the absence of an agreement to the contrary, deviations from statutory law though a collective agreement, apart from some provisions related to industrial relations, work councils, and trade unions' rights.[16]

5 Some Conclusions

Most reforms have weakened the normative function of collective bargaining through policies encouraging disorganized decentralization to the company level. One manifestation of this trend is the increasing role of the employer to unilaterally regulate the terms of employment, often replacing the collective agreement at the company level for a potentially indefinite period. By removing or weakening these self-regulatory mechanisms, labour law reforms have created gaps in law and practice that are likely to put some fundamental labour rights at risk.

While multi-employer collective bargaining is still seen as the backbone of the industrial relations system in most EU Member States and at the level of the European social partners, some CEE EU Member States have adopted policies that both directly and indirectly dismantle national and sectorial collective bargaining. EU candidate states have so far opted to preserve their national tripartite or bipartite agreements, generally with the support of the social partners. These agreements have universal application, and thus serve an important normative role complementary to the law. However, their binding nature has often being challenged by nonmembers of the signatory employers' organizations.

Decentralization of collective bargaining has been accompanied by the legal recognition of elected workers' representatives in collective negotiations at the company level. Despite the growing attention they have recently received, the involvement of elected representatives in collective bargaining has proved to be sporadic and less effective than that of trade unions. In some cases, complicated solutions for determining the bargaining powers of workers' representatives (as

[15] Labour law includes the Labour Code and secondary legislations, as well as collective agreements in force; the opt out does not apply to the Labour Code.

[16] CEELex database, www.CEELex, ILO.

established by law) have created legal and practical uncertainties at the company level.

Atypical agreements have replaced more traditional ones, often deviating from the principle of favorability through individual negotiations or through collective bargaining with *ad hoc* elected workers' representatives under more flexible conditions. Reportedly meant to expand the scope of collective bargaining, such solutions have not so far led to this result.

More stringent legal requirements, including higher thresholds for representativeness and restrictive conditions for extension, have translated into lower collective bargaining coverage. This is even the case where the number of company collective agreements has increased. Generally, workers employed in companies with less than 20 employees remain outside the scope of collective bargaining.

It appears that the last decade labour reforms have created various degrees of imbalance between the employment policy objective of increasing flexibility on the labour market and the general public policy goal to secure inclusive access to decent work.

What would then be an effective policy intervention ensuring that the employment relationship is indeed the place where all workers fully enjoy labour rights and decent working conditions and employers benefit from the certainty, predictability and social peace it brings?

At the EU level, there is a longstanding need for clear and consistent policy and legislative intervention to provide unitary rules regarding collective bargaining and to address shortly some regulatory gaps:

- the absence of consistent and unitary definitions of the concepts of "worker" and "employment relationship" throughout the EU legislation.[17] Although partially addressed by the case law of the European Court of Justice, it still raises legal and practical challenges to classification of workers in national legislations of the EU CEE Member states
- the lack of an European framework of collective bargaining, which is left up to the national legislators, practice, culture and industrial relations traditions, and thus results in legal and practical inconsistencies.

References

Barnard C (2012) EU employment law. Oxford University Press

CEELex. Available at: www.esap.online and https://www.ilo.org/budapest/lang%2D%2Den/index.htm

Chivu L, Ciutacu C, Dimitriu R (2013) The impact of legislative reforms on industrial relations in Romania. ILO, Budapest

[17] Freedland and Kountouris (2011), Barnard (2012), Davies (2018).

Czarzasty J (2024) 20 years after. Changing perspectives on industrial relations in Central and Eastern Europe two decades after EU enlargement: from transition to transformation. ETUI, published online

Davies P (2018) Employment law in the European Union. Cambridge University Press

European Commission (2010) DG Employment and Financial Affairs. Surveillance of Intra-Euro-Area Competitiveness and Imbalances

European Commission (2012) Labour Market Developments in Europe

European Council (2011) Presidency conclusions. Brussels

European Court of Justice, Summary of the Judgment: Union *Européenne* de l'artisanat et des petites et moyennes entreprises (UEAPME) v Council of the European Union, Case T-135/96 (1996)

Freedland M, Kountouris N (2011) The legal construction of personal work relations. Oxford University Press

Gyulavari T, Kartias G (2012) The hungarian labour law reform: the great leap towards full employment? Dereito 21(2):167–188

Kahancova M, Martiskova M (2011) Bargaining for social rights: redefining representativeness in Central and Eastern Europe. Central European Labour Studies Institute

Mihes C (2020) A comparative overview of drivers and outcomes of labour law and industrial relations reforms in selected Central and Eastern European countries. ILO

NORMLEX. Available at www.ilo.org

Vaughan-Whitehead D (2013) Public sector shock: the impact of policy retrenchment in Europe. Edward Elgar Publishing

Non-discrimination and Equal Treatment

The Principle of Non-Discrimination in the Workplace: Judgments of the Court of Justice in Polish Cases

Dagmara Skupień

1 Introduction: Historical Background

The Polish regulations on equal treatment and the principle of non-discrimination significantly precede the date of Poland's accession to the European Union. According to Article 95 of the 1921 Constitution,[1] the first fundamental law adopted in the independent Polish state after the partition period (1795–1918),[2] the Republic of Poland was to provide full protection of life, liberty, and property to all persons within its borders without distinction of origin, nationality, language, race, or religion. In addition, Article 96 of the 1921 Constitution stipulated that all citizens are equal before the law. In the subsequent constitution proclaimed in the period of independency (1918–1939), namely the 1935 Constitution,[3] the principle of non-discrimination was not that clearly expressed. The emphasis in the 1935 Constitution, which was characterised by an authoritarian approach to the state system, was placed on the duties of individuals towards the State rather than on their rights.[4] However, Article 7(2) of the 1935 Constitution stated that powers of a given citizen

[1] See Ustawa z dnia 17 marca 1921 r. - Konstytucja Rzeczypospolitej Polskiej (Act of 17 March 1921 – Constitution of the Republic of Poland), Dziennik Ustaw (Polish Journal of Laws – later Dz. U.) of 1921, No. 44, item 267.

[2] See more about the 123 years' partition period: Encyclopedia Britannica (2024).

[3] Ustawa Konstytucyjna z dnia 23 kwietnia 1935 r. (Constitutional Law of 23 April 1935), Dz. U. of 1935, No. 30, item 227.

[4] Bardach et al. (1998), p. 502.

D. Skupień (✉)
Department of European, International and Collective Labour Law, Faculty of Law and Administration, University of Lodz, Lodz, Poland
e-mail: dskupien@wpia.uni.lodz.pl

K. Koldinská et al. (eds.), *Labour Law and Social Security Law in Central and Eastern Europe*, European Union and its Neighbours in a Globalized World 26,
https://doi.org/10.1007/978-3-032-04496-9_3

(depending on their level of effort and contribution to public good) to influence public affairs cannot be restricted on grounds of origin, religion, sex, or nationality.

After World War II and the communist takeover of the state in Poland, the Constitution was enacted in 1952.[5] The 1952 Constitution established a new political order, namely, people's democracy based on the dominant role of workers and farmers [Article 1(1) and (2)] and introduced a new name for the country: The Polish People's Republic (*Polska Rzeczpospolita Ludowa*, PRL). Formally, the 1952 Constitution enshrined a catalogue of civic rights. Among others, it expressed the principle of equality between men and women in all spheres of economic and social life, including equality in work and pay [Article 66(1) and (2)], and equality of rights for all citizens regardless of race, nationality, and religion. The PRL has ratified the ILO Convention No. 111 that prohibits discrimination in the field of employment and occupation[6] as well the United Nations Covenants: on Civil and Political Rights[7] and on Economic, Social and Cultural Rights.[8] In practice, the communist regime which governed Poland in years 1944-1989 violated civic rights. In the worst cases, communist functionaries committed crimes against humanity.[9] Workers and farmers were exploited and there was no true equality between men and women.[10]

The political transformation towards a democratic state started in 1989. The currently binding Constitution of 1997[11] is founded on the principle of the democratic rule of law (Article 2). It guarantees to all people equality before the law, and the right to equal treatment by public authorities [Article 32(1)]. The Constitution also establishes the prohibition of discrimination in political, social, or economic life for any reason [Article 32(2)]. Furthermore, Article 33 of the Constitution guarantees the equality of rights for men and women, including in employment.

It should also be indicated that in 1992 Poland ratified the European Convention for the Protection of Human Rights and Fundamental Freedoms,[12] what constituted an important step in the democratization of the country and guaranteeing equality and non-discrimination of citizens.[13] In 2004, Poland ratified the 1983 ILO Vocational Rehabilitation and Employment (Disabled Persons) Convention (No. 159), establishing the principle of equal opportunity between disabled workers and

[5] Konstytucja Polskiej Rzeczypospolitej Ludowej uchwalona przez Sejm Ustawodawczy w dniu 22 lipca 1952 r., [Constitution of the Polish People's Republic adopted by the Legislative Sejm on July 22, 1952], Dz. U. of 1952, No. 53, item 232.

[6] Dz. U. of 1961, No. 42, item 218.

[7] Dz. U. of 1977, No. 38, item 167.

[8] Dz. U. of 1977, No. 38, item 169.

[9] Davies (2023), p. 63 or Kuczyńska (2022), pp. 123–139.

[10] See for example Leszczyński (2020), pp. 477–523 or Mrozek (2019), pp. 257–282.

[11] Konstytucja Rzeczypospolitej Polskiej z dnia 2 kwietnia 1997 r., Dz. U. of 1997, No. 78, item 483.

[12] Dz. U. of 1993, No. 61, item 284.

[13] Dz. U. of 1993, No. 61, item 284.

workers with no disabilities; while allowing positive actions in favour of disabled persons.[14]

Obviously, in this context it is not possible to assert that the foundations for the anti-discrimination law in Poland were established at the moment of the accession to the European Union (EU) in 2004. However, the prevention and combating of discrimination at the workplace were significantly strengthened in our country under the influence of EU law. Poland's accession to the EU has entailed an obligation to respect anti-discrimination provisions resulting from the EU primary law as well as to transpose anti-discrimination directives.

The EU work-related anti-discrimination directives were initially transposed by Poland only by incorporating new corresponding provisions into the Labour Code. Especially Article 11^3 establishing the principle of non-discrimination in employment and the new Chapter IIa, fully dedicated to the enforcement of equal treatment and combating discriminations, were inserted into the Labour Code.[15] However, this transposition method was not sufficient due to the limitation of the personal scope of protection for employees in the strict sense of the Labour Code.[16]

In order to fully adapt Polish legislation to EU anti-discrimination law, the Law of 3 December 2010 on the transposition of certain provisions of EU law regarding equal treatment[17] was enacted. This latter act is complementary to the anti-discrimination provisions of the Labour Code. It regulates legal measures and claims pursued by self-employed persons and persons employed under civil law contracts.[18] According to Article 4(2) of the above-mentioned Law on Equal Treatment, this law shall apply, among others, to the conditions for taking up and pursuing economic or professional activities, including, in particular, in the context of an employment relationship or work performed under a civil law contract.

According to the current prevailing interpretation both of the Polish courts and expressed in the legal doctrine, Article 18^{3a} § 1 of the Labour Code, in its present version after amendments,[19] sets out an open catalogue of criteria on grounds of which discrimination is prohibited.[20] On the contrary, the law on equal treatment

[14] Dz. U. of 2005, No. 43, item 412. See Walczak (2021), pp. 64–65.

[15] Ustawa z dnia 24 sierpnia 2001 r. o zmianie ustawy - Kodeks pracy oraz o zmianie niektórych innych ustaw (Act of 24 August 2001 amending the Act - Labour Code and amending certain other acts), Dz. U. of 2001, No. 128, item 1405, modified by the Act of 14 November 2003 amending the Act- Labour Code and amending certain other acts (ustawa z dnia 14 listopada 2003 r. o zmianie ustawy - Kodeks pracy oraz o zmianie niektórych innych ustaw), Dz. U. of 2003, No. 213, item 2081.

[16] See Skupień (2010), pp. 167–169.

[17] Ustawa o wdrożeniu niektórych przepisów Unii Europejskiej w zakresie równego traktowania (later called 'the Law on Equal Treatment'), Dz. U. of 2010, No 254, item 1700, consolidated version: Dz. U of 2023, item 970.

[18] Cf. Skupień (2021), p. 163.

[19] Ustawa z dnia 16 maja 2019 r. o zmianie ustawy - Kodeks pracy oraz niektórych innych ustaw (Act of 16 May 2019 amending the Act - Labour Code and amending certain other acts), Dz. U. of 2019, item 1043.

[20] Góral (2021), p. 31 or Tyc (2023), p. 75.

defines a closed catalogue of discrimination grounds, namely gender, racial or ethnic origin, religion, nationality, political beliefs, ethnic origin, confession, or sexual orientation.[21]

The Court of Justice of the European Union (CJEU) in Polish cases decided on application of the principle of non-discrimination in light of Article 157 TFEU, Directive 200/78,[22] Directive 2006/54[23] as well as Directive 1999/70.[24]

The legal problems addressed in the aforementioned case law concerned both the interpretation of the concept of discrimination (judgment in case VL[25]) or its material scope (judgments in cases: J.K.,[26] Nierodzik,[27] Commission v. Poland[28] or K.L.[29]). This caselaw has been selected as it solves various legal problems concerning the interpretation of the EU anti-discrimination directives, such as especially the material and personal scope of these acts.

The purpose of this publication is to analyse the Court of Justice jurisprudence in Polish cases concerning the compliance of Polish legislation or employers' practice with EU anti-discrimination law and to assess to what extent these judgments contribute to ensuring effective protection against discrimination in the workplace.

2 Combating Discrimination: In Search of a Comparator

The assessment of whether an unequal treatment of a person has occurred based on a certain characteristic is usually carried out by the courts comparing their situation in employment with that of another person with comparable work experience and

[21] Skupień (2021), p. 163.

[22] Council Directive 2000/78/EC of 27 November 2000 establishing a general framework for equal treatment in employment and occupation, *OJ L 303, 2.12.2000, p. 16–22.*

[23] Directive 2006/54/EC of the European Parliament and of the Council of 5 July 2006 on the implementation of the principle of equal opportunities and equal treatment of men and women in matters of employment and occupation (recast), *OJ L 204, 26.7.2006, p. 23–36.*

[24] Council Directive 1999/70/EC of 28 June 1999 concerning the framework agreement on fixed-term work concluded by ETUC, UNICE and CEEP, *OJ L 175, 10.7.1999, p. 43–48.*

[25] Judgment of the Court (Grand Chamber) of 26 January 2021 in Case C-16/19 VL v. Szpital Kliniczny im. dra J. Babińskiego Samodzielny Publiczny Zakład Opieki Zdrowotnej w Krakowie [Dr J. Babiński Clinical Hospital, Independent Public Healthcare Institution in Kraków, Poland], ECLI:EU:C:2021:64.

[26] Judgment of the Court (Second Chamber) of 12 January 2023 in Case C-356/21 J.K. v. TP S.A. ECLI:EU:C:2023:9.

[27] Judgment of the Court (Eighth Chamber) of 13 March 2014 in Case C-38/13, Nierodzik v. Samodzielny Publiczny Psychiatryczny Zakład Opieki Zdrowotnej im. dr. Stanisława Deresza w Choroszczy, ECLI:EU:C:2014:152.

[28] Judgment of the Court (Grand Chamber) of 5 November 2019, in Case C-192/18 European Commission v. Republic of Poland, ECLI:EU:C:2019:924.

[29] Judgment of the Court (Grand Chamber) of 20 February 2024 in Case C-715/20 K.L. v. X sp. z o. o., ECLI:EU:C:2024:139.

length of service, with the main difference between the two persons being the 'protected ground'.[30] The CJEU made a breakthrough in this approach to the problem of discrimination in the above-mentioned judgment in case C16/19 V.L. The dispute in the main proceedings was triggered by the employer's practice aimed at encouraging workers to submit a certificate attesting their disability. The purpose of this practice was to eliminate the burden on the employer, a public hospital, of payments to the State Fund for the Rehabilitation of Persons with Disabilities (PFRON). According to Article 21(1) of the Law of 27 August 1997 on Vocational and Social Rehabilitation and Employment of Persons with Disabilities[31] employers employing 25 or more workers, in terms of full-time equivalents, shall, as a principle, pay monthly contributions to the Fund equivalent to 40.65% of average pay multiplied by the number of employees equal to the difference between the number of employees that ensures compliance with the employment index of 6% of persons having a disability in the workforce and the actual number of disabled persons employed.

However, according to Article 21(2) of the same law, employers employing persons having a disability for at least 6% of their workforce shall be exempt from payment of the above-mentioned contribution. The essence of the contribution system in force under the aforementioned Article 21(1) is the application of financial burdens to entities that do not employ a statutorily defined ratio of persons with disabilities.[32]

In order to encourage employees with disabilities to submit a disability certificate, the hospital's director organized a meeting with employees in the second half of 2013 and then offered to grant a monthly allowance in an amount of 250 Polish zlotys (PLN) (approximately EUR 60) to workers who would have submitted disability certificates after the date of the meeting. Accordingly, the allowance, for which Polish law did not make provision, was granted by unilateral decision of the Hospital's director to 13 employees, specifically those who had submitted a disability certificate on a date after the staff meeting. On the other hand, no financial reward was provided to those workers who reported their disability to the employer prior to the meeting. VL was one of 16 persons who, due to the fact that they had submitted their disability certificate before the date of the said meeting, did not receive any allowance for the above-mentioned reason.

According to VL, she was treated discriminatorily compared to other employees who submitted their disability certificates after the date of the above-mentioned meeting. She initiated a judicial proceeding, claiming payment of the said monthly allowance as well as compensation for the harm suffered as the result of a breach of the principle of equal treatment in employment. Her case was dismissed in the first instance. The *Sąd Okręgowy w Krakowie* (Regional Court in Kraków, Poland). to which the V.L.'s appeal was lodged, referred the case to the Court of Justice for

[30] European Union Agency for Fundamental Rights and Council of Europe (2018), p. 45 or Halmos (2023), p. 29.

[31] Ustawa z dnia 27 sierpnia 1997 r. o rehabilitacji zawodowej i społecznej oraz zatrudnianiu osób niepełnosprawnych, Dz. U. of 1997, No 123, item 776, as subsequently amended.

[32] See also Klimkiewicz (2011), p. 23.

preliminary ruling. It raised doubts about the possible classification of the above practice as discriminatory in the context of Article 2 of Directive 2000/78. The Polish court asked the Court of Justice, in essence, whether Article 2 of Directive 2000/78 should be interpreted as meaning that the practice adopted by an employer and consisting of the exclusion of workers with disabilities, who have already submitted disability certificates to that employer before the date chosen by that employer for the submission of such a certificate, from receiving an allowance paid to workers with disabilities can be covered by the ‘concept of discrimination’ referred to in that provision.

The atypical character of the case consists in the fact that the complainant in the main proceedings finds herself subject to less favourable treatment compared not to persons who do not have disabilities but compared to persons who also have disabilities.

The Court of Justice underlined in this case that directive 2000/78, intended to establish a general framework for combating discrimination on the grounds, inter alia, of disability, is thus a specific expression, within the field that it covers, of the general principle of non-discrimination enshrined in Article 21 of the Charter of Fundamental Rights of the European Union (CFREU).[33]

The CJEU further argued that the protection granted by Directive 2000/78 would be diminished if it were considered that a situation where such discrimination occurs within a group of persons, all of whom have disabilities, is, by definition, not covered by the prohibition of discrimination laid down thereby solely on the ground that the difference in treatment at issue occurs between persons with disabilities.[34]

The Court underlined that although Article 1 and Article 3(4) of Directive 2000/78, as well as recitals 11 and 12, make generic references to discrimination ‘on the grounds’ or ‘based on’, inter alia, disability, they do not specify in any way the person or group of persons that can be used as a benchmark to assess whether there is such discrimination.[35]

Although it was ultimately up to the national court to determine whether the practice at issue in the main proceedings constitutes discrimination prohibited by Directive 2000/78, the Court of Justice gave guidance regarding possible qualification of the above-described practice as direct or indirect discrimination.

According to the reasoning of the CJEU, direct discrimination on the grounds of disability would be considered if less favourable treatment occurred due to a cause that is inextricably related to the disability. In this case, the referring court therefore had to determine whether the temporal condition imposed by the employer to receive the allowance in issue in the main proceedings, that is, the submission of the disability certificate after a date chosen by that employer, constitutes a criterion that is inextricably linked to the disability of the workers who were denied that

[33] See paragraphs 32-33 of the CJEU in Case C-16/19. Cf. Quirico (2024), p. 46.

[34] See paragraph 35 of the CJEU judgment in Case C-16/19.

[35] See paragraph 30 of the CJEU judgment in Case C-16/19.

allowance.[36] The Court of Justice suggests that one of the indicators supporting such a qualification would be that the disability certificate gives rise to specific rights that the worker can rely on against the employer, which are directly derived from that worker's status as a worker with a disability.[37]

An analysis of whether indirect discrimination is at stake in a given case is founded on the grounds that, in factual circumstances, the disadvantaged position of certain employees is linked to the application of an apparently neutral criterion, namely the submission of a disability certificate after a meeting. The Court suggests that the element to be considered by the national court in this context is whether the employees who submitted the certificate earlier are not characterised by a more visible disability or a more severe form of it, which required reasonable accommodation, and thus the disclosure of the disability to the employer took place at an early stage of employment.

In any event, in defence against a charge of indirect discrimination, as defined in Article 2 (2) point b (i) of Directive 2000/78, the employer was required to prove that the practice applied 'is objectively justified by a legitimate aim and the means to achieve that aim are appropriate and necessary'. The Court of Justice indicates that, in any case, it is apparent from the intended purpose of the practice at issue in the main proceedings, which is to save money, that the conditions for such justification are not satisfied, which is for the referring court to verify, where appropriate.[38]

To summarise, the CJEU decided that the practice adopted by the employer in the main proceedings consisting of the payment of an allowance to workers with disabilities who have submitted their disability certificates after a date chosen by that employer, and not to workers with disabilities who have submitted those certificates before that date, may constitute direct discrimination if it is established that the above-mentioned practice is based on a criterion that is inextricably linked to disability, inasmuch as it is such as to make it impossible for a clearly identified group of workers, consisting of all workers with disabilities whose disabled status was necessarily known to the employer when that practice was introduced, to satisfy that temporal condition.

Alternatively, that practice, although apparently neutral, may constitute discrimination indirectly based on disability if it is established that, without being objectively justified by a legitimate aim and without the means of achieving that aim being appropriate and necessary, it puts workers with disabilities at a particular disadvantage depending on the nature of their disabilities, including whether they are visible or require reasonable adjustments to be made to working conditions.

The CJEU judgment in the case VL is very innovative.[39] It presents a bold approach that allows for more effective protection against discrimination, including when comparing the situation of an alleged victim of unequal treatment with persons characterized by the same protected characteristic.

---

[36] See paragraph 51 of the CJEU judgment in case C-16/19.

[37] Paragraph 52 of the CJEU judgment in Case C-16/19.

[38] Paragraph 59 of the judgment in Case-16/19.

[39] Compare Mitrus (2021), p. 10.

3 Protection Against Discrimination and Atypical Forms of Work

3.1 Discrimination of Self-Employed Persons

Directive 2000/78 has a wider scope of application than the EU social policy directives adopted on the basis of Article 153(2)(b) TFEU.[40] This directive aims to combat discrimination, which concerns, among others, not only 'conditions for access to employment', but also 'self-employment or occupation.[41] On the other hand, unlike Directive 2000/43, it does not apply to 'access to and supply of goods and services available to the public'.[42] The European Commission has proposed the adoption of an amending directive that would extend the material scope of Directive 2000/78, in particular to the access and supply of goods and other services that are available to the public, but the new directive has not been adopted so far and the work on it has stalled.[43]

The J.K. case in the main proceedings concerned the termination of cooperation with J.K., a self-employed audio-visual editor, who had worked for TP SA (a company which operates a nationwide public television channel in Poland) for a long period of time, namely 7 years, on the basis of consecutive short-term contracts for a specific work. In December 2017, J.K. published a video clip on YouTube in which he and his partner presented a song promoting the celebration of Christmas by same-sex couples. According to him, this public affirmation of homosexual unions resulted in the contractor's abrupt withdrawal from cooperation and the failure to enter into another contract for specific work, despite the fact that he had already set dates for shifts in the next period of cooperation for TP SA.

According to the plaintiff, a refusal of TP SA to renew a contract with him constituted discrimination based on sexual orientation. As a consequence, J.K. initiated legal proceedings against TP SA before *Sąd Rejonowy dla m. st. Warszawy w Warszawie* (the District Court for the capital city of Warsaw in Warsaw) for discrimination on the grounds of sexual orientation and claimed compensation for damage.

---

[40] See Skupień (2022), pp. 280–281 and 283.

[41] Cf. Article 3(1)(a) of Directive 2000/78.

[42] Cf. Article 3(1)(h) of Council Directive 2000/43/EC of 29 June 2000 implementing the principle of equal treatment between persons irrespective of racial or ethnic origin, *OJ L 180, 19.7.2000, p. 22–26.*

[43] See Article 3(1)(d) of the Proposal for a Council Directive on implementing the principle of equal treatment between persons irrespective of religion or belief, disability, age or sexual orientation {SEC(2008) 2180} {SEC(2008) 2181}, COM/2008/0426 final.

In the judicial proceedings, TP SA invoked the freedom of contracting in the course of its business. It contended that the compensation action should be dismissed, submitting, inter alia, that the law did not guarantee the renewal of the contract for specific work which it had concluded with the applicant. The defendant party relied on Article 5(3) of the Law on Equal Treatment, which stipulates that this law shall not apply to the freedom of choice of parties to a contract as long as that choice is not based on sex, race, ethnic origin, or nationality.

The referring court, namely the District Court in Warsaw, had doubts about the compatibility of Article 5(3) of the Law on Equal Treatment with Article 3(1)(a) and (c) of Directive 2000/78. The subject of the Polish court's preliminary question in this case was, in fact, whether the material scope of the directive's application extends to the sphere of cooperation on the basis of other contracts than an employment contract, such as a contract for a specific work, and specifically whether the refusal to renew a civil law contract falls within the scope of Article 3 (1)a) of Directive 2000/78, that is, within the 'conditions for access to self-employment or occupation' and Article (1)(c), namely, 'employment and working conditions, including dismissals and pay'.

The CJEU confirmed in this judgment that Directive 2000/78 is not an act of EU secondary legislation such as those based, in particular, on Article 153(2) TFEU, which seek to protect only workers as the weaker party in an employment relationship, but aims to eliminate, on grounds related to social and public interest, all discriminatory obstacles to access to livelihoods and to the capacity to contribute to society through work, irrespective of the legal form in which it is provided.[44] Apart from the fact that the above-mentioned provision expressly refers to self-employment, it also follows from the terms 'employment' and 'occupation', understood in their usual sense, that the EU legislature did not intend to limit the scope of Directive 2000/78 to posts occupied by a 'worker', within the meaning of Article 45 TFEU.[45]

However, the CJEU found it necessary to distinguish activities that fall within the scope of Directive 2000/78 from those consisting of the mere provision of goods or services to one or more recipients and which do not fall within that scope.[46] According to the CJEU, in order for occupational activities to fall within the scope of Directive 2000/78, these activities should be genuine and pursued in the context of a legal relationship characterised by a degree of stability.[47]

In the next step of its reasoning, the CJEU argued that it was obvious from the order for reference that the activity pursued by the applicant constituted a genuine and effective occupational activity, carried out on a personal and regular basis for

[44] See paragraph 43 of the judgment in Case C-356/21.

[45] Paragraph 37.

[46] Paragraph 44.

[47] Paragraph 45.

the same recipient, enabling the applicant to earn his livelihood, in whole or in part. For this reason, the question whether the conditions for access to such an activity fall within Article 3(1)(a) of Directive 2000/78 do not depend on the classification of that activity as 'employment' or 'self-employment', since the scope of that provision and, accordingly, the scope of that directive must be construed broadly.[48]

The CJEU next concluded that the phrase 'conditions for access' to self-employment covers circumstances or facts the existence of which is essential for a person to be able to pursue a particular self-employed activity.[49] Therefore, in order for a person such as J.K. to be able to pursue his occupational activity effectively, the conclusion of a contract for specific work constitutes a factor the existence of which may be essential. As a consequence, the concept of "conditions of access" to self-employment, within the meaning of Article 3(1)(a) of Directive 2000/78, can include the conclusion of a contract such as that at issue in the main proceedings. Consequently, the refusal to conclude a contract for specific work with a contractor engaged in an independent economic activity on grounds related to the sexual orientation of that contractor falls within the scope of the above-mentioned provision of Directive 2000/78.[50]

Furthermore, the CJEU also presented a broad interpretation of the concept 'employment and working conditions', including dismissals [...] as provided in Article 3(1)(c) of Directive 2000/78. In this context, the CJEU relied on the assumption that Directive 2000/78 aims at eliminating discriminative obstacles to access to livelihoods and to the capacity to contribute to society through work, irrespective of the legal form in which it is provided. Therefore, the protection conferred by Directive 2000/78 cannot depend on the formal categorization of a contract on the basis of which the work is carried out.[51] According to the CJEU that agrees with Advocate General Ćapeta on this aspect,[52] Article 3(1)(c) of Directive 2000/78 refers to 'dismissal' only by means of an example of 'employment and working conditions' and covers, inter alia, unilateral termination of any activity referred to in Article 3(1)(a) of that directive. Therefore, the fact that in December 2017, the J.K. was unable to complete any of the one-week shifts provided for in the contract for specific work which he had concluded with TP SA. appears to constitute an involuntary termination of activity of a self-employed person, which may be assimilated to dismissal of an employee.

The CJEU in case J.K. also underlined that protection conferred by Directive 2000/78 cannot be jeopardized by the freedom to choose a contracting party. It is indisputable that fundamental freedom to conduct a business, enshrined in Article 16 of the CFREU (Freedom to conduct a business), covers the freedom to exercise

48 Paragraph 47.

49 Paragraph 49.

50 Paragraph 51.

51 Paragraphs 54-55.

52 Cf. Opinion of the Advocate General Ćapeta delivered on 8 September 2022, point 102, ECLI:EU:C:2022:653.

an economic or commercial activity, freedom of contract, and free competition, and encompasses, in particular, the freedom to choose with whom to do business. However, the freedom to conduct a business is not absolute but must be viewed in relation to its social function. Accepting that freedom of contract allows a refusal to contract with a person based on that person's sexual orientation would simply remove Article 3(1)(a) of Directive 2000/78 of its practical effect.[53]

In consequence, the CJEU decided that Article 3(1)(a) and (c) of Directive 2000/78 must be interpreted as precluding national legislation which has the effect of excluding, on the basis of the freedom of choice of contracting parties, from the protection against discrimination to be conferred by that directive, the refusal, based on the sexual orientation of a person, to conclude or renew with that person a contract concerning the performance of specific work by that person in the context of the pursuit of a self-employed activity.

The above presented judgment in case J.K. is not only an important ruling in the battle for equal treatment of LGBTIQ+ persons[54] but also for the more effective protection of self-employed people against discrimination based on various grounds, not necessarily on sexual orientation. The CJEU has applied a very broad interpretation of the material scope of Directive 2000/78, extending it to self-employed persons who have concluded civil law contracts with another party.[55] The Court placed particular emphasis on the protection of people who perform work in person, regardless of the type of contract concluded.[56]

It is particularly important in light of the official statistics that showed that in June 2023, 2,332,500 people performed work based on mandate contracts and related contracts (contractors) in Poland and that 2/3 of the contracts concluded by Polish employers with foreigners in 2023 were civil law contracts.[57]

The logical consequence of the judgment for Polish legislation should be the modification of Article 5(3) of the Law on Equal Treatment in a sense that precludes refusal to conclude a contract for discriminative reasons and not restricted to certain grounds only. However, in light of the visible distinction operated by the CJEU between occupational activities, including those carried out by self-employed workers to earn their livelihood, and the mere provision of goods or services to one or more recipients, the protection of self-employed persons is not complete. For this reason, the Commission's proposal to extend the scope of Directive 2000/78, in particular, to 'access to and supply of goods and services that are available to the public' should be revived.

---

[53] Paragraphs 75 and 77 of the CJEU judgment in Case C-356/21.

[54] Covington (2023).

[55] Křičková and Fellerová Palkovská (2023).

[56] Hajn (2024), p. 24.

[57] Główny Urząd Statystyczny - Statistics Poland (2024), p. 1, Ministerstwo Rodziny, Pracy i Polityki Społecznej (2024), p. 4.

3.2 *Discrimination on the Grounds of Fixed-Term Employment*

The question of whether the notice period in the event of dismissal falls within the scope of Directive 1999/70 was the subject of the CJEU judgment in Case C-38/13 Nierodzik, which led to a change in Polish legislation.[58]

The background of the dispute in the main proceedings concerned a specific provision provided for in the Law of 17 December 1998 on pensions from the Social Insurance Fund[59] which is still in force, namely Article 103a which states that entitlement to a pension shall be suspended irrespective of the amount of income earned by the pensioner from employment continued without prior termination of the employment relationship with the employer for whom a given person was employed immediately before the date of acquisition of the right to a pension fixed in the decision of the pension authority (the Social Insurance Institution—ZUS).

As a consequence, a person who intends to work for their employer simultaneously perceiving pension benefits should request the employer to terminate the existing employment relationship and propose to establish a new one. The abovementioned provision gives thus the employer the freedom to shape the new employment conditions according to his interests and needs, and the employee is in a less favourable negotiating position being at risk of losing their employment.

Ms. M. Nierodzik had been employed in the hospital for almost 24 years. Wishing to perceive her pension entitlement, she requested her employer to terminate the open-ended employment contract, and on the following day after the termination of this contract, the parties concluded a new fixed-term contract for a period of 5 years. Shortly after the conclusion of this contract, the hospital dismissed Ms. Nierodzik with no justification and with 2 weeks' notice only, which was consistent with the legislation in force at that time.

In light of the provisions in force at the date of the facts, termination of a fixed-term contract was possible only if the contract was concluded for a period longer than 6 months, but the notice period was the same regardless of seniority and amounted to only 2 weeks in each case (ex Article 33 of the Labour Code). As it concerns open-ended contracts, the length of the notice period depended on the length of service of the worker with the employer concerned and varied from 2 weeks to 3 months, respectively (ex Article 36 § 1 of the Labour Code).

The CJEU in this case first argued that the term 'employment conditions' included conditions for the termination of a fixed-term contract. The CJEU then indicated that there were no objective reasons that would justify establishing a rigid 2 weeks' notice period for fixed-term contracts. The CJEU decided that Clause 4(1) of the Framework Agreement on fixed-term work concluded on 18 March 1999, which is annexed to Council Directive 1999/70 (later: The Framework Agreement

---

[58] Skupień (2015), p. 87.

[59] Ustawa z dnia 17 grudnia 1998 r. o emeryturach i rentach z Funduszu Ubezpieczeń Społecznych, consolidated version: Dz. U., 2023, item 1251, 1429, 1672.

on fixed-term work) must be interpreted as precluding a national rule, such as that at issue in the main proceedings, which provided that, for the termination of fixed-term contracts of more than six months, a fixed notice period of two weeks may be applied regardless of the length of service of the worker concerned, while the length of the notice period for contracts of indefinite duration is fixed in accordance with the length of service of the worker concerned and may vary from two weeks to three months, where those two categories of workers are in comparable situations.

As a result of this judgment, the Polish Labour Code was modified in order to align the duration of the notice periods in the case of fixed-term contracts with the respective duration in the case of open-ended contracts.[60] Recently, in 2023,[61] an obligation of employers to justify the termination of fixed-term contracts with the notice period was also introduced,[62] that aligns Polish Labour Code with Article 30 of the CFREU (Protection in the event of unjustified dismissal). In the previous state of the law, the employer, when terminating the fixed-term employment contract, was not obliged to indicate the reasons for the dismissal. This made it difficult for the employee to effectively defend their rights in subsequent judicial proceedings. The amendment to the Labour Code preceded the CJEU judgment in the Polish case K.L, in which the CJEU decided that Clause 4 of the Framework Agreement on Fixed-Term Work must be interpreted as precluding national legislation according to which an employer is not required to state, in writing, the reasons for the termination of a fixed-term employment contract with a notice period, although it is bound by such an obligation in the event of termination of an employment contract of indefinite duration.

These legal changes, together with the previous reform aimed at combating the overuse of fixed-term contracts[63] contribute to eliminate inequalities in the legal status of workers employed on the basis of fixed-term contracts in Poland. Hopefully, the legislative changes undertaken under the influence of the EU will diminish the scope of fixed-term employment in Poland. The percentage of fixed-term contracts in overall employment is still high and amounted to 26 % of total employment in 2022.[64]

[60] Cf. Article 36 § 1 of the Labour Code.

[61] Ustawa z dnia 9 marca 2023 r. o zmianie ustawy - Kodeks pracy oraz niektórych innych ustaw, Dz. U. 2023 item 641.

[62] Compare Article 45 § 1 of the Labour Code.

[63] Skupień (2015), pp. 85–96 or Pisarczyk (2012), p. 257 et seq.

[64] Eurostat (2023).

4 Concept of 'Remuneration' Under Article 157 TFUE

The CJEU judgment in Case C-192/18 Commission v. Poland is part of the larger framework of the Court's case law on breach of the rule of law and underminement of judicial independence by the governmental reform of the judiciary in Poland in recent years.[65] However, it is also important for its wide interpretation of the material scope of the principle of equal pay for men and women.[66]

The European Commission has initiated proceedings for infringement of EU law against Poland regarding amendments to national measures providing regulating age of retirement for judges of ordinary courts, judges of the Supreme Court, and of public prosecutors. The statutory retirement age of this group, namely, the age of 67 was lowered by introducing the age of 65 for men and 60 for women. At the same time, the possibility of continuing to carry out the duties of judge of the ordinary courts beyond the newly set age by authorisation of the Minister for Justice was introduced. In this case, the European Commission presented the opinion that the above-mentioned amendments constituted a breach of Article 157 TFEU and Article 5(a)—prohibition of discrimination on grounds of sex in occupational social security schemes and 9(1)(f) of Directive 2006/54—discriminatory measure of the occupation social security scheme, consisting of fixing different retirement ages, as well as Article 19(1), second subparagraph TEU (Effective judicial protection in the fields covered by EU law).

The Court of Justice shared the view of the European Commission. On the one hand, the CJEU declared that, in granting, pursuant to Article 1(26)(b) and (c) of the Law amending the Law on the system of ordinary courts and certain other laws of 12 July 2017,[67] Polish Minister for Justice the right to decide whether or not to authorise judges of ordinary Polish courts to continue to carry out their duties beyond the new retirement age of those judges, as lowered by Article 13(1) of that law, the Republic of Poland has failed to fulfil its obligations under the second subparagraph of Article 19(1) TEU.

On the other hand, the CJEU also declared that, in establishing, by Article 13(1) to (3) of the above mentioned law, a different retirement age for men and women who are judges in ordinary Polish courts and the Sąd Najwyższy (Supreme Court, Poland) or are public prosecutors in Poland, the Republic of Poland has failed to meet its obligations under Article 157 TFEU and Articles 5(a) and 9(1)(f) of Directive 2006/54.

According to Article 7(2) of Directive 2006/54, a pension scheme for public servants falls within the scope of the principle of equal pay if the benefits payable under the scheme are paid to the worker due to his employment relationship with the

[65] Compare CJEU judgment in case C-619/18, Commission v. Poland (Independence of the Supreme Court), ECLI:EU:C:2019:531.

[66] See also Coli (2019).

[67] Ustawa z dnia 12 lipca 2017 r. o zmianie ustawy — Prawo o ustroju sądów powszechnych oraz niektórych innych ustaw, Dz. U. of 2017, item 1452.

public employer, despite the fact that such scheme is part of a general statutory scheme.[68]

The Court of Justice distinguished between pensions for old age and retirement that fell under the material scope of Article 7(1)(a) of Directive 79/7[69] and benefits that should be qualified as 'remuneration' under Article 157(2) TFEU. It clarified the boundary between public social security schemes governed by Directive 79/7,[70] and professional occupational pension schemes governed by Directive 2006/54.

The Court of Justice, relying on its previous case-law[71] explained that a pension which concerns only a particular category of workers, which is directly related to the period of service completed and whose amount is calculated by reference to the final salary, is within the scope of Article 157 TFEU.[72] According to the CJEU, the three pension schemes that the action of the Commission concerns satisfy those conditions with the result that they fall within the material scope of equal treatment in occupational social security schemes (Chapter 2 of Title II of Directive 2006/54).

Furthermore, the Court of Justice did not approve the reasoning of the Polish government explaining that lowering the retirement age for women, judges, or prosecutors to the age of 60 years, namely a decrease by 5 years in comparison to the retirement age for men, could constitute a positive action in favour of women in the labour market. According to the Court, even though Article 157(4) TFEU authorises the Member States to maintain or adopt measures providing for specific advantages in order to prevent or compensate for disadvantages in professional careers, with a view to ensuring full equality between men and women in working life, it cannot be inferred that such a provision permits the setting of such age conditions that differ according to sex. The national measures covered by that provision must, in any case, contribute to helping women conduct their professional life on the same footing as men.[73] Setting for retirement a different age condition based on sex does not compensate for the disadvantages to which the careers of female public servants are exposed by helping these women in their professional life and by providing a remedy for the problems they may encounter in the course of their professional career.[74] The clarification of the concept of 'pay' in the above-mentioned judgment will also be relevant under the Directive (EU) 2023/970 of the European Parliament and of

[68] See also Recital 14 of Directive 2006/54/EC.

[69] Council Directive 79/7/EEC of 19 December 1978 on the progressive implementation of the principle of equal treatment for men and women in matters of social security, *OJ L 6, 10.1.1979, p. 24–25.*

[70] It should be noted, that Article 7(1)(a) of Directive 79/7/EEC provides for the right of Member States to exclude from the directive's scope the question of determination of pensionable age for the purposes of granting old-age and retirement pensions.

[71] Compare judgments: of 26 March 2009, Commission v Greece, C-559/07, EU:C:2009:198, paragraph 42 and the case-law cited, and of 15 January 2019, E.B., C-258/17, EU:C:2019:17, paragraph 46 and the case-law cited.

[72] The CJEU judgment in Case C-192/18, paragraph 60.

[73] The judgment in case C-192/18, paragraph 80.

[74] The CJEU judgment in case C-192/18, paragraph 81.

the Council of 10 May 2023 to strengthen the application of the principle of equal pay for equal work or work of equal value between men and women through pay transparency and enforcement mechanisms.[75]

5 Conclusions

The analysed jurisprudence of the Court of Justice in Polish cases presents a broad interpretation of the EU anti-discrimination provisions strengthening the protection of workers—including those in atypical relationships—against discrimination.

The case law of the Court of Justice has contributed to eliminating from Polish legislation provisions that discriminate against persons employed on a fixed-term basis; or against women holding positions in the judiciary or the prosecution service. It has also limited the scope of freedom to conclude civil law contracts in cases where the refusal to conclude a contract is based on discriminatory grounds. The CJEU also adopted an innovative approach for the protection of people with disabilities in employment and the combat of discriminatory practices by employers. The role of the EU's anti-discrimination legislation and its favourable interpretation by the Court of Justice for working people, irrespective of the legal form of contract binding them with the other party, cannot be overestimated. The prohibition of discrimination had been established by international or national laws before the legal developments of the EU. However, the adoption of anti-discrimination directives in the EU with a whole range of preventive and supportive measures for victims of discrimination provided in these acts, as well as the Court's control over their correct implementation and application in the Member States, is an effective tool to prevent and combat this negative phenomenon. The overview of the Court of Justice rulings in Polish cases illustrates difficulties that are bound with the proper implementation of EU anti-discrimination law in the Member States, as well as with enshrining of good practices in the workplaces. The wide interpretation of EU provisions by the Court of Justice in Polish cases has especially a positive effect on the situation of more vulnerable workers, such as persons with disabilities, workers employed on the basis of temporary or civil law contracts, as well as 'solo' self-employed. The effects of the analysed judgments will extend beyond Polish workplaces and help to better protect workers against discrimination in the EU Member States.

References

Bardach J, Leśniodorski B, Pietrzak M (1998) Historia ustroju i prawa polskiego (History of the Polish political system and law), Warszawa

[75] OJ L 132, 17. 5. 2023, pp. 21–44.

Coli M (2019) The Judgment of the CJEU in Commission v. Poland II (C-192/18): the resurgence of infringement procedures as a tool to enforce the rule of law? Diritti Comparati https://www.diritticomparati.it/judgment-cjeu-commission-v-poland-ii-c-192-18-resurgence-infringement-procedures-tool-enforce-rule-law/. Accessed 30 Oct 2024

Covington (2023) CJEU Recognizes Rights of Self-Employed LGBTIQ Persons in Landmark Judgment, 12 January 2023, https://www.cov.com/en/news-and-insights/news/2023/01/cjeu-recognizes-rights-of-self-employed-lgbtiq-persons-in-landmark-judgment. Accessed 30 Oct 2024

Davies N (2023) Serce Europy (The heart of Europe), 3th edn. Kraków

Encyclopedia Britannica (2024) Partitioned Poland, https://www.britannica.com/place/Poland/Accommodation-with-the-ruling-governments. Accessed 30 Oct 2024

European Union Agency for Fundamental Rights and Council of Europe (2018) Handbook on European non-discrimination law, Luxembourg

Eurostat (2023) Temporary Employment – Statistics, May 2023, https://ec.europa.eu/eurostat/statistics-explained/images/4/4d/Temporary_employment_by_age_and_country_%28in_%25_of_total_employment%2C_2022%29.png. Accessed 30 Oct 2024

Główny Urząd Statystyczny - Statistics Poland (2024) Wykonujący pracę na podstawie umów zlecenia i pokrewnych w Polsce w czerwcu 2023 r. (Persons performing work on the basis of contract of mandate and related contracts in Poland in June 2023), 14 March 2024, https://stat.gov.pl/statystyki-eksperymentalne/kapital-ludzki/wykonujacy-prace-na-podstawie-umow-zlecenia-i-pokrewnych-w-polsce-w-czerwcu-2023-r-,16,2.html. Accessed 30 Oct 2024

Góral Z. (2021) Różne oblicza dyskryminacji w zatrudnieniu – uwagi wstępne (Different faces of discrimination in employment – introductory remarks). In: Carby-Hall JR, Góral Z, Tyc A (eds) Różne oblicza dyskryminacji w zatrudnieniu (Different faces of discrimination in employment), Warszawa

Hajn Z (2024) Zakres i warunki ochrony przed dyskryminacją w zakresie zatrudnienia i pracy w świetle wyroków Trybunału Sprawiedliwości w sprawie Ligebehandlingsnavnet przeciwko HK/Danmark, HK/Privat (C-587/20) oraz w sprawie J. K. przeciwko TP S.A. (C-356/21) [Scope and conditions of protection against discrimination in employment and occupation in the light of the judgments of the Court of Justice in Ligebehandlingsnavnet v HK/Danmark, HK/Privat (C-587/20) and in J.K. v TP S.A. (C-356/21)], Praca i Zabezpieczenie Społeczne No. 5

Halmos S (2023) "It's All Relative?" role of comparison in terms of equality in employment under EU law. In: Carby-Hall JR, Góral Z, Tyc A (eds) Discrimination and Employment Law. International Legal Perspectives, Oxon-New York.

Klimkiewicz L (2011) Wpłaty na Państwowy Fundusz Rehabilitacji Osób Niepełnosprawnych (Payments to the State Fund for Rehabilitation of Persons with Disabilities), Warszawa

Křičková L, Fellerová Palkovská I (2023) Battling the hydra in EU anti-discrimination law: ECJ judgment raises more questions about discrimination against self-employed workers, VerfBlog, 1/31, https://verfassungsblog.de/battling-the-hydra/. Accessed 30 Oct 2024

Kuczyńska H (2022) Odpowiedzialność karna Polskiej Zjednoczonej Partii Robotniczej (PZPR) za tzw. "zbrodnie komunistyczne" (Criminal responsibility of the Polish United Workers' Party (PZPR) for so-called "communist crimes"). In: Grzebyk P (ed) Zbrodnie komunistyczne. Odpowiedzialność państwa oraz jednostek (Communist crimes. Responsibility of the State and of individuals), Warszawa

Leszczyński A (2020) Ludowa historia Polski (People's history of Poland). Warszawa

Ministerstwo Rodziny, Pracy i Polityki Społecznej (2024), Informacja o zatrudnieniu cudzoziemców w Polsce, Warszawa

Mitrus L (2021) Specyfika zakazu dyskryminacji ze względu na niepełnosprawność w prawie pracy Unii Europejskiej (uwagi dotyczące skutków wyroku TSUE w sprawie C-16/19 VL przeciwko Szpitalowi Klinicznemu im. dra J. Babińskiego w Krakowie) [Specific nature of the prohibition of discrimination based on disability under European Union labour law (remarks concerning the effects of the CJEU judgment in case C-16/19 VL v. Szpital Kliniczny im. dra

J. Babińskiego in Kraków)], Praca i Zabezpieczenie Społeczne/Labour and Social Security Journal No. 9

Mrozek J (2019) Przemiany pozycji kobiet w PRL-u – wybrane konteksty (Transitions of Women's Position in the Polish People's Republic – Selected Contexts), Studia Edukacyjne No. 54

Pisarczyk Ł (2012) Fixed-term Employment Contracts in Poland: In Search of Equilibrium between Flexibility and Protection. In: Davulis T, Petrylaitė D (eds) Labour regulation in the 21st century: In Search of Flexibility and Security, Newcastle-upon-Tyne

Quirico O (2024) Implementing international disability law in the european Union. A substantive and procedural appraisal. Oxon-New York

Skupień D (2010) The prohibition of age discrimination in labour relations. In: Petrykowska-Lewaszkiewicz B (ed) Rapports polonais, XVIIIe Congrès international de droit comparé, Washington 25 VII- 1 VIII 2010, Łódź

Skupień D (2015), Reform of the fixed-contract regulations in Poland. In: Morávek J, Pichrt J (eds) Atypická zaměstnání - cesta k vyšší zaměstnanosti?, Praha

Skupień D. (2021), Workplace whistleblower protection in Poland: Current Situation and Perspectives. In: Skupień D (ed) Towards a Better Protection of Workplace Whistleblowers in the Visegrad Countries, France and Slovenia, Łódź-Warszawa

Skupień D (2022) Praca na własny rachunek w ramach Unii Europejskiej w świetle prawa i orzecznictwa (Self-employment in the European Union in the light of legal regulations and case law), Studia z Zakresu Prawa Pracy i Polityki Społecznej, 29(3)

Tyc A (2023) The "Other" discriminatory criteria unregulated in the Polish labour code but clarified by case law. In: Carby-Hall JR, Góral Z, Tyc A (eds) Discrimination and employment law. International legal perspectives, Oxon-New York

Walczak K (2021) Zasada niedyskryminacji w świetle prawa międzynarodowego (MOP) [Principle of non-discrimination under international law (ILO)]. In: Carby-Hall JR, Góral Z, Tyc A (eds) Różne oblicza dyskryminacji w zatrudnieniu [The different faces of discrimination in employment], Warszawa

The Evolution of Polish Antidiscrimination Laws in the Workplace: A Labour Law Perspective in the Context of European Union ('EU') Regulations

Marcin Wujczyk

1 Introduction

Protection against discrimination has evolved in the provisions of the Labour Code since its adoption in 1974. However, it is Poland's accession to the European Union that has had the greatest impact on the evolution of regulations governing non-discrimination in employment relationships. This article aims to show how the evolution of the concept of discrimination has been reflected in the regulations of Polish law. I would like to place particular emphasis in this paper on the relationship between changes in EU regulations and their implementation in the Polish legal order and the change in the perception of the prohibition of discrimination as a tool for the protection of employees.

2 Concepts of Non-Discrimination

The principle of equality and non-discrimination is not uniform in the European Union. This is due to the fact that it has developed over many years in different areas, often producing only partial solutions. The lack of uniformity is also due to the influence on anti-discrimination regulations of the solutions of individual Member States, which differ strongly both in their specific solutions and in the concept of equality and non-discrimination. Finally, it is worth noting that the concept of non-discrimination in EU legislation grew out of efforts to eliminate unequal

M. Wujczyk (✉)
Department of Labour Law and Social Policy, Jagiellonian University, Kraków, Poland
e-mail: marcin.wujczyk@uj.edu.pl

K. Koldinská et al. (eds.), *Labour Law and Social Security Law in Central and Eastern Europe*, European Union and its Neighbours in a Globalized World 26,
https://doi.org/10.1007/978-3-032-04496-9_4

treatment between men and women. This has translated into giving the principle of equal treatment irrespective of gender a special role.

Consequently, it is possible to speak on the basis of treaty regulations of formal and substantive, individual and group equality, as well as equal treatment and equality of results.[1] This division should be overlaid with a prohibition of differentiation on the basis of certain characteristics, namely: sexual orientation, religion, age, disability, race and ethnic origin and gender.

In trying to define the concept of equality and non-discrimination in EU law, one can draw on the division proposed by Ch. McCrudden and S. Prechal.[2] Although the concept has been presented some years ago it still rightly describes approaches to equality. It seems that the CJEU continues to develop and refine equality concepts through case law, building on the foundations described by McCrudden and Prechal. Recent cases like Tesco Stores (C-624/19) from 2021 and BVAEB (C-405/20) from 2022 show the ongoing application and evolution of equality principles in EU jurisprudence. The scope of non-discrimination law has continued to expand in line with the framework described by McCrudden and Prechal.

They distinguished four basic ways of understanding this principle:

(1) equality as an imperative for rational differentiation;
(2) equality as a duty to ensure equal access to specially protected goods;
(3) equality as a prohibition of discrimination on the basis of certain legally protected characteristics;
(4) equality as a duty to actively work towards equal opportunities.

Re (1) above. The first understanding of equality in EU legislation derives from the Aristotelian assumption that one should "treat the same in the same way and different in a different way". The principle of equality allows for differentiation between persons in the same situation but requires that this differentiation is not arbitrary and must instead be reasonably justified. It is therefore not necessary that there are special circumstances justifying a departure from equal treatment, but only that the differentiation can be considered to be justified in the given circumstances.[3] Within the framework of this concept, it is often pointed out that it is also necessary to demonstrate the proportionality of the measures taken to the objective pursued by the provisions introducing the differentiation.[4]

Re (2) above. The second concept of equality focuses on ensuring equality of access to certain goods (e.g. the right to free movement of capital). It plays a role in

---

[1] Śledzińska-Simon (2011), p. 50.

[2] McCrudden and Prechal (2009), pp. 11–50. The concept presented nu these authors has been qand followed uoted in many laters papers, e.g. **"Connecting the Dots, Taking a Stand: Universities, Democracy and Gender Equality Policies"** by Diana Elena Neaga (2024) or **"Gender Inequality and Growth in Europe"** by Stephan Klasen and Anna Minasyan (2017). Also EU bodies follows the division proposed by McCrudden and Prechel, see **"Equality between men and women"** by the European Parliament (2024).

[3] Ibid, p. 12.

[4] Ibid, p. 15.

the framework of the functioning of the internal market and the protection of fundamental rights.[5] Here, the focus is on the equal distribution of goods and less on the characteristics of their recipients. The prohibition of discrimination on the basis of nationality plays a central role in the understanding of equality analysed. In this model, non-domestic goods, services and capital must be treated in the same way as their domestic counterparts.[6]

Re (3) above. According to the third understanding of equality, no distinction must be made on the basis of characteristics considered to be legally protected, which are considered irrelevant or otherwise unacceptable, unless there is a justification for the differentiation. These characteristics are, in particular, nationality, gender, racial and ethnic origin, disability, age, religion or views or, finally, sexual orientation. EU legislation introduces a higher standard of judicial protection in such situations.[7] The prohibition of unequal treatment in this case is not linked to the granting of fundamental rights. Consequently, the order for equal treatment is broad in nature and allows all spheres of life to be enjoyed without discrimination.[8]

Re (4) above. Finally, equality is seen as an obligation to take measures to equalise social opportunities and consequently ensure substantive equality.[9] In this case, it is therefore not sufficient to refrain from actions that are considered discriminatory, but it is necessary both to counteract discrimination that has already occurred and, more importantly, to introduce solutions that prevent discriminatory situations from arising and ensure equality of opportunity for all.

3 Personal Scope of the Prohibition of Discrimination Under EU Law

EU directives on non-discrimination are universal in scope. They apply to both private and public sector employers. It should only be noted that the prohibition of discrimination under EU law applies to all forms of work activity: under employment and non-employment, civil and administrative laws. The prohibition of discrimination also covers the self-employed. In the EU context, an "employer" is the party who *engages* and *manages* the employee and is legally responsible for complying with anti-discrimination rules. Although precise definitions can vary by Member State, the above framework guides interpretation under EU anti-discrimination directives. Covering different types of engagement (including

[5] Bossuyt (1976), pp. 68–69.

[6] Kadelbach (2003), pp. 486–487.

[7] Judgment of the CJ of 9 September 2003 in Case C-25/02 *Katharina Rinke v. Ärztekammer Hamburg*, [2003] ECR, p. I-08349; judgment of the CJ of 14 December 1995 in Case C-444/93 *Ursula Megner and Hildegard Scheffel v. Innungskrankenkasse Vorderpfalz, now Innungskrankenkasse Rheinhessen-Pfalz*, [1995] ECR, p. I-04741.

[8] Śledzińska-Simon (2011), pp. 52–53.

[9] Howard (2008), European Law Journal, no. 14, p. 168.

self-employed) by the anti-discriminations rules is the result of broad understanding of worker under EU laws. The CJEU has consistently held that the term "worker" covers any person who performs services *for and under the direction of another person* (the employer) *in return for remuneration.*

A further differentiation in the personal scope of protection against discrimination under EU law concerns third-country nationals. Directive 2000/78/EC indicates that the prohibition of discrimination should also apply to third-country nationals, but it will not cover their access to employment and occupation.[10] Directive 2000/43/EC excludes all treatment linked to the legal status of the third-country nationals concerned (Article 3(2)). However, this formulation does not warrant a complete exclusion of this group from the protection against discrimination regulated by the Directive. The preamble to Directive 2000/43/EC states that the prohibition of discrimination should also apply to third-country nationals, but does not cover differences of treatment on grounds of nationality and is without prejudice to the provisions governing the entry and residence of third-country nationals and their access to employment and to occupation.[11] By contrast, the protection of third-country nationals is not excluded by Directive 2006/54/EC.

Doubts have arisen as to whether the prohibition of gender discrimination in pay applies only to the prohibition of differentiation between employees or whether it also applies to self-employed persons. Until 2004, under Article 157 TFEU governing the right to equal pay, the Court of Justice did not rule on how the concept of worker used in this provision should be understood. The Court addressed this issue in the *Allonby* case. In that judgment it indicated that, for the purposes of Article 157(1) TFEU, a worker is to be understood as a person who performs services for and under the direction of another person for a certain period of time in return for which he receives remuneration.[12] Referring to the definition of remuneration in Article 157(2) TFEU, it further pointed out that it follows from the definition of this concept that the authors of the Treaty did not intend that the concept of worker within the meaning of Article 157(1) should include independent service providers who do not have a relationship of subordination with the person to whom the services are provided.[13] At the same time, however, the Court pointed out that the formal recognition of a person as self-employed under national law does not change the fact that a person must be classified as a worker within the meaning of Article 157(1) TFEU if his or her independence is fictitious. The judgment broadened the understanding of the term employee by emphasising that in determining how the term is to be understood, it is not so much the formal determination of the nature of the legal relationship between the parties to the legal relationship that is relevant,

---

[10] According to recital 12 of Directive 2000/78/EC, the prohibition of discrimination should also apply to third-country nationals, but it will not cover differences of treatment on grounds of nationality, without prejudice to provisions concerning the entry and residence of third-country nationals and their access to employment and to occupation.

[11] Mitrus (2010).

[12] Judgment of the CJ in Case C-256/01 *Allonby*, paragraph 67.

[13] Ibid, paragraph 68.

but above all its content, which determines the employee nature of the relationship.[14]

4 Substantive Scope of the Prohibition of Discrimination Under EU Law

An analysis of the EU Directives makes it clear that the prohibition of discrimination extends to all working conditions, including hiring and firing.

Protection against discrimination includes, firstly, access to employment (Article 3(1)(a) of Directive 2000/43/EC, Article 3(1)(a) of Directive 2000/78/EC, Article 14(1)(a) of Directive 2006/54/EC). This concept should be understood as both the possibility to take up employment in a given occupation and the employer's obligation to formulate objective selection criteria.

The prohibition of discrimination in access to employment covers not only disadvantages suffered by a particular group because it possesses a legally protected characteristic, but also instances of protection of such a group which lead in practice to a restriction of the rights of those protected. For this reason, the jurisprudence of the Court of Justice considers it inadmissible to prohibit the employment of women in night work (while allowing for certain exceptions in this respect) when men are not prohibited from undertaking this type of work.[15] Also, fear of the possible consequences of pregnancy cannot be a ground for refusing employment. This was confirmed by the Court of Justice in the *Dekker* judgment.[16] In this ruling, it considered cases of indirect discrimination where an employer refused to employ a female candidate (deemed suitable for the job) because of fear of the adverse consequences of employing a pregnant woman. This action was motivated by legislation adopted by the public authorities which equated incapacity for work due to pregnancy and childbirth with incapacity for work due to illness.

The duty to comply with the principle of equal treatment in access to employment also extends to statements made by an employer regarding the conditions under which it makes employment for a position conditional. Therefore, a public declaration by an employer that it will not employ persons with a particular legally protected characteristic (e.g. persons of a certain ethnic or racial origin) has the appearance of discrimination. Moreover, the Court of Justice indicated in one of its judgments that "Such statements being likely strongly to dissuade certain candidates from submitting their candidature and, accordingly, to hinder their access to

---

[14] Barnard (2012), p. 299.

[15] Judgment of the CJ of 25 July 1990 C-345/89 *Criminal proceedings against Alfred Stoeckel*, ECLI:EU:C:1991:324.

[16] Judgment of the CoJ of 8 November 1990 in Case C-177/88 *Elisabeth Johanna Pacifica Dekker v. Stichting Vormingscentrum voor Jong Volwassenen (VJV-Centrum) Plus*, ECLI:EU:C:1990:383.

the labour market. The existence of such direct discrimination is not dependant on the identification of a complainant who claims to have been the victim."[17]

The prohibition of discrimination regulated by EU law also applies to working conditions, including dismissal and pay (Article 3(1)(c) of Directive 2000/43/EC, Article 3(1)(c) of Directive 2000/78/EC, Article 14(1)(c) of Directive 2006/54/EC). These conditions should be understood in a broad sense. In the *Meyers* judgment,[18] the Court of Justice refused to limit the notion of working conditions to those conditions laid down in the employment contract or applied by the employer to the employee's employment. Therefore, in the Court's view, benefits such as family loan must be treated as conditions of employment within the meaning of EU law.

The discrimination rules dictate, inter alia, that there should be no differentiation in the rights of men and women insofar as they perform maternity duties.[19] For this reason, the Court of Justice considered that the child-feeding break should be granted equally to the employee father and mother of young children who are in a comparable situation with regard to the need to care for the child. As noted by the Court, "[…] the evolution of the national legislation and its jurisprudential interpretation has progressively broken the link between the granting of the break known as a 'breastfeeding break' and the biological fact of breastfeeding […] It follows that the break is granted to workers in their capacity as parents of the child. It cannot therefore be regarded as enabling the protection of the biological condition of the woman in the period following pregnancy or the protection of the special relationship between the mother and her child".[20] EU anti-discrimination legislation opposes a national measure which provides that female workers who are mothers and have the status of an employed person may benefit in various forms from a break during the first nine months after the birth of that child, whereas male workers who are fathers and have the same status may benefit from that break only if the mother of the child also has the status of an employed person.

The prohibition of discrimination also covers working conditions in terms of pay. This issue will be considered later in this chapter, hence it should be noted at this point that the particular importance of ensuring equality in the area of equal pay is already reflected in the regulation of this issue in the Treaty on the Functioning of the European Union. According to Article 157(1) TFEU, each Member State shall ensure the application of the principle of equal pay for male and female workers for equal work or work of equal value.

Protection against discrimination under EU equal treatment legislation also applies to the conditions under which an employee is terminated.[21] Termination is

---

[17] Judgment of the CJ in Case C-54/07 *Feryn NV*.

[18] *Judgment* of the CJ of 13 July 1995 in Case C-116/94 *Jennifer Meyers v. Adjudication Officer*, ECLI:EU:C:1995:247.

[19] Szczerba-Zawada (2015), p. 107.

[20] Judgment of the CJEU of 30 September 2010 in Case C-104/09 *Pedro Manuel Roca Álvarez v. Sesa Start España ETT SA*, [2010] ECR I-08661.

[21] CJEU judgment of 12 September 2013 in Case C-614/11 *Niederösterreichische Landes-Landwirtschaftskammer v. Anneliese Kuso*, ECLI:EU:C:2013:544.

understood broadly and includes the termination of the employment relationship between an employee and his or her employer, even as a result of a voluntary redundancy arrangement. The Court of Justice has taken the view that the concept of termination of the employment relationship does not include the non-renewal of a fixed-term employment contract if the period for which it was concluded has ended. However, it can be considered whether discrimination in the employment would come into play in such a case.

In a number of judgments, the Court of Justice has emphasised that it constitutes discrimination to set a different retirement age for women and men if the attainment of that age can be a single ground for dismissal.[22] The Court has stated that "[...] a general policy of dismissal (termination of employment) which involves the dismissal (termination of an employment contract) of an employee (female employee) on the sole ground that she has reached or exceeded the age for the acquisition of pension rights, which is different for men and women under national law, introduces discrimination on grounds of sex".[23]

The prohibition of discrimination in employment also extends to rules for determining the amount of severance pay due on termination of employment. They should not lead to differentiation between employees on the basis of one of the legally protected characteristics. Similarly, it has been recognised that discrimination may occur when differentiating compensation for unjustified termination.[24]

The Directives also refer to the prohibition of discrimination as regards access to all types and levels of vocational guidance, vocational training, further training and retraining of workers, including practical experience (Article 3(1)(b) of Directive 2000/43/EC, Article 3(1)(b) of Directive 2000/78/EC, Article 14(1)(b) of Directive 2006/54/EC). The Court of Justice has adopted a broad understanding of vocational guidance and vocational training in its case law. In the *Gravier* case[25] it indicated that "[...] any form of education which makes it possible to obtain a qualification for a given profession, trade or occupation or which provides the necessary skills for such a profession, trade or occupation is vocational training, whatever the age or level of training of the pupils or students, even if the training programme includes a general education component".

Finally, the anti-discrimination directives apply to all persons in respect of membership and undertaking activities in an organisation of workers or employers or any organisation whose members carry on a particular profession, including the benefits provided by such organisations (Article 3(1)(d) of Directive 2000/43/EC, Article 3(1)(d) of Directive 2000/78/EC, Article 14(1)(d) of Directive 2006/54/EC).

---

[22] Case C-46/07, Commission v. Italy, Case C-559/07, Commission v. Greece (2009).

[23] CJEU judgment in Case -C356/09 *Pensionsversicherungsanstalt v. Christine Kleist.*

[24] Judgment of the CJ of 9 February 1999 in Case C-167/97 *Regina v. Secretary of State for Employment, ex parte Nicole Seymour-Smith and Laura Perez,* [1999] ECR I-00623.

[25] Judgment of the CJ of 13 February 1985 in Case C-293/83 *Françoise Gravier v. City of Liège,* [1985] ECR p. 00593.

5 Exceptions to Non-Discrimination Under EU Law

Exceptions to the prohibition of discrimination have been allowed under EU law. They are divided in the literature into: exceptions to the prohibition of discrimination *stricto sensu* (general and specific), positive action and reasonable accommodation.

Exceptions to the prohibition of discrimination *stricto sensu of* a general nature are provided for indirect discrimination. According to the anti-discrimination directives, indirect discrimination does not exist if a provision, criterion or practice is objectively justified by a legitimate (lawful) aim and the means of achieving that aim are appropriate and necessary (Article 2(2)(b) of Directive 2000/78/EC, Article 2(2)(b) of Directive 2000/43/EC, Article 2(1)(b) of Directive 2006/54/EC). This exception was discussed earlier in this chapter when analysing the concept of indirect discrimination.

Exceptions to the prohibition of discrimination *stricto sensu of* a specific nature include occupational requirements (provided for in Directive 2000/43/EC, Directive 2000/78/EC and Directive 2006/54/EC) and the justification for a difference in treatment on grounds of age (provided for in Directive 2000/78/EC).

As indicated, the *stricto sensu* exceptions to the prohibition of discrimination include those provisions of the Directives which allow for differentiation on the basis of substantial and determining occupational requirements. This exception is provided for in Article 4(1) of Directive 2000/78/EC. According to this provision, Member States may provide that a difference of treatment based on a characteristic related to one of the grounds (unlawful differentiation) does not constitute discrimination where, by reason of the nature of the particular occupational activities or of the context in which they are carried out, a characteristic constitutes a genuine and determining occupational requirement, provided that the objective is legitimate and the requirement is proportionate. A similar provision is included in Article 4 of Directive 2000/43/EC, under which Member States may provide that a difference of treatment which is based on a characteristic related to racial or ethnic origin does not constitute discrimination where, by reason of the nature of the particular occupational activities or of the context in which they are carried out, a characteristic constitutes a genuine and determining occupational requirement, provided that the objective is legitimate and the requirement is proportionate. The application of this exemption to the principle of non-discrimination requires several criteria. First, it must be established whether the difference in treatment is based on a characteristic related to one of the discriminatory criteria. Secondly, it must be assessed whether the characteristic constitutes a substantial and determining occupational requirement. Thirdly, it must be determined whether the requirement is legally justified. Fourthly, it is necessary to verify whether the requirement is proportionate.[26] The current wording of the anti-discrimination directives allows for the application of

[26] Cf. judgment of the CJEU of 12 January 2010 in Case C-229/08 *Colin Wolf v. Stadt Frankfurt am Main*, [2010] ECR, p. I-00001.

the analysed exception to the prohibition of discrimination when the differentiation is made on the basis of a characteristic related to an anti-discrimination criterion and not on the basis of that criterion.[27] This understanding of the exception to the prohibition of discrimination was adopted by the Court of Justice in the case of *Wolf*,[28] in which the subject matter of the decision was the refusal by the authorities to take into consideration Mr Wolf's application for employment in the technical fire service at intermediate level on the ground that he was over the age limit of 30. The Court held that, under Article 4(1) of Directive 2000/78/EC, a difference of treatment based on a characteristic related to one of the grounds listed in Article 1 of Directive 2000/78/EC does not constitute discrimination where, by reason of the nature of the particular occupational activities or of the context in which they are carried out, a characteristic constitutes a genuine and determining occupational requirement, provided that the objective is legitimate and the requirement is proportionate. Consequently, it is not the reason giving rise to the difference in treatment but the characteristic associated with that reason that must constitute a substantial and determining occupational requirement. For that reason, the Court considers that, in order to determine whether the difference in treatment on grounds of age contained in the legislation at issue in the main proceedings is justified, it must be ascertained whether physical fitness constitutes an age-related characteristic and is a substantial and determining occupational requirement in relation to the occupational activity in question or its exercise, provided that the aim pursued by that legislation is legitimate and the requirement is proportionate.[29] A more critical view was expressed by the Court in *Prigge et al. V. Deutsche Lufthansa AG*,[30] which concerned the provisions of a collective agreement providing for the compulsory retirement of pilots over the age of 60. The Court stated that, as far as airline pilots were concerned, it was fundamental that they possessed, among other things, specific physical abilities, as physical deficiencies in this profession could have serious consequences. The ECJ submitted that it was undeniable that these abilities deteriorate with age. It concluded its considerations in this regard by pointing out that the fact of possessing specific physical abilities may be regarded as a "substantial and determining occupational requirement" within the meaning of Article 4(1) of Directive 2000/78/EC in order to exercise the profession of airline pilot and that the possession of such abilities is linked to age. Despite taking this position, the Court found that the provisions of the collective agreement introducing a compulsory retirement for pilots were discriminatory. It was prevailed in this case by the fact

[27] So, for example, in Council Directive 79/7/EEC on the progressive implementation of the principle of equal treatment for men and women in matters of social security.

[28] CJEU judgment in Case C-229/08 *Colin Wolf v. Stadt Frankfurt am Main*.

[29] See also CJEU judgment of 13 September 2011 in Case C-447/09 *Reinhard Prigge and Others v. Deutsche Lufthansa AG*, ECLI:EU:C:2011:573; CJEU judgment of 13 November 2014. in Case C-416/13 *Mario Vital Pérez v Ayuntamiento de Oviedo*, ECLI:EU:C:2014:2371 CJEU judgment of 15 November 2016 in Case C-258/15 *Gorka Salaberria Sorondo v. Academia Vasca de Policía y Emergencias*, ECLI:EU:C:2016:873.

[30] CJEU judgment of 13 September 2011 in Case C-447/09 *Prigge*.

that national and international regulations allow this activity, under certain conditions, until the age of 65. Thus, the requirements under the agreement were considered disproportionate.

With regard to employment in the military services the Court has not ruled out that the need to ensure full operational efficiency may justify the employment of men only.[31] That positions has not changed since then.

A specific exception to the prohibition of discrimination based on professional requirements concerns the professional activities of churches and other public or private organisations whose ethos is based on religion or belief. This is regulated by Article 4(2) of Directive 2000/78/EC, according to which, in the case of occupational activities of churches or other public or private organisations the ethos of which is based on religion or views, a difference of treatment based on a person's religion or views shall not constitute discrimination where, by reason of the nature of these activities or of the context in which they are carried out, a person's religion or views constitute a genuine, legitimate and justified occupational requirement, having regard to the organisation's ethos. The reference to ethics indicates that this exception will not apply to personal beliefs or convictions. Such differential treatment should, as stated in the Directive, respect the constitutional principles and provisions of the Member States and the general principles of Union law and should not be an excuse for discrimination based on other grounds. It is therefore only permissible to treat differently on the grounds of religion or views, but this exception cannot be extended to other criteria for unlawful differentiation, such as gender or ethnic origin.

The anti-discrimination directives provide for exceptions to the prohibition of unequal treatment on grounds of age. Article 6(1) of Directive 2000/78/EC provides that Member States may provide that a difference of treatment on grounds of age does not constitute discrimination if, within the framework of national law, it is objectively and reasonably justified by a legitimate aim, in particular employment, labour market and vocational training policy objectives, and if the means of achieving that aim are appropriate and necessary. Age may therefore be a basis for differentiation provided that three conditions are met:

(1) the purpose of the differential treatment on grounds of age can be objectively and reasonably justified;
(2) the measures to treat differently on the basis of age are in accordance with the legislation;
(3) that measures aimed at differential treatment on grounds of age are appropriate and necessary.

The Court of Justice has indicated that Member States are not required by national legislation to specify exhaustively the aims which may justify the

[31] Judgment of the CJEU of 26 October 1999 in Case C-273/97 *Angela Maria Sirdar v. The Army Board and Secretary of State for Defence*, ECLI:EU:C:1999:523.

exception contained in Article 6(1) of Directive 2000/78/EC.[32] Based on the Court's jurisprudence, it is possible to identify the objectives that justify differentiation between workers on the grounds of age. These will include[33]: protection of acquired rights and legitimate expectations with regard to the evolution of wages in the future[34]; creation of meaningful savings for pensions[35]; protection of employees with significant length of service in the company and support for their reintegration into the labour market, implemented by the severance payment[36]; compensation for the employee's longer experience, which allows him to perform his professional duties better[37]; preventing possible disputes over a worker's ability to perform a job after a certain age[38]; promoting the exchange of experience and innovation by mixing generations of workers[39]; optimising human resources management[40]; ensuring a balance between political, economic, social, demographic or budgetary considerations[41]; promoting access to employment through a better distribution of employment between generations.[42]

With regard to the condition of the legitimacy of the aim of differentiation on grounds of age, the Court of Justice emphasised that, in order to be legitimate, such an aim must be related to employment, labour market or vocational training policy.[43] Therefore, ensuring flight safety was not considered to be a permissible objective. Furthermore, the Court emphasised that a 'legitimate' objective is one which is not of a purely individual nature related to the situation of the employer concerned (e.g. increasing competitiveness or reducing costs), but is in the general interest.[44]

---

[32] Judgment of the CJ of 5 March 2009 in Case C-388/07 *The Queen, on the application of The Incorporated Trustees of the National Council for Ageing (Age Concern England) v. Secretary of State for Business, Enterprise and Regulatory Reform*, ECLI:EU:C:2009:128; judgment of the CJ of 16 October 2007 in Case C-411/05 *Félix Palacios de la Villa v. Cortefiel Servicios SA*, ECLI:EU:C:2007:604.

[33] Cf. in more detail T. Dudek, *Permissible derogations...*, pp. 278–279.

[34] CJEU judgment of C-476/11 in HK Danmark acting on behalf of Glennie Kristensen v Experian A/S.

[35] CJEU judgment of 26 September 2013 in Case C-476/11 *HK Danmark v. Experian A/S*, ECLI:EU:C:2013:590.

[36] CJEU judgment of 12 October 2010 in Case C-499/08 *Ingeniørforeningen i Danmark v. Region Syddanmark*, ECLI:EU:C:2010:600.

[37] Judgment of the CJEU of 8 September 2011 in the joined cases *Sabine Hennigs (C-297/10) v Eisenbahn-Bundesamt and Land Berlin (C-298/10) v. Alexander Mai*, ECLI:EU:C:2011:560.

[38] Judgment of the CJEU of 21 July 2011 in Joined Cases *Gerhard Fuchs (C-159/10) and Peter Köhler (C-160/10) v. Land Hessen*, ECLI:EU:C:2011:508.

[39] Ibid; Gosseries (2014), pp. 75–76.

[40] CJEU judgment in the joined cases of *Gerhard Fuchs (C-159/10) and Peter Köhler (C-160/10).*

[41] CJEU judgment of 12 October 2010 in Case *C-45/09 Gisela Rosenbladt v. Oellerking Gebäudereinigungsges. mbH*, ECLI:EU:C:2010:601.

[42] Judgment of the CJ in Case C-411/05 *Palacios de la Villa.*

[43] CJEU judgment of 10 March 2011 in Case C-109/09 *Deutsche Lufthansa AG v. Gertraud Kumpan*, ECLI:EU:C:2011:129; CJEU judgment of 13 September 2011 in Case C-447/09 *Prigge.*

[44] CJEU judgment in the joined cases of *Gerhard Fuchs (C-159/10) and Peter Köhler (C-160/10).*

With regard to the requirement that differentiation on the basis of age must be appropriate and necessary, the measure in question must not appear unreasonable in terms of the objective pursued and must be based on information whose probative value is assessed by the national court.[45] In addition, consideration must also be given to the consequences that the measure will have for society and the benefits that are associated with it for individuals. The Court indicated that States have a certain degree of discretion in assessing whether a measure is appropriate or necessary to achieve the objective justifying the age-based differentiation. However, that discretion should not be so wide that the protection against discrimination is apparent.[46]

The Court found that measures that cannot be considered appropriate and necessary include provisions that allow, without limitation, fixed-term employment contracts to be concluded with employees over the age of 52[47] or provisions in a collective agreement that set the salary of a public sector contractual employee at the time of his or her employment, within a particular grade, only according to the age of that employee.[48] By contrast, the Court considered appropriate and necessary provisions on automatic termination of employment contracts on the basis of the employee reaching retirement age.[49]

It should be mentioned that Directive 2000/78/EC provided for an exception to the prohibition of age discrimination in matters relating to employee social security schemes. Article 6(2) of Directive 2000/78/EC indicates that Member States may provide that the fixing, for employee social security schemes, of ages for the granting or acquisition of rights to old-age or invalidity benefits, including the fixing, within those schemes, of different ages for employees or groups or categories of employees, and the use, within those schemes, of age criteria for calculating benefits, does not constitute discrimination on the grounds of age, provided that it does not constitute discrimination on the grounds of sex. While this provision should be interpreted restrictively, it applies to all types of social security schemes which cover the risk of old age and invalidity.[50]

A special exception to the prohibition of differentiation on the basis of one discriminatory criterion are so-called positive actions. They aim at identifying and eliminating situations that lead to or perpetuate inequalities in the workplace. The possibility to introduce positive action is provided for in Article 5 of Directive 2000/43/EC, Article 7(1) of Directive 2000/78/EC and Article 3 of Directive 2006/54/EC. The anti-discrimination directives indicate that positive action may continue, without a charge of discriminatory policy, as long as a state of equality of

---

[45] Ibid.

[46] Schlachter (2011), p. 290.

[47] Judgment of the CJ in Case C-144/04 *Mangold*.

[48] CJEU judgment in the joined cases of *Sabine Hennigs (C-297/10) v. Eisenbahn-Bundesamt and Land Berlin (C-298/10)*.

[49] CJEU judgment in Case *C-45/09 Gisela Rosenbladt v. Oellerking Gebäudereinigungsges. mbH*.

[50] CJEU judgment in Case C-476/11 *HK Danmark v. Experian A/S*.

treatment is not achieved with regard to the treatment of persons belonging to the group at which the positive action was directed.[51]

Advocate General Tesauro,[52] referring to the situation of women, distinguished three groups of provisions as a basis for positive action. The first concerns the removal of barriers that create difficulties in the enjoyment of opportunities; this group includes, inter alia, measures to encourage women to participate in upskilling training. The second group aims at sharing family responsibilities and redistributing professional opportunities between women and men (issues of working hours, childcare arrangements, taking into account family responsibilities in social and fiscal policies will come into play here). The third group is made up of measures to remove the effects of permanent and long-term discrimination by giving preferential treatment to a disadvantaged group, in particular through a quota system.

In the *Kalanke* and *Marshall* judgements,[53] the Court of Justice indicated the most relevant principles on which positive action should be implemented in terms of sex discrimination. They pointed out that positive action is a specific measure which, although discriminatory, in fact seeks to eliminate or reduce existing inequalities that may exist in the reality of social life. However, giving automatic priority to a particular group for employment or promotion, in sectors where that group is underrepresented, cannot be considered legitimate. On the other hand, it will be legitimate to give priority to such persons, provided that this is not done automatically, and that the national legislation guarantees to candidates outside this group an objective assessment of their competence, taking into account all the criteria specific to candidates.

Many doubts were raised about the possibility of introducing so-called quota systems as positive action. Such solutions can lead to situations where groups not covered by positive action are disadvantaged. For this reason, the Court considered that, in the case of employers where women are particularly under-represented, in the context of proven under-representation, a limited number of subsidised, affordable childcare places, a limited number of subsidised pre-school places reserved only for women could be regarded as permissible positive action, provided that men caring for children themselves would be entitled to use those places under the same conditions as women.[54] In contrast, the Court held that provisions giving absolute and unconditional priority to certain categories of women could not be justified as positive action.[55]

---

[51] Świątkowski, Świątkowski (2008), p. 142.

[52] Judgment of the CJ of 17 October 1995 in Case C-450/93 *Eckhard Kalanke v. Freie Hansestadt Bremen*, [1995] *ECR, p. I-03051.*

[53] Judgment of the CJ of 2 August 1993 in Case C-217/91 *M. Helen Marshall v. Southampton and South-West Hampshire Area Health Authority*, [1993] ECR, p. I-4367.

[54] Judgment of the CJ of 19 March 2002 in Case C-476/99 *H. Lommers v. Minister van Landbouw, Natuurbeheer en Visserij*, ECLI:EU:C:2002:183.

[55] Judgment of the CJ of 30 September 2004 in Case C-319/03 *Serge Briheche v. Ministre de l'Intérieur, Ministre de l'Éducation nationale and Ministre de la Justice*, ECLI:EU:C:2004:574.

A specific form of positive action is provided for in Article 7(2) of Directive 2000/78/EC. According to this provision, with regard to persons with disabilities, the principle of equal treatment shall not prevent the right of Member States to maintain or adopt provisions on the protection of health and safety at the workplace or measures aimed at creating or maintaining provisions or facilities to protect or promote their integration into the working environment. Such measures include, inter alia, percentage targets for the employment of persons with disabilities between 15 and 50% or the adoption of a code of good practice for the employment of persons with disabilities.[56]

6 Measures of Protection Against Discrimination Under EU Law

In order to ensure the effective implementation of the principle of non-discrimination, the EU legislator has introduced measures to provide protection for those discriminated against or assisting them.

In accordance with Article 15 of Directive 2000/43/EC, Member States shall lay down the rules on penalties applicable to infringements of the national provisions adopted pursuant to this Directive and shall take all measures necessary to ensure that they are implemented. The sanctions, which may compel the payment of compensation to the victim, must be effective, proportionate and dissuasive. An analogous regulation is introduced in Article 17 of Directive 2000/78/EC. A more information how the remedies to ensure compliance with anti-discrimination law should be implemented might be found in Article 17 of Directive 2006/54/EC, which provides that Member States shall ensure that all persons who consider themselves wronged by failure to apply the principle of equal treatment may pursue their claims under this Directive through the courts, possibly with the assistance of other competent authorities, and, if they consider it appropriate, after a conciliation procedure, even after the relationship in which the discrimination is alleged to have occurred has ended.

It should first be noted that EU law has left considerable discretion to Member States as to the type of sanctions to be applied in the event of a breach of the prohibition of discrimination. Sanctions including fines, imprisonment, prohibition to carry out certain activities, non-award of a contract or dissolution of an organisation have been considered acceptable in the literature. However, it is rightly pointed out that such criminal law sanctions may not fulfil the requirements imposed by the Directives, due to the fact that the reverse burden of proof rule, which should be considered unacceptable in criminal law, will not be applied when imposing them. A further limitation of the discretion in defining sanctions for violations of the

[56] Thus Council Recommendation 86/379/EEC of 24 July 1986 on the employment of disabled people in the Community, OJ L 255, 12.12.1986, p. 43.

prohibition of discrimination has been made by the case law of the Court of Justice. The *Johnston* judgment[57] indicates that it is not permissible for Member States to completely exclude judicial review of the implementation of the principle of equal treatment. In the subsequent *Coote* judgment, the Court made it clear that Article 17 of Directive 2006/54/EC, interpreted in the light of the general rule, confers on all persons the right to obtain effective protection before a competent court against actions deemed to infringe the principle of equal treatment.

The most common protective measure introduced to ensure the effectiveness of protection against discrimination is the right to claim compensation by the discriminated person. Based on the wording of the Directives and the position expressed by the Court of Justice, several features can be identified that distinguish discrimination compensation. First, it should fully compensate for the damage suffered. It would seem that where the legal system of a Member State provides for the possibility of claiming compensation for non-material damage, it should also be possible to compensate for this type of non-material damage. Secondly, compensation should not be capped. It would not be a correct implementation of the requirements of EU law to introduce a lump sum amount of compensation or to set an upper limit for such compensation.[58] It should be noted, however, that Directive 2006/54/EC allowed for the possibility of setting a maximum value for the compensation that a person discriminated against may claim, but only in relation to cases in which the employer can prove that the damage suffered by the job applicant as a result of the discrimination consists only in the fact that there was a refusal to consider his/her job application. Thirdly, compensation should constitute an annoyance for the discriminator and thus have a preventive function. The requirement that the compensation must be aggravating is introduced by Article 15 of Directive 2000/43/EC and Article 17 of Directive 2000/78/EC.[59] This rationale has also appeared in some judgments of the Court in the context of the need to deter further discriminatory acts.[60] The amount of compensation should take into account the fact that the value of the amount corresponding to the damage decreases over time. Therefore, the Court considered it necessary to take into account the award of interest based on the provisions of national law.[61]

Effective protection against discrimination under EU law also includes countering instances of retaliation. This was pointed out by the Court of Justice in the already cited *Coote* case, (later explicitly expressed in Article 24 of Directive

---

[57] Judgment of the CJ of 15 May 1986 in Case C-222/84 *Marguerite Johnston v. Chief Constable of the Royal Ulster Constabulary*, [1986] ECR, p. 01651.

[58] Judgment of the CJ in Case C-217/91 *Marshall.*

[59] Case C-30/19, Braathens Regional Aviation (2020), M. Bell, 'Anti-Discrimination Law and the European Union'.

[60] CJ judgment of 10 April 1984 in Case C-14/83 *Sabine von Colson and Elisabeth Kamann v. Land -NordrheinWestfalen*, ECLI:EU:C:1984:153; CJ judgment in Case C-217/91 *Marshall.*

[61] CJ judgment in Case C-217/91 *Marshall*; M. Domańska, *Discrimination against an employee; pursuing compensation claims. Glosa to the SN judgment of 14.02.2013, III PK 31/12*, PiP 2006, z. 2.

54/2006/EC) indicating that Member States are required to introduce into their national legal systems not only such measures as are necessary to protect employees, including those who are employees' representatives, provided for by national legislation or practice, against dismissal or other adverse treatment by the employer in response to a complaint within the undertaking or any legal proceedings aimed at ensuring compliance with the principle of equal treatment.

The anti-discrimination directives also draw attention to the need to cooperate with organisations supporting victims of discrimination (e.g. Article 17(2) of Directive 2006/54/EC).

In addition, some Directives require Member States to establish bodies for the promotion, analysis, monitoring and support of equal treatment of all persons (Article 20 of Directive 2006/54/EC; Article 13 of Directive 2000/43/EC). Taking Directive 2006/54/EC as an example, Member States should ensure that the competences of these bodies include:

(1) Providing independent assistance to victims of discrimination in bringing discrimination complaints;
(2) conducting independent research on discrimination;
(3) publishing independent reports and making recommendations on all problems related to such discrimination;
(4) exchanging available information with the relevant European bodies, such as the future European Institute for Gender Equality.

An important element to facilitate protection against discrimination is the introduction of a reversed burden of proof in discrimination cases. As provided for in Directive 2006/54/EC, Member States should introduce arrangements to ensure that, where persons who consider themselves wronged because the principle of equal treatment has not been applied to them establish, before a court or other competent authority, facts from which it may be presumed that there has been direct or indirect discrimination, it is for the respondent to prove that there has been no breach of the principle of equal treatment (Article 19(1)). The provisions of the Directives, therefore, do not relieve the complainant of the obligation to prove the truth of its allegations. He or she is obliged to prove circumstances which make discrimination plausible. This includes, first and foremost, the obligation to show that he/she has been treated differently from other persons in a similar situation. Only by demonstrating these circumstances does the burden of proof shift. In the practical operation of this solution, it has repeatedly been argued that it is not entirely clear at what point it can be considered that the evidence presented by the discriminated employee shifts the burden of proof to the employer.[62] In some cases, the circumstances of the case will justify shifting the burden of proof to the employer from the outset. These types of cases are referred to as *prima facie* cases.[63] Such

[62] Barnard, p. 307.

[63] Judgment of the CJ of 27 October 1993 in Case C-127/93 *Dr. Pamela Mary Enderby v. Frenchay Health Authority and Secretary of State for Health*, ECLI:EU:C:1993:859.

cases may arise if relevant statistics confirm differential treatment of employees in comparable situations. However, it is necessary to indicate that the case is of this nature.

The employer, on whom the burden of proof has been shifted, must show that the actions alleged to be discriminatory were justified by objective reasons or were not discriminatory. The employer can therefore show that there were special needs of the company or that the differentiation was justified by non-discriminatory factors.[64] By contrast, the Court of Justice has indicated that intent to discriminate or the lack thereof is not subject to examination in evidence.

7 The Origins of the Explicit Prohibition of Discrimination in Polish Domestic Law

By virtue of the Act of 2 February 1996 amending the Labour Code and certain acts, the preamble, which at that time was already a relic of the previous regime, was deleted from the Code. At the same time, the catalogue of basic principles of labour law was expanded by adding the provisions of Articles 11(1)–11(3) in the first section. Thus, it explicitly obliged the employer to respect the dignity and other personal goods of the employee. The employee's dignity is undoubtedly the source of his/her numerous rights. The reference to this value in the labour legislation has clearly emphasised that certain behaviours of the employer, e.g. unequal treatment, harassment, discrimination, may violate the employee's dignity. Article 11(2) of the Labour Code introduced the principle of equal treatment of employees in employment relations. In particular, as in Article 33 of the Constitution of the Republic of Poland, emphasis was placed on equal treatment of women and men. At the same time, Article 11(3) of the Labour Code enunciated the prohibition of discrimination, which initially included explicitly the criteria of gender, age, disability, race, nationality, beliefs, especially political or religious beliefs, and trade union membership, but it should be emphasised that this was already an open catalogue at that time.

These provisions were based on the concept of Equality before the Law, described above. They emphasised that there should be no differentiation between employees on the basis of gender or other criteria for prohibited differentiation.

---

[64] Judgment of the CJ of 26 June 2001 in Case C-381/99 *Susanna Brunnhofer v. Bank der österreichischen Postsparkasse AG*, ECLI:EU:C:2001:358.

8 Development of Polish Antidiscrimination Laws During Preparation for Membership in EU Structures

The next stage in the development of anti-discrimination legislation came in the first half of the 2000s, when Poland was preparing to sign the Accession Treaty in order to join the EU. The Act of 24 August 2001 amending the Labour Code and certain other acts introduced a chapter to the Code entitled 'Equal treatment of women and men'. This was in response to the requirements set out in the National Programme of Preparation for Membership in the European Union for 2000–2002. The purpose of the amendment to the Labour Code was to implement the gender equality standard set by the provisions of: Directive 75/117/EEC on the approximation of the laws of the Member States relating to the application of the principle of equal pay for men and women; Directive 76/207/EEC; Directive 92/85/EEC on the introduction of measures to encourage improvements in the safety and health at work of pregnant workers and workers who have recently given birth or are breastfeeding; Directive 97/80/EC on the burden of proof in cases of discrimination based on sex; Directive 96/34/EC on the framework agreement on parental leave concluded by UNICE, CEEP and the ETUC.

The provisions introduced in the Labour Code established the obligation to treat women and men equally in all aspects of employment. This obligation was extended to the stage of establishment of the employment relationship, changes in its content, access to promotion and training, and the stage of termination of the relationship. Moreover, the wording of Articles 11(2)–11(3) was amended to cover labour in general and not just employment relationships, thus broadening the scope of the principles. The nullity, by operation of law, of provisions of collective bargaining agreements and other acts of labour law based on the law, as well as of employment contracts that violate the principle of equal treatment of representatives of both sexes, was also adopted. For the first time, the concept of indirect discrimination was introduced into the Code. In addition, an information obligation was imposed on the employer towards employees regarding the provisions on the principle of equal treatment of women and men in employment. A right to compensation for breaches of the principle of equal treatment between men and women in an amount equal to at least the minimum wage and no more than six times that wage was also provided for. For fuller protection, the prohibition of retaliation against an employee who exercises anti-discrimination rights is also regulated.[65]

The incomplete transposition of the Directives in 2001 and the adoption of several new acts by the EU bodies in the meantime made it necessary for the Polish legislator to adopt another act—the Act of 14 November 2003 amending the Act—Labour Code and some other acts. This extended the catalogue of discriminatory criteria set out in Article 18(3a) § 1 of the Labour Code to include age, disability,

[65] Koutrakos (2003), Modern Law Review, vol. 66, p. 765.

race, religion, nationality, political beliefs, trade union membership, ethnic origin, religion, sexual orientation (analogously, the catalogue set out in Article 11(3) of the Labour Code was also extended). Thus, the provisions of Chapter IIa of Section One were extended to equal treatment in general, not only in the context of gender (this change was reflected in the rewording of the name of the chapter). The same Act defined direct discrimination and modified the definition of indirect discrimination. The original definition of indirect discrimination indicated that it existed "when there are disparities in terms and conditions of employment to the disadvantage of all or a significant number of employees of one sex, if they cannot be objectively justified on grounds other than sex." In the amended legislation, the definition was already more expansive: "Indirect discrimination exists where, as a result of an apparently neutral provision, criterion applied or action taken, there is a disproportion in terms of conditions of employment to the disadvantage of all or a significant number of employees belonging to a group distinguished on one or more of the grounds referred to in § 1, if the disproportion cannot be justified on other objective grounds. First of all, indirect discrimination ceased to refer exclusively to cases of gender-based differentiation. Secondly, its scope of application has been broadened by indicating that it can be caused not only by a specific provision, but also by an operating practice. The legislation also introduced an exception for employment in churches and trade unions and organisations whose purpose is directly related to religion or beliefs.

Importantly, the employer's duty to prevent discrimination in employment is explicitly established. This last element should be considered particularly important. It shows a shift from viewing the prohibition of discrimination as an obligation to refrain from unjustified differentiation between employees to taking proactive action to eliminate instances of non-discrimination. It is thus a manifestation of a shift towards a conception of the prohibition of discrimination understood as an obligation to ensure equality of access to specially protected goods.[66]

The sources of anti-discrimination law in employment, apart from the Labour Code and the general provisions of the Polish Constitution, should be sought in at least a few special laws. First of all, it is worth mentioning the Act of 9 July 2003 on the employment of temporary workers. This act introduces a prohibition of less favourable treatment of temporary employees in comparison with regular employees directly employed by the user employer. The prohibition does not apply to access to training to improve professional qualifications organised by the user employer if the temporary worker has been working for that user employer for less than six weeks. The Act provides for the right to compensation from the temporary employment agency in the event of violation of the said prohibition by the user employer, under the rules set out in the Labour Code.

[66] Dudek (2015), p. 270.

9 Changes Introduced in Antidiscrimination Law After Poland's Accession to the EU

A new premise prohibiting discrimination was introduced into the Labour Code by an amendment in the form of the Act of 24 August 2007 amending the Act - Labour Code and certain other acts, which introduced the institution of telework into the Polish legal order. The Act prohibited treating a teleworker less favourably than a regular employee and any discrimination on the grounds of performing or refusing to undertake telework. The telework provisions have now been repealed. As a side note, it should be noted that an analogous regulation, with regard to the remote employee, was introduced by the Act of 1 December 2022 amending the Act - Labour Code and certain other acts.[67]

The Polish legislator returned to the process of implementation of EU anti-discrimination legislation in 2008, when the European Commission accused Poland of improper transposition of several directives. By means of the Act of 21 November 2008 amending the Act—Labour Code, changes were made to the definitions of indirect discrimination, harassment and sexual harassment. These definitions were made more specific, giving them wording that is still valid today. In addition, a prohibition of negative consequences for an employee who submits to or opposes harassment and sexual harassment was introduced. With regard to the latter, it was pointed out that harassment is only an action that is unwelcome in nature; it was also stressed that in order to speak of harassment, it is not enough to merely violate dignity but it is also necessary to "violate the employee's dignity and create an intimidating, hostile, degrading, humiliating or derogatory atmosphere towards him/her."

The scope of protection for an employee exercising his or her rights for breach of the principle of equal treatment against him or her and the scope of protection for an employee who provides support to an employee exercising such rights has also been clarified. In particular, it was pointed out that the protection includes not only the prohibition of termination or unfavourable treatment but also "must not result in any negative consequences for the employee". The same amendment provided an employee returning from maternity leave with the right to take up a job in the same or an equivalent position.

The Act of 3 December 2010 on the Implementation of Certain Provisions of the European Union on Equal Treatment incorporated anti-discrimination provisions into the provisions of the Act of 27 August 1997 on Professional and Social Rehabilitation and Employment of Persons with Disabilities. Pursuant to these regulations, an employer is obliged to provide necessary reasonable accommodation to a disabled person who is in an employment relationship with the employer, participating in the recruitment process or undergoing a training, internship, vocational preparation or apprenticeship or graduate training. These reasonable accommodations consist of making the necessary changes or adjustments to the specific needs notified to the employer as a result of the disability, provided that making such

---

[67] Górnicz-Mulcahy (2016), MPP, No. 9.

changes or adjustments would not result in a disproportionate burden being imposed on the employer. Failure to make such reasonable accommodation is considered a breach of the principle of equal treatment in employment within the meaning of the Labour Code.

The principle of equal treatment in employment was also expressed in the provisions of the Act of 20 April 2004 on promotion of employment and labour market institutions, which replaced the previously binding Act of 14 December 1994 on employment and counteracting unemployment. In the case of this Act, it was also the Equality Act that introduced the provision enshrining the principle of equal treatment in employment, however, it should be noted that individual institutions regulated by the Act already included the prohibition of discrimination in their wording before the 2010 amendment. We are talking, for example, about job placement services, vocational guidance or the organisation of training provided by labour offices. Interestingly, in the case of the various services described in the Act, the legislator provided for different discriminatory criteria and within closed catalogues, i.e. differently than in the general regulations of the Labour Code.[68]

In 2011, a further amendment was made in an attempt to clarify the principles of the exception to the prohibition of discrimination in respect of religion and beliefs. To a large extent, this premise was narrowed, indicating that it does not constitute a violation of the principle of equal treatment for churches and other religious associations, as well as organisations whose ethos is based on religion, beliefs or worldview, to restrict access to employment, on the basis of religion, beliefs or worldview if the nature or character of the exercise of the activities of churches and other religious associations and organisations results in **religion, beliefs or worldview being a genuine and determining occupational requirement of the employee, proportionate to the achievement of the legitimate objective of differentiating the situation of that person**; In view of the previous phrase that religion should constitute a substantial, legitimate and justifiable occupational requirement, this represented a narrowing of the applicability of this condition. At the same time, it also added that the exception justifies requiring employees to act in good faith and loyalty to the ethics of a church, other religious association and organisations whose ethics are based on religion, beliefs or worldview.[69]

In 2019, the prohibition of discrimination was *de facto* aligned with the prohibition of unequal treatment by introducing an open catalogue of grounds for discrimination. This was a very significant change that completely altered the concept of discrimination. *De facto*, almost any unequal treatment in the absence of an objective justification started to be treated as a discriminatory action. This was undoubtedly the moment when it could be considered that Polish legislation started to treat this obligation as a duty to actively work towards equal opportunities. Another step in this direction was the addition, in 2023, of the right to claim compensation for discrimination by employees who, when exercising their rights under the

[68] Szabłowska-Juckiewicz (2019), pp. 41–71.

[69] Babińska (2011) PiZS, no. 3; Gromaszek (2011), in: Niedbała (ed.).

prohibition of discrimination or assisting them, encountered retaliatory actions. In the same year, the *de facto* situation of fixed-term and permanent contract employees was equalised.

The above was the result of the implementation of the following into Polish law: Directive (EU) 2019/1152 of the European Parliament and of the Council of 20 June 2019 on transparent and predictable working conditions in the European Union (Official Journal of the EU L 186 of 11.07.2019, p. 105), and Directive (EU) 2019/1158 of the European Parliament and of the Council of 20 June 2019 on work-life balance for parents and carers and repealing Council Directive 2010/18/EU (Official Journal of the EU L 188 of 12.07.2019, p. 79).

10 Incompatibility of Polish Anti-Discrimination Regulations with the EU Standards

The assessment of the implementation of EU law into the Polish national order is not unequivocal.[70]

For the most part, EU regulations on discrimination in employment have been implemented into Polish law. However, certain issues raise doubts. Firstly, it should be noted that Article 18^{3a} § 3 of the Labour Code indicates that unequal treatment can be said to exist if an employee is treated less favourably than other employees. Meanwhile, EU law assumes that for discrimination to be recognised, it is sufficient for inferior treatment to be established in relation to another (one) person. At the same time, it is worth noting that in judicial practice the plural used in Article 18^{3a} § 3 of the Labour Code is not considered binding.[71]

The Polish legislation also recognises that for direct discrimination it is sufficient that an employee may be treated less favourably. At the same time, however, the Polish legislator did not take into account that part of the EU definition, from which it follows that discrimination occurs when a person is treated less favourably than another person in a comparable situation is, has been or would be treated because of a specific protected characteristic. Thus, this may lead to the view that, for discrimination to be deemed to have occurred, a sufficient basis will be a situation of potential differential treatment of an employee which has not yet occurred, but which the employee believes may soon occur.[72]

The regulation of the issue of shifting the burden of proof on the employer is also questionable. The Labour Code uses the formula: "unless the employer proves that it was motivated by objective reasons". Such a general formulation of the key issue of procedural facilitation in discrimination proceedings for EU directives may result in a lower level of protection than required by EU law. These concerns are

[70] Mitrus (2006); S. Samol (2011) in: Niedbala (Ed.).

[71] Boruta (2004), *MPP*, no. 2.

[72] Kędziora et al. (2018), in: Śmiszek (Ed.), pp. 27–28.

confirmed by some court decisions in which the issue of shifting the burden of proof is not adequately addressed.

One may also have doubts as to the proper implementation of the regulations concerning the prohibition of discrimination in remuneration. Indeed, Article 18^{3c} of the Labour Code, which refers to this issue, does not indicate that the prohibition of unequal treatment in remuneration arising from this provision applies when the differentiation is based on one of the legally protected characteristics. While this is the prevailing position, the issue is worth clarifying.

Finally, doubts arising in the context of regulating the right to compensation for violation of the prohibition of discrimination should be highlighted. Despite the amendment of Article 18^{3d} of the Labour Code, which regulates this issue, it is still not clear from it that compensation, as required by EU regulations, should be effective, proportionate and dissuasive. There are also doubts as to what type of losses such compensation should cover (only material or also non-material).

It is worth noting that the Polish legislator has decided, unlike the EU legislator, to formulate an open catalogue of grounds for unlawful differentiation. The level of protection is thus broader than that resulting from the anti-discrimination directives. It may be doubted whether such a solution does not distort the purpose for which anti-discrimination legislation was established, i.e. sanctioning and eliminating the most socially unacceptable cases of differentiation, and thus educating society in respect for other social groups.

According to Article 2(2)(c) of Directive 2006/54, discrimination on grounds of sex includes "any less favourable treatment of a woman related to pregnancy or maternity leave within the meaning of Directive 92/85/EEC". As noted in recital 23, "unfavourable treatment of a woman related to pregnancy or maternity constitutes direct discrimination on grounds of sex", a consequence of the view expressed by the CJEU in the Dekker judgment. Adopting this understanding of unequal treatment on the grounds of maternity allows one to conclude that, in such a case, the comparison with a so-called comparator should be abandoned, even though it is a structural element of direct discrimination. This specificity is somewhat noted by the Implementation Act in Article 12(1), stating that in the event of unequal treatment in connection with pregnancy or parental rights, claims under the Act are available. Nevertheless, the onus is on the practice of applying the law to properly interpret the gender condition for unequal treatment on the grounds of maternity.

It should be pointed out, moreover, that, with regard to the scope in question, Directive 2006/54 pays particular attention in Article 4 to the principle of equal pay for equal work or work of equal value. This is in fact a reference to Article 157(1) of the Treaty on the Functioning of the European Union, according to which 'each Member State shall ensure the application of the principle of equal pay for male and female workers for equal work or work of equal value'. This principle has been transposed into the Polish national legislation through Article 183c §1 of the Labour Code granting employees the right to equal pay for equal work or work of equal value. The personal scope of the Polish legislation may raise doubts. Due to the location of the right to equal remuneration for equal work or work of equal value in the Labour Code, it is only granted to employees within the meaning of Article 2 of the Labour Code, i.e. persons employed on the basis of an employment contract, appointment, election, nomination or cooperative employment contract. The problem in this case is the concept of employee, which is autonomous in EU law. According to the jurisprudence of the CJEU, an employee is any person who performs actual and effective work, with the exception of what may be considered marginal and ancillary work, for a certain period of time for and under the direction of another person, for which he or she receives remuneration. This means that, in the reality of the Polish labour market, some persons providing work on the basis of civil law contracts may have the status of an employee in the EU context, which is what the equal treatment provisions are, even if they are not entitled to it under national law.

The analysis of the provisions of the Implementation Act and the Labour Code in the light of the secondary legislation indicated at the beginning shows that, in principle, the Polish legislator has correctly implemented the forms of unequal treatment. Nevertheless, several specific remarks should be made in this regard. Firstly, in the definition of direct discrimination in Article 183a §3 of the Labour Code, an erroneous hypothetical comparative perspective was adopted in connection with the phrase "(…) or could be treated in a comparable situation less favourably than other employees", while the Directives in the area of equal treatment use the term "(…) or another person would be treated in a comparable situation". This apparent error has been recognised in the case law of the national courts, which, despite the wording of the national provision, interpret the concept of direct discrimination in accordance with the terminology used in the Directives. In connection with this approach to the interpretation of Article 183a §3 of the Labour Code, there can therefore be no accusation of incorrect transposition of the relevant Directives into the national legal order.

Secondly, it is noteworthy that the definition of indirect discrimination in Article 183a §4 of the Labour Code refers to a particularly unfavourable situation "in relation to all or a significant number of employees belonging to a group distinguished on the basis of one or more" characteristics, whereas the directives relating to the sphere of employment only refer to a particularly unfavourable situation for persons distinguished on the basis of a given characteristic without establishing, unlike in Article 183a §4 of the Labour Code, an appropriate proportion. However, the wording of the quoted provision seems to be a consequence of the interpretation adopted by the CJEU.

11 Concluding Remarks

In conclusion, it should be stressed that the system of anti-discrimination law in employment in force in Poland is extensive and heterogeneous. We find in it both norms of national law, partially codified and contained in special laws, as well as norms having their source in international obligations. At this point it is worth noting that EU legislation has had the greatest impact on the shape of Polish anti-discrimination law. To illustrate this phenomenon, one can point to Directive (EU) 2023/970 of the European Parliament and of the Council of 10 May 2023, which reinforces the principle of equal pay for men and women. Despite such a long tradition of this principle in the international, European and Polish systems, Poland will have to implement new rules related to transparency and enforcement mechanisms of this principle in the coming years precisely because of the activity of the EU legislator.

References

Babińska R (2011) Measures of individual legal protection against discrimination in employment. PiZS, no. 3

Barnard C (2012) EU employment law. Oxford, Oxford University Press, p 299

Boruta I (2004) Prohibition of discrimination in employment - new concepts. PiZS, no. 2

Bossuyt M (1976) L'interdiction de la discrimination dans le droit international des droits de l'homme. Establissements Emile, Bruxelles

Dudek T (2015) Permissible derogations from the prohibition of discrimination in EU law. In: Szczerba-Zawada A, Zawidzka-Łojek A (eds) Anti-discrimination Law of the European Union., WuroPrawo, Warsaw

Górnicz-Mulcahy A (2016) The transfer of a workplace to another employer and the principle of equal pay treatment in the light of Supreme Court case law. MPP, no. 9

Gosseries A (2014) What makes age discrimination special? A philosophical look at the ECJ case law. Netherlands J Legal Philosophy 43(1)

Gromaszek M (2011) Controversies regarding compensation for violations of the principle of equal treatment in employment. In: Niedbała Z (ed) Law on discrimination in social, economic, and political life, Difin, Warsaw

Howard E (2008) The European year of equal opportunities for all-2007: is the EU moving away from a formal idea of equality? Eur Law J 14

Kadelbach S (2003) Union citizenship. Jean Monnet Working Paper

Kędziora K, Mazurczak A, Śmiszek K (2018) The EU prohibition of discrimination and polish law: an analysis of anti-discrimination provisions in the practice of polish courts. In: Śmiszek K (ed), Difin, Warsaw

Koutrakos P (2003) How far is far enough? EC law and the organisation of the armed forces after Dory. Mod Law Rev 66

McCrudden Ch, Prechal S (2009) The concepts of equality and non-discrimination in Europe: a practical approach. EU, Brussels

Mitrus L (2006) The impact of community regulations on polish labour law, Zakamycze, Krakow

Mitrus L (2010). Equal treatment (prohibition of discrimination) in employment. In: Hajna Z (ed) System of EU law, vol. 15. Freedom of Movement for Workers within the European Union., C.H. Beck, Warsaw

Samol, S. (2011). Discrimination in employment in Poland in the light of EU regulations. In: Niedbała Z (ed) Law on discrimination in social, economic, and political life., Difin, Warsaw

Schlachter M (2011) Mandatory retirement and age discrimination under EU law. Int J Comp Labour Law Ind Relat 27(3)

Śledzińska-Simon A (2011) The principle of equality and non-discrimination in EU law. Studia BAS 2:47

Świątkowski AM (2008) Migrant workers' right to equal treatment. Pol Społ 11–12

Szabłowska-Juckiewicz M (2019) Employer's liability for violations of the principle of equal treatment, Wolters Kluwer, Warsaw

Szczerba-Zawada A (2015) Areas covered by the prohibition of discrimination in European Union law. In: Szczerba-Zawada A, Zawidzka-Łojek A (eds) Anti-discrimination Law of the European Union., EuroPrawo, Warsaw

Maternity and Parental Leave Management as a Tool for Work-Life Balance

Lucie Matějka Řehořová

1 EU Legislation on Work-Life Balance

Over the years it's become quite clear, that work-life balance is one of the key priorities of the European Union. The EU legislation is based in particular on the Charter of Fundamental Rights of the European Union (specially Article 23 and 33, which govern equality between men and women and protection of the family). Work-life balance is also one of the principle of the European Pillar of Social Rights.[1]

To further implement the Pillar principles the Council adopted new directive on work life balance: Directive (EU) 2019/1158 of the European Parliament and of the Council of 20 June 2019 on work-life balance for parents and carers and repealing Council Directive 2010/18/EU (Work-life balance Directive, WLB Directive). The new rules are set in addition to the rights under Directive 92/85/EEC of 19 October 1992 on the introduction of measures to encourage improvements in the safety and health at work of pregnant workers and workers who have recently given birth or are breastfeeding (Directive 92/85) and it completes the rules laid down by the Directive (EU) 2019/1152 of the European Parliament and of the Council of 20 June 2019 on

[1] While not legally binding, the European Pillar of Social Rights sets out 20 principles, including several relevant to work-life balance: **Principle 2**: Gender equality; **Principle 9**: Work-life balance, emphasizing rights to parental leave and flexible working arrangements; and **Principle 10**: Fair working conditions, including adequate rest periods and a balance between work and private life.

L. Matějka Řehořová (✉)
Charles University, Faculty of Law, Labour Law and Social Security Law Department, Prague, Czech Republic
e-mail: rehorol@prf.cuni.cz

K. Koldinská et al. (eds.), *Labour Law and Social Security Law in Central and Eastern Europe*, European Union and its Neighbours in a Globalized World 26,
https://doi.org/10.1007/978-3-032-04496-9_5

transparent and predictable working conditions in the European Union (Directive on Transparent and Predictable Working Conditions, TPWC Directive).

The WLB Directive was based on the following figures:

- the overall employment rate for women is still 11.6% lower than for men;
- 31,5% of working women work part-time, compared to 8.2% of working men;
- just over 50% of women work full-time, compared with 71.2% of men;
- almost 20% of economically inactive women are driven to their choice by caring responsibilities, compared to less than 2% of men.[2]

Even though the equality between men and women is a fundamental principle of the EU, across European Union women remain considerably underrepresented in the labour market and in management. In particular, this new initiative seeks to promote a more equitable distribution of caregiving responsibilities between women and men. The general objectives of the WLB Directive are to ensure the application of the principle of equal opportunities between women and men in the labour market and equal treatment in the workplace; and to enable parents and persons with caring responsibilities to better reconcile their work and caring responsibilities.

Several other EU legal instruments complement the Work-Life Balance Directive to support the reconciliation of work and personal life. These legal frameworks address related aspects such as working time, gender equality, and non-discrimination. Some of the key legal instruments are as follows:

- Directive 2003/88/EC of the European Parliament and of the Council of 4 November 2003 concerning certain aspects of the organization of working time (Working Time Directive)—establishes minimum safety and health requirements for working hours to ensure a better balance between work and personal life;
- Directive 2006/54/EC of the European Parliament and of the Council of 5 July 2006 on the implementation of the principle of equal opportunities and equal treatment of men and women in matters of employment and occupation (Equal Treatment Directive)—promotes gender equality in employment and occupation and supports work-life balance by ensuring equal opportunities and treatment for men and women in accessing jobs, training, and promotions; and by prohibiting discrimination on grounds of sex, which could include unequal access to flexible work arrangements.
- Directive 2010/18/EU of 8 March 2010 implementing the revised Framework Agreement on parental leave (Parental Leave Directive)—even though it was replaced by the Work-Life Balance Directive it is still relevant for historical context, when it provided the framework for parental leave and established the principle of non-transferable leave for both parents.
- Directive 89/391/EEC of 12 June 1989 on the introduction of measures to encourage improvements in the safety and health of workers at work (Health and Safety Framework Directive)—ensures that employers take measures to adapt

[2] Available on: https://www.consilium.europa.eu/en/policies/work-life-balance/.

working conditions to the needs of employees, including those with family responsibilities; and encourages workplace adaptations to reduce stress and improve mental health, indirectly supporting work-life balance.
- Regulation (EU) 2021/241 of the European Parliament and of the Council of 12 February 2021 establishing the Recovery and Resilience Facility (Recovery and Resilience Facility)—is part of the EU's NextGenerationEU program, this regulation includes funding and reforms that indirectly support work-life balance, such as: investments in childcare and elderly care facilities and programs to improve gender equality in the labour market.
- Council Recommendation of 22 May 2019 on High-Quality Early Childhood Education and Care Systems—promotes access to childcare to enable parents, especially women, to return to work; and encourages Member States to invest in infrastructure and support for early childhood education, easing the burden of caregiving on parents.
- Directive 2022/2041 of the European Parliament and of the Council of 19 October 2022 on adequate minimum wages in the European Union (Adequate Minimum Wages Directive)—supports work-life balance indirectly by improving economic stability for workers, ensuring they can reduce excessive working hours and prioritize family responsibilities.

2 Reconciliation Instruments

Motherhood and childcare are major precarization factors in the career path of women. Typical measures to support maternity and parental leave and to help achieving work-life balance of employees include support for childcare in the form of allowances or the establishment of a company nursery, adjusting working hours and allowing part-time work, maintaining contact with the parent, e.g. by allowing participation in educational events, teambuilding, etc.

In general the tools for reconciliation are different:

- part-time jobs;
- flexible working hours (other working time arrangements - compressed week);
- job sharing;
- teleworking;
- atypical forms of employment;
- maternity and parental leave management.

These measures are of great importance because in the Czech Republic women leave the labour market for an exceptionally long time and returning to work could therefore be a lot more difficult and stressful for both employees and employers.

Even though the above stated efforts of the European Union is to ensure equal opportunities for men and women and a better reconciliation of work and family life, it is clear that there are major differences between Member States considering access to maternity and parental leave, which is of course based, among other things, on the historical experiences, legacy and development of the particular country.

3 Maternity Leave and Parental Leave in the Czech Republic

3.1 Development of the Parental Support

Historically, the financial security of the mother in the Czech Republic was realized through the maternity allowance (the terminology reflected the beneficiary and the contemporary pattern of childcare—the mother cares, therefore the maternity allowance). The right to a maternity allowance was based on similar conditions as today—a woman had to have worked at least 270 days in the last 2 years. The support period lasted one year, after which the woman returned to work and the child was placed in a nursery.[3]

Two years after the law was adopted, the original law was repealed and replaced by Act No. 107/1971 Coll., which extended the length of the maternity allowance support period to two years. In the 1980s, the maternity allowance was then extended to 3 years and the amount of the allowance was gradually increased in the following years.

The first post-revolutionary legislation changed the terminology and introduced the concept of parental allowance, thus opening up the possibility for fathers to care for their children personally for a full day and in a proper manner, while being entitled to material security from the state. The upper limit for the parental allowance was set up to 3 years of age of the child (a seven-year support period was set in the case of caring for a severely disabled child who required extraordinary care). Parents were allowed to work (with a certain upper limit on the income limit for eligibility to receive the allowance).[4]

In 1995, the Act on State Social Support[5] was adopted, which newly extended the support period for parental allowance to 4 years of age. The amount of the allowance was derived from the parent's subsistence level. One of the more significant amendments in 2006 fundamentally changed the calculation of parental allowance—it was based on the average monthly wage in the non-business sector (calculated as 40% of the average wage). Relatively soon afterwards, another conceptual amendment to the State Social Support Act was adopted, which exempted the

[3] Act No. 154/1969 Coll., on Maternity Allowance.

[4] Act No. 382/1990 Coll., on Parental Allowance.

[5] Act No. 117/1995 Coll., on State Social Support (hereinafter referred to as the State Social Support Act).

parental allowance from being linked to other nominal variables and established the exact amount of the parental allowance, including three rates of drawdown.[6]

Currently, we distinguish 2 basic forms of benefits through which a parent is provided for the period of childcare in the Czech Republic: maternity allowance and parental allowance.[7] Both of these benefits are based on different social security principles; the persons entitled to them, the method of drawing them and their amount differ.

3.2 Maternity Leave and Maternity Allowance in the Czech Republic

According to the Labour Code[8] maternity leave in the Czech Republic is reserved for women employees in connection with advanced pregnancy, childbirth and care of the newborn child. The father may only take paternity leave (2 weeks) or parental leave.

Maternity leave shall be granted to a female employee for a period of 28 weeks. If the employee gives birth to 2 or more children at the same time (multiple birth), she is entitled to maternity leave for 37 weeks. Czech legislation does not favour single mothers when taking maternity leave, nor does it take into account 3 or more births. The employer is obliged to provide the employee with excused leave without wage or salary compensation. During the period of maternity leave, the employee is usually covered by a sickness insurance benefit, specifically maternity allowance, depending on the fulfilment of the conditions laid down in the social security legislation.

Maternity allowance is one of the sickness insurance benefits and as such is governed by the Sickness Insurance Act.[9] In terms of the personal scope of the benefit, not everyone in the Czech Republic is covered by the sickness insurance system since it is obligatory only for employees (who earn the minimum income[10]). Therefore, typically self-employed women are not entitled to maternity allowance unless they voluntarily participate in an insurance as self-employed or entrepreneurs. The basic purpose of maternity allowance is to compensate for lost earnings during the earliest childcare period, Czech legislation provides maternity allowance

[6] Up to 2 years of age of the child it could be drawn at an increased rate of CZK 11.400 (approx. 456 EUR), up to 3 years of age of the child at the basic rate of CZK 7.600 (approx.304 EUR) and up to 4 years of age of the child at a reduced rate of CZK 3.800 (approx.152 EUR).

[7] A special benefit is **paternity allowance**, which the father of the child is entitled to for 2 weeks during the first 6 weeks after the birth of the child.

[8] Act No. 262/2006 Coll., Labour Code (hereinafter referred to as the Labour Code).

[9] Act No. 187/2006 Coll., Sickness Insurance Act (hereinafter referred to as the Sickness Insurance Act).

[10] The minimum income for employees to participate in the sickness insurance is 4.000 CZK (approximately € 160) a month.

in the amount of 70% of the reduced income.[11] To qualify for maternity allowance the fundamental condition is participation in the sickness insurance system for at least 270 calendar days in the last two years before taking the maternity leave. The self-employed person must also meet the condition of having been insured for at least 180 days in the last year before the date on which the period of the allowance begins. The child's father or the mother's husband can claim the maternity allowance if he has entered into a written agreement with the mother to care for the child, or if the child's mother is unable or unavailable to care for the child.[12]

3.3 Parental Leave and Parental Allowance in the Czech Republic

Parental allowance is governed by the State Social Support Act. Through this non-insurance based and untested social security benefit, the state participates in covering the costs of nutrition and other basic personal needs of families with small children.

The parental allowance is granted to a parent who personally cares for the youngest child in the family for a full day and properly for the entire calendar month until the total amount of CZK 350,000 (EUR 14.000) is exhausted, but no longer than until the child is 3 years old. If the youngest child in the family is 2 or more children born at the same time, the parent is entitled to up to a total of CZK 525,000 (EUR 21.000).[13] The amount of the benefit is the same for all claimants, regardless of their income. The parent is not restricted in economic activity and the child could be places in a crèche, kindergarten or other similar facility for children. If the child is under two years of age, he/she may not attend these facilities for more than 92 hours in a calendar year; for older children, the children's attendance at these facilities is not monitored.[14]

While maternity benefits are sickness insurance benefits that replace income lost as a result of maternity leave (i.e. important personal impediment to work), the parental allowance, as a state social support benefit paid from the state budget, serves more as a type of state contribution to the upbringing of a child, or as a certain 'social wage'. This regulation of parental allowance is undoubtedly in line with the guarantee of social rights. The conditions for entitlement to parental allowance

---

[11] The employee's income is not counted in full for the purposes of calculating the allowance, but is reduced through a fairly complex and complicated system (there are 3 reduction limits up to which the employee's daily income is counted).

[12] Details in Czech Republic and its social protection of parents with young children (2024), pp. 61–72.

[13] With effect from January1, 2024 the parental allowance has been increased and its maximum support period has been aligned with the length of parental leave (i.e. 3 years).

[14] Section 31 of the State Social Support Act.

are, as above-mentioned, very loose. Basically, anyone who has children can draw parental allowance, regardless of their financial, social or work situation.[15]

One of the interesting features of the parental allowance in the Czech Republic is the possibility of its flexible withdrawal, depending on the level of the parent's income (in other words, the higher the parent's income, the faster the budget can be exhausted). The choice of the amount of parental allowance can be changed once every three months.

4 International Comparison with Selected EU Countries

When comparing the institutional state support for parents during the period of their care for young children, there are significant differences across the EU Member States. Below are presented findings of a comparative study conducted by a team from the Faculty of Law of Charles University in 2023 that dealt with the legal regulation of maternity and parental leave in selected EU Member States (Table 1).[16]

Regarding the maternity leave generally the length of maternity leave differs between the period before and after childbirth and of course depends on the number of born children. The shortest maternity leave is granted in Belgium, Germany, Sweden and Slovenia (only 14 resp. 15 weeks). In France the maternity leave is 16 weeks long. Poland and Hungary have longer maternity leave as of 20 and 24 weeks long.

Regarding the parental leave it is clear that different countries take different approaches. As can be seen from the table the legal systems set the maximum age of the child up to which parental leave may be taken, and they also determine the length of the leave in terms of weeks or even days. One of the shortest parental

Table 1 Comparison of the length of maternity leave and parental leave

	Maternity leave	Parental leave	
CR	28w	3y	
Belgium	15w	4m	(8y)
France	16w	1y (×2)	(3y)
Hungary	24w	44d	(3y)
Germany	14w	3y	
Slovenia	15w	160d	
Sweden	14w	18m	(8y)
Poland	20w	41w	(6y)

[15] Details in Czech Republic and its social protection of parents with young children (2024), pp. 61–72.

[16] Analysis of the Legal Regulation of Maternity and Parental Leave in Selected EU Member States (2023). Available at: https://www.spcr.cz/images/2023/analyzy/Analyza_MD_a_RD_KA4.pdf.

leaves is in Belgium and is set at 4 months. Hungary also has very short parental leave, which lasts 44 working days and can be taken until the child is 3 years old. France allows parental leave for 1 year and parental leave could be extended twice (it ends when the child is 3 years old). According to Polish law each parent is entitled to 41 weeks' parental leave (could be taken until the child is 6 years old). The standard duration of parental leave in Germany is 1 or 2 years (depends on the type of allowance) but can be prolonged to 3 years (the last year there is however no entitlement to parental allowance). In Slovenia, the regulation is quite modern, each parent is entitled to 160 days of parental leave. In Sweden there are several types of parental leave—depending on whether it is accompanied with the allowance, and it also depends on the extent to which the parental leave is taken with respect to working time of the employee.

It is evident from the above stated that the Czech approach is somewhat isolated. Even though the Czech institutional state support is one of the longest in the European Union (this applies to both maternity leave and parental leave), the financial support during these impediments to work is insufficient. Simply put we keep the parents at home longer, but for less money.

For example, except for Slovakia, the basic maternity leave in other countries is shorter than in the Czech Republic, however the financial compensation during maternity leave is higher than that granted in the Czech Republic. The majority of the analysed and compared legal regulations guarantee the employee 100% of the average earnings that the employee earned before taking maternity leave for the duration of the maternity leave. This represents the full extent of the employee's material security in France, Hungary, Germany, Poland and Slovenia. The legislation of other countries, while not compensating the employee for earnings up to the original amount, continues to grant the employee a higher level of security than the Czech legislation. In Belgium, the employee is entitled to a benefit of 82% of gross wages; in Slovakia, maternity pay is 75% of the daily assessment base.

As for the parental allowance in most countries, the main source of security during parental leave is usually a benefit from the public social security system (typically from social insurance). This means that participation in the insurance scheme is a condition for entitlement to the benefit. Of course, there are also countries where parental allowance is not linked to participation in the insurance scheme. For example, the German regulation of parental allowance is similar to the Czech model. Parental allowance is provided here as a family benefit, financed from the state budget.[17]

The prevailing trend towards reconciliation of work and family life across the European Union can be traced in countries that are successful in supporting the effective reconciliation of work and family life, where there are usually quite high parental benefits for a shorter period of time, which are then followed by guaranteed opportunities for flexible work and sufficient capacity of affordable childcare

[17] Another future challenge for the Czech legislator is the implementation of the requirement for the non-transferability of the right to at least 2 months of parental leave to the other parent, as regulated in Article 5 WLB Directive.

services.[18] It is a firm believe of the author of this chapter that an increase in the material security of employees during maternity leave in the Czech Republic may, with an appropriate combination of adjustments to the length of the support period, contribute to an increase in the birth rate and a more satisfactory financial situation of the caring parents. The same applies for the parental leave, which is currently unnecessarily long and inadequately funded (compared to the above selected European countries). The suitable combination of the support period and the amount of benefit together with the sufficient places in pre-school facilities and the flexibility of the labour market, will bring the desired work-life balance. However, this state is not possible to be achieved without support and reassurance from the state as well as the employers.[19]

5 The Future Challenges and Conclusions

If we look at the beginning, from the historic point of view the parental leave has served in the Czech Republic as a tool to increase birth rates and regulate women's employment in the labour market (e.g. in the 1990s as a solution to structural unemployment). Research shows that 38% of mothers of three-year-olds took advantage of the newly stated extension of the length of the support period to four years in 1995, i.e. more than a third of women stayed at home for at least a year longer and their children therefore did not enter pre-school education at three years. This had several implications, including an increase in unemployment among women raising four- and five-year-olds, which ceased to be noticeable once the children reached the age of six, as most women had already returned to work (unless they were on further maternity/parental leave) once they started school.[20]

---

[18] Analysis of the Legal Regulation of Maternity and Parental Leave in Selected EU Member States (2023). Available at: https://www.spcr.cz/images/2023/analyzy/Analyza_MD_a_RD_KA4.pdf.

[19] In several EU Member States, the Recovery and Resilience Facility (RRF) established by Regulation (EU) 2021/241 played a significant role in improving conditions for achieving work-life balance. For instance, Germany, France, and Italy used RRF funding to expand early childhood care capacity, digitize social services, and promote gender equality in the labour market. These investments were part of broader structural reforms aimed not only at post-pandemic recovery but also at addressing long-standing barriers to labour market participation for parents, especially mothers.

These measures are crucial in providing practical tools that enable parents—particularly women—to return to the labour market more quickly without having to choose between career and caregiving responsibilities. This approach also contributed to higher female employment rates and a more equitable distribution of caregiving duties between parents, in line with the objectives of the European Pillar of Social Rights.

[20] Maminka nebo školka? Dopady prodloužení čerpání rodičovského příspěvku na budoucí vzdělání a pracovní uplatnění dětí (2021).

The Czech Republic thus from original length of 1 year ended up with one of the longest parental leaves in Europe,[21] which has of course many consequences for the working life of the parent (usually woman):

- a woman can drop out of the workplace for 3 years as a result of maternity and childcare—in the case of multiple children and subsequent maternity and parental leave, it is not uncommon in the Czech Republic for a woman to interrupt her career for 6 or more years;
- over such long period the woman herself, her needs and life priorities change, just as the workplace change, the working team change, and therefore the woman may even be reluctant to return to work due to concerns about coping with work responsibilities and balancing childcare and work.
- loss of potential (and subsequent lower contributions to the public budget).

There are some typical features of the Czech labour market which need to be taken into consideration when assessing the topic of work-life balance. The gender employment gap in the Czech Republic is most critical when women have young children. The Czech Republic has a low female employment rate at the typical age of parenthood and has long been one of the worst countries in the EU in terms of the gender employment gap between women and men aged 20–64.[22] The proportion of children under three years old enrolled in formal childcare (5% in 2022 up to 29 hours per week, 1.8% from 30 hours per week) is below the EU average.[23] Only a negligible percentage of men in the Czech Republic take parental leave (2%), even though the parental allowance can be taken flexibly by both parents. Women work longer than men, but unfortunately spend more time in unpaid work. There is typical high labour market segregation (women work in different occupations than men) – the segregation is both horizontal and vertical (for horizontal segregation the typical example is teaching staff/nurses/IT and construction; for vertical segregation the pyramid is classically depicted where women are kept at the lower levels of the organisational pyramid and their numbers decrease as they move up—glass ceiling or sticky floor phenomenon).

In approaching the topic and the challenges outlined above, it is necessary to accept that this is a complex issue that in the future requires multidisciplinary research—labour law, social security law, economic and social studies etc. Support for parents in caring for their children and reconciling work and family life is also closely linked to the issue of equal pay. Money is generally a sensitive issue for most families and when deciding who stays at home with the children, the choice often falls on the woman, who usually earns a lower wage. And while the

---

[21] Act No. 154/1969 Coll., on Maternity Allowance; Act No. 117/1995 Coll., on State Social Support.

[22] Eurostat. Gender employment gap. Available at https://ec.europa.eu/eurostat/databrowser/view/TESEM060/bookmark/table?lang=en&bookmarkId=aefb3ecf-3dcc-4009-b77e-9a7c76e73159.

[23] Eurostat. Children in formal childcare or education by age group and duration - % over the population of each age group. Available at https://ec.europa.eu/eurostat/databrowser/view/ilc_caindformal__custom_14867362/default/table?lang=en.

male-colleagues move up in their career ladder, the woman returns to work after parental leave to the same remuneration she was getting a few years ago before she went on parental leave (in the Czech Republic there is no direct obligation to make up the financial remuneration from the original salary level, which the woman left). Leaving women permanently on a lower remuneration level. In addition to this, the caring role of the woman goes further in her personal life, because when she stops caring for her children, she can start caring for her aging parents and then her grandchildren (sandwich generation). Finally, women's career paths will culminate in a pension pay gap, as lower earnings in economically active life lead to a lower retirement pension.

To summarize it is obvious that the Czech society still faces a number of challenges in the area of reconciliation, especially in the area of the length of parental leave and financial support during childcare with the aim of greater involvement of the other parent and better reconciliation of work and family life. The question is rather complex, any reduction in the duration of parental leave must be accompanied by adequate pre-school capacity and employers' willingness to use flexible employment instruments to support the employment of parents of young children.

The author of the chapter is out of opinion that in the area of work-life balance the impact of the European union has definitely been beneficial for the Czech legal environment (because as we could see on the comparative chart, the Czech legal system is quite extraordinary and unique), nevertheless there are still many challenges ahead of the Czech legislator to make up for the deficits in work life balance in the Czech Republic and to ensure favourable conditions for working parents.

References

Bičáková A, Kalíšková K, Zapletalová L (2021) Maminka nebo školka? Dopady prodloužení čerpání rodičovského příspěvku na budoucí vzdělání a pracovní uplatnění dětí. Národohospodářský ústav AV ČR, v. v. i., 2021. https://www.consilium.europa.eu/en/policies/work-life-balance/

Eurofound (2024) Social governance of the Recovery and Resilience Facility: involvement of national social partners. Publications Office of the European Union, Luxembourg. Available at: https://www.eurofound.europa.eu/en/publications/2024/social-governance-recovery-and-resilience-facility-involvement-national-social

Eurostat. Gender employment gap. Available at https://ec.europa.eu/eurostat/databrowser/view/TESEM060/bookmark/table?lang=en&bookmarkId=aefb3ecf-3dcc-4009-b77e-9a7c76e73159

Eurostat. Children in formal childcare or education by age group and duration - % over the population of each age group. Available at https://ec.europa.eu/eurostat/databrowser/view/ilc_caindformal__custom_14867362/default/table?lang=en

Koldinská K, Matějka Řehořová L (2024) Czech Republic and its social protection of parents with young children in: Promoting labour market participation of parents with young children across the EU. Kopp Mária Institute for Demography and Families (KINCS), Budapest, pp 61–72

Koldinská K, Pichrt J, Morávek J, Štefko M, Matějka Řehořová L (2023) Analysis of the legal regulation of maternity and parental leave in selected EU Member States. SPČR. Prague. Available at: https://www.spcr.cz/images/2023/analyzy/Analyza_MD_a_RD_KA4.pdf

The Work-Life Balance in EU Law and the Quest for Substantive Gender Equality in Reconciling Work with Family Responsibilities

Aleksandar Ristovski

1 Introduction

Work and family represent two different sides of one same coin—people's lives. Paid work is a necessity, which enables a dignified human life.[1] Unpaid work related to caring for children or other dependent family members, on the other hand, is a biologically and morally driven duty, which is "non-negotiable".[2] Working people are more willing to "sacrifice the earnings necessary for living"[3] rather than forsaking or putting the people they care for at risk. The competing demands of work and family domains[4] create a tension that manifests as work-family conflict or imbalance, with their resolution or reconciliation constituting what is termed 'work-family' or 'work-life balance'. The term "work-family balance" primarily refers to the need to establish policies and legal provisions aimed at reconciling the inherent tensions in juggling people's work commitments and family responsibilities.[5] The term "work-life balance" in turn, is a broader term, which in addition to traditional family responsibilities is also aimed at non-family responsibilities and demands,

[1] Guess (2021), p. 15.

[2] Caracciolo di Torella and Masselot (2010), p. 9.

[3] Collins et al. (2012), p. 370.

[4] Greenhaus and Singh (2004), pp. 687–697.

[5] Caracciolo di Torella and Masselot (2010), p. 5.

A. Ristovski (✉)
Ss. Cyril and Methodius University, "Iustinianus Primus" Law Faculty, Skopje, North Macedonia
e-mail: a.ristovski@pf.ukim.edu.mk

K. Koldinská et al. (eds.), *Labour Law and Social Security Law in Central and Eastern Europe*, European Union and its Neighbours in a Globalized World 26,
https://doi.org/10.1007/978-3-032-04496-9_6

such as study, commitment to travel or the like[6] as well as at personal lifestyles of workers in general.[7]

The issue of work-family, i.e. work-life balance is intrinsically related to the issue of gender (in)equality in the broadest sense.[8] The roots of this relationship can be traced back to the period of the early stages of industrialization, the transition from an agrarian to an industrial society and the separation of the household from the workplace.[9] The Industrial Revolution's rigid demarcation between employment (the public sphere) and family life (the private sphere) precipitated fundamental transformations in gender roles within both labour markets and domestic settings. This binary restructuring not only redefined the social positions of men and women, but also fundamentally altered the conceptualization of work itself—irrespective of whether such work occurred in productive or reproductive spheres. Such a gendered dichotomy has historically privileged men's dominance in the public sphere of paid employment while systematically excluding women from labour markets or confining them to marginalized positions, thereby reinforcing their prescribed role in unpaid domestic and care work within the private sphere.[10] Paid employment—formally structured through employment contracts—became institutionalized as a productive social function performed in exchange for wages. Conversely, unpaid domestic labour—primarly associated with the contract of marriage—was systematically framed as unproductive[11] or socially reproductive[12] function akin to leisure, completely separate and independent from employment and as such was regarded outside the scope of labour law.[13] By removing formal and informal prohibitions on women's employment (such as certain norms that obliged married women to leave the labour market after marriage or other direct and indirect forms of discrimination that discouraged women's access to employment and strengthened their economic dependence on men in the family) during the 40 s and 50 s of the last century, the participation rate of married women in the labour markets gradually increased.[14] In its early stages, this configuration largely preserved the foundational assumptions of the prevailing 'gender contract,'[15] leaving intact its gendered allocation of productive and reproductive roles. Such paradigms were mirrored in the social role of *men*

[6] Brough et al. (2020), pp. 1–15.

[7] Kalamatiev and Ristovski (2017), pp. 100–112.

[8] Feminist scholars point out that the term "work-family" is more appropriate than the term "work-life" balance, because it implies the combination between paid and unpaid work, and thus includes a gender perspective. Lewis (2009), p. 15.

[9] Hein (2005).

[10] Hayers (2017), p. 2.

[11] Freedman and Fudge (2016), p. 233.

[12] Social reproduction may be defined as renewal of and care for human life (and thus human labour power) across generations. Ferguson (2018).

[13] Caracciolo di Torella and Masselot (2010), p. 8.

[14] Freedman, Fudge (2016), p. 235.

[15] The term "gender contract" is defined as a normative and material basis around which sex/gender divisions of paid and unpaid labour operate in a given society. Rubery (1998), p. 23.

as family breadwinners who establish a standard employment relationship and earn a family wage and of women as *family caregivers* who perform unpaid work and possibly earn a secondary wage.[16] The feminization of the workforce, which gained momentum during the 60s and 70s of the last century, inevitably began to affect the gender contract,[17] replacing the traditional "*male breadwinner/female caregiver*" with a "*male and female (dual) breadwinners/female caregiver*" model.[18] The growing demand for women's productive work has necessitated parallel policy interventions aimed at advancing gender equality in employment—including equal pay regulations and prohibitions against sex-based discrimination. For decades, these measures and policies concentrated solely on enhancing women's labour market participation—prioritizing workplace gender equality—while systematically neglecting interventions to redress gender disparities outside of employment, that is in unpaid work in the family.[19] However, a truncated conception of gender equality—one limited to parity in employment while excluding equitable participation in unpaid care work—fundamentally undermines the attainment of the ideal of substantive gender equality. Today, despite the fact that the "*male and female (dual) breadwinners*" model is by and large a common practice in the EU member states women still bear the bulk of unpaid care work and other domestic work in the households compared to men.[20]

This double burden faced by women—to be productive workers in the employment sphere and main "bearers" of the responsibilities related to unpaid work in the family sphere, not only puts their physical and psychological health at risk,[21] but also compromises their prospects to achieve substantive gender equality on both sides of the equality spectrum (labour market and family). Namely, the greater the disproportion in the sharing of unpaid care and other family work between men and women, the lower the chances of a more even involvement in the labour market and income of women (for example, due to not looking for a job and career interruption or part-time employment and performing other forms of casual and less paid work in order to adapt professional obligations to family responsibilities) against men. Concomitantly, the unequal division of responsibilities in the family followed by the parallel detachment of women from the labour market puts additional pressure on them to increase

[16] Vosko (2006), p. 55.

[17] Fudge and Owens (2006), pp. 14–15.

[18] Fudge (2014), p. 3.

[19] Eurofound (2020), p. 2.

[20] According to the European Institute for Gender Equality (EIGE) research on gender inequalities in care, a significantly higher proportion of women (93 per cent), than men, (53 per cent), are involved in unpaid care work at least several times a week (EIGE 2021a, p. 16). Of those involved in unpaid care work on a daily basis, the time spent by employed women on at least one activity among childcare, long-term care and housework is one and a half times higher (3.9 h per day) compared to the time spent by employed men (2.6 h per day) (EIGE 2021a, p. 17).

[21] For example, according to the 2020 Eurofound study, the strain caused by the work-life conflicts, more seriously affect the mental health of women compared to men. In that direction, a significantly higher number of women than men with children up to 17 years of age stated that they feel tension (23% vs. 19%), loneliness (14% vs. 6%) or depression (14% vs. 6%). (Eurofound 2020c, p. 17).

unpaid care and other family work, perpetuating gender stereotypes and creating a "vicious circle" between inequalities in employment and family life.[22]

Contemporary labour law must no longer be subjugated to the dualism resulting from the classical economic understanding of the distinction between "productive" and "unproductive" labour.[23] By continuing to disregard the gendered allocation of paid versus unpaid work—while considering caregiving disparities as merely private choices of men and women—current frameworks perpetuate structural inequalities that demand legal intervention.[24] The potential of the "latest" in the "generation" of models of work and family life (the so-called "*dual breadwinners/dual caregivers*" model) defined as a social and economic arrangement in which men and women have a symmetrical engagement both in terms of paid work in the labour market and in terms of unpaid work in the domestic sphere,[25] can only be fulfilled if the increased participation of women in labour markets is followed by a proportional participation of men in family responsibilities.[26] The adoption of Directive 2019/1158 on Work-Life Balance as the first legal instrument that explicitly addresses the issue of work-life balance as a stand-alone concept and puts care and care-related responsibilities on the EU agenda is a right step in the direction of promoting these values.

2 Gender Equality and Reconciliation of Professional with Family and Private Life (a Brief Overview of the EU Legislative Framework and Theoretical Discourses)

Work-life balance measures and policies are one of the most important components for achieving gender equality in the EU. Consequently, gender equality remains unachievable without both societal valorization and legal institutionalization of work-life reconciliation measures that holistically address workers' dual professional and caregiving responsibilities.[27] The genesis of the interaction between the issue of gender equality and the work-life balance within the EU can be traced back to the initial introduction of the principle of equal pay between men and women in the Treaty of Rome in 1957.[28] However, it then served more the purpose of

---

[22] Arabadjieva (2022), pp. 9, 18.

[23] Beneria (1999), p. 287.An ILO 2018 study shows that if unpaid care services were valued on the basis of an hourly minimum wage, they would have amounted to 9 per cent of global GDP, corresponding to US$11 trillion (purchasing power parity 2011). See ILO, Care Work and Care Jobs for the Future of Decent Work, (International Labour Office, 2018), xxix.

[24] Freedman, Fudge, op.cit., 235.

[25] Gornick and Meyers (2001).

[26] Caracciolo di Torella (2020).

[27] Lomazzi et al. (2019), p. 2.

[28] The principle of equal pay for equal work or work of equal value between men and women is regulated by art. 157 of the Treaty on the Functioning of the European Union (former art. 141 of

preventing distortions of the (former) common (now single market),[29] than the need to elevate gender equality as a social goal, in itself.[30] The actual intersection between gender equality and work-family, i.e. work-life balance takes place for the first time in the Social Action Program of 1974.[31] With the adoption of this document, "*reconciling family responsibilities with job aspirations*" is placed on the EU's agenda. From this foundation, a succession of legislative reforms, policy initiatives, and institutional measures has developed, informed by diverse regulatory approaches, feminist theoretical perspectives, and evolving conceptions of equality.

In the period until the entry into force of the Treaty of Amsterdam in 1997,[32] measures and policies for reconciling work with family life in the European Community/European Union were mainly developed within the regulatory context of employment policy[33] in light of the need to establish gender equality in the sphere of employment ("*male and female/dual breadwinners*" model). This period saw the introduction of both soft law measures and directives, indirectly or directly impacting reconciliation of work with family life. Key examples include: Directive on Equal Treatment of men and women 76/207/EEC[34]of 1976, the Pregnant Workers Directive 92/85/EEC of 1992[35] and the Parental Leave Directive 96/34/EC of 1996.[36] The common denominator of such measures, in essence, is their orientation towards a single direction: to prohibit discrimination against women in employment. These measures either explicitly aim to protect women (as with pregnancy, maternity leave, and breastfeeding provisions) or are designed in ways that implicitly encourage their primary use by women (as seen in parental leave frameworks). They neither fundamentally oppose the stereotype of women as the primary caregiver in the family, nor do they substantially promote the concept of equal parenting. On the

---

the Treaty establishing the European Community), but it dates back to the Treaty establishing the European Economic Community of 1957 (art. 119).

[29] Lomazzi, Israel, Crespi, op.cit, 3.

[30] Gender equality was elevated to the level of a fundamental principle of the EU with the decision of the EU Court of Justice in the "Defrenne 2" case from 1976. The Court gave both vertical and horizontal direct effect of (the then) article 119, which extended its enforceability not merely between individuals and the government, but also between private parties. See Gabrielle Defrenne v Société anonyme belge de navigation aérienne Sabena, Case 149/77.

[31] Council Resolution of 21 January 1974 concerning a social action programme, *Official Journal C 013, 12/02/1974 P. 0001 – 0004.*

[32] Treaty of Amsterdam amending the Treaty on European Union, the Treaties establishing the European Communities and certain related acts, *Official Journal C 340, 10/11/1997.*

[33] Bercusson (1996), p. 210.

[34] Council Directive 76/207/EEC on the implementation of the principle of equal treatment for men and women as regards access to employment, vocational training and promotion, and working conditions, *Official Journal L 039.*

[35] Council Directive 92/85/EEC on the introduction of measures to encourage improvements in the safety and health at work of pregnant workers and workers who have recently given birth or are breastfeeding, *Official Journal L 348.*

[36] Council Directive 96/34/EC on the framework agreement on parental leave concluded by UNICE, CEEP and the ETUC, *Official Journal L 145.*

other hand, the issue of care for other dependent persons, including adult family members, remains outside the scope of reconciliation measures. Hence, two key criticisms are attributed to the measures: the first refers to the problem of stereotyping the role of women, and the second, to the tendency to cover only the care of children, but not of other dependent persons, including adult family members. This situation, in a certain way, corresponds to an (older) current of feminist theories,[37] which is based on the understanding of the "*sameness*" of women with men, highlighting the need to establish policies to implement such "sameness" through strengthening and equalizing the position of women with the position of men in the labour market[38]. Driven by the desire to attain equality in employment, some 1980s feminist scholars advocated equating pregnancy—a biologically female-specific condition—with gender-neutral work absences like illness or disability. This approach sought to normalize maternal absence by framing it as analogous to other forms of temporary incapacity.[39] EU legislative approaches to work-family reconciliation prior to the 1997 Amsterdam Treaty were fundamentally grounded in the model of formal equality. The aim of this model is to protect the dignity and autonomy of individuals regardless of their personal attributes or characteristics (for example, sex, race and the like). It is based on the concept of prohibiting direct discrimination and promoting the principle of "meritocracy"—the different treatment between individuals may be justified by having different merits, but not by stereotypes related to their belonging to a certain protected group.[40] The Amsterdam Treaty strengthenes the concept of gender equality by transforming policies prohibiting discrimination into policies promoting opportunities.[41] The employment regulatory context within which work-family reconciliation measures were mainly developed has been replaced by a different normative course, in which reconciliation begins to be regulated as an independent and integrative concept that belongs equally to mothers, fathers and carers general.[42] Confirmation for such a transformative course can be found in the Charter of Fundamental Rights of the EU from 2000,[43] that is, from 2007,[44] through which the right to reconcile professional and family life[45] has been elevated to the level of a fundamental human right. The European legislator gradually becomes more aware of the limitations of the feminist

---

[37] Davies (2009), p. 105.

[38] Gornick and Meyers (2001), p. 2.

[39] Vinković (2023), p. 134.

[40] Barnard (2012), p. 289.

[41] Blanpain (2013), pp. 254–258.

[42] Caracciolo di Torella and Masselot (2010), pp. 15, 26.

[43] Charter of Fundamental Rights of the European Union, Official Journal of the European Communities C 364/1.

[44] Charter of Fundamental Rights of the European Union, Official Journal of the European Communities C 303/17.

[45] Article 33 of the Charter of Fundamental Rights of the EU reads: To reconcile family and professional life, everyone shall have the right to protection from dismissal for a reason connected with maternity and the right to paid maternity leave and to parental leave following the birth or adoption of a child.

theories of the 80s, which ignore the need for special rights for women (such as those related to pregnancy and maternity) whose guarantee is a necessary precondition for actual gender equality in labour markets.[46] In that regard, the feminist theory of "sameness" is increasingly giving way to the theory of "*difference*" which extends beyond the sphere of employment by recognizing and valuing gender "differences" in performing unpaid care work in the family where women have a dominant role, and calls for the establishment of measures and policies to address such differences.[47] At the same time, the perception and regulation of reconciliation measures and policies are beginning to take shape through the model of the so-called substantive equality. This model emerges as a response to critiques of formal equality—particularly its failure to address women's real circumstances as primary family caregivers, and its reliance on finding an equivalent male comparator to establish discrimination—a requirement which proves unworkable in cases of pregnancy-based unequal treatment. The substantive equality model approaches the question of equality through the prism of the disadvantages faced by members of a certain group. It is oriented towards achieving equality in terms of the result.[48] While grounded in the prohibition of indirect discrimination, this model extends beyond such constraints by employing special measures—including positive action and even positive discrimination—to rectify systemic underrepresentation or disadvantage affecting particular groups . EU legislation following the Amsterdam Treaty should also be understood in this intended sense.

Measures to reconcile work and family life adopted in the last two and a half decades include various soft law instruments (such as the Resolution on the balanced participation of women and men in family and working life from 2000[49] and the Work-Life Balance Package from 2008[50]), but also certain directives (such as the Directive 2006/54/EC for equal opportunities and equal treatment of men and women in matters of employment and occupation (recast) from 2006[51] and the Parental Leave Directive 2010/18/EU[52] repealing and replacing the eponymous Directive of 1996). All the while, the affluent case law of the Court of Justice has played a huge role. The latest stage in the development of measures and policies to

---

[46] Conaghan (2013), p. 81.

[47] Gornick and Meyers (2001), p. 2.

[48] Barnard, op.cit, pp.291–293.

[49] Resolution of the Council and of the Ministers for Employment and Social Policy, on the balanced participation of women and men in family and working life, *Official Journal C 218.*

[50] This Package, among other things, provided for Proposals for amendments to existing directives such as the Directive for self-employed workers 86/613/EEC and for pregnant workers 92/85/EEC. While amendments to the first directive were successfully adopted through Directive 2010/41/EU, attempts to amend the second directive failed and were withdrawn in 2015. https://ec.europa.eu/commission/presscorner/detail/en/MEMO_08_603.

[51] Directive 2006/54/EC of the European Parliament and of the Council on the implementation of the principle of equal opportunities and equal treatment of men and women in matters of employment and occupation (recast), *Official Journal L 204.*

[52] Council Directive 2010/18/EU implementing the revised Framework Agreement on parental leave concluded by BUSINESSEUROPE, UEAPME, CEEP and ETUC and repealing Directive 96/34/EC, Official Journal of the European Union L 68/13.

reconcile work with family, i.e. private life, was marked by the adoption of the European Pillar of Social Rights in 2017, which provided a new impetus in the development of such measures and policies.[53] Under its auspices, the new Directive on Work-Life Balance for Parents and Carers was finally proposed and then in 2019 adopted by the European Parliament and the Council.

3 Reconciling Work with Family Responsibilities and the Special Protection of Women in Case of Pregnancy and Maternity (a One-Way Reconciliation?)

The special protection of women in the field of employment once seen as a legitimate reason for safeguarding a weaker human being[54] is obsolete, because such an approach is now perceived as form of disguised discrimination, having adverse effects on equality of opportunity in employment.[55] Instead of special measures for their "general" protection as women, female workers enjoy special protection in exceptional cases such as pregnancy and maternity. However, the issue of drawing a line where special protection ends[56] and where discrimination against women or the imbalance of equal treatment at the expense of men begins is a complex issue. In EU law, pregnancy and maternity rights are addressed through various instruments that establish a complex horizontal linkage. On the one hand, there are the directives in the field of equal treatment and opportunities (of which the Equal Treatment Directive 76/207/EEC, including its 2002 amendments through Directive 2002/73/EC[57] and the Recast Directive 2006/54 are of particular importance), and on the other hand the Directive on Pregnant Workers 92/85/EEC.

3.1 The Approach of the Equality Directives

The original text of the Equal Treatment Directive 76/207/EEC does not provide for special provisions, i.e. positive rights for women in case of pregnancy and maternity, but rather refers to the protection of pregnancy and maternity as an *exception*

[53] Interinstitutional Proclamation on the European Pillar of Social Rights, OJ [2017] C428/10.

[54] Starova (2009), p. 346.

[55] Birk (2007), pp. 218–219.

[56] Grgurev (2014), p. 139.

[57] Directive 2002/73/EC of the European Parliament and of the Council amending Council Directive 76/207/EEC on the implementation of the principle of equal treatment for men and women as regards access to employment, vocational training and promotion, and working conditions, *OJ L 269*.

to the principle of equal treatment between men and women.[58] A more detailed explanation of the justification for such an exception, i.e. different treatment is given by the European Court of Justice in the "*Hofmann*" case, where it refers to two legitimate goals of the protection of pregnancy and maternity, namely: (1) the protection of woman's *biological condition* during pregnancy and thereafter until such time as her physiological and mental functions have returned to normal after childbirth and (2) the protection of the *special relationship between a woman and her child* over the period which follows pregnancy and childbirth, by preventing that relationship from being disturbed by the multiple burdens which would result from the simultaneous pursuit of employment.[59] The biological particularity and uniqueness of pregnancy and maternity creates inherent tensions within comparator-based discrimination models.[60] Therefore, the literal application of the concept of equal treatment by comparing the condition of a pregnant women or women who has recently given birth to a similarly-situated male comparator is an artificial legal exercise.[61] The first significant judgment through which the Court of Justice addresses this impracticality filling the legal anomaly is the "Dekker" case.[62] The Court ruled that since pregnancy only affects women, decisions made on the ground that a women is pregnant are a form of sex discrimination without the need to make comparisons. This approach is also confirmed by Directive 2002/73/EC amending Directive 76/207/EC,[63] and further by the Recast Directive 2006/54/EC.[64] The difference between the Equal Treatment Directive 76/207/EC including its amendments through Directive 2002/73/EC and the Recast Directive 2006/54/EC is that, while the former retain a passive approach to regulating the special protection of women during pregnancy and maternity *as an exception* to the principle of equality between men and women, the latter abandons such a formula by which approaches the ideal of substantive gender equality.

---

[58] This Directive shall be without prejudice to provisions concerning the protection of women, particularly as regards pregnancy and maternity. Art 2(3).

[59] See Case 184/83 *Hofmann v Barmer Ersatzkasse* [1984] ECR 3047.

[60] Ellis and Watson (2012), pp. 333–338.

[61] Barnard (2012), p. 403.

[62] "Dekker" case is about an employer who refuses to enter into a contract of employment with a pregnant candidate (Ms. Dekker) whom he considers to be suitable for the job, on the grounds that the employer's insurers refused to cover the costs of her maternity leave. The Court, *inter alia*, said that a refusal to employ a women on account of her pregnancy could not be justified on the grounds of the financial loss which an employer who appointed a pregnant women would suffer for the duration of her maternity leave. See Case 177/88, *Dekker v Stichting Vormingscentrum voor Jong Volwassenen* [1990] ECR I–3941.

[63] See Art.2, (7).

[64] See Art.2, (2), c.

3.2 *The Approach of the Pregnant Workers Directive*

The Pregnant Workers Directive 92/85/EEC was adopted as the tenth individual directive of Directive 89/391/EEC on the general framework for the safety and health of workers at work.[65]

It contains definitions of the terms "pregnant worker", "worker who has recently given birth" and "worker who is breastfeeding", but a closer explanation of the concept of "pregnancy" and the personal scope of application of the Directive can be found in the jurisprudence of the Court of Justice of the EU.[66] The Directive is based on the assumption that employed expectant and new mothers must be considered a particularly sensitive risk group and protected against the dangers which specifically affect them. However, despite the principal role of the safety and health regulatory context, the Directive does not neglect the context of equal treatment either.[67]

One of the most significant rights from the Pregnant Workers Directive is the right to a continuous period of maternity leave of at least 14 weeks.[68] The Directive implicitly distinguishes two periods of leave resulting from the total maternity leave: compulsory leave of at least 2 weeks and optional leave up to the remaining 14 weeks. Compulsory leave is considered as a non-waivable period of leave, while the use of the optional leave depends on the woman's personal choice, but in any case, the employer is not allowed to put pressure on the woman to waive her right to the full length of leave.[69] The Pregnant Workers Directive also contains certain rights that are related, but at the same time can be considered to be beyond the narrower context of safety and health at work. They refer to the *prohibition of dismissal* and the *exercise of employment rights*. The prohibition of dismissal includes the period from the beginning of pregnancy to the end of maternity leave. Exceptions to this prohibition may be allowed only in exceptional cases not connected to the worker's condition and if they are permitted under national legislation and/or practice, and where applicable, provided that the competent authority has given its consent.[70] As "exceptional cases" that justify dismissal, cannot be considered the cases where a pregnant worker *is not available to perform her duties* during the period for which she is needed, regardless of whether the main reason for her initial

[65] Blanpain (2013), p. 738.

[66] E.g., the Court included a "*subordinated member of a board of directors of a company* (Case C-232/09, *Dita Danosa v LKB Līzings SIA* [2010] I-11405) and "*workers who are on childcare leave* at the time they seek a right to maternity leave" (Case C-116/06 *Sari Kiiski v Tampereen kaupunki* [2007] I-07643) under the definition of a "pregnant worker", but excluded a worker who despite having had a successful in vitro fertilization (IVF) procedure resulting with the creation of embryos, at the time she requested dismissal protection stating that she was pregnant, the embryos were still not implanted to her uterus (Case C-506/06 *Mayr* v. *Bäckerei und Konditorei Gerhard Flöckner* [2008] I-1017).

[67] Kenner (2003), p. 156.

[68] Art 8 (1).

[69] Kovacs and Heissl (2015), p. 301.

[70] Art.10.

employment was a replacement for another worker who uses maternity leave (the Webb case[71]) or because the worker concluded a fixed-term employment contract (Tele Denmark case[72]). A confirmation that the unilateral termination of the employment contract of a pregnant worker, regardless of whether she is employed for a fixed or indefinite period of time, will be considered contrary to the prohibition of dismissal, can also be found in "Melgar".[73] Finally, in "Paquay",[74] the Court extends the protection against dismissal to those cases in which the employer takes preparatory steps for dismissing the employee on the grounds of pregnancy and/or of the birth of a child, such as searching for and finding a permanent replacement for the relevant employee, before the end of that period. Concerning the *employment rights*, Directive 92/85/EC firstly obliges the Member States to guarantee workers who, for reasons related to the protection of safety and health are forced to work under modified working conditions, to another job or to be granted a leave, the exercise of the employment rights relating to the employment contract including the *maintenance of a payment to, and/or entitlement to an adequate allowance*. During maternity leave, on the other hand, the workers should receive either payment or an adequate allowance which is at least equivalent to that which they would receive in case of sick leave. In both cases, the exercise of the entitlements may depend on the fulfillment of eligibility conditions, which by no means, may require previous employment longer than 12 months counted from the date of confinement.[75]

---

[71] In "Webb", it is about an EMO Air Cargo Ltd. employee (Ms Webb), who was employed initially to replace another employee, who was about to go on maternity leave, but then to continue working on the return to work of the absent employee. Shortly after starting work, Ms. Webb announced that she was pregnant too and was dismissed due to her unavailability to work during the period for which she was needed. See Case C-32/93 Carole Louise Webb v EMO Air Cargo (UK) Ltd. [1994] I-1963.

[72] Tele Danmark, concerns a women (*Ms Brandt-Nielsen*) who entered into a fixed term employment contract knowing that she was pregnant and that she would not be able to perform the job for certain period of time, while she did not inform the employer of this fact. See: Case C-109/00 Tele Danmark A/S v Handels-og Kontorfunktionærernes Forbund i Danmark (HK) [2001] I-06993.

[73] In the "Melgar" case, it is about a pregnant worker (Ms Melgar) who is seeking protection due to the non-renewal of her employment contract, which had previously been extended several times. The Court determined that the non-renewal of a fixed-term employment contract when such contract has come to the end of its stipulated term and is not subsequently renewed, cannot be considered a dismissal for which a prohibition is stipulated in accordance with Article 10 of Directive 92/85/EEC. However, if the reason for the non-renewal of the fixed-term contract is motivated by the pregnancy of the worker concerned, this would constitute direct discrimination based on sex contrary to the Recast Directive 2006/54. See: Case C-438/99 *Jiménez Melgar* v. *Ayuntamiento de Los Barrios* [2001] I-6915.

[74] In "Paquay", the employer notified the employee (Ms Paquay) of her dismissal when she returned to work after maternity leave. The Court found the the employer took preparatory steps for such a decision (such as placing an advertisement in a newspaper offering permanent recruitment for her post) while Ms. Paquay was on maternity leave. See: Case C-460/06 *Paquay* Nadine Paquay v Société d'architectes Hoet + Minne SPRL [2007] I-8511.

[75] Art.11 of the Directive.

4 Reconciling Work with Family Responsibilities (a Working Fathers' and Carers' Perspective)

4.1 The Situation Before the Adoption of the Work-Life Balance Directive

For decades, EU work-family reconciliation policies systematically marginalized paternal roles, constructing childcare as an almost exclusively maternal responsibility within the policy framework. Interestingly, this situation was "bolstered" by certain judgments and interpretations of the Court of Justice that strengthened the gender division of the roles of women (as primary caregivers) and man (as primary breadwinners) even further.[76] However, over time, the Court has become more willing to scrutinize whether a period of leave is genuinely designed to protect women who have just given birth, or it refers to the need to provide longer-term care for children which can be provided by both parents.[77] Thus, in the "Roca Alvarez" case[78] a subject of assessment by the Court of Justice was a leave scheme for feeding babies in Spain which allowed each parent 1 h of leave from work until the child is 9 months old. Such a right to leave was granted to all employed mothers (regardless of whether the fathers of the children have the status of employees), but only to the employed fathers (if the mothers of the children have the status of employees). The Court held that such a situation perpetuates a traditional distribution of the roles of men and women in relation to the exercise of their parental duties and on that view, the leave should be afforded to men on the same terms as it was afforded to women.

The involvement of fathers in policies and measures to reconcile work with family life, usually appears in two forms: paternity leave and parental leave.[79] The right to paternity leave was beyond the regulatory framework of EU labour law for many years.[80] It is mentioned only in two instruments in the field of equality (the Directive

[76] E.g, in the "*Hofmann*" case, the claim of the plaintiff (Mr Hofmann) for payment of child-care allowance for the period between the expiry of the statutory protective period of 8 weeks which was available to the mother and the day on which the child reached the age of 6 months (a period, in which he took care of the child while the mother continued her employment) was rejected. The Court of Justice stated that Directive 76/207 is not designed to settle questions concerned with the organization of the family, or to alter the division of responsibility between parents. Another similar example is the "*Abdoulaye*" case, where the Court of Justice held that the payment of FRF 7500 by Renault only to pregnant women commencing a maternity leave to offset the occupational disadvantages inherent in maternity leave is not discriminatory against men. See Case C-218/98 Oumar Dabo Abdoulaye and Others v Régie nationale des usines Renault SA [1999] I-05723.

[77] Davies (2012), p. 137.

[78] See Case C-104/09 Pedro Manuel Roca Álvarez v Sesa Start España ETT SA [2010] *I-08661*.

[79] More on paternity and parental leave see in Eurofound (2019).

[80] It should be noted that the first draft of the Pregnant Workers Directive provided for two unpaid days of paternity leave related to the birth of the child. However, such a proposal not only that was not included in the adopted and still existing Directive of 1992, but was also not included in the

2002/73/EC amending the Equal Treatment Directive[81] and the Recast Directive 2006/54[82]). These instruments, however, do not provide for the right to paternity leave as a positive right granted for fathers. They merely provide the same level of protection of paternity and adoption leave compared to maternity leave, if Member States have already introduced such rules into national law. This means that fathers' rights within the framework of the Equality Directives have the status of "optional" and not "individual" and thus mandatory rights for the Member States.[83]

Parental leave, on the other hand, is granted to both parents to enable them to take care of their child.[84] This right was regulated for the first time by the Parental Leave Directive 96/34/EC of 1996 implementing the Framework Agreement on Parental Leave concluded between the European social partners. Directive 96/34/EC introduced an individual right to at least 3 months of parental leave on the grounds of the birth or adoption of a child to both men and women workers[85] and provided for the right to taking time off from work on grounds of force majeure for urgent family reasons in cases of sickness or accident to all workers.[86] If Parental Leave Directive 96/34/EC is the first directive adopted by means of social dialogue implementing a Framework Agreement between the representative social partners at Union level, the Parental Leave Directive 2010/18/EU of 2010 (repealing Directive 96/34/EC) is the first directive implementing a revision of a Framework Agreement.[87] Directive 2010/18/EU introduced three key rights in the context of reconciling work with family and private life. The first one, was the *right to parental leave* granted to each parent, i.e. man or women worker for at least a period of 4 months, with the possibility of being used until a given age of the child up to 8 years,[88] where at least one of the 4 months is non-transferable.[89] The second one, was the right *to request changes to the working hours and/or patterns*[90] which the worker could exercise only when returning to work after previously taking parental leave.[91] Finally, the third one, was the right *to time off from work* on grounds of force majeure for urgent family reasons in cases of sickness or accident making the

Proposal for its amendment of 2009, which was also never adopted. Paternity leave is for the first time introduced and regulated by Directive 2019/1158 (EU) on Work-Life Balance from 2019.

[81] Art.2 (7).

[82] Art.16.

[83] Caracciolo di Torella (2017), pp. 187–198.

[84] Case 519/03, Commission of the European Communities v Grand Duchy of Luxemburg [2005] I-03067.

[85] Clause 2 (1).

[86] Clause 3 (1).

[87] Houwerzijl (2015), pp. 493–494.

[88] See Clause 2 (1).

[89] See Clause 2 (2).

[90] See Clause 6 (1).

[91] See Davies. A.C.L, op.cit, 138.

immediate presence of the worker indispensable,[92] which applied not only to working parents, but indirectly to all working carers and was intended for all urgent situations related not only to the care of children, but also of other persons (e.g., a partner, an elderly or another dependent relative).[93]

4.2 *The Situation After the Adoption of the Work-Life Balance Directive*

Directive 2010/18/EU has been repealed and replaced by the most recent Work-Life Balance Directive 2019/1158. The Work-Life Balance Directive constitutes both an extension and substantive enhancement of the regulatory framework established under Directive 2010/18/EU. It not only *reinforces current entitlements but also extends new rights to parents and carers.*[94] With the explicit mention of "carers" already in its title, Directive 2019/1158 no longer perceives the issue of "reconciliation", i.e. "balance" just as a problem of women or parents, but as something that can and will affect most workers.[95] The introduction of gender-neutral language (parents and careres was motivated by positive efforts to address uneven distribution of unpaid care work and achieve gender equality.[96] The Directive's main objective remains to be gender equality which could be achieved by promoting the participation of women in the labour market, the equal sharing of caring responsibilities between men and women, and the closing of the gender gaps in earnings and pay.[97] Directive 2019/1158 applies to a broader range of persons compared to previous Directives on parental leave. Its **personal scope** includes all workers who have an employment contract or employment relationship, *taking into account the case-law of the Court of Justice*,[98] regarding the criteria for determining the status of a worker.[99] It is a significant step forward in terms of greater inclusiveness because it obliges Member States possibly with more restrictive definitions of employment contracts and employment relationships in the national labour law systems to align with the case law of the CJEU possibly with a broader interpretation of the personal scope of application of the rights covered by the Directive.[100] By explicitly referring

[92] See Clause 7 (1).

[93] Kenner.J, op.cit, 274.

[94] See Recital 15 of the Directive.

[95] Caracciolo di Torella, Revue de Droit Comparė du Travail et de la Sėcuritė Social, 2/2020.

[96] Vinkoviċ, op.cit., p. 135.

[97] Recital 6 of the Directive.

[98] Art.2 of the Directive.

[99] See Recital 17 of the Directive.

[100] Chieregato (*International Journal of Comparative Labour Law and Industrial Relations*, Volume 36, Issue I, 2020), pp. 12–13.

to the CJEU case-law regarding the established criteria for determining the status of a worker, the personal scope of application of Directive 2019/1158 can implicitly be extended to the most vulnerable categories of workers (such as: domestic workers, on-demand workers, intermittent workers, voucher based-workers, platform workers, trainees and apprentices) provided that they fulfil those criteria. Anyway, this legal approach could still be short of inclusivity, because certain non-standard dependent workers, such as platform workers, may still fail to be considered workers in accordance to national and EU law.[101]

The most significant part of the Directive consists in its **material scope**. In that regard, the Directive contains four individual rights, namely: *the right to paternity leave, the right to carers' leave, the right to parental leave and the right to request flexible working arrangements*.[102] While the former two are rights that are regulated for the first time by an EU directive, the latter two have their roots in the repealed Parental Leave Directives, but are simultaneously strengthened and deepened by the new Work-Life Balance Directive. Each of these rights is significant not only in terms of the aim to improve the balancing of work with family responsibilities of parents and workers with caring responsibilities,[103] but also in terms of the quest for substantive gender equality, reflected in the goal of an equal share of caring responsibilities between men and women, which *inter alia* assumes an equal take up of leaves and other work-life balance arrangements by fathers.[104]

Paternity leave is defined as leave from work for fathers or, if recognised by national law, for equivalent second parents, on the occasion of the birth of a child for the purpose of providing care.[105] It can amount to 10 working days that can be taken partly before or only after the birth of the child, as well as in flexible ways.[106] Similar to maternity leave, it is provided as an unconditional right, i.e. right, the exercise of which shall not be made subject to period of work qualification or to a length of service qualification, and employers cannot refuse or postpone the worker's request to use it. Another indicator of the similarity with maternity leave is the amount of its payment or allowance that should be at least equivalent to a sick leave compensation and may be preconditioned by previous employment not exceeding 6 months prior to the expected date of the birth of the child.[107] The effectiveness of paternity leave incentives is undermined by structural inconsistencies across Member States, particularly regarding compensation levels that frequently align with suboptimal sick pay schemes rather than equitable remuneration standards,

[101] Arabadjieva (2022), p. 26.

[102] Art.1 of the Directive.

[103] See Recital 10 of the Directive.

[104] See Recital 11 of the Directive.

[105] Art.3, 1 (a).

[106] Art.4 (1).

[107] Ibidem.

creating divergent economic dis/incentives for fathers' uptake.[108] The scope of paternity leave rights extends beyond biological fathers to include equivalent second parents (if they are recognized under national law), with such entitlements being granted ex lege irrespective of marital or family status as defined by national law.[109] With such an approach, the Directive acknowledges the plurality of family units in contemporary societies, making it possible the right to be acquired by families of same-sex parents (so-called rainbow families) or of persons with constantly changing identities (so-called fluid families) who take care of children. However, it fails to address or specifically refer to single parent families (mostly composed of women) who are arguably in even more vulnerable position. Other criticisms can also be attributed to the Directive in the context of the regulation of the right to paternity leave. Therefore, although it carries the name 'work-life balance,' it not only completely overlooks the issue of maternity but also does not establish greater parity in the length of paternity and maternity leave (the latter remaining substantially longer than the former). Another point of criticism is that, unlike the mandatory portion of maternity leave, paternity leave is not compulsory in any way.[110]

Parental leave is leave from work for parents on the grounds of the birth or adoption of a child with the purpose of taking care of that child.[111] The Work-Life Balance Directive addresses the following aspects related to the exercise of the right to parental leave: the structure and duration of the right, the age of the child up to which the right can be exercised, the (non)transferability, the flexibility in use, the payment and the eligibility. The right to parental leave is *structured* as an individual right for each parent with a duration of 4 months.[112] The time frame until which parental leave can be used is related to reaching a certain age of the child specified in national law, *up to eight years of age*.[113] Such a limitation ignores the work-life balance needs of parents of children in early school age (up to 12 years).[114] In comparison with the former Parental Leave Directive 2010/18/EU which defined it as "in principle" *non-transferable right*, the Work-Life Balance Directive formally structures the right to parental leave as an individual right that cannot be transferred from one parent to another. However, even the new Directive does not significantly depart from framing (at least) part of this entitlement as a family right—meaning it can be transferred between parents. Unlike the repealed Directive 2010/18/EU, under Directive 2019/1158/EU, only two of the 4 months of guaranteed parental

[108] According to the data of the European Commission from 2018, only 13 member states out of the then 28 provided for "well-paid" paternity leave (in the amount of at least 66% of previous earnings). See European Commission, Paternity and parental leave policies across the European Union, Assessment of current provision, 2018, 5.

[109] Art.4, (3).

[110] Caracciolo di Torella, Revue de Droit Comparė du Travail et de la Sėcuritė Social, 2/2020.

[111] Art.3, (1) b.

[112] See Art.5, (1).

[113] See Art.5, (1).

[114] ETUC (2022), p. 22.

leave per parent are non-transferable.[115] With that, the portion of non-transferable leave between parents increases from one to 2 months, and if such portion is not used, it is lost. The question of the (non)transferability of the right to parental leave is of crucial importance for the extent to which working fathers are involved in caring responsibilities. This may depend on factors based on "values" and/or "economic costs."[116] Under the prevailing influence of traditional socio-cultural factors—such as entrenched gender stereotypes and employer resistance—allowing parental leave to be transferable risks creating pressure for male workers to transfer their leave entitlement to female partners.[117] Of course, one of the most significant reasons for the "resistance" to such "interference" is the economic implications that would result from the potentially reduced income of the family as a consequence of the uptake of parental leave by the higher-earning parent (usually the man whose income from work is greater compared to women's incomes, especially when it comes to households with lower incomes). Hence, it becomes evident that the introduction of the right to parental leave as a fully non-transferable right (so-called quota system) would achieve the ultimate goal of substantive gender equality if, among other measures and policies, its uptake is compensated with an income the amount of which will not make (significant) difference in relation to the user's regular income.[118] The Work-Life Balance Directive does not explicitly mention and is not limited to the modalities for using parental leave provided for in previous directives[119] but it guarantees *the right of workers to request to take parental leave in flexible way* while providing an obligation for employers to consider and respond to such requests, taking into account the needs of both the employer and the worker.[120] The possibility of using parental leave in flexible ways could inevitably contribute to an increased uptake of parental leave by men. However, it is interesting that, in certain flexible ways (such as the joint and simultaneous use of leave by both parents), there is a risk that the desired goal of increasing equality in parenting will not be achieved, because one parent (usually the father) is significantly less active in providing care compared to the other (usually the mother).[121] Finally, one of the most significant elements of parental leave that concerns the need for equal uptake of the leave by men and women, are the elements related to its *compensation* and *eligibility*. The Work-Life Balance Directive stipulates for the first time that the right to parental leave should be *paid*.[122] However, such payment or allowance covers only two out of the four months of parental leave and applies to the non-trans-

[115] See Art.5 (1) and (2).

[116] Pircher et al. (2023), p. 5.

[117] Oliveira et al. (2020), p. 305.

[118] Arabadjieva (2022), p. 24.

[119] E.g. on full-time basis, part-time basis (for example, half-time over 6 months), in a fragmented way (for example, a few hours at a time over a certain period) or in the form of a time-credit system (for example, 1 month per yerar). See European Trade Union Confederation (2011), p. 23.

[120] Art.5, (6).

[121] EIGE, *Gender inequalities in care and consequences for the labour market*, 2021, 34–35.

[122] See Art.8, (1).

ferable months of each parent.[123] On the other hand, unlike the compensation levels for maternity and paternity leave, compensation level for parental leave is not specified (for example, in the amount of payment or allowance at the level of sick leave) and is left entirely to the national level, in that it should facilitate the take-up by both parents.[124] Certain expressions that can serve as an orientation for determining the level of payment and as a sound legal ground for an interpretation by the Court of Justice, can be found in the non-binding recitals of the Directive.[125] In any case, the Directive's abstention from introducing a provision that stipulates a firm financial incentive (particularly for the uptake of parental leave by fathers) may limit the prospects for greater equality in the sharing of care-related responsibilities. Criticisms of the Work-Life Balance Directive are attributed also in relation to the *eligibility* for exercising the right to parental leave, because it is not regulated as an automatic and unconditional right of the holders similar to maternity and paternity leave. Its acquisition may be subject to certain conditions regulated by national law, such as a period of work qualification or length of service qualification, which shall not exceed 1 year.[126] Qualification periods can be a major barrier for accessing the right to parental leave, particularly when it comes to workers who have recently changed jobs or who have worked on temporary contracts with breaks between them.[127]

One of the most significant achievements of the Work-Life Balance Directive is the introduction of **the right to carers' leave**. In fact, the Directive recognizes for the first time the provision of care as a responsibility which does not consist only of care of children (i.e. parental leave) by a working parent, but also of personal care or support by the worker (i.e. carer) to a relative (child, parent, spouse or partner in civil partnership, where such partnerships are recognized by national law) or to a person who lives in the same household as the worker, and who is in need of significant care or support for a serious medical reason.[128] Carers' leave is defined as an individual right of each working carer and amounts to five working days per year,[129] but compared to maternity, paternity and even parental leave, this right does not have the status of paid leave from work. The introduction of carers' leave as a guaranteed right—independent of employer discretion and with dismissal protection for workers who exercise it[130]—represents in itself a significant advancement under the

---

[123] See Art.5 (2).

[124] See Art.8 (3).

[125] For example, Recital 29 states that "workers should be provided with a right to an adequate allowance while on leave", while Recital 31, which emphisizes the payment or allowance for the minimum non-transferable period of parental leave, states that it should be "sufficiently well remunerated, with a view to allowing for a decent living standard".

[126] Art.5 (4).

[127] Arabadjieva (2022), p. 27.

[128] Art.3, (1) c, d, e.

[129] Art.6 (1).

[130] See Art.12 (1).

Work-Life Balance Directive.[131] However, its status as an unpaid entitlement can affect the extent of its use, especially by men. On the other hand, the limited duration of 5 working days might be sufficient to provide short-term care or support, or to find other and more sustainable options for the dependent person, but it is certainly insufficient to provide regular and continuous help over a longer period of time.[132] The relatively limited range of persons for whose personal care and support the leave can be used is also subject to criticism. The modest quality and quantity of entitlements attached to the right to carers' leave, however, does not call into question its significance for workers who are in need of it, because without this right, they would either depend on the goodwill of their employer[133] or use days from their annual leave or other periods of leave, for caregiving. In parallel with the establishment of the new right to leave for carers, the Work-Life Balance Directive also retains the "old" right to unpaid time off from work due to force majeure for urgent family reasons in the case of illness or accident from the repealed Directives.[134] Although there are certain similarities between the rights to leave for carers and for urgent family reasons, such as their focus on the family in a wider sense and not just on children, the main difference is that the former is intended for providing long-term care, while the latter, to address urgent and immediate situations.[135]

Completing the quartet of individual rights established by the Work-Life Balance Directive is **the right to request flexible working arrangements**.[136] The most important improvements in the regulation of this right concern the scope of persons (since it is no longer an exclusive right of working parents, but also of working carers) as well as its purpose (since it is no longer based on purely economic motives of employers for flexible employment of workers, but a self-standing right related to the concept of work-life balance).[137] Hence, the right to request flexible working arrangements is intended both for workers with children up to at least eight years of age and for carers, for caring purposes.[138] Flexible working arrangements refer to the options available to workers to adjust their working patterns, which may include remote working arrangements, flexible working schedules, or reduced working hours.[139] The worker's request entails the obligation of the employer to consider and

[131] See Art.12 (1).

[132] For example, in its binding provisions, the Directive does not mention additional persons who may fall under the category of "relatives", such as siblings and grandparents, which on the other hand, are mentioned in Recital 27 of the Directive.

[133] Oliveira et al. (2020), p. 309.

[134] See Art.7.

[135] Caracciolo di Torella (2017), p. 7.

[136] The introduction of this right within the family-friendly/work-life balance legislation in the EU draws inspiration from the statutory right of employees with young children or children with disabilities to request flexible work arrangements in UK employment law. Sargeant and Lewis (2010), pp. 277–279.

[137] Caracciolo di Torella (2020).

[138] See, Art.9 (1).

[139] Art.3, (1) f.

respond to such a request within a reasonable period of time, and to provide reasons for any refusal or postponement. Consequently, even under the new Directive, the right to request flexible working arrangements does not constitute an absolute entitlement, but rather merely a right to make such a request.[140] When deciding on the request, including a possible negative decision, it is necessary to consider the balancing of interests between the two parties (both the employer and the worker), i.e. to take into account their needs.[141] As to eligibility conditions, the Directive allows Member States to subject this right to either a work qualification period or service length requirement, provided this shall not exceed 6 months.[142] In addition to criticisms about its nature as simply enabling workers to request (without guaranteeing approval of) flexible arrangements,[143] the Directive's approach to regulating this right draws further criticism. It is considered to leave too much discretion to employers to determine whether workers can exercise the right because it does not specify the reasons on the basis of which employers could refuse a workers' request. What also remains unclear is to what extent the obligation to "*take into consideration*" the interests of workers when submitting a request for flexible working arrangement, can limit the space for employers to refuse that request.[144] Flexible working arrangements undoubtedly allow parents and carers (especially women) to better reconcile the tensions between work and family responsibilities, as they allow the preservation of human capital in periods of accentuated needs and obligations in the family.[145] However, the risks of perpetuating the gender "status quo" should not be underestimated, particularly if working women make use of them more than working men.

5 Reconciling Work with Family and Private Life in the Macedonian Legislation

The regulation of work-family or work-life balance in North Macedonia's labour legislation continious to leg significantly behind both contemporary legislative approaches in EU member states, and the measures mandated by the EU Work-Life Balance Directive. The core provisions for special protection of pregnancy, maternity and parenthood in North Macedonia have remained substantially unaltered since the country's first (now repealed) Labour Relations Law of 1993[146] enacted

---

[140] Waddington and Bell (2021), p. 510.

[141] Art.9 (2).

[142] Art.9 (4).

[143] Baranard, op.cit.,p. 423.

[144] Arabadjieva (2022), pp. 28–29.

[145] EIGE, op.cit., 30.

[146] Law on Labour Relations, Official Gazette of Republic of Macedonia, no.80/93.

after the independence, with their legal foundations tracing back to the legislation of the former Socialist Federal Republic of Yugoslavia (SFRY), of which the Socialist Republic of Macedonia was a constituent federal unit. This is particularly relevant to gender equality measures and policies related to unpaid care work in the family.

The current Law on Labour Relations of 2005[147] (hereinafter LLR) nominally contains a provision that obliges *employers to enable workers to more easily reconcile family and professional obligations*.[148] Yet, the regulatory framework governing 'special protection'—which includes specific measures for safeguarding pregnant workers' health and safety, maternity, parental and childbirth-related rights and workplace protections—ultimately reinforces the traditional 'male and female/dual-breadwinner - female caregiver' model. Simultaneously, the legislation remains deficient in flexibility measures accommodating workers with family responsibilities—whether concerning flexible ways of using leaves or flexible working arrangements. The concept of leaves is based on the so-called "leave from work due to pregnancy, childbirth and parenting" that can be used uninterruptedly for a period of 9 months for the birth of one child and 15 months for the birth of two or more children at once, and its primary holder is the mother.[149] The total leave period comprises two components: (1) a mandatory portion that must be utilized, and (2) an optional portion that may be exercised facultatively.[150] The mandatory portion spans: no later than 28 days prior to the expected delivery date (earliest permissible leave commencement), through a minimum of 45 days after confinement (constituting the earliest permissible termination of leave, after which the mother may return to work).[151] The optional portion encompasses: the prenatal period preceding the mandatory leave (exercisable no earlier than 45 days before the expected delivery date), and the postnatal period following the mandatory portion of the leave, i.e. after the 45th day of confinement.[152] The leave entitlement provides full salary compensation, calculated at 100% of the beneficiary's average monthly earnings over the 12-month period preceding leave commencement.[153]

The Law on Labour Relations formally stipulates that the right to leave due to pregnancy, childbirth and parenting can be used by the father as well.[154] However, the father can use the leave only if it is not used by the mother. The Law neither

[147] Law on Labour Relations, Official Gazette of Republic of Macedonia, no.62/05.

[148] LLR, Art. 161, para 2.

[149] See LLR, Art. 165, para 1.

[150] Kalamatiev et al. (2011), p. 65.

[151] See LLR, Art.165, para 2 and Art.166, para 1.

[152] Ibidem.

[153] See LLR, Art.170, para 1 and Law on Health Insurance, (Official Gazette of Republic of Macedonia, no. 25/2000), Art.16, para 1 and Art.17, para 2.

[154] See LLR, чл.167.

explicitly specifies the earliest date when the father may commence leave (despite the evident conclusion—given the mandatory maternity leave period—that he may only commence leave after the completion of the mother's mandatory portion, that is, at least 45 days after confinement), nor establishes procedural details for its implementation including mechanisms for transferring leave entitlements from mother to father, nor mandates any compulsory quota of total leave reserved exclusively for fathers.

The amendments to the LLR from 2013[155] have introduced the right to "unpaid parental leave", the purpose of which is absence from work and care for the child after the expiration of the regular paid leave for pregnancy, childbirth and parenting.[156] With these changes, a partial and inadequate "attempt" is made to comply with the (already at that time) repealed Parental Leave Directive 96/34/EC of 1996. This finding stems from the fact that the amendments provide for parental leave of 3 months in total (instead of 3 months individually for each parent as provided for in the repealed Directive, which are in principle non-transferable[157]) that can be used in the period until the child reaches the age of three.[158] Furthermore, the right to unpaid parental leave (reserved exclusively for female workers) can be characterized as discriminatory[159]—both against male workers, who are explicitly excluded, and against female workers themselves, as it exacerbates gender disparities in the unpaid caregiving responsibilities within families.[160]

The regulation of the right to leave due to pregnancy, childbirth and parenting under North Macedonia's labour legislation—when examined against European directives—gives rise to critical dilemmas. First, it remains unclear whether the law properly distinguishes between 'maternity leave' and 'parental leave' or defines their structural parameters. Second, the extent to which this framework aligns with EU standards, particularly the Work-Life Balance Directive (2019/1158/EU), requires scrutiny. Third, the legal position of working fathers in exercising childcare-related leave compared to mothers' entitlements presents unresolved disparities. The response to the first dilemma requires a broader perspective on EU Law, including the case law of the Court of Justice of the EU. Ever since its ruling in the "Hofmann" case in 1984 and onward, the Court of Justice has consistently interpreted the right to maternity leave as being primarily tied to the protection of women's health in the period following pregnancy and childbirth (i.e., the biological necessity), and only secondarily to the objective of reconciling professional and

155 Law on supplementing and amending the LLR, (Official Gazette of Republic of Macedonia, no.137/2013).

156 See Right of Youth at the Workplace in a Macedonian Context - a national adaptation of the ILO Guide and Toolkit "Rights at Work for Youth, (ILO, 2018), 121.

157 See Parental Leave Directive 96/34/EC, Clause 2 (1).

158 See LLR, Art.170-a.

159 Ibid; Kalamatiev and Ristovski (2017).

160 Ibid; Kalamatiev and Ristovski (2017).

family life (i.e., the social necessity). When maternity leave is 'extended' beyond the biologically necessary recovery period surrounding childbirth, its purpose shifts toward adressing the social necessity to care for the child during its early development. Overemphasizing such a social necessity, however, can perpetuate gender stereotypes and reflect negatively on gender equality in parenting. Conversely, parental leave has an exclusively social purpose. It is designed to facilitate parental childcare responsibilities. The leave due to pregnancy, childbirth and parenting in Macedonian labour legislation neither defines nor differentiates between the purposes for which "maternity" and "parental" leave are used. That being said, given that the father's exercise of this leave right is rendered purely formalistic—as the law explicitly designates the mother as its primary holder—the legal nature of this entitlement remains ambiguous. It is unclear whether it constitutes, "extended maternity leave", "individual parental leave of the mother that can be transferred to the father" or "family leave intended for both parents". Concerning the **second dilemma**, it can be concluded that the leave due to pregnancy, childbirth and parenting is aligned with the Pregnant Workers Directive, but not with the Work-Life Balance Directive. According to the way it is designed, the right to leave due to pregnancy, childbirth and parenting corresponds to the "compulsory" part of the maternity leave (at least 2 weeks allocated before and/or after confinement[161]) and the "optional" part of the maternity leave (the remaining period up to at least 14 weeks allocated before and/or after confinement[162]) provided for in the Pregnant Workers Directive. It also corresponds to the obligation to ensure the leave is adequately paid (at least equivalent to that which the worker concerned would receive in the event of a sick leave[163]) as well as with the eligibility to exercise this right (previous employment for no longer than 12 months immediately before the expected date birth[164]). However, when comparing leave entitlements for pregnancy, childbirth, and parenthood with the parental leave provisions under the Work-Life Balance Directive, fundamental discrepancies emerge in their legal nature—particularly since the Directive expressly establishes parental leave as an individual, non-transferable right for each parent.[165] The answer to the **third dilemma** is already clear. LLR neither sets for an individual, mandatory part of the leave intended for fathers, nor does it reserve any other kind of quota for the involvement of fathers in unpaid parental care in the family.

LLR is also not compliant with the Work-Life Balance Directive with regard to the **right to paternity leave**. A legal provision that most closely resembles the right to paternity leave is the *right to paid leave due to certain personal or family*

---

[161] See PWD, Art.8 (2).

[162] See PWD, Art.8 (1).

[163] See PWD, Art.11 (3).

[164] See PWD, Art.11 (4).

[165] See WLBD, Art.5 (1).

circumstances.[166] It includes elements of "broader" work-life balance (since it can be used on the occasion of a marriage or the death of a close relative), but also of "narrower" work-family balance (since it can be used by the father for the birth of a child). However, the Law does not specify the minimum number of days off that can be taken by the father in the occasion of a birth of a child. It is left to the collective agreements that usually provide for this right in the amount of 2 days. Consequently, North Macedonia's paternity leave provisions fail to achieve full harmonization with the Work-Life Balance Directive, as national legislation does not guarantee the minimum 10-working day period required under EU law.[167] The short duration of the right to "paternity leave" in the Macedonian legal framework calls into question the very purpose of this right, which is to support mothers throughout recovery after childbirth, care for the newborn and another older child, registering the child in registry books and other unpaid work in the family.[168]

The LLR overlooks **the right to carers' leave** as a specific right with a distinctive purpose which is providing personal care or support for a dependent member of the family or household. The same is true for the rights to request flexible ways of using **the right to leave due to pregnancy, childbirth and parenting and flexible working arrangements**. The right to paid leave due to pregnancy, childbirth and parenting is used uninterruptedly (as a full-time leave) and it usually ends before the expiry of or around the ninth or 15th month after the birth of the newborn/s. Neither the law nor the collective agreements provide for a different and more adjusted way for its use that will better meet the needs of the parents (e.g. as a part-time leave, in several parts, and the like). Certain flexibility exists in the case of using the right to unpaid parental leave. This kind of parental leave can be used in three parts of 1 month until the child reaches the age of three.[169] On the other hand, LLR does not recognize the right to request a flexible working arrangement. One of the many weaknesses of the legal framework that regulates part-time work is that it doesn't provide for the right to change working hours from full-time to part-time and vice versa at the request of the worker.[170] The LLR similarly fails to regulate telework. Consequently, any spatial flexibility must be derived from the more traditional framework of homework arrangements—an approach that presents several systemic shortcomings.[171]

---

[166] See LLR, Art.146, para 1.

[167] See WLBD, Art. 4 (1).

[168] EIGE, op.cit., 32.

[169] LLR, Art.170-a, para 1.

[170] Mojsoska Blazhevski et al. (2021), p. 35.

[171] See more on this in Mihes and Ristovski (2020), pp. 7–11.

6 Conclusion

The concept of reconciling work with family responsibilities, i.e., work-life balance, has undergone a long and evolving process of development within both the hard and soft law of the EU, as well as in the case law of the Court of Justice of the European Union (CJEU). Initially inspired by the need to advance gender equality in employment and enhance women's economic contribution to society, work-life balance measures were primarily directed toward mothers, enabling them to maintain employment while caring for young children. However, the double burden borne by women—to be both productive workers and devoted mothers—fundamentally contradicts the principle of substantive gender equality. This ideal requires equal sharing of parental responsibilities and unpaid domestic work between women and men. With the adoption of the 2019 Work-Life Balance Directive, the issue of reconciliation or work-life balance has not only extended to fathers, deepening their involvement in childcare, but has also begun encompassing other caregivers. In any case, from an instrument carrying the title 'work-life balance', it was expected to also address the issue of the position of mothers, which continues to be regulated by the Pregnant Workers Directive—adopted more than 30 years ago. Considering the regulatory framework for paternity and parental leave, we may once again conclude that mothers retain their status as primary caregivers for children. A similar conclusion can be drawn regarding the regulation of carers' leave rights. When examining the definitions of carers and conditions warranting caregiving, along with the overall quality and scope of attached provisions, it remains debatable whether—and to what extent—this right will trigger substantive changes in EU Member States' national legislations. A critical perspective can also be applied to the right to request flexible working arrangements, as it still lacks the status of an absolute right and remains subject to employer approval. While the Directive may fall short of fully realizing its transformative potential for gender equality (particularly in redistributing unpaid familial care), it nevertheless represents a paradigm-shifting instrument with ripple effects extending across EU member states and beyond. North Macedonia, which lags significantly in meaningfully regulating work-life balance issues, could derive valuable lessons from the EU discourse examining the interplay between work-life balance measures and substantive gender equality between men and women. This trajectory demands profound systemic reform in conceptualizing North Macedonia's work-life balance framework—particularly in reimagining the design and implementation of maternity, paternity, and parental leave policies.

Official Documents and Directives

Charter of Fundamental Rights of the European Union, OJ C 364/1; OJ C 303/17.
Council Directive 76/207/EEC; 92/85/EEC; 96/34/EC.
Directive 2002/73/EC; 2006/54/EC; 2010/18/EU; 2019/1158 (EU).

Treaty of Amsterdam, OJ C 340, 10/11/1997.
European Commission (2018). *Paternity and parental leave policies across the EU.*
European Institute for Gender Equality (EIGE), 2021.
Interinstitutional Proclamation on the European Pillar of Social Rights, OJ [2017] C428/10.
Law on Labour Relations, Official Gazette of Republic of Macedonia, no.80/93, 62/05, 137/2013.

References

Arabadjieva K (2022) Reshaping the Work-Life Balance Directive with Covid-19 lessons in mind. ETUI, pp 9, 18, 24, 26, 27, 28–29
Barnard C (2012) EU employment law, 4th edn. Oxford University Press, pp 289, 291–293, 403, 423
Beneria L (1999) The enduring debate over unpaid labour. Int Labour Rev 138:287
Birk R (2007) European social charter. Wolters Kluwer, pp 218–219
Blanpain R (2013). European labour law. Wolters Kluwer, pp 254–258, 738
Brough P, Timms C, Chan XW, Hawkes A, Rasmussen L (2020) Work–life balance: definitions, causes, and consequences. In: Theorell T (ed) Handbook of socioeconomic determinants of occupational health. Springer, pp 1–15
Caracciolo di Torella E (2017) An emerging right to care in the EU: a "new start to support work-life balance for parents and carers". ERA Forum 18:187–198
Caracciolo di Torella E (2020) One more step along the way: the 2019 Work Life Balance Directive Revue de Droit Comparé du Travail et de la Sécurité Sociale, 2/2020
Caracciolo di Torella E, Masselot A (2010). Reconciling work and family life in EU law and policy. Palgrave MacMillan, pp 5, 8, 15, 26
Collins H, Ewing KD, McColgan A (2012) Labour law. Cambridge University Press, p 370
Davies ACL (2009) Perspectives on labour law. Cambridge University Press, p 105
Davies ACL (2012) EU labour law. Edward Elgar Publishing Limited:137–138
Ellis E, Watson P (2012) EU anti-discrimination law. Oxford University Press:333–338
Eurofound (2019) Parental and paternity leave – uptake by fathers. Publications Office of the European Union, Luxembourg
European Trade Union Confederation (2011) The Revised Parental Leave Framework Agreement. An ETUC Interpretation Guide, p 23
Eurofound (2020) Women and labour market equality: Has COVID-19 rolled back recent gains? Publications Office of the European Union, Luxembourg, p 2
Ferguson S (2018) Social reproduction: what's the big idea? Pluto Press
Freedman S, Fudge J (2016) The contract of employment and gendered work. Oxford University Press, pp 233–235
Fudge G, Owens R (2006) Precarious work, women, and the new economy: the challenge to legal norms. Hart Publishing:14–15
Gornick JC, Meyers MK (2001) Building the dual earner/dual carer society: policy developments in Europe. Rethinking social protection conference. Harvard University
Greenhaus J, Singh R (2004) Work and family. Encyclopedia of Applied Psychology, pp 687–697
Guess R, (2021) A Philosopher Looks At Work. Cambridge University Press
Hayers L J B (2017) Stories of Care: A Labour lf Law. Palgrave MacMillan
Hein C (2005) Reconciling work and family responsibilities: practical ideas from global experience. International Labour Office

Kalamatiev T, Ristovski A (2017) Labour legislation and policies aimed at reconciling employee's professional commitments with their personal and family life. Aktualni Problemi na Trudovoto i Osiguritelnoto Pravo, Tom IX, pp 100–112

Kalamatiev T, Mitrevski Ž, Ristovski A (2011) Handbook on employment relationship rights of women and youth in Republic of Macedonia. Friedrich Ebert Stiftung, Skopje, p 65

Kenner J (2003) EU employment law: from Rome to Amsterdam and beyond. Hart Publishing, pp 156, 274

Kovacs E, Heissl C (2015) 92/88/EEC: maternity protection. Wolters Kluwer, p 301

Lewis J, (2009) Work-family balance, gender and policy. Edward Elgar Publishing Limited Cheltenham

Mihes C, Ristovski A (2020) Legal analysis of the regulation and implementation of "telework" in Macedonian labour law context. ILO, pp 7–11

Oliveira A, De la Corte-Rodríguez M, Lütz F (2020) The new directive on work-life balance: towards a new paradigm of family care and equality? Eur Law Rev 45(3):305

Pircher B, de la Porte C, Szelewa D (2023) Actors, costs and values: the implementation of the Work-Life Balance Directive. West European Politics. https://doi.org/10.1080/01402382.2023.2181504

Rubery J (1998) Women in the labour market: a gender equality perspective. OECD, Paris, p 23

Sargeant M, Lewis D (2010) Employment law. Pearson Education Limited, pp 277–279

Vinković M (2023) Leading or breeding: gender segregation in the labour market. Gender Persp Priv Law 4:133–135

Waddington L, Bell M (2021) The right to request flexible working arrangements under the work-life balance directive—a comparative perspective. Eur Labour Law J 12(4):510

Social Rights of the Elderly: Analysis from the Viewpoint of EU Social Policy, the Market and the Hungarian Law

Henriett Rab and Márton Leó Zaccaria

1 Problem Statement

The problem of the ageing workforce can be observed as a common phenomenon in the labour market of all Member States of the European Union (hereinafter: EU), including the countries that joined with the 2004 enlargement.[1] This social (demographic) phenomenon cannot be interpreted in isolation and exclusively in the present, since it had a clearly identifiable history in previous decades and is difficult to treat in isolation from many other challenges European societies face.[2] In this context, reference should be made to social changes and challenges which, on the one hand, are not independent of the negative economic processes affecting individual countries,[3] and on the other hand, they have a major impact on employment and the

The chapter's text is based on a research, which contains some parts in Hungarian. Some of these Hungarian parts were translated with DeepL Translate. These parts include separate sentences of the full text. These parts include separate sentences of the full text. The authors reviewed the translation for accuracy.

[1] Bíró and Elek (2019), pp. 164–166.

[2] Pecinovsky (2019), pp. 44–45, 65–66.

[3] Schreurs (2023), pp. 346–348, 357–358.

H. Rab · M. L. Zaccaria (✉)
University of Debrecen, Faculty of Law, Debrecen, Hungary
e-mail: rab.henriett@law.unideb.hu; zaccaria.marton@law.unideb.hu

K. Koldinská et al. (eds.), *Labour Law and Social Security Law in Central and Eastern Europe*, European Union and its Neighbours in a Globalized World 26,
https://doi.org/10.1007/978-3-032-04496-9_7

transformation of labour law across Member States.[4] It is also necessary to refer to e.g. the decrease in birth rates, since the ageing labour market cannot be treated as a general problem alone, since employment legislation cannot remain neutral in the long run against the difficulties of recruiting workforce within the Member States, which is also a characteristic of Europe.

All these problems could be solved essentially within national borders, i.e. at national labour market level, but this cannot be done effectively for two reasons. Firstly, the free movement of workers and the economic community represented by the EU (also) link the Member States in this field, meaning that solutions that are effective or less effective in a given case can send out ripples that have an impact in several Member States. That is, from this point of view, national solutions can only partially solve these problems, in other words, they are more of a symptomatic treatment, definitely in the short and medium term. Secondly, we cannot ignore the EU spirit and legislative trend, which does not fundamentally exclude closer social and labour law (social policy) cooperation between Member States, along the lines of economic cooperation.[5] Its primary objective is to address effectively and jointly such and similar labour market and social problems (see: adaptive workforce and high-level social protection at the same time).[6] In this context, it is mainly new legal solutions and new labour market phenomena that have emerged, either as a result of the European Pillar of Social Rights (hereinafter: EPSR)[7] or in the case law of the Court of Justice of the European Union (hereinafter: CJEU).

Therefore, our study examines the main research question from a market, legislative and enforcement perspective: how the crucial social rights of older workers can be effectively enforced in these changing labour market conditions. In the following, particular attention will be paid to the employment rights of older people, based on the relevant fundamental rights and case law of the CJEU. In addition, the challenges generated by the digitalisation of work are reflected in our work, and we explore the essential economic and social factors—paralleled by the guarantees of social rights protection—which may prevent employees from actually spending their retirement years at the end of their active careers in a way that respects their human dignity and their social rights are not violated.

---

[4] Liukkunen (2020a), pp. 19–21, 37–38. (Accessed 26 May 2024).

[5] Rainone (2024), pp. 2–3, 7.

[6] European Commission – Directorate-General for Employment, Social Affairs and Inclusion (2014) Labour law and working conditions. Social Europe guide, vol 6. Publications Office of the European Union, Luxembourg, pp 9–14, 24–25. https://codecizietineri.files.wordpress.com/2014/04/7a-social_europe_guide.pdf (Accessed 26 May 2024).

[7] The European Pillar of Social Rights: where are we now and where are we going? (2019) ETUI. https://www.etui.org/about-etui/news/the-european-pillar-of-social-rights-where-are-we-now-and-where-are-we-going (Accessed 26 May 2024).

2 Guarantees Under EU Law: The Importance of the Fundamental Rights Context

While in general there are several levels of protection against discrimination,[8] and legislators mostly seek to ensure that workers are not subject to disproportionate, objectively unjustified discrimination based on a personal characteristic,[9] we believe that the Charter of Fundamental Rights of the European Union (hereinafter: CFREU) is of prime importance in this area. On the one hand, direct references to the CFREU appear from time to time in judgments of the CJEU,[10] which is explained by the importance of secondary legislation in the field of anti-discrimination legislation, so that the fundamental rights prescriptions necessarily show a close link with the individual directives and, through them, with the labour law rules of the Member States. On the other hand, bearing in mind other relevant sources of law, such as the European Social Charter (hereinafter: ESC)[11] or the European Convention on Human Rights (hereinafter: ECHR),[12] the CFREU appears to be the most important in primary law in terms of guaranteeing the fundamental rights of workers, not counting the universal equality clauses in the Treaties.[13] In the light of this, the content and legal nature of Article 25 of the CFREU that we will discuss below.

2.1 Equal Treatment Based on Age: Principle or Right?

Citing *Delfino*'s problem statement[14] and the classification system that can be derived from it,[15] we believe that it is not unreasonable to ask the above question even if the CFREU naturally provides for fundamental rights and not for principles.[16] However, this distinction is still necessary to outline the basis of our analysis, because, on the one hand, some articles of the CFREU may have a different legal nature, even by their wording.[17] On the other hand, in the light of the relevant

[8] Gyulavári (2007), pp. 30–32.

[9] Schlachter (2011), pp. 287–299.

[10] Papa (2015), pp. 190–191, 203–205.

[11] Article 7 (right of children and young persons to protection) and Article 12 (right to social security) of the European Social Charter (ESC), Article 23 of the Revised European Social Charter (right of elderly persons to social protection).

[12] Article 14, European Convention on Human Rights (ECHR) (Prohibition of discrimination).

[13] Articles 2–3, Treaty on the European Union (equality, aims of the EU) and Article 10, Treaty on the Functioning of the European Union (combatting discrimination).

[14] Delfino (2015), pp. 86–92.

[15] Delfino, Ibid, pp. 87–91.

[16] Alaimo and Caruso (2010a), p. 88. (Accessed 26 May 2024).

[17] Article 21, Charter of Fundamental Rights of the European Union (CFREU): "Any discrimination based on...shall be prohibited." Article 30, Charter of Fundamental Rights of the European

secondary legislation,[18] the prohibition of age discrimination is part of a framework in EU law that already in itself applies a variety of legal instruments against discrimination in the labour market. An example of this regulatory approach can be the negative and positive approach to equal rights in regulation,[19] the reversed (shared) burden of proof,[20] or the normative nature of the specific but narrow scope of justification based on age.[21]

In our opinion—following the logic of the above reasoning—it can be concluded that the prohibition of age discrimination is a fundamental principle of EU law,[22] enshrined in the general commitment to equal rights in the Treaties,[23] and the fact that the legal guarantees supporting it are reflected in EU law from several sides. At the same time, since this matter of principle is not included in the CFREU as a fundamental social or solidarity right in the narrow sense,[24] it is enshrined in the legislation and in the practice of the CJEU as a fundamental right to be guaranteed to EU citizens. Article 25 itself seems clear in this respect, since—read together with the anti-discrimination framework under Article 21—it guarantees the dignity of older people by protecting their rights, with a special emphasis on participation in social life, of which the world of work is of course, an integral part. Article 25 of the CFREU reads as follows:

> The Union recognises and respects the rights of the elderly to lead a life of dignity and independence and to participate in social and cultural life.[25]

However, it cannot be ignored that this fundamental right is based, on the one hand, on a general prohibition, a legislative prohibition, i.e. some kind of restriction of conduct,[26] and, on the other hand, that the limits of the content of the fundamental

---

Union (CFREU): "Every worker has the right to protection against unjustified dismissal…" The latter is connected anti-discrimination by the clear prohibition of unjustified dismissal, which means that even a hidden, underlying reason for dismissal pointing in the direction of age discrimination, is against EU law and infringes fundamental social rights. Moreover, Article 21 and 30 – as fundamental rights – form a significant barrier in regard to the workers' social protection, speaking not only of discrimination.

[18] Council Directive 2000/78/EC of 27 November 2000 establishing a general framework for equal treatment in employmentand occupation.

[19] Articles 1–2, Directive 2000/78/EC: "(1) For the purposes of this Directive, the 'principle of equal treatment' shall mean that there shall be no direct or indirect discrimination whatsoever on any of the grounds referred to in Article 1."

[20] Article 10, Directive 2000/78/EC.

[21] Article 6, Directive 2000/78/EC.

[22] Article 10, Treaty on the Functioning of the European Union (TFEU).

[23] Articles 2–3, Treaty on European Union (TEU).

[24] See Chapter III on Equality.

[25] Article 25, Charter of Fundamental Rights of the European Union (CFREU).

[26] Paragraph (1) of Article 21, Charter of Fundamental Rights of the European Union (CFREU): "Any discrimination based on any ground such as sex, race, colour, ethnic or social origin, genetic features, language, religion or belief, political orany other opinion, membership of a national minority, property, birth, disability, age or sexual orientation shall be prohibited."

right itself are difficult to draw. The commentary to Article 25 points out that the Member States themselves have such an extensive practice and legislative tradition in this area,[27] that in some cases it may be questionable whether a discriminatory conduct falls within the scope of Article 25—or indeed Article 21—at all. This dilemma is also a recurrent point of interpretation in the case law of the CJEU, and—drawing on Articles 1 and 2 of Directive 2000/78/EC—it can be stated that the prohibition of age discrimination in employment and labour law should be applied as widely as possible,[28] although certain exceptions are legitimate.[29] Moreover, the tangible legal framework for this legislation is perhaps still relatively young compared to the field of gender equality used as a model,[30] thus the CJEU should continue to work on the development and clarification of such key age-specific concepts as indirect discrimination,[31] effective legal protection[32] or special justification rules.[33]

2.2 *The Legal Nature of Article 25 of the Charter of Fundamental Rights of the European Union and the Scope of Legal Protection*

As mentioned above, Article 25 and the Directive are general standards, allowing only narrow exceptions or derogations from age-neutral labour market regulations or practices. At the same time, the means of achieving equality are varied, bearing in mind that Article 21 is a classic imperative prohibition, stating only that discrimination on grounds of age is prohibited.[34] It follows from this general statement alone that this fundamental right should be applied to all types of labour law facts and problems, and it is in fact "enforced" by the Directive and Article 25 of the CFREU, which also does not discriminate between potentially discriminatory facts or conduct. Consequently, in relation to the right to work, conditions of access to work, job applications, working conditions, remuneration, the right to a career, termination of employment, any benefits linked to employment (pension, length of service, etc.), the rule of non-discrimination on the grounds of age must be respected.

This is also of great importance for the rest of our analysis, since some of the labour market and labour law disadvantages that we sometimes seem to take for granted are, mainly, in conflict with these prohibitions. At the same time, our analysis would be one-sided if we did not pay at least as much attention to the general and

[27] Veneziani (2006), pp. 203–210.
[28] Takács (2021), p. 36.
[29] Hungler (2021).
[30] 1970s and 2000s.
[31] Hős (2014), pp. 52–53.
[32] Articles 9–10, Directive 2000/78/EC.
[33] Schlachter (2011), pp. 39–40.
[34] Veneziani (2006), pp. 203–204, 208.

special exemption rules that may still make age discrimination, where appropriate, in the labour market or in employment conditions and terms of employment lawful. In order to interpret these, some important components of recent case law of the CJEU are in the following.

3 Fragments from Recent CJEU Case Law on the Interpretation of Age Discrimination in the Workplace (in the Labour Market)

The importance of the case law of the CJEU as the guardian of these rights is paramount, since if the above-mentioned guarantees—or their absence—are (almost) solely dependent on the conduct and discretion of the employers, the employment of older people may become unpredictable and lack transparency. In light of this, reintegration into the labour market will not be effective without strengthening the basic social protection rules guaranteed by the CFREU[35] and the EPSR, and the CJEU's interpretation of the law can also serve this purpose in the current market circumstances.

By age discrimination, we do not only mean discrimination in the "traditional" sense,[36] but also disadvantaged situations against younger persons, typically e.g. young people starting their careers. Although the most basic source of law in this area, Directive 2000/78/EC, does not contain specific provisions adapted to each age group,[37] fundamental differences between the two discrimination situations can be detected. In this study, we focus exclusively on scope of age discrimination against older people, mainly for reasons of space and conceptual reasons, and based on the hypothesis that discrimination against older people in the labour market is still clearly demonstrably higher today. Although this sample is not necessarily representative due to differences in the Member States' regulations and labour markets, we believe that the case law of the CJEU is a faithful reflection of these trends, especially since the labour market crisis caused by ageing societies is a common phenomenon in the Member States. Surely, the above conclusion can reasonably be drawn from this.

In the following, we will briefly attempt to analyse old-age discrimination in the labour market in the light of the labour law and fundamental rights context discussed in the first part of the study, and then draw conclusions based on the results

---

[35] Berke (2013), pp. 8–14.

[36] Hepple (2003).

[37] Contrary, for example, to the Hungarian Labour Code (LC): LC Section 4 (special provisions applied to young workers), LC Sections 114 and 119 (special provisions applied to young workers regarding working time and rest periods), point a) Paragraph (1) of LC Section 294 (definition of young worker); Paragraph (4) of LC Section 66 (special provisions applied in the case of termination of workers' employment relationship close to old-age pension), and point g) of Paragraph (1) of LC Section 294 (definition of retired worker).

of the analysis on the effectiveness and trends in the protection against age discrimination. The primary tool for this will be a jurisprudential analysis of the key provisions of Directive 2000/78/EC, which are also prominent in the case law of the CJEU. The question can therefore be posed in this context as to which types of labour law situations and which categories of workers fall under the umbrella of the rights guaranteed by the Directive. Although a broad interpretation is necessary in this context, the case law of the CJEU has from time to time clarifies the types of facts that fall within this concept.[38]

We consider judgment C-644/19 to be a case with a somewhat specific factual situation, but also suitable for drawing a general conclusion.[39] According to the judgement, Articles 1 and 2 of the Directive do not apply to retired employees if, after reaching retirement age, their employment in the same job as before is only possible if an additional condition is met. In the specific case of university lecturers, they can only remain in their former posts after retirement if they are also doctoral supervisors; otherwise, they can only be employed for a limited period with a lower-level remuneration.[40] In our view, it is noteworthy that the CJEU treats employment during retirement according to essentially different principles, even if in this specific case age is not necessarily the sole criterion for the organisation of employment, since the tasks of a doctoral supervisor do not necessarily correspond to age. Furthermore, since they are retired employees, the strict prohibition under the Directive cannot be applied to them unchanged.

In support of this necessarily broad interpretation of the Directive, we refer to the Case C-587/20,[41] according to which, under Article 3 (1) (a) and (d) of the Directive, the protection guaranteed by the Directive must be granted to a person holding or standing for the office of president of an employees' organisation where the constitution of the organisation provides for an age limit. On this basis, positions related to employee representation and activities cannot be exempted from the prohibition of age discrimination, unless there is an objective reason consistent with the Directive's exemption.

Judgement C-301/21[42] reflects the problem of the scope of the Directive in several respects, pointing out that the prohibition of age discrimination is not inconsistently applicable to all situations, which may be in any way related to the age of the employee in terms of the disadvantage suffered by the employee. The legitimacy of a difference in the remuneration of judges appointed before and after a certain legislative date is at issue in the underlying national case,[43] in which the injury to employees was caused by the fact that the remuneration of employees (judges) appointed after a certain date were lower than the colleagues' appointed before that

[38] Gyulavári and Hős (2013), pp. 290–293.

[39] Case C-644/19, FT v Universitatea "Lucian Blaga" Sibiu and Others.

[40] Case C-644/19, point 19 and conclusions.

[41] Case C-587/20, Ligebehandlingsnævnet acting on behalf of A v HK/Danmark and HK/Privat.

[42] Case C-301/21, Curtea de Apel Alba Iulia and Others.

[43] Case C-301/21, points 24–34.

date. The labour market problem posed by this case is therefore given, and at the same time it also points out a general contradiction, since it may be questionable how much leeway the employer or the legislator—taking into account the prohibition of age discrimination—has in determining the wages of employees when a given date marks a clear caesura in this respect. Although it is conceivable that there may be a substantial age difference between colleagues doing the same work for different enumeration because of the time differences, the CJEU interprets this as not in itself a reason that follows from Article 1 of the Directive, since "...Directive 2000/78 must be interpreted as meaning that it precludes discrimination only where that discrimination is based on one of the grounds that it lists expressly in Article 1."[44] In other words, age is not the basis of discrimination in this case, since, in our view, younger employees could fill the given position earlier and older employees could fill it later. This way, Article 2 (1) and (2) do not apply to such facts, as there is nothing to be exempted if there is no ground for discrimination (protected characteristic) under Article 1. In our view, this type of interpretation of the law reinforces the need for labour market flexibility discussed earlier.

4 Labour Market Adaptability Versus Legal Protection: The Risks of Employing Older People

Because of the above, it can be concluded that rules protecting older employees are in place and that fundamental norms are of prime importance in this area. In addition, if we look at the collision of the governing legislation and the labour market problems outlined earlier, primarily ageing, we can see that market opportunities and challenges in many cases have the potential to undermine the effectiveness of non-discriminatory employment. Moreover, the related processes are divergent, as the market reality in fact prioritises the most active and extensive involvement of older employees,[45] extending the retirement age, where appropriate, but at least making "lifelong employment" more legitimate and beneficial for the employee. At the same time, discrimination against older people in employment law and in the labour market still persists, as it can be seen partly through regulation and partly through principles of jurisprudence.[46] In our opinion, there are problems with different roots behind this dichotomy.

It is clear that European societies now need not to prepare for these phenomena, but to live with them, and if it is possible to resolve the economic and legal tensions they cause. By this we mean, first of all, that employers—or even decision-makers—sometimes still seem to take for granted the market situation that all employees can be replaced, if necessary, and of course typically by younger, better qualified

[44] Case C-301/21, point 69.

[45] Manfredi and Vickers (2013), pp. 251–260.

[46] Hungler, pp. 6–7, 13–15.

employees (who, because of their younger age and less work experience, may do the same job for less remuneration, according to the general labour market assumption). Today, this is only true in a very narrow circle and by no means, in general in the labour market, in addition there are no real arguments for "replacing" older employees, or even refusing to employ them, even if the use of objective age limits may be legitimate in certain jobs (see the justification method below).[47] However, it follows a contrario, that if such objective circumstances do not exist, we are certainly talking about a discriminatory employer practice or rule, which therefore violates primary EU law,[48] secondary EU law,[49] human rights guarantees[50] and of course, national law in some cases.[51] The opposing processes should therefore—presumably—lead to more flexible solutions required from both the law enforces, and the legislator, which protect the employees' interests but ensure labour market adaptation properly.

Nevertheless, of course, the other side of the labour market reality cannot be ignored either: older employees are not in principle suited to all types of work, and here we do not necessarily mean just the physical characteristics. An important role in creating a labour market balance for older generations is to ensure that this part of the workforce can also become adaptive, that they do not suffer labour market disadvantages because of technological achievements, new ways of working, and digitalisation in general, due to their adaptability and flexibility. However, beyond a rational measure, it is very difficult for legal regulation to help, as both employees and employers have a great responsibility in this area, and the conflicting interests and processes mentioned above are difficult to reconcile.

A concrete manifestation of this labour market problem is the basic expectation of reintegration of older people, even at retirement age, into the labour market. A good example of this can be the Hungarian solution,[52] but overall, this is a typical phenomenon in the EU. On the one hand, the regulation itself can be worrisome, since even if the employment of pensioners appears only as an option, it can still be harmful, even on a social level. On the other hand, these labour law guarantees actually work in the opposite direction to what is typically the legislative objective (see e.g. Article 25 of the CFREU). Namely, in this sense, the employment of older generations, even full-time employment, is made possible solely on the basis of market interests, without the appropriate legal guarantees, their right to equality is likely to be violated, as they will be at a disadvantage in the labour market in many

[47] Hendrickx (2013), pp. 82–83.

[48] Articles 2–3, Treaty on European Union (TEU), Article 10, Treaty on the Functioning of the European Union (TFEU), and Articles 21 and 25, Charter of Fundamental Rights of the European Union (CFREU).

[49] Article 2, Directive 2000/78/EC.

[50] Article 14, European Convention on Human Rights (ECHR).

[51] See the Hungarian example: Section 8 (concept of direct discrimination and protected characteristics) and Section 9 (concept of indirect discrimination) of the Act on Equal Treatment and Promotion of Equal Opportunities.

[52] Ferencz (2015), p. 68, Sipka and Zaccaria (2017), pp. 24–25.

respects compared to younger generations. In this way, the prohibition of discrimination may be rendered meaningless, and it is precisely the fact that the economic mechanism that necessarily employs older employees for as long as possible and in as large number as possible does not include real legal guarantees that will constitute a violation of their dignity and their right to equality. Thus, for example, the directive guarantees can also become secondary, since both the definite prohibition of direct and indirect discrimination may lose its function, but also the special exemption system in terms of its essence, because economic necessity seems to override these principles and rights.

5 Labour Law in the Service of Older People: Occupational Safety and Health, Compliance, Social Protection and Their Reasonable Limits

Based on the above, it is clear that as the employees get older, they have to face more and more problems in the labour market. The importance of age is present in both younger and older age in the employment framework, but while so far, we have examined the issue from an equal treatment perspective, in the following we return to the issue of age regarding justified differentiation and preference. The issue of justified differentiation has already been discussed in the context of justified discrimination on the grounds of the nature of the work, but there are also a number of cases that do not necessarily appear to be justified because of labour law and equal treatment rules.

5.1 Working Conditions as a Stable Framework for Older Workers

First, it is worth highlighting the distinction arising from the nature of the working time schedule. During the course of their lives, the employees perform work in many cases in different life situations, possibly of the same value. Depending on the generation, these days, the young employee at the beginning of their career mainly strives to maximize their free time.

In this case, the young employee prefers a work schedule that means longer working hours per day combined with more rest days. This, of course, also requires good stamina and endurance due to their age. However, at a similar age, a young person with children has different needs: likes to be at home at night and spend weekends with their family. Older employees can and do work longer hours again, and only their health and motivation determine the limits of their working hours. Is the distinction that an employer makes when they select employees to join an existing work schedule, thus differentiating between employees based on age, a justified distinction?

We need a different approach to answer this question from a legal and HR (Human Resource Management) perspective. As far as labour law is concerned, it is sufficient to start from the assumption that in the case of the employee, the employment contract is concluded and the employment is based on the mutual agreement of the parties,[53] while the guarantees of working time are provided by labour law.[54] Therefore, if the employee accepts a task and acknowledges the working time schedule, the employer only has to employ the employee. A slightly more informed approach is to include compliance,[55] within that, labour law compliance in our investigation. After all, how much is it enough to rely on the employment contract and the agreement of the parties if the framework for continuity is not ensured due to labour law guarantees[56] such as the ban on night work for young children, limits on working hours for young employees or the protection of older workers' health at work? It is pointless for an employer to employ a sufficient number of workers to carry out a particular task if, because of labour law requirements, special operating conditions such as night work, 12-hour working hours or uninterrupted working hours are not guaranteed. In our view, conscious workforce planning and the security of supply of tasks may be reason enough to ensure a justified distinction, if it is based on truly rational reasons and continuity of operations cannot be ensured otherwise.

The importance of occupational health examinations increases with age, and it is a natural process that, as health deteriorates; the risk parameters for work also gradually deteriorate in some elements. The planning of this and the management of the risks arising from the activity are also the extraordinary task of the employer, along with this, the necessary occupational safety regulations and the avoidance of the risk of health deterioration arising from the work can also be assessed in advance, a compliance[57] activity within the framework of labour law. If the basic operation involves a health risk, it is necessary to be prudent in the organisation of work when setting daily working hours, breaks and additional health and safety regulations. In other words, behaviour—a commitment that is stricter than labour law regulations—also appears in the employer's activities, which we evaluate as part of the signs of CSR (Corporate Social Responsibility) operation.[58] Without prejudice to financial planning, employment with a reallocation of costs and a focus on prevention is already compliant and socially responsible corporate behaviour. The significance of what we have described may be that labour market actors often criticise labour legislation for providing too many costly guarantees for the protection of

[53] Berke (2013), pp. 105–122.

[54] See, for example, the regulation of irregular work schedule in the Hungarian Labour Code (LC).

[55] Wu and van Rooij (2019), pp. 579–591.

[56] Berke (2013), pp. 42–46.

[57] See regarding the development of the compliance mindset: Ambrus and Farkas (2019).

[58] Kun (2011), p. 24. Rab (2018), pp. 202–217.

employees, which are not needed on the employees' side (supported by the growing atypical forms of employment). As described here, the demand may also come from the part of the employer, if they consider long-term employment.[59]

5.2 *Considerations from the Side of Human Resource Management*

HR perspectives add a new dimension to the issue. In the aforementioned labour market environment of labour shortages, the retention of workforce cannot be ensured solely through the forward-looking design of labour legislation, as the importance of subjective human needs should not be ignored. It is no coincidence that in the context of Industry 4.0, the importance of motivation and workforce retention precedes recruitment.[60] However, in addition to the motivational toolbox, new aspects have also emerged in the recruitment framework, which now have relevance for labour law. Here we think of the requirement of equal treatment. When the employer, for reasons relevant to them, looks for an older or younger employee for a position during the selection process, the employer does not make their decision according to the logic of the law of opportunity. The question to be examined is whether this constitutes a justified distinction. For the employer, the distinction is objectively justified, because the security of production/task supply presupposes that they entrust the task to colleagues who are also compatible in personality at group level.

Generational differences[61] have been shown to cause internal tensions in the body. Thus, if the existing group of employees is older/younger, this is the target group that the employer will target when selecting other employees.[62] If an employer excludes a target group with a protected characteristic in the selection procedure, the employer violates the rules of equal treatment. There is therefore only one legal way of this practice: if we accept production and operational interests as a justified distinction. The role of the law is to provide guarantees for individuals in need of protection, but in this case, the protection creates an artificial situation where the protection provided based on a protected characteristic may result an unfair situation for the individual, where the appropriate working environment and social needs are not provided. This means that the employee will be legally protected, but their

[59] The demand for long-term employment can also be part of the market culture, for example in Far-Eastern societies. It is also possible that this demand is forced by the labour market itself because of the labour shortage, urging employers to try to keep their workforce. See in detail: Fehér (2007), pp. 11–21.

[60] Pataki-Magyar (2024). (Accessed 26 May 2024).

[61] Balogh et al. (2021), pp. 59–67. (Accessed 27 May 2024). Fluktuáció és generációs különbségek (2023). (Accessed 27 May 2024).

[62] Ungureanu (2024).

labour market situation will be rather unstable and the social rights of the new generation[63] will be marginalised.

We can also face the opposite direction operation of equal treatment in relation to generational differences in employment. After all, a number of national, EU-level motivational solutions appear to promote the employment of the elderly—in this case, pensioners–, all of which can be examined from the point of view of equal treatment in the context of ensuring the possibility of preferential treatment. Among the Hungarian rules, cooperative employment—with tax benefits—for retired people in a similar way to students' employment is the case like this, and the provision of different levels of training for older people, including even higher education, to catch up with their peers or to support lifelong learning. This is essentially aimed at ensuring the active presence of the older generation in society—in our context, in the labour market.[64] This issue also leads to the question of how to solve the problems of the pension system, which could be the subject of a separate study. However, we can say that the creation of an active role for the older, retired generation is a consequence of an ageing society and is aimed at reducing the level of dependency rates, naturally along with social reasons. CSR and compliant thinking are essential to help reduce the level of interference in the social order through state regulators, when labour market actors manage these types of situations through preliminary consideration of the processes involved, either based on their own responsibility or in the interests of their employers.

Digitalisation adds a new dimension and challenges to the situation, as the emergence of AI intensifies generational differences, and the problem of ageing is already appearing at the generational level for Generation X and even Generation Y, since their relationship with information technology tools is very different from that of Generation Z or Generation Alpha. Several researches investigate[65] what employment solutions and conditions are needed to treat the symptoms of digitalisation and robotisation: The EU[66] and the International Labour Organization (ILO)[67] are also working in a number of ways to promote continuous training and the adaptation of labour market actors to the dynamic advance of digitalisation and artificial intelligence. However, in relation to training and catching up, we must not forget that this is an artificial intervention in the labour market processes, helping to reduce discrimination between generations. It is still premature to judge the results and significance of the programme, but it can be concluded that all this is a conscious defensive

[63] See Article 5 (secure and adaptable employment) or Article 9 (work-life balance) of the European Pillar of Social Rights (EPSR).

[64] Article 25, Charter of Fundamental Rights of the European Union (CFREU).

[65] See for example: Kopp (2019), Richards and Smart (2016), Ződi (2018), p. 184, Kirov and Thill (2018), pp. 297–313.

[66] European Social Partners Framework Agreement on Digitalisation.22.06.2020. https://ec.europa.eu/social/main.jsp?catId=521&langId=en&agreementId=5665 (26/05/2024).

[67] ILO – Global Commission on the Future of Work (2019) Work for a brighter future. Geneva, p 35. https://www.ilo.org/wcmsp5/groups/public/%2D%2D-dgreports/%2D%2D-cabinet/documents/publication/wcms_662410.pdf (Accessed 26 May 2024).

reaction in order to reduce the disadvantage, which would basically result discriminatory situations on the labour market.

6 Conclusion

Overall, it can be concluded that the international and EU development of social rights plays a major role in the construction of anti-discrimination rules, how we treat individuals with certain protected characteristics is a key issue in an advanced society. Whether it is women, elderly persons, persons with disabilities, but in general it is also true that, given the level of development of a certain society and legal system, virtually all personal characteristics are entitled to legal protection, taking into account in particular the traditions of that legal system. A well-developed body of relevant case law underpins this system of non-discrimination, which derives from our fundamental human rights.

In the first part of our study, we dealt with these current rules and trends in legal interpretation by addressing the question of how protection against age discrimination can be assessed and applied with sufficient effectiveness in the current social and societal context. However, during the evaluation, in addition to the classical social law aspects, we also pointed out the possibility of a market-driven interpretation. The basic aim of anti-discrimination rules is—from an employee's point of view—to correct imbalances resulting from a weaker position. However, in cases where the discrimination also takes into account the social interests of the discriminated parties, it may be questionable whether these types of social interests can legitimise discrimination. In answering this question, we have highlighted situations that arise in the labour market and in the context of work organisation and labour law, and that can be regarded from a different perspective of discrimination than the way market solutions reflect on these situations. The significance of the problem is that the labour market perception of the older generation is mixed. There are a number of key principles and EU legal measures to promote active ageing, in the interest of keeping older people in or re-entering the labour market. However, the labour market is more sensitive to this situation, focusing on the efficiency aspect. There are solutions to protect the interests and rights of older workers, just as the importance of life-long learning is not in question, and long-term learning and development can be given increased importance in the context of digitalisation and AI. However, other relevant aspects—such as generational differences, occupational health issues, physical workload, and ideal work organisation solutions—point rather towards solutions that discriminate older workers. All of this can even lead to a new approach to legitimate age-based (justified) different treatment.

Finally, it should be noted that the labour market reacts to the above problem of age discrimination and the collision of labour market effectiveness according to the extent of labour shortages in the labour market and how labour law instruments can address these. This type of direct market perspective can be reconciled with the issue of discrimination if organisational sociological reasons are taken into account in the justified distinction, for which there is currently no relevant and well-developed legal practice, as these are not the main focus of anti-discrimination cases. In fact, the market tends to mask these reasons in order to reduce the risk of discrimination. The former aspects promote economic sustainability, while the latter point to the human rights values that derive from the idea of equality and are at the heart of the European social and legal systems of our time. The way to strike a balance between the two is therefore not yet known, but strict, consistently interpreted anti-discrimination standards and employers acting in economic (market) interests should work together to achieve this goal in the near future as soon as possible.

References

Alaimo A, Caruso B (2010a) Dopo la politica i diritti: l'Europa 'sociale' nel Trattato di Lisbona. WP C.S.D.L.E. 'Massimo D'Antona', INT 82/2010, p 88

Berke G (2013) A munkaszerződés és a vállalkozás szabadsága a munkajogban. Pécsi Munkajogi Közlemények 2011(2):105–122

Bíró A, Elek P (2019) Az idősödés munkapiaci összefüggései. In: Fazekas K, Elek P, Hajdu T (eds) Munkaerőpiaci tükör. KRTK, Budapest, pp 164–166

Delfino M (2015) The court and the charter – A "consistent" interpretation of fundamental social rights and principles. Eur Labour Law J 2015(1):86–92

Ferencz J (2015) A szociális szövetkezetek tagjának munkaviszonya. Magyar Munkajog 2015(1):68

Hendrickx F (2013) Active and healthy ageing. Eur Labour Law J 2013(2):82–83

Hős N (2014) Az általános jogelvek és az Alapjogi Charta szerepe az Európai Bíróság életkoron alapuló hátrányos megkülönböztetéssel kapcsolatos joggyakorlatában. Magyar Munkajog E-Folyóirat 2014(1):52–53

Hungler S (2021) A szociális integráció alapjogi kérdései – A szociális partnerek korlátozott szerepe az életkor szerinti diszkriminációval szembeni küzdelemben. Állam- és Jogtudomány 2021(4):8–9

Kun A (2011) Vállalati társadalmi felelősség – a munkajogon túl, a munkajog helyett, avagy a munkajog által? Munkaügyi Szemle 2011(1):24

Liukkunen U (2020a) The ILO and transformation of labour law. In: Halonen T, Liukkunen U (eds) International Labour Organization and global social governance, pp 19–21, 37–38

Manfredi S, Vickers L (2013) Meeting the challenges of active ageing in the workplace: is the abolition of retirement the answer? Eur Labour Law J 2013(4):251–260

Papa V (2015) The dark side of fundamental rights adjudication? The court, the charter and the asymmetric interpretation of fundamental rights in the AMS case and beyond. Eur Labour Law J 2015(3):190–191, 203–205

Pecinovsky P (2019) EU economic governance and the right to collective bargaining: Part 2. From imposed restrictions of the right by EU Member States towards a social economic governance. Eur Labour Law J, 2019(1):44–45, 65–66

Rab H (2018) A CSR szemlélet munkajogi vetületei. Pro Publico Bono – Magyar Közigazgatás 2018(4):202–217

Rainone S (2024) EU social dialogue revitalisation: Between rhetoric, new rights, political commitments and historical caution. Eur Labour Law J, 2024 (online first), 2–3, 7

Schlachter M (2011) Mandatory retirement and age discrimination under EU law. Int J Comp Labour Law Ind Relat 2011(3):287–299

Schreurs S (2023) EU social policy and the subsidiarity principle: the end of an illusion? Eur Labour Law J 2023(2):346–348, 357–358

Sipka P, Zaccaria ML (2017) A szövetkezeti tagi munkaviszony jogi kockázatai, különös tekintettel az alapvető munkavállalói jogokra. Munkajog 2017(1):24–25
Takács D (2021) Az életkori alapú antidiszkrimináció szabályozási háttere. Közjogi Szemle 2021(3):32–33, 36
Veneziani B (2006) Non-discrimination (Article 21). In: Bercusson B (ed) European labour law and the EU Court of Justice fundamental rights. Nomos, Baden-Baden, pp 203–210
Wu Y, van Rooij B (2019) Compliance dynamism: capturing the polynormative and situational nature of business responses to law. J Bus Ethics 2019(3):579–591

Oficial Documents

European Commission – Directorate-General for Employment, Social Affairs and Inclusion (2014) Labour law and working conditions. Social Europe guide, vol. 6. Publications Office of the European Union, Luxembourg, pp 9–14, 24–25
The European Pillar of Social Rights: Where are we now and where are we going? (2019) ETUI

Online Sources

Alaimo & Caruso (2010b). https://csdle.lex.unict.it/sites/default/files/Documenti/Articoli/2010-2_Alaimo-Caruso.pdf. Accessed 26 May 2024
Liukkunen (2020b) The ILO and transformation of labour law. https://www.ncbi.nlm.nih.gov/pmc/articles/PMC7562826/. Accessed 26 May 2024
Pataki-Magyar (2024) A negyedik ipari forradalom hatása a munkaerőpiacra. https://olm.hu/negyedik-ipari-forradalom-2resz/. Accessed 26 May 2024
Ungureanu (2024) Generational gap at work, insights and how to improve. https://www.linkedin.com/pulse/generational-gap-work-insights-how-improve-ioana-ungureanu. Accessed 26 May 2024

Separate and Unequal: Persistent Segregation of Roma Children in Czech Republic and Eastern Europe

Jakub Tomšej

1 Introduction

The European Union's role in combating racial discrimination represents one of the most significant supranational efforts to establish comprehensive anti-discrimination frameworks in contemporary history. The adoption of the Race Equality Directive (2000/43/EC) marked a watershed moment in European anti-discrimination law, establishing a robust legal framework that prohibits both direct and indirect discrimination based on racial or ethnic origin across multiple spheres of public life, including education.[1] This directive, alongside Article 21 of the Charter of Fundamental Rights of the European Union and the broader equality principles embedded in EU treaties, has created a multi-layered system of protection against discrimination that extends far beyond the traditional scope of EU economic integration.[2] The framework's particular significance lies in its comprehensive approach, encompassing not only prohibitive measures against discrimination but also requiring member states to establish specialized equality bodies, implement positive action measures, and ensure effective judicial remedies for victims of discrimination.[3]

For the Eastern European countries that joined the EU in 2004, including the Czech Republic, Hungary, and Slovakia, the implementation of EU

[1] Crowley (2022), pp. 52–59.

[2] Eklund and Kilpatrick (2021).

[3] Tomšej et al. (2023).

J. Tomšej (✉)
Law Faculty, Department of Labour and Social Security Law, Charles University, Prague, Czech Republic
e-mail: tomsej@prf.cuni.cz

K. Koldinská et al. (eds.), *Labour Law and Social Security Law in Central and Eastern Europe*, European Union and its Neighbours in a Globalized World 26,
https://doi.org/10.1007/978-3-032-04496-9_8

anti-discrimination law represented a fundamental challenge to existing institutional practices and social attitudes, including with regard to existing schemes regarding the treatment of Roma communities. The accession process itself served as a crucial catalyst for legal and institutional reforms, as these countries were required to adopt the EU's equality acquis as a prerequisite for membership. However, the formal transposition of EU directives into national law revealed a stark disconnect between legal frameworks and social reality.[4] In the Czech Republic, for example, the adoption of the local Anti-Discrimination Act was one of the last milestones on the way to conformity with the EU law, and it happened only 5 years after the accession.[5] The persistence of segregation practices in education, particularly affecting Roma children, highlighted the limitations of legal reforms in addressing deeply entrenched discriminatory practices. This tension between EU legal requirements and national implementation has become especially evident in the education sector, where despite formal compliance with EU anti-discrimination law, systemic discrimination continues through various indirect mechanisms, including geographical segregation.[6] The ongoing challenge of Roma segregation in these countries underscores a critical question about the effectiveness of EU legal instruments in promoting substantive equality, particularly in contexts where discrimination is deeply embedded in institutional practices and social attitudes.

While segregation commonly evokes historical images of African American racial segregation in the American South or South African apartheid—practices now universally condemned[7]—the contemporary reality of racial segregation in Czech education presents a more complex and contentious social challenge. Unlike these historical examples, the segregation of Roma children in the Czech education system remains a contemporary issue that has yet to achieve similar societal consensus regarding its condemnation. From an anti-discrimination law perspective, however, the illegality of such practices is unambiguous, warranting not a balanced analysis of pros and cons, but rather a critical examination of this persistent social ailment and potential remedies.[8]

Educational segregation in the Czech context manifests in two distinct forms.[9] The first involves the disproportionate placement of Roma minority students in facilities designed for pupils with special healthcare needs. This systemic issue stems from assessment procedures that systematically evaluate ethnic minority members as unsuitable for mainstream education, resulting in their placement in special schools or specialized classes intended for students with specific educational needs (particularly those with intellectual disabilities). This form of segregation

[4] Nehudková (2018).

[5] Boučková (2009).

[6] Farkas (2007).

[7] Thornberry (2016), p. 235.

[8] Tomšej (2024).

[9] Sýkora (2007).

gained international attention through the landmark European Court of Human Rights case D.H. and Others v. Czech Republic.

The second form involves the overrepresentation of Roma minority members in certain mainstream primary schools. This pattern emerges from the intersection of socially excluded localities with school district boundaries and various social phenomena, notably including "white flight"—where increased enrollment of minority students triggers an exodus of majority students, creating a spiral effect of increasing segregation.[10] While in the first case, Roma students are effectively treated as individuals with mild mental disabilities, in the second case, they remain within the standard educational system but in segregated schools that typically experience degraded educational quality and other adverse effects.

Recent statistical data from 2021–2022 reveals the persistent nature of Roma segregation in Czech education.[11] While Roma children constitute approximately 3% of the total population, their distribution across Czech schools shows clear patterns of segregation. Out of 4273 primary schools in the Czech Republic, approximately 130 schools have a Roma student population exceeding 33%. The segregation manifests in two distinct patterns:

- Approximately 60 schools with high Roma concentration are designated for students with various disabilities, including mental, physical, visual, or hearing impairments, severe speech defects, developmental learning disorders, behavioral disorders, multiple disabilities, or autism (as defined under Section 16(9) of the Czech Education Act)
- According to the Public Defender of Rights Office (2022–2023), 26.2% of Roma children are educated under the Framework Educational Program for Basic Education with reduced educational output requirements due to mild mental disability.

Particularly troubling is the fact that these statistics remain largely unchanged from the 2016/2017 academic year, indicating a lack of progress in addressing segregation despite various policy interventions and legal obligations.

The fight against educational segregation has deep historical roots, exemplified by the landmark U.S. Supreme Court decision in Brown v. Board of Education (1954).[12] A significant development occurred in April 2024, when the European Committee of Social Rights (ECSR) issued its decision in ERRC v. Czech Republic.[13] The Committee emphasized that states have a duty to collect data when certain categories of families might face discrimination, and that the absence of such data collection can itself contribute to indirect discrimination. The Czech Republic was found to have failed to adequately assess the over-representation of

[10] Renzulli and Evans (2005), pp. 398–418.

[11] Group of authors (2024); The Public Defender of Rights (2022).

[12] United States Supreme Court decision of May 17, 1954, Brown v. Board of Education of Topeka, 347 U.S. 483.

[13] European Committee of Social Rights (ECSR) Decision in the case of ERRC v. Czech Republic; Complaint No. 190/2020.

Roma children in public care, with the Committee noting that indirect discrimination may arise by failing to take adequate steps to ensure that rights are genuinely accessible to all families, including Roma families.

This chapter aims to critically examine the concept of segregation as it manifests in contemporary Eastern European education systems, with particular focus on the Czech Republic, but taking into consideration the situation in Slovakia and Hungary. Through analysis of recent developments, legal frameworks, and persistent challenges, I seek to answer a fundamental question: Is enhanced EU intervention necessary to address the persistent segregation of Roma children in these member states? The continued documentation of segregation practices, confirmed by the recent decision of the European Committee of Social Right as well as a recent call to action from the European Commission, suggests that this question has become increasingly pertinent.

2 Segregation in Education in International and European Law Including Key Case Law

This section will briefly summarise the regulation on international and European law, their transposition in the national law, and it will then focus on applicable case law. The legal framework prohibiting educational segregation rests on multiple international, European, and national instruments. The 1960 UNESCO Convention against Discrimination in Education provided an early definition of discrimination that explicitly included segregation and the establishment of separate educational systems. While Czechoslovakia ratified this convention in 1963, its direct applicability in the Czech Republic remains contested due to procedural issues regarding its publication in the official collection of laws.

At the international level, the International Convention on the Elimination of All Forms of Racial Discrimination, to which the Czech Republic is a party, explicitly condemns racial segregation (Article 3) and extends protection to the right to education (Article 5).[14] The European Convention on Human Rights, while not explicitly addressing segregation, prohibits discrimination based on race and national minority status (Article 14), and its Additional Protocol enshrines the right to education.[15]

The European Union's Race Equality Directive (2000/43/EC) represents a cornerstone of anti-discrimination protection, prohibiting discrimination based on race or ethnic origin in education, though it does not explicitly address segregation.[16] The Czech Republic has implemented this directive through its Anti-Discrimination Act, which prohibits both direct and indirect discrimination in access to and provision of

---

[14] Thornberry (2016), p. 235.

[15] Bell (2002), pp. 10–12.

[16] Bell (2002), p. 8.

education.[17] Notably, the Czech legislation extends protection against discrimination in education beyond the grounds specified in EU legislation.

The Czech Education Act (No. 561/2004 Coll.) further reinforces these principles by establishing non-discrimination and equal access to education as fundamental principles, applying to both Czech and EU citizens.[18] However, like many of the aforementioned instruments, it does not explicitly address segregation. This legislative framework demonstrates both the comprehensive nature of anti-discrimination protection and its potential limitations in addressing educational segregation specifically, as evidenced by the persistent challenges faced by Roma children in the Czech education system.

The European Court of Human Rights' judgment in D.H. and Others v. Czech Republic represents a landmark decision in the fight against educational segregation of Roma children.[19] The case, brought by 18 Roma children from the Ostrava region, challenged their placement in special schools, arguing this constituted discrimination in their right to education based on their ethnic origin. While the initial Chamber judgment found no violation of the Convention (with a 6-1 vote), the Grand Chamber's subsequent reversal marked a transformative moment in European human rights jurisprudence.

The judgment's significance lies in several groundbreaking principles:

First, the Court established that discrimination based on skin color is of an "especially odious" nature, requiring absolute prohibition and admitting no possible justification in contemporary democratic society. This categorical approach strengthened the protection against racial discrimination in education.

Second, the Court made crucial determinations regarding evidence of indirect discrimination. It accepted statistical evidence as valid proof of indirect discrimination when such statistics prove reliable and significant upon critical examination. Importantly, the Court also emphasized that indirect discrimination could be proven through other means, even in the absence of statistical data.

Third, and perhaps most significantly for practical application, the Court rejected the Czech government's defense that parents had consented to their children's placement in special schools. The Court reasoned that members of a vulnerable community, often lacking adequate education themselves, could not be expected to fully comprehend the consequences of such consent. This recognition of the structural barriers facing Roma parents marked an important shift from formal to substantive equality.

These principles continue to shape both judicial interpretation and policy development across Europe, particularly in addressing the persistent challenges of Roma segregation in educational systems. The judgment's emphasis on substantive equality and recognition of structural discrimination provides a crucial framework for evaluating contemporary segregation practices and developing effective remedies.

---

[17] Tomšej et al. (2023), pp. 14–17.

[18] Tomšej et al. (2023), p. 283–293.

[19] Devroye (2009), pp. 81–101.

The ECHR concluded that the placement of Roma pupils in schools for children with mental disabilities, where a significantly simplified curriculum was taught, did not indicate actual mental disorders among these students. Rather, it revealed that the testing procedures for student placement were inadequate and failed to consider the unique characteristics of the Roma community. As a result, it found indirect racial discrimination.

The European Court of Human Rights (ECHR) has ruled on school segregation several times beyond the D.H. and Others case. A notable recent judgment is the Szolcsán case, which addressed spatial segregation in Hungarian primary education within regular schools.[20] This case involved a Roma student with a hearing impairment who attended a segregated school in his catchment area. When his request to transfer to another school he deemed more suitable for his health condition was rejected, he attributed it to racial discrimination.[21]

The ECHR ruled that if the applicant was educated in a segregated school, the state had an obligation to take positive measures towards rectification, which should have involved transferring the applicant to a non-segregated school. The Court emphasized that inclusive education is the most appropriate means of ensuring the fundamental principles of universality and non-discrimination in exercising the right to education.

The Court mandated that measures taken following the judgment must ensure the end of segregation of Roma pupils in the school in question and, more broadly, develop a policy against segregation in education and take steps to eliminate it.

This ruling, from last year, serves as a cautionary note for other countries. It suggests that from the perspective of preserving students' rights under the Convention, it is insufficient to focus solely on implementing the D.H. judgment and rectifying the system targeting educational facilities for students with disabilities. Even spatial segregation within regular schools presents a problem that needs to be addressed.

3 Current Practice in the Czech Republic

The D.H. judgment continues to hold significant relevance for Czech society, even 16 years after its pronouncement by the Grand Chamber. The process of aligning Czech practices with the Convention's requirements remains ongoing. Major changes in the Czech education system only occurred with the amendment to the Education Act, effective from January 1, 2016, which promoted educational inclusion.[22]

---

[20] Decision of the First Section of the European Court of Human Rights of 30 March 2023, application number 24408/16.

[21] Leisure (2023).

[22] Záhumenský and Tomšej (2018), pp. 69–75.

Despite these undeniable shifts, particularly strengthening the position of students with disabilities, the situation of Roma students has not significantly improved. The Public Defender of Rights' recommendation on the joint education of Roma and non-Roma children from 2017 provides a still relevant description of the situation.[23] Some key observations from this report include:

1. The persistence of segregation of Roma pupils into former "special schools" or separate classes within mainstream schools, based on ethnicity and socio-economic status rather than actual educational needs.
2. Misdiagnosis and over-representation of Roma children in "programs for pupils with mild mental disabilities," leading to their segregated education.
3. The concentration of Roma pupils in certain schools due to residential segregation, attendance zoning policies, and parents' free choice, resulting in ethnically homogeneous schools or classes.
4. A lack of effective desegregation measures and concepts by schools and municipal authorities to prevent and address segregation.
5. The persistence of prejudices, lack of training, and low expectations from pedagogical staff regarding Roma pupils' abilities.

These issues contribute to broader negative impacts facing Czech society, including increased social exclusion, difficulties in breaking the poverty cycle, and rising social tensions. A World Bank study suggests that the Czech Republic loses 367 million EUR annually due to insufficient Roma integration and low education levels.[24]

In December 2023, the Czech Republic submitted an Action Plan for the execution of the D.H. judgment to the Committee of Ministers of the Council of Europe. This plan reflects the current approach of the Ministry of Education, Youth and Sports to ensuring equal access to education for Roma pupils, including planned measures to be implemented in the coming years according to a set schedule. The measures are thematically divided into three project cards focusing on school support, counseling system reform, and ethnic desegregation.

In March 2024, an oral review of the execution of the D.H. judgment took place at the meeting of the Committee of Ministers of the Council of Europe. The Committee generally welcomed the proposed measures and called for their swift implementation according to the stated schedule.

Based on this decision, the Czech Republic is required to submit a comprehensive report on the adoption of all announced measures to the Committee of Ministers by the end of 2025. Additionally, by the end of 2024, it must submit an analysis of the reasons for low participation of Roma children in preschool education and present a plan of measures to improve the situation.

[23] Public Defender of Rights (2018).

[24] The World Bank (2010).

The Czech Supreme Court has made a significant ruling in a case involving educational segregation.[25] This decision came in response to an appeal by Roma plaintiffs who had previously been unsuccessful in their claims of segregation in education. The case centered on a primary school that operated two educational programs in separate buildings, named "Three Steps into Life" and "We Want to Be Successful". While the school claimed the programs differed mainly in language and IT instruction, the plaintiffs argued this was a facade for ethnic segregation.

In its decision, the Supreme Court affirmed that segregation is a "special form of discrimination" and is legally unacceptable. The Court's reasoning provides important clarifications on the nature of discrimination in education. It elaborated on the concepts of direct and indirect discrimination, emphasizing that disadvantage is inherent in the very act of differential treatment or separation. Crucially, the Court stated that such separation is discriminatory and stigmatizing in itself, regardless of the quality of education provided.

This ruling establishes that racial segregation cannot be justified by claiming segregated students had equal educational opportunities. This marks a significant shift in legal thinking. The Court's decision suggests that to prove discrimination, it is sufficient to demonstrate disproportionate representation of an ethnic minority in a particular school or class using official or credible unofficial statistics. While plaintiffs can still argue about unequal educational conditions, this is no longer necessary to prove discrimination.

The impact of this ruling on future cases could be substantial. While the lower courts initially dismissed the case, the Supreme Court's reasoning gives the plaintiffs a high chance of success. Although the final outcome is not yet known, this ruling sets an important precedent that could lead to more inclusive educational practices and greater equality in Czech schools. It represents a significant development in the interpretation and application of anti-discrimination law in the context of education in the Czech Republic.

4 Current Practice in Slovakia

The situation regarding the segregation of Roma pupils in the Slovak education system is particularly concerning, with statistical data revealing an even more severe problem than in some neighboring countries. Almost half (47%) of children from marginalised communities aged from 6 to 15 in mainstream education have only Roma classmates, while 32% of these children attend a school with exclusively Roma pupils.[26]

---

[25] Czech Supreme Court judgment of 5 May 2022, file no. 25 Cdo 473/2024.

[26] Durbáková (2024), pp. 48–49.

Attempts to address this problem through legislative means have faced significant obstacles. A proposal for an amendment to the Schools Act, which aimed to tackle educational segregation, failed to get sufficient support in the Slovak Parliament. This legislative setback highlights the political challenges in addressing this deeply entrenched issue.

One particularly problematic aspect of Roma education in Slovakia is the "two-shift system," which affects some of the segregated schools.[27] This system often results in Roma children attending school in separate shifts from non-Roma children, further exacerbating their isolation and limiting opportunities for integration.

The European Commission has taken note of these issues and has been increasingly pushing Slovakia to address them. In 2015, the Commission initiated an infringement procedure against Slovakia due to its failure to effectively address the segregation of Roma children in education. This procedure is a formal step the Commission can take against EU member states that are not complying with EU law.

Following the lack of significant progress, in 2019, the European Commission issued a Reasoned Opinion urging Slovakia to comply with EU equality rules. This step represented an escalation of the infringement procedure and signaled the Commission's growing impatience with the lack of effective action by Slovak authorities.

Despite these warnings and the passage of time, the Slovak government's response appears to have been insufficient. As a result, in 2023, the European Commission took the significant step of referring Slovakia to the Court of Justice of the European Union (CJEU) for failing to effectively tackle the issue of segregation in its education system. This referral to the CJEU represents a serious escalation and could potentially lead to legal consequences for Slovakia if the Court finds it in breach of EU law.

This sequence of events—from the initiation of the infringement procedure in 2015 to the referral to the CJEU in 2023—demonstrates the persistent nature of educational segregation in Slovakia and the challenges in addressing it. It also highlights the role of EU institutions in attempting to enforce anti-discrimination norms and promote inclusive education practices across member states.

Despite the challenging situation in Slovakia, there is one positive development worth noting: a landmark judgment by the Slovak Supreme Court, delivered approximately a year after the Czech Supreme Court's ruling on segregation. This case is particularly interesting because the plaintiff sought not monetary compensation for non-material harm, but rather the imposition of an obligation on the defendant to develop a so-called desegregation plan.

The case concerned the establishment of a modular primary school in a socially excluded locality in Stará Ľubovňa, which was attended exclusively by Roma pupils. The Slovak Supreme Court approached the matter similarly to its Czech counterpart, stating that segregation constitutes a special form of discrimination.

[27] Durbáková (2024), p. 54.

The Court drew inspiration from countries like Bulgaria and Romania, which explicitly define segregation as a distinct form of discrimination.

In its ruling, the Slovak Supreme Court rejected the lower courts' opinion that claims of discrimination could be refuted by arguing that the school was established due to insufficient capacity or that education legislation doesn't prevent pupils from choosing schools outside their residential district. The Court determined that segregation had occurred in this case, and although a discriminatory motive wasn't proven and a legitimate aim of providing education close to children's residences was claimed, the construction of the school in this situation was not a suitable and proportionate means to achieve this goal. The Court emphasized that it is the state's duty to act in the best interests of the child and to take effective measures to prevent segregation.

Regarding the burden of proof, the Slovak Supreme Court slightly diverged from the Czech ruling. It stated that once it was established that the school provided education for an ethnically homogeneous Roma community, it was up to the defendant to prove that the segregation was not caused by the means they used.

The Court's decision to consider ordering a desegregation plan as a remedy is particularly noteworthy. This approach offers a more forward-looking and potentially more effective solution than mere monetary compensation. It addresses the root of the problem and aims to prevent future segregation, rather than simply compensating for past harm.

While this ruling specifically pertains to the Slovak context, the concept of court-ordered desegregation plans may serve as an inspiration for addressing similar issues in other countries. This approach could potentially lead to more meaningful and systemic changes in educational practices and policies across the region.

5 Current Practice in Hungary

In Hungary, Roma children face significant challenges related to educational segregation, mirroring issues seen in other Central European countries. The European Commission has initiated infringement proceedings against Hungary, as it has against the Czech Republic and Slovakia, for violations of Council Directive 2000/43/EC, which implements the principle of equal treatment regardless of racial or ethnic origin.

The European Court of Human Rights (ECtHR) has delivered two significant judgments against Hungary, both of which deemed the practices of placing Roma pupils in segregated schools or classes as discriminatory. The first case, Horváth and

Kiss v. Hungary, was decided in 2013.[28] This case addressed the long-standing issue of misdiagnosis of Roma children as having mental disabilities and their subsequent placement in special schools. The Court found that this practice resulted in de facto segregation and discrimination.

More recently, in 2023, the ECtHR ruled on the case of Szolcsán v. Hungary.[29] This judgment further reinforced the Court's stance against educational segregation of Roma children, emphasizing the state's obligation to take concrete steps to end discriminatory practices in education.

At the national level, Hungarian courts have also made significant rulings addressing Roma segregation in schools. A landmark decision came from the Hungarian Supreme Court in 2020, which upheld a lower court's ruling that Roma children from the town of Gyöngyöspata were entitled to compensation for school segregation. This case attracted considerable attention and sparked debates about integration and educational equality in Hungary.

Another noteworthy case involved the city of Kaposvar. In this instance, domestic courts took a proactive approach to addressing segregation. They prohibited the city from admitting Roma pupils to first grade in certain circumstances, mandated changes to school district boundaries, and ordered the creation and public disclosure of a desegregation plan. The court required this plan to be published on the websites of both the school's founding body and the school itself.[30]

These judicial decisions at both the European and national levels highlight the ongoing struggle against educational segregation in Hungary. They also demonstrate an evolving legal approach that goes beyond merely identifying discrimination to ordering specific, actionable steps towards desegregation.

However, despite these legal interventions, the implementation of court decisions and the actual desegregation of schools remain significant challenges. The persistence of segregation indicates deep-rooted societal issues, including residential segregation, socio-economic factors, and sometimes resistance from both Roma and non-Roma parents to integration efforts.

The situation in Hungary underscores the complexity of addressing educational segregation, where legal victories, while important, are only one step in a broader process of social and systemic change. It also highlights the need for comprehensive, long-term strategies that address not only education but also broader issues of social inclusion and equality for the Roma community.

---

[28] Decision of the Second Section of the European Court of Human Rights of 29 January 2013, application number 11146/11.

[29] Decision of the First Section of the European Court of Human Rights of 30 March 2023, application number 24408/16.

[30] Kádár (2021), p. 145.

6 Next Steps?

The over-reliance on judicial intervention to address educational segregation represents a fundamental weakness in current anti-discrimination efforts. It seems that court (both through decisions like D.H. and Others v. Czech Republic, as well as by way of a reference to both Supreme Court rulings discussed above) play a key role in addressing segregation in education, but it is problematic that they remain the primary drivers of desegregation efforts. This judicial-centric approach fails to address the systemic nature of educational segregation and places an undue burden on affected communities.

The Czech Anti-discrimination Act provides various legal remedies, including the right to demand cessation of discrimination and elimination of its consequences. In cases of Roma segregation within schools or classes, plaintiffs can request courts to order specific desegregation measures.[31] These may include requiring school authorities to:

1. Develop and publish desegregation plans with concrete statistical targets
2. Implement measures ensuring all students, regardless of ethnicity, enter mainstream education
3. Revise school district boundaries
4. Allocate necessary financial resources for desegregation
5. Explicitly declare anti-discrimination policies in school educational programs
6. Develop teacher training programs for managing heterogeneous classrooms
7. Establish supportive school counseling services
8. Create an inclusive school climate free from racial discrimination

However, it is fundamentally problematic to rely solely on courts as agents of change in educational desegregation. While judicial interpretation may be necessary for complex legal questions, the existence of clear precedents like the D.H. case and subsequent Supreme Court decisions should obviate the need for constant judicial intervention. The continued inaction of schools and their governing bodies, forcing affected parties to seek judicial remedies, is particularly problematic for two reasons:

First, it places an unreasonable burden on the judicial system's capacity. And more importantly, it imposes significant obstacles on segregation-affected students and families, for whom accessing justice through courts can be exceptionally challenging due to financial, social, and cultural barriers.

The current situation, where local practices fail to be put in compliance with the case law requirements under the assumption that affected parties will lack the motivation, strength, or financial means to pursue legal action, represents a fundamental failure of institutional responsibility. This passive approach to compliance not only

[31] Tomšej et al. (2023), p. 287–288.

perpetuates discrimination but also undermines the basic principles of equal access to education and justice.

7 Conclusions

Recent developments in the Czech Republic may signal potential progress, particularly through the Action Plan for the implementation of the D.H. and Others judgment, submitted to the Committee of Ministers of the Council of Europe in December 2023. This initiative demonstrates renewed governmental commitment to addressing segregation issues. The project documentation on ethnic desegregation outlines specific measures, including the possibility of initiating procedures to abolish identified school districts where local authorities prove unwilling to participate in more moderate solutions.

However, these developments must be viewed with cautious optimism. The measures' anchoring solely at the action plan level makes them somewhat vulnerable, particularly given the approaching 2025 elections, which may bring a government with different priorities. While the action plan itself mentions amending the Education Act as one of its measures, the fact that adequate remedy has not been achieved in the 16 years since the D.H. judgment suggests that legislative changes are indeed necessary to ensure lasting impact on desegregation efforts and combat the persistent stigmatization of Roma pupils.

Sixteen years after the landmark D.H. and Others v. Czech Republic judgment, the landscape of educational segregation in Central and Eastern Europe presents a sobering reality. Despite the European Court of Human Rights' clear stance against discriminatory practices, similar patterns of Roma pupils' segregation persist across multiple Member States, suggesting that domestic and existing EU mechanisms have proven insufficient to address this fundamental rights violation.

The parallel experiences of the Czech Republic, Slovakia, and Hungary demonstrate that this is not merely a localized issue but rather a systemic challenge requiring a coordinated supranational response. In all these countries, Roma children continue to face both direct segregation through placement in separate classes or schools and indirect segregation through seemingly neutral criteria that disproportionately affect Roma pupils. The persistence of these practices, despite numerous national strategies and action plans, reveals the limitations of purely domestic approaches and soft law instruments.

As this topic seems to affect several member state where time is flying but improvements achieved on national level are insufficient, this systemic failure calls for a paradigm shift in the EU's approach to educational segregation. While the Race Equality Directive (2000/43/EC) provides a general framework for combating discrimination, experience has shown that its broad provisions have not generated sufficient pressure for concrete desegregation measures. The time has come for a specific EU regulation directly addressing educational segregation, one that would leave no room for ambiguity or selective implementation.

Such a regulation should contain several key elements. First, it must explicitly define and prohibit both direct and indirect forms of educational segregation, moving beyond the current framework's general anti-discrimination provisions. This definition should encompass not only obvious forms of separation but also more subtle mechanisms that lead to de facto segregation, such as catchment area manipulation or the misuse of special education diagnostics.

Second, the regulation should mandate that Member States develop and implement comprehensive desegregation plans with clear timelines and measurable objectives. These plans must include:

- Detailed mapping of segregated educational facilities
- Specific measures for gradual desegregation
- Resources allocation mechanisms
- Monitoring and evaluation frameworks
- Provisions for meaningful consultation with affected communities

Third, and perhaps most crucially, the regulation must establish a robust enforcement mechanism with clear sanctions for non-compliance. The current infringement procedures have proven too slow and politically sensitive to effectively address educational segregation. A dedicated enforcement framework, possibly including financial consequences linked to EU funding, would provide the necessary incentive for Member States to prioritize desegregation efforts.

Critics might argue that such a regulation would infringe upon Member States' competence in educational matters. However, this argument overlooks the fundamental nature of the right to non-discriminatory education and the EU's obligation to ensure equal treatment across all Member States. The regulation would not dictate educational content or methods but rather ensure that educational systems operate without discrimination—a core EU value and competence.

Moreover, the regulation's implementation could draw upon the wealth of experience and good practices developed over the past decades. From successful local desegregation initiatives to effective monitoring mechanisms, there exists a substantial body of knowledge about what works in promoting inclusive education. The regulation would provide the legal framework necessary to scale up these proven approaches.

The moral imperative for such action is clear. Each year of delay means another cohort of Roma children denied their fundamental right to equal educational opportunities. The social and economic costs of continued segregation—in terms of reduced human capital, social cohesion, and economic potential—affect not only the Roma communities but European society as a whole.

The timing for such an initiative is particularly apposite. As the EU grapples with questions of social inclusion and equality in the post-pandemic recovery, addressing educational segregation could demonstrate concrete commitment to these values.

Looking ahead, the adoption of such a regulation would represent a decisive step toward fulfilling the promise of equal education made in numerous EU documents and court decisions. While it would undoubtedly face implementation challenges, the current situation—where systemic discrimination persists despite clear legal prohibitions—demands bold action. The question is no longer whether such intervention is necessary, but rather how much longer Europe can afford to wait.

The D.H. judgment's legacy should not be merely as a landmark decision that articulated principles of non-discrimination, but as a catalyst for concrete institutional change. As we mark two decades of EU membership for these countries—years that have brought significant economic development, legal harmonization, and integration into the European common market—the persistent segregation of Roma pupils stands as a reminder of unfinished business in the realm of fundamental rights. These 20 years have demonstrated that EU membership provides both opportunities and obligations; while these nations have successfully adapted to numerous demanding EU regulations in areas from environmental protection to consumer safety, the basic right of equal access to education remains elusive for one of Europe's most vulnerable minorities. Looking ahead to the next decades of EU membership, the time has come for the Union to move beyond monitoring and recommendations to establish binding obligations that will finally transform anti-discrimination principles into reality. The success or failure to address educational segregation will serve as a litmus test for the EU's capacity to ensure that economic integration is matched by genuine social inclusion and respect for fundamental rights across all Member States.

References

A Group of authors (2024) Výzkumná zpráva: Analýza příčin vyššího podílu romských žáků vzdělávajících se dle RVP ZV UV ve třídách zřízených podle § 16 odst. 9 školského zákona a návrh souboru opatření pro oblast vzdělávání a další relevantní oblasti. Available at: edu.cz

Bell M (2002) Combating racism through European laws: a comparison of the Racial Equality Directive and Protocol 12. In: Chopin I, Niessen J (eds) Combating racial and ethnic discrimination: taking the European legislative agenda further. Commission for Racial Equality, Brussels

Boučková P (2009) Antidiskriminační zákon: konec diskriminace v Čechách? Právní rozhledy 13:II

Crowley N (2022) To name and address the underlying problem: Structural discrimination on the ground of racial or ethnic origin. Publications Office of the European Union, Luxembourg

Devroye J (2009) The Case of D.H. and Others v. the Czech Republic. North West J Int Hum Rights 7(1):81–101

Durbáková V (2024) Country report non-discrimination Slovakia 2024. Publications Office of the European Union, Luxembourg

Eklund H, Kilpatrick C (2021) Article 21 EU charter of fundamental rights. EUI AEL Working Paper; 2021/01

Farkas L (2007) Segregation of Roma children in education. Addressing structural discrimination through the race equality directive. Office for Official Publications of the European Communities, Luxembourg

Kádár A (2021) Hungary – country report non-discrimination 2018. Publications Office of the European Union, Luxembourg, p 145

Leisure P (2023) Avoiding the perpetuation of discrimination in education: individual positive measures versus broad anti-segregation policy in Szolcsán v. Hungary, 17 May 2023. Available at: StrasbourgObservers.com

Nehudková E (2018) Diskriminace v přístupu k tržnímu bydlení z důvodu etnického původu. Právní rozhledy 10:354
Public Defender of Rights (2018) Recommendation of the Public Defender of Rights on the joint education of Roma and non-Roma children. File no. KVOP-53237/2018. Available at: eso.ochrance.cz
Public Defender of Rights (2022) Naplňování práva na rovné zacházení a ochrany před diskriminací. Monitorovací zpráva 2022. File no. KVOP-21621/2026. Available at: eso.ochrance.cz
Renzulli LA, Evans L (2005) School choice, charter schools, and white flight. Soc Probl 52(3):398–418
Sýkora L (ed) (2007) Segregace v České republice: stav a vývoj, příčiny a důsledky, prevence a náprava. Univerzita Karlova, Praha
The World Bank (2010) Roma inclusion: an economic opportunity for Bulgaria, Czech Republic, Romania and Serbia. Available at: documents.worldbank.org
Thornberry P (2016) The international convention on the elimination of all forms of racial discrimination: a commentary, Oxford commentaries on international law. Oxford University Press
Tomšej J et al. (2023) Antidiskriminační zákon a související předpisy. Praktický komentář (Anti-Discrimination Act and connected legislation. Practical Commentary), Wolters Kluwer, Prague
Tomšej J (2024) Country report non-discrimination Czech Republic 2023. Publications Office of the European Union, Luxembourg
Záhumenský D, Tomšej J (2018) Country report non-discrimination Czech Republic 2018. Publications Office of the European Union, Luxembourg

Specific Challenges for Social Protection

Cross-Border Healthcare Law Development: Connecting Points Between Slovenian and EU Law

Grega Strban

1 Introductory Observations

Cross-border healthcare has been available for insured persons under the Slovenian mandatory health insurance also before Slovenia's accession to the EU in May 2004. The Healthcare and Health Insurance Act (ZZVZZ)[1] from 1992 enshrined the right to healthcare abroad.[2] More specific provisions could be found in the Rules of Mandatory Health Insurance from 1994.[3] Not only could an insured person access cross-border healthcare when working abroad, during business and private travelling or studies, temporary or permanent settlement abroad, but also when planning medical treatment outside of Slovenia. However, the latter was only possible when treatment in Slovenia has been exhausted and with cross-border healthcare healing or improving the health condition or preventing of its deterioration could be reasonably expected. Additionally, minor children had the right to be escorted by an adult. Medicine and medical appliances could also be purchased abroad, if not available in Slovenia. At all this instances, cross-border treatment was not limited to the Member States of the EU, since Slovenia was not yet among them.

[1] *Zakon o zdravstvenem varstvu in zdravstvenem zavarovanju* (ZZVZZ), Official Gazette RS 9/92 with amendments.

[2] Article 23 ZZVZZ.

[3] *Pravila obveznega zdravstvenega zavarovanja*, Official Gazette RS, No. 79/94 with amendments.

G. Strban (✉)
Faculty of Law, University of Ljubljana, Ljubljana, Slovenia

University of Johannesburg, Johannesburg, South Africa
e-mail: grega.strban@pf.uni-lj.si

K. Koldinská et al. (eds.), *Labour Law and Social Security Law in Central and Eastern Europe*, European Union and its Neighbours in a Globalized World 26,
https://doi.org/10.1007/978-3-032-04496-9_9

Next to such unilateral social security coordination measures, promoted also by the (initial and revised) European Social Charter,[4] Slovenia was party to numerous bilateral social security agreements with countries within and outside of the EU.[5] They provided for urgent healthcare when staying on the territory of the contracting party or for the reimbursement of costs for urgent medical treatment. Among multilateral instruments, Slovenia was bound by the Equality of Treatment (Accident Compensation) Convention, 1925 (No. 19), covering also medical treatment for accidents at work abroad. All mentioned unilateral, bilateral and multilateral legal solutions are still in force after the EU accession.

However, by joining the EU more legal possibilities of cross-border healthcare are offered. Next to national and international legal instruments mentioned above, there are a couple of possibilities under the EU law. One is governed by the rules of linking (coordinating) of public, social security systems of the Member States, including public health systems,[6] and the other by the rules of free movement of (medicinal) goods and (health) services, as construed by the Court of Justice of the EU (CJEU) and codified by the Union legislator.[7]

Slovenian mandatory health insured persons seem to be well aware of cross-border healthcare options also due to information provided by the Health Insurance Institute of Slovenia (*Zavod za zdravstveno zavarovanje Slovenije*, ZZZS). According to the ZZZS yearly report for 2023,[8] there were 92.274 cases of cross border healthcare outside of Slovenia (amounting to almost 45 million Euro) and 68.151 cases in Slovenia (amounting to almost € 38 million). The numbers are noticeable, since there are just over two million of insured persons in Slovenia and mandatory health insurance budget amounted to € 4.3 billion in 2023.[9] Hence all cross-border healthcare costs amounted to over one percent of that budget.[10]

It should be noted that the Slovenian Constitution acknowledges not only the right to social security, whereby expressly mentioning mandatory health insurance as one of social insurance branches, but also the right to healthcare, which concerns more the delivery side of healthcare. Healthcare from public funds (taxes and social

[4] See Article 12 Paragraph 4 (initial and revised) European Social Charter.

[5] More on bilateral social security agreements, Strban (2018), p. 129.

[6] Regulation No (EEC) 883/2004 on the coordination of social security systems, OJ L 166 30.4.2004 as amended and Regulation No (EC) 987/2009, OJ L 284, 30.10.2009 as amended.

[7] Directive 2011/24 on the application of patients' rights in cross-border healthcare, OJ L 88, 4.4.2011. It is legally binding for the EU and EEA States, but not for Switzerland.

[8] ZZZS (2024), p. 32–34.

[9] ZZZS (2024), p. 110.

[10] In comparison, in the EU the total amount of introductions for the reimbursement of cross border healthcare under the Coordination Regulations amounted to € 4.6 billion in 2022. For unplanned necessary cross-border healthcare the share in total healthcare spending amounted to 0.1 percent. The number of healthcare reimbursement claims is expected to show a strong correlation with the number of tourist arrivals. For instance, in 2022 more than 200 million trips to another Member State were made. Moreover, around 2.1 million persons resided in a Member State other than the competent Member State. More than 70 percent of this group were cross-border workers and almost 30% were pensioners. De Wispelaere et al. (2024), p. 20.

security contributions) must be regulated by law. Slovenian Constitution is thereby establishing a distinction between public and private healthcare delivery. It is the duty of the State to guarantee all forms of access to (public) health care, among them geographic, financial, timely, informational and procedural access to high quality healthcare to everyone.[11] For instance, if geographical or timely access could not be readily offered, cross-border healthcare might come into play.

In the present paper the questions of when cross border healthcare is required and how it can be provided to the Slovenian mandatorily health insured person within the EU is explored. It has already been established that the possibilities of cross-border healthcare have been enlarged after the EU accession. Moreover, the question is whether only the EU is playing a role for the Slovenian legislature, or does the same apply vice versa, and the Slovenian health legislation and practice are influencing the EU law as well?

2 Cooperation of Public Healthcare Systems in the EU

2.1 Application and Scope of the Social Security Coordination Regulations

International cooperation of public healthcare systems within the EU takes a form of social security coordination and dates to the very beginnings of the current EU. The first Social Security Coordination Regulations, i.e. Regulation No 3 concerning the social security of migrant workers[12] and Regulation No 4 (implementing regulation) of 1958, are applicable since 1959. The text on linking social security systems of the six EU founding Member States has been agreed upon and an international convention was proposed. To avoid the time-consuming procedure of ratification, it was agreed to pass those rules in a form of a regulation. Interestingly, it was the first real (substantive) legal instrument in the (current) EU.[13] They already entailed the right to cross-border healthcare, although only in the case of urgent treatment[14] and when moving residence to another Member State.[15]

Later on, social security coordination, including cross-border healthcare (also planned treatment in another Member State) was enshrined in Regulation (EEC)

[11] Strban (2024b), p. 10.

[12] Regulation (EEC) 3/1958 on social security rights of migrant workers, OJ 30, 16.12.1958.

[13] Regulations No. 1 and 2 dealt with the use of languages and the form of the *laisser passer* to the Members of the European Parliament, respectively.

[14] Only when (temporarily) staying in another Member State (Ger. *bei einem vorübergehenden Aufenthalt im Hoheitsgebiet eines anderen Mitgliedstaats)* benefits in case of urgent medical treatment, including hospitalisation were provided (Ger. *Leistungen, wenn sein Zustand sofort ärztliche Betreuung einschließlich Krankenhauspflege erforderlich macht*). It might be worth mentioning that English was not an official language at that time.

[15] Article 19 Regulation (EEC) No 3/1958.

1408/71[16] and its implementing Regulation (EEC) 574/72. Both were constantly developed by the CJEU and the legislature, and became one of the most complex Union legal instruments.

In 1998 the process of modernisation and simplification of social security coordination law began with the publication of the proposal for a new Regulation by the European Commission,[17] which resulted in passing of the new Social Security Coordination Regulations. Interestingly, the Regulation (EC) 883/2004 was passed only a couple of days before the largest enlargement of the EU so far. The 15 Member States agreed on the wording of the Regulation on the 29 April 2004, and it was published in the official journal a day later.[18] Only another day later, i.e. on the first of May 2004 the 10 States joined the EU and the unanimity of 25 (and later 27) Member States would have been required. Hence, rushing with a legislative procedure might be understandable, but also some provisions might have been passed in a hasty manner and without thorough debate.

The implementing Regulation was passed only in 2009, as Regulation (EC) 987/2009,[19] due to the required unanimity of 27 Member States at the time. Hence, the Regulation (EC) 883/2004 could only be applied after entering into force of the implementing regulation, i.e. since May 2010. Also, this regulation is constantly being amended by legislative acts and construed by the CJEU decisions. Even though unanimity requirement and the right to a veto of each Member State has been modified (no requirement in the Council, but according to so called alarm procedure the decision might be taken by the European Council, deciding by unanimity) Member States do not find it easy to agree on the proposed amendments to the Social Security Coordination Regulations.[20]

Even though, Member States remain competent to determine the scope of protected persons, kinds and levels of benefits, obligations of the beneficiaries and procedures to enforce the rights, coordination of social security systems is achieved with a regulation, which is a unifying measure. Hence, not substantive, but rather a part of formal social security law, governing the application of the substantive social security law in cross-border situations, is unified among all Member States. The attribute of direct applicability is linked to the doctrine of supremacy. It is not open

[16] Article 22 Regulation (EEC) No 1408/71 on the application of social security schemes to employed persons and their families moving within the Community, OJ L 149, 5.7.1971.

[17] COM (1998) 779 final, Brussels, 21.12.2008.

[18] Regulation (EEC) No 883/2004 on the coordination of social security systems, OJ L 166, 30.4.2004 as amended, is legally binding also for the EFTA States (EEA and Switzerland), based on special agreements.

[19] OJ L 284, 30.10.2009. More on Social Security Coordination Regulations, Fuchs and Janda (2025) and Eichenhofer (2025).

[20] The latest proposal for the revision of Coordination Regulations was presented in December 2016. Strasbourg, 13.12.2016, COM(2016) 815 final. Revision concerns among others long-term care, family and unemployment benefits. With latter a certain tension between East and West of the EU could be detected.

to Member States to interfere with the direct application of a regulation in the national legal order.

Social Security Coordination Regulations nevertheless influence the substance of national social security systems. For instance, Member States ensuring protection to all residents are obliged to broaden the personal scope of their social security system also to the Union migrant workers (even if they reside in another Member State).[21]

Moreover, a special rule applies for healthcare of worker's family members. Social Security Coordination Regulations apply an EU definition of members of a family by referring to national law.[22] As a rule, family members are defined by the legislation of the competent Member State, which is providing benefits. However, for healthcare (sickness benefits in kind), family (or household) members are defined by the legislation of the Member State of their residence.[23] This might lead to unequal results, when personal scopes of national legislations are diverse. For instance, a same-sex partner could reside in a Member State not recognising such partnerships. Even if another partner would be subject to the legislation of the competent Member State (by working there), who would cover same-sex partner, the first one might not have access to healthcare as a family member.[24] The reverse situation, e.g. when a competent Member State not recognising same-sex partnerships would have to reimburse healthcare costs for a same-sex partner residing in another Member State (covered as a family member there) healthcare is provided to a broader personal scope than the one under pure national law of the competent Member State.

As to their material scope of application, Social Security Coordination Regulations cover traditional social security schemes, including mandatory health insurance or National Health Service. Hence, social and medical assistance is excluded from their material scope.[25] However, if the notion of social assistance is rather clear and could be distinguished from social security,[26] the concept of medi-

---

[21] The leading principle for determining the legislation applicable for economically active persons is the *lex loci laboris*. Article 11 Regulation (EC) No 883/2004.

[22] If there is no national definition, for instance if all residents are covered, regardless of their family relations, EU law might offer one, e.g. in Article 1(i)2 Regulation (EC) 883/2004. If the legislation of a Member State which is applicable does not make a distinction between the members of the family and other persons to whom it is applicable, the spouse, minor children, and dependent children who have reached the age of majority shall be considered members of the family.

[23] Article 1(i)1(ii) Regulation (EC) No 883/2004. It might not always be easy to determine the place of residence. See Article 11 Regulation (EC) No 987/2009 and e.g. case C-255/13 – *I*, EU:C:2014:1291 (receiving healthcare in another Member State for over a decade, does not necessarily establish residence there).

[24] Possible solutions have already been provided by the CJEU, although in other areas of law (e.g. also relating to free movement). Case C-673/16 - *Coman and Others*, ECLI:EU:C:2018:385. More in Strban et al. (2020), p. 36.

[25] Article 3(5)(a) Regulation (EC) No 883/2004.

[26] CJEU clarified the notion of social assistance under social security coordination Regulations and Free Movement Directive (or Residence Directive), i.e. Directive 2004/38. Verschueren (2014).

cal assistance might cause more difficulties. It could be assumed that medical care and assistance is always provided when so required by the individual's state of (ill) health. CJEU tried to mirror a distinction between social security and social assistance also when distinguishing between sickness (social security) benefits in kind and medical assistance.[27] The Court argued that medical assistance is dependent on an individual assessment of the personal need. It probably meant medical need of a social assistance recipient (or other recipient in financial, i.e. social assistance need).

2.2 Cross-Border Healthcare Under Public Systems

Under the Social Security Coordination Regulations there are several options for receiving healthcare outside of the competent Member State. Benefits in kind, also those in case of sickness or injury cannot be exportable as such, since e.g. healthcare is provided for in the Member State of residence or stay. However, the right to healthcare as such is in a way subject to export rules. Healthcare may be provided in another Member State and paid for by the competent Member State. By allowing medical treatment in another Member State, residence clauses are waived and the right to healthcare is exported.[28] Moreover, in the Member State where healthcare is provided the equal treatment of all (resident and moving) patients comes to the forefront.[29]

Rules on receiving healthcare outside of the competent Member State were agreed among the Member States. In general, we could distinguish between three situations. In the first one a person resides outside of the competent Member State. Entitlement to healthcare is opened not only in the competent Member State (e.g. the one of work), but also in the Member State of residence, according to the rules applicable there, on the account of the health insurance carrier in the Member State of insurance. Hence, the competent Member State, e.g. Austria, would issue an S1 form[30] and ZZZS would issue a Slovenian health insurance card. When costs would incur, they would be reimbursed by Austria.

Second situation is, when a person temporarily stays in another Member State for non-medical purposes, e.g. for tourist, business, family or study reasons, and health condition necessitates medical care. Such person will be entitled to healthcare in the Member State of stay, on the account of the Member State of insurance, but with certain limitations. Only the necessary treatment will be provided, as

---

[27] CJEU case C-535/19 - *A*, EU:C:2021:595. The Court found that the benefit in case was social security benefit, as it was granted without any individual and discretionary assessment of personal needs, to recipients based on a legally defined position and (cumulatively) related to one of the risks expressly listed in Article 3(1) of Regulation (EC) 883/2004.

[28] See also Jorens and Van Overmeiren (2009), p. 69.

[29] Strban (2013), p. 391.

[30] S forms relate to Sickness, https://europa.eu/youreurope/citizens/work/social-security-and-benefits/social-security-forms/index_en.htm

established by medical practitioners in the Member State of stay. Necessary care covers more than urgent medical care. It must consider the nature of the benefits and the expected length of stay. In addition, the Administrative Commission for the Coordination of Social Security Systems established a list of medical benefits related to necessary specialist medical care which for practical reasons require prior agreement between the moving person and the healthcare provider. The continuity of treatment of a person during stay in another Member State has to be guaranteed.[31]

Since 2004 necessary medical treatment may be invoked by the European Health Insurance Card (EHIC). It was rather a step back for Slovenia, where a smart health insurance card was in operation and EHIC was just a plastic card. Still, EHIC is not like a credit card, although in some cases it was attempted to be used as such. In Slovenia there are well known cases of planned childbirths in Austria, for which the costs have tried to be settled by EHIC. Slovenian Supreme Court did not recognise necessary treatment for such planned childbirth in Austria.[32] For some period, it seems that reimbursement of cross-border childbirths has been restricted in the Union at large. However, childbirth as such shall not be excluded from necessary treatment as it may also happen unpredictable in another Member State.[33]

The third situation deals with the planned cross-border medical treatment. The insured person has to obtain a prior authorisation from the competent institution in the Member State of insurance, before going for a treatment to another Member State. This authorization must be issued, if the treatment is among the benefits provided in the person's own health care system, but cannot be provided there within a time limit which is medically justifiable, taking into account his or her current state of health and the probable course of the illness.[34] In this case a person is entitled to benefits in kind in another Member State (according to the rules applied there and paid or reimbursed according to the tariffs in the Member State of treatment). Hence, if waiting times are too long (and waiting lists have to be managed

[31] Article 19 Regulation (EC) 883/2004 and Article 25 of the implementing Regulation (EC) 987/2009. A non-exhaustive list in the Annex to the Decision No S3 of 12 June 2009 defining the benefits covered by Articles 19(1) and 27(1) of Regulation (EC) No 883/2004 of the European Parliament and of the Council and Article 25(A)(3) of Regulation (EC) No 987/2009 of the European Parliament and of the Council (OJ C 106, 24.4.2010, pp. 40–41, applicable as of 2014), mentions kidney dialysis, oxygen therapy, special asthma treatment, echocardiography in case of chronic autoimmune diseases, chemotherapy.

[32] E.g. Slovenian Supreme Court decisions SI:VSRS:2012:VIII.IPS.182.2011 and SI:VSRS:2012:VIII.IPS.47.2012.

[33] The Decision S3 of the Administrative Commission for the Coordination of Social Security Systems (OJ C 106, 24.4.2010, in force since 2014) stipulates that healthcare shall include benefits provided in conjunction with chronic or existing illnesses as well as in conjunction with pregnancy and childbirth, but not when the objective of the stay in another Member State is to receive these treatments.

[34] On the procedure for issuing such authorization case C-56/01 *Inizan*, EU:C:2003:578, case C-372/04 *Watts*, EU:C:2006:325.

individually, not administratively)[35] there is a right to cross-border healthcare,[36] regardless of the reason.[37] In exceptional cases of urgent cross-border treatment, prior authorisation might be waived and reimbursement provided also without authorising such cross-border healthcare in advance.[38]

Of course, for cross-border healthcare to work in practice, social security administrations must cooperate sincerely and mutually trustworthy. A special program of Electronic Exchange of Social Security Information, EESSI) has been established.[39] However, for a direct digital experience between a citizen and an institution in a Member State, another solution called European Social Security Pass, is being piloted and delivered its first results in 2022. In the future, also EHIC should be in a digital form, presentable to a public healthcare provider in another Member State and linked with the respective national public healthcare institution in the competent Member State.[40]

3 EU Healthcare Market

3.1 Free Movement of Goods and Services

The CJEU has not only construed the Social Security Coordination Regulations but has also relied directly on the Treaty provisions on (active and passive)[41] free movement of (medical) services and (medicinal) goods to enable medical treatment in another member state. Introduction of a complementary route for exporting the right to healthcare started with the judgments in the cases *Kohll* and *Decker* in 1998[42] and was further developed since.[43] Although judgments are binding *erga omnes* (interpreting the EU law for all), they are passed with having an actual case at hand in mind (in an *ad hoc* manner), and Member States could still distinguish their situation from the one in the judgment (and disregard it in their specific situation). In the same vein, the Slovenian social courts delivered their first judgment on free

[35] Case C-372/04 - *Watts*, EU:C:2006:325. Bieback (2015), p. 244.

[36] Article 44b ZZVZZ reiterates the rules of the Social Security Coordination Regulations.

[37] Case C-268/13 - *Petru*, EU:C:2014:2271

[38] Case C-777/18 - *Vas Megyei Kormányhivatal*, EU:C:2020:745.

[39] On the repository of national institutions https://ec.europa.eu/social/social-security-directory/pai/select-country/language/en. It might be mentioned that first electronic documents were officially exchanged between Slovenian and Austrian pension institutes in 2019.

[40] More at https://ec.europa.eu/social/main.jsp?catId=1545&langId=en. See also UNU (2022).

[41] Passive free movement was confirmed in cross-border healthcare (joined) cases C-286/82 (and C-26/83) *Luisi and Carbone*, EU:C:1984:35. They were not very alarming for the Member States, since no reimbursement from the public healthcare system was claimed for private healthcare abroad.

[42] Cases C-158/96 *Kohll*, EU:C:1998:171 and C-120/95 *Decker*, EU:C:1998:167.

[43] Strban (2023a), p. 337.

movement of cross-border medical services only at the end of 2009, despite the EU law being applicable already since the beginning of May 2004.[44]

Moreover, the judgments have been ignored by the Member States not only at a national, but also at a Union level. The EU legislature did not consider CJEU case law on cross-border healthcare in passing the new Social Security Coordination Regulation in 2004, although many cases had been decided by then.

Argumentation that judgments do not apply in certain cases and there is only one possibility of cross-border healthcare, i.e. by coordination of the public health systems, is no longer possible. The rules developed by CJEU were codified in a Directive in 2011.[45] It is called a Cross-Border Healthcare Directive, although it is not the only Union legal instrument enabling cross-border healthcare. Nevertheless, the Directive had to be transposed into national law, whereas a regulation applies directly. Hence, the reader of national law might be aware of the Directive rules, but less so of the Regulation rules, since it must be studied in addition to national law. It might also avoid national legislative and legal terminological procedure, making its text not always straightforwardly understandable. The rules of the Cross-Border Healthcare Directive had to be transposed into national law (by the 25 October 2013), whereas the Social Security Coordination Regulations are directly applicable since May 2010. Yet, many more discussions developed when the Directive had to be transposed and only a few (if any) when the new Social Security Coordination Regulations became applicable. Moreover, many Member States were late in transposing the Directive,[46] and, not all were in favour of the Directive in the first place.[47]

Slovenia transposed the Cross-Border Healthcare Directive with only slight delay of 11 days (on the 5 November 2013). This was even more important from the Slovenian than the EU perspective. Slovenian Constitutional Court[48] established that according to the Slovenian Health Care and Health Insurance Act (ZZVZZ), the payment of health care services of at least 90 percent of the value of medical care abroad is guaranteed to persons insured under the mandatory health insurance. Until the amendments to ZZVZZ, transposing the Cross-Border Healthcare Directive to Slovenian legal order, there were no legislatively defined conditions that would limit this right, neither was there a procedure in which it would be decided whether medical care is justified. The Court argued that there was no authorisation given by the law for ZZZS to limit the scope of the right to cross-border healthcare in the Rules of Mandatory Health Insurance. The determination of the conditions for the

---

[44] See cases Ps 2203/2007, 15. 5. 2009, in relation to Psp 425/2009, 17. 12. 2009, SI:VDSS:2009:PSP.425.2009.

[45] Directive 2011/24/EU on the application of patients' rights in cross-border healthcare, OJ L 88, 4.4.2011.

[46] After the transposition deadline, the Commission launched 26 infringement procedures for late or incomplete notification of transposition measures. Following this process, all Member States finally notified their complete transposition measures. European Commission (2018).

[47] The Austrian, Polish, Portuguese and Romanian delegations voted against the Directive and the Slovak delegation abstained. Council of the European Union, Brussels, 28. 2. 2011, 7056/11.

[48] Decision No Up-1303/11, U-I-25/14, 21.3.2014, SI:USRS:2014:Up.1303.11.

exercise of the right to healthcare (abroad) and the manner of its exercise are according to the Slovenian Constitution explicitly reserved for a legislative act. The Court found breach of the constitutional articles on the right to social security (Art. 50) and to healthcare (Art. 51).

After annulling the Rules of Mandatory Health Insurance several questions were opened, like is the right to cross-border healthcare (in and outside of the EU) unlimited and encompasses also benefits not covered by the Slovenian legislation (only these benefits can be claimed cross-border under the EU healthcare law). At the time of decision, the ZZVZZ had already been amended and cross-border healthcare regulated by a legislative act, also due to the transposition deadline of the Cross-Border Healthcare Directive. Hence, the decision of the Slovenian Constitutional Court applied to a limited number of pending cross-border healthcare cases.

3.2 Cross-Border Healthcare in the Union Common Market

The system of prior authorisation for cross-border healthcare is according to the Social Security Regulations a rule for planned treatment. However, according to the Cross-border Healthcare Directive it is an exception and should be construed narrowly. Under certain conditions it may be introduced also under the Directive, although not every Member State has actually introduced it.[49] It should be limited to what is necessary and proportionate to the objective to be achieved, and may not constitute a means of arbitrary discrimination or an unjustified obstacle to the free movement of patients.[50] It is only admissible for hospital and highly specialized treatment, when it involves particularly risky treatments, or give rise to serious and specific concerns relating to the quality or safety of the care. The question remains what is risky and what not, and who is to judge the health care systems of other Member States.[51] Moreover, there is no obligation to cover non-healthcare costs under the Directive.

Prior authorisation for hospital treatment under the Cross-Border Healthcare Directive might cause certain difficulties. Since the Directive does not distinguish between planned and unplanned cross-border healthcare a paradox situation might emerge. For instance, cross-border tourist may break a leg while skiing and is brought by a medical helicopter to a private clinic. EHIC under the Regulation cannot be applied, since it is a private hospital. Moreover, no blanc or ex-post authorisation is foreseen by the Directive. It might be a blind spot of EU cross-border healthcare law.[52] This clearly shows that the Directive was initially intended to cover

[49] Olsson et al. (2021), p. 22, van Seben et al. (2022), p. 30.

[50] Article 8 Directive 2011/24/EU.

[51] Strban (2023a), p. 348.

[52] Strban et al. (2017), p. 38.

(only) planned cross-border healthcare. Problem could be solved by not applying the Directive to unplanned healthcare and leave it to the Social Security Coordination Regulations and purely national law where reimbursement may be foreseen also for private urgent healthcare abroad. Another option would be to expressly stipulate that prior authorisation may not be required for necessary or even urgent treatment under the Directive. Hence, more clarity in this respect could be desired for.[53]

Even if Member States might have used the same procedures for granting prior authorisation under the Social Security Coordination Regulations and the Cross-Border Healthcare Directive, a distinction has been clearly outlined by the CJEU, referring also to the scope of social security coverage, i.e. level of covered costs for cross-border healthcare. Under the Regulations cross-border healthcare is covered according to the prices in the Member State of treatment, equally as for public patients insured by that legislation. Under the Directive the level of reimbursement is limited to the prices in the Member State of affiliation (and not exceeding actual costs of treatment).[54] Actually, direct (co-)payments might be covered under the Regulations[55] and under the Directive but shall never exceed actual healthcare costs.

Therefore, prior authorisation might be justified under the Regulations (in order not to disturb the financial balance of social security system) but becomes more difficult to justify it under the Directive (where costs according to home tariffs are reimbursed). CJEU clarified that whether equal or equally effective treatment can be given in the Member State of residence, constitutes an objective medical assessment. Therefore, Regulations exclusively consider patient's medical condition, not personal choices of medical care. Moreover, not considering religious beliefs (difference in treatment indirectly based on religion) for refusing prior authorisation under the Regulations may be a justified and proportionate measure. Conversely, due to systemic difference of the reimbursement system under the Directive, prior authorisation in the Member State of affiliation cannot be refused in such case and cross-border healthcare must be allowed and (partially) reimbursed. Indirect discrimination based on religion cannot be justified under the Directive (whereby also the provisions of the Charter of Fundamental Rights of the EU has to be considered).[56]

The CJEU is allowing a combination of both legal instruments when deciding on prior authorisation. Cross-border medical assessment of equal or equally effective healthcare may be performed according to the Directive, although, it is a condition for covering cross-border healthcare under the Regulations. Setting an additional condition of medical assessment from national public health system (next to healthcare being among the benefits and not available in due time) is a condition beyond the requirements of the Regulations and disproportionately limits free movement of

---

[53] Ibid., p. 7.

[54] Article 7(4) Directive 2011/24/EU. Not so clear from the operative part in English language of the case C-173/09 - *Elchinov*, EU:C:2010:581, but very clear in other languages (also Bulgarian, language of the case).

[55] If national costs are lower than actual costs. Article 26(7) Regulation (EC) 987/2009 (reminiscence of decision in case C-368/98 - *Vanbraekel and Others*, EU:C:2001:400).

[56] Case C-243/19 - *Veselības ministrija*, EU:C:2020:872.

services under the TFEU. Even more importantly, the Court is advancing quality of treatment and its results, since proposed cross-border medical treatment might not cause invalidity.[57]

Some questions remain open, i.e. whether a personal physician, who may act as a gatekeeper to public healthcare, like in Slovenia, could be chosen in another Member State? According to the Cross-Border Healthcare Directive the administrative requirements could remain but should not be discriminatory.[58]

Another question might be how cross-border patients should be treated in the Member State providing healthcare. Such patient will have to comply with the same standards in the Member State of treatment, including possible waiting list. The situation might get complicated, when the same healthcare provider offers the same medical services for public and private patients. A tendency of the healthcare provider might arise to treat cross-border patients as private patients. The advantage for a patient might be that there are no waiting lists, and they could be treated immediately in a nicer setting and the personnel might invest a bit more effort due to direct payment. The reasons for acting as a private patient may vary. Private healthcare provision might have a better reputation, investments in public facilities might be slowed down and salaries of medical and supporting professions lowered or stagnating, which was especially the case in some Member States during the time of the recent economic recession. This might lead to shortages even in basic medical supplies and infrastructure.[59] Moreover, patients may desire to exercise consumer control over providers. If no third party (social health insurance or national health service) is involved in the transaction, this makes the provider accountable directly to the patient, and the provider responds accordingly.[60]

However, such direct payment of a private patient is generally less convenient for most patients and may be afforded only by a limited number of well-off private patients. The prices for private patients are set distinctively as for public patients and are as a rule higher than the agreed prices for public healthcare provision. A specific problem may exist when direct payments are informal. Although much of the evidence of such covert or hidden payments is anecdotal, since it is illegal in many countries, experts acknowledge that such payments exist in some countries.

The question of steering (the behaviour of) patients towards private healthcare provision is not relevant only for national patients, but even more so for cross-border patients. Possibility of visiting purely private providers and be publicly reimbursed was created by the CJEU and the Cross-Border Healthcare Directive. Limiting informational access to healthcare is a consequence of the asymmetry of information. For instance, in some Member States (like in Croatia, where many Slovenians make summer holidays) private ambulatories for tourists operate within

---

[57] Case C-538/19 - *Casa Naţională de Asigurări de Sănătate and Casa de Asigurări de Sănătate Constanţa*, EU:C:2021:809.

[58] Article 7, Paragraph 7 Directive 2011/24/EU.

[59] See *e.g.*, *Petru*, C-268/13, EU:C:2014:2271.

[60] Strban et al. (2017), p. 74.

public primary care centres, but are outside of the public network.[61] However, mid July 2024 some of the public health centres have opened 36 ambulatories for tourist with the agreement of national health insurance carrier and EHIC could be used in the future.[62] Complexity of (foreign) healthcare systems pronounces even more the asymmetry of information. Therefore, providing straightforward, actual and transparent information is essential for proper functioning of the EU cross-border healthcare law.

Moreover, reimbursing of cross-border private healthcare while not reimbursing of such care within the competent Member State may cause healthcare providers to establish themselves just across the border and may lead to a so-called reverse discrimination of national patients.[63]

4 Slovenia at a Crossroad: Public or Market Healthcare?

There are distinctive points, where public and private healthcare could be distinguished. It might be at the point of public or private health insurance, determining personal and material scope of public (social) insurance and leaving the rest to the health insurance market. But it might also be at the point of healthcare delivery. It should be mentioned that one of the oldest legal relations in healthcare is contractual relation between a patient and a medical doctor. At first it was an exchange relation, where a patient demanded, and a medical doctor provided healthcare. Medical doctor promised to deliver a service and a patient paid for it. Such payment was not considered as a sinalagmatic obligation but was treated separately. Medical service was delivered "honeste" (honourably) and without payment. In line with medical art the wellbeing of patients and not gaining of money was at the forefront. In Roman law, medical doctor was rewarded with voluntary payment, so called "honorarium".[64]

With (r)evolution[65] of public, social healthcare systems, which may be administered as (centralised or decentralised) national health service or social health insurance (reimbursing healthcare costs or providing healthcare in natura, like in Slovenia), the patient-doctor relation evolved. Further legal relations between socially insured patients and social insurance carriers and the later and healthcare providers are established. Socially insured person may claim healthcare rights at the healthcare provider included in the public network. The infrastructure of such public network must be provided by local communities and the State. Social health

[61] See https://zdravlje.gov.hr/zdravstveni-turizam-5532/turisticke-ambulante/6211

[62] See https://zdravlje.gov.hr/vijesti/turisti-mogu-dobiti-zdravstvenu-uslugu-na-36-lokacija-pri-domovima-zdravlja/6479

[63] More on whether there is discrimination of providers or reverse discrimination of patients (or merely a better law can be chosen) Strban (2023b), p. 317.

[64] Gurgel (2000), str. 5.

[65] Strban (2024c), p. 201.

insurance utilises it by contracting (public and private) providers in the public network, with a purpose of providing healthcare to socially insured patients.

One of the most powerful interest groups in every society are medical doctors. We all not only respect, but to a certain extent also fear and even envy them and are crossed if not all aspects of access to healthcare are guaranteed.[66] Therefore, at the end of 2024 the amendments to the health services act are publicly discussed.[67] Questions are, whether not only general conditions (like medical licence and registration) that apply to all healthcare providers shall be regulated, but also specific conditions for those included in the public network (like special permission, respecting the principle of economical provision of healthcare with expert supervision, digital connectivity, training on mandatory health insurance and awareness that medical doctors under public network are acting on both, the demand and the supply side of healthcare). The question is also whether public network should operate on a non-profit bass[68] and how much are public doctors (organised as self-employed providers of medical services or as private companies) allowed to work for profits within the public sector and outside of it. If they are allowed to be both, employed in a public sector and provide the same services on the healthcare market, they may be tempted to prolong the waiting times under the public network and steer patients towards private provision of healthcare.

It goes without saying that both, public and market healthcare are required and there is enough space for both. The question is only how much, if at all they should be mixed without producing socially negative effects (such as jumping the ques. or prolonging waiting times and hence limiting timely access to healthcare).

5 Concluding Thoughts

Cross-border healthcare has been legislated under the Slovenian, international and EU law already before the Slovenian accession to the European Union. However, in the 20 years of membership many things have changed. More legal options for cross-border patients have opened. Next to cooperation of public (social security) healthcare systems, more market-oriented possibility of reimbursement of cross-border healthcare costs exists.

Such rules have influenced the shaping of national public healthcare systems and were at the same time shaped by the national rules and practices. Concerning

[66] Medical doctors in Slovenia are on strike since 15 January 2024 (now already more than 11 months), with the sole argument of raising the salaries.

[67] More at https://www.gov.si/zbirke/javne-objave/javna-obravnava-osnutka/, November 2024. In May 2025 amendments to the Health Services Act were passed, Official Journal RS, No. 32/2025.

[68] Decisions of the Slovenian Constitutional Court were at first focused on the organisational aspects of healthcare provision but are later turning towards its substance. See decisions U-I-194/17, SI:USRS:2018:U.I.194.17, and U-I-59/18, SI:USRS:2022:U.I.59.18.

Slovenia, this may be visible by the cross-border childbirth cases and decisions of the Slovenian Constitutional Court.

Member States remain in charge of social security law and organisation of their respective public healthcare systems. Every change in national law may have implications to the EU social security coordination law. Therefore, agreements in the EU on how national social security systems should be coordinated and to what extent healthcare shall be provided on the common market have to be reviewed when loopholes in protection are detected. However, due to many (and sometimes diverging) interests, it is not easy to agree on the new social security coordination rules. The same goes for the free movement of medical services and medicinal goods rules, which are also not perfect.

Considering national rules of cross-border healthcare, bilateral and international social security agreements next to the EU cross-border healthcare law, the legal landscape has become very complex. This presents difficulties not only to national administrations but foremost to cross-border patients. They are hardly able to be fully informed about national, foreign and EU rules.

The question then is whether it is really in the interest of the Member States and their social security systems to have an open market of medical benefits? Will everyone ever have equal access to all medical benefits in all Member States? Or are the more informed, more mobile and wealthier persons, as well as Member States with more developed healthcare systems (again) profiting the most? Is really the best healthcare provided only if we directly pay for it or is there still need for social solidarity providing equal and equitable[69] access to high-quality healthcare to all?[70]

References

Bieback K-J (2015) Article 20 Regulation 883/2004. In: Fuchs M, Cornelissen R (eds) EU social security law: a commentary on EU Regulations 883/2004 and 987/2009. C.H. Beck, Hart, Nomos, pp 238–252

De Wispelaere F, De Smedt L, Pacolet J (2024) Intra-EU mobility and the use of private health insurance: trivial or substantial?. Working paper. HIVA KU Leuven

Eichenhofer E (2025) Sozialrecht der Europäischen Union, 9th edn. ESV

European Commission (2018) Report from the Commission to the European Parliament and the Council on the operation of Directive 2011/24/EU on the application of patients' rights in cross-border healthcare. COM(2018) 651 final, Brussels, 21.9.2018

Fuchs M, Janda C (2025) Europäisches Sozialrecht, 9th edn. Nomos

Gurgel DS (2000) Die Entwicklung des Vertragsärztlichen und Vertragszahnärztlicher Vergütungssystems nach dem zweitem Weltkrieg. Schaker Verlag

Jorens Y, Van Overmeiren F (2009) General principles of coordination in Regulation 883/2004. Eur J Soc Secur 11(1–2):47–79

[69] See article 3 of the Convention on Human Rights and Biomedicine (Oviedo Convention).

[70] Is social security (including healthcare) still about social risks or is it merely a benefit for contributions paid? More in Strban (2024a), p. 143.

Olsson, J., De Smedt, L., & De Wispelaere, F. (2021). Data on cross-border patient healthcare following Directive 2011/24/EU, Reference year 2020. European Commission
Strban G (2013) Patient mobility in the European Union: between social security coordination and free movement of services. ERA Forum 14(3):391–407
Strban G (2018) Member States' approaches to bilateral social security agreements. Eur J Soc Secur 20(2):129–147
Strban G (2023a) Cross-border healthcare and social security rights. In: Pennings F, Vonk G (eds) Research handbook on European social security law. Edward Elgar Publishing, pp 332–352
Strban G (2023b) Cross-border healthcare and reverse discrimination: An (un)solved issue? In: Aranguiz A, Bednarowicz B, Quené M, Vanheule D (eds) Pioneering social Europe, Lieber Amicorum Herwig Verschueren. die Keure, pp 317–324
Strban G (2024a) Social risks and their development. In: Mocella M, Sychenko E (eds) The quest for labour rights and social justice, work in a changing world. Franco Angeli, pp 143–160
Strban G (2024b) Dostop do zdravstvenih storitev in medicinskih stvari (Access to medical services and medicinal goods). Delavci in delodajalci (Employees and Employers) XXIV(1):9–30
Strban G (2024c) (R)evolution of social security law in a changing world: from protecting the poor to the workers and finally every member of society? In: Accetto M, Škrubej K, Weiler JHH (eds) Law and revolution past experiences, future challenges. Routledge, pp 201–215
Strban G, Berki G, Carrascosa Bermejo D, Van Overmeiren F (2017) Access to healthcare in cross-border situations. FreSsco Analytical Report 2016. EU, Brussels
Strban G, Spiegel B, Schoukens P (2020) The application of the social security coordination rules on modern forms of family. MoveS Report, European Commission. Retrieved from https://ec.europa.eu/social/main.jsp?langId=en&catId=1098&moreDocuments=yes
UNU (2022) Case studies on digital transformation of social security administration and services. Case Study European Union, United Nations University, Operating Unit for Policy-Driven Electronic Governance, ILO Publishing
van Seben, R. et al. (2022). Study on enhancing implementation of the cross-border healthcare directive 2011/24/EU to ensure patient rights in the EU. Final Report, Directorate General for Health and Food Safety, Publications Office of the EU
ZZZS (2024) Letno poročilo ZZZS 2023 (Yearly Report ZZZS 2023). ZZZS, Ljubljana

Legal Regime of the Social Security Certificate from the Perspective of the CJEU Case Law

Martin Štefko

1 Introduction

One of the key requirements for the free movement of workers is their protection of social rights. Not accidently, this is one of fundamental freedoms the EU is based on. Individuals rendering services in different parts of the European Union shall not lose some or even all accrued welfare rights simply because of their cross-border economic activities. To ensure such a goal, the EU has created so called coordination regulations. These regulations constitute, according to the settled case law of the CJEU, a complete and uniform system of conflict rules and their aim is to ensure that workers moving within the EU are subject to the social security scheme of only one Member State, to prevent the system of legislation of more than one Member State from being applicable and to avoid the complications which may result from that situation.[1] The law at the same time ensures that the persons covered by Regulation No 883/2004[2] are not left without social security cover because no legislation applies to them. The main tool used by the EU law in this regard is so called E 101 s and later PD A1s (hereinafter "PDs A1"). It is PDs A1 that create a presumption that the worker concerned is properly affiliated to the social security

[1] See Case 19-67, C-2/89 Kits van Heijningen [1990] ECR I-1755, paragraph 12; Case C-425/93 Calle Grenzshop Andresen [1995] ECR I-269, paragraph 9; Case C-131/95 Huijbrechts [1997] ECR I-1409, paragraph 17, and Case C-275/96 Kuusijärvi [1998] ECR I-3419, paragraph 28).

[2] Regulation No 883/2004 on the coordination of social security systems as amended (hereinafter "Regulation 883/2004").

M. Štefko (✉)
Faculty of Law, Department for Labour Law and Social Security law, Charles University, Prague, Czech Republic
e-mail: stefkom@prf.cuni.cz

K. Koldinská et al. (eds.), *Labour Law and Social Security Law in Central and Eastern Europe*, European Union and its Neighbours in a Globalized World 26,
https://doi.org/10.1007/978-3-032-04496-9_10

scheme of the Member State whose competent institution has issued those certificates.

This article analyses enforceability of PDs A1 concerning the applicable legislation.[3] We ask whether the rule of PDs A1 has grown up to become a useful tool to rely upon? As it will be shown, PDs A1 are real figures of law; there are around 4.6 million issued every year from 2022.[4] Employees and their employers apply for them. Immigration police carries out regular checks, especially in Austria, France, and Switzerland. If PDs A1 certificate are missing, this can have unpleasant consequences for the travellers as well as for their employers.[5] But at the same time, the EU legislator has identified cases when some national legislators had not obeyed EU law on regular bases.[6] In legal words: although PDs A1 are binding on the competent institution and the courts of the Member State in which that worker is working, there are exceptions, because this was the only way how to appease opposing Member states; and they are many of them.

For demonstrational purposes, let us consider here a case of employers operating in international goods transport who used the essence of the business to maintain a fictitious seat in a low-wage Eastern European Member State, such as the Czech Republic, Latvia or Poland. PDs A1 were issued as proofs for their drivers that there are insured in low wage countries.[7] Although this sector of industry with a high degree of mobility is crucial for the smooth functioning of the EU internal market, it is obvious that national legislative systems not only generally exclude short periods from certain social benefits (periods spent by drivers in Member State highways), but also have a problem with undertaking to place the core of their business outside of the state of their seat.[8]

Today, when there are more PDs A1 issued for individuals working in two or more states (the Czech Republic included) than PDs A1 issued by Czech social security administration as the competent institution, we can at least to certain degree state that we bear the costs of EU coordination as well.

2 PDs A1

In a long-term view, it would be better to not limit the freedom of services by EU social security dimension, but it has never been an option. The coordination of social security must have been introduced as a soothing measure for those western

[3] From resent published articles cf.: Froger-Michon and Cai (2018); KPMG International (2020); Fragomen (2024); Réseau Fiscalité et Nomadisme (RFN) (2005); Ius Laboris (2019).

[4] Cf. Coordination of social security systems at a glance 2023 Statistical Report.

[5] E.g. fines, denial of entry, problems during return travel, social security payments according to the law of the country of stay, denial of benefits from accident insurance after a work accident, etc.

[6] Cf. directive 2020/1057, preamble point 19.

[7] Those drivers are not temporary agency workers. Cf. C-784/19.

[8] See for instance France by Article L 114–15-1 of 'Code de la sécurité sociale'.

European countries, which started to view not only, but also Eastern European workers as the threat to their welfare. Ideally, a driver should be subject to the same social security regulations anywhere in the European Union.[9] Since this has not been possible so far, given the low level of economic interpenetration[10] and high national differences in the field of national welfare (not to be speaking about tax policy, which is still out of EU coordination regulations), the EU legislator has given rise to a single system of conflict of laws that upholds the applicability of the one determined social security. This was particularly the objective of Regulation No. 3[11] of the Council which, as of 1 October 1972, has been substituted by Regulation No 1408/71 and as from May 2010 by Regulation No 883/2004.

Certain level of formalization in coordination processes has been needed. Dispatched drivers from other Member States have to prove being on a business trip or relocation to defend encroachments on their wages done by host state authorities. They must have evidence that they are covered by only one social security system and determine which one is it. For that purpose, PDs A1 has also been used. PDs A1 are issued on the basis of regulations, which are described in more detail in Sect. 3.

2.1 Scope

EU citizens are covered by coordination of social security schemes and may be subject to PDs A1. Third-country nationals may be subject of PD A1 as well provided that they are legally staying and working in the territory of the Member States.[12]

PDs A1 are usually relevant only in the event of the application of the rules for determining the social security legislation applicable to the workers concerned. As ruled in the A-Rosa case, CJEU concluded that PDs A1 is binding on both the social security institutions of the Member State in which the work is carried out and the courts of that Member State, even where it is found by those courts that the conditions under which the worker concerned carry out his activities do not fall within the material scope of that provision of Regulation No 1408/71.[13]

In *Grana-Novoa*, the Court held that social security conventions concluded between a single Member State and one or more third States fall out of the scope of

---

[9] As the French delegation demanded. See Morsa (2019), p. 140. For French statement cf.: Commission européenne. *Document de travail des services de la Commission – Évaluation d'impact – Initiative visant à améliorer la législation sociale dans les transports routiers*, SWD(2017) 186 final, Bruxelles, 31 mai 2017. Disponible sur: https://eur-lex.europa.eu/legal-content/FR/TXT/?uri=CELEX:52017SC0186

[10] Manpower, cited above, paragraph 10.

[11] Regulation No 3, 1958, OJ 561.

[12] Cf. C 477/17, paragraph 44 et seq.

[13] Cf. C-620/15, paragraph 53.

Regulation No 1408/71.[14] In those cases, PDs A1 cannot find its application. As ruled in Rhine agreement cases, a certificate issued by an institution of a Member State confirming that a worker classified as a Rhine boatman is subject to the legislation of that Member State, such as the certificates at issue in the main proceedings, cannot be regarded as being an E 101 certificate.[15]

2.2 *The Issuance of PDs A1*

The legal predecessor of PDs A1 was the E-101, which was entitled 'certificate concerning the applicable legislation'. It was a model form prepared by the Administrative Commission on Social Security for migrant workers.[16] Under Regulations No. 883/2004 the E 101 certificates have from 1 May 2010 become portable documents A1 (PDs A1). Said certificates are standard forms issued by the social security institution of the Member State with whom a worker is registered. They aim to prove that the worker pays social contributions in another EU country, particularly in the case of posting or working in several countries at the same time. In connection with PDs A1, CJEU concluded that the EU law should not be considered in isolation, but that in cases of doubt, it should be interpreted and applied in the light of the versions existing in the other three languages.[17]

PDs A1 is not an act that provides rights to a worker but is only declaratory. Even so, it is binding upon the institutions and courts of the host Member State including where, following a request for reconsideration and withdrawal sent by the competent institution of that latter Member State to the issuing institution, that institution has declared that it has provisionally suspended the binding effects of that certificate until it decides definitively on that request.[18] CJEU reasoned this aspect of interpretation with the opinion that if that were not so, the principle that self-employed persons are to be covered by only one social security system would be undermined,

[14] CJEU judgment of the Court of 2 August 1993, C-23/92.

[15] Een though it may come in the same form and irrespective of whether it was issued by the institution designated by the competent authority of a Member State within the meaning of Regulation No 1408/71 for issuing that type of certificate. Cf. Inspecteur van Rijksbelastingdienst (C-72/14), and T. A. van Dijk v Staatssecretaris van Financiën (C-197/14).

[16] Referred to in Title IV of Regulation No 1408/71. See Administrative Commission Decision No 202 of 17 March 2005 on model forms necessary for the application of Council Regulations (EEC) No 1408/71 and (EEC) No 574/72 (E 001, E 101, E 102, E 103, E 104, E 106, E 107, E 108, E 109, E 112, E 115, E 116, E 117, E 118, E 120, E 121, E 123, E 124, E 125, E 126 and E 127) (2006/203/EC) (OJ 2006 L 77, p. 1). Under the new Regulations (EC) No 883/2004 of the European Parliament and of the Council of 29 April 2004 on the coordination of social security systems (OJ 2004 L 166, p. 1) and (EC) No 987/2009 of the European Parliament and of the Council of 16 September 2009 laying down the procedure for implementing Regulation No 883/2004 (OJ 2009 L 284, p. 1), the E 101 certificate has from 1 May 2010 become portable document A1.

[17] CJEU Case 9/79, P. 353.

[18] Cf. Joined Cases C-410/21 and C-661/21.

as would the predictability of the system to be applied and, consequently, legal certainty. In cases in which it was difficult to determine the system applicable, each of the competent institutions of the two Member States concerned would be inclined to take the view, to the detriment of the self-employed person concerned, that their social security system was applicable.[19]

The issuing institution is required to carry out a proper assessment of the facts relevant to the application of the rules relating to the determination of the legislation applicable in the matter of social security and, consequently, to ensure the correctness of the information contained in that certificate.[20]

PDs A1 establishes a presumption that posted workers are properly affiliated with the social security system of the Member State in which the undertaking that posted those workers is established. PDs A1 proves that the social security legislation of the issuing Member State applies and confirms that the person concerned has no obligations to pay social security contributions in another Member State, mainly in the host state. On that certificate, the competent institution of the Member State in which an undertaking employing the workers concerned is established declares that its social security system will remain applicable to those workers. By the principle that workers must be covered by only one social security system, the certificate thus necessarily implies that the other Member State's social security system cannot apply.[21] PDs A1 may have a retroactive effect.[22]

The current legal framework provides that the employer or the person concerned must inform the competent institution about their planned transnational activities, whenever possible before these activities take place. As Estonia reports regularly, it is here where the AI was put into service when "a robot registers all A1 certificates issued by Estonia and checks if there are overlapping periods with Finnish pension insurance or that every worker working on a site is either insured in Finland or has a valid A1 certificate according to the official register); and creates tasks for the handlers when errors or overlapping periods occur."[23]

Competent institutions must carry out a diligent examination of the application of their social security system. It is necessary to deduce from all the circumstances

---

[19] Case C-178/97. Point 41, (Fitzwilliam Executive Search, paragraph 54).

[20] See C-115/11, paragraph 45; FTS, paragraph 51; and Case C-178/97 Banks and Others, paragraph 38.

[21] CJEU judgment of 26 January 2006, *Herbosch Kiere*, C-2/05, EU:C:2006:69, paragraph 21 and the case-law cited.

[22] CJEU implicitly acknowledged that the E 101 certificate may produce retroactive effects when it held that the option which Article 17 of Regulation No 1408/71 confers on Member States to agree, in the interest of a worker, to apply a legislation different from that designated by Articles 13–16 also applies in respect of periods that have already expired (Case 101/83 Raad van Arbeid v Brusse [1984] ECR 2223, paragraphs 20 and 21; Case C-454/93 Rijksdienst voor Arbeidsvoorziening v Van Gestel [1995] ECR I-1707, paragraph 29). Articles 11 and 11a of Regulation No 574/72 also provide that, in such a situation, an E 101 certificate is to be issued. Cf. C-178/97, see paras 43, 48, 53–54, 57, operative part 2–3.

[23] Commission: Fraud and error in the field of EU social security coordination, Reference year 2021, p. 15.

of his employment whether he is under the authority of that establishment.[24] The duty follows from the principle that the institutions of the other Member States are entitled to expect the institution of the Member State concerned to fulfill that obligation. For example, Belgium has developed Osiris, a monitoring and reporting application used to monitor all files processed by inspection bodies/institutions and to report to the Social Research and Information Service (Service d'Information et de Recherche Sociale—SIRS), in the form of an electronic platform, and to political bodies. An issuing institution can withdraw PDs A1 on its initiative and not only based on a request for review and withdrawal from the competent institution of another Member State. In Zakład Ubezpieczeń Społecznych Oddział w Toruniu,[25] CJEU underscores that the institution issuing an A1 certificate has an ongoing obligation to regularly assess the worker's situation since the A1 certificate holds binding authority across Member States, and other institutions cannot revoke it. Article 5 of Regulation No 987/2009 does not foresee any procedure that the issuing institution must comply with when withdrawing an A1 certificate on its initiative.

CJEU clarifies that the dialogue and conciliation procedure apply only to the withdrawal of the A1 certificate following a request for review made by the competent institution of another member state.

2.3 Trust vs. Fraud

Somewhere along the way, the PDs A1 started to be falsified. Those certificates necessarily imply that the other Member State's social security system, especially the host state's, cannot apply. They are the proof and, at the same time, thus may constitute a tool to cover fraud in the form of non-payment of insurance premiums to the host country's system. Such fraud may be, speaking of nature, a simple one or a sophisticated one. For simple frauds, the falsification of documents is done by a false PDs A1 or by false social security data, without the holder being present and having paid contributions to another social security scheme within the European Union and the EEC. For more complex frauds, the real relationship between the social security scheme to which the employee or self-employed person is subject under PD A1 and the host State is undermined.

Under the principle of sincere cooperation, laid down in primary EU law,[26] which also entails the principle of mutual trust, means that the host state is bound by issued PDs A1. As CJEU several times stated the host state cannot assume the competence to decide which social security is applicable as Belgium did. CJEU concluded: "*In the second place, it is clear from settled case-law that a Member State may not rely on the fact that other Member States have also failed to perform their obligations to*

[24] Case 19–67, point 354.

[25] CJEU Case C-422/22, Zakład Ubezpieczeń Społecznych Oddział w Toruniu v TE.

[26] Article 4(3) TEU.

justify its failure to fulfill its obligations under the FEU Treaty. In fact, in the EU legal order established by the Treaty, the implementation of EU law by the Member States cannot be made subject to a condition of reciprocity."[27]

EU has defined its policy against fraud in several legal documents.[28] Actions to combat fraud and error are considered to be an inherent part of the proper implementation of Regulations (EC) No 883/2004. The key factor is proclaimed closer and more effective cooperation between competent authorities and institutions which shall be based on principles of public service, efficiency, active assistance, rapid delivery, and accessibility.[29]

That procedure has been elaborated on and now it consists of three steps. The first is sometimes called by CJEU as the channel of dialogue. Because increasing report and information duties[30] is not enough, decision No. A1 formalized a dialogue and conciliation procedure concerning the validity of PDs A1.

The issuance of wrong PDs A1 may be simply a mistake. Therefore, the Social Security Administration (CSSA) obtains information from the State Labour Inspectorate Office, including lists of employees who often submit incomplete or otherwise suspicious PD A1 forms. The CSSA then contacts national competent institutions, to verify those cases.

If social security institutions of different Member States disagree as to the social security legislation applicable to a worker, they must settle the issue following the dialogue and conciliation procedure set out in Article 76(6) of Regulation No 883/2004 and Article 5, 6 and 16 of Regulation No 987/2009. This procedure is the second step. In such cases when Member States cannot reach an agreement, in particular regarding the classification of laws or schemes within the scope of social security coordination they may turn to the Administrative Commission. Decision No 181 specifies that the competent institutions may submit to the Administrative Commission, through their government representative, a note that will be examined at the first meeting following the 20th day after its submission to reconcile the opposing views on the legislation applicable to the case.[31] CJEU upheld the channel of dialogue and the conciliation procedure as mandatory steps before the host state

---

[27] Cf. case C-356/15, paragraph 106. For further guidance *Commission* v *Finland*, C-118/07, EU:C:2009:715, paragraph 48 and the case-law cited.

[28] Cf. decision No H5 of 18 March 2010 concerning cooperation on combating fraud and error within the framework of Council Regulation (EC) No 883/2004 and Regulation (EC) No 987/2009 of the European Parliament and the Council on the coordination of social security systems.

[29] Cf. Decision No A1 of 12 June 2009 concerning the establishment of a dialogue and conciliation procedure concerning the validity of documents, the determination of the applicable legislation and the provision of benefits under Regulation (EC) No 883/2004 of the European Parliament and of the Council.

[30] Done by within the system for the Electronic Exchange of Social Security Information.

[31] 2001/891/EC: Decision No 181 of 13 December 2000 concerning the interpretation of Articles 14(1), 14a(1) and 14b(1) and (2) of Council Regulation (EEC) No 1408/71 on the legislation applicable to posted workers and self-employed workers temporarily working outside the competent State.

authorities questioned PDs A1's validity.[32] However, published data[33] and experts' opinions are not very optimistic about the real efficiency of the conciliation.[34] In Altun and Others, CJEU confirmed that competent courts or tribunals of the host state may assess the validity and content of PDs A1, in respect of which decisions of the Administrative Commission for Coordination of Social Security Systems have only the status of an opinion.[35]

If that commission does not succeed in reconciling the points of view of the Member States on the question of the legislation applicable, it is, for the Member State doubting the correctness of a declaration by another Member State to tell the Commission or, as a last resort, bring proceedings under Article 259 TFEU for the Court to examine, in the context of those proceedings, the question of the applicable legislation.[36] This is the third step.

For some time, there were thoughts about whether the third step is mandatory or whether the host state may go to its courts instead. EU law gives the national court sole responsibility for determining whether PDs A1 were issued in violation of EU law or not.[37] Because PDs A1 is binding not only on the competent institution of the Member State to which those workers are posted[38] but also well the person who calls on that worker's services not to act upon that certificate, host state authorities started formal administrative or even criminal procedure in their courts. The host state's authority is obliged to inform the competent institution about its actions.[39] Provided that the host state authorities do not recognize PDs A1 issued by another Member State, a court of the host Member State is not entitled to scrutinize the validity of PDs A1.[40] CJEU decided that the legal authorities or jurisdictions of a member state cannot refuse to recognize PDs A1 awarded by another member or associated state as long as the certificate has not been withdrawn or declared invalid.

[32] Cf. CJEU C-620/15, paragraph 56.

[33] Annual reports of European Labour Authority and Administrative Commission. Cf. European Commission, *Fraud and Error in the Field of EU Social Security Coordination – Reference Year 2023* (Report, 2024) https://ec.europa.eu/social/BlobServlet?docId=27421&langId=en accessed 2 June 2025. European Labour Authority, *ELA Report on Construction Sector: Issues in Information Provision and Enforcement* (Report, 2023) https://globalabc.org/resources/publications/ela-report-construction-sector-issues-information-provision-enforcementaccessed 2 June 2025. European Commission, *Annual Report on Intra-EU Labour Mobility 2024* (Report, 2025) https://employment-social-affairs.ec.europa.eu/policies-and-activities/moving-working-europe/facts-and-figures-intra-eu-labour-mobility-and-eu-social-security-coordination_en accessed 2 June 2025.

[34] Morsa (2019), p. 140.

[35] Case 19-67, p. 355.

[36] See, to that effect, judgment in Banks and Others, EU:C:2000:169, paragraph 44.

[37] See *Cilfit and Others* (283/81, EU:C:1982:335) and *Intermodal Transports*, C-495/03, EU:C:2005:552, paragraph 37, and case law cited there.

[38] CJEU Herbosch Kiere, C-2/05, EU:C:2006:69, paragraph 24.

[39] Cf. CJEU Banks and Others, C-178/97, EU:C:2000:169, paragraph 42 and 47.

[40] See, to that effect CJEU *Herbosch Kiere*, C-2/05, EU:C:2006:69, paragraph 32 and C-620/15, paragraph 49.

However, there is a so-called criminal exception as ruled on in Altun and Others. If the host state institution puts before the institution that issued the PD A1 concrete evidence that suggests that those certificates were obtained fraudulently, it is the duty of the latter institution, by the principle of sincere cooperation, to review, in the light of that evidence, the grounds for the issue of those certificates and, where appropriate, to withdraw them.[41] Provided that there is evidence, collected in the course of a judicial investigation, that supports the conclusion that PDs A1 were fraudulently obtained or relied on, and the issuing institution fails to consider that evidence to review the grounds for PDs A1. In such a case, a national court may, in the context of proceedings brought against persons suspected of having used posted workers ostensibly covered by PDs A1, disregard those certificates if, based on that evidence and with due regard to the safeguards inherent in the right to a fair trial which must be granted to those persons, it finds the existence of such fraud.[42] PDs A1 are disregarded for criminal proceedings provided that, first, a reasonable period has elapsed without the issuing institution having reconsidered the grounds for issuing that certificate and having adopted a decision on the specific evidence submitted by the competent institution in the host Member State, which gave rise to the view that that certificate had been obtained or invoked fraudulently, as the case may be, by cancelling or withdrawing the certificate in question and, second, that the guarantees inherent in the right to a fair trial which must be afforded to those persons have been respected.[43]

2.4 *Data*

The European Commission publishes statistical reports on intra-EU labour mobility and EU social security coordination.[44] According to these data, a total of 4.6 million A1 certificates were issued in 2022. Speaking of which, three million A1 certificates were issued to persons who were relocated to another Member state as specified by Article 12 of Regulation No. 883/2004 and 1.4 million A1 certificates issued to persons who pursue an activity in two or more Member States (ie., covered by Article 13). The trend is clear and can be seen on comparison of figures form 2012 and 2022. Between said years, the number of A1 issued more than tripled, or increased by more than three million A1. Among all member states, both Poland and Germany have consistently issued by far the most PDs A1. Together, these two Member States issued 50% of all PDs A1 in 2022.[45]

[41] CJEU case C-359/16, paragraph 54 as is clear from the case-law referred to in paragraph 43 of the present judgment.

[42] See, to that effect, judgment of 6 February 2018, Altun and Others, C-359/16, EU:C:2018:63, paragraph 36 and the case-law cited.

[43] Joined Cases C-410/21 and C-661/21.

[44] Cf. Coordination of social security systems at a glance 2023 Statistical Report.

[45] De Wispelaere (2023), p. 12.

The Czech Republic is the country where the number of PDs A1 issued in other States outnumbered A1 endorsements issued by the Czech competent institution in 2022. In terms of numbers, the vast majority of PDs A1 issued were issued by the German institution, followed by A1 certificates issued by the Slovak Social Insurance Institution.[46]

Because the number of PDs A1 issued is increasing, the trend of an increasing number of interconnected relationships between businesses from different EU Member States can be confirmed.[47] Even so, the veracity of these A1 data may not be entirely consistent with the number of employees posted and arriving in the host country. Experts point out that authorities are not always informed about these transnational activities. Consequently, there might be a discrepancy between the number of PDs A1 issued and the actual number of persons being sent abroad. However, this difference has likely narrowed in recent years. Indeed, some Member States have laid down sanctions in their national legislation for not having a PD A1 and/or carrying out far more inspections on having a PDs A1. In addition, the communication of competent authorities concerning the application for a PDs A1 when making a 'business trip' to another EU/EFTA country may also have a direct impact.

3 Determining the Place of Work for International Transport

The guiding principle of coordination has always been the avoidance, in the interests both of workers and employers and of national social funds, of any unnecessary plurality or confusion of benefits and liabilities arising from the simultaneous alternative application of several legislations,[48] because only in this manner the freedom to provide services could be promoted. Hence, the EU legislator's intervention was and still is needed and necessary. But to be honest because, the main criterion of identification of the respective social security in EU legislation does not function well.[49] There is a high level of misuse and distrust in the inter-member-state

[46] Out of the 69,505 PDs A1 issued by Czechia in 2022, 11.1% were issued under Art. 12 BR (i.e., posted workers), 87.4% under Art. 13 BR (i.e., active in two or more Member States), and 1.4% under other categories. According to Art. 12 BR, Czechia received 73,088 PDs A1 in 2022. Almost three out four PDs A1 under Art. 12 BR were issued by Germany (73.5%) and 9% were issued by Slovakia. De Wispelaere et al. (2023), p. 54.

[47] These are cases of unused PDs A1s as well as cases where PD A1s are forgotten.

[48] As CJEU held in judgment of 5 December 1967, Case 19/67, Van der Vecht, Rec. 1967, p. 445.

[49] Therefore, the multilateral quota system of the European Conference of Ministers of Transport is one of the main instruments regulating access to the Union market by third-country operators and access to third country markets by Union operator.

commerce and PDs A1 are used as another tool to help drivers[50] in their difficult situation.[51]

The basic rule for our case in international transport is contained in Article 13 of Regulation 883/2004[52] governing the pursuit of activities in two or more Member States, which applies to a person who habitually works as an employed person in two or more Member States.[53] Such a person is subject to the legislation of the Member State in whose territory he/she resides if he/she carries out a substantial part (at least 25% of his/her remuneration or activity) of his/her activity in that Member State or, if he/she does not carry out a substantial part of his/her activity in the Member State in whose territory he/she resides, to the legislation of the Member State in whose territory the registered office or place of business of the undertaking or employer is situated, if he/she is employed by a single undertaking or employer. The first criterion requires two conditions to be met simultaneously: residence in the territory of the Member State in which the driver carries out a substantial part of his activity. A substantial part of the activity is at least 25% of the working time or remuneration spent in that State. The definitions of person, residence, and employment in Regulation 883/2004 are key to the assessment of the situation. "Residence" means habitual residence (Article 11 of Regulation 987/2009) and, as stated above, for this article, we assume that the drivers do not reside in the State where they spend a substantial part of their working time as the employer's drivers. In assessing the "substantial part of the activity" of drivers in international transport, it is generally accepted in practice that working time is the most appropriate criterion on which to base a decision. However, it must be recognized that the division of activity between two or more Member States may not always be as obvious to a transport worker as it is to a worker in "standard" cross-border employment (e.g., regulations on working time records in member states varies; in come countries like in the Czech Republic, working time records do not contain and convey the place of work). Accordingly, a more detailed examination of the working arrangements may be necessary to determine the applicable legislation in such cases where it is difficult to estimate the working time in the Member State of residence.

It is clear from case law, that the exception derogating from the rule that a worker is to be subject to the legislation of the Member State in whose territory he is employed applies to undertakings providing temporary personnel only if, those

---

[50] Directive 2020/1057, preamble point 22.

[51] For the purpose of this article we ignore other certificates, such as S1 certificate of entitlement to healthcare, S2 Authorisation to obtain planned health treatment in another EU or EFTA country, S3 certificate of entitlement to healthcare in your former country of employment, U1 statement of insurance periods to be taken into account when calculating an unemployment benefit, U2 authorisation to continue receiving unemployment benefit while looking for a job in another country, U3 warning to the employment services of the country paying benefits, DA1 certificate of entitlement to medical treatment under special conditions reserved for accidents at work and occupational diseases in another EU country, and/or P1 summary of pension decisions taken.

[52] We consider Article 12 of Regulation No 883/2004 as inappropriate to be applied to intrastate transport of goods.

[53] CJEU names this place as the State of employment rule.

undertaking normally pursue their activity in the territory of the State in which they are established and workers employed by undertakings normally carrying on their business in the territory of the State in which they are established.[54] In a case concerning taxation (Case C-73/06 Planzer Luxembourg),[55] the CJEU held that the term 'place of business' means the place where the essential decisions concerning the general management of a company are taken and where the functions of its central administration are exercised. The Court clarified this as follows: '*'The determination of the place of business requires taking into account a set of factors, among which are, in the first place, the company's registered office, the place of its central administration, the meeting place of the company's directors and the place, usually identical, where the general policy of the company is decided. Other elements may also be taken into account, such as the residence of the principal directors, the place where general meetings are held, the place where administrative and accounting documents are kept, and the place where most financial, particularly banking, transactions are carried out.*"

The EU legislator searched for balanced sector-specific rules on posting that are based on the existence of a sufficient link between the driver and the service provided, and the territory of a host Member State. While international carriage in transit across the territory of a Member State does not constitute a posting situation; a combined transport operation does provided that the nature of the service provided during the initial or final road leg is not closely linked with the Member State of establishment if the road leg on its own is cross-trade operations. By contrast, when the transport operation during the road leg is carried out within the host Member State or as a non-bilateral international transport operation, there is a sufficient link with the territory of a host Member State. Therefore, the posting rules should apply. When a driver engages in bilateral transport operations from the Member State where the undertaking is established (the 'Member State of establishment') to the territory of another Member State or a third country or back to the Member State of establishment, the nature of the service is closely linked with the Member State of establishment. On the contrary, where a driver performs other types of operations, notably cabotage operations[56] or non-bilateral international transport operations, there is a sufficient link to the territory of the host Member State. In DRV Intertrans BV, CJEU concluded that a community license for road transport issued by the competent authorities of a Member State does not constitute irrefutable proof that that company's registered office is in that Member State.[57]

[54] Therefore, there is a necessary link between the undertaking providing temporary personnel and the posted worker, in so far as the posted worker must normally be attached to the undertaking which posted him to another Member State. See judgment in Manpower, cited above. In paragraphs 16 and 23 of that judgment.

[55] EU coordination does not cover taxes, what is a big obstacle for our case and free movement of services as well.

[56] Usually understood as domestic transport operations for hire or reward carried out temporarily on the territory of a Member State by an operator established in another Member State.

[57] CJEU cases C-410/21 and C-661/21.

We can add form labour law perspective that Directive 2020/10572 lays down specific rules concerning Directive 96/71/EC3 and Directive 2014/67/EU4, both of which are legislative acts concerning the posting of workers in the framework of the provision of services. It distinguishes between types of transport operations to which rules on posting should apply and those to which posting rules should not apply. The general criterion for such distinction is the degree of connection with the territory of the host Member State.

The decision of the CJEU of 16 July 2020, C-610/18, concerning a case that was referred to the CJEU requesting a preliminary ruling in a dispute between a company in Cyprus, AFMB, and the authorities of the Netherlands. The Dutch authorities claimed in a case before a national court in the Netherlands that several of the lorry drivers who according to their employment contracts were employed by AFMB were nevertheless subject to the Netherlands' social security legislation. According to the CJEU, the decisive element of the assessment, conversely, had to be the objective working situation of drivers based on a determination of the actual circumstances of the drivers and the link to AFMB and the Dutch transport companies. In that regard, the CJEU, like the Dutch authorities, stated that the relevant assessment criteria are: which undertaking exercises the effective authority management over the workers concerned; which undertaking bears the wage costs of drivers' work; and which has the actual power to dismiss the workers. In this specific case, it had been stated that the drivers were fully at the disposal of the Dutch transport companies. Before their employment, the drivers had also been selected by the Dutch transport companies, which could also decide whether the drivers should be made redundant by AFMB. Finally, the actual cost of the drivers' wages was effectively borne, via the commission paid to AFMB, by the transport companies; AFMB only formally paid their wages. The CJEU suggested that these elements were likely to lead to drivers being covered by the Dutch legislation on social security. However, it was for the referring national court to rule on the specific dispute between AFMB and the Dutch authorities in light of the assessment criteria established by the CJEU.

3.1 Brass Plate

The EU rules, as well as the case law, repeatedly refer to so-called 'fictitious residences'. It is a general principle that formally constituted establishments, whose physical presence is practically limited to a label on the office door ('brass plate'), where the social security jurisdiction of the employees is linked to a purely administrative company without any delegation of real decision-making powers, do not usually satisfy the conditions of a company's registered office. Application practice has then followed the case law of the CJEU to define the criteria for establishing a fictitious registered office.

According to the refined definition in Article 14(5a) of Regulation No 987/2009, the institution of the place of residence could take into account the following criteria based on the information available or in close cooperation with the institution in the Member State where the employer has its registered office or place of business:

- the place where the undertaking has its registered office and its administration,
- the length of time the undertaking has been established in the Member State,
- the number of administrative staff working in that office,
- the place where the majority of contracts with customers are concluded,
- the office that determines company policy and operational matters, the place where the main financial functions, including banking, are located,
- the place designated under EU regulation as the place responsible for managing and maintaining records relating to the regulatory requirements of the particular industry in which the company is involved; and
- the place where the recruitment of staff takes place.

From the point of view of the case under consideration, it should be understood that the more criteria defined in Article 14(5a) of Regulation No 987/2009 are not fulfilled by the driver's employer, the more likely the competent institution may conclude that the employer's residence in the state designed by PDs A1 is only fictitious. If the registered office is a formal establishment ("brass plate"), then the competent institution should refuse to issue PDs A1, which would mean that the host state authorities could argue that the drivers are subject to the legislation of the Member State in which the establishment with which that person has the closest connection in terms of employment activity is located. That undertaking would then be considered for the Regulation to be the seat or place of business of the undertaking employing the drivers.

Competent authorities require to be lodged drivers:

- the work schedule for the period under review (i.e. since the start of the employment relationship);
- the routes that the drivers have/had to travel; and
- estimated journey times.

The person requesting the determination of the applicable legislation should provide substantiated facts (e.g. by providing service rosters travel plans or other information) to distinguish between the time spent working in the state of residence and the time spent working in other Member States. Where working time spent in the Member State of residence is not available or where it is not clear from the overall circumstances that a substantial part of the activity is carried out in the Member State of residence, a method other than the working time method may be used to determine whether or not a substantial part of the activity is carried out in the Member State of residence. In this context, it is proposed that the activity be divided into different elements or events and that the extent of activity in the state of residence is determined based on the number of elements occurring there as a percentage of the total number of events in the period. The assessment should be based, where possible, on the distribution of work over 12 months.

Provided that data shows that the drivers' employer performs work in different Member States and none of these countries, especially not in the host state, they do not simultaneously live and perform activities within the scope of 25%. If this is the case, then the rule that the laws of the Member State in whose territory the head office or place of business of the undertaking or employer is located shall apply to the seat of the drivers 'employer if they do not carry out a substantial part of their activity in the Member State in whose territory he resides if he is employed by the same undertaking or employer.[58]

3.2 *The Unacceptable Unification of Powers*

However, as time went by, it became obvious that the proper implementation of coordination rules that were enacted to avoid administrative complications commanded, the increase of EU bureaucracy. Although the coordination should be aimed at overcoming obstacles likely to impede the freedom of movement of workers, the EU had to increase the level of formal administration to meet the increasing needs of administration barriers developed by Member States' authorities. Therefore, the Administrative Commission for Coordination of Social Security Systems[59] was created. Although the consensus to constitute the European Labour Authority has not been reached yet, the rationalization and optimization of both EU and Member States institutional environment has always been and is needed.

After 10 years there are still loopholes in the existing provisions of Regulation 883/2004 and deficiencies in their enforcement. There are discrepancies between Member States in the interpretation, application, and implementation of those provisions, creating a heavy administrative burden for drivers and operators. This creates legal uncertainty, which is detrimental to the social and working conditions of drivers and the conditions for fair competition for operators in the sector,[60] was supposed to be solved by a proposal amending Regulation No. 883/2004.[61]

In 2016, it was prepared by the European Commission that "*grants new implementing powers to the Commission in accordance with Article 291 Treaty on the Functioning of the European Union ("TFEU") to further specify a uniform approach to the issuance, verification and withdrawal of the Portable Document A1 (a certificate concerning the social security legislation which applies to the holder).*"[62]

[58] Accordingly, then, within the context of point 5a of Article 14 outlined above, the place of business of the Client shall, for these purposes, be the Czech Republic.

[59] Coordination Regulation No 3/58 Chapter 8, Title III Art. 43 and 44.

[60] Preamble of Directive 2020/1057.

[61] Proposal for a REGULATION OF THE EUROPEAN PARLIAMENT AND OF THE COUNCIL amending Regulation (EC) No 883/2004 on the coordination of social security systems and regulation (EC) No 987/2009 laying down the procedure for implementing Regulation (EC) No 883/2004.

[62] European Commission, 'Proposal for a Regulation of the European Parliament and of the Council amending Regulation (EC) No 883/2004 on the coordination of social security systems and Regulation (EC) No 987/2009 laying down the procedure for implementing Regulation (EC) No

The envisioned solution was seen in the upgrade of the Commission's competences and powers. The commission should rule on and specify the uniform conditions and procedures for PDs A1. The Commission should set forth

- the issuance, the format and the contents of PDs A1,
- the determination of situations in which PDs A1 shall be issued,
- the elements to verified before PDs A1 can be issued,
- the withdrawal of PDs A1 when its accuracy and validity is contested by the competent institution of the Member State of employment.

For various reasons the proposal was opposed by of Member States which blocked the proposal. One of two strong negative opinions that fuel the refusal was the unwanted EU dominancy over PDs A1.[63]

In 2021, the European Parliament called for the creation of a European Social Security Card (ESSP), which would allow for real-time digital verification of workers' social security, thereby simplifying procedures relating to the application, issue and verification of PD A1 forms in order to combat fraud.[64]

4 Conclusions

There is no doubt about that PDs A1 have become an important pillar of coordination and their existence facilitates the freedom of movement. The purpose is to avoid any simultaneous application of national legislative systems which might result in a purposeless increase in the social security contributions of both the worker and the employer.[65] CJEU has already held on many occasions that the PDs A1[66] issued by the competent institution of a Member State to show that a worker moving within the European Union is affiliated to that Member State's social security scheme is binding on both the competent institution and the courts of the host Member State, with the result that the worker cannot, therefore, be made subject to the social security scheme of the latter Member State.

PDs A1 constitute a sign of the economic reality, in which rich welfare states need hefty contributions done by every existing taxpayers. However, high taxes or social security contributions mean high prices of labour, goods, and services, and those who can put in use cheaper labour gain a big advantage in such an economy. Some undertakings avail themselves of high labour costs by sending workers from

883/2004' COM (2016) 815 final, 13 December 2016 https://eur-lex.europa.eu/legal-content/EN/TXT/?uri=CELEX:52016PC0815 accessed 2 June 2025.

[63] Cf. Azevedo (2018); European Commission (2022); European Parliament (2023); Pölös (2025).

[64] European Parliament, 'Resolution of 25 November 2021 on strengthening the protection of workers through digital tools (2021/2007(INI))' [2021] OJ C81/156 https://eur-lex.europa.eu/legal-content/EN/TXT/?uri=CELEX:52021IP0473 accessed 2 June 2025.

[65] CJEU case 19–67, point 354.

[66] CJEU case C-178/97, point 41.

low-wage countries to Member States other than that in which they are established. They make inappropriate statements of domestic activity, establish letterbox companies, proclaim bogus self-employment, or declare such wrong statuses of the relocated personnel. In short, those are circumventing the application of Article 12 (false evidence that Article 13 instead of Article 12 or fraudulent use of Article 13) because there is no direct relationship between the relocated workers and the employers nor substantial activities in the sending Member States are maintained, and those employers only misuse posting or relocations. It is therefore not surprising that even today[67] some institutions still question the binding nature of PDs A1.[68] However, where the institutions of other Member States raise doubts as to the correctness of the facts on which the certificate is based or as to the legal assessment of those facts and, consequently, as to the conformity of the information contained in the certificate, the issuing institution must re-examine the grounds on which the certificate was issued and, where appropriate, withdraw it.[69]

As long as it has not been withdrawn or declared invalid by the authorities of the Member State which issued it, PDs A1 bind the competent institution and the courts of the Member State in which the drivers are posted, unless there is the so-called criminal exception as ruled on in Altun and Others. Not even the court of the host Member State is not entitled to scrutinize the validity of PDs A1 as regards the certification of the matters based on which such a certificate was issued, in particular the existence of a direct relationship between the undertaking established in a Member State and the workers which it has posted to another Member State, during the period of their posting,[70] unless the so-called criminal exception is fulfilled. A criminal judge may disregard PDs A1 provided that PDs A1 constitute fraud based on evidence and with due regard to the safeguards inherent in the right to a fair trial.

Gradually, a robust system for eliminating mistakes between the competent institutions of the Member States has been established. If the host-state competent institution cannot rectify the error, the host State has the option of requesting enhanced consultation or may request conciliation from the Administrative Commission for Coordination of Social Security Systems. Shall the conciliation process and other soft approaches not satisfy the host state authorities, CJEU can be requested to intervene. Another exception was adjudicated by CJEU in so called criminal exception. Thus, it is for criminal judges to balance between enhancing social and working conditions for drivers and facilitating the exercise of the freedom to provide road transport services based on fair competition between national and foreign operators in most obvious cases of fraud. CJEU shown clairvoyance when it approved so called criminal exception in most vivid breaches of law. Because the best solution

---

[67] Spoken on behalf of PDs A1 issued in the Czech Republic, they are questioned by the Belgian authorities in 2024.

[68] Fraud and error in the field of EU social security coordination Reference year: 2019, p. 17.

[69] Case C-202/97.

[70] Case C-2/05.

which was envisioned in the 2016 European Commission's Labour Mobility Package has not been acceptable for some Member States.

The current compromise is obviously the maximum that can be asked for without the unification of substantive laws or centralization of competent institutions on the EU level. Unless one of those is available, host authorities will continue not only to check the existence of A1s but also question the veracity of the alleged facts that led the competent authority to issue PDs A1. The described system may not be the most efficient, but it has some advantages as well. It is decentralized; it enhances democracy because it pushes Member States to ongoing cooperation that is for a longer period more sustainable than simple ordered solutions.

Acknowledgments This chapter has been written and published thanks to the financial support of the grant project COOPERATIO/LAW.

References

Azevedo JL (2018) Amending social security coordination – challenges of the Regulations (EC) No. 883/2004 and No. 987/2009. UNIO – EU Law J

Banks and Others (C-178/97, EU:C:2000:169)

CJEU Case 19-67, European Court Reports 1969 I-00525

CJEU Case 9/79 of 5 February 1981, Case C-9/79, European Court Reports 1981 I-00207

CJEU C-2/89 Kits van Heijningen ECR 1990 I-1755

CJEU judgment of the Court of 2 August 1993, C-23/92, European Court Reports 1993 I-04875

CJEU Case C-425/93 Calle Grenzshop Andresen ECR 1995 I-269

CJEU C-131/95 Huijbrechts ECR 1997 I-1409

CJEU C-275/96 Kuusijärvi ECR 1998 I-3419

CJEU C-178/97 Fitzwilliam Executive Search of 10 February 2000, Case C-178/97, European Court Reports 2000 I-00883

CJEU C-784/19 (Grand Chamber) of 3 June 2021, Case C-784/19, European Court Reports 2021 I-0427

CJEU Joined Cases C-410/21 and C-661/21 of 2 March 2023, Joined Cases C-410/21 and C-661/21, European Court Reports 2023 I-0138

De Wispelaere F, De Smedt L, Pacolet J (2023) Coordination of social security systems at a glance, vol 12. Statistical Report HIVA-KU Leuven

European Commission (2022) Fraud and error in the field of eu social security coordination

European Parliament (2023) Social security cover in other EU Member States. Fact Sheets on the European Union

Fragomen (2024) The importance of A1 certificates. Fragomen Insights. https://www.fragomen.com/insights/the-importance-of-a1-certificates.html. Accessed 2 June 2025

Fraud and error in the field of EU Social Security Coordination Reference year: 2019

Froger-Michon C, Cai H (2018) A1 form: presentation and latest case-law developments. CMS Francis Lefebvre. https://cms.law/en/chn/publication/a1-form-presentation-and-latest-case-law-developments. Accessed 2 June 2025

Herbosch Kiere (C-2/05, EU:C:2006:69)

Ius Laboris (2019) New guidance on A1 social security certificates for business trips. Ius Laboris. https://iuslaboris.com/insights/new-guidance-on-a1-social-security-certificates-for-business-trips. Accessed 2 June 2025

KPMG International (2020) A1 certificate for social security. KPMG. https://assets.kpmg.com/content/dam/kpmg/sk/pdf/2o2o/A1-certificate-for-social-security.pdf. Accessed 2 June 2025
Morsa M (2019) The European regulations on social security coordination from the perspective of the Belgian authority. Revue Belge de securite sociale - 1e Trimestre:140
Pölös Z (2025) Romanian hauliers reject EU social security proposal. Trans.INFO
Réseau Fiscalité et Nomadisme (RFN) (2005) A1 certificate: when, how, and for whom? RFN. https://www.rfn.fr/en/news/a1-attestation-when-how-and-for-who. Accessed 2 June 2025

The Digital Europe Programme and Its Impact on the Hungarian Health Care System, with Special Regard to the EESZT

József Hajdú

1 Introduction

The Digital Europe Programme (DIGITAL) is focused on bringing digital technology to businesses, citizens and public administrations.[1] In line with the EU digital programs it is an important strategic goal for Hungary to modernize its public administration (including health care system) and to increase the use of modern information and communication technologies in the interactions between state institutions themselves as well as between state institutions and citizens.[2]

The digitalised elements of the social security system will improve the exchanges of information within Hungary and/or other EU MS's social security institutions and speed up the recognition and granting of eligible benefits across borders.[3,4] It will thus make it easier for EU citizens to live, work and travel abroad, for companies to do business in other EU MSs, and for national administrations to coordinate social security across borders.[5]

Furthermore, Hungary's current Artificial Intelligence Strategy, which looks ahead to 2030, identifies the healthcare sector as one of the priority areas for the application of AI technology. The Strategy's objective is "to strengthen the

[1] Bıçakcı (2024).

[2] The Digital Europe Programme (2016).

[3] Hadzic (2023).

[4] Digital Europe (2024).

[5] Towards a more digital social security coordination: Commission proposes steps to make it easier for Europeans to live, work and travel abroad (2023).

J. Hajdú (✉)
University of Szeged, Szeged, Hungary
e-mail: hajdu@juris.u-szeged.hu

K. Koldinská et al. (eds.), *Labour Law and Social Security Law in Central and Eastern Europe*, European Union and its Neighbours in a Globalized World 26,
https://doi.org/10.1007/978-3-032-04496-9_11

responsible use of the existing and growing healthcare data assets in Hungary, in consultation and cooperation with relevant stakeholders, to strengthen the use of AI in diagnostics and therapeutics, to develop and implement AI-supported medical decision-making and medical devices, and to actively contribute to an efficiently functioning healthcare sector".[6]

This paper deals with a significant social security related IT developments: the National eHealth Infrastructure (in Hungarian: Elektronikus Egészségügyi Szolgáltatási Tér (EESZT); hereinafter the Hungarian abbreviation will be used: EESZT).[7] It is a central IT platform which has set the foundations for ensuring communication between healthcare service providers and patients. The system overhauling the Hungarian health care system aims at maximising the speed, efficiency and service-oriented approach of public health care. The key to this is continuous contact between health care institutions, therapists and pharmacies, ensuring that information is consistent and accessible to all eligible participants.[8]

The aim of this article is to introduce the legal framework and the operational scope of the EESZT. The followed research method is a qualitative research method to collecting and analyzing non-numerical data relating to the Hungarian medical professionals', service providers' and patients' perception of digitalisation and its influence on effectiveness of health insurance law, with special regards to the EESZT.

2 Hungarian Digitalisation Strategy and the EESZT

The Hungarian EESZT is designed to combine new digital technology with international best practices in healthcare, a similar model to digital healthcare systems in Estonia, Ireland and the United Kingdom.[9]

The digitalization of the healthcare providers system is part of the government-led Hungarian Digital Success Programme (Digitális Jólét Program: DJP).[10] Within it the Hungarian government has initiated the digitalization of the health system through its EESZT system.[11] It is a central IT hub, which ensures communication between almost all health care service providers and patients.[12,13]

The EESZT connects both public and private healthcare services (e.g. hospital, outpatient clinics, GP services, pharmacies, etc.) and the citizens/patients across

[6] Matits (2024).

[7] Mi az EESZT? (2024).

[8] EESZT (2024).

[9] Electronic Health Service Space.

[10] Digitális Jólét Program (2024).

[11] The Hungarian government has already initiated the digitalization of the health system through its national patient record in 2017. The national patient record is now accessible through the National eHealth Infrastructure - Elektronikus Egészségügyi Szolgáltatási Tér (EESZT).

[12] Digitális Jólét Program (2024).

[13] eHealth in Hungary (2024).

Hungary. The shared patient data will help to make faster, more accurate diagnoses and better targeted treatment.

The EESZT is a fully digital system that facilitates information flow and makes it easier and faster for the data sent to the system to reach the relevant professionals. It is an integrative platform, available 24 h a day systems with the appropriate authorisation.[14]

The scale of the robust data set in the EESZT is well illustrated by the data from the Health Sector Strategy (2021), which states that the amount of health data stored and accessible in the system has already exceeded 500 million. According to the same strategy, the number of e-Prescriptions issued on a typical weekday exceeds 800,000.[15] Furthermore, in Hungary, 75 million healthcare documents (such as lab results, outpatient records, discharge summaries) and nearly 180 million doctor-patient encounters are recorded online in the EESZT annually. This averages to 300,000 healthcare documents per day in the system.

It is essential for modern healthcare that all patient data be readily accessible to every therapist from one single source, regardless of whether the health services used by the patient were from a publicly funded or private healthcare service. The services of the EESZT provide more information to health professionals about the patient, allowing them access to information about any medicines, referrals or medical records prescribed by other therapists.[16]

3 The Gradual Expansion of the Institutional Scope of the EESZT

The EESZT started operating on November 1, 2017. Initially, general practitioners, state outpatient and inpatient healthcare institutions, as well as all pharmacies joined the system.By November 1, 2018, the National Ambulance Service and some private healthcare providers were also included.[17] By January 1, 2020, the system expanded to include all privately funded healthcare providers with a medical or dental operating license. Starting from September 1, 2021, medical device distributors with health insurance reimbursement contracts were also incorporated into the EESZT.

The relatively rapid spread of the system was greatly facilitated by the fact that doctors and pharmacists continued to use the same computer systems in their work

[14] The Role of the EESZT in Hungarian Healthcare (2023).

[15] Matits (2024).

[16] The Role of the EESZT in Hungarian Healthcare (2023).

[17] Electronic provision of rescue control data to hospitals, additional rescue control development (2020) https://e-egeszsegugy.gov.hu/web/eeszt-information-portal/ambulance-service

as they did before the EESZT. They did not need to purchase new equipment or learn a new program.[18]

The expansion of the EESZT greatly improves the quality and effectiveness of healthcare: unnecessarily repeated examinations can be avoided and health professionals get a much more accurate picture of their patient which promotes a more definite diagnosis and faster recovery. Meanwhile, citizens have access to more and more data concerning their medical treatment through a single centralised interface.

4 The Expansion of the EESZT's Functions

The functions available in the EESZT have been continuously expanding since its introduction. In 2024, a total of 18 different activities were available. These are briefly introduced as follows:

1. *E-prescription.* The e-prescription system allows users to query electronic prescriptions issued by doctors. Prescriptions are displayed on separate pages, showing both those that have already been filled and those still awaiting fulfillment. Detailed information about the e-prescriptions can be viewed. However, prescriptions issued on paper (the traditional method) will only appear in the system among those that have been filled, as pharmacists enter these prescriptions into the system during the dispensing process.[19]
2. *Health documents.* These include digital health documents created in healthcare institutions after the connection to the EESZT. Medical records, outpatient sheets, discharge summaries, and other documents generated during healthcare services can be viewed and downloaded at any time.[20]
3. *Event Catalog.* This is where all events are recorded when a patient receives healthcare services in outpatient and inpatient facilities, or at general practitioner services. These data are uploaded by the healthcare institutions. They allow both the patient and their treating doctor to know precisely, even years later, when and where a specific examination took place, and who was the treating physician at that time.[21]
4. *eReferral.* The eReferral prescribed by the doctor can be viewed in the EESZT system. The platform allows patient to query both valid and used eReferrals.[22]
5. *eProfile.* The healthcare data uploaded by the patient's treating physician, which rarely or never changes, is included. These data can be life-saving in case of

[18] EESZT Információs portál (2024).

[19] E-prescription has completely replaced traditional prescriptions (2022).

[20] Event catalogue, Health documents (2023).

[21] Article 12, of the 39/2016.(XII. 21.) EMMI Decree on the detailed rules related to the Electronic Health Service.

[22] Sándor Tünde (2023).

emergency care. Examples of such health information include details about allergies, drug sensitivities, blood type, pregnancy, implanted devices, etc.[23]

6. *Digital self-determination.* it provides the opportunity to regulate access to health data managed by the EESZT. It is possible to continuously track who has requested access to a patient's data. The data displayed to healthcare providers depends on the settings, permissions, and restrictions made during self-determination. The patient's data can only be viewed by the family doctor and treating physician, with particularly sensitive data, such as information about sexually transmitted diseases, psychiatric or addiction treatment, being accessible only to specialists in those fields.[24]

   The settings for digital self-determination can only be overridden in life-threatening situations, which are listed in the Decree 52/2006 (XII. 28.) of the Ministry of Health on Certain urgent health services. Beyond this, the patient may only voluntarily, without any external influence, give consent to override the set restrictions for a single day (24 h). If the patient does this in the EESZT, they can specify disease categories (e.g., Gynecology, Urology, Addiction Treatment, etc.); however, this is not possible if the patient does so on paper.[25]

7. *The enforcement of patient rights.* Patient rights include, among others, the right to access healthcare documentation, which means that the patient is entitled to familiarize themselves with the contents of the healthcare documentation made about them. In this way, the use of the EESZT also helps in the enforcement of patient rights.[26]

8. *Digital Image Transfer.* If the connected data controller meets the technical requirements necessary to use the service, the image created by an imaging diagnostic procedure can be recorded in the healthcare information system, and data may be provided to the registry maintained by the operator of the EESZT concerning the digital image transfer service.

   Under the digital image transfer service, only authorized sector users who are permitted to access the service can retrieve imaging diagnostic records or other digital image data of the subject based on the specified National Health Insurance Fund (TAJ) number, or another identifier registered in the EESZT if the TAJ number is unavailable.

   The digital image transfer can also be used for the secure transmission of data between connected data controllers. In such cases, the EESZT provides technical assistance for the implementation of data transmission among the connected data controllers. Data transmission will only be performed by the EESZT to a sector user who is authorized to access the data according to the EESZT's identification and access control records, and self-determination registry data.

[23] EESZT (2024).

[24] Mit jelent a teljesen tiltó állapot és hogyan állítható be az EESZT-ben? (2021).

[25] Alexin Zoltán (2022).

[26] EESZT- Elektronikus Egészségügyi Szolgáltatási Tér (2024).

The data processing related to the use of the service is logged. The details of the data processing can be accessed by the patient via the direct access interface of the EESZT. If the patient has set up notifications, they will receive an email alert when the image transfer occurs.[27]

9. *Electronic (Remote) Consultation.* Only doctors who are separately registered in the EESZT system are authorized to initiate and accept an electronic remote consultation request. When initiating an electronic remote consultation, the requesting doctor compiles a list of the healthcare documents (including images from diagnostic imaging procedures) that they wish to share with the consulting doctor during the consultation. If the consulting doctor accepts the request, the EESZT will provide them access to the listed documents, provided that this does not conflict with any declaration made in the patient's self-determination record. The consulting doctor will transmit their medical opinion to the requesting doctor via the EESZT platform. However, acceptance of the request for an electronic remote consultation is not mandatory.[28]
10. *Electronic Disease Registry.* Data submission to the electronic disease registry, managed via the EESZT, can only be completed through the electronic data submission form. The authority managing the disease registry is responsible for designing the template for this form. The formal and technical requirements for the data submission form, as well as the data templates necessary for the design of the form, are determined by the operator and made available to connected data controllers.

    If a data template required for the design of the data submission form has not yet been published by the operator, the authority managing the disease registry can request the operator to create and publish the required data template within 30 working days. The data in the disease registries, which is stored in a way that does not allow for personal identification, can be accessed by any connected data controller.

    Regarding the EESZT, the amount of data entering the event log will approximately triple. Instead of the previous sixteen types of records, doctors providing patient care are now required to report on fifty-three different types of appearances. The exact list can be found in Annex 1 of the 2016/39. (XII. 21.) EMMI Decree.[29]
11. *The preventive role of the EESZT.* The EESZT system includes a section for screening tests, which displays public health screening recommendations based on age and gender. For example: a) For women, breast screening is recommended every 2 years between the ages of 45 and 65. b) Cervical screening is recommended every 3 years between the ages of 25 and 65. c) Both genders should undergo colorectal and rectal screenings every 2 years between the ages of 50 and 70.

[27] Radics (2018).

[28] Radics (2022).

[29] Minden egyes bitre szüksége van az államnak a betegekről (2020).

In addition, individuals over the age of 65 are provided with the most comprehensive list of recommended tests, including e.g. bone density measurement, ankle-brachial index determination, lung screening, and vision acuity tests, etc. The application provides brief information about each of these tests, explaining which specialist should perform them and how often they should be done.[30]

12. *Checking Social Security Status*. In the "Social Security Lamp" menu, the patient can verify the validity of his/her social security identification number (TAJ card) and the status of his/her social security relationship.[31] This function is updated daily, allowing his/her to check in real-time whether his/her health care coverage status is in order. It also helps to verify whether employers are paying the social security contributions for their employees.[32]

    The "Social Security Lamp" menu contains several color categories: 1. Green Lamp: This means the social security number (TAJ number) is valid, and the social security status is in order. 2. Red Lamp: The TAJ number is valid, but the social security status is not in order. 3. Blue Lamp: This appears for those who are insured abroad and are paying contributions in another country. 4. Brown Lamp: The TAJ number is invalid. 5. Yellow Lamp: The TAJ number is valid, but health care services can only be accessed with certain restrictions.[33]
13. *Electronic service order*. In the case of an electronic service order, the requesting doctor issues a paper-based certificate of the electronic service order upon the request of the patient involved in the healthcare service. The certificate contains the data of the electronic service order and the EESZT identifier of the electronic service order, in both barcode and human-readable text formats.

    The healthcare provider (data controller) connected to the system views and verifies the electronic service order via the EESZT and records the usage of the electronic service order and the completion of the healthcare service through the EESZT. If the data recording fails for any reason, the healthcare provider (data controller) is required to record the data within 24 h after the service has been provided.[34]
14. *Electronic appointment scheduling*. The requesting doctor can, simultaneously with the electronic service request, or within the validity period of the electronic service request, schedule an appointment via the EESZT interface, with the data controller providing the service. The connected data controller can publish available time slots for the services it offers via the EESZT in order to

[30] Koncsek (2024).

[31] Ernőfy (2024).

[32] Újabb funkcióval bővült a 2,6 millió magyar által használt egészségügyi alkalmazás (2024) https://www.portfolio.hu/gazdasag/20240116/ujabb-funkcioval-bovult-a-26-millio-magyar-altal-hasznalt-egeszsegugyi-alkalmazas-663207 (downloaded: 12.11.2024)

[33] Új funkcióval bővül az EgészségAblak alkalmazás: már azt is látjuk, rendben van-e a tb-nk (2024) https://medosz.hu/hir/uj_funkcioval_bovul_az_egeszsegablak_alkalmazas_mar_azt_is_latjuk_rendben_van-e_a_tb-nk (downloaded: 12.11.2024).

[34] Fazekas (2023), p. 96.

facilitate appointment scheduling. In case of modification or cancellation of the reserved appointment, the healthcare provider is obligated to notify the patient and arrange a new appointment.[35]

15. *Cross-border healthcare information exchange*. The operator of the EESZT ensures information exchange with the national contact points of other member states through an IT connection to uphold the rights related to cross-border healthcare. The information exchange covers the following healthcare services: 1. healthcare treatment of a patient in another member state, 2. prescription medication dispensation in another member state, 3. healthcare treatment of a patient from another member state in Hungary, and 4. Dispensation of medication prescribed in another member state in Hungary.

    For data protection guarantees, the operator only transfers the patient's data to the national contact point of another member state if the patient has given their consent within the framework of their digital self-determination.[36]

16. *Student (pupil) Absence Documentation*. Starting from September 1, 2024,[37] in the case of a child's illness, the medical certificate required to justify school absences will be sent directly from the medical doctor to the KRÉTA[38] educational system via the EESZT. This means that when the doctor records the child's illness details on the EESZT platform, the medical certificate will automatically be transferred to the KRÉTA system as well. As a result, parents no longer need to handle this process, as it will be carried out directly between the doctor and the school. The aim is to minimize administrative work for educational institutions and ensure that they receive information about the child's condition in the shortest possible time, with the added assurance that the medical certificate's authenticity is beyond doubt, thanks to this technical solution.

    In practice, the absence must be reported to the family doctor on the first day of illness, but parents can do this by phone or email. If the parent deems it necessary, a personal consultation can be arranged in the following days. If the child has not recovered by the previously determined end date, a new certificate will be required for the extended period. This can again be requested via email or in person, depending on the child's condition.[39]

[35] Radics (2024).

[36] Egészségügyi adatok határon átnyúló továbbításáról is nyilatkozhatunk az EESZT-ben (2022); https://adozona.hu/altalanos/Mar_egeszsegugyi_adatok_hataron_atnyulo_tov_38S1RO (downloaded: 12.11.2024).

[37] 1997. évi XLVII. törvény 27/A. § alapján.

[38] The Neptun KRÉTA (Public Education Registration and Curriculum Base System)—hereinafter referred to as KRÉTA—is an IT system supporting the tasks of the educational organisers of public education institutions, which cooperates with other systems of public education in an integrated and adaptive way.

[39] Orvosi igazolások eljuttatása iskolai hiányzásról KRÉTA rendszerbe EESZT-n keresztül (2024) https://www.healzz2.hu/hirek/orvosi-igazolasok-eljuttatasa-iskolai-hianyzasrol-kreta-rendszerbe-eeszt-n-keresztul (downloaded: 12.11.2024).

17. *Kindergarten kids Absence Documentation.* Since September 1, 2024, it has become mandatory for kindergartens to use the oviKRÉTA (in other words: kindergartenKRÉTA) system. With the integration of EESZT and KRÉTA (originally for pupils), the issue of medical certificates has been resolved, as the system fully replaces the previous paper-based medical certificates. An additional advantage of the system is that in cases of prolonged illness, the teacher can see that the doctor has reassigned the child and extended the treatment.[40]
18. *Personal medical data access.* It can be accessed on the citizen portal of the EESZT, after using Client Gate authorisation. The portal contains all medical data uploaded after 1 November 2017 by institutions who joined the cloud. The data exchanges allow for a more thorough understanding of the patient's health background and medical history, electronic recording and making available of health data facilitates the flow of information and reduces administrative burdens, and institutions can transfer medical documents related to patient care more accurately, safely and faster to one another.[41]

5 Potential Development in the Future

The already cited Healthcare Sector Strategy regards the EESZT digital data assets as a unique yet underutilized opportunity at the European level.[42]

This can be integrated into strategic thinking with an amendment to the law approved by the National Assembly, which, starting January 1, 2026, will open the doors of the EESZT, considered a treasure trove of health and related personal data. Since these are highly sensitive data, the use of such data is strictly purpose-bound under the law. It is only allowed for training, testing, and evaluation of artificial intelligence algorithms, and the development of medical devices and digital health applications.[43]

According to the plans, developers will be able to work with data from the EESZT in a so-called "secure processing environment," primarily anonymous (i.e., stripped of personal data), and only those who have received permission from the operator of the EESZT (currently the Minister of the Interior) will be allowed to do so. In addition to the permission, the details of the cooperation must be clarified in an agreement with the Minister of the Interior.

[40] Így működik az új igazolási rendszer az óvodákban és az iskolákban (2024) https://vira.hu/2024/09/05/igy-mukodik-az-uj-igazolasi-rendszer-az-ovodakban-es-az-iskolakban/ (downloaded: 12.11.2024).

[41] The Role of the EESZT in Hungarian Healthcare (2023) https://e-egeszsegugy.gov.hu/web/eeszt-information-portal/the-role-of-the-eeszt-in-hungarian-healthcare (downloaded: 12.11.2024).

[42] Digital Health, Digital Services Act package (2024) https://www.pgeu.eu/digital-health/

[43] Megnyitják az EESZT-t az AI-fejlesztők előtt (2024) https://medicalonline.hu/informatika/cikk/megnyitjak_az_eeszt_t_az_ai_fejlesztok_elott (downloaded: 12.11.2024).

The Minister's approval can only be granted to those who have first obtained approval from the relevant professional-ethical committee of the Health Science Council for the research (this body gives the green light to many studies in the healthcare field, including clinical trials, and has significant authority in this area).[44]

The magnitude of the change is difficult to predict in advance; what is certain is that significant professional expectations precede the change. Based on data generated by technology in the future, we will be able to gain a more accurate picture of the real effectiveness of medicine therapies, the healthcare characteristics of the Hungarian population (even broken down by region), and, in certain cases, even which diseases Hungarian drug development and trade should focus on in the future.[45]

Many questions also arise regarding how the amendment will fit into the dynamically changing digital regulatory framework. Answering these is a task for lawyers. GDPR compliance holds a prominent place in the approved draft law. However, how it aligns with the EU's artificial intelligence regulation remains uncertain at this point.[46]

In addition to the above, the National Health Insurance Fund can offer many opportunities in areas such as screening tests, care activities, telemedicine, patient education, database analysis, etc. What is certain is that digitalization already plays a crucial role in modern healthcare today and will increasingly do so in the near future.[47]

Many fear that the rise of information technology will push personal interactions to the background in healthcare. However, in my opinion, this fear is unfounded, as it simply represents a new communication tool that, when used effectively, can make doctor-patient encounters more meaningful. Through the active involvement of patients, the quality of care can be significantly improved, and it can lead to greater success in encouraging healthier lifestyles.

Regarding the spread of digital health, there will undoubtedly be significant differences between age groups and social classes. However, I believe that with proper consideration and regulation, the right balance can be found between traditional medicine and digitalization.[48]

---

[44] Szabó Bálint (2024).

[45] A magyar egészségügy jövője: forradalmat hozhat a mesterséges intelligencia (2024) https://www.vg.hu/kozelet/2024/11/a-magyar-egeszsegugy-jovoje-forradalmat-hozhat-a-mesterseges-intelligencia#google_vignette (downloaded: 12.11.2024).

[46] Matits (2024).

[47] Pákozdyné Bőcz (2024), pp. 57–73.

[48] Rosta (2020).

6 The Benefits of the EESZT

The benefits of the EESZT are evident from its relatively short history. One of the main advantages is that, in the short term, all patients will experience faster healthcare delivery. Healthcare providers can access patient data, test results, e-referrals, and e-prescriptions with just one click. Patient data is stored in a highly secure, five-tier security system, and patients can track who accessed their data, when, and from which institution. Even if a patient forgets their prescription at home, they can still retrieve it from the system.

Another key development is that medical records and test results from the past 5 years are now included in the system, meaning that even lost or forgotten medical history will be available to the treating physician. This allows for more accurate diagnoses and more effective treatments.[49]

The EESZT enables a shift towards data-driven healthcare, where decisions in medical diagnostics, research, and public health are increasingly based on data. This is already the case today, but due to limited time, resources, and capacity, it is apparent that certain healthcare sectors—both globally and in Hungary—may face serious challenges in the next 5–10 years.

For example, in Hungary, there are approximately 65 million GP-patient consultations annually, with an average of only 5–7 min per patient. This is very little time. Therefore, it is crucial that GPs receive support to make the best decisions within this limited time frame, using the most comprehensive information available. Instead of sifting through multiple pdf files results or healthcare documents for a single piece of data or a trend in a specific parameter over time, GPs should be able to access structured data with a single query. These solutions are being developed and steadily improving, paving the way for data-driven healthcare delivery.[50]

As mentioned earlier, the patient has the right to access their health documentation and to be informed about their condition. According to Hungarian healthcare law, this access involves complex cognitive functions such as perception, comprehension, and understanding, meaning that the patient not only has the right to view their radiological images and read their reports, but also—with appropriate assistance—must be involved in interpreting these images, in the process of diagnosing, and in the development of the necessary therapy. These points clearly emphasize the need for continuous doctor-patient communication, and they directly highlight that all information and data provided to the patient—whether verbal, written, or otherwise—must be understandable and interpretable by them. This line of thought leads to the conclusion that simply making a patient's health data and documentation electronically available does not mean they actually possess the relevant information. In fact, it can be argued that interpreting medical reports without the guidance

[49] EESZT Információs portál (2024) https://e-egeszsegugy.gov.hu/lakossagi-szolgaltatasok (downloaded: 12.11.2024).

[50] Joó (2024).

of a doctor could lead to misinterpretation, which may negatively affect further communication.[51],[52]

The extensive and high-level use of digital health technologies is an essential prerequisite for effective medical decision-making and personalized care. Digitalization clearly impacts the issue of healthcare providers' legal liability, with both potential negative and positive consequences. It can increase a healthcare provider's liability due to easier proof of negligence or failure to meet expected duties, or from a funding responsibility perspective, it allows for better tracking of unnecessary or overfunded treatments. At the same time, the EESZT enables faster, more accurate diagnoses and treatments tailored to them, improving patient safety and satisfaction, potentially reducing the number of lawsuits.[53]

The EESZT played a positive role during the COVID-19 pandemic.[54] Following the outbreak of the pandemic in mid-March 2020, the role of telemedicine became more prominent, which was reinforced by Government Decree 15/2020 (IV.29). The fact that telemedicine consultations could be implemented in practice, and that the number of in-person doctor-patient encounters could be minimized, was largely due to the fact that ePrescriptions were already operational. During the pandemic, the patient flow in general practitioners' offices did not decrease significantly, as patients still needed medication, but in most cases, this no longer required physical visits.

At the same time, the pandemic led to several important developments and changes within the EESZT system, some of which had already been anticipated. For example: a) The prescription validity for medications requiring specialist recommendations was automatically extended. b) It became possible to log into the EESZT not only with a personal ID card but also via a mobile application. c) Certain medical aids (such as test strips for blood glucose measurement, diapers, etc.) could now be prescribed as ePrescriptions, and so on.[55]

7 Some Critical Remarks

A criticism of the EESZT is that if a patient grants general consent, this applies to all documents (e-Prescription, events, health records), granting unlimited access for an indefinite period of time. A more sensible approach would be to make the

[51] Angyal Miklós: Az egészségügyi dokumentáció tartalmi és formai követelményeiről; http://www.szoszolo.hu/06tanulmanyaink/231013kommentar_angyal.htm (downloaded: 12.11.2024).

[52] Csák Réka Borbála - Feith Helga Judit (2024).

[53] Csák Réka Borbála - Feith Helga Judit (2024).

[54] PWC Kihívásból lehetőségek az egészségügyben Az ellátórendszer újragondolása (nem csak) a COVID-19 járvány apropóján; https://www.pwc.com/hu/hu/szolgaltatasok/kozszolgalati-tanacsadas/Kihivasbol_lehetosegek_az_egeszsegugyben.pdf (downloaded: 12.11.2024).

[55] Rosta László (2020).

specific document, necessary for the given treatment, available to the doctor before starting the examination.[56]

Furthermore, the EESZT allows the patient to object to data processing under the right to (apparent) self-determination. However, institutions are legally obliged to record the data. The patient may object to the doctor's access to their data, but not to access by state authorities. Doctors can access all confidential data by pressing the "urgent case" button, although they must justify the reason for access on the online platform. However, there is no public information on where this justification is stored or who receives notifications about it. The patient cannot request immediate notification via email about who has accessed their data. The system only allows the patient to search the access logs, with the exception of data requests from investigative authorities (which are prohibited by law from notifying the individuals concerned).[57]

In practice, teleconsultations were conducted through various channels depending on the infrastructure of the healthcare system (phone, SMS, email, Facebook, video sharing platforms, etc.), which, however, are often questionable in terms of data security. Hospitals and professional societies also attempted to assist, with two good examples being the Gottsegen György National Cardiological Institute, which provided 24-h phone consultations for patients, and the Hungarian Diabetes Society, which offered online consultation opportunities between general practitioners and diabetologists on its website.[58]

In my opinion, it would be justified to create a more unified communication network to ensure secure connections between healthcare systems, healthcare providers, and patients.

Regarding the EESZT, a concern that arises is the violation of medical confidentiality. The system identifies specialists as the patient's primary care physician, regardless of whether they are actually the treating physician. As a result, specialists, who may be unfamiliar to the patient, are granted access to sensitive data with the same privileges as the treating physician when they access the patient's record. Critics argue that this may lead to a breach of medical confidentiality. Simply by recording data in the EESZT, healthcare professionals may unintentionally share it with individuals outside the healthcare system, without fully realizing the implications.[59]

In addition, the Act C of 2012 on the Criminal Code does not contain a section that would punish the violation of medical confidentiality. The provision on the misuse of personal data (Section 219 of the Criminal Code) is formulated in such a way that it is not applicable to the breach of confidentiality regarding medical data.[60]

---

[56] Alexin Zoltán (2022).

[57] Mi az EESZT https://e-egeszsegugy.gov.hu/lakossagi-szolgaltatasok (downloaded: 12.11.2024).

[58] Kardiológusokkal lehet nonstop telefonon konzultálni (2020) https://gokvi.hu/hir/2020/10/29/kardiologusokkal-lehet-nonstop-telefonon-konzultalni (downloaded: 12.11.2024).

[59] Ferincz Jenő (2019).

[60] Btk. 219. § Személyes adattal visszaélés (2024) https://buntetojog.info/kulonos-resz/btk-219-%C2%A7-szemelyes-adattal-visszaeles/ (downloaded: 12.11.2024).

As for data protection issue, the platform transfers the health data of every patient to a central database which the various health professional can consult through the corresponding hospital, general practitioner or The main data-protection challenges identified in connection with Hungary's EESZT platform and related health-data processing:

a) *Legislative and enforcement gaps*. Despite Hungary's General Data Protection Regulation (GDPR) alignment, the sheer complexity of EESZT's statutory framework makes full compliance difficult. In particular, inconsistent enforcement of Infotv. (Hungary's Privacy Act) and GDPR principles has been flagged as a major hurdle, slowing down the adoption of robust data-protection safeguards across all participating providers.[61]
b) *Insufficient transparency and patient awareness*. Surveys show that many citizens remain unaware of their rights within EESZT (e.g. access, rectification, objection), which undermines meaningful consent. Low user awareness leads to inadequate exercise of data-subject rights and hampers trust in the system.[62]
c) *Secondary use and AI-driven processing*. From 2026, legislation will permit case-by-case AI access to EESZT data. Without comprehensive Data Protection Impact Assessments (DPIAs) and strict algorithmic-transparency measures, this risks violating GDPR's principles of purpose limitation and fairness.[63]

To address these data protection challenges, all EESZT stakeholders should conduct regular DPIAs, strengthen technical security (e.g., multi-factor authentication, encryption at rest), roll out comprehensive patient-information campaigns, and establish clear governance for any secondary/AI-based use of health data.

8 Conclusion

Nowadays, digitalization appears in almost every area of life. The goal of the EESZT aimed at renewing Hungary's healthcare is to provide the population with faster, more efficient, and service-oriented care. The key to this lies in the continuous connection between healthcare institutions, treating physicians, pharmacies, and patients. Due to the EESZT, the information is unified and accessible to all authorized participants.

[61] Péter Takács (2022) Privacy and Data Security Challenges in the Hungarian Health Sector at the Beginning of the twenty-first Century, https://bm-tt.hu/wp-content/uploads/2022/02/TakacsP_Security_Challenges_in_the_21st_Century_web-40.pdf?utm_source=chatgpt.com

[62] Tibor Roskó, Gergő József Szőllősi (2020) Behind passwords: An analysis of preliminary results in order to understand how users protect their privacy; https://firstmonday.org/ojs/index.php/fm/article/download/10616/10202?utm_source=chatgpt.com#author

[63] Helga Bíró, Mate Laczko Toth, Baker McKenzie AI Developers to Access Hungarian Health Data by 2026; https://www.lexology.com/library/detail.aspx?g=7b6b7ecf-4c57-4671-a381-6417e36a4207&utm_source=chatgpt.com

As part of a project funded by both Hungarian and European Union sources, under the current legal framework, all healthcare providers in Hungary are required to connect to the EESZT and provide data as stipulated by law. The system is continuously evolving and improving, but the criticisms mentioned above are valid and still require solutions, particularly in terms of patient rights, data protection, and the prevention of abuse.

According to my opinion, one of the most important development directions remains ensuring the highest level of data protection and security, guaranteeing data integrity, and preventing fraud and abuse. This approach aligns with the goals set out in the European Digital Decade policy framework.

Overall, the entire Hungarian society benefits from the EESZT, but many still feel that their entire patient journey is being exposed against their will, and they fear the depersonalization of care.

References

A magyar egészségügy jövője: forradalmat hozhat a mesterséges intelligencia (2024). https://www.vg.hu/kozelet/2024/11/a-magyar-egeszsegugy-jovoje-forradalmat-hozhat-a-mesterseges-intelligencia#google_vignette

Angyal Miklós: Az egészségügyi dokumentáció tartalmi és formai követelményeiről. http://www.szoszolo.hu/06tanulmanyaink/231013kommentar_angyal.htm

Biçakci S (2024) Digital Europe Program: nurturing technological sovereignty for a resilient European digital ecosphere; https://www.swp-berlin.org/publications/products/fachpublikationen/Digital_Europe_Program_Salih_B.pdf

CSÁK Réka Borbála - FEITH Helga Judit (2024) Dokumentációs kötelezettség a digitalizálódó egészségügyben, Orvosok Lapja. https://mok.hu/orvosoklapja/jogikerdesek/dokumentacios-kotelezettseg-a-digitalizalodo-egeszsegugyben

Digital Europe (2024). https://www.euro-access.eu/en/programs/9/Digital-Europe

Digitális Jólét Program (DJP) – áttörés a digitális fejlesztésekben (2024). https://digitalisjolet-program.hu/

EESZT- Elektronikus Egészségügyi Szolgáltatási Tér (2024). https://magyarorszag.hu/szuf_ugyleiras?id=5aba2115-f461-48e4-80da-9ff6d762ecce

EESZT Információs portál (2024). https://e-egeszsegugy.gov.hu/lakossagi-szolgaltatasok

Egészségügyi adatok határon átnyúló továbbításáról is nyilatkozhatunk az EESZT-ben (2022). https://adozona.hu/altalanos/Mar_egeszsegugyi_adatok_hataron_atnyulo_tov_38S1RO

eHealth in Hungary (2024). https://gnius.esante.gouv.fr/en/international-digital-health-systems/ehealth-hungary

Electronic Health Service Space. https://webtown-group.com/hu/national-ehealth-infrastructure-case-study

E-prescription has completely replaced traditional prescriptions (2022). https://hirlevel.egov.hu/2022/11/28/az-e-recept-teljesen-kiszoritotta-a-hagyomanyos-venyeket/

Ernőfy N (2024) Bemutatjuk a magyarok leghasznosabb applikációját. https://index.hu/belfold/2024/07/18/egeszsegugy-egeszsegablak-applikacio-idopontfoglalas-e-recept-digitalis-leletek/?token=2ec98ae49059013aab0ab54404332d07

Event catalogue, Health documents (2023). https://egeszsegvonal.gov.hu/ellatorendszer/eeszt/2094-esemenykatalogus-egeszsegugyi-dokumentumok.html

Fazekas M (2023) Az egészségügyi közigazgatás szervezetrendszerének változásai és az egészségügyi ellátórendszer átalakítása; KRE ÁJK Budapest, Glossa Iuridica X. évfolyam, 7. szám p. 96
Ferincz Jenő (2019) Mindent tudnak rólunk. https://nepszava.hu/3030256_mindent-tudnak-rolunk
Hadzic D (2023) European Union – new steps towards digital social security. https://kpmg.com/xx/en/our-insights/gms-flash-alert/flash-alert-2023-174.html
Így működik az új igazolási rendszer az óvodákban és az iskolákban (2024). https://vira.hu/2024/09/05/igy-mukodik-az-uj-igazolasi-rendszer-az-ovodakban-es-az-iskolakban/
Joó T (2024) Adatgyarmat leszünk, vagy magunk hasznosítjuk egészségügyi adatainkat? https://medicalonline.hu/informatika/cikk/adatgyarmat_leszunk__vagy_magunk_hasznositjuk_egeszsegugyi_adatainkat
Kardiológusokkal lehet nonstop telefonon konzultálni (2020). https://gokvi.hu/hir/2020/10/29/kardiologusokkal-lehet-nonstop-telefonon-konzultalni
Koncsek R (2024) Leomlottak a falak - Nagy előrelépés történt a betegellátásban. https://www.economx.hu/belfold/meditech-orvos-egeszsegugy-innovacio-szocska-miklos-adat-vagyok-belugyminiszterium-digital-health.784437.html
Matits K (2024) Adatforradalom az egészségügyben – megnyílik a magyar egészségügyi adatbázis az AI-fejlesztők előtt. https://www.portfolio.hu/gazdasag/20240617/adatforradalom-az-egeszsegugyben-megnyilik-a-magyar-egeszsegugyi-adatbazis-az-ai-fejlesztok-elott-692261
Megnyitják az EESZT-t az AI-fejlesztők előtt (2024). https://medicalonline.hu/informatika/cikk/megnyitjak_az_eeszt_t_az_ai_fejlesztok_elott
Mi az EESZT? (2024). https://e-egeszsegugy.gov.hu/mi-az-eeszt
Minden egyes bitre szüksége van az államnak a betegekről (2020). https://www.tisztessegesadatkezeles.org/2020/11/minden-egyes-bitre-szuksege-van-az-allamnak-a-betegekrol/
Mit jelent a teljesen tiltó állapot és hogyan állítható be az EESZT-ben? (2021). https://gdpr.news.hu/cikkek/mit-jelent-a-teljesen-tilto-allapot-es-hogyan-allithato-be-az-eeszt-ben/
Orvosi igazolások eljuttatása iskolai hiányzásról KRÉTA rendszerbe EESZT-n keresztül (2024). https://www.healzz2.hu/hirek/orvosi-igazolasok-eljuttatasa-iskolai-hianyzasrol-kreta-rendszerbe-eeszt-n-keresztul
Pákozdyné Bőcz I (2024) Digitális közszolgáltatások, e-egészségügy Magyarországon - Az EESZT bevezetése és fejlesztései, az e-egészségügy digitális jövője. Közigazgatási és Infokommunikációs Jogi PhD Tanulmányok 5(1):57–73
PWC Kihívásból lehetőségek. az egészségügyben Az ellátórendszer újragondolása (nem csak) a COVID-19 járvány apropóján; https://www.pwc.com/hu/hu/szolgaltatasok/kozszolgalati-tanacsadas/Kihivasbol_lehetosegek_az_egeszsegugyben.pdf
Radics Z (2018) Változások az elektronikus vény és az elektronikus adattovábbítás kapcsán. https://orvosivallalkozas.hu/cikk/valtozasok-az-elektronikus-veny-es-az-elektronikus-adattovabbitas-kapcsan
Radics Z (2022) Mire jó az Elektronikus Egészségügyi Szolgáltatási Tér? https://jogkoveto.hu/tudastar/elektronikus-egeszsegugyi-szolgaltatas
Radics Z (2024) A járóbeteg-szakellátási digitális időpontfoglaló rendszer. https://jogkoveto.hu/tudastar/a-jarobeteg-szakellatasi-digitalis-idopontfoglalo-rendszer-bevezetese
Rosta L (2020) Egy háziorvos gondolatai az EESZT-ről. https://mok.hu/orvosoklapja/aktualis/egy-haziorvos-gondolatai-az-eeszt-rol
Sándor T (2023) Jön az e-beutaló, csökkennek a várólisták – csúcskonferenciázik a magyar egészségügy. https://www.vg.hu/vilaggazdasag-magyar-gazdasag/2023/11/jon-az-e-beutalo-csokkennek-a-varolistak-csucskonferenciazik-a-magyar-egeszsegugy#google_vignette
Szabó B (2024) Elektronikus Egészségügyi Szolgáltatási Tér. https://webtown.hu/en/web/guest/eeszt-esettanulm%C3%A1ny
The Digital Europe Programme (2016). https://digital-strategy.ec.europa.eu/en/activities/digital-programme
The Role of the EESZT in Hungarian Healthcare (2023). https://e-egeszsegugy.gov.hu/web/eeszt-information-portal/the-role-of-the-eeszt-in-hungarian-healthcare

Towards a more digital social security coordination: Commission proposes steps to make it easier for Europeans to live, work and travel abroad (2023). https://ec.europa.eu/commission/presscorner/detail/en/ip_23_4263
Újabb funkcióval bővült a 2,6 millió magyar által használt egészségügyi alkalmazás (2024). https://www.portfolio.hu/gazdasag/20240116/ujabb-funkcioval-bovult-a-26-millio-magyar-altal-hasznalt-egeszsegugyi-alkalmazas-663207
Zoltán A (2022) Nem veszik komolyan az önrendelkezést egyes orvosok; https://www.tisztessegesadatkezeles.org/2022/11/nem-veszik-komolyan-az-onrendelkezest-egyes-orvosok/

Social Europe, Free Movement and the Phenomenon of Reverse Social Dumping

Luka Mišič

1 Introduction

As the European Union (hereinafter: the EU) grapples with balancing economic and social integration and free movement and social rights, tensions between socially and economically diverse Member States (hereinafter: MS) have become increasingly evident. The concept of social Europe, which promotes social rights, equal opportunities and equal treatment across the EU, is facing strain as MSs navigate, each on their own, the complexities of free movement and social protection under EU law.

In this context, the chapter examines the phenomenon of *reverse social dumping*. In this practice, wealthier MSs, rather than employers or businesses, which is the more common case with social dumping, exploit lower social standards in poorer MSs to minimise their financial obligations or achieve other goals. Conversely, poorer MSs may even apply higher social standards than usual to gain an advantage over richer MSs or promote the best interests of their workers. Both represent institutional and commonly strategic manipulation of social security rules. On the one hand, unlawful practices can undermine EU social policies and the level of social integration. On the other hand, they constantly challenge the European legislator

This research is part of the project *Analysis of Social Security Systems for Specific Groups of Workers in Hungary and Slovenia* (N5-0339), funded by the Slovenian Research and Innovation Agency.

L. Mišič (✉)
Faculty of Law, Department for Labour Law and Social Security Law, University of Ljubljana, Ljubljana, Slovenia
e-mail: luka.misic@pf.uni-lj.si

K. Koldinská et al. (eds.), *Labour Law and Social Security Law in Central and Eastern Europe*, European Union and its Neighbours in a Globalized World 26,
https://doi.org/10.1007/978-3-032-04496-9_12

and can, if purely domestic social agendas are set aside, make the enforcement of social and free movement rights more resilient.

2 Social Europe: A State of Social Fatigue?

The notion of *social Europe* is best described as a body of EU law that, on the one hand, establishes supranational social policies and, on the other hand, affects social rights and social policies in MS. It leads to the protection and extension of social rights using positive integration and market-correcting or restricting policies. It also intervenes in national social policies to enforce the market and promote free movement, free competition and non-discrimination.[1] Its history extends from the failed Social Action Programme in the 1970s, the open method of coordination following the Lisbon Strategy from 2000, all the way to the Lisbon Treaty in 2009, when the EU Charter of Fundamental Rights, which also contains social rights, obtained the same legal status as the Treaties.[2] However, the first European provisions on social security coordination date back to 1958, when Regulations No. 3 and 4 were passed, whilst it was the Treaty of Rome which introduced equal pay for women and men and free movement rights for workers as early as 1957. More recently, the now very diverse EU has declared the European Pillar of Social Rights, delivering 20 principles promoting a strong social Europe.

Despite these efforts, it appears that, similar to enlargement fatigue,[3] MSs are suffering from social fatigue or an unwillingness to implement or exercise the protection and extension of social rights through positive integration. They often wish to reap the benefits of the common market without carrying the burdens associated with free movement, residence and non-discrimination rights or the principle of equal treatment. The two types of fatigue are, of course, interlinked, as any EU enlargement makes the European community less socio-economically homogeneous and can thus lead to MSs' greater reluctance to cooperate.

Several authors have already highlighted the problematic relationship between Europe's East and West or between the old and new MSs concerning social and free movement rights guaranteed to citizens under EU law. These lie at the heart of European integration. The Regulation (EC) No 883/2004 of the European Parliament and of the Council of 29 April 2004 on the coordination of social security systems affords protection of social security benefits to EU citizens, stateless persons and refugees residing in an MS, who are or have been subject to the legislation of one or more MSs, as well as to their family members and survivors. More precisely, by protecting social security rights in cross-border situations, the Regulation enables the free movement of persons. Without a coordination mechanism in place, they

[1] Martinsen, Vollaard (2014), pp. 679–680.

[2] Dawson, De Witte (2012), pp. 45 ff.

[3] See, for example, Szołucha (2010), pp. 2 ff.

could experience a loss, reduction or suspension of their social security benefits if moving across borders. They could also become subject to double or multiple taxation for social security purposes. From this perspective, the law on the coordination of social security systems represents the cornerstone of free movement in the EU, generally transgressing the idea of a common market by granting rights to both economically active and inactive EU citizens or persons.

The Regulation is closely linked to Directive 2004/38/EC of the European Parliament and of the Council on the right of citizens of the Union and their family members to move and reside freely within the territory of the Member States. However, the so-called Citizens' Rights Directive prevailed over the Regulation with respect to special non-contributory cash benefits (hereinafter: SNBCs), creating an exclusionary mechanism concerning residence rights or, put differently, the right to belong, even if the links of belonging are pre-assigned rather than chosen.[4]

The European Court of Justice (hereinafter: CJEU) treated SNCBs as social assistance benefits in *Brey* (C-140/12) and subsequent case law, even though they represent a special category of benefits under the Regulation. In *Commission v. UK* (C-308/14), the *Brey* and in *Dano* (C-333/13), its case law was extended to a broader range of benefits falling under the material scope of application of the Regulation than solely SNCBs.[5]

According to the Directive, EU citizens may only claim income support benefits if they meet permanent residence conditions. If not, they may face expulsion as an extreme measure taken by the host MS. Under the Regulation, SNBCs are not considered to be social assistance benefits, which lie beyond the material scope of application and are exempt from the coordination mechanism. They are regarded as benefits of a mixed nature. They aim to increase the amount of social security (insurance) benefits. They are coordinated but not exported. A person who is moving from one MS to another will not be able to export an SNBC, e.g. an allowance serving as a supplement to their pension, but may claim such benefits in the host MS if available under its domestic legislation. From the perspective of the Directive and the now infamous case law of the CJEU, such an allowance would, as mentioned, count as income support under the free movement law. This creates friction between rights and obligations under the Regulation and the Directive, even if both pieces of legislation are aimed at facilitating the free movement of persons and/or EU citizens and were even passed at the same time. Nevertheless, both create different circles of solidarity within the European communities. They partially converge on the economically active persons, e.g. workers or self-employed persons,[6] but diverge on the economically inactive EU citizens due to the *sufficient resources* condition enshrined in the Directive but not yet found in the Regulation.[7] This applies to international

---

[4] See Spaventa (2017), p. 209. On the burdens of national citizenship, obtained within a theoretical lottery procedure, see Mišič (2020), pp. 53 ff.

[5] Pennings (2022), pp. 202 ff.

[6] For the social security of economically active persons, also their social assistance entitlements, see Verschueren (2016) pp. 187 ff.

[7] For the proposal to include such condition in the Regulation see Pennings (2022), pp. 207–208.

social security law as well, since social assistance is generally excluded from the scope of application of international coordination agreements.[8]

According to Vonk, the present EU law on social security coordination is based upon two distinctions between social security schemes. One is between social security (insurance) benefits and SNBCs, the other is between SNBCs and social assistance benefits.[9] The place of minimum subsistence benefits under EU law is thus shrouded in controversy. MSs are reluctant to grant tax-funded benefits to mobile EU citizens at home, let alone to those moving to other parts of the EU.[10] Put differently, they have no interest in providing social assistance benefits to their citizens or permanent residents, let alone to other EU citizens. Even if there is little evidence that migration within the EU is inspired by welfare tourism,[11] MSs' objectives concerning the protection of their national welfare states constantly compete with the EU's objectives of free movement, equal treatment and equal opportunities, and the fight against poverty and social exclusion. As mentioned, some of these make up the notion of a *social Europe*. Shuibhne argues that the notion of EU citizenship has evolved into something less than what citizenship in normative terms requires, needs or deserves, claiming that the EU generates a version of pseudo-citizenship at best, draping a thin veil of self-serving rhetoric over its formative and enduring economic ancestry.[12] The question is whether the EU is *citizenship-capable*[13] since it ascribes little, if any, income support obligations on the host MS, just like *real* national citizenships do. By excluding non-nationals and short-term residents from income support coupled with the fear of expulsion, EU law creates what Minderhoud and Mantu describe as a narrow type of solidarity, which is available only for those who do not need it and when they do not need it,[14] i.e. for economically active person or persons, who possess sufficient resources not to become a (disproportionate) burden on the social assistance scheme of the host MS, and for all who either belonged to the first and/or second category of EU citizens in a period long enough that a right to permanent residence was granted.

If, on the one hand, the care for the sustainability of national welfare states' budgets and restricted access to benefits seems rational and legitimate concerning tax-funded social rights, where a sufficient link between the beneficiary and the

---

[8] Vonk, Walsum (2012), p. 17.

[9] Vonk (2020), p. 139.

[10] *Ibid.*, pp. 138–140.

[11] See Verschueren (2015), pp. 29 ff. Nevertheless, the European Commission has already proposed the introduction of residence criteria stemming from Directive 2004/38/EC in Regulation (EC) No 883/2004. See COM(2016) 815 final from 13. 12. 2016. According to Golynker (2020), p. 123, its aim was to protect Member States against welfare tourism. However, as observed by Golynker, the Parliament was concerned with the rights of economically inactive migrants as EU citizens and their enjoyment of human rights, whilst the decision of the Council showed that Member States also prioritised the rights of EU citizens over welfare tourism concerns.

[12] Shuibhne (2010), p. 1597.

[13] *Ibid.*, p. 1598.

[14] Minderhoud, Mantu (2017), p. 206.

anonymous taxpayers is often lacking, it should be considered redundant concerning contribution-funded benefits. These are usually provided and financed within a two-sided social insurance relationship of mutual obligation between two parties, i.e., the socially insured person and the social insurance carrier. The insurance relationship itself creates the link missing when tax-funded rights of economically inactive persons are at stake. Nevertheless, the complex relationship between MSs or their policy goals and the policy goals of the EU extends to the field of social insurance as well. The term *social fatigue* might not even describe the situation best, since MSs or their competent institutions often actively compete with one another or against EU law to gain financial or other advantages.

3 Free Movement Creates Conflict

Pennings, for example, described the state of affairs concerning the coordination of unemployment benefits as a battlefield between the East and the West.[15] According to the author, the coordination of unemployment benefits has two significant issues. First, job-seekers do not move symmetrically but mostly from poorer to richer MSs and from East to West. This means that, on the one hand, richer MSs bear the costs associated with the aggregation of periods, i.e. insurance records from MSs with generally lower wages and unemployment benefits lead to entitlement in MSs with generally higher wages and unemployment benefits. On the other hand, low-income MSs commonly finance job searches in high-income MSs with limited means of control.[16] This correlates to the second major issue. The supervision of job-seeking activities, mandatory for unemployment benefits recipients to remain entitled, is carried out by the host MS, not the MS paying the benefits.[17] As described by Grabbe, the complicated relationship between closed welfare states and EU migration flows has made the coordination of social security benefits difficult, with opposition from Western European policymakers concerning the reform of the current regulations.[18] It is these and other policy issues that refute the notion that national policy positions in the field of social security coordination are less problematic than when accessing social assistance benefits. On the contrary, the field of social security coordination might be even more prone to diverse and/or unlawful practices by competent institutions from different MSs. Unlike the field of social assistance, where little EU law regulation is in place, at least concerning economically inactive persons with no special legal status, social security coordination is governed by the Regulation alone.

---

[15] Pennings (2020).

[16] See footnote no. 10 on welfare tourism.

[17] See Pennings (2020), p. 149.

[18] Grabbe (2023), pp. 23–24.

When providing unemployment benefits, high-income MSs may, for example, treat regular cross-border workers as frontier workers to apply special rules according to which unemployment benefits are paid under the competence of the MS of residence (*lex loci domicilii*) instead of the MS of last employment (*lex loci laboris*).[19] Low-income MS might apply special provisions in national law that provide higher unemployment benefits for frontier workers. Similarly, competent MSs might use different rules on the aggregation of periods, disregarding periods from MSs in which no social security contributions were paid since persons were not insured in the field of unemployment insurance, even if such periods would have been considered had they fulfilled in the territory of the competent MS, which is the rule of the Regulation.[20] Since competent institutions have to consider only the last professional income received by the unemployed persons, this may either go in favour of or against the financial interest of the worker.[21] If becoming unemployed in a low-income MS after more extended periods of employment in a high-income MS, this will generally worsen their economic situation and *vice versa.* This also applies to the competent institutions, which sometimes have to pay higher unemployment benefits, considering only the last professional income but not the average received by the unemployed person over a longer period.[22]

In the field of posting, where one of the most important exceptions to the *lex loci laboris* principle applies, Rennuy points to several gaps between the law and its actual application.[23] According to Article 12 of the Regulation, sending MS remains competent in the field of social security even if work is performed on the territory of a different MS, provided the statutory conditions are met. This enables the free movement of services and is of the most significant benefit to consumers or clients, who receive cheaper services within the common market. To prevent the establishment of letter-box companies,[24] informal agency work, and the associated phenomenon of social dumping, the employer must usually carry out its activities in the territory of the sending MS; the posting must be of a temporary nature; the posted worker, who must preserve a genuine link with their employer from the sending MS, ought not to replace another posted worker, and so on.[25]

In light of the principle of sincere cooperation, the competent issuing institutions of the sending MS must carry out a proper assessment of the facts relevant to the

---

[19] Mišič, Strban (2024), p. 13.

[20] See Pennings (2022), pp. 328 ff.

[21] *Ibid.*

[22] On the proposal for the revision of the Regulation see *Ibid.,* pp. 337 ff.

[23] Rennuy (2020), p. 218.

[24] See, for example, Verschueren (2020), p. 485.

[25] The conditions are further determined in Article 14 of the Regulation (EC) No 987/2009 of the European Parliament and of the Council of 16 September 2009 laying down the procedure for implementing Regulation (EC) No 883/2004 on the coordination of social security systems as well as the Decision No A2 of 12 June 2009 concerning the interpretation of Article 12 of Regulation (EC) No 883/2004 of the European Parliament and of the Council on the legislation applicable to posted workers and self-employed workers temporarily working outside the competent State.

application of the rules determining the applicable social security legislation and, consequently, to guarantee the correctness of the information contained in the PD A1.[26] Since PD A1 is binding on the host MS and cannot be unilaterally disregarded even by courts,[27] non-compliance enables employers and self-employed persons to choose the applicable legislation, thus opting out of and into mandatory social security schemes and depriving the competent MS of social security contributions.[28] They may also falsely trigger the competence of the sending MS to gain an advantage over their competitors from a richer MS. Even more so since MSs enjoy an essential margin of discretion in designing the Portable Document (hereinafter: PD) A1 granting procedure,[29] in which the posting conditions are examined and the competence of the sending MS as opposed to the competence of the receiving MS in the field of social security is thus determined. Some MSs seem not to carry out any assessment of the relevant facts at all,[30] whilst the verification of the posting conditions generally varies significantly from one country to another.[31] This may lead to misuse that favours the sending MS and their employers. Until Slovenia faced charges before the CJEU for promoting social dumping and unlawful competition, social security contributions for posted workers were paid from their Slovenian (minimum) salaries instead of their actual salaries, commonly obtained in Austria and Germany.

However, it appears that no MS is innocent in the field of social security coordination, and that free movement rights act as one of the leading conflict creators in the EU.[32] Austrian authorities supposedly targeted Slovenian posted craftsmen with labour inspection procedures and, more famously, adjusted the amount of family benefits such as the family allowance paid in cross-border situations according to the living standard (price of consumer goods and services) of the MS in which the child resides.[33] Under the cloak of neutrality, adjusting the number of benefits both according to the living standard of higher-income MSs and low-income MSs, they discriminated against workers and their family members from countries like Czechia, Hungary, Slovakia, or Slovenia, for example.

According to Kukovec, the social claims of the *periphery* are almost non-existent in the current discourse. Unlike free movement and social considerations in the European centres, which are often perceived as natural or less problematic, the periphery's claims are frequently viewed as harmful due to the fear of social

---

[26] Jorens, De Wispelaere (2019), p. 120. In-depth in Rennuy (2020), p. 217.

[27] See, for example, Verschueren (2020), pp. 488 ff. See *Altun* (C-359/16), *Alpenrind* (C-527/16), *Vueling Airlines* (C-370/17 and C-37/18) or in respect to criminal procedures DRV Intertrans and Others (C-410/21 and C-661/21) and, more recently and with reference to the said case-law in Ministère public and Others (C-628/22).

[28] Rennuy (2020), p. 219.

[29] See Jorens and De Wispelaere (2019), p. 119.

[30] Rennuy (2020), p. 217.

[31] Jorens, De Wispelaere (2019), p. 120.

[32] Mišič, Strban (2023), pp. 430 ff.

[33] For family benefits see Marhold, Ludvik (2020), pp. 273 ff.

dumping. Conversely, EU law is not concerned with goods dumping within the internal market, which, as Kukovec points out, has enormous potential to harm the periphery's industry, employment levels, capital, and brand recognition.[34]

This article introduces *reverse social dumping* as a new form of (social) dumping. On the one hand, it is a result of applying free movement rights in a socially and economically diverse EU landscape. On the other hand, it helps to reaffirm these differences while deepening the *centre-periphery* divide and the divide between the *(un)conditionally deserving* and *undeserving* EU citizens.[35]

4 Reverse Social Dumping: A Working Definition

Reverse social dumping describes the practice whereby competent institutions from high-income MS take advantage of lower amounts of social security benefits paid in a low-income MS, for example by transferring competence to that MS. Unlike social dumping, where employers from low-income MS usually take advantage of their lower amounts of pay, working conditions, etc., against the interests of their workers and competition, it is the high-income MSs taking such advantage to protect their financial interests against the interest of the workers from low-income MSs. It entails an act of "competence shopping".[36]

As mentioned, high-income MSs hosting cross-border workers who became unemployed in their territory might treat them as unemployed frontier workers instead of regular cross-border workers to shift competence. By attributing the special status of a frontier worker, they might, however, risk a social or administrative dispute. Nevertheless, taking legal action is not likely due to language, economic and other barriers that prevent unemployed persons from seeking justice in another MS. They also receive unemployment benefits, only in a different MS and generally in lower amounts. Additionally, unemployment benefits are commonly paid as short-term social security benefits, with unemployed persons being reemployed sooner or later. Despite the risk, the attribution of such legal status is one of the two possible ways of transferring the competence to the MS of residence, which now applies its domestic law (calculation base, calculation percentages, upper and lower thresholds, duration of entitlement, etc.) when granting unemployment benefits. In such cases, the MS of last employment only reimburses the associated costs for a limited period from 3 to 5 months, depending on the person's insurance records from its territory and up to the amount of the benefits that would have been paid under its applicable legislation. If the competence shifts to a low-income MS, the high-income MS in which the cross-border worker became unemployed saves the difference between the amount of benefits that would have been paid under its

[34] Kukovec (2015), pp. 419 ff.

[35] See Mišič (2020), pp. 62–63.

[36] Mišič, Strban (2024), p. 14.

applicable legislation and the amount paid under the relevant legislation of the now competent MS of residence. This applies even though social security contributions were paid in the MS of the last employment. Presumably, wholly unemployed frontier workers possess better chances of becoming reemployed in their MS of residence than in the MS of their last employment.

According to Article 65 of the Regulation, wholly unemployed frontier workers should thus register with the employment services and claim unemployment benefits in the MS of residence (*lex loci domicilii*), not the MS of last employment, whilst other unemployed cross-border workers, i.e. cross-border workers, who do not return to the MS of residence at least once a week, may either claim unemployment benefits in the MS of last employment (*lex loci laboris*) or return and claim these benefits in the MS of residence. By returning and claiming benefits there, they also trigger the competence of the MS of residence.

Nevertheless, competent institutions in high-income MS might not take the abovementioned risk of actually attributing the special legal status of a frontier worker to regular cross-border workers, indicating that the person returned to the MS of residence at least once a week. Still, they may encourage them to claim unemployment benefits in their MS of residence instead of the primary competent MS, in effect losing this right in the MS of last employment.[37] This scenario seems more plausible since it brings less risk in cases of a dispute, and it resolves the issue of proving the (non-)existence of the frontier worker status. At the same time, the advice offered to the unemployed cross-border worker to return to the MS of residence and claim unemployment benefits there might even be considered as assisting the weaker party in the two-sided social insurance relationship. Of course, not concerning the amount of benefits but the advice that they are entitled to such benefits in their home country, where it might be more practical for the unemployed person to exercise their rights. However, a shift of competencies makes it more difficult for job-seekers to look for work in a different MS, including the MS of their last employment, since unemployment benefits can, when exported, be used as a means of income support.[38] This makes their free movement rights and the functioning of the common market less effective.

In 2021, the Slovenian legislature amended the Market Regulation Act, which now includes two upper limits set on the amount of unemployment benefits. The general limit is set at only 892.50 EUR, whilst the double applies to persons permanently residing in the territory of Slovenia, who drive daily or weekly to another MS where they perform work—i.e. a casuistic description of frontier workers by the Slovenian lawmaker—is set at 1.785 EUR which coincidently roughly mirrors, as mentioned, the upper limit set in Austrian legislation where the great majority of Slovenian-resident frontier workers are employed. The period in which the increased unemployment benefits are paid under the Market Regulation Act mirrors the period

[37] For the interplay between Austrian and Slovenian competent institutions see Mišič, Bagari (2021), pp. 80 ff.

[38] See Pennings (2020), p. 149.

of either 3 or 5 months in which the MSs of the last employment have to reimburse these benefits under Articles 65(6) and 65(7) of the Regulation.

The Slovenian case differs in that it eliminates the adverse effects of Article 65 of the Regulation and its competence and reimbursement rules, which favour high-income MS of last employment. From this perspective, the Regulation itself represents a framework for reverse social dumping by neglecting the general *lex loci laboris* principle and applying the special *lex loci domicilii* principle. By doing so, the European periphery has fought against the Regulation, which supports the European centres and their financial interests, even if it risks action by Austria or other high-income MS or the European Commission. The legislative action is also supported by the proprietary understanding of social insurance rights, as social security contributions in Austria were generally paid from higher wages, for which the low general limit set at € 892.50 is completely disproportional and diminishes the principle of insurance. This also applies to Slovenian-resident unemployed persons, whose unemployment benefits could also reach the specific upper limit of € 1785, thus raising the issue of unequal treatment within the national context.

5 From Reverse to Institutional Social Dumping?

The inventive way in which the Slovenian legislator bypassed EU rules in the field of social security coordination could represent a specific type of reverse social dumping, calling for a more general definition of the notion or, conversely, for defining two distinct types of reverse social dumping.

In a broad sense, reverse social dumping can describe any practice whereby a competent institution from one MS takes advantage of competence (i.e., competence shopping) or other social security rules to gain a financial or other benefit, commonly at the expense of another MS.

What makes this an act of *social dumping* is the fact that differences in social law standards between MSs are required and used to gain an advantage. What makes a case of social dumping *reverse* is the fact that either higher standards are applied at the expense of another MS (reversed application of standards), or that lower standards are used, however not by low-income MSs to gain a competitive advantage in the common market but by high-income MSs protecting their position against low-income MSs (reversed notion of dumping).

In the case of the Slovenian legislator, it is the application of higher social law standards that makes the dumping *reverse*, in other cases, it is the fact that lower social law standards are not seen as a threat but as an opportunity for the competent high-income MS. Since competent institutions cannot set up subsidiaries in low-income MS, they have to rely on competence rules or the presence of a cross-border element to gain financial or other advantage. Cases similar to the Austrian case of adjusting family benefits to the standard of living in another MS, or the potential cases of treating cross-border workers as frontier workers may be better described as *institutional social dumping* which is sometimes also *reversed* from the perspective that higher social law standards are applied, e.g. in the case of the Slovenian Market Regulation Act.

A form of institutional social dumping (reversed notion of dumping) could theoretically occur in the field of planned healthcare if, for example, high-income MSs, their public officers or physicians would promote the Directive 2011/24/EU of the European Parliament and of the Council of 9 March 2011 on the application of patients' rights in cross-border healthcare among insured persons, claiming healthcare in low-income MS instead of MS of insurance. This could be achieved either by soft measures, such as enhanced promotion and information exchange, or by legal measures, such as not requiring prior authorisation when accessing complex health services.[39] In such cases, the social insurance carriers from the competent high-income MS would generally reimburse a lower amount of healthcare costs that would have been paid or compensated in the MS of insurance due to typically lower prices in the MSs in which treatment was provided. This could apply, for example, to Austrian, German or Italian patients exercising their patient rights during their summer holidays in Croatia, either with private or public providers. The case for reverse social dumping is, of course, stronger with respect to public providers with fixed prices. However, it is far less likely that cross-border patients will seek and obtain timely planned treatment within the public healthcare system of any host MS. Nevertheless, in such cases, the high-income MS would not only save money but also other resources that could be spent on domestic patients not invoking the right to planned healthcare under the Directive. Berki, discussing the European Healthcare Fund, notes that MSs might be motivated to outsource their patients to countries with good quality care but much cheaper treatments to save money.[40] Such cases could also be considered cases of reversed social dumping (reversed application of standards) if it were low-income MSs promoting patients' rights under the Patients' Rights Directive. They would still have to reimburse the patients up to the amounts paid under its applicable legislation with the insured persons covering the differences, however, the latter could, at least theoretically, enjoy better access to better quality care in a high-income MS. Similar reasoning could also be applied to both the field of unplanned as well as planned treatment under the Regulation.

In the first and less likely case, MSs could promote the use of the European Health Insurance Card to the extent that patients would claim *false unplanned* treatment in another MS under Article 19 of the Regulation, rather than lawfully claim planned treatment under the Directive, where they may have to bear part of the costs themselves due to differences in prices, or in a purely national context. In such cases, the act of reverse social dumping could occur when treatment would be claimed in a low-income MS, for example, following advice by a public officer. Similarly, and more likely, high-income MSs may be tempted to send their patients

[39] For the general rules of the Directive see Strban (2013), pp. 393 ff. or Mišič, Strban (2023), pp. 441–443.

[40] Berki (2019), p. 76.

to low-income MSs with good quality healthcare under Article 20 of the Regulation whenever treatment is not timely accessible in the MS of insurance.

Discussing the different forms or definitions of social dumping may seem redundant since all the practices described here could be considered rights abuses and nothing more. However, an attempt to define or categorise a type of practice in a more specific way may reveal different, previously less discernible dynamics between MSs in the field of social security law.

6 Conclusion: Change as the Only Way Forward

The Regulation, which for most social security lawyers represents the cornerstone of free movement in the EU and thus lies at the heart of what we consider *social Europe*, is a living instrument. It has to adapt to the changed circumstances in society, e.g. with respect to mobility patterns, new social risks, new forms of work and work organisation. Even so, competent institutions, employers, workers, and self-employed persons may find novel ways to bypass its provisions. Some to gain a competitive advantage in the common market, others to safeguard their public finances or reach labour market, policy or political goals of protecting their national welfare states. Either way, the current social security coordination framework is faced with new challenges that might require further legislative action shortly, even if old issues such as the problematic provisions on wholly unemployed frontier workers or other cross-border workers have not yet been resolved due to the power struggles between the East and the West. With future enlargement, this might become even more difficult due to the further diversification of the purchasing power, social, labour and living standards, as well as national policies in Europe. On the one hand, MS governments are bound by domestic social contracts, which make it difficult to shrink welfare commitments without running the risk of losing national electoral support. On the other hand, ever since the 1980s, eurozone MSs especially have become bound by a pervasive programme of European market integration which increasingly exposes their now semi-sovereign welfare states to regulatory competition.[41] Additionally, current European peripheries, feared and at the same time needed by the European centres due to their competitive advantage in the common market or willingness or ability of their work-forces to take on scarce jobs, might re-establish themselves as the new or at least second-best centres in Europe, bringing new political dynamics to the table.

Among less theoretical and more recent issues in the field of social security coordination, the phenomenon of remote work has to be highlighted. If, following the Administrative Commission's 2022 Guidance Note on telework, the 25% criterion used under Article 13 of the Regulation and Article 14 of the Implementing Regulation, were to become exclusively applicable to teleworking, then employers

[41] Corti, Hemerijck (2024), p. 244.

from high-income MSs might become tempted, taking advantage of the example set in the field of unemployment benefits, to make remote work mandatory for, say, at least 8 days per month or 90 days per year. By doing so, they might trigger a shift in competence for social security purposes from the high-income MS of employment to the low-income MS of residence, where at least 25% of activities would have to be carried out. The application of this conflict rule, namely, means that for workers who spent 25% or more of their working time teleworking from home, the legislation of their MS of residence becomes fully applicable, including the duty to pay social security contributions.[42] This would, of course, benefit their employers if they were willing to take on the administrative burden of being associated with another MS's social security system. Still, not the workers or the MSs of employment, left with no social security contributions in the bank. Due to the higher 50% threshold set in the Framework Agreement on social security for cross-border telework,[43] this now seems less likely.

This is just an example to show how quickly the current regulation needs to be adapted in some cases. At the same time, it is challenging to precisely identify the areas where future circumstances will necessitate new changes. What is clear is that change or adaptation is the only way forward. As mentioned, MS' unlawful practices can, on the one hand, undermine EU social policies and the level of social integration but can, on the other hand, make the enforcement of social and free movement rights more resilient if the European legislator amends the applicable legislation without paying too much attention to national social policies or at least by paying attention to all interests, both the interests of the European centres as well as of the periphery.

Acknowledgments This chapter has been written and published thanks to the financial support of the ARIS Bilateral Research Project N5-0339 Analysis of social security systems for specific groups of workers in Hungary and Slovenia.

References

Berki G (2019) Patient mobility in the EU – a playground for all of us? Revue Belge de securite-sociale 1E trimestre:65–79

Corti F, Hemerijck A (2024) Social Europe in a bind, again? In: Hemerjick A, Matsaganis M (eds) Who's afarid of the welfare state now? Oxford University Press, Oxford, pp 241–267

Dawson M, De Witte M (2012) The EU legal framework of social inclusion and social protection: between the Lisbon strategy and the Lisbon Treaty, in Cantillon B (et al) (eds) Social inclusion and social protection in the EU: interactions between law and policy. Cambridge, Intersentia:41–70

---

[42] Mišič, Strban (2024), p. 14.

[43] For a recent discussion on the Framework Agreement see, for example, Rewucha (2024), pp. 448 ff.

Golynker O (2020) EU coordination of social security from the point of view of EU integration theory. Eur J Soc Secur 22(2):110–137
Grabbe C (2023) Free movement and access to social security in the EU: the challenge of exporting unemployment benefits. Eur J Soc Secur 25(1):20–40
Jorens Y, De Wispelaere F (2019) Intra-EU posting: looking for solutions: a Herculean or a Sisyphean Task? Belgisch tijdschrift voor sociale zekerheid 1E trimester 2019:113–138
Kukovec D (2015) Law and the periphery. Eur Law J 21(3):406–428
Marhold F, Ludvik CP (2020) Thoughts about indexing family benefits: Are authorities permitted to apply the Austrian indexation of family benefits? The primacy of EU law and the right/obligation to request a ruling from the Court of Justice of the European Union. Eur J Soc Secur 22(3):273–286
Minderhoud P, Mantu S (2017) Back to the roots? No access to social assistance for Union citizens who are economically inactive. In: Thym D (ed) Questioning EU citizenship. Judges and the limits of free movement and solidarity in the EU. Hart Publishing, Oxford, pp 191–207
Mišič L (2020) Equality of opportunity in the EU: rethinking of the European pillar of social rights in light of free movement as a supranational principle of justice. Zbornik znanstvenih razprav 80:41–75
Mišič L, Bagari S (2021) Koordinacija dajatev za brezposelnost v Evropski uniji: kdo pije, kdo plača? Podjetje in delo 47(1):80–104
Mišič L, Strban G (2023) Social security and free movement: why EU mobility will always come at a price. In: Jorens Y (ed) The lighthouse function of social law, Proceedings of the ISLSSL XIV European Regional Congress Ghent 2023. Springer, Cham, pp 421–447
Mišič L, Strban G (2024) Atypical work and residence in cross-border situations: the coordination of unemployment benefits. Eur J Soc Secur 0(0):1–18
Pennings F (2020) The discussion on the revision of the coordination rules of unemployment benefits – a battlefield between East and West. Eur J Soc Secur 22(2):148–162
Pennings F (2022) European social security law, 7th edn. Intersentia, Cambridge
Rennuy N (2020) Posting of workers: enforcement, compliance and reform. Eur J Soc Secur 22(2):212–234
Rewucha A (2024) Crossing borders and moving frontiers: Coordinating European social security for modern cases of global mobility. Eur J Soc Secur 26(4):434–455
Shuibhne N (2010) The resilience of EU market citizenship. Common Mark Law Rev 47(6):1597–1628
Sindbjerg Martinsen D, Vollard H (2014) Implementing social Europe in times of crises: reestablished boundaries of welfare? West Eur Polit 37(4):677–692
Spaventa E (2017) Earned citizenship - Understanding union citizenship through its scope. In: Kochenov D (ed) EU citizenship and federalism. The role of rights. Cambridge, Cambridge University Press, pp 204–225
Strban G (2013) Patient mobility in the European Union: between social security coordination and free movement of services. ERA Forum 14:391–407
Szołucha A (2010) The EU and enlargement fatigue: why has the European Union not been able to counter enlargement fatigue? J Contemp Eur Res 6(1):1–16
Verschueren H (2015) Free movement of EU citizens. Including for the poor? Maastricht J Eur Comp Law 22(1):10–34
Verschueren H (2016) Being economically active: how it still matters. In: Verschueren H (ed) Residence, employment and social rights of mobile persons. On how EU law defines where they belong. Intersentia, Cambridge, pp 187–214
Verschueren H (2020) The CJEU's case law on the role of posting certificates: a missed opportunity to combat social dumping. Maastricht J Eur Comp Law 27(4):484–502
Vonk G (2020) The EU (non) co-ordination of minimum subsistence benefits: What went wrong and what ways forward? Eur J Soc Secur 22(2):138–147
Vonk G, Walsum Van S (2012) Access denied. Towards a new approach to social protection for formally excluded migrants. In: Vonk G (ed) Cross-border welfare state. Immigration, social security and integration. Intersentia, Cambridge, pp 17–60

Long-Term Care: Not a Nightmare in the EU?

Kristina Koldinská

1 Introduction

The demographic trend of population aging in Europe presents a critical challenge for long-term care (LTC) systems. By 2050, it is projected that nearly 30% of Europeans will be aged 65 or older, compared to 20% in 2020, as highlighted by Eurostat.[1] This shift reflects increasing life expectancy and declining birth rates across the continent. According to the European Commission's 2021 Ageing Report, the old-age dependency ratio—measuring the number of individuals aged 65 and over relative to those of working age—is set to rise from 32% in 2020 to 57% by 2100.[2] This dramatic increase underscores the growing demand for long-term care services to support an aging population.

Furthermore, the 2024 Ageing Report argues that one half of future gains in life expectancy will be spent in good health and the other half in disability. Public LTC expenditure in the EU is projected to increase from 1.7% of GDP in 2022 to 2.6% of GDP in 2070, an increase of 48%.[3] Population aging will considerably raise the

This work was supported by the European Regional Development Fund project "Center for Inequality and Open Society" (no.: CZ.02.01.01/00/23_025/0008690).

[1] Eurostat (2024).

[2] European Commission (2021a).

[3] European Commission (2024a).

K. Koldinská (✉)
Faculty of Law, Department of Labour Law and Social Security Law, Charles University, Prague, Czech Republic
e-mail: koldinsk@prf.cuni.cz

K. Koldinská et al. (eds.), *Labour Law and Social Security Law in Central and Eastern Europe*, European Union and its Neighbours in a Globalized World 26,
https://doi.org/10.1007/978-3-032-04496-9_13

share of the population that relies on long term care. According to recent prognoses, care demand will grow most in Southern and Eastern Europe, where populations are aging fast and disabilities are widespread among the elderly. Kotschy and Bloom predict, average increase in care demand of 47 percent with the largest increases in Southern and Eastern Europe.[4]

In September 2018, the EU Commission published a study on long-term care called 'Challenges in long-term care in Europe - A study of national policies 2018'.[5] The publication analyses the national long-term care policy in 35 European countries, with a focus on long-term care for the elderly (65 years or older).

According to the study, there is a clear trend towards home care and community-based care. As a result of this development, the number of residential nursing homes in some countries has fallen in the last 25 years. Particularly in the Nordic countries, which have a long tradition of residential care, there has been a discernible process of de-institutionalizing care services. A completely different picture can be seen in Eastern and Southern Europe, where residential care is growing. Another trend is the growing privatisation and commercialisation of care services.

Apart from this, national long-term care arrangements for people aged 65+ are substantially different in terms of organisation, funding and access to care services. Common challenges emerge in terms of quality assurance and informal care, which is mainly provided by women across all countries.

The report identifies four challenges which are common to all European countries:

- access and adequacy of long-term care services,
- quality of formal home care and residential services,
- the employment of informal carers, and
- the financial sustainability of national long-term care systems.

The implications of these trends are far-reaching for long-term care systems. They demand a re-assessment of current frameworks to accommodate a growing number of elderly individuals requiring assistance with daily living and healthcare. It's key element—emphasizing prevention and rehabilitation measures as promising avenues to promote individual wellbeing and absorb pressure from long-term care systems by improving the health of the elderly.[6]

At the same time, it's crucial to introduce effective measures of robust social protection in wider sense of the term, so that a complex system of health care, social services, social benefits and adequate labour law measures would be in place in next decades, when ageing of European populations will become an even hotter issue, than it is today.

LTC is a significant issue across Europe, highlighting notable differences between Eastern and Western European approaches. The growing demand for LTC

[4] Kotschy and Bloom (2022).

[5] Baeten et al. (2018).

[6] Kotschy and Bloom (2022).

raises critical concerns regarding gender equality, as caregiving responsibilities disproportionately fall on women, and challenges the integration of modern concepts in social and healthcare services. This chapter explores these dimensions and examines whether a unified European response to LTC challenges is both necessary and beneficial, especially given the substantial divergence between Central and Eastern European practices and Western policies.

To address this, selected long-term care insurance systems from various countries will be analysed, with a particular focus on determining whether these models can be effectively adapted and implemented in Central and Eastern European contexts. In this connection, a recently adopted complex Italian legislation on people with LTC needs will be introduced. The European Care Strategy as an EU response will be discussed in concluding part of this chapter.

2 LTC: Some Sources of Nightmare

There are already few comparative studies, which identify problems, that might be connected with LTC.

A very old and problematic one seems to be a fragmentation of LTC. According to Spasova, Baeten and Vanhercke access to and affordability of services can be hindered by the fragmentation of LTC. Their study argues, that in general, LTC provision and funding are split horizontally and vertically, i.e. between health care and social care as well as between territorial entities. Fragmentation of provision between health care services and social services often leads to a lack of coordination between entities, which in turn affects waiting periods and administrative procedures, or regional disparities in LTC provision.[7]

Second, there are access issues related to the underdevelopment of formal services, both for home care and community based LTC and residential care.

In connection to LTC, emphasis has been put on de-institutionalisation in research literature already from 1990s.[8] The Spasova's paper argues, that there are significant differences among EU countries. Home and community-based services are most developed in the Nordic countries (DK, FI, IS, NO, SE) and some Continental European countries (e.g. AT, BE, DE, FR, LU, NL). Eastern European countries (e.g. BG, CZ, EE, LV, LT, MK, PL, RO, RS, SI, SK) face insufficient availability of home care provision, or provision often targeted at persons with a high degree of dependency. In Eastern Europe, has been a slight but steady fall in the number of residential beds since the 2000s e.g. in LV, while in other countries there has been a certain increase in the number of residential beds (e.g. BG, EE, LT, RO). In both Southern and Eastern Europe, demand strongly exceeds supply for both institutional and home care provision.

[7] Spasova et al. (2018), pp. 7–12.

[8] Anttonen and Sipilä (1996), 87–100; Mansell and Ericsson (1996).

The quality of LTC is key to maintaining and improving the quality of life of frail older people, both in residential and home care settings. However, the requirements in place vary substantially according to the type of care, i.e. residential care or home care. Whereas the home care sector remains mostly unregulated, residential care is governed by stricter requirements. These quality control measures seem to be a first step to ensuring quality commitment, but in some countries there are problems in implementation due to limited resources, a lack of qualified inspectors and/or a lack of transparency in the process.

One of the main solutions proposed in national policy making and EU discourse is to develop access to home-based services in order to enable older people to live independently at home as long as possible.

In this connection, it should be recalled, that already in 1996 the Revised European Charter of Social Rights enshrined in its Art. 23 the right of elderly persons to "choose their life-style freely and to lead independent lives in their familiar surroundings for as long as they wish and are able, by means of provision of housing suited to their needs and their state of health or of adequate support for adapting their housing; b the health care and the services necessitated by their state."[9]

Availability and affordability of home-based services is a significant issue in most EU countries. In many cases, a person in need of LTC simply does not find a service, which would suit to own needs and preferences. As this chapter will later demonstrate, the shortage of services raises critical issues such as equal access to social security schemes for domestic workers and the right to freely choose a service provider. Relevant and noteworthy perspectives from the CJEU will be quoted in this regard.

There is a high incidence of informal care in most European countries. The main reasons for the high incidence of informal LTC are the shortage of accessible formal LTC facilities, the poor quality of LTC, the non-affordability of LTC, and, finally, the traditional model of intergenerational and family relations.[10]

Grages, Eggers and Frau-Effinger found out, that "against the background of demographic ageing and increasing female labour market participation, many European welfare states restructured their long-term care (LTC) policies for persons of age and persons with disabilities by strengthening social rights to receive publicly funded care and extending care infrastructure since the 1990s. Despite this trend, care by family members remains a relevant factor in care provision." The authors of the study argue that the position of welfare states reflects how far LTC policies may be associated with poverty risks, opportunities to exercise active citizenship and potential for gender equality.[11] In fact, LTC is gaining on importance in

---

[9] A detailed commentary of this important document available: Lukas (2021)

[10] Spasova et al. (2018).

[11] Grages et al. (2021).

a very intense way, so that also other authors use the concept of LTC to identify welfare state typology.[12]

LTC appears to be a highly dynamic field that, in many ways, reflects the recent trends and developments within European societies, particularly in the realm of social rights. One notable trend is the increasing significance of the gender dimension across various sectors, and LTC is no exception.

3 LTC: An Issue with Strong Gender Dimension

According to the study enacted in 2021, most European welfare states introduced new benefits or other forms of social security support for care-giving family members.[13] Most of them are women. The question remains, whether these instruments are robust enough to guarantee a real possibility to care after own family member. 1 in 3 Europeans are estimated to have caring responsibilities and over 9.1 million people, mostly women, work in the care sector. Unpaid care responsibilities keep around 7.7 million of women in Europe away from participating in the labour marked compared to only 450,000 men—almost all women in the EU are regular carers and 81% are daily carers.

In several countries where the social services network is underdeveloped, families are often left to manage the care of their dependent relatives on their own. Home care and assistance, in particular—due to the limited availability of institutional services—tend to fall predominantly on women, many of whom are migrants from third countries. This "informal solution" is especially prevalent in Italy and Spain. While less common, similar situations also exist in countries that joined the EU in 2004. However, many of these home caregivers operate under precarious conditions, often working semi-legally or without legal residence in the country they perform work.

Some years ago, Spain introduced a special social security scheme for domestic workers to improve their social situation and guarantee social protection to those workers. However, this scheme was brought to CJEU, as it did not provide access to all social protection measures to domestic workers. A female domestic worker, who was enrolled in the Special Scheme for Domestic Workers, has been prevented from contributing to unemployment scheme in order to obtain protection in respect of unemployment. Therefore, the domestic worker appealed against the decision of national authority, claiming, that the Spanish legislation gives rise to indirect discrimination on grounds of sex in social security matters as regards female domestic workers, who comprise almost all of that group of workers. Since the situation of domestic workers who have lost their jobs is not the same as that of workers who are

---

[12] Ariaans et al. (2021), pp. 609–617. This study identifies six types of welfare state on the basis of LTC concept: residual public system, private supply system, public supply system, evolving public supply system, need-based supply system, evolving private need-based system.

[13] Grages et al. (2021).

covered by social security, exclusion from unemployment protection means that those workers are also unable to obtain any other benefit or allowance that is dependent on entitlement to unemployment benefit having come to an end. According to the claimant, national legislation places those workers in a situation of social distress, which takes the form not only, directly, of not being able to obtain unemployment benefit, but also, indirectly, of not being able to obtain other types of social assistance.

CJEU confirmed the legal opinion of the claimant in this case and ruled that "a national provision that excludes unemployment benefits from the social security benefits granted to domestic workers by a statutory social security scheme, where that provision places female workers at a particular disadvantage in relation to male workers and is not justified by objective factors unrelated to any discrimination on grounds of sex."[14] Indirect gender discrimination has been therefore found to be in place.

This landmark ruling brought some optimism in a research debate on possibilities of EU law and its interpretation in favour of domestic workers and their social situation. Chieregado, for instance, argues, that „This case, therefore, meaningfully clarifies the potential of EU law in challenging any unjustified differential treatment of domestic workers, well beyond the scope of social security."[15] She concluded that "the judgment highlights that EU law can be a promising legal avenue to address the long-standing exclusion of domestic workers from national law, thus contributing to bringing national legislation more in line with the ILO Domestic Workers Convention and advancing domestic workers' demands for decent working conditions and full social protection.".[16]

In fact, the ILO Domestic Workers Convention seems to be an instrument of international law to be followed, especially in Europe, where the position of domestic workers in general is not satisfactory at all, due to precarious working conditions, inequalities and mistreatment. That is why, the author of this chapter already some time ago argued, that the EU shall consider a more intense encouraging of its Member States to ratify ILO Domestic Workers Convention.[17] In 2025, there are just 8 EU countries plus 2 EFTA countries, which ratified the Convention. None of them is from the group of Member States new in 2004. In combination with other instruments of the EU law, it could significantly contribute to social rights guarantees to domestic workers and as a result also to an improved situation of people in need of care.

In connection with assistance provided at home, another CJEU recent ruling[18] shall be recalled shortly as well. In the case where a ruling was published in December 2024 CJEU has been asked in principal, about how to find a balance

---

[14] Case C-389/20, *CJ v Tesorería General de la Seguridad Social (TGSS)*, ECLI:EU:C:2022:120.

[15] Chieregato (2022).

[16] Ibid.

[17] Koldinská (2018), pp. 420–431.

[18] Case C-518/22, *AP Assistenzprofis*, ECLI:EU:C:2023:956.

between protection against age discrimination, on the one hand, and protection against discrimination based on disability, on the other. A company specialising in providing assistance and advice to persons with disabilities was seeking personal assistants to help a 28-year-old female student in all areas of her everyday life. The job advertisement stated a preference for persons 'between 18 and 30 years old'. A candidate whose age is not within that range and whose job application was rejected felt discriminated against based on her age. In its judgment, the Court of Justice pointed out that the preference for personal assistants within a certain age range expressed by the disabled person is likely to promote respect for that person's right to self-determination and age requirement in this specific case did not constitute discrimination based on age. The Court ruled that: „taking account of the preference for a certain age range expressed by the disabled person in receipt of personal assistance services is likely to promote respect for that person's right to self-determination in the provision of those personal assistance services, inasmuch as it appears reasonable to expect that a person within the same age range as the disabled person will fit more easily in that person's personal, social and university circle."[19]

This ruling holds significant relevance to the topic of LTC, primarily because it marks the first time the CJEU applied the principle of self-determination in the provision of personal assistance services within the framework of EU anti-discrimination law. The case involved a conflict between two forms of the right to equal treatment, and the CJEU established a preference for the individual in a more vulnerable position—specifically, someone requiring assistance, or, in other words, long-term care.

4 LTC Public Insurance: An European "National" Solution

In connection with the above, it shall be mentioned, that in 2021, nursing professionals, home-based personal care workers were among the 19 occupations with high magnitude shortages in several EU Member States. Across Europe, there are challenges for care systems with respect to shortages of care workers, increasing skill requirements for care workers, barriers to universal and equitable access to care, and cost containment subject to adequate care quality. Most national LTC policies have shown to be insufficient to significantly reduce unmet needs for personal care. Moreover, a number of all people potentially in need of long-term care across the EU stands at 30.8 million people and is projected to rise by more than seven million people by 2050. Conversely, generous pensions are significantly associated with lower unmet needs, underscoring the importance of considering the likely adverse effects of future pension reforms.[20] At the same time, long-term care seems to be a still not fully discovered opportunity to boost economy.

[19] Ibid, para 65.

[20] Szenkurök et al. (2024).

In reaction to the above, several European countries have established public insurance systems specifically aimed at providing long-term care—long term care insurance (hereinafter "LTCI"). These systems vary significantly in their design, funding mechanisms, and the scope of services they cover. This diversity reflects each country's unique social, economic, and political context, as well as their healthcare infrastructure and policy priorities.

Although the LTCI system is considered a relatively effective tool in state policy for long-term care, only a small number of countries in Europe have implemented this system: specifically, Germany, the Netherlands, Luxembourg, Belgium (Flanders), and recently Slovenia. A short description of each of the existing LTCI systems follows, while some analytical comments will be provided at the end of this section.

4.1 Germany (Pflegeversicherung)

The longest experience with LTCI is apparently behind Germany, which introduced the LTCI in 1995. In a recent report of the German Ministry of Labour and Social Affairs, several scenarios of further financial development of the system are analysed, while the report concluded, that "social long-term care insurance should continue to cover the risk of needing long-term care as an independent, general risk of life, regardless of age. It should continue to ensure a long-term level of needs-based support for people in need of long-term care. The objectives that accompanied the introduction of long-term care insurance in 1995, and the principles on which social long-term care insurance is based continue to apply and are supplemented by the new principles of intergenerational equity, sustainability and demographic stability."[21]

The German long-term care insurance system, known as "Pflegeversicherung," is a mandatory insurance scheme introduced in 1995—Book XI of the German Social Code (Sozialgesetzbuch, SGB).[22] It provides comprehensive coverage for individuals requiring long-term care services due to illness, disability, or old age. Funded through contributions from both employees and employers, the system offers a range of benefits, including financial support for professional care, home care services, and assistance with daily activities.

The system is almost entirely financed by contributions and premiums. Contributions are income dependent. Anyone who is covered by statutory health insurance is legally covered by statutory LTCI. Anyone who is insured by a private health insurance company must take out private long term care insurance.

[21] Bundesregierung (2024).

[22] Sozialgesetzbuch, Elftes Buch, Soziale Pflegeversicherung. Availible via https://www.sozialgesetzbuch-sgb.de/sgbxi/1.html

LTC is managed by a number of LTCI funds. Remunerations for services are negotiated in advance between the "costbearers" and the service providers and not by the government. Formal care services are almost entirely provided by private for-profit and non-profit providers who have been contracted by LTCI funds. Semi-residential home providers are overwhelmingly private, with non-profit originations representing over half of all such homes. LTC in kind is only provided by those who are licensed and contracted by LTC insurers. The Arbitration board (Schiedsstelle) inspects annually the quality of home care and residential providers.

Eligibility for public LTC benefits is based on a qualifying period of at least 2 years of LTCI contribution within a decade prior to application. It is not dependent on the age of the person needing long-term care but is based on the level of need for long-term care. The need for long-term care is defined as exhibiting health-related restrictions to independence or abilities that require the help of others.

Long-term care insurance provides benefits both for care at home or in residential care homes by relatives or nursing services and for care in an inpatient facility by nursing staff.[23] Benefits can include benefits in cash and benefits in kind.

According to 2017 study, the program is widely accepted among citizens and has achieved many of its original goals: ensuring access to LTC services and reducing reliance on the locally-funded safety-net social assistance program, which can be used to cover nursing home costs.[24]

4.2 Netherlands

Long-term care insurance has a long tradition in the Netherlands, as the Netherlands was one of the first countries to introduce it—origins of long-term care insurance combined with health insurance lay already in 1960s. The current system is based on the 2015 reforms, when this insurance became independent from other types of public insurance.

The Dutch system for the provision of long-term care has been reformed from a national scheme covered by one law, the Exceptional Medical Expenses Act (Algemene Wet Bijzondere Ziektekosten, AWBZ) to create a system that is divided up among the municipal domain (the Social Support Act and Youth Act) for which municipalities receive a budget from the state; the national domain of the Long-term Care Act, which has a similar construction to the AWBZ; and the domain of the health insurers (Health Insurance Act), which is funded by health insurance premiums.[25]

In principle, the public national long-term care is funded by social security premiums and co-payments. The contribution is not fixed percentage of income as in

[23] Gesund.bund.de (2024).

[24] Nadash et al. (2017), pp. 588–597.

[25] Eurocareers (2023a).

other countries, but is calculated on the basis of the client's income, wealth, household, age and the type of care received.[26] The system is subsidised by the State.[27]

The system is administered by 32 regional care offices, which perform several functions, including the contracting of private provider organisations and the material control of provider organisations.[28]

The right to care is determined by the Care Assessment Center in an indication decision at the request of the insured. The right to care that is established in the indication decision is in line with the needs of the insured. Most care is delivered in kind, but clients can also choose to contract care through a personal budget scheme.[29]

The sustainability of the Dutch LTC system has been debated for quite some time. On one hand the system provides comprehensive coverage of long-term care expenditures, on the other hand, the system as such is very expansive, according to OECD probably most expansive in the world.[30] However, this primacy is probably due to the fact that formal care is used much more than informal care in the Netherlands, and the cost of informal care is not included in the total cost of LTC.[31] In fact, authors from the Netherlands in their report from 2023 argue that: "The findings reveal that no other country spends more per capita on publicly financed formal care than The Netherlands. A potential reason is that the threshold to receive formal care appears to be lower in the Netherlands than in other countries. Still, a considerable share of the adult population provides informal care. Caregiving is concentrated in specific demographic groups. The costs of informal care provision are considerable, but as a share of total spending on long term care they are smaller than in most developed countries. Adding the costs of informal care to formal care expenditures changes the view on who bears the costs of long-term care."[32] This, in fact, highlights the previously mentioned issue of gender imbalance in LTC, particularly concerning the provision of day-to-day care—whether in the formal care sector or as informal care provided at home. A 2018 report prepared for the European Commission emphasized the need to acknowledge the limitations of informal care and advocated for strategies to both enhance support for informal caregivers and ensure the provision of high-quality professional care where required, all while operating within budgetary constraints.[33] Moreover, Mot pleads for focusing on sustainability of the LTC as such, including sustainability of the insurance system. The fact that the system is universal and based on principle of solidarity is a great achievement for people in need of LTC.[34]

---

[26] Kelders and de Vaan (2018).

[27] European Commission (2021b).

[28] Eurocareers (2023a).

[29] Ibidem.

[30] OECD (2020).

[31] Bakx et al. (2023).

[32] Ibid.

[33] Ibid.

[34] Mot (2010).

4.3 Luxembourg

Luxembourg was one of the pioneering European countries in the development of an explicit pillar of LTCI.[35] It was indeed created in 1999—Book V of Luxembourg Social Security Code (Code de la Sécurité Sociale, CSS)—and was adapted in 2005,2017 and 2018. The goal of the insurance is to provide compensation for the expenses generated through third-party assistance to perform daily living activities.

The system prioritises rehabilitation measures over long-term care, at-home care over institutional care and in-kind services over cash benefits.

Contribution to the LTCI is mandatory. All (active or retired individuals) pay a dedicated contribution of 1.4% of all their income (i.e., wages, revenue, pension, income from an inheritance). This contribution is topped up by a State's participation (40% of the total expenditure) and by an obligatory contribution from the electricity sector. LTCI is managed by the National Health Fund of Luxembourg (Caisse Nationale de Santé).

Any person enrolled in health insurance scheme is fully insured against the risk of dependency, as are family members. Eligibility is based on need, with no conditions of income or age. To be eligible, a dependent person must be in a significant and a constant need of assistance from a third party for carrying out activities of daily living. The need for assistance must account for a minimum of 3.5 h per week, last at least 6 months and be indefinitely. The level of dependency is expressed in 15 levels, based on the amount of care required per week expressed in minutes and is determined by the attending physician.

Cash benefits are claimed by 79% of home care beneficiaries (16% opt only for cash benefits while 63% prefer a mixed scheme). Cash benefits do not exceed 10% of total expenditure on LTC. Some 67% of LTC expenditure goes on residential care and 33% on home care—the exact opposite of the number of beneficiaries (33% in residential care and 67% in home care).

Although the LTCI insurance for the elderly is defined at a high level of social protection, efficiency, cost containment and adequacy of care raise growing concerns among providers and trade unions.[36]

[35] Eurocareers (2023b).

[36] Eurocareers (2023b).

4.4 Belgium (Flanders)

Unlike in the other Belgian regions, long-term care insurance in Flanders is a separate insurance. Long-term care insurance is included in the so-called Flemish social protection system, in the Decree on Flemish social protection (Decreet houdende de Vlaamse sociale bescherming).[37]

Flemish social protection is funded through contributions and state support. In 2024, the amount of contribution is 62 euros (or 31 euros for people with a low income).[38] The amount is paid to one of the 6 recognized healhcere funds. It is mandatory for people aged 26 and above living in the Flemish Region and optional for inhabitants of the Brussels-Capital Region.[39] The Flemish government supplements the income from the care premiums with more than 2 billion euros (mainly to pay for care and personnel costs in elderly care, rehabilitation hospitals and facilities).

The core body of Flemish social protection is Flemish Social Protection Agency. The agency is responsible for financing a large part of the healthcare and personnel costs in elderly care (residential care centers, day care centers, etc.), provides policy support and develops regulations, recognizes, subsidizes and monitors the various healthcare funds etc.[40] The long insurance is administered by six funds, one of them established by the Flemish government.

To be eligible for a care budget for the severely dependent persons or for a care budget for elderly persons requiring care, the insured person must have resided 10 years (of which 5 years continuously) 5 years in the Flemish region or in the Brussels-Capital region and be member of an agreed insurance fund.[41] The beneficiary must also, depending on the intervention, either have a reduced self-sufficiency capacity within a residential, semi-residential or outpatient framework or have a recognised disability or be at least 65 years of age with a disability or a reduction in self-sufficiency. Medical examinations for the care budget for elderly needing assistance are still conducted at the federal level.

People in need of care receive a "care budget" which is a monthly allowance. There are different categories for the healthcare budget.

Healthcare budget for those in serious need of care is a healthcare budget of 140 euros/month for people who need a larger amount of care. These are, for

[37] Decreet Houdende de Vlaamse Sociale bescherming (2018). Availible via https://codex.vlaanderen.be/PrintDocument.ashx?id=1029649&geannoteerd=false#H1087890. Accessed 2 Jan 2025.

[38] Departement Zorg Over de Vlaamse Sociale bescherming. Availible via https://www.departementzorg.be/nl/over-de-vlaamse-sociale-bescherming. Accessed 2 Jan 2025

[39] Joining the Flemish Social Protection. In: Flanders.be. https://www.vlaanderen.be/en/joining-the-flemish-social-protection. Accessed 2 Jan 2025.

[40] Agentschap Vlaamse Sociale bescherming. In: Vlaanderen.be. https://www.vlaanderen.be/organisaties/administratieve-diensten-van-de-vlaamse-overheid/beleidsdomein-welzijn-volksgezondheid-en-gezin/departement-zorg/afdeling-vlaamse-sociale-bescherming/agentschap-vlaamse-sociale-bescherming. Accessed 2 Jan 2025

[41] European Commission (2024b).

example, elderly people who stay in a residential care center or people of all ages who need a lot of (possibly professional) support at home.

Care budget for the elderly with a care need is a budget for people over 65 with a care need. The amount of this budget depends on the income and the care burden of the older person. Care budget for people with disabilities is a monthly budget for both children and adults with a recognized disability who meet certain conditions. It is awarded automatically.

4.5 *Slovenia*

Long-term care insurance was introduced in Slovenia in 2023, when the new Long-Term Care Act (zakon o dolgotrajni oskrbi, ZDO)[42] came into force. The long-term care law was already prepared in 2021, but the referendum delayed its adoption.

The Slovenian LTCI establishes a budgetary source for financing long-term care and a contribution from employees and employers. Funds for LTC insurance will be collected similarly to health insurance contributions, whereby each (that is, employer and employee) will contribute 1% of the worker's salary. Special provisions apply to particular employment arrangements, for example, self-employed persons. Additionally, €190 million (approximately 0.4% of Slovenia's GDP) will be added annually from the State budget.[43]

LTC insurance is obligatory for all people insured in health insurance after they have reached the age of 18.[44] This could also apply for people under the age of 18, if they are required to have health insurance. The insurance is administered by Slovenian Health Insurance Institute (ZZZS).

According to some analysis, major challenge to the implementation of the Act in full is the timely and effective upgrade or establishment of LTC services foreseen in the Act, especially strengthening capacity for home care.[45]

Eligibility for benefits under the Long-Term Care Insurance (LTCI) system in Slovenia is granted to individuals who have been insured under LTCI for a minimum of 24 out of the preceding 36 months, have either permanent or temporary residency in Slovenia, and require assistance with basic or supportive daily activities for a period of no less than 3 months or on a permanent basis. Upon meeting these criteria, the beneficiary is classified into one of five levels of dependency or self-care limitations based on a points-based evaluation conducted by a long-term care consultant.

---

[42] Zakonodolgotrajnioskrbi(ZDOsk-1).Availibleviahttps://pisrs.si/pregledPredpisa?id=ZAKO8819

[43] World Health Organization (2023).

[44] Zavod za zdravstveno zavarovanje Slovenije. Vključitev v obvezno zavarovanje za dolgotrajno oskrbo. https://zavarovanec.zzzs.si/vkljucitev-v-obvezno-zavarovanje-za-dolgotrajno-oskrbo/. Accessed 2 Jan 2025

[45] World Health Organization (2023).

The insured has the right to non-monetary benefits, which may consist of e.g. day care in an institution or home care, or monetary benefits.

According to government estimates, the full set of services and the full costs of the new system will be apparent in 2026.[46] Total LTC expenditure is estimated to increase from 1.45% of GDP in 2020 to 1.72% of GDP in 2026. Private expenditure as a share of total LTC expenditure is expected to decrease from 24.1% to 18.7%.

4.6 LTCI: A Right Way?

The analysis of existing national long-term care insurance (LTCI) systems highlights several key considerations for the ongoing debate about whether LTCI represents the optimal approach to addressing long-term care needs or merely one relatively expensive component of a broader, necessary evolution of LTC.

The dual challenges of affordability and efficiency in meeting the increasing demand for long-term care must remain at the forefront of this discussion. While LTCI systems may indeed be costly, their significance cannot be understated, particularly when viewed through the prism of high-cost care scenarios—an area where valuable lessons can be drawn from health insurance systems.

A critical takeaway is the need to emphasize efficiency within these systems. Long-term care services have the potential to become as economically significant as health care, with their predictable cost structures offering a distinct advantage. However, achieving this potential will require targeted improvements in the financing of home care, ensuring higher quality and a broader range of options. These enhancements are essential not only to address present-day needs but also to prepare for the demands of the future in a sustainable and effective manner.

By leveraging the insights gained from health insurance and committing to efficient and comprehensive long-term care systems, countries can build a foundation for a more equitable and resilient care framework. In this context, LTCI is likely to serve as one of several interconnected components of an advanced and efficient LTC system. The Italian experience in implementing such a comprehensive approach, as detailed in the subsequent section of this chapter, merits close attention and thoughtful consideration.

[46] World Health Organization (2023).

5 A Complex Solution for Future LTC: Example of Italy

It seems to be clear that amending single pieces of national law or adding here or there a new benefit or service does not provide a complex response to all demands that the LTC need represents. The new law,[47] adopted in 2023 in Italy introduces the National System for the Non-Self-Sufficient Elderly Population (hereinafter "SNAA"). The law pursues important objectives, such as overcoming the current fragmentation of measures in this area and defining new intervention models, designed starting from the conditions of the elderly and their families and, therefore, able to respond appropriately to their complex and changing needs.

The SNAA provides—at central, regional and local level—for the integrated planning of all measures for non-self-sufficiency, divided between health, social services and monetary benefits. It is foreseen that in practice, the public actors involved jointly plan how to use all the dedicated resource. Recomposing fragmentation is a key objective.

The benefit ("elderly bonus") provided for in the Decree, has remained almost unchanged, but it is associated with an additional amount (850 euros per month per user). This respects an ancient Italian tradition of not reforming but adding something to the existing, leaving it as it is and layering the new on top of the old. Not only a high need for assistance but also reduced economic resources are required to receive the temporary service. The principle is thus introduced that one can benefit from assistance for non-self-sufficiency provided that, in addition to being in this state, one is also poor, while through welfare it is also necessary to support the middle classes. The extension of the benefit would have an exorbitant cost: 10.2 billion per year to provide it to all 80+ recipients of the accompanying allowance, 14.3 billion to all those 65+.

The Decree No. 29 defines the role of caregivers, identifies the methods of relationship with the operators of the social, social health and health services system at the various times and interventions that concern the non-self-sufficient relative, establishes the tasks of the Regions and provides for the involvement of caregiver associations in regional and national planning. Overall, a rather solid set of general indications emerges. Decree 29 does not provide for further acts called upon to translate them into practice—Decrees, Guidelines or anything else—because the subsequent steps on the subject will be part of the process of the Framework Law on Family Caregivers, currently under discussion.

The last objective consists in expanding the offer, in particular of personal services, which is rather scarce in Italy. The reform would require an additional 6–8 billion per year when fully operational. Still, first opinions on this reform argue, that the decisive junction consists in the ability to redesign welfare to enable it to respond effectively to the growing presence of non-self-sufficient elderly people, in

[47] Legge 23 marzo 2023, n. 33 "Deleghe al Governo in materia di Politiche in favore delle persone anziane".

increasingly complex conditions.[48] The new Italian system is worth close attention in the future.

6 EU Response so far…

In 2022, the European Commission has presented the European Care Strategy to ensure quality, affordable and accessible care services across the European Union and improve the situation for both care receivers and the people caring for them, professionally or informally.[49]

When reading the European LTC strategy, it's interesting to notice that there is no proposal to further develop work-life balance legislation. In fact, the WLB directive of 5 days of care leave for people with caring responsibilities seems to be insufficient.

The strategy considers not only elderly care, but also child care. Both types of care are reflected together, as there are many aspects in common.

In its document, the Commission proposed concrete actions to support Member States in increasing access to high-quality and affordable care services, while improving working conditions and work-life balance for carers.

The proposed measures are as follows:

- Ensuring that long-term care is timely, comprehensive and affordable, allowing a decent standard of living for people with long-term care needs;
- Increasing the offer and mix of professional long-term care services (homecare, community-based care and residential care), close territorial gaps in the access to long-term care, roll-out accessible digital solutions in the provision of care services, and ensure that long-term care services and facilities are accessible to people with disabilities;
- Ensuring high-quality criteria and standards for long-term care providers;
- Supporting informal carers, who are often women and relatives of care receivers, through training, counselling, psychological and financial support; and
- Mobilising adequate and sustainable funding for long-term care, including by using EU funds.

[48] Patto per un Nuovo Welfare sulla Non Autosufficienza (2024).

[49] In connection with the „Europeanisation"of the debate on LTC, Tinos and Valvis are proposing to introduce a simple new 4-scale measure of care needs which, by combining the two metrics of ADL (Activities of Daily Living) and GALI (Global Activity Limitation Index), introduces some gradation of the intensity of care. Using a consistent measure incorporating intensity, such as the one proposed, will facilitate international comparisons, improve long-term expenditure projections, and aid policy discussion, including the transfer of best practice. See https://www.tandfonline.com/doi/full/10.1080/08959420.2022.2110810

To improve working conditions[50] and attract more people—in particular men—to the care sector, Member States are recommended to:

- promote collective bargaining and social dialogue with a view to improving wages and working conditions
- ensure the highest standards of occupational health and safety
- design continuous education and training for care workers
- tackle gender stereotypes around care and launch communication campaigns
- ratify and implement ILO Convention 189 on domestic worker

The Commission's proposals for Council Recommendations are being discussed by Member States with a view to adoption by the Council. According to the Commission proposals, Member States should inform the Commission on measures to implement the Recommendations 1 year after adoption. For each Recommendation, the Commission shall publish an in-depth report within 5 years to give an overview of the state of play of implementation.[51]

Even if the European Care Strategy is just a strategy and therefore there are no binding legal measures foreseen in the near future, it's significant that the topic of long term care has a dedicated document at the EU level. Underlining attention to LTC services and, especially, the work conditions of paid care workers, together with equality principle and gender dimension seems to be a positive and concrete step forward. It helps especially to start an European reflection on this very important topic and provide a concise EU policy in the future, instead of fragmented and isolated solutions across European countries.[52] Also Caracciolo Di Torella and Masselot argued, that the regulation of care by the EU is crucial because it enables the development of a broad range of policies. It contributes to the sustainability of society and ultimately it enables individuals to flourish.[53]

The research literature providing first analysis and evaluation of the European Care strategy points out, that ECS considers the broader infrastructure—especially from the perspective of a service mix—but it is largely accepting the status quo in regard to social protection and deep systemic reliance on informal care and unpaid carers. Daly says for instance, that the European Care Strategy is adjudged to rely on an economistic approach. This sees it suggest some important measures for better services and working conditions for care workers but not enough on social protection rights and too little to disrupt the reliance on unpaid carers. Comparing the European Union approach with that of several United Nations entities—the International Labour Organization, World Health Organization and UN Women—indicates that other approaches are possible, though all need improvement.[54] UN

[50] In this connection. Trojansky points out, there might be some serious risks for working conditions of platform workers working in LTC sector. See https://www.eesc.europa.eu/sites/default/files/files/qe-02-20-092-en-n.pdf

[51] European Commission (2022).

[52] Zacharenko and Elomäki (2022), pp. 1314–1335.

[53] Caracciolo di Torella and Masselot (2020).

[54] Daly (2023), pp. 1–16.

organisations focus much more strongly on social protection and reforming the broader care configuration (though it must be said that their remit allows them to be more light touch in regard to the details and implementation of provision).

Dely concludes by suggesting to promote a 'care-first' perspective, which would move towards a society wherein people would give and receive care on the basis of their capacities and needs, and where there would be action from governments at all levels to support and value care as labour activity and a relational orientation.[55] The above mentioned example from Italy seems to opt, as least partially, for this approach.

7 Conclusions: LTC not a Nightmare, but an Opportunity

Long-term care (LTC) presents a growing challenge for European societies, but it also offers an opportunity to create more inclusive, sustainable systems of care that better reflect the demographic realities of an aging population. While introducing long-term care insurance (LTCI) in various countries can be a critical step toward improving access and coverage, it is far from a comprehensive solution. A holistic approach that addresses multiple dimensions of care provision is essential for ensuring effective and equitable LTC across the European Union.

A truly European approach to LTC requires more than comparative studies—it demands coordinated action. While initial steps, such as the 5-day carer's leave introduced in the Work-Life Balance Directive, offer some support to families balancing work and caregiving responsibilities, this is insufficient. Greater efforts are needed to enable meaningful reconciliation of professional and caregiving roles, especially as informal care will remain a crucial element of LTC for the foreseeable future.

Furthermore, enhancing the position of domestic workers, who often bear the brunt of informal care provision, is essential. The International Labour Organization (ILO) has laid important groundwork in protecting domestic workers' rights, but the EU is well-positioned to strengthen these protections further, ensuring fair treatment and decent working conditions.

Equally important is planning for a substantial expansion of home care—both formal and informal—as well as developing community-based care options for individuals who, for various reasons, cannot or do not wish to remain in their homes. Such models can provide flexibility, preserve dignity, and reduce the pressure on institutional facilities.

Health care reform is another critical component of this comprehensive approach. Too often, health and social services operate in silos, which can lead to a premature or unnecessary dependency on long-term care services. Bridging this gap through

[55] Ibid.

integrated health and social care systems can prevent dependency and promote greater autonomy among elderly and vulnerable populations.

Lastly, consideration should be given to introducing the concept of social rehabilitation. After acute care needs have been addressed, combining health and social services to restore a person's self-sufficiency can significantly reduce long-term dependency. The exchange of good practices and increased cooperation on the EU level could play a key role in fostering innovation and effective solutions in this area.

In conclusion, while long-term care may currently seem like a looming nightmare for Europe, it need not remain so. With a comprehensive, coordinated, and forward-thinking approach, the EU can transform this challenge into an opportunity—ensuring that aging populations are met with dignity, autonomy, and well-supported care systems. By addressing the shortcomings in insurance, domestic work protections, care integration, and social rehabilitation, Europe can pave the way for a future where long-term care is no longer a burden, but a testament to social solidarity and shared responsibility.

References

Anttonen A, Sipilä J (1996) European social care services: is it possible to identify models? J Eur Soc Policy 6(2):87–100

Ariaans M, Linden P, Wendt C (2021) Worlds of long-term care: a typology of OECD countries. Health Policy 125:609–617. https://doi.org/10.1016/j.healthpol.2021.02.009

Baeten R, Coster S, Ghailani D et al (2018) Challenges in long-term care in Europe: a study of national policies. Publications Office of the European Union, Luxembourg

Bakx P, Van Doorslaer E, Wouterse B (2023) Long-term care in the Netherlands. National Bureau of Economic Research. https://doi.org/10.3386/w31823

Bundesregierung (2024) Bericht der Bundesregierung Zukunftssichere Finanzierung der sozialen Pflegeversicherung – Darstellung von Szenarien und Stellschrauben möglicher Reformen. Availible via https://www.bundesgesundheitsministerium.de/fileadmin/Dateien/5_Publikationen/Pflege/Berichte/Bericht_Zukunftssichere_Finanzierung_der_SPV-2024.pdf. Accessed 2 Jan 2025

Caracciolo di Torella E, Masselot A (2020) Caring responsibilities in European law and policy: Who cares? Routledge, Abingdon

Chieregato E (2022) The role of EU law in challenging the unjustified differential treatment of domestic workers: An analysis of the court of justice decision in CJ V Tesorería general de la seguridad social (TGSS) (C-389/20). SSRN Electron J. https://doi.org/10.2139/ssrn.4259778

Daly M (2023) Long-term care as a policy issue for the European Union and United Nations organisations. Int J Care Caring 9:1–16. https://doi.org/10.1332/239788221x16887213701095

Departement Zorg Over de Vlaamse Sociale bescherming. Availible via https://www.departement-zorg.be/nl/over-de-vlaamse-sociale-bescherming. Accessed 2 Jan 2025

Eurocareers (2023a) The Netherlands. Availible via https://eurocarers.org/country-profiles/netherlands/. Accessed 2 Jan 2025

Eurocareers (2023b) Luxembourg. Availible via https://eurocarers.org/country-profiles/luxembourg/. Accessed 2 Jan 2025

European Commission (2021a). The 2021 ageing report: economic and budgetary projections for the EU Member States (2019–2070). Availible via https://economy-finance.ec.europa.eu/publications/2021-ageing-report-economic-and-budgetary-projections-eu-member-states-2019-2070_en. Accessed 2 Jan 2025

European Commission (2021b) Long-term care report: trends, challenges and opportunities in an ageing society, Country profiles, vol II. Publications Office of the European Union, Luxembourg. Availible via https://op.europa.eu/en/publication-detail/-/publication/b39728e3-cd83-11eb-ac72-01aa75ed71a1
European Commission (2022) A European care strategy for caregivers and care receivers. In: Employment, social affairs and inclusion. https://employment-social-affairs.ec.europa.eu/news/european-care-strategy-caregivers-and-care-receivers-2022-09-07_en. Accessed 2 Jan 2025
European Commission (2024a) Belgium. In: Employment, social affairs and inclusion. https://employment-social-affairs.ec.europa.eu/policies-and-activities/moving-working-europe/eu-social-security-coordination/your-rights-country-country/belgium_en. Accessed 12 Jan 2025
European Commission (2024b) The 2024 ageing report: economic and budgetary projections for the EU Member States (2019–2070). Availible via https://economy-finance.ec.europa.eu/publications/2024-ageing-report-economic-and-budgetary-projections-eu-member-states-2022-2070_en. Accessed 2 Jan 2025
Eurostat (2024) Statistics explained. Population structure and ageing. Availible via https://ec.europa.eu/eurostat/statistics-explained/index.php?title=Population_structure_and_ageing#Past_and_future_population_ageing_trends_in_the_EU. Accessed 2 Jan 2025
Gesund.bund.de (2024) Long-term care insurance: coverage for people who need long-term care. In: Long-term care insurance: coverage for people who need long-term care. https://gesund.bund.de/en/long-term-care-insurance#benefits. Accessed 2 Jan 2025
Grages C, Eggers T, Pfau-Effinger B (2021) Long-term care regimes in Europe. EUROSHIP Working Paper No. 6, Oslo. https://doi.org/10.6084/m9.figshare.16782868. https://euroship-research.eu/publications
Kelders Y, de Vaan K (2018) ESPN thematic report on challenges in long-term care – Netherlands. Availible via https://ec.europa.eu/social/BlobServlet?docId=19861&langId=en. Accessed 2 Jan 2025
Koldinská K (2018) ILO pioneering on domestic workers – migrant women issues. Hung J Leg Stud 59:420–431. https://doi.org/10.1556/2052.2018.59.4.6
Kotschy R, Bloom DE (2022) A comparative perspective on long-term care systems. IZA – Institute of Labor Economics, Bonn. Availible via https://docs.iza.org/dp15228.pdf. Accessed 2 Jan 2025
Lukas K (2021) The revised European social charter: an article by Article Commentary. Edward Elgar Publishing Limited, Cheltenham. https://www.e-elgar.com/shop/gbp/the-revised-european-social-charter-9781789903638.html?srsltid=AfmBOoqpa8X%2D%2D2_lepIa9fkRMCxsuAPTFNpUfJ9W_3eJbk04MwBwZ4Lw
Mansell J, Ericsson K (1996) Deinstitutionalization and community living: intellectual disability services in Britain. Chapman & Hall, Scandinavia
Mot E (2010) The Dutch system of long-term care. Centraal Planbureau, Den Haag. Availible via https://www.cpb.nl/sites/default/files/publicaties/download/dutch-system-long-term-care.pdf. Accessed 2 Jan 2025
Nadash P, Doty P, von Schwanenflügel M (2017) The German long-term care insurance program: evolution and recent developments. Gerontologist 58:588–597. https://doi.org/10.1093/geront/gnx018
OECD (2020) Spending on long-term care. Availible via https://www.oecd.org/en/publications/spending-on-long-term-care_e1f00970-en.html. Accessed 2 Jan 2025
Patto per un Nuovo Welfare sulla Non Autosufficienza (2024) Alla ricerca del futuro - La riforma dell'assistenza agli anziani non autosufficienti. Availible via https://www.pattononautosufficienza.it/wp-content/uploads/2024/10/VOLUME_PATTO_online_definitivo.pdf Accessed 2 Jan 2025
Spasova S, Baeten R, Vanhercke B (2018) Challenges in long-term care in Europe. Eurohealth Observer 24:7–12. Available via https://iris.who.int/bitstream/handle/10665/332533/Eurohealth-24-4-7-12-eng.pdf. Accessed 2 Jan 2025

Szenkurök V, Weber D, Bilger M (2024) Informal and formal long-term care utilization and unmet needs in Europe: examining socioeconomic disparities and the role of social policies for older adults. Int J Health Econ Manag 25:87. https://doi.org/10.1007/s10754-024-09378-z

World Health Organization (2023) European Observatory on Health Systems and Policies. Adoption of a new Long-Term Care Act. Avalible via: https://eurohealthobservatory.who.int/monitors/health-systems-monitor/analyses/hspm/slovenia-2022/adoption-of-a-new-long-term-care-act-(2023). Accessed 2 Jan 2025

Zacharenko E, Elomäki A (2022) Constructions of care in EU economic, social, and gender equality policy: care providers and care recipients versus the needs of the economy? Soc Polit Int Stud Gender State Soc 29:1314–1335. https://doi.org/10.1093/sp/jxac014

Social Rights of Temporary Protected Persons in the EU: Current Challenges and Further Perspectives

Alla Fedorova

1 Introduction

Russian large-scale military aggression against Ukraine has caused the largest internal and external influx of displaced persons since World War II and has changed the situation with the ensuring human rights of displaced persons in Europe dramatically and fundamentally. The first several months of Russian invasion turned Ukraine into a world leader by the numbers of people who left its territory. Indeed, during only the first 12 days of the war more than two million people entered the EU

The material is prepared within the implementation of the project "The Approximation of Ukrainian Social and Labour Legislation to EU Law" (ID number 1233330) at the Faculty of Law, Palacký University in Olomouc (Czech Republic) under supervision of Ondrej Hamuľák. This project has received funding through the MSCA4Ukraine project, which is funded by the European Union. Views and opinions expressed are however those of the author only and do not necessarily reflect those of the European Union or any other organisations and institutions where the author is a member. Neither the European Union nor the MSCA4Ukraine Consortium as a whole, nor any individual member institutions of the MSCA4Ukraine Consortium as well as other organisations can be held responsible for them.

A. Fedorova (✉)
Faculty of Law, Palacký University, Olomouc, Czechia

Institute of International Relations, Taras Shevchenko National University of Kyiv, Kyiv, Ukraine
e-mail: alla.fedorova@upol.cz

K. Koldinská et al. (eds.), *Labour Law and Social Security Law in Central and Eastern Europe*, European Union and its Neighbours in a Globalized World 26,
https://doi.org/10.1007/978-3-032-04496-9_14

fleeing the war in Ukraine.[1] By the end of April 2024 (2 years since the beginning of the war) six million people have been recorded in European countries, including more than 4.2 million people who have obtained temporary protection in the EU states.[2] Figures show that the total number of people that fled the war in Ukraine to Europe is more than the population of almost every second EU state, such as Finland or Denmark, Croatia[3] and this numbers could increase, taking into account the continuation of the war and free visa regime for Ukrainians with the EU.

Moving across the borders and seeking protection on the territory of other countries, people can apply for different types of protection, including temporary protection. Despite the type of protection requested, one of the main questions that arose for the majority of displaced persons beyond safety reasons is protection and realisation of their basic social rights, such as rights to housing or shelter, food, medical care, social assistance etc. Considering the activation of the EU Temporary Protection Directive, the ability and obligations of EU countries to protect and ensure social rights of millions of temporary protected persons (hereinafter, "TPPs") fled the war in Ukraine received a significant concern in Europe and become a burning issue in the region for the discussion and scrutinization.

Being provided at national level, temporary protection is understood as more uncertain and unclear form of protection in case of mass influxes of displaced persons with a variety of different regimes established and regulated by states themselves. It has never been a point of particular attention of scholars, especially in the sphere of social rights of temporary protected persons and the existence or potential scope of international states' obligations to protect TPPs social rights, despite several publications on this issue in general aspect[4] and several researches devoted to the peculiarities of national regimes of temporary protection in different countries. For example, protection for Syrians in Turkey,[5] temporary protection for displaced persons from Balkan countries during the war in former Yugoslavia[6] or possibility of the implementation and activation of the Temporary Protection Directive 2001/55/EC.[7]

Russia's full-scale military aggression against Ukraine radically changed not only the real life of at least the whole Europe, but also the theoretical views and approaches on temporary protection, including those related to feasibility of the EU Temporary Protection Directive's activation. Despite the raise of academics'

---

[1] Operational data portal. Ukraine refugee situation. Ukraine. Flash update # 1.8 March 2022. Available at: https://data.unhcr.org/en/situations/ukraine

[2] UNHCR, Operational data portal. Ukraine refugee situation. Updated 19 April 2024. Available at: https://data.unhcr.org/en/situations/ukraine

[3] Eurostat. The number of persons having their usual residence in a country on 11/07/2022. Available at: https://ec.europa.eu/eurostat/databrowser/view/TPS00001/bookmark/table?lang=en&bookmarkId=c0aa2b16-607c-4429-abb3-a4c8d74f7d1e

[4] Ineli-Ciger (2018), Ineli-Ciger (2016), Durieux (2021), Marston (2003).

[5] Zenginkuzucu (2021), pp. 385–410

[6] Fitzpatrick (2000), pp. 279–306.

[7] Bauloz et al. (2015); Ineli-Ciger (2016); Kresic (2020).

general interest to the issue and publishment of the new papers and rare researches,[8] the social aspect is still underestimated.[9] Considering the amount of temporary protected persons in the EU countries, unexpected heavy burden to their national social security systems, challenges to both their social policy and EU social and asylum policies, social issues of temporary protection in Europe have been brought into the focus. At the same time the EU Directive gives states broad margin of appreciation, underlined only minimum scope of EU states' obligations to assist and support temporary protected persons that actualise the necessity of their interpretation according to the EU Directive and compare obligations under the Directive with obligations under international human rights treaties in this sphere, considering their ratification by the vast majority of the EU states.

Therefore, the purpose of this article is to analyse the social obligations that the EU states have under the EU Temporary Protection Directive, taking into consideration the key tendencies and current changes in national legislation and policy of the EU countries through the lens of its implementation. The article also focuses on international obligations that the EU states could have under international instruments in the context of TPPs social protection, including the European Social Charter and their correlation with the scope of social rights that EU states guarantee to TPPs in accordance with the EU Directive. Moreover, taking into account the maximum duration of temporary protection under the EU Directive, the perspectives of elaboration the approaches to further social support of TPPs after 2025 should also be outlined.

Consequently, the article has several main parts. The first part examines the social obligations under the EU Temporary Protection Directive, examples of national legislation adopted due to the regulation of temporary protection for people fleeing the war in Ukraine and the changes that have been already made within the 2 years. The second part is devoted to other states' obligations in the sphere of social rights according to the international treaties, in particular, the European Social Charter. The correlation of international obligations and the assessment of the national legislative tendencies helps to outline the ways of evolution of EU states' social obligations for TTPs protection and formulate the conclusions on the minimum implicit obligations and conformity of current national legislation with the EU Directive and international standards as well as underline the slippery path for the EU countries and the EU itself due to reduction of social support of TPPs and the necessity of providing further social support for vulnerable TPPs.

---

[8] Carrara et al. (2022).

[9] Only few papers were published that not covered all aspects of the topic. For example Motte-Baumvol et al. (2022).

2 EU States' Social Obligations Under the EU Temporary Protection Directive

Considering the understanding of temporary protection as exceptional measures in case of unexpected mass influxes that states provide at national level, at the end of previous century some EU countries granted the temporary protection status for some categories of people from former Yugoslavia (Bosnians and later, for people from Kosovo) at their national level which was characterised by application of various criteria, different scope of rights and regimes[10] etc.

This variability of temporary regimes within the EU territory inevitably led to the elaboration of the EU common approach of temporary protection that was enshrined in the EU specific Temporary Protection Directive 2001/55/EC. Later, in spite of several official attempts of its activation initiated by Italy and Malta during the migration crises in EU (in particular in some countries of the EU such as Italy, Greece, Malta), the appropriate decision had not been adopted.[11] Scientists had identified at least several reasons for EU negative decisions on activation of the Directive. Meltem Ineli-Ciger underlined that the EU officials and national governments of the majority of EU member states did not recognize the situations with refugees in 2011 or 2015 as the mass influx, moreover, the states that were not affected by the arrived refugees, consequently had not been ready to share the burden, had been afraid of potential "pull factor" of the Directive for migrants, that made abundantly clear inability to find the qualified majority of votes for the activation decision as well as solidarity among the EU countries on this issue.[12] She also logically presumed that "under the current asylum trends in Europe, the chances of the Directive being implemented in the future are slim".[13] It would be necessary to fully agree with such an assertion, but only before the full-scale Russia's military aggression against Ukraine.

After the first hours of the beginning of Russian large-scale military invasion of Ukraine, thousands of people have been moving to Ukrainian boarders with the EU countries. 4 March 2022, 10 days from the beginning of the war, the Temporary Protection Directive 2001/55/EC has been activated by the Council's decision for the first time since its adoption in 2001 as the only choice to protect Europe from massive humanitarian catastrophe. Indeed, this form of protection became the quickest and the most effective EU reaction to mass influx of displaced people from Ukraine and the most appropriate solution for the protection of the EU from the refugee and humanitarian crisis in Europe that EU has never encountered in its entire history.

In paragraph 6 of the Council Implementing Decision initial estimation of the potential numbers of displaced people was given as "between 2,5 million and 6,5

---

[10] Koser and Black (1999), p. 535.

[11] Fedorova (2022), pp. 333–362.

[12] Ineli-Ciger (2015), pp. 241–242.

[13] Ibid., p. 242.

million as a consequence of the armed conflict, of whom it is anticipated that between 1,2 and 3,2 million would be persons seeking international protection". The estimation of the United Nations High Commissioner for Refugees under the worst-case scenario was also added, showing the maximum amount of four million persons fleeing the territory of Ukraine.[14] However, all potential assessments had been underestimated. During only the first 12 days of the war more than two million people entered the EU fleeing the war in Ukraine.[15] Two years since the beginning of the war, 4.3 million Ukrainians have become the temporary protected persons in different EU countries.[16]

During this period a range of questions has arisen in both theoretical and practical sides, such as the possibility to obtain temporary protection or other status for people who stayed in the EU without appropriate permission before the war had started, persons who violated the migration rules before or for persons from Ukraine with the citizenship of one of the EU countries (as it was in cases of Ukrainian Roma people with Hungarian citizenship in the Czech Republic[17]) etc. However, the vast majority of issues that have arisen in the context of temporary protected persons from Ukraine as well as of any other group of displaced persons, concerned social support and protection. Considering the fact that many of TPPs have lost everything due to the war, they need a safe and adequate place to live, clothing, food, means of livelihood, accession to medical care, possibility to attend the local schools for children, or find jobs for workable age adults etc. The most important issues for staying in dignity for every TPP concerns primarily the social sphere and social rights.

Therefore, host states have to guarantee a range of social rights for people who have been granted the status of TPP. And the realisation of the basic rights of three categories of persons displaced from Ukraine at least at minimum level according to the Council decision became one of the key issues for the EU states in addition to granting of the appropriate temporary permission to stay within the territory of the host EU state.

The minimum states' obligations in the social sphere were clearly specified in the EU Temporary Protection Directive. According to the Directive, the EU states must ensure at least: access to suitable accommodation or receiving the means to obtain housing (para. 1 Article 13); medical care at least emergency care and essential treatment of illness (para. 2 Article 13); necessary assistance in terms of social

[14] Council Implementing Decision (EU) 2022/382 of 4 March 2022 establishing the existence of a mass influx of displaced persons from Ukraine within the meaning of Article 5 of Directive 2001/55/EC, and having the effect of introducing temporary protection, *OJ L 71, 4.3.2022, p. 1–6.* Available at: https://eur-lex.europa.eu/legal-content/EN/TXT/?uri=celex:32022D0382

[15] Operational data portal. Ukraine refugee situation. Ukraine situation. Flash update # 1.8 March 2022. Available at: https://data.unhcr.org/en/situations/ukraine

[16] Eurostat, Number of temporary protected people at 4.3 million. 8 March, 2024. Available at: https://ec.europa.eu/eurostat/web/products-eurostat-news/w/ddn-20240308-3

[17] See, for example, Zdeněk (2022).

welfare and means of subsistence (para 2 Article 13).[18] At the same time, all mentioned social assistance and allowance benefits in the Directive would be provided for TPPs without sufficient resources (Article 13). The same restricted approach can be defined in the context of housing due to obtaining the means for it by the TPPs in case of necessity, that can be understood as a lack of state obligation to guarantee appropriate housing for all temporary protected persons.

The Directive also includes the right to access to labour market of the host country and self-employed activities, taking into account their ability to meet their own needs (article 13); right to education on the same conditions that nationals have (article 14); right to medical and other assistance for persons with special needs and some other rights as the right to family reunification.

Given the interpretation of "adequate protection", the Commission underlined in the Operational guidelines that according to "the respect for human dignity, a dignified standard of living has to be ensured in respect of everyone",[19] including access to means of subsistence and accommodation, emergency care and adequate care for minors. This is the only provision related to social rights in the Guidelines. The special attention in the Guidelines was also drawn to the children's rights in line with the UN Convention on the Rights of the child, the EU Strategy on the rights of the child and relevant EU acquis. It was stated that "full protection to the specific rights of children, including… wellbeing of all children fleeing from the Ukrainian conflict, must be ensured by the host state".[20]

Therefore, no explanations have been given to the brief provisions of the Directive on social rights of TPPs. Presumably, this might be due EU competence in social issues. Considering the fact that social sphere is commonly understood as a national phenomenon, this sphere belongs to EU competence to take measures to ensure coordination of Member States' social policies and, in some limited issues, it is a shared competence between the EU and its Member States.[21] In general, this means that social policy has continued to be predominantly the responsibility of EU countries themselves, as evidenced by a variety of national social security and pension systems.

[18] Council Directive 2001/55/EC of 20 July 2001 on minimum standards for giving temporary protection in the event of a mass influx of displaced persons and on measures promoting a balance of efforts between Member States in receiving such persons and bearing the consequences thereof. *OJ L 212, 7.8.2001, p. 12–23.* Available at: https://eur-lex.europa.eu/legal-content/en/TXT/?uri=celex:32001L0055

[19] European Commission (2022) Communication from the Commission on Operational guidelines for the implementation of Council implementing Decision 2022/382 establishing the existence of a mass influx of displaced persons from Ukraine within the meaning of Article 5 of Directive 2001/55/EC, and having the effect of introducing temporary protection 2022/C 126 I/01, *OJ C 126I, 21.3.2022, p. 1–16.* Available at: https://eur-lex.europa.eu/legal-content/EN/TXT/?uri=CELEX%3A52022XC0321%2803%29

[20] Ibid.

[21] Consolidated version of the Treaty on the Functioning of the European Union, articles 4–6. 2007. *Official Journal C 326, 26/10/2012 P. 0001–0390.* Available at: https://eur-lex.europa.eu/legal-content/EN/TXT/?uri=celex%3A12012E%2FTXT

Naturally, aforementioned issues were reflected in the variable social packages for TPPs. In the first year of the war, Bulgaria provided TPPs with accommodation and meals in hotels that agreed to this program with a compensation from the state[22]; in Austria, in addition to social allowance, TPPs were offered free accommodation and meal either at an organised federal government accommodation or regional centers[23]; long term providing of housing, social support and free medical insurance were proposed for TPPs in the Czech Republic,[24] while Greek and Slovak governments that decided not to provide TPPs with social housing at all, allowed TPPs to apply for different forms of housing that exist in the country, mostly on payable conditions.[25] Social allowance for TPPs in Germany in the amount of up to 459 euro per person was provided exclusively depending on the needs and status of the temporary protected person; in the Netherlands TPPs had the right to receive 260 euro during the period of only 3 months; the financial assistance of circa 115 euro per month during 3 months for temporary protected persons was organized in Romania.[26] Unique approach for granting the social benefit was implemented in Bulgaria. In order to receive social assistance in the amount of 20 euro per day in this county a temporary protected workable age person had to perform community service for at least 4 h during 14 days per month.[27] Some states, as Spain, provided TPPs without resources only with free lunch and dinner services in public canteens.[28] After activation of the Directive each state has elaborated its own mechanism of TPPs social

[22] Check-list of the minimum standards for the social protection of the displaced persons from third countries who cannot return to their country of origin that are guaranteed by the members states of the European Union and the Council of Europe within their European integration obligations. Analysis prepared by the male and female experts of the Non-Governmental Organisation “Ukrainian Centre for Social and Legal Research”: Myroslava Buk, Volodymyr Burak, Mariia Vashchyshyn, Oksana Hirnyk-Ivanochko, Iryna Lasko, Tetiana Parpan, Olena Rym, Svitlana Synchuk, Oksana Stasiv (2022).

[23] Ukrainische Flüchtlinge – Krankenversicherung, 2022. Available at: https://www.gesundheitskasse.at/cdscontent/?contentid=10007.884366&portal=oegkportal

[24] Lex Ukrajina, Zákon o některých opatřeních v souvislosti s ozbrojeným konfliktem na území Ukrajiny vyvolaným invazí vojsk Ruské federace, Available at: https://www.zakonyprolidi.cz/cs/2022-65/monitor?g=12129955

[25] FRA, National legislation implementing the EU Temporary Protection Directive in selected EU Member States (October 2022 Update). Available at: https://fra.europa.eu/en/publication/2022/national-legislation-implementing-eu-temporary-protection-directive-selected-eu-0

[26] Ibid.

[27] Bulgaria for Ukraine, Assistance for displaced persons from Ukraine. Social support. Available at: https://ukraine.gov.bg/social-support/

[28] Check-list of the minimum standards for the social protection of the displaced persons from third countries who cannot return to their country of origin that are guaranteed by the members states of the European Union and the Council of Europe within their European integration obligations. Analysis prepared by the male and female experts of the Non-Governmental Organisation “Ukrainian Centre for Social and Legal Research”: Myroslava Buk, Volodymyr Burak, Mariia Vashchyshyn, Oksana Hirnyk-Ivanochko, Iryna Lasko, Tetiana Parpan, Olena Rym, Svitlana Synchuk, Oksana Stasiv—within the Council of Europe Project “Continued support to promoting social human rights in Ukraine” (2022).

protection, promptly adopted special Laws (e.g., in the Czech Republic, Italy, Germany), governmental or ministerial acts (Poland, Slovakia, France) or decisions of administrative authority (Malta).[29] Usually, for legal regulation of the detailed procedure, granting social rights and benefits specific legislative documents have been adopted by states, including Switzerland, Norway.

It has to be stressed that such a diversity of the approaches from generous social benefits, free of charge housing to place in special refugees' camps and the variability of social packages is in conformity within the obligations under the Directive and its minimum standards.

Moreover, after half a year of Russian large-scale invasion of Ukraine, EU states commenced the adoption of amendments to national legislation that reducing types, size of social payments and limiting of the scope of social rights and support. The housing compensation program for TPPs in Poland has been discontinued and only the unprotected categories of TPPs could count on 4 months of free housing and food, during which they have to find a job and means of subsistence.[30] Free of charge medical insurance as well as emerging housing in the Czech Republic were limited to 150 days by the amendments to the special Law Lex Ukraine that regulates all main aspects of TPPs status in the country.[31] Many charity funds and programs in different EU countries have also run out of available free resources, including accommodation. Undoubtedly, despite reducing the level of protection, the EU states continue to perform their obligations under the Directive.

At the beginning of the third year of the war, the reduction of programs and benefits for TPPs became prevalent all over Europe. From September 2024, the maximum period of stay in free housing will be shortened to 90 days for all TPPs, including vulnerable persons in Czechia.[32] In Poland, from July 2024, a one-time allowance upon arrival, free accommodation and food for 120 days (with some exceptions) will be terminated; additional criteria were established for children's allowances.[33] In Germany, despite the increasement of the size of main social payments for 12% for TPPs,[34] some payments will be available only after receiving the so-called "reduced" benefit for 36 months, the set of free medical services for its recipients has also been significantly reduced as well as social payments in case of providing the person with free housing and meal. Moreover, special investigation of social security fraud of people with Ukrainian passports and the citizenship of one

[29] EUAA (2023) Providing Temporary Protection to Displaced Persons from Ukraine: A Year in Review..

[30] Majumdar (2022).

[31] Lex Ukrajina, Zákon o některých opatřeních v souvislosti s ozbrojeným konfliktem na území Ukrajiny vyvolaným invazí vojsk Ruské federace, Available at: https://www.zakonyprolidi.cz/cs/2022-65/monitor?g=12129955

[32] Simochko (2024).

[33] Pushenko (2024).

[34] Assistance to Ukrainian refugees in Germany: the amount of payments in 2024. Facty, 5 March, 2024. Available at: https://fakty.com.ua/ru/ukraine/suspilstvo/20240305-dopomoga-ukrayinskym-bizhenczyam-u-nimechchyni-rozmir-vyplat-u-2023-roczi/

of the EU states was conducted.[35] At the beginning of 2024, all regions of Germany agreed on a single standard for bank cards that will be used to pay benefits for temporary protected, refugees, asylum seekers. Restrictions on cash withdrawals, prohibition of transfer of such funds to other cards, using them outside the state and other restrictions have been established.[36] German approach shows the establishment of tighter control over social payments and their beneficiaries.

In general, the trend of limitations and reduction of social support of TPPs is clear and becoming increasingly common. The huge numbers of TPPs, deterioration of general economic situation, inflation in many EU countries, cost of living increases and continuation of the war negatively affected the social policy for TPPs of many EU countries and the gradual depletion of available resources in Europe for millions of TPPs is acutely felt. At the same time, almost all states are providing all TPPs in need with at least accommodation in shelters, emergency medical care and some social benefits, that are exactly enshrined in the Directive as the minimum guarantees. Thus, the reduction of social support for TPPs should be limited, at least by the minimum social standards provided by the EU Directive.

Analysing the scope of EU social standards for TPPs, it is necessary to scrutinise the minimum standards according to different international documents that potentially could be applied to this category of persons.

3 Do EU States Have Social Obligations of TPPs Rights Protection According to International Universal and European Human Rights Instruments?

The above analysed EU Directive prescribed states' obligations on social rights protection of TPPs in general terms, giving them wide margin of appreciation since EU limited competence in the sphere of social policy. Consequently, the EU states are able to create different schemes of TPPs social protection (e.g., compensation for rent of housing, special social allowance or just providing TPPs in need with free meals in public or charity canteens and shelter in a special camps), change their national rules and regulations, discontinue any social program, terminate social payment and guarantee only minimum protection of basic needs. In this context, minimum social obligations of the EU states under different international instruments ought to be scrutinised for a better comprehensive understanding of EU states' obligation of TPPs social rights protection and the role of these obligations under the EU Directive.

---

[35] Sozialbetrug mit ukrainischen Pässen – Tausende Verdachtsfälle, WELT, 23.02.2024. Available at:https://www.welt.de/politik/deutschland/article250242930/BAMF-Sozialbetrug-mit-ukrainischen-Paessen-Tausende-Verdachtsfaelle.html

[36] Bohdan'ok (2024).

3.1 Universal Human Rights instruments and Their Applicability to TPPs

A wide range of social human rights such as rights to decent standard of living, social security, social assistance, health, medical care and assistance, housing etc., were enshrined in international universal and regional documents, including the Universal Declaration on Human Rights, the International Covenant on Economic, Social and Cultural Rights, ILO conventions, the European Social Charter and the Social Charter revised, the EU Charter of fundamental rights, Additional protocol to the American Convention on Human Rights etc. Social rights, enshrined in general international treaties must be extended to all persons without any discrimination and guaranteed by States Parties. However, it should be noted that despite the provisions about guarantees of social rights to everyone in some of the mentioned international treaties, the personal scope of many of those doesn't expand to full extent to every person under jurisdiction of the State Parties and would depend on many factors, including citizenship, permanent residence, legal status, previous contributions to social security funds, etc. At the same time, the global migration processes, refugee crisis make international monitoring bodies to think about broader interpretation of personal scope of the international social human rights treaties, extending some minimum set of social rights to non-nationals, including illegal ones.

In this context, the special attention for the scrutinisation of obligations to protect social rights of TPPs, that the EU states could have under international universal instruments, should be paid to the International Covenant on Economic, Social and Cultural Rights as an element of the International Bill of Human Rights and as a key treaty in the sphere of social rights ratified by more than 170 States parties, including all European countries, and its Committee of Economic, Social and Cultural Rights that adopts the general comments on any issue affecting economic, social and cultural rights to which States parties should devote more attention.

Unfortunately, it must be assumed that neither international universal treaties nor regional ones contain special provisions on the protection of the rights of temporary protected persons. No special treaty has ever been adopted either. Considering elaboration of the International Guidelines on temporary protection within UN High Commissioner for Refugees and the International Law Association, their analysis also would be necessary for the understanding of universal approach to the idea of states' commitments in the sphere of TPPs' social rights.

3.1.1 International Covenant on Economic, Social and Cultural Rights

The International Covenant on Economic, Social and Cultural Rights declares the right to social security, an adequate standard of living, including adequate food, clothing and housing, the enjoyment of the highest attainable standard of physical and mental health and other social rights to everyone.[37] Detailing the state obligations in the context of business activities, the Committee in the General Comment 24, adopted in 2017, noted that asylum seekers and undocumented migrants are at particular risk of facing discrimination in the enjoyment of Covenant rights due to their precarious situation.[38] Moreover, earlier in 2009 in its General Comment No 20 on non-discrimination in economic, social and cultural rights, the Committee stressed that all children have to have access to education, adequate food and affordable health care despite their nationality and legal status, including illegal migrant and undocumented children.[39] In this Comment the Committee also quoted the position of another universal treaty body—the Committee on the Elimination of All Forms of Racial Discrimination, which also analysed states' obligations in the sphere of prohibition of discrimination and emphasised the importance of the application the Covenant's rights to everyone, "including non-nationals, such as refugees, asylum-seekers, stateless persons, migrant workers and victims of international trafficking, regardless of legal status and documentation".[40]

On the other side, despite this broad approach to the personal scope of the extension of social rights to everyone, the Committee on Economic, Social and Cultural Rights repeated that the provision of article 2 para 3 of the Covenant which allows developing countries to determine "to what extent they would guarantee the rights recognized in the present Covenant to non-nationals."[41] Claire Lougarre, analysing the extent of recognition and protection of non-nationals' social rights under all UN treaties paid attention to ambiguities in this context for middle-income countries, considering their policy during Covid time and made conclusion on opaque protection of these rights to non-nationals.[42]

Generally, the international human rights committees and institutions use different formulations for states' obligations in the sphere of social rights. UN High Commissioner for human rights noted that governments shall take progressive measures to the extent of their available resources to protect the rights of everyone—regardless of citizenship, including social security, an adequate standard of living

[37] International Covenant on Economic, Social and Cultural Rights, adopted 16 December 1966, General Assembly resolution 2200A (XXI).

[38] General comment No. 24 (2017) on State obligations under the International Covenant on Economic, Social and Cultural Rights in the context of business activities, Adopted by the Committee on Economic, Social and Cultural Rights at its sixty-first session, (29 May-23 June 2017), para 8.

[39] Committee on economic, social and cultural rights (2009).

[40] Committee on the Elimination ofRacial Discrimination (2004).

[41] See for example, para.30 of the General comment of the Committee on economic, social and cultural rights No. 20 Non-discrimination in economic, social and cultural rights (art. 2, para. 2, of the International Covenant on Economic, Social and Cultural Rights), Forty-second session, Geneva, 4–22 May 2009, E/C.12/GC/20, 2 July 2009: "This paragraph is without prejudice to the application of art. 2, para. 3, of the Covenant, which states: "Developing countries, with due regard to human rights and their national economy, may determine to what extent they would guarantee the economic rights recognized in the present Covenant to non-nationals."

[42] Lougarre (2020), p. 252–290.

etc.[43] The Committee on Economic, Social and Cultural Rights stated in its comments and observations that states must guarantee, ensure the right to adequate housing, minimum standard of living regardless of citizenship.[44] The Committee on the Elimination of Racial Discrimination will encourage states to include non-citizens in national health insurance systems.[45] Analysing human rights of non-citizens, UN High Commissioner for human rights paid attention to such categories of people as stateless persons, refugees, asylum-seekers, non-citizen workers and their families.

Unfortunately, TPPs were neither directly listed among other categories of non-nationals in the mentioned comments, nor a special recognized group of displaced persons in the context of human rights of non-nationals at universal level, possibly due to extraordinary and rare cases of granting people temporary protection status, its regulation exclusively at national level etc. Moreover, the scope of social rights of this category of displaced people who are granted the legal status by the host state, has not been outlined at UN treaties and documents of the monitoring bodies. However, despite the possibility of TPPs consideration as non-nationals in the context of non-discrimination, the issue on states' obligations to broaden extension of some scope of social rights for non-nationals at universal level according to the concept of their belonging to everyone (that means TPPs as well) remains rather vague and controversial. On the other hand, considering the legal status of TPPs, they should have more social protection and support as illegal migrants. At the same time, the issue of correlation of the social rights of TPPs and other groups of non-nationals remains ambiguous.

3.1.2 International Guidelines on Temporary Protection

The activities of development of principles for temporary protection at the universal level have been appeared after providing by some EU states the temporary protection regimes for several categories of people fleeing the war in former Yugoslavia at the end of previous century and adoption of the EU Temporary Protection Directive. As a result, in 2002 the International Law Association elaborated the Guidelines on Temporary Protection aimed at the pragmatic regulation of the situation in cases of mass influx of people when the providing of refugee status on individual bases would be not possible. The range of minimum social rights which should be guaranteed to TPPs by the host states was listed in this document. First of all, it was

[43] The rights of non-citizens. Office of the UN High Commissioner for human rights. 2006, United Nations publication, New York and Geneva, p. 25, ISBN-13: 978-92-1-154175-5.

[44] See, e.g., General Comment No. 4 of the Committee on Economic, Social and Cultural Rights; International Covenant on Economic, Social and Cultural Rights, art. 2 (2); Committee on Economic, Social and Cultural Rights, concluding observations on the third periodic report of Ukraine.

[45] Committee on the Elimination of Racial Discrimination, concluding observations on the initial and second periodic reports of Saudi Arabia (para. 206)

stressed that TPPs "shall be treated in accordance with human rights standards and, where applicable, the guarantees of the 1951 Convention Relating to the Status of Refugees".[46] According to the Guidelines, states should ensure at least the right to an adequate standard of living including adequate food, clothing and housing, rights to adequate health care, education, access to employment in cases of prolonged stay, family reunification, freedom of movement which, to the extent possible, should not be restricted, and TPPs should be protected against discrimination. The disclaimer of the expression of solely the authors or publishers' views of and do not reflection those of UNHCR, the United Nations and its Member States was specially made to emphasise the role and nature of the document.

Within the UN, the Guidelines on Temporary Protection or Stay Arrangements were adopted by UN High Commissioner for Refugees in 2014, more than a decade after the International Law Association's Guidelines and the EU Directive. Despite the broader list of TPPs rights, UN Guidelines prescribe almost the same list of social rights that was enshrined in the mentioned Guidelines, e.g., guarantees of shelter/housing, access to health and other basic services and education. The special attention was paid to special care for separated and unaccompanied children, persons with special needs etc.[47] Specifying the list of TPPs rights, both Guidelines recalled the Executive Committee Conclusion on Protection of Asylum-Seekers in Situations of Large-Scale Influx 1981,[48] which includes basic sanitary and health facilities as well as the states' obligation to grant TPPs all necessary facilities to obtain a satisfactory durable solution etc.

In general, the approach to elaborate the Guidelines on temporary protection instead of a treaty is completely understandable and seems like the approach for protection of internally displaced persons whose rights and states' obligations were enshrined in the Guiding Principles on internal displacement. Therefore, based on the provided analysis of the ICESCR, the textual absence of special provisions on TPPs' rights in international treaties and the non-binding nature of the UN High Commissioner for Refugees' Guidelines on Temporary Protection or Stay Arrangements, it could be noted that, despite the existence of millions of TPPs,[49] no special legally binding obligations for the states regarding the protection of TPPs' social rights have been elaborated at international universal level.

---

[46] Guidelines on Temporary Protection. Resolution 5/2002 on Refugee Procedures 6 April 2002, 5/2002, adopted by the 70th Conference of the International Law Association held in New Delhi, India, 2–6 April 2002 /International Law Association, para 10.

[47] UNHCR (2014), para 16.

[48] UNHCR, ExCom, Protection of Asylum-Seekers in Situations of Large-Scale Influx, No. 22 (XXXII), 21 October 1981.

[49] Considering the lack of general data of TPPs in the world due to various regulations in the states, that provide this status (for instance, the US can grant temporary protection status to some categories of arrivals, the UK proposes a special temporary protection schemes for Ukrainians), only EU states gave temporary protection to more than four million people (the detailed data see at https://ec.europa.eu/urostat/statistics-explained/index.php?title=Temporary_protection_for_persons_fleeing_Ukraine)

3.2 *Social Rights of Temporary Protected Persons Within the Council of Europe*

3.2.1 European Social Charter

In Europe, the main treaty that enshrined the broadest range of social rights is a counterpart of the European Convention on Human Rights—the European Social Charter (hereinafter, "ESC") which also is called the Social Constitution of Europe. However, unlike the majority of other human rights international treaties, the rights enshrined in the Charter are not applicable to all persons under the jurisdiction of the States Parties.[50] The Appendix to the European Social Charter 1961 and the Charter revised 1996 defines the limitations of its personal scope to nationals of States Parties lawfully resident or work regularly within the territory of the Party concerned.[51]

Nevertheless, according to the case law of the European Committee of Social Rights (hereinafter, "ECSR"), the personal scope limitation prescribed by the Appendix cannot be interpreted to deny the protection of the most basic rights offered by the Social Charter. Therefore, in some exceptional situations the personal scope can be expanded to other categories of persons regardless their status.[52] Moreover, due to refugee crises in Europe, the ECSR provided the interpretation of the implementation of Charter's rights to refugees and asylum seekers "where their situation corresponds to that defined in the 1951 Convention".[53] One of such exceptional situations was analysed by the European Committee of Social Rights in the case "International Commission of Jurists and European Council for Refugees and Exiles v. Greece",[54] which concerned the deprivation of protection of migrant children in Greece, lack of housing or placement in overcrowded institutions and/or detention facilities, restrictions on access to medical care etc. It was stipulated that the application of the Charter's provisions to irregular migrants become rather exceptional, but "social rights directly related to the right to life and human dignity, and which are part of a "non-derogable core" of rights, must be guaranteed" to refugees, asylum seekers etc.[55] The Committee also stated that refugees and stateless persons lawfully staying in the territory of States Parties should be granted no less favourable treatment than prescribed by other international treaties ratified by the host State or as favourable as possible and in any case according to the para 2 of the

[50] Valette (2016).

[51] European Social Charter (revised), 3 May 1996. ETS No. 163. Appendix. Scope of the Revised European Social Charter in terms of persons protected. Available at: https://rm.coe.int/168007cde4

[52] Smusz-Kulesza, Manasyan, Fedorova (2021).

[53] Valette (2016).

[54] ECSR, International Commission of Jurists (ICJ) and European Council for Refugees and Exiles (ECRE) v. Greece, application 173/2018, Available at: https://hudoc.esc.coe.int/eng?i=cc-173-2018-dmerits-en

[55] Ibid.

Appendix, and at least the provisions identified in the case-law of Committee as those that are applicable to these categories of persons.[56]

Moreover, in some situations the Committee has asked states to add information about personal scope for the fulfilment the obligations, for example, concerned social and medical assistance (Article 13 para 1). In the Committee's conclusions for Denmark, published in 2022, analysis of social assistance for foreign nationals lawfully and unlawfully present in the territory and the information on entitlement to emergency hospital treatment in some cases to everyone, even to non-residents under temporary stay in Denmark, was mentioned. The Committee once again repeated its legal position about "a legally recognised right to the satisfaction of basic human material need (food, clothing, shelter) in situations of emergency to cope with an urgent and serious state of need."[57] It was also stressed that states must guarantee the effective realisation of these rights in practice. The same position that was formulated in the decision "European Federation of National Organisations working with the Homeless (FEANTSA) v. the Netherlands"[58] was repeated in the Conclusions for several other states, e.g., Estonia, Luxemburg.

Despite the different approaches of the extension of Charter's rights to refugees, asylum-seekers, migrants and other categories of non-nationals and outlining some "non-derogable core" Charter's rights, the rights of TPPs have not been the subject of the Committee's direct consideration as well as the interpretation of personal scope of the Charter for temporary protected persons, except several mentions, e.g., ECSR Conclusions 2023 on article 31 para 1 for Türkiye includes the analysis of information on general amount of Syrian TPPs, providing foreigners under international protection and temporary protection with cash assistance during the Covid-19 crisis.[59]

Hence, given that all EU member states are parties to the European Social Charter (either the revised or the 1961), their obligations under the Charter to guarantee core rights to TPPs are obvious; however, the potential scope of these rights remains unclear. Undoubtedly, TPPs' status differs from asylum seeker, refugee statuses, illegal migrants or worker migrants, but the current situation with millions of TPPs from Ukraine is unique due to the compliance of Ukrainian TPPs with the rule of personal scope enshrined in the Appendix to the Charter. Indeed, the large-scale Russian military aggression was the trigger for EU "resuscitation" of temporary protection by adoption of the Council implementing decision 4 March 2022. The vast majority of Ukrainian TPPs in the EU meet two key requirements for extension

[56] European Committee of Social Rights, International Federation of Human Rights Leagues (FIDH) v France, No. 14/2003, dec. 3 November 2004.

[57] European Committee of Social Rights, Conclusions XXII-2 - Denmark - Article 13-1.

[58] European Committee of Social Rights, European Federation of National Organisations working with the Homeless (FEANTSA) v. the Netherlands, Complaint No. 86/2012, decision on the merits of 2 July 2014, §187.

[59] European Committee of Social Rights, Conclusions 2023 - Türkiye - Article 31-1.

of the Charter's rights to foreigners in the host country[60]: citizenship of one of State Party of the ESC due to ratification of the Charter revised by Ukraine in 2006 and legal status on the territory of the host state.

Does it mean that temporary protected Ukrainian nationals should have all rights as other States Parties nationals who are lawfully resident and work in the territory of a State Party of the Charter, for instance, migrant workers? Or in other words, do the standards of the European Social Charter have to be guaranteed to TPPs in the same way as to other nationals of States Party taking into consideration ratified articles and provision of the ESC by the host state? As of today, there are no direct answers to such questions.

Moreover, foreigners who are citizens of the participating states and legally reside or work in the territory of another Party and are low-income, must enjoy the individual right to appropriate assistance on an equal basis with citizens,[61] without the need to apply the principle of reciprocity.[62] Member States are also obliged to provide non-resident foreigners with low-income—regardless of whether they are in the country legally or not—emergency social (accommodation, food, clothing) and medical assistance (emergency medical care) according to the individual's specific state of health.[63] Minor migrants living in the country even with illegal status have the right to receive full medical and psychological care.[64] At the same time, according to the practice of the ECSR, states are not obliged to apply guaranteed income mechanisms within their social protection systems for non-residents.[65]

Due to uncertain status of temporary protection, there hadn't been a necessity for such interpretations of TPPs rights and states' commitments for this category of people under the Charter before the beginning of the Russian aggression against Ukraine and the first time activation of the EU Temporary Protected Directive.

In spite of periodically mentioned rights of people who stay temporarily in the territory of country by states parties in the context of national legislation,[66] to date, there is no jurisprudence of the European Committee of Social Rights on the violation of TPPs rights. Theoretically, in the future, states could include the information

---

[60] Only 4 European countries are not parties of the ESC: Liechtenstein, Monaco, San Marino and Switzerland.

[61] ESCR, Digest of the ESC, Conclusions XIII-4 (1996), Statement of interpretation 13§2. Available at:

[62] ESCR, Digest of the ESC, Conclusions VII (1981), Statement of interpretation 13§4. Available at:

[63] ECSR, Conclusions XX-2, Czech Republic - Article 13§4, Available at: https://hudoc.esc.coe.int/eng?i=XX-2/def/CZE/13/4/EN, Conclusions 2013, Sweden - Article 13-4. Available at: https://hudoc.esc.coe.int/eng?i=2013/def/SWE/13/4/EN

[64] ECSR, Defence for Children International (DCI) v. Belgium, app. no. 69/2011, decision on the merits 23 October 2012. Available at: https://hudoc.esc.coe.int/eng/?i=cc-69-2011-dmerits-en

[65] ECSR, Digest, Conclusions XIII-4 (1996), Statement of interpretation, article 13.

[66] For example, in ECSR's Conclusions 2017 for Bulgaria it was stated that according to the national report, national legislation does not contain any longer the term "temporary protection" and "there are no limitations as regards the access of refugees and persons enjoying humanitarian protection to social services…as they have equal rights as Bulgarian citizens": Conclusions 2017, Bulgaria - Article 14-1.

on the protection of TPPs' social rights in their national reports, or they could be asked to provide this information by the ECSR. There is also a possibility to launch a collective complain versus state whose legislation or practice is not in conformity with Charter's standards. However, the potential applicants for the protection of TPPs rights are unclear. Hardly any national or international trade unions would lodge a collective complaint for protection of TPPs. Presumably, it could be international non-governmental organisations which have a special participatory status with the Council of Europe, but most of them were established for protection rights of specific group or categories of people or professions. In case of launching collective complaints on TPPs rights or rising of this topic within the states report procedure, the European Committee could meet the necessity to interpret the Charter's personal scope for temporary protected persons, considering their legal residency and rights at the EU states.[67] Therefore, these is some room for further interpretation of the Charter in the context of TPPs rights, nevertheless, at the beginning of the third year of TPPs in Europe, the scope of their social rights under ESC remains vague.

3.2.2 European Convention on Human Rights

The analysis of EU states' obligations in the sphere of TPPs social rights protection cannot be considered comprehensive enough without the analysis of possible protection of TPPs' social rights under the Convention for the protection of Human Rights and Fundamental Freedoms (hereinafter, "European Convention on Human Rights", "Convention"). Despite the textual absence of social rights in the text of the Convention and its protocols, evolutive interpretation of many Conventional provisions by the European Court of Human Rights allows to include a broad range of social issues to the Conventional mechanism.[68] The Court managed to form quite detailed approaches to protection of social rights and the same time, obligations to guarantee all rights prescribed in the Convention and protocols to everyone under State Parties jurisdiction without exceptions (e.g., foreigners, legal or illegal migrants, asylum seekers, refuges etc.). Considering armed conflicts in different European regions, some cases were devoted to protection of the rights of internally displaced persons, although there have been adopted only a few judgements on temporary protection issues. In 2021, the Grand Chamber of the Court adopted judgement in the case "M.A. v. Denmark" which concerned 3 year waiting period

[67] All EU states ratified the ESC or ESC revised.

[68] This topic has been the subject of research of many academics in various publications, for instance: López-Jacoiste (2020); Brems (2007), pp. 135–167; Warbrick (2007); Leijten (2018), pp. 25–58; Slingenberg and Leijten (2023); Fedorova (2012), pp. 241–251. Moreover, the Registry of the European Court of Human Rights prepared and periodically updated the Guide on the case-law of the European Convention on Human Rights related to Social Rights, where the analysis and summary of the case-law relating to social rights is provided.

for temporary protected person in Denmark[69] for family reunification while other categories of people who obtained international protection, did not have such kind of restrictions.[70] Analysing the national legislation, the Court draw attention to the argumentation of the Danish Government that explained non acceptance of many refugees with threats for the social cohesion due to obligations to provide all persons granted international protection in Denmark with social benefits and allowances, as well as housing, language training and employment initiatives. It underlined the importance and key role of social issues in different aspects of international protection and the related rights of such people even within the right to family reunification. In this judgment, the European Court also mentioned the EU Temporary Protection Directive amongst other international sources, stating that it had never been implemented (para. 159). Moreover, the European Court compared the general practice of introducing waiting periods for persons granted subsidiary protection and persons granted temporary protection and gave rise to concern and criticism of the difference.[71]

In general, there were only several cases on temporary protection and the subjects were not related to social rights. Nevertheless, rather overarching legal positions on minimum social needs have been framed for asylum seekers, refugees, and other categories of non-nationals. For instance, in the case “M. S. S v. Belgium and Greece” the European Court of Human Rights noticed that very often asylum seekers had nowhere to live, slept on the streets, in certain parks in Athens, they had “permanent state of fear of being attacked and robbed, and of complete destitution generated by their situation (difficulty in finding food, no access to sanitary facilities, etc.)”.[72] It was also noticed that a special card for asylum seekers (“pink card”) didn’t provide such kind of persons with social benefits, assistance or even free medical treatment; and furthermore, they couldn’t obtain the work permit because of different bureaucratic obstacles as a necessity to have tax number what was impossibly without a permanent place of living. The Court found that living on the street, without resources or access to sanitary facilities, any means of providing for essential needs considered that “the applicant has been the victim of humiliating treatment showing a lack of respect for his dignity” that constitute violation of the Article 3 of the Convention.[73]

Considering the main direction of the European Convention and having already included everyone in its ratione personae, hardly worth waiting for appearance of

---

[69] According to national legislation of Denmark, temporary protection status could be granted to persons whose need for protection is based on a particularly serious situation in their country of origin in connection with an armed conflict or a similar situation (European Court of Human Rights, M.A. v. Denmark, application no. 6697/18, judgment of the Grand Chamber 9 July 2021).

[70] European Court of Human Rights, M.A. v. Denmark, application no. 6697/18, judgment of the Grand Chamber 9 July 2021.

[71] Ibid., para 151–154.

[72] European Court of Human Rights, M. S. S v. Belgium and Greece, app. 30,696/09, judgment of the European Court of Human Rights 21 January 2011.

[73] Ibid.

profound changes in Court's interpretation and earlier formulated position of states' positive obligations in social sphere for TPPs support.

4 The Key Perspectives of Further Evolution of Social Obligations of the EU States for TTPs Protection

The European Court of Human Rights and international treaties' bodies formulated broad approaches on extension of human rights to refugees, illegal migrants and other different groups of non-nationals, including their social basic rights as right to shelter, food, emergency medical care etc. Calling upon states to guarantee the right to adequate housing, minimum standard of living for every person or providing broad range of social rights to refugees, the Committee on Economic, Social and Cultural Rights, UN High Commissioner for human rights have never drawn particular attention to temporary protected persons. The European Court of Human Rights formulated well established case-law on social rights of different groups of displaced persons, including illegal migrants or internally protected people, has not dealt with TPPs social rights likewise. The European Committee of Social Rights has done analogously. Providing a broad interpretation of personal scope of the European Social Charter, the Committee outlined basic social needs and "non-derogable core" of rights that must be guaranteed by States Parties for everyone, emphasizing on states' obligations to children, not distinguishing a group of temporary protected persons.

The brief analyses of possible protection of TPPs social rights under different international treaties proved not only the lack of regulation of this issue and lack of interpretation by relevant monitoring bodies, but also discovered the necessity to initiate the discussion of applicability human rights treaties to some extent to TPPs as to non-nationals according to existed interpretative practice, underlying the obvious states' obligations to provide temporary protected persons with much broader range of guarantees than must be guaranteed to illegal migrants. In other words, TPPs should be granted with wider set of social rights that, for example included in the "non-derogable core" of social rights under European Social Charter, taking into account legal status of TPPs in the EU countries according to the EU Directive, national legislation and states' obligations under international human rights treaties. It is obvious from interpretation of personal scope of international human rights instruments that states ought to have implicit international commitments with regard to TTPs as special categories of vulnerable persons who legally stay under the jurisdiction of the host country. However, the main responsibilities on the social rights protection of TPPs still remain at national level and should be brought in accordance only with the unclear minimum standards of the EU Temporary Protection Directive.

Although, it might be assumed that among European human rights treaties, the European Social Charter has the greatest potential of inclusion TPPs' social rights issues to the subject of its consideration.

Taking into account the reduction of social programs and benefits for TPPs by many EU countries, it can lead to inclusion only shelter as a minimum obligation in the sphere of housing for TPPs in need. That could be a place in special buffer centers according to a new Bulgarian governmental plan or proposition of emergency accommodation for short period of time in Italy. It means that the minimum housing standard and other social standards of the EU Directive can be compared with interpretations of states obligations for illegal non-nationals. Moreover, minimum obligations in the sphere of medical care according to the Directive which cover only emergency care, also correspond with minimum obligations towards different non-nationals under international human rights treaties. Taking into account implemented limited free of charge periods of medical insurance in Bulgaria and the Czech Republic or the possibility to find some medical institutions which could provide free of charge assistance for TPPs in Italy could lead to possibility of providing only free of charge emergency medical care for TPPs.

The most difficult aspect for comparison between obligations under the EU Directive and international human rights instruments is social benefits and assistance for TPPs. While the Committee on Economic, Social and Cultural Rights encourages states to ensure the right to adequate housing and minimum standard of living for everyone, the European Court of Human Rights considered that most cases on the amount of pension or social benefits are very sensitive and usually found appropriate applications inadmissible due to lack of evidence of leading insufficient benefits to "degradation incompatible with human dignity".[74] Despite the lack of protection of social right such as right to work, right to free medical assistance or right to claim minimum financial assistance, the Court also emphasized that person's living conditions that reached the minimum level of severity could be considered within the ambit the Article 3.[75]

Analysing the scope of TPPs social protection and substance of the social assistance under the Temporary Protection Directive, Julia Motte-Baumvol, Tarin Cristino Frota Mont'Alverne, Gabriel Braga Guimarães drew attention to the word "necessary" in the Article 12 for assistance that pointed to the limitation of the scope of TPPs protection and linked to the idea of survival.[76] Taking into account preparatory documents for the EU Directive, including Rapporteur's statement to the Parliament, they included access to at least essential health care, basic shelter and housing, water and sanitation, foodstuffs, and the most basic forms of education—"that necessary for humans to survive, including nutrition, shelter and health"—as a minimum safety net or minimum core of TPPs rights.

Generally, such an understanding of TPPs social rights can put them on the same line with illegal migrants. At the same time, the definition of temporary protection that was given in the EU Directive includes a broad margin of appreciation for States and allows them to adopt different approaches to the concept of temporary

[74] ECtHR, Budina v. Russia (dec.), application 45603/05, decision 18.6. 2009.

[75] ECtHR, Anna Pančenko against Latvia (dec.), application no. 40772/98, 28 October 1999.

[76] Motte-Baumvol et al. (2022).

protection and to the minimum social support that should be guaranteed to this group of people. Thus, the EU States can increase this level according to their national legislation and policy or provide TPPs with the set of social rights only for survival. In the last case, the access to labour market makes them easy target for discrimination, labour exploitation, trafficking etc. In other words, the sphere of protection of TPPs social rights remains "a grey zone". Taking into account that the maximum duration of temporary protection under the EU Directive will be expired in March 2025, the further EU states' social obligations provoke even more uncertainties and variabilities of national approaches. Despite the preliminary consent to continue temporary protection by the EU states and waiting for EU decision, many states have already started to elaborate other solutions that can be proposed for different groups of TPPs, e.g., temporary residence permit for economically active TPPs.

5 Conclusions

Temporary protection of displaced people had never played a crucial role as a form of international protection, mostly being a specific national regime to regulate refugee crisis in extraordinary case of mass influx of displacement and not having specific provisions on this issue neither at universal nor European level till the beginning of twenty-first century. As it has been already mentioned, the elaboration of national temporary protection regimes by some EU countries for people fleeing the war in former Yugoslavia motivated the EU to adopt a special Directive that led to elaboration of UN High Commissioner for Refugees' Guidelines on Temporary Protection or Stay Arrangements and International Law Association's Guidelines on Temporary Protection. In the last two decades, Europe faced several large-scale migration crises, nevertheless, the Directive had not been activated and international monitoring bodies had not examined the cases of TPPs human rights violations, except several cases considered by the European Court of Human Rights, that were not devoted to social rights. Thus, the scope of states' obligations in the sphere of TPPs social rights protection was hardly defined and could be distinguished from general obligations raised within the issue of human rights protection of refugees, asylum seekers and other categories of non-nationals, relevant interpretation of monitoring bodies of different international human rights instruments.

However, the beginning of Russian military invasion of Ukraine in February 2022 led to first time activation of the EU Temporary Protection Directive that launched "a new life" for temporary protection at international level and started a new stage of the development of international protection of displaced people. All EU states, except Denmark,[77] were obliged by its provisions and since the activation

[77] Only Denmark from EU member States refused to be bound by the Temporary Protection Directive according to it opt-out nature. However, in March 2022, the special law on granting a special residence permit to persons fleeing the war in Ukraine was adopted that reflected EU

of the Directive on March 4, they have had to guarantee minimum rights for at least 3 groups of people according to Council Implementing Decision. At the same time, states' minimum obligations in the sphere of social rights remain vague and are still waiting for the clarification even 2 years since the beginning of mass influx of people fleeing the war in Ukraine.

Taking into account variability of national approaches and systems of TPPs social rights protection elaborated by the EU states and the clear common tendency of gradually reduction of their social support, the question of the minimum scope of EU states' social obligations is becoming increasingly important for both host EU states and TPPs. In this context, the correlation of obligations to protect social basic rights of TPPs under the EU Directive and international human rights treaties could play a crucial role, despite the total lack of specialised international treaties regarding the protection of the rights of temporarily protected.

The provided research showed that means of subsistence and necessary assistance for TPPs according to the EU Directive are correlated with the set of non-derogable core of social rights or basic social needs for everyone, as it was understood within international treaties, including the European Convention on Human Rights and the European Social Charter. It underlined the ambiguousness of the scope of social states' obligations and a broad margin of appreciation for them. Indeed, states are obliged to provide TPPs without resources with minimum social support that have to be enough to cover their basic needs that include food, water, sanitation, shelter and emergency health care. Consequently, the EU states have already had almost the same scope of social obligations for TPPs protection under international human rights treaties before the activation of the EU Directive. And its activation granted people fleeing the war in Ukraine with the temporary permission to stay and work and with minimum social guarantees that can be. There are no obligations under the EU Directive to provide TPPs with the set of social rights, access to national social or housing programs that nationals or even refugees have. Undoubtedly, such ambiguity of TPPs rights and further social support leave TPPs in complete uncertainty and under permanent stress.

In this context, further interpretation of minimum social guarantees under the EU Directive should be provided. This explanation could help avoid massive poverty and homelessness among thousands TPPs without income in EU territory or even with minimum income which would be insufficiently in many EU countries to cover housing and other social basic needs without access to different social assistance and benefits such as, for example, partial compensation of housing rent and/or services.

Being perfectly aware that the ideal solution for TPPs social rights in form of development of a new European treaty or elaboration of the special recommendations, guidelines on temporary protection within the Council of Europe or adoption of amendments to international human rights treaties in force seems implausible in

---

approach and provided Ukrainian refugees even referable status in comparison with other refugees. See in details at: https://ec.europa.eu/migrant-integration/news/new-danish-law-those-fleeing-ukraine-mirrors-eu-temporary-protection-directive_en

short or medium-time perspectives. The evolutive broad interpretation of personal scope of international human rights treaties in parallel with the amendments to Operational Guidelines for applying the EU Temporary Protection Directive[78] could be the workable prompt solution for the third year of temporary protection under the EU Directive and benchmarks for searching pathways of social support of millions of Ukrainians in EU after 2025.

References

Bauloz C, Ineli-Ciger M, Singer S, Stoyanova V (2015) Seeking asylum in the European Union: selected protection issues raised by the second phase of the Common European Asylum System. Brill

Brems E (2007) Indirect protection of social rights by the European Court of Human Rights. In: Exploring social rights: between theory and practice. Hart, pp 135–167

Carrara S, Ineli-Ciger M, Vosyliute L, Bruman L (2022) EU grants temporary protection for people fleeing war in Ukraine: time to rethink unequal solidarity in EU Asylum Policy. CEPS Policy Insights No 2022-09

Durieux JF (2021) Temporary protection and temporary refuge. In: Costello C, Foster M, McAdam J (eds) The Oxford handbook of international refugee law. Oxford Academic

Fedorova A (2012) Protection of social rights within the European Convention on Human Rights. Law Ukraine 11-12:241–251. [Федорова, А. (2012). Захист соціальних прав в рамках Європейської Конвенції з прав людини. *Право України*, (11-12), 241-251]

Fitzpatrick J (2000) Temporary protection of refugees: elements of a formalized regime. Am J Int Law 94(2):279–306

Ineli-Ciger M (2016) Time to activate the temporary protection directive: why the directive can play a key role in solving the migration crisis in Europe. Eur J Migr Law 18:1–33

Koser K, Black R (1999) Limits to harmonization: the “temporary protection” of refugees in the European Union. Int Migr 37(3):535

Leijten I (2018) The ECHR and socio-economic rights protection. In: Core socio-economic rights and the European Court of Human Rights. Cambridge University Press, Cambridge, pp 25–58

López-Jacoiste E (2020) Chapter 8: Social rights in the case law of the European Court of Human Rights. In: Research handbook on international law and social rights. Edward Elgar Publishing, Cheltenham. https://doi.org/10.4337/9781788972130.00018

Motte-Baumvol J, Mont’Alverne TCF, Guimarães GB (2022) Extending social protection for migrants under the European Union’s temporary protection directive: lessons from the war in Ukraine. Oxford University Comparative Law Forum. Available at: https://ouclf.law.ox.ac.uk

Slingenberg L, Leijten I (2023) Chapter 2: Social security in the case law of the European Court of Human Rights. In: Research handbook on European social security law. Edward Elgar Publishing, Cheltenham. https://doi.org/10.4337/9781800886353.00008

Valette MF (2016) Protection and promotion of migrants’ social rights by the European Committee of Social Rights. Rev Eur Migr Int 32(3–4) Available at: http://journals.openedition.org/remi/10420

Warbrick C (2007) In: Baderin M, McCorquodale R (eds) Economic and social interests and the European Convention on human rights in economic, social, and cultural rights in action

[78]Communication from the Commission on Operational guidelines for the implementation of Council implementing Decision 2022/382 establishing the existence of a mass influx of displaced persons from Ukraine within the meaning of Article 5 of Directive 2001/55/EC, and having the effect of introducing temporary protection 2022/C 126 I/01.

Meltem, Ineli-Ciger (2016) A Temporary Protection Regime in Line with International Law: Utopia or Real Possibility? International Community Law Review 18(3-4) 278-316 10.1163/18719732-12341332

Dikran M., Zenginkuzucu (2021) A Comparative Analysis on International Refugee Law and Temporary Protection in the Context of Turkey The Age of Human Rights Journal (17) 385-410 10.17561/tahrj.v17 10.17561/tahrj.v17.6297

Esra, Yılmaz Eren (2019) Is Temporary Protection Eternal? The Future of Temporary Protection Status of Syrians in Turkey Border Crossing 9(2) 125-134 10.33182/bc.v9i2.718

Mario, Krešić (2020) Analiza europskog instituta privremene zaštite Analysis of the European Institute of Temporary Protection Godišnjak Akademije pravnih znanosti Hrvatske 11(1) 97-118 10.32984/gapzh 10.32984/gapzh.11.1.6 Reports and Official Publications

EUAA (2023) Providing temporary protection to displaced persons from Ukraine: a year in review. Publications Office of the European Union, Luxembourg. Available at: https://euaa.europa.eu

European Commission (2022) Communication on operational guidelines for the implementation of council implementing decision 2022/382 establishing the existence of a mass influx of displaced persons from Ukraine. OJ C 126I, 21.3.2022, pp 1–16. Available at: https://eur-lex.europa.eu

European Committee of Social Rights (2023) Conclusions 2023 - Türkiye - Article 31-1. Available at: https://hudoc.esc.coe.int

European Social Charter (revised). ETS No. 163. Available at: https://rm.coe.int/168007cde4

FRA (2022) National legislation implementing the EU temporary protection directive in selected EU Member States. Available at: https://fra.europa.eu

UNHCR (2014) Guidelines on temporary protection or stay arrangements. Available at: https://www.unhcr.org/542e99fd9.pdf

UNHCR (2022) Operational data portal: Ukraine refugee situation. Available at: https://data.unhcr.org/en/situations/ukraine

Legislation and Case Law

Council Directive 2001/55/EC of 20 July 2001 on Minimum Standards for Giving Temporary Protection in the Event of a Mass Influx of Displaced Persons. OJ L 212, 7.8.2001, pp. 12–23. Available at: https://eur-lex.europa.eu

Council Implementing Decision (EU) 2022/382 of 4 March 2022 Establishing the Existence of a Mass Influx of Displaced Persons from Ukraine. OJ L 71, 4.3.2022, pp 1–6. Available at: https://eur-lex.europa.eu

European Court of Human Rights (1999) Anna Pančenko against Latvia. Application No. 40772/98, Decision, 28 October 1999

European Court of Human Rights (2009) Budina v. Russia. Application No. 45603/05, Decision, 18 June 2009

European Court of Human Rights (2011) M.S.S. v. Belgium and Greece. Application No. 30696/09, Judgment, 21 January 2011

European Court of Human Rights (2021) M.A. v. Denmark. Application No. 6697/18, Judgment of the Grand Chamber, 9 July 2021

International Instruments

Committee on Economic, Social and Cultural Rights (2009) General comment no. 20: non-discrimination in economic, social and cultural rights. E/C.12/GC/20, 2 July 2009

Committee on the Elimination of Racial Discrimination (2004) General comment no. 30 on non-citizens

International Covenant on Economic, Social and Cultural Rights. Adopted 16 December 1966, General Assembly Resolution 2200A (XXI)

Employment of Persons with Disabilities: How Far Is Ukraine from European Equality Standards?

Olena Rym and Yana Simutina

1 Introduction[1]

Ukraine's European dream came closer to reality in June 2022 when it was granted EU candidate status. Despite the ongoing war with Russia and prolonged martial law, Ukraine has demonstrated its ability to carry out the necessary reforms required by the EU accession process.[2] Although the war is forcing policymakers to make significant adjustments to domestic socio-economic development priorities,

[1] While this book was being prepared for publication, the draft law "On Amendments to Certain Laws of Ukraine on Ensuring the Right of Persons with Disabilities to Work" (Reg. No. 5344-d), which we analyse in this chapter, was adopted in the version under consideration and became Law of Ukraine No. 4219-IX. Currently, in preparation for its entry into force on 1 January 2026, active rule-making work is underway at the level of bylaws to ensure the effective implementation of its provisions in practice.

[2] Commission staff working document. Ukraine 2023 Report. Accompanying the document Communication from the Commission to the European Parliament, the Council, the European Economic and Social Committee and the Committee of the Regions 2023 Communication on EU Enlargement policy. Available at: https://op.europa.eu/en/publication-detail/-/publication/a0f3eaa6-7eee-11ee-99ba-01aa75ed71a1/language-en.

O. Rym (✉)
Department of Social Law, Ivan Franko National University of Lviv, Lviv, Ukraine
e-mail: olena.rym@lnu.edu.ua

Y. Simutina
Koretsky Institute of State and Law of the National Academy of Sciences of Ukraine, Kyiv, Ukraine

University of Bristol, Bristol, UK
e-mail: yana.simutina@bristol.ac.uk

K. Koldinská et al. (eds.), *Labour Law and Social Security Law in Central and Eastern Europe*, European Union and its Neighbours in a Globalized World 26,
https://doi.org/10.1007/978-3-032-04496-9_15

overcoming social inequalities, particularly in the employment of disabled people, remains a state policy priority.

The rationale behind this assertion is illustrated by the statistics below. In this, it is important to note that, even prior to the Russian invasion of Ukraine in 2022, Ukraine already had a considerable number of people with disabilities. As a result of more than three years of hostilities and the large number of military personnel with disabilities due to combat injuries, the number of people with disabilities in Ukraine has increased significantly. The Wall Street Journal, citing the German prosthesis manufacturer Ottobock, notes that in just 17 months of war, about 50,000 Ukrainians have lost limbs and need prosthetics.[3] According to official data, since the beginning of the full-scale invasion, more than 300,000 people have been recognised as persons with disabilities.[4] As of the beginning of 2023, more than 2.7 million people were registered as having a disability, and this figure has now exceeded 3 million.[5] However, given that many people have not yet registered their disability status, the actual number may be even higher.[6] The government must therefore act now to ensure that these people are able to return to work and are given the chance to live a full and dignified life. In this context, the authors aim to highlight Ukraine's achievements and challenges in improving social protection and the inclusion of persons with disabilities, particularly by ensuring their right to work.

2 Current Situation of People with Disabilities' Employment in Ukraine

The problem of employment of persons with disabilities is not new and affects a significant number of the Ukrainian population. According to the data published on the official website of the Ministry of Reintegration of the Temporarily Occupied

[3] Pancevski, B. (2023). In Ukraine, Amputations Already Evoke Scale of World War I. Wall Street Journal. Available at: https://www.wsj.com/articles/in-ukraine-a-surge-in-amputations-reveals-the-human-cost-of-russias-war-d0bca320.

[4] В Україні налічується 3 мільйони людей з інвалідністю – Жолнович, 19.09.2023. Укрінформ. [There are 3 million people with disabilities in Ukraine - Zholnovych 19.09.2023, Ukrinform.] [In Ukrainian]. Available at: https://www.ukrinform.ua/rubric-society/3763345-v-ukraini-nalicuetsa-3-miljoni-ludej-z-invalidnistu-zolnovic.html.

[5] Борсукова, О. За півтора року кількість людей з інвалідністю в Україні зросла на 300 тисяч – Мінсоцполітики [Borsukova, O. Over a year and a half, the number of people with disabilities in Ukraine has increased by 300 thousand - Ministry of Social Policy]. 19.09.2023 [In Ukrainian]. Available at: https://life.pravda.com.ua/society/2023/09/19/256633/.

[6] Черновол, К. З 2022 року кількість людей з інвалідністю в Україні зросла на сотні тисяч, - міністр [Chernovol, K. Since 2022, the number of people with disabilities in Ukraine has increased by hundreds of thousands, - Minister]. 28.11.2024 [In Ukrainian]. Available at: https://www.unian.ua/health/z-2022-roku-kilkist-lyudey-z-invalidnistyu-v-ukrajini-zrosla-na-sotni-tisyach-ministr-12834306.html.

Territories of Ukraine, there are currently 3 million people with disabilities in Ukraine.[7] The actual numbers were and are probably much closer to the international figure of 16% of people with disabilities. It is believed that this category potentially includes more than one million women of working age and 20% of the 11.3 million Ukrainian pensioners who are not covered by official statistics.[8] This means that there are more than 6 million people with disabilities in Ukraine.[9] If we compare these figures with the total population of Ukraine, which is steadily declining and, according to estimates by the International Monetary Fund, stands at around 33 million in 2025 approximately one in six people has a disability.[10] The above reveals a poor state system of collecting statistical data on the problems of persons with disabilities, which ultimately deprives the state itself of the ability to formulate and implement relevant state policies adequately. Thus, today in Ukraine, there are no clear regulations on the procedure for collecting appropriate data, the database does not cover all persons with disabilities, there are no accurate statistics covering specific types of disabilities, and there are no obligations to collect data disaggregated by gender and age. The database includes only people who have been officially assigned one of the three disability groups. Although in 2011 Ukraine established the Centralised Information System on Disability,[11] an automated database containing information on persons with disabilities, children with disabilities and other persons entitled to rehabilitation services and assistive technologies, its scope remains limited. Persons with functional impairments who have not undergone a formal disability assessment procedure are not covered by the system, resulting in a significant underrepresentation of the true extent and diversity of disability in the country. Those persons with disabilities who have not received official status are not included in the statistics at all. At the same time, the statistics of the Ministry of Health of Ukraine differ from the statistics of the Ministry of Social Policy of Ukraine, as the latter keeps records only of those who have applied for a disability pension. Court statistics on cases involving persons with disabilities are also incomplete and imperfect. The State Statistics Service of Ukraine collects data on the

[7] There are three million individuals with disabilities in Ukraine, 25.09.2023. Available at: https://unity.gov.ua/en/2023/09/25/there-are-three-million-individuals-with-disabilities-in-ukraine/.

[8] UN Policy Paper on Disability. Ukraine. Available at: https://ukraine.un.org/sites/default/files/2021-12/UN%20Policy%20Paper%20on%20Disability_ENG_FINAL.pdf.

[9] Roundtable dialogue on humanitarian support for persons with disabilities in Ukraine. 23.05.2023. Available at: https://www.who.int/europe/news/item/23-05-2023-roundtable-dialogue-on-humanitarian-support-for-persons-with-disabilities-in-ukraine.

[10] International Monetary Fund. World Economic Outlook Database: April 2025. Ukraine. Available at: https://www.imf.org/en/Publications/WEO/weo-database/2025/april/weo-report?c=926,&s=LUR,LP,&sy=2023&ey=2030&ssm=0&scsm=1&scc=0&ssd=1&ssc=0&sic=0&sort=country&ds=.&br=1.

[11] Положення про централізований банк даних з проблем інвалідності, затверджене постановою Кабінету Міністрів України від від 16.02.2011 № 121 [Regulation on the Centralised Data Bank on Disability, approved by the Cabinet of Ministers of Ukraine on 16.02.2011, № 121] [In Ukrainian]. Available at: https://zakon.rada.gov.ua/laws/show/121-2011-%D0%BF#Text.

number of all plaintiffs with disabilities by type of complaint (administrative and civil). Still, there is no data on the type of complaint and the types of violations mentioned in the complaints.[12] As a result, it is currently not possible to obtain reliable disaggregated data (e.g. by type of disability, gender, age, region or employment status). Thus, despite the existence of some registries, Ukraine still lacks a centralised and functional disability data infrastructure, which makes it difficult to develop, monitor and evaluate inclusive policies in line with obligations under the UN Convention on the Rights of Persons with Disabilities and EU standards.

In this context, the UN Committee on the Rights of Persons with Disabilities, after analysing Ukraine's implementation of the UN Convention on the Rights of Persons with Disabilities, even commented on the need to introduce an adequate mechanism for collecting relevant statistics in Ukraine. Based on the detailed data collected, measures should be developed and implemented at the state level to realize and protect the rights of persons with disabilities.[13] The situation with data collection has become more complicated since the beginning of the war.

According to the State Statistics Service and the Social Protection Fund for the Disabled, every second person with a disability is of working age and needs rehabilitation and further employment.[14] In the context of employment for people with disabilities, the numbers are even more impressive. According to the Ministry of Social Policy of Ukraine, only 17% of people with disabilities were employed in 2021.[15] However, according to experts, these figures are overstated, as the employment of people with disabilities often exists only 'on paper'. A more realistic figure is 13%.[16] The International Labour Organization (ILO), guided by Convention No. 159 and Recommendation No. 168, emphasizes the importance of promoting decent work and ensuring the full participation of persons with disabilities in the labour market. At the same time, it has consistently emphasised that the persistently low

[12] Smusz-Kulesza, M. (2021). Draft of the Report on the Needs Assessment with Respect to Policy and Legal Framework Revision in the Area of Rights of People with Disabilities in Ukraine. Available at: https://rm.coe.int/final-report-eng-1-/16809f31b5.

[13] UN Policy Paper on Disability. Ukraine. Available at: https://ukraine.un.org/sites/default/files/2021-12/UN%20Policy%20Paper%20on%20Disability_ENG_FINAL.pdf.

[14] Працевлаштування осіб з інвалідністю – зареєстровано доопрацьований законопроект. 30 листопада 2022 [Employment of Persons with Disabilities - a revised draft law has been registered. November 30, 2022]. [In Ukrainian]. Available at: https://www.coe.int/uk/web/kyiv/-/draft-law-on-employment-of-persons-with-disabilities-has-been-registered.

[15] Абдулліна, М. Адаптація робочих місць для людей з інвалідністю. Як держава допомагає у працевлаштуванні людей з інвалідністю і про що говорить міжнародний досвід? 06.03.2023 *Економічна правда.* [Abdullina, M. Adaptation of workplaces for people with disabilities. How does the state help in the employment of people with disabilities and what does international experience show? 06.03.2023. *Ekonomichna Pravda.*] [In Ukrainian]. Available at: https://www.epravda.com.ua/columns/2023/03/6/697696/.

[16] Коваленко, Н. В Україні люди з обмеженими можливостями потерпають від безробіття, 11.10.2011. [Kovalenko, N. People with disabilities suffer from unemployment in Ukraine, 11.10.2011] [In Ukrainian]. Available at: https://www.radiosvoboda.org/a/24364674.html.

employment rate among persons with disabilities is unacceptable and must be urgently and significantly improved.[17]

Thus, the current situation in the field of employment of persons with disabilities requires urgent improvement of the regulatory framework that ensures the realization of their right to employment. The right to employment for people with disabilities is guaranteed by the Constitution of Ukraine, first and foremost. In addition, Ukraine has ratified a number of international conventions that are intended to prevent discrimination against persons with disabilities in the workplace. These include ILO Convention No. 159 on Vocational Rehabilitation and Employment (Disabled Persons) and No. 173 on Protection of Workers' Claims (Employer's Insolvency), the UN Declaration on the Rights of Mentally Retarded Persons, the UN Declaration on the Rights of Disabled Persons, the UN Declaration on Standard Rules on the Equalization of Opportunities for Persons with Disabilities and UN Convention on the Rights of Persons with Disabilities. Thus, on the one hand, people with disabilities have all the same labour rights as people without disabilities. On the other hand, the state provides a number of guarantees for people with disabilities aimed at their inclusion in the labour market. For example, the Labour Code of Ukraine regulates special labour regimes, working hours, and other conditions. According to its provisions, employers must organize working conditions for such employees in accordance with their individual rehabilitation program, organize training, retraining, and employment of persons with disabilities in accordance with medical recommendations, and establish part-time or part-time work at their request. Persons with disabilities of groups I and II are entitled to an annual basic leave of 30 calendar days, and persons with disabilities of group III—26 calendar days. Such persons may apply for an unpaid leave, which is granted at the request of the employee on a mandatory basis: for persons with disabilities of group III—for up to 30 calendar days annually and for persons with disabilities of groups I and II—for up to 60 calendar days annually. Restrictions are established on the involvement of persons with disabilities in overtime and night work. Such involvement is not allowed without their consent. At the same time, according to the Labour Code, disabled employees may be dismissed on a general basis.

The Law of Ukraine "On Rehabilitation of Persons with Disabilities in Ukraine," mentions two types of workplaces for people with disabilities: regular and special.[18]

The main legal act in Ukraine that defines the basis for the social protection of persons with disabilities is the Law of Ukraine "On the Fundamentals of Social Protection of Persons with Disabilities in Ukraine" (LFSPPD), which recognises

[17] New ILO database highlights labour market challenges of persons with disabilities. June 13, 2022. Available at: https://ilostat.ilo.org/blog/new-ilo-database-highlights-labour-market-challenges-of-persons-with-disabilities/.

[18] Закон України «Про реабілітацію осіб з інвалідністю в Україні» від 06.10.2005 № 2961-IV [The Law of Ukraine "On Rehabilitation of Persons with Disabilities in Ukraine" of 06.10.2005 No. 2961-IV] [In Ukrainian]. Available at: https://zakon.rada.gov.ua/laws/show/2961-15#Text.

employment as one of the guarantees of such protection.[19] According to the Article 18 of this Law, employers are obliged to allocate and create workplaces for the employment of persons with disabilities, including separate (special) workplaces, organize appropriate working conditions for them, taking into account individual rehabilitation programs, and provide other social and economic guarantees established by applicable law. In addition, pursuant to Article 19 of the Law, employers are required to set a standard of 4% of the average number of full-time employees on the payroll for the year, and if they employ 8 to 25 people, one workplace.

Unfortunately, the quota system, as one of the main characteristics of the Ukrainian state policy on the employment of persons with disabilities, which is reflected in the regulatory definition of the number of workplaces that employers are obliged to create to ensure the employment of persons with disabilities, does not work. It is ineffective, primarily for the people for whom it was made. Instead, it is an example of the inefficiency of the system of creating and allocating workplaces for persons with disabilities, as it allows unfair employers to avoid paying administrative and economic sanctions by not employing persons with disabilities. Finally, the application of these sanctions in practice is also an ineffective way to accumulate funds for the Social Protection Fund for Persons with Disabilities, which should be used for its intended purpose—supporting the employment of persons with disabilities and creating new workplaces.

In addition, the LFSPPD defining the subjects of the social obligation to employ persons with disabilities, contains discriminatory conditions. The point is that the entire scope of social responsibility in the field of promoting the employment of persons with disabilities, including for failure to meet the standard for employment and creating appropriate working conditions in the workplace, is assigned to private sector employers. The LFSPPD does not establish such an obligation for state or municipal institutions. Therefore, the state, declaring the status of a welfare state, has legally exempted itself (did not provide for itself) from the same obligation to employ persons with disabilities.[20]

The current legislation lacks effective tools for efficient state support of employers and their motivation to employ persons with disabilities. It does not provide for a differentiated approach to the employment of different categories of persons with disabilities. In this regard, the association of social enterprises (to promote the employment of persons with disabilities) exclusively with enterprises founded by organizations of persons with disabilities looks strange. At the same time, in

---

[19] Закон України «Про основи соціальної захищеності осіб з інвалідністю» від 21.03.1991 № 876- XII [The Law of Ukraine "On the Fundamentals of Social Protection of Persons with Disabilities" of 21.03.1991 No. 876-XII] [In Ukrainian]. Available at: https://zakon.rada.gov.ua/laws/show/875-12?find=1&text=дота#w1_4.

[20] Пилипенко, П., Бурак, В., Рим, О. (2023) Стандарти соціального захисту осіб з інвалідністю: новели законодавства України. *Юридичний науковий електронний журнал*. № 11/2023. С. 223 [Pylypenko, P., Burak, V., Rym, O. Standards of social protection of persons with disabilities: novelties of Ukrainian legislation. *Legal scientific electronic journal*. № 11/2023. P. 223.] [In Ukrainian]. Available at: http://www.lsej.org.ua/11_2023/51.pdf.

European countries, these forms can have different expressions - from the establishment of enterprises by the private sector to the creation of such enterprises by persons with disabilities.

The mechanism for obtaining assistance for reasonable accommodation is highly complicated, which leads to the private sector's refusal to apply for the relevant subsidies. Aid recipients mainly include enterprises of public organizations of disabled people.

The above shortcomings of the current system of employment of persons with disabilities do not facilitate the employment of these persons but rather create obstacles to their employment. Consequently, the current social legislation of Ukraine does not contain effective mechanisms for implementing state policy in the field of ensuring the right to work for persons with disabilities and their employment, especially in the open labour market. According to the data, in 2021, no special workplace for the employment of persons with disabilities was funded in Ukraine.[21] Therefore, the problem of job accessibility and reasonable accommodation remains open, and there has been no progress in recent years.

With the aim of facilitating access to the labour market for disabled people and removing barriers in the workplace in August 2023 the Government introduced a programme to compensate employers for making workplaces accessible to people with disabilities.[22] Under the programme, an employer who accomodates a workplace for a person with a group 1 disability by purchasing equipment, furniture, appliances, etc., will receive compensation of 15 minimum wages. The compensation for a workplace adapted for a person with a group 2 disability is 10 minimum wages.[23]

Ukraine has pledged to comply with the status of a welfare state and has ratified a number of international documents in this regard.[24] All of this necessitates the development of an effective mechanism for the employment of persons with disabilities as the most effective form of their proactive social protection. Moreover, in the context of the ongoing process of EU integration, Ukraine faces the challenge of

---

[21] Пояснювальна записка до проєкту Закону України «Про внесення змін до деяких законів України щодо забезпечення прав осіб з інвалідністю на працю». 18 листопада 2022 [Explanatory Note to the Draft Law of Ukraine "On Amendments to Certain Laws of Ukraine on Ensuring the Rights of Persons with Disabilities to Work". November 18, 2022] [In Ukrainian]. Available at: https://itd.rada.gov.ua/billInfo/Bills/pubFile/1549495.

[22] Work without barriers: 10,000 jobs for people with disabilities to be created by employers at state expense in 2024. Ministry of Economy of Ukraine, 13 December 2023. Available at: https://www.kmu.gov.ua/en/news/robota-bez-barieriv-10-000-robochykh-mists-dlia-liudei-z-invalidnistiu-zmozhut-oblashtuvaty-robotodavtsi-za-koshty-derzhavy-u-2024-rotsi.

[23] Minimum wage increase increases compensation for workplace equipment for employees with disabilities. April 1, 2024. Available at: https://okna.ua/en/news/20240401/minimum-wage-increase-increases.

[24] UN Convention on the Rights of Persons with Disabilities (ratified on 16 December 2009), ILO Human Resources Development Convention № 142 (ratified in 1979), European Convention on Human Rights (ratified on 17 July 1997), European Social Charter (revised) (ratified on 14 September 2006).

the aligning its national legislation with the EU acquis in the social and employment sphere. In order to understand where Ukraine is now in implementing international and European equality standards, it is necessary to highlight the main of them as well as the current European policy on the employment of people with disabilities.

3 International and European Standards on Employment of Disabled People

3.1 UN and Council of Europe standards

The UN Convention on the Rights of Persons with Disabilities (CRPD, Convention), adopted in 2006 (entered into force for the EU on 23 January 2011), was the first legally binding international instrument setting minimum standards for the rights of persons with disabilities.

Article 27 of the CRPD defines "the right of persons with disabilities to work on an equal basis with others; this includes the right to the opportunity to gain a living by work freely chosen or accepted in a labour market and work environment that is open, inclusive and accessible to persons with disabilities."[25] In 2015, Ukraine submitted its First Periodic Report on the Implementation of the Convention on the Rights of Persons with Disabilities to the UN Committee on the Rights of Persons with Disabilities.[26] Public associations of persons with disabilities submitted to the Committee an Alternative Report of Public Organisations on the Implementation of the UN Convention on the Rights of Persons with Disabilities.[27] With a view to further implementation of the Convention in Ukraine, the Committee provided concluding observations on Ukraine's initial report on the implementation of the UN Convention on the Rights of Persons with Disabilities. With regard to labour and employment (Art. 27), the Committee expressed concern that the employment quota requirement was not being properly implemented and that most persons with disabilities remained unemployed. Furthermore, the Committee is concerned about the lack of employment opportunities for persons with mental and psychosocial disabilities and the absence of policies or programmes for supported employment in the open labour market. The Committee called on the Ukrainian government to ensure the effective implementation of constructive measures and to strengthen

[25] UN Convention on the Rights of Persons with Disabilities. Available at: https://social.desa.un.org/issues/disability/crpd/article-27-work-and-employment.

[26] UN Committee on the Rights of Persons with Disabilities (CRPD), Consideration of reports submitted by States parties under article 35 of the Convention, Initial reports of States parties due in 2012: Ukraine, CRPD/C/UKR/1, 12 November 2014. Available at: https://www.refworld.org/reference/statepartiesrep/crpd/2014/en/106638.

[27] CRPD, Alternative report on compliance with the UN Convention on the Rights of Persons with Disabilities, 5 June 2015. Available at: https://www.slideshare.net/slideshow/alternative-report-ukraine/49033184.

incentives for businesses and the public sector to employ people with disabilities. The Committee also recommended taking measures to ensure supported employment for people with intellectual and psychosocial disabilities in the open labour market.[28]

By ratifying the CRPD in December 2009, Ukraine joined an internationally agreed effort to guarantee the fundamental rights of persons with disabilities. The National Action Plan for the Implementation of the Convention on the Rights of Persons with Disabilities for the period up to 2020 was approved by the Cabinet of Ministers of Ukraine on 1 August 2012. The Plan aimed to promote, protect and ensure the full and equal enjoyment of all human rights and fundamental freedoms by persons with disabilities in all areas of public life, taking into account the provisions of the Convention, as well as to take measures to ensure respect for their inherent dignity.[29] In April 2021, the Plan was renewed for the period up to 2025.[30]

Ukraine has been a member of the Council of Europe since 1995 and has ratified its core human rights instruments, including the European Convention on Human Rights (ECHR) and the European Social Charter (revised) (ESCr), thus it is worthwhile to start this section by looking at the standards proclaimed by them. Indeed, the Council of Europe documents play a particularly important role among European standards in the field of employment of people with disabilities, as all EU Member States are members of the Council of Europe and have ratified both documents.

The ECHR provides the fundamental framework for the Council of Europe Member State to protect and promote human rights for all, including the rights of people with disabilities. The European Court of Human Rights (ECtHR) has developed these rights in its case law. Despite the fact that the case law of the ECtHR contains only a few decisions dealing with the issue of employment or access to education of disabled people and the denial of reasonable accommodation in this regard, the ECtHR has overall played an important role in encouraging states to ensure equality rights of people with disabilities.

In the case of *Çam v Turkey,* 23 February 2016, the Court found a violation of Article 14 in conjunction with Article 2 of Protocol No. 1 because the relevant

[28] CRPD, Concluding Observations in relation to the initial report of Ukraine, CRPD/C/UKR/CO/1, 4 September 2015. Available at: https://www.refworld.org/policy/polrec/crpd/2015/en/107065.

[29] Постанова Кабінету Міністрів України від 01.08.2012 № 706 "Про затвердження Державної цільової програми "Національний план дій з реалізації Конвенції про права осіб з інвалідністю" на період до 2020 року [Resolution No. 706 of 1 August 2012 on the approval of the State Target Programme "National Action Plan for the Implementation of the Convention on the Rights of Persons with Disabilities' for the period up to 2020" [In Ukrainian]. Available at: https://zakon.rada.gov.ua/laws/show/706-2012-%D0%BF#Text.

[30] Розпорядження Кабінету Міністрів України від 07.04.2021 № 285-р Про затвердження Національного плану дій з реалізації Конвеції про права осіб з інвалідністю на період до 2025 року" [Order of the Cabinet of Ministers of Ukraine dated 07.04.2021 No 285-r on approval of the National Action Plan for the implementation of the Convention on the Rights of Persons with Disabilities for the period until 2025 [In Ukrainian]. Available at: https://zakon.rada.gov.ua/laws/show/285-2021-%D1%80#Text.

domestic authorities had at no stage attempted to identify the applicant's needs (they refused to enroll a blind person in the Music Academy even though she had passed the examination) or to explain how her blindness could have impeded her access to a musical education. Nor had the authorities ever considered that reasonable accommodation might have enabled her to be educated in the Music Academy (the domestic authorities at no stage considered special accommodations to meet any special educational needs resulting from the applicant's blindness). Although the applicant was entirely qualified for admission to the academy, the refusal to enrol her was based solely on the fact that she was blind. Furthermore, the Court considered that the discrimination on grounds of disability also extended to the refusal to make reasonable accommodation to facilitate access by persons with disabilities to education. Such accommodation was vital for the exercise of human rights. By refusing to enrol the applicant without considering the possibility of accommodating her disability, the national authorities had prevented her, without any objective and reasonable justification, from benefiting from musical education in breach of the Convention.[31]

In the case *Enver Şahin v. Turkey*, 30 January 2018 the impossibility for a paraplegic person to gain access to the university buildings for his studies owing to the lack of suitable facilities was examined. The applicant complained in particular that he had been obliged to give up his studies owing to the refusal of his request for the facilities to be adapted. The Court held that there had been a violation of Article 14 (prohibition of discrimination) of the Convention read in conjunction with Article 2 (right to education) of Protocol No. 1, finding that the Turkish Government had not demonstrated that the national authorities, and in particular the university and judicial authorities, had reacted with the requisite diligence in order to ensure that the applicant could continue to enjoy his right to education on an equal footing with other students. The Court noted in particular that a proposal by the rector's office to provide a person to assist him had not been made following an assessment of the applicant's actual needs and an honest appraisal of the potential impact on his safety, dignity and independence. Furthermore, the domestic courts had not ascertained whether a fair balance had been struck between the competing interests of the applicant (his educational needs) and society as a whole. They had also omitted to look for possible solutions that would have enabled the applicant to resume his studies under conditions as close as possible to those provided to students with no disability, without imposing an undue or disproportionate burden on the administration.[32]

In the case *Bayrakcı v. Turkey*, 5 February 2016, the applicant, who was employed as a tax official, had one leg amputated and was registered as 60% disabled. He complained that his management had not complied with the legislation on disabilities because of the lack of suitable toilet facilities installed at his workplace. The Court rejected the applicant's complaint for failure to exhaust domestic remedies,

[31] Case of *ÇAM v. Turkey* (application no. 51500/08), 23 February 2016. Available at: https://hudoc.echr.coe.int/eng-press?i=003-5307099-6607283.

[32] Case of *Enver Şahin v. Turkey*, (application no. 23065/12), 30 January 2018. Available at: https://hudoc.echr.coe.int/eng-press?i=003-5989451-7665919.

finding that he had not brought an action in the Turkish courts against the State authorities for failure to comply with the statutory provisions on disabilities, and declared his application inadmissible. However, ECtHR noticed that the lack of suitable toilet facilities at his workplace could admittedly have had real and serious consequences for the applicant's daily life, such as arousing feelings of humiliation and distress that could impinge on the quality of his private life.[33]

The ESCr is the primary legal document defining the Council of Europe's standards in the field of social and economic rights and, in particular, the right of persons with disabilities to independence, social integration and participation in the life of the community. An essential element of Article 15 of the ESCr is its second paragraph, which directly relates to employment and provides that the Parties undertake to promote their access to employment through all measures tending to encourage employers to hire and keep in employment persons with disabilities in the ordinary working environment and to adjust the working conditions to the needs of people with disabilities or, where this is not possible because of the disability, by arranging for or creating sheltered employment according to the level of disability. Such measures may sometimes require recourse to specialised placement and support services. Under this provision, Parties must aim to develop a coherent policy for people with disabilities. The provision takes a modern approach to how the protection of disabled people shall be carried out, for example, by providing guidance, education, and vocational training whenever possible in the framework of general schemes rather than specialised institutions. It not only provides the possibility but, to a large extent, obliges Parties to adopt positive measures for the disabled. It is understood that the term "sheltered employment" in paragraph 2 also covers working co-operatives.[34]

The European Committee of Social Rights (ECSR) plays an important role in interpreting the provisions of the ESCr. In its numerous conclusions, the ECSR has repeatedly emphasised that Article 15§2 requires States Parties to promote equal and effective access to employment on the open labour market for persons with disabilities. It applies to persons with physical and/or intellectual disabilities.

The effective exercise of the right of persons with disabilities to vocational training and rehabilitation requires specific measures to be taken, which may if need be, take the form of positive action designed to improve the "employability" of disabled persons and their access to and ability to remain in employment. Employment policy for disabled people must allow them to use their skills by offering them jobs corresponding to their employment potential within the ordinary working environment. In addition, particular emphasis must be put on the protection of persons who are disabled as a result of an occupational accident or illness.

The specific account taken of disabilities in working life implies the responsibility of all its participants: the State, employers, and trade unions. The aim of this

[33] Case of *Bayrakcı v. Turkey* (application no. 2643/09), 5 February 2016. Available at: https://hudoc.echr.coe.int/eng-press?i=003-6628750-8799234.

[34] Explanatory Report to the European Social Charter (Revised) Strasbourg, 3.V.1996. Available at: https://rm.coe.int/16800ccde4.

provision of the Charter is therefore to achieve equal employment opportunities for persons with disabilities by not only rethinking the disability itself but also obtaining the participation of disabled persons in the life of the community on an equal footing.[35]

States Parties enjoy a margin of discretion concerning the other measures they take to promote access to employment for persons with disabilities. Article 15§2 does not require the introduction of quotas, but when such a system is applied, its effectiveness is taken into consideration when assessing conformity with Article 15§2.[36]

Article 15§2 of the ESCr requires that persons with disabilities be employed in an ordinary working environment, except where this is not possible due to the nature of the disability. In such exceptional cases, provision may be made for sheltered employment. They should aim to assist their beneficiaries to enter the open labour market.[37]

People working in sheltered employment facilities where production is the main activity are entitled to the basic provisions of labour law, particularly the right to fair remuneration and trade union rights.[38]

The ECSR, when assessing whether the situation in a state complies with Article 15 § 2 of the ESCr, focuses on three areas: employment of persons with disabilities, anti-discrimination norms and measures to promote the employment of persons with disabilities. In assessing whether the situation in a state complies with Article 15 § 2 of the ESCr and whether persons with disabilities have adequate equal access to work, the ECSR takes into account not only the relevant legislation, including judicial and non-judicial remedies provided for in the event of discrimination on the grounds of disability but also its fairness and practical aspects, for example, figures concerning the total number of persons with disabilities, including those in the age of working; those employed (on the open market and in sheltered employment); those benefiting from employment promotion measures; those seeking employment; those that are unemployed as well as the general transfer rate of people with disabilities from sheltered to open market employment.[39]

An essential step of the Council of Europe was adopting the Council of Europe Disability Strategy 2017-2023. The overall goal of this Strategy was to achieve equality, dignity, and equal opportunities for people with disabilities, which requires

---

[35] Conclusions XIV-2 (1998), Statement of Interpretation on Article 15. Available at: https://hudoc.esc.coe.int/eng#{%22sort%22:[%22escpublicationdate%20descending%22],%22escdcidentifier%22:[%22XIV-2_Ob_V1-11/Ob/EN%22]}.

[36] Conclusions XIV-2 (1998), Belgium. Available at: https://hudoc.esc.coe.int/eng?i=XIV-2/def/BEL/15/2/EN.

[37] Conclusions 2005, Estonia. Available at: https://hudoc.esc.coe.int/eng?i=2005/def/EST/15/2/EN.

[38] Conclusions XVII-2 (2005), Czech Republic. Available at: https://hudoc.esc.coe.int/eng?i=XVII-2/def/CZE/15/2/EN.

[39] Conclusions XX-1 (2012), Czech Republic. Available at: https://hudoc.esc.coe.int/eng?i=XX-1/def/CZE/15/2/EN; Conclusions 2012, Cyprus. Available at: https://hudoc.esc.coe.int/eng?i=2012/def/CYP/15/2/EN.

ensuring independence, freedom of choice, and full and effective participation in all spheres of life and society, including community life. The Strategy focuses on five priority areas (equality and non-discrimination; awareness raising; accessibility; equal recognition before the law; freedom from exploitation, violence and abuse) and is directed at five cross-cutting themes (participation, cooperation and collaboration - coordination; universal design and reasonable accommodation; gender equality perspective; multiple discrimination; education and training). In the context of employment of persons with disabilities, the Strategy focuses on the need for effective anti-discrimination measures and ensuring proper vocational training and education of persons with disabilities.[40]

3.2 EU Standards

The identification of EU standards relating to the employment of people with disabilities cannot be separated from the evolution of a legal framework at the EU level for the rights of people with disabilities in general. These standards in the field of disability rights did not emerge overnight, and their development has been quite a long process.

The rights of people with disabilities have been enshrined in the EU Treaties since 1997. However, the primary law of the European Union became explicitly inclusive of persons with disabilities with the entry into force on 1 May 1999 of the Amsterdam Treaty, which inserted an article into the Treaty (now Article 19 in the Treaty on the Functioning of the European Union (TFEU) allowing the Council of Ministers to take appropriate measures to combat discrimination on the ground of disability (among other grounds).[41] The current TFEU entered into force on 1 December 2009, adding a new provision (Article 10 TFEU) that stipulates that "in defining and implementing its policies and activities, the Union shall aim to combat discrimination based on sex, racial or ethnic origin, religion or belief, disability, age or sexual orientation."[42]

The Charter of Fundamental Rights of the European Union, adopted in 2000 and given legal effect by the Lisbon Treaty on its entry into force in December 2009, prohibits discrimination on the grounds of disability (Article 21) and recognises and

[40] Council of Europe Disability Strategy 2017-2023. Available at: https://www.coe.int/en/web/disability/strategy-2017-2023.

[41] Consolidated versions of the Treaty on European Union and the Treaty on the Functioning of the European Union - Consolidated version of the Treaty on the Functioning of the European Union - Protocols - Annexes - Declarations annexed to the Final Act of the Intergovernmental Conference which adopted the Treaty of Lisbon, signed on 13 December 2007. Available at: https://eur-lex.europa.eu/legal-content/EN/TXT/HTML/?uri=CELEX%3A12012E%2FTXT.

[42] Ibid.

respects the right of persons with disabilities to independence, social and occupational integration and participation in society (Article 26).[43]

To guarantee the rights of persons with disabilities to employment, the EU has Directive 2000/78/EC, which establishes general conditions for equal treatment in employment and occupation. It is the only EU non-discrimination directive of direct relevance to people with disabilities adopted so far under Article 13 of the EC Treaty (now Article 19 TFEU). The Directive obliges the Member States to take measures to prohibit direct and indirect discrimination and harassment on the grounds of disability (among other grounds) with regard to employment (including recruitment) and vocational training. Article 5 regulates the provision of reasonable accommodation for persons with disabilities, placing employers under obligation to provide workplace adjustments if needed.[44] The obligation on employers to provide reasonable accommodation became a conceptual novelty.[45] The Directive defines the concept of reasonable accommodation as 'appropriate measures, where needed in a particular case, to enable a person with a disability to have access to, participate in, or advance in employment, or to undergo training'. The wording 'where needed in a particular case' underlines the individual nature of this measure. However, there is no absolute obligation to provide reasonable accommodation, as the provision contains a limitation concerning the costs/burdens of the measures, spelt out unless such measures would impose a disproportionate burden on the employer.[46]

In the field of health and safety in the workplace, EU law recognises the need for particular measures to protect workers with disabilities. "Workplaces must be organised to take account of handicapped workers, if necessary. This provision applies in particular to the doors, passageways, staircases, showers, washbasins, lavatories and workstations used or occupied directly by handicapped persons".[47]

It should also be noted that disputes and conflicts arising in the area of disability discrimination are subject to review by the EU Court of Justice (ECJ), the highest level of the EU's judicial system. The Court has clarified that Directive 2000/78/EC must be interpreted in line with the CRPD and has done so in many cases. This fact allows to consider the CRPD as one of the most influential human rights instruments on the case law of the ECJ.[48]

[43] Charter of Fundamental Rights of the European Union. OJ C 364, 18.12.2000. Available at: https://www.europarl.europa.eu/charter/pdf/text_en.pdf.

[44] Council Directive 2000/78/EC of 27 November 2000 establishing a general framework for equal treatment in employment and occupation. Available at: http://data.europa.eu/eli/dir/2000/78/oj.

[45] Implementation of the Employment Equality Directive in light of the UN CRPD. European Implementation Assessment. Available at: https://www.europarl.europa.eu/RegData/etudes/STUD/2020/654206/EPRS_STU(2020)654206_EN.pd.

[46] Ibid.

[47] Council Directive 89/654/EEC of 30 November 1989 concerning the minimum safety and health requirements for the workplace (first individual directive within the meaning of Article 16 (1) of Directive 89/391/EEC. Available at: https://eur-lex.europa.eu/eli/dir/1989/654/oj.

[48] Liu, K., O'Cinneide, C. (2019), The ongoing evolution of the case-law of the Court of Justice of the European Union on Directives 2000/43/EC and 2000/78/EC: a legal analysis of the situation in EU Member States, European Commission, pp. 7, 44.

Given the significant role of ECJ case law in interpreting the provisions of Directive 2000/78/EC, some cases are worth mentioning. For example, in the *HK Danmark* decision[49] the ECJ interpreted Article 5 of Directive 2000/78/EC. In this case, two employees were dismissed from their jobs on short notice due to their absence from work due to health problems. The employer denied that the concept of disability covered the applicants' health condition. The Court stated that "Directive 2000/78 must, as far as possible, be interpreted in a manner consistent with this UN CRPD'. As a result, the Court, in this case, noted that "the term 'disability' should be understood as referring to a limitation which, in particular, results from a physical, mental or psychological impairment which, when interacting with various barriers, may hinder a person's full and effective participation in occupational life on an equal basis with other workers." This means that disability does not necessarily mean complete exclusion from work or professional life.

Furthermore, the ECJ has held that under Article 5 of the Directive, equality of access means that employers are obliged to take appropriate measures to enable a disabled person to access, participate in or be promoted in work. The Court referred to the broad definition of reasonable accommodation in Article 2 of the CRPD.

In this case, the Court also noted that, under the Directive and Article 2(2) of the CRPD on reasonable accommodation, measures in this regard are not limited to specific material adaptations but may include organisational measures. Thus, it was held that reducing working hours may be considered a reasonable accommodation measure if the reduction enables the employee to continue working. The ECJ left the matter to the national Court to assess whether the reduction in working hours in this particular case represented a disproportionate burden on the employer.

Legal literature has widely discussed the ECJ's ruling in *HK Danmark*. It is considered a "particularly rich and important judgment for understanding how the Directive 2000/78/EC addresses disability discrimination, and, more generally, the relevance of the CRPD for the interpretation of EU law in the context of disability".[50]

In the C-270/16 *Ruiz Conejero* ruling the concept of absenteeism versus protection of persons with disabilities was interpreted.[51] The Spanish Court referred the case to the ECJ for a preliminary ruling, asking whether the provision in the Spanish labour law that allows employees to be dismissed after accumulated sickness absences was in conformity with Directive 2000/78/EC. This provision, aimed at combating absenteeism, which is reportedly a significant cause for concern in Spain, is phrased neutrally because it applies to all workers, with or without disabilities.

---

[49] CJEU, C-335/11 and C-337/11, HK Danmark, acting on behalf of Jette Ring v. Dansk almennyttigt Boligselskab and HK Danmark, acting on behalf of Lone Skouboe Werge v. Dansk Arbejdsgiverforening, acting on behalf of Pro Display A/S, 11 April 2013. Available at: https://curia.europa.eu/juris/liste.jsf?num=C-335/11&language=EN.

[50] Implementation of the Employment Equality Directive in light of the UN CRPD. European Implementation Assessment, p.16. Available at: https://www.europarl.europa.eu/RegData/etudes/STUD/2020/654206/EPRS_STU(2020)654206_EN.pd.

[51] CJEU, C-270/16 Carlos Enrique Ruiz Conejero v Ferroser Servicios Auxiliares SA and Ministerio Fiscal, 18 January 2018.

When the plaintiff, who had an officially recognised disability, was dismissed following intermittent periods of sick leave, he challenged the decision, arguing that his absences were directly linked to his disability and that his dismissal constituted discrimination based on disability. It should be noted that the employer was not aware of the disability at the time of dismissal. The ECJ held that combating absenteeism at work may be regarded as a legitimate aim, instancing also the direct and indirect costs absenteeism entails for companies. However, it argued that it was for the referring Court to assess the appropriateness of the measures implemented and to ascertain that these were within what was necessary to attain the aim pursued. The Court found that the provision in question was liable to 'place workers with a disability at a disadvantage, and so to bring about a difference of treatment indirectly based on disability' within the meaning of Directive 2000/78/EC, arguing that workers with a disability have the additional risk of being absent by reason of an illness connected with the disability. In this respect, the ECJ cited its earlier *HK Danmark* ruling. The Court held that the Directive must be interpreted as 'precluding national legislation under which an employer may dismiss a worker on the grounds of his intermittent absences from work, even if justified, in a situation where those absences are the consequence of sickness attributable to a disability'. The referring Spanish Court subsequently ruled that the challenged dismissal of Mr Ruiz Conejero was null and void because it constituted indirect disability discrimination.[52]

The ratification of the CRPD by the EU in 2010 catalysed more disability-related legislation in the field of accessibility. At that stage, it was considered a milestone in the history of human rights as it was the first time ever that the EU became a party to an international human rights treaty. The EU framework's mandate encompasses areas of EU competence. It serves as a complement to the national frameworks and independent mechanisms, which bear the primary responsibility for the promotion, protection and monitoring of the CPRD within the Member State.[53]

To lay the ground for the implementation of the CRPD in the EU, the European Disability Strategy 2010-2020: A Renewed Commitment to a Barrier-Free Europe,[54] which has the overall objective to achieve full empowerment and participation of persons with disabilities in society, was adopted in 2010.[55] It aimed to enable people with disabilities to enjoy their rights fully and participate in society and the economy on an equal level with others. The main focus of the Strategy was the elimina-

---

[52] Ibid.

[53] Baciu, E.L. et al. (2015). Where do We Stand on Disability? European and Romanian Policy Developments Regarding the Inclusion and Protection of Disabled Persons, Over the Last Quarter of Century, Revista de Asistenţă Socială, anul XIII, nr. 1/2015, pp. 43–58.

[54] European Disability Strategy 2010-2020: A Renewed Commitment to a Barrier-Free Europe. Available at: https://eur-lex.europa.eu/LexUriServ/LexUriServ.do?uri=COM%3A2010%3A0636%3AFIN%3Aen%3APDF.

[55] The predecessor of the European Disability Strategy was the European Disability Action Plan 2004 – 2010, adopted by the Commission during the 2003 European Year of Persons with Disabilities.

tion of barriers in eight key areas: accessibility, participation, equality, employment, education and training, social protection, health, and external action.

Moreover, the labour inclusion of persons with disabilities is addressed in the European Pillar of Social Rights (EPSR), launched in November 2017 as a (legally non-binding) reform compass for economic and social convergence. The 2017 EPSR Ehas proclaimed the equal opportunities and inclusion of persons with disabilities as one of the fundamental principles. Presented as the highest commitment to social rights in the EU to date, the Pillar has raised the expectations for consistent disability mainstreaming as well as disability-specific instruments at both the EU and national levels. Principle 17 of the Pillar underlines that persons with disabilities have the right to income support that ensures their living in dignity, services that enable them to participate in the labour market and society, and a work environment adapted to their needs.[56] However, the Pillar is not legally binding. Regardless of how promising EPSR may seem, it cannot be enforced in court, nor can the European Commission initiate infringement proceedings against Member States that do not comply with the Pillar's standards. As Garben points out, this is a slightly uncomfortable reality, which some could consider a disappointment especially in light of the prominent reference to social rights: the Pillar spites its own name.[57] From another perspective, the EPSR's significance lies in its impact on the relationship between the EU and its member states. The EPSR and the 'convergence process' in the field of social rights that it encourages could reveal the need for new European Union legislative initiatives.[58]

On 3 March 2021, the European Commission adopted its 2021-2030 Strategy for the rights of persons with disabilities, which seeks to make progress on ensuring that all persons with disabilities in the EU, regardless of their sex, racial or ethnic origin, religion or belief, age or sexual orientation: enjoy their human rights; have equal opportunities and equal access to participate in society and the economy; are able to decide where, how and with whom they live; move freely in the EU regardless of their support needs; no longer experience discrimination.[59]

Based on the lessons drawn from the previous Strategy, the new one takes account of the diversity of disability comprising long-term physical, mental, intellectual or sensory impairments (in line with Article 1 of CRPD), which are often invisible. The Strategy calls on Member States to: establish, by 2024, targets for increasing

---

[56] European Pillar of Social Rights. Available at: https://commission.europa.eu/system/files/2017-11/social-summit-european-pillar-social-rights-booklet_en.pdf.

[57] Garben, S. (2020), The European Pillar of Social Rights and the European social Charter. Europe des droits & libertés/Europe of Rights & Liberties. 2020 (1), pp. 65–78. Available at: https://www.europedeslibertes.eu/article/the-european-pillar-of-social-rights-and-the-european-social-charter/.

[58] De Schutter, O. (2018). The European Pillar of Social Rights and the Role of the European Social Charter in the EU Legal Order. The study prepared at the request of the Secretariat of the European Social Charter and of the CoE-FRA-ENNHRI-Equinet Platform on Economic and Social Rights, Council of Europe, 14 November 2018. Available at: https://rm.coe.int/study-on-the-european-pillar-of-social-rights-and-the-role-of-the-esc-/1680903132.

[59] Union of Equality: Strategy for the Rights of Persons with Disabilities 2021-2030. Available at: https://ec.europa.eu/social/main.jsp?catId=738&langId=en&pubId=8376&furtherPubs=yes.

the employment rate of persons with disabilities and reducing employment rate gaps between persons with and without disabilities to help achieve the 2030 headline employment target proposed in the Action Plan to implement the European Pillar of Social Rights for endorsement by the European Council; strengthen the capacities of employment services for persons with disabilities and enhance work with social partners and organisations of persons with disabilities to that end; facilitate self-employment and entrepreneurship, including for persons with intellectual and psychosocial disabilities, through providing support on legal and business matters, including by using the EU funds.[60]

A package of measures on integrating people with disabilities into the labour market was published on 20 September 2022. This disability employment package should help Member States ensure that people with disabilities enjoy social inclusion and economic autonomy through their employment. In December 2022, the Council of the EU adopted conclusions regarding the inclusion of people with disabilities in the labour market, calling on Member States to implement the guidelines in the package. It covers six areas of action: strengthening the capacities of employment and integration services; promoting hiring perspectives through affirmative action and combating stereotypes; ensuring reasonable accommodation at work; retaining persons with disabilities in employment; preventing disabilities associated with chronic diseases; securing vocational rehabilitation schemes in case of sickness or accidents, and; exploring quality jobs in sheltered employment, and pathways to the open labour market.[61]

Based on the abovementioned overview of the European standards and EU policies on equality and inclusion of persons with disabilities, the next paragraph will present the progress made by Ukraine in developing its national policy on employment of persons with disabilities and its compatibility with the European ones.

4 Ukraine's State Policy Priorities for the Employment of Persons with Disabilities

Today, Ukraine has taken a course toward a barrier-free society—as a new social norm that it strives for and that is gradually being established in state policy. The main guideline for the expected changes is the National Strategy for the Creation of a Barrier-Free Space in Ukraine for the period until 2030, which was adopted in 2021.[62] It provides for the creation of a barrier-free space in Ukraine in 6 main directions:

[60] Ibid.

[61] Disability Employment Package to improve labour market outcomes for persons with disabilities. Available at: https://ec.europa.eu/social/main.jsp?catId=1597&langId=en.

[62] Національна стратегія із створення безбар'єрного простору в Україні на період до 2030 року, схвалена розпорядженням Кабінету Міністрів України від 14.04.2021 № 366-р. [National Strategy for Creating a Barrier-Free Environment in Ukraine until 2030, approved by the

- social and civil accessibility, which involves ensuring equal opportunities for the participation of all people and social groups in the life of communities and the state;
- educational accessibility—a creation of equal opportunities and free access to education, including lifelong education;
- economic accessibility—provision of conditions and opportunities for employment, entrepreneurship of youth, women, the elderly people, people with disabilities, etc.;
- information accessibility—conditions under which people, regardless of their functional impairments or communication capabilities, have access to information in various formats and using technologies that take into account their needs and abilities;
- physical accessibility—the creation of an environment in which public buildings and public places, transport, and services are physically accessible to all social groups;
- digital accessibility—providing access to information, communication, and public and other online services for all social groups, including the elderly, people with disabilities, people living in rural areas, etc.

To implement this Strategy, on April 25, 2023, the Government approved the Action Plan for 2024–2025 for the implementation of the National Strategy for the Formation of a Barrier-Free Space in Ukraine until 2030.[63] The plan defines four priority areas of work: barrier-free space, goods, services, and information. It is expected that the phased and combined implementation of the Strategy's measures will address challenges in the employment policy for people with disabilities.[64]

In fact, the problems faced by Ukraine in the way of employment of persons with disabilities are not unique only to our society. On the contrary, they are characteristic of many states.[65] In this context, the entire international community has been making efforts for a long time to solve these problems and to develop practical steps

---

Ordinance of the Cabinet of Ministers of Ukraine No 366-r, 2021.] [In Ukrainian] Available at: https://zakon.rada.gov.ua/laws/show/366-2021-%D1%80#Text.

[63] Розпорядження Кабінету Міністрів України від 25.04.2023 № 372-р "Про затвердження плану заходів на 2023-2024 роки з реалізації Національної стратегії із створення безбар'єрного простору в Україні на період до 2030 року" [Order of the Cabinet of Ministers of Ukraine dated 25.04.2023 No. 372-p On Approval of the Action Plan for 2023-2024 for the Implementation of the National Strategy for Creating Barrier-Free Space in Ukraine for the Period up to 2030] [In Ukrainian]. Available at: https://zakon.rada.gov.ua/laws/show/372-2023-%D1%80#Text.

[64] Yaroshenko, O.M. et al. (2024), National Strategy for a Barrier-Free Environment: Problems, Tolerance and Implementation. International Social Work, 67(1), pp. 226–241. Available at: https://doi.org/10.1177/00208728221126002.

[65] Оверчук, В.А. (2018). Міжнародний досвід у сфері працевлаштування осіб з інвалідністю. *Науковий вісник Ужгородського національного університету*. Випуск 22, частина 3, с. 14-17. [Overchuk, V.A. International experience in the field of employment of persons with disabilities. *Scientific Bulletin of Uzhhorod National University*. Issue 22, part 3, pp. 14-17] [In Ukrainian].

to overcome them. To this end, Ukraine's strategic partners—the Council of Europe and the European Union—have developed a number of legal acts that oblige member states to act in a certain way. Ukraine is a member of the Council of Europe and, as a candidate country for European Union accession, aspires to become a full member in the future. This promising status determines the vector of domestic legal reforms, especially in the area of equality and non-discrimination. Therefore, on our path to European integration, we must use European standards of social protection for persons with disabilities.

It should be emphasized that the relevant normative design work is underway in Ukraine. Here, it is worth paying attention to the European integration draft law "On Amendments to Certain Laws of Ukraine Regarding Ensuring the Rights of Persons with Disabilities to Work" (No. 5344-d), which the Committee of the Verkhovna Rada of Ukraine on Social Policy and Protection of Veterans' Rights recommended to the Verkhovna Rada of Ukraine to adopt in the second reading and in general.[66] The purpose of this draft law is to ensure the realization by persons with disabilities of their right to work at an appropriate level, taking into account the experience of EU countries and international labour standards.

The draft law No. 5344-d proposes to create favorable conditions for the employment of persons with disabilities, including by implementing approaches approved in other countries to the development of incentive mechanisms for employers and expanding opportunities for persons with disabilities. Among the main innovations of draft law No. 5344-d is the introduction of a target contribution payment instead of administrative and economic sanctions for non-fulfilment of the employment standard. Analysis of the draft law's content allows us to conclude that its developers have refused to adopt a legal approach that substantiates the negative obligation to punish employers for non-compliance with normative legislation regarding the employment of persons with disabilities. Instead, the draft law proposes the concept of economic stimulation for employers to employ persons with disabilities and introduces a control mechanism to ensure the proper employment of persons with disabilities and the maintenance of their labour rights. The new mechanism's basis is employers' payment of insurance contributions to support the employment of persons with disabilities (Article 18-2 of the draft law). Additionally, the minimum number of employees required to calculate the size of these contributions is determined to be eight or more. At the same time, we note that Council Recommendation No. 86/379/EEC of 24.07.1986 on the employment of persons with disabilities in the Community draws attention to the fact that such a minimum can be from 15 to 50 workers.[67] Therefore, the draft law even states a lower limit of the minimum number of employees than recommended at the EU level, which is taken as the basis for establishing the obligation to pay a contribution to support the employment of

[66] Горбунова, О. Право на працю за європейськими зразками, 19 січня 2024 [Horbunova, O. The right to work according to European standards. January 19, 2024] [In Ukrainian] Available at: http://www.golos.com.ua/article/376390.

[67] Council Recommendation No. 86/379/EEC of 24 July 1986 on the employment of disabled people in the Community. Available at: https://eur-lex.europa.eu/eli/reco/1986/379/oj/eng.

persons with disabilities. As a result, the employer will be able to choose to employ persons with disabilities in specially equipped workplaces or to pay a targeted contribution to support their employment to a special fund of the state budget (the funds of which will be spent in a targeted manner).

The provisions of Article 15§2 of the ESCr, which require states to promote access to employment on the open labour market for people with disabilities, are also reflected in the draft law. The practice of the ECSR proves that the successful fulfilment of this obligation by the state will be considered the following:

- adoption of legislation prohibiting discrimination based on disability in employment;
- the same legal obligation to employ persons with disabilities for private and public sector employers;
- measures protecting employees with disabilities from dismissal and the employer's obligation to continue the employment of a person who received a disability as a result of industrial injury or illness;
- compliance with the obligation to provide reasonable accommodation.[68]

All of the above has been reflected in the draft law No. 5344-d.[69] The provisions of the draft law correspond to the practice of the ECSR regarding Article 15 of the ESCr and prescribe the following: the prohibition of discrimination based on disability in the field of employment (Article 2 of the draft law); the extension of the legal obligation to employ persons with disabilities to employers, regardless of the organizational and legal form and form of ownership (Part 2, Article 1 of the draft law); the protection of employees—persons with disabilities from dismissal due to health conditions, and the obligation of employers to ensure the right to work to a person who received a disability as a result of an accident at work or an occupational disease (Article 18 of the draft law).

Moreover, the draft law complies with the social principles of the CRDP by enshrining in it the main principles of the Convention (Article 3), such as respect for the inherent dignity of a person, their independence, in particular, the freedom to make their own choice; non-discrimination; full and effective involvement and inclusion in society; respect for the characteristics of persons with disabilities and acceptance of them as a component of human diversity and a part of humanity; equality of opportunity; accessibility.[70]

The authors of the draft law also did not ignore certain aspects of the general obligations of the member states of the CRDP, in particular regarding the

[68] Ibid. https://eur-lex.europa.eu/eli/reco/1986/379/oj/eng.

[69] Законопроект № 5344-д «Про внесення змін до деяких законів України щодо забезпечення прав осіб з інвалідністю на працю» (редакція, доопрацьована комітетом). 23.03.2023 [Draft Law of Ukraine No. 5344-d "On Amendments to Certain Laws of Ukraine on Ensuring the Rights of Persons with Disabilities to Work" (version revised by the Committee). 23.03.2023.] [In Ukrainian]. Available at: https://itd.rada.gov.ua/billInfo/Bills/pubFile/1704626.

[70] UN Convention on the Rights of Persons with Disabilities. Available at: https://social.desa.un.org/issues/disability/crpd/article-27-work-and-employment.

consideration of persons with disabilities in all strategies and programs for the protection and promotion of human rights; conducting or encouraging experimental and design development of goods, services, equipment, and objects of universal design (which is defined in Article 2 of the Convention), the adaptation of which to the specific needs of a person with a disability would require as little adaptation and minimal costs as possible, promotion of their availability and use, as well as promoting the idea of universal design during the development of standards and guidelines; encouraging the teaching of professionals and staff working with persons with disabilities on the rights recognized in the Convention in order to improve the provision of assistance and services guaranteed by these rights.

In the context of Ukraine's obligation to implement Directive 2000/78/EC on establishing general rules of equal treatment in the field of employment and professional activity, the draft law contains norms designed to prevent the social exclusion of persons with disabilities. In particular, it is proposed to extend the effect of relevant anti-discrimination requirements to both the private and public sectors (state authorities, local self-government bodies, law enforcement agencies, etc.). It is determined that an employer, for the purposes of the draft law, shall be considered a legal entity regardless of its organizational and legal form, a form of ownership, and subordination, as well as a natural person - an entrepreneur who uses the labour of persons under the terms of an employment contract (contract), a service contract or on other conditions stipulated by law.

In order to ensure a barrier-free society for persons with disabilities in the sphere of realization of the right to work, international documents, for example, Article 27 of the CRPD, define a social standard - reasonable accommodation. Article 17-1 of the draft law proposes a range of effective and practical measures that the employer must take to adapt the workplace to the needs of a person with a disability in the context of compliance with the standard of reasonable accommodation. Within this standard, a mechanism has been developed to ensure the individual needs of a person with a disability during employment. The range of these measures, in particular, includes the implementation of modifications and corrections to buildings and premises with the aim of bringing them to a state where they can be used by persons with disabilities, narrowing the content or reducing the scope of work duties for the position held by a person with disabilities, equally as well as changes in the work or study schedule of a person with a disability and others.

The social standard of 'reasonable accommodation during the employment of a person with a disability' is defined in the draft law to ensure the comprehensiveness of social protection for persons with a disability. In particular, Article 17-1 of the draft law provides that social services are provided as part of the standard 'reasonable accommodation during the employment of a person with a disability', in addition to labour guarantees for employees with disability. Clause 9 of the mentioned Article specifies that, if necessary, an employee with disability is provided with an assistant at the workplace or the social service of a personal assistant is engaged, or other employees are engaged to assist in the performance of work duties. All these measures are components of social support for employees with disabilities in the workplace. Separately, the provision of sign language translation services is defined as an element of reasonable accommodation (if necessary). Funding of social services within the framework of the social standard 'reasonable accommodation during the employment of a person with a disability' is planned to be carried out at the expense of the Fund for the Social Protection of Persons with a Disability, which fully complies with Art. 27 of the Law of Ukraine "On Social Services".[71]

According to the draft law No. 5344-d, the legal guarantee of compliance with the standard 'reasonable accommodation of the workplace of a person with a disability' is also to encourage employers to use more funds from state sources through a guaranteed return of what they spent within the limits of reasonable accommodation of the workplace of a person with a disability. In particular, the draft law envisages the employer's right to apply for compensation or a subsidy for reasonable accommodation costs to the Fund for Social Protection of Persons with Disabilities. This norm reflects the implementation of the principle of joint responsibility of society in the field of social protection of persons with disabilities.

The draft law also expands the category of enterprises that can benefit from financial support from the state, such as protected employment enterprises, which will not aim to make a profit but to provide work for people with severe functional limitations. In particular, it refers to Articles 19-1 and 19-2 of the draft law, which provide for the creation of enterprises or entrepreneurs of labour integration or enterprises of protected employment. The specified norms enable the implementation of the principle of a differentiated approach to employers' fulfilment of the obligation to employ persons with different categories of disabilities. These norms were implemented to fulfill Ukraine's obligations under the ESCr, namely, part 2 of Article 15, which defines the provision of access to work for persons with disabilities and the need to adjust working conditions to their needs or, if this is impossible due to disability, to create sheltered employment according to the level of disability.

In addition, the draft law No. 5344-d provides for:

- creation of a special state budget fund to support the employment of persons with disabilities;
- the employer's liability for misuse of funds of the social protection fund for persons with disabilities in double amount;
- the preservation of employment relations with the employer is guaranteed for the employee where the employee has an accident at work/occupational disease;
- the employer's right to the guarantees provided by the Law "On Employment of the Population" in the case of employment of a person with a disability, regardless of his registration as unemployed;
- involvement of private employment agencies in the promotion of employment and employment of persons with disabilities.

A critical analysis of the draft law No. 5344-d "On Amendments to Certain Laws of Ukraine Regarding Ensuring the Rights of Persons with Disabilities to Work"

[71] Закон України «Про соціальні послуги» від 17.01.2019 № 2671-VIII [Law of Ukraine "On Social Services" of 17.01.2019 No. 2671-VIII] [In Ukrainian]. Available at: https://zakon.rada.gov.ua/laws/show/2671-19#Text.

reveals that its content represents a novel conceptual framework in the field of social protection for persons with disabilities and their alignment with international and European social standards.

5 Conclusions

The importance of Ukraine's European and Euro-Atlantic course cannot be overstated, especially in the context of protecting disability rights. Implementing European equality standards is a crucial step towards creating a barrier-free society. It is imperative to study and analyze the mechanisms for supporting the employment of persons with disabilities developed by the international community. This not only creates conditions for the realization of the rights of persons with disabilities but also demonstrates Ukraine's reliability as a potential candidate for European Union membership.

An overview of the challenges facing Ukraine in improving social protection and integration of persons with disabilities, in particular by ensuring their right to work, shows that at this stage, Ukrainian legislation is far from European standards of equality. The main shortcomings of the current Ukrainian legislation in this area, namely discrimination by private sector employers (compared to the public sector) and the lack of reasonable accommodation, are seen as serious obstacles to the proper realization of the rights of persons with disabilities.

However, the main priorities of the state policy on promoting the employment of persons with disabilities have led to the draft law No. 5344-d "On Amendments to Certain Laws of Ukraine on Ensuring the Right of Persons with Disabilities to Work" (2023). Comparing the proposed changes with European standards, we can conclude that the state paradigm for the employment of persons with disabilities has changed. Ensuring compliance with legislation on the rights of people with disabilities and the compliance of the restored infrastructure with the standards of an accessible environment is in line with international and European social standards, contributing to proactive social protection in post-war Ukraine.

The draft law No. 5344-d holds significant potential to determine the possibility of employing a person with a disability on a permissive basis—'all types of work are allowed, except for those expressly prohibited by a medical certificate.' This could enhance the prestige of the employer as a representative of socially responsible business, engender a novel culture of perception of persons with disabilities, and engage the state and business in ensuring the accessibility of the workplace. It is therefore to be hoped that the successful adoption of draft law No. 5344-d and the implementation of the initiatives and measures to support the employment of persons with disabilities will be forthcoming. Consequently, an assessment of the state of Ukrainian legislation compliance with European equality standards reveals that a trajectory aligned with European norms will inevitably result in the equalisation of legal guarantees. Nevertheless, the time required to achieve this goal is perceived as a challenge, as the necessary changes are considered to be urgent.

Legislation and Case Law

Case of ÇAM v. Turkey (application no. 51500/08), 23 February 2016. Available at: https://hudoc.echr.coe.int/eng-press?i=003-5307099-6607283

Case of Enver Şahin v. Turkey, (application no. 23065/12), 30 January 2018. Available at: https://hudoc.echr.coe.int/eng-press?i=003-5989451-7665919

Case of Bayrakcı v. Turkey (application no. 2643/09), 5 February 2016. Available at: https://hudoc.echr.coe.int/eng-press?i=003-6628750-8799234

Charter of Fundamental Rights of the European Union. OJ C 364, 18.12.2000. https://www.europarl.europa.eu/charter/pdf/text_en.pdf

CJEU, C-270/16 Carlos Enrique Ruiz Conejero v Ferroser Servicios Auxiliares SA and Ministerio Fiscal, 18 January 2018.

Conclusions XIV-2 (1998), Statement of Interpretation on Article 15. Available at: https://hudoc.esc.coe.int/eng#{%22sort%22:[%22escpublicationdate%20descending%22],%22escdcidentifier%22:[%22XIV-2_Ob_V1-11/Ob/EN%22]}

Conclusions XIV-2 (1998), Belgium. Available at: https://hudoc.esc.coe.int/eng?i=XIV-2/def/BEL/15/2/EN

Conclusions 2005, Estonia. Available at: https://hudoc.esc.coe.int/eng?i=2005/def/EST/15/2/EN

Conclusions XVII-2 (2005), Czech Republic. Available at: https://hudoc.esc.coe.int/eng?i=XVII-2/def/CZE/15/2/EN

Conclusions XX-1 (2012), Czech Republic. Available at: https://hudoc.esc.coe.int/eng?i=XX-1/def/CZE/15/2/EN

Conclusions 2012, Cyprus. Available at: https://hudoc.esc.coe.int/eng?i=2012/def/CYP/15/2/EN

Consolidated versions of the Treaty on European Union and the Treaty on the Functioning of the European Union - Consolidated version of the Treaty on the Functioning of the European Union - Protocols - Annexes - Declarations annexed to the Final Act of the Intergovernmental Conference which adopted the Treaty of Lisbon, signed on 13 December 2007. Available at: https://eur-lex.europa.eu/legal-content/EN/TXT/HTML/?uri=CELEX%3A12012E%2FTXT

Council Directive 2000/78/EC of 27 November 2000 Establishing a General Framework for Equal Treatment in Employment and Occupation. Available at: http://data.europa.eu/eli/dir/2000/78/oj.

Council of Europe Disability Strategy 2017-2023. Available at: https://www.coe.int/en/web/disability/strategy-2017-2023

Council Recommendation No. 86/379/EEC of 24 July 1986 on the employment of disabled people in the Community. Available at: https://eur-lex.europa.eu/eli/reco/1986/379/oj/eng

European Disability Strategy 2010–2020. Available at: https://eur-lex.europa.eu/LexUriServ/LexUriServ.do?uri=COM%3A2010%3A0636%3AFIN%3Aen%3APDF.

European Convention on Human Rights (ratified on 17 July 1997) Available at: https://www.echr.coe.int/documents/d/echr/convention_ENG

European Pillar of Social Rights. Available at: https://commission.europa.eu/system/files/2017-11/social-summit-european-pillar-social-rights-booklet_en.pdf.

European Social Charter (revised) (ratified on 14 September 2006) Available at: https://rm.coe.int/168048a5e8

ILO Human Resources Development Convention № 142 (ratified in 1979) Available at: https://normlex.ilo.org/dyn/nrmlx_en/f?p=NORMLEXPUB:12100:0::NO::P12100_ILO_CODE:C142

UN Convention on the Rights of Persons with Disabilities. Available at: https://social.desa.un.org/issues/disability/crpd/article-27-work-and-employment.

Union of Equality: Strategy for the Rights of Persons with Disabilities 2021-2030. Available at: https://ec.europa.eu/social/main.jsp?catId=738&langId=en&pubId=8376&furtherPubs=yes

UN Policy Paper on Disability in Ukraine. Available at: https://ukraine.un.org/sites/default/files/2021-12/UN%20Policy%20Paper%20on%20Disability_ENG_FINAL.pdf

Закон України «Про реабілітацію осіб з інвалідністю в Україні» від 06.10.2005 № 2961-IV. [The Law of Ukraine "On Rehabilitation of Persons with Disabilities in Ukraine" of 06.10.2005 No. 2961-IV] [In Ukrainian]. Available at: https://zakon.rada.gov.ua/laws/show/2961-15#Text

Закон України «Про основи соціальної захищеності осіб з інвалідністю» від 21.03.1991 № 876-XII [The Law of Ukraine "On the Fundamentals of Social Protection of Persons with Disabilities" of 21.03.1991 No. 876-XII] [In Ukrainian]. Available at: https://zakon.rada.gov.ua/laws/show/875-12?find=1&text=дота#w1_4

Закон України «Про соціальні послуги» від 17.01.2019 № 2671-VIII [Law of Ukraine "On Social Services" of 17.01.2019 No. 2671-VIII] [In Ukrainian]. Available at: https://zakon.rada.gov.ua/laws/show/2671-19#Text

Національна стратегія із створення безбар'єрного простору в Україні на період до 2030 року, схвалена розпорядженням Кабінету Міністрів України від 14.04.2021 № 366-р. [National Strategy for Creating a Barrier-Free Environment in Ukraine until 2030, approved by the Ordinance of the Cabinet of Ministers of Ukraine No 366-r, 2021.] [In Ukrainian]. Available at: https://zakon.rada.gov.ua/laws/show/366-2021-%D1%80#Text

Положення про централізований банк даних з проблем інвалідності, затверджене Постановою Кабінету Міністрів України від 16.02.2011 № 121 [Regulation on the Centralised Data Bank on Disability, approved by the Cabinet of Ministers of Ukraine on 16 February 2011, № 121] [In Ukrainian]. Available at: https://zakon.rada.gov.ua/laws/show/121-2011-%D0%BF#Text

Постанова Кабінету Міністрів України від 01.08.2012 № 706 "Про затвердження Державної цільової програми "Національний план дій з реалізації Конвенції про права осіб з інвалідністю" на період до 2020 року [Resolution No. 706 of 1 August 2012 on the approval of the State Target Programme "National Action Plan for the Implementation of the Convention on the Rights of Persons with Disabilities' for the period up to 2020" [In Ukrainian]. Available at: https://zakon.rada.gov.ua/laws/show/706-2012-%D0%BF#Text

Розпорядження Кабінету Міністрів України від 07.04.2021 № 285-р Про затвердження Національного плану дій з реалізації Конвенції про права осіб з інвалідністю на період до 2025 року" [Order of the Cabinet of Ministers of Ukraine dated 07.04.2021 No 285-r on approval of the National Action Plan for the implementation of the Convention on the Rights of Persons with Disabilities for the period until 2025 [In Ukrainian]. Available at: https://zakon.rada.gov.ua/laws/show/285-2021-%D1%80#Text

Розпорядження Кабінету Міністрів України від 25.04.2023 № 372-р "Про затвердження плану заходів на 2023-2024 роки з реалізації Національної стратегії із створення безбар'єрного простору в Україні на період до 2030 року" [Order of the Cabinet of Ministers of Ukraine dated 25.04.2023 No. 372-р On Approval of the Action Plan for 2023-2024 for the Implementation of the National Strategy for Creating Barrier-Free Space in Ukraine for the Period up to 2030] [In Ukrainian]. Available at: https://zakon.rada.gov.ua/laws/show/372-2023-%D1%80#Text

Reports and Online Sources

Commission staff working document. Ukraine 2023 Report. Accompanying the document Communication from the Commission to the European Parliament, the Council, the European Economic and Social Committee and the Committee of the Regions 2023 Communication on EU Enlargement policy. Available at: https://op.europa.eu/en/publication-detail/-/publication/a0f3eaa6-7eee-11ee-99ba-01aa75ed71a1/language-en

De Schutter, O. (2018). The European Pillar of Social Rights and the Role of the European Social Charter in the EU Legal Order. The study prepared at the request of the Secretariat of the European Social Charter and of the CoE-FRA-ENNHRI-Equinet Platform on Economic and Social Rights, Council of Europe, 14 November 2018. Available at: https://rm.coe.int/study-on-the-european-pillar-of-social-rights-and-the-role-of-the-esc-/1680903132

Digest of the case law of the European committee of social rights, Council of Europe, June 2022. P. 138-139. Available at: https://rm.coe.int/digest-ecsr-prems-106522-web-en/1680a95dbd

Disability Employment Package to improve labour market outcomes for persons with disabilities. Available at: https://ec.europa.eu/social/main.jsp?catId=1597&langId=en

Explanatory Report to the European Social Charter (Revised) Strasbourg, 3.V.1996. Available at: https://rm.coe.int/16800ccde4

International Monetary Fund. World Economic Outlook Database: April 2025. Ukraine. Available at: https://www.imf.org/en/Publications/WEO/weo-database/2025/april/weo-report?c=926,&s=LUR,LP,&sy=2023&ey=2030&ssm=0&scsm=1&scc=0&ssd=1&ssc=0&sic=0&sort=country&ds=.&br=1

Minimum wage increase increases compensation for workplace equipment for employees with disabilities. April 1, 2024. Available at: https://okna.ua/en/news/20240401/minimum-wage-increase-increases

New ILO database highlights labour market challenges of persons with disabilities. June 13, 2022. Available at: https://ilostat.ilo.org/blog/new-ilo-database-highlights-labour-market-challenges-of-persons-with-disabilities/

Pancevski, B. (2023). In Ukraine, Amputations Already Evoke Scale of World War I. *Wall Street Journal*. Available at: https://www.wsj.com/articles/in-ukraine-a-surge-in-amputations-reveals-the-human-cost-of-russias-war-d0bca320.

Roundtable dialogue on humanitarian support for persons with disabilities in Ukraine. 23.05.2023 Available at: https://www.who.int/europe/news/item/23-05-2023-roundtable-dialogue-on-humanitarian-support-for-persons-with-disabilities-in-ukraine

There are three million individuals with disabilities in Ukraine, 25.09.2023. Available at: https://unity.gov.ua/en/2023/09/25/there-are-three-million-individuals-with-disabilities-in-ukraine/

Work without barriers: 10,000 jobs for people with disabilities to be created by employers at state expense in 2024. Ministry of Economy of Ukraine, posted 13 December 2023. Available at: https://www.kmu.gov.ua/en/news/robota-bez-barieriv-10-000-robochykh-mists-dlia-liudei-z-invalidnistiu-zmozhut-oblashtuvaty-robotodavtsi-za-koshty-derzhavy-u-2024-rotsi

Абдулліна, М. Адаптація робочих місць для людей з інвалідністю. Як держава допомагає у працевлаштуванні людей з інвалідністю і про що говорить міжнародний досвід? 06.03.2023 Економічна правда. [Abdullina, M. Adaptation of workplaces for people with disabilities. How does the state help in the employment of people with disabilities and what does international experience show? 06.03.2023. Ekonomichna Pravda.] [In Ukrainian]. Available at: https://www.epravda.com.ua/columns/2023/03/6/697696/

Борсукова, О. За півтора року кількість людей з інвалідністю в Україні зросла на 300 тисяч – Мінсоцполітики [Borsukova, O. Over a year and a half, the number of people with disabilities in Ukraine has increased by 300 thousand - Ministry of Social Policy]. 19.09.2023 [In Ukrainian]. Available at: https://life.pravda.com.ua/society/2023/09/19/256633/

В Україні налічується 3 мільйони людей з інвалідністю – Жолнович, 19.09.2023, Укрінформ. [There are 3 million people with disabilities in Ukraine - Zholnovych 19.09.2023, Ukrinform.] [In Ukrainian]. Available at: https://www.ukrinform.ua/rubric-society/3763345-v-ukraini-nalicuetsa-3-miljoni-ludej-z-invalidnistu-zolnovic.html

Горбунова, О. Право на працю за європейськими зразками, 19 січня 2024 [Horbunova, O. The right to work according to European standards. January 19, 2024] [In Ukrainian] Available at: http://www.golos.com.ua/article/376390

Законопроект № 5344-д «Про внесення змін до деяких законів України щодо забезпечення прав осіб з інвалідністю на працю» (редакція, доопрацьована комітетом). 23.03.2023 [Draft Law of Ukraine No. 5344-d "On Amendments to

Certain Laws of Ukraine on Ensuring the Rights of Persons with Disabilities to Work" (version revised by the Committee). 23.03.2023.] [In Ukrainian]. Available at: https://itd.rada.gov.ua/billInfo/Bills/pubFile/1704626

Коваленко, Н. В Україні люди з обмеженими можливостями потерпають від безробіття, 11.10.2011. [Kovalenko, N. People with disabilities suffer from unemployment in Ukraine, 11.10.2011] [In Ukrainian]. Available at: https://www.radiosvoboda.org/a/24364674.html

Особам з інвалідністю. Офіційний сайт Міністерства соціальної політики України [For persons with disabilities. Official website of the Ministry of Social Policy of Ukraine] [In Ukrainian]. Available at: https://www.msp.gov.ua/timeline/invalidnist.html

Пояснювальна записка до проекту Закону України «Про внесення змін до деяких законів України щодо забезпечення прав осіб з інвалідністю на працю». 17.11.2022 [Explanatory Note to the Draft Law of Ukraine "On Amendments to Certain Laws of Ukraine on Ensuring the Rights of Persons with Disabilities to Work". November 17, 2022] [In Ukrainian]. Available at: https://itd.rada.gov.ua/billInfo/Bills/pubFile/1549495

Працевлаштування осіб з інвалідністю – зареєстровано доопрацьований законопроект. 30.11.2022 [Employment of Persons with Disabilities - a revised draft law has been registered. 30.11.2022]. [In Ukrainian]. Available at: https://www.coe.int/uk/web/kyiv/-/draft-law-on-employment-of-persons-with-disabilities-has-been-registered

Черновол, К. З 2022 року кількість людей з інвалідністю в Україні зросла на сотні тисяч, - міністр [Chernovol K. Since 2022, the number of people with disabilities in Ukraine has increased by hundreds of thousands, - Minister]. 28.11.2024 [In Ukrainian]. Available at: https://www.unian.ua/health/z-2022-roku-kilkist-lyudey-z-invalidnistyu-v-ukrajini-zrosla-na-sotni-tisyach-ministr-12834306.html

References

Baciu, E.L., Alexiu, T.M., Birneanu, A.G. (2015) Where do we stand on disability? European and Romanian policy developments regarding the inclusion and protection of disabled persons over the last quarter of a century. Revista de Asistență Socială 13(1):43–58

Garben, S. (2020) The European pillar of social rights and the european social charter. Europe des droits & libertés/Europe of Rights & Liberties 2020(1):65–78. Available at: https://www.europedeslibertes.eu/article/the-european-pillar-of-social-rights-and-the-european-social-charter/

Liu, K., O'Cinneide, C. (2019) The ongoing evolution of the case-law of the Court of Justice of the European Union on Directives 2000/43/EC and 2000/78/EC: a legal analysis of the situation in EU Member States, European Commission. Available at: https://op.europa.eu/s/z5DQ

Smusz-Kulesza, M. (2021) Draft of the Report on the Needs Assessment with Respect to Policy and Legal Framework Revision in the Area of Rights of People with Disabilities in Ukraine. Available at: https://rm.coe.int/final-report-eng-1-/16809f31b5

Yaroshenko, O.M. et al (2024) National strategy for a barrier-free environment: problems, tolerance and implementation. Int Soc Work 67(1):226–241. Available at: https://doi.org/10.1177/00208728221126002

Оверчук, В.А. (2018) Міжнародний досвід у сфері працевлаштування осіб з інвалідністю. *Науковий вісник Ужгородського національного університету.* Випуск 22, частина 3, с. 14-17. [Overchuk, V.A. International experience in the field of employment of persons with disabilities. Scientific Bulletin of Uzhhorod National University. Issue 22, part 3, pp. 14–17] [In Ukrainian]

Пилипенко, П., Бурак, В., Рим, О. (2023) Стандарти соціального захисту осіб з інвалідністю: новели законодавства України. Юридичний науковий електронний журнал. № 11/2023 [Pylypenko, P., Burak, V., Rym, O. (2023) Standards of social protection of persons with disabilities: novelties of Ukrainian legislation. *Legal scientific electronic journal*. № 11/2023.] [In Ukrainian]. Available at: http://www.lsej.org.ua/11_2023/51.pdf

Labour Law

Lost in Space: CEE Countries Workforce and 20 Years of Enlargement

Mario Vinković and Tena Konjević

1 Introduction

Within the European Union (hereinafter: EU), three discernible patterns of labour mobility have emerged over time: firstly, migration to another Member State, including the phenomenon of daily or weekly mobility, which is supported by the freedom of movement of workers as regulated in Article 45 of the Treaty of the Functioning of the European Union[1] (hereinafter: TFEU), and, secondly, by the freedom of establishment stipulated in Article 49 of the TFEU. The final pattern includes temporary mobility, facilitated mainly through the posting of workers,

[1] Consolidated version of the Treaty on the Functioning of the European Union (TFEU), Official Journal of the EU, C 326, 26 October 2012.

This chapter is a product of work that has been fully supported by the Faculty of Law Osijek Josip Juraj Strossmayer University of Osijek under the project nr. IP-PRAVOS-3: *Labour law and the challenges of the 21st century; transformation, humanization, discrimination and equality.*

M. Vinković (✉)
Faculty of Law Osijek, Josip Juraj Strossmayer University of Osijek, Osijek, Croatia

Member, European Committee of Social Rights, Strasbourg, France
e-mail: mvinkovi@pravos.hr

T. Konjević
Faculty of Law Osijek, Josip Juraj Strossmayer University of Osijek, Osijek, Croatia

Central European Academy, Budapest, Hungary

Member, European Committee of Social Rights, Strasbourg, France
e-mail: tkonjevic@pravos.hr

K. Koldinská et al. (eds.), *Labour Law and Social Security Law in Central and Eastern Europe*, European Union and its Neighbours in a Globalized World 26,
https://doi.org/10.1007/978-3-032-04496-9_16

which is established by the freedom to provide services according to Article 56 of the TFEU.[2] Therefore, the notion of intra-EU labour mobility is not limited only to 'permanent' cross-border mobility or commuting, but it also encompasses all 'temporary' cross-border labour mobility forms in the EU.[3] However, generally speaking, intra-EU labour mobility has undergone a notable increase over the past decade.[4] Historical events such as the 2004,[5] 2007[6] and 2013[7] EU enlargement, economic downturns, migration crises, the Brexit process, and the recent global health crisis have collectively exerted unprecedented pressure on EU free movement law. The migration patterns subsequent to the enlargements demonstrated greater dynamism compared to previous experiences, particularly in states with significant social and wage disparities compared to the established 'old Member States',[8] especially in the scope of temporary labour migration (hereinafter: TLM), which will be the further focus.

TLM has become a widespread phenomenon that involves working in a host country for a certain time, after which the worker returns to the home country. Despite challenges in quantifying its scale, research consistently shows its significance and growing trend. Scholars address the challenges following the TLM, mainly including poverty and exploitation, by advocating for extending rights to temporary migrant workers, including special rights for their unique circumstances.[9] Going into the past, already since the 1970s, posting arrangements, as a form of temporary labour migration, have been applied to dispatch highly skilled or specialised personnel abroad. This utilisation of posting has typically generated limited controversy,[10] due to the ability of national governments to levy taxes and social insurance contributions on all domestic employers without facing challenges from foreign competitors operating under different social and labour costs, or from domestic manufacturers evading obligations by relocating production abroad ('offshoring'). This dynamic shifted as European Integration advanced toward a unified Internal Market, characterised by 'negative integration' that eliminated barriers to trade and factor mobility across Europe.[11] Namely, upon the integration of Spain and Portugal into the EU in 1986,[12] two nations with notably lower wage structures compared to 'old EU members' joined the bloc. This event marked the inception of

[2] Barnard (2012), p. 143.; Bottero (2021), p. 23.; De Wispelaere and Pacolet (2016), p. 9.

[3] De Wispelaere et al. (2022), p. 8.

[4] De Wispelaere and Pacolet (2020), p. 34.; See more: Hassan et al. (2023).

[5] Treaty of Accession of the Czech Republic, Estonia, Cyprus, Latvia, Lithuania, Hungary, Malta, Poland, Slovenia and Slovakia, Official Journal of the EU, L 236, 23 September 2003.

[6] Treaty of Accession of the Republic of Bulgaria and Romania, Official Journal of the EU, L 157, 21 June 2005.

[7] Treaty of Accession of the Republic of Croatia, Official Journal of the EU, L 112, 24 April 2012.

[8] O'Leary and Iglesias (2021), s. 507.

[9] Alasia Nuti (2018), p. 203.

[10] Arnholtz and Lillie (2020), p. 5.

[11] Eichhorst (1998), p. 8.

[12] Treaty of Accession of Spain and Portugal, Official Journal, L 302, 15 November 1985.

ongoing political discourse regarding the influx of posted workers from these countries. This influx initiated the initial phase of labour market competition and prompted national regulatory adjustments.[13]

This period witnessed a series of landmark judgements from the European Court of Justice (hereinafter: CJEU) about posted work practices, meaning that, for an extended period, the CJEU played a pivotal role in shaping the legal framework governing posted workers employed in a Member State distinct from their company's primary operational base. Key judgements, such as the *Webb* decision from 1981,[14] followed by the *Seco* and *Dequenne* as well as *Giral* rulings in 1982,[15] established the criteria for determining wage levels, legal standards, and minimum conditions as per the host State's regulations.[16] The *Rush Portuguesa*[17] case in 1990, post-dated Spain and Portugal's accession to the EU, further refined this jurisprudence. Here, the CJEU determined that provisions for the free movement of workers will not be applied to posted workers, with the main explanation that they would return to their sending country after finishing their work, without access to the host States' labour market.[18] This evolving legal context culminated in Directive 96/71/EC,[19] codifying the status of posted workers in EU law. Before this Directive, only social security affiliation issues were covered by EU legislation and the legal framework for posted workers was primarily guided by the Rome Convention,[20] which had been ratified by the majority of Member States.[21] The initial version of the PWD 96 sought to strike a balance between the freedom to provide services and ensuring social protection for posted workers while preventing social dumping, unfair competition and exploitation.[22] Also, it permitted the mobility of employment contracts from the sending country while granting host states the authority to enforce specific elements of their labour laws on posted workers. Adopted following extensive political debates, the PWD 96 represented a delicate compromise accommodating various interests. Its ambiguous nature led to diverse interpretations. When the

---

[13] Arnholtz and Lillie (2020), p. 5.

[14] Judgment of the Court of 17 December 1981, Criminal proceedings against Alfred John Webb, Case 279/80, ECLI identifier: ECLI:EU:C:1981:314.

[15] Judgment of the Court of 3 February 1982, Société anonyme de droit français Seco and Société anonyme de droit français Desquenne & Giral v Etablissement d'assurance contre la vieillesse et l'invalidité, Joined cases 62 and 63/81, ECLI identifier: ECLI:EU:C:1982:34.

[16] Richard (2014), p. 1.

[17] Judgment of the Court (Sixth Chamber) of 27 March 1990, Rush Portuguesa Ldª v Office national d'immigration, Case C-113/89, ECLI identifier: ECLI:EU:C:1990:142.

[18] Houwerzijl and Verschueren (2024), p. 194.

[19] Directive 96/71/EC of the European Parliament and of the Council of 16 December 1996 concerning the posting of workers in the framework of the provision of services, Official Journal L 18, 21 January 1997.

[20] Convention on the Law Applicable to Contractual Obligations (Rome Convention) 80/934/EEC, Official Journal L 226, 9 October 1980.

[21] Alsos and Eldring (2008), p. 443.

[22] Eichhorst (1998), p. 17.

PWD 96 was reviewed in 2003, there was reluctance to challenge this established compromise by proposing its revision.[23] Afterwards, the matter concerning posted workers, specifically the political initiatives aimed at standardising the employment law status of workers sent abroad by their employers to provide services, has become a pivotal and contentious issue in contemporary European social policy. The previously established legal framework permitted the utilisation of more lenient foreign labour laws, particularly concerning minimum wages, during the workers' assignments abroad. However, in response to flaming concerns regarding competitive cost pressures from workers from accessing Central and Eastern European Member States (hereinafter: CEE), governments of host EU member states and trade unions have instigated regulatory actions at both European and national levels.[24] In the following, the authors will in more detail explain, on one side, the impact of the CEE countries from their accession to the EU to the last amendment of the PWD of the phenomenon of posting of workers, and the impact of EU legislation on the position of CEE posted workers on the EU labour market, on the other.

2 CEE Enlargement Impact on the Evolution of Posting of Workers within the EU

The accession of CEE countries, coupled with the subsequent significant rise in intra-EU labour mobility, reinvigorated discussions around posting within the EU.[25] Firstly, the inclusion of eight CEE countries ('EU8') into the EU in 2004, followed by the accession of Romania and Bulgaria ('EU2') in 2007, and finally Croatia in 2013, symbolised a pivotal moment in European integration by bridging a continent previously divided since the conclusion of the World War II. This expansion facilitated the broader application of the free movement of capital, goods, services and people across Central and Eastern Europe. However, due to significant economic disparities, concerns arose in Western Europe regarding potential large-scale migration from the new Member States, which could adversely affect labour markets and welfare systems in the recipient countries.[26] Consequently, except for the United Kingdom, Ireland and Sweden, most countries implemented transitional measures to regulate the freedom of movement of workers.[27] The limitations on labour mobility were similarly applied during all three latest accession phases, consequently

[23] Arnholtz and Lillie (2020), p. 5.

[24] Eichhorst (1998), pp. 5–6.

[25] Dølvik and Eldring (2015).

[26] Galgóczi and Leschke (2012), pp. 5–6.

[27] Since the 2004, 2007, and 2013 EU enlargements, transitional arrangements have restricted the free movement of workers and effectively allowed Member States to limit the employment of Central and Eastern European citizens for up to seven years. These restrictions included complex procedures such as work permit requirements, national quotas, proof of suitability, and other domestic regulatory measures. See: Konjević (2023), pp. 123–124.

restricting an influx of CEE workers.[28] Despite those limitations, the high unemployment rates and comparatively low wages in the new Member States created a strong economic incentive for their citizens to seek other opportunities in the 'old Member States'.[29] Many mobile citizens from Eastern Europe have chosen to engage in temporary migration to established EU nations through seasonal and circular patterns, frequently moving between their home country and the host state(s).[30] Consequently, posting emerged as a favoured method for bringing CEE workers to Western Europe,[31] since the freedom of movement of services hasn't been involved in the 'transitional periods' restrictions.[32] The primary distinction between posted and mobile workers lies in the fact that, unlike mobile workers are governed by the EU's free movement of workers, posted workers do not integrate into the labour market of the host state. As a result, they are not entitled to the same equal treatment rights as workers permanently residing in the other Member State.[33] Therefore, the CEE EU enlargements significantly influenced the scale of intra-EU labour mobility, particularly in the realm of intra-EU posting. The temporary restrictions on the free movement of workers (effectively closing 'the front door') while leaving the free movement of services unrestricted ('the back door' remained open) likely contributed to the notable increase in the number of posted workers migrating from Eastern to Western European Member States.[34] This opportunity proved financially appealing for both Eastern European undertakings and workers, as well as for Western European companies operating in labour-intensive and price-sensitive sectors.[35]

The transitional provisions governing the free movement of workers for individuals from EU8 countries were in effect for a maximum period of seven years, concluding specifically on 30 April 2011.[36] Given this context, one might anticipate a decline in the attractiveness of posting as a means of facilitating the free movement of services post-transition.[37] However, even after the expiration of these transitional measures associated with Article 45 TFEU, posting continued to be favoured over the free movement of workers for cost-effective labour recruitment. This pref-

[28] De Wispelaere and Pacolet (2020), p. 34.

[29] Arnholtz and Lillie (2020), p. 5; Wagner and Hassel (2016), pp. 125–158.

[30] Nuti (2018), p. 205.

[31] An illustrative example of circumventing transitional restrictions through the posting of workers, influenced by the EU enlargement and highlighting tensions between national and EU regulations, can be observed in the 'Norwegian shipbuilding case'. See more in: Alsos and Mette Ødegård (2020), p. 50.

[32] Arnholtz and Lillie (2020), p. 5; Wagner and Hassel (2016), pp. 125–158.

[33] Houwerzijl and Berntsen (2020), p. 163.

[34] European Commission (2006) Report on the functioning of the transitional arrangements set out in the 2003 accession treaty (period 1 May 2004–30 April 2006). Brussels: COM (2006), p. 48.; De Wispelaere et al. (2022), p. 31; De Wispelaere and Pacolet (2016), p. 9.

[35] De Wispelaere et al. (2022), p. 31.

[36] Konjević (2023), pp. 123–124.

[37] De Wispelaere and Pacolet (2020), p. 34.

erence could be attributed to the comprehensive equal treatment mandates of Article 45 TFEU, which cover aspects such as wages, labour standards, and social benefits.[38] Therefore, contrary to initial expectations, the post-transition landscape witnessed an increase in the use of posting as a labour mobility tool.[39] Empirical data reveals a rising trajectory in intra-EU posting since 2011, following a period of relative stagnation between 2007 and 2010,[40] while between 2010 and 2014, there was a notable annual growth rate of 8.3% in posted workers within the EU. During this period, there was a significant increase in the issuance of PDs A1[41] to posted workers from Slovenia, Poland, Greece and Bulgaria. Concurrently, Germany, Belgium, Estonia and Slovenia experienced a substantial rise in the receipt of PDs A1 for posted workers. Notably, approximately 86% of the PDs A1 issued for posted workers were intended for activities in the EU15 Member States, while 44% originated from the EU13 Member States.[42,43] Poland emerged as the leading 'exporter' of posted workers within the EU in 2011, surpassing Germany and France. As a host country, Germany had the highest number of received posted workers in 2011, followed by France.[44] Further analysis reveals distinct patterns in the types of posting. A significant 70.2% of workers posted from EU13 Member States are employed in the industrial sector, compared to 53.4% from EU15 Member States. This distinction leads to the differentiation of two primary forms of posting: low to medium-skilled workers posted from low-labour-cost to high-labour-cost Member States, predominantly in labour-intensive sectors, and medium to high-skilled posted workers occupying qualified positions.[45] Research suggested that nationals from EU8 countries primarily compete with non-European immigrants for low-skilled jobs rather than with native workers.[46] Given that low-skilled jobs often come with low wages, temporary labour migrants are at risk of poverty and marginalisation. Additionally, many of these migrants find themselves overqualified for the roles they undertake. This situation gives rise to social immobility and 'brain waste', interconnected issues that pose challenges not only for individual migrants, whose career aspirations likely diverge from their current roles but also for their countries of origin.[47]

---

[38] Houwerzijl and Berntsen (2020), pp. 149–150.

[39] Richard (2014), p. 3.

[40] De Wispelaere and Pacolet (2020), p. 34.

[41] A narrow interpretation of posting typically relies on A1 certificates issued by the sending Member State under Regulation (EC) No. 883/2004 on the coordination of social security systems. However, as noted by various studies, this concept differs from the definition of posting in Directive 96/71/EC (PWD), which governs applicable labour law rules. As a result, A1 data only offer an approximate view of actual posting levels. See: Houwerzijl, Berntsen (2020) p. 151.

[42] Pacolet and Wispelaere (2015), p. 40.

[43] Kahanec (2012), pp. 21–22.

[44] Richard (2014), pp. 3–4.

[45] De Wispelaere and Pacolet (2016), pp. 9–10.

[46] Kahanec (2012), pp. 21–22.

[47] Nuti (2018), p. 205.

Hence, the unexpected trajectory of the posting trend during the post-transition period can be attributed to two primary factors. Firstly, employer-driven posting is closely tied to economic expansion, particularly in the cross-border trade of services. This results in a significant correlation between service exports and the utilisation of intra-EU posting, which often necessitates the physical presence of posted workers. Secondly, the notable surge in intra-EU posting may signify a deliberate mobility strategy, favoured for its advantages over permanent relocation. In this context, the traditional 'once and forever' migration approach may be becoming outdated, with temporary labour mobility, including intra-EU posting, gaining prominence.[48] Besides these reasons, it is important to acknowledge that the number of PD A1s issued may not provide a comprehensive representation of intra-EU posting activities due to inherent statistical limitations. Therefore, the insight may be limited to tracking the issuance of PDs A1 rather than accurately capturing the entire landscape of intra-EU posting.[49] Additionally, the provisions outlined in Directive 96/71/EC (hereinafter: PWD 96) ensured that posted workers received either equal or, often, higher remuneration compared to what they would earn in their home Member State. This income disparity was particularly pronounced for workers posted from EU13 to EU15 Member States, given the substantial variations in average and minimum wages between 'high-wage' EU15 and 'low-wage' EU13 Member States. Notably, the wage disparity between Member States has widened consistently since 1996, escalating from a minimum wage ratio of 1:3 to 1:10, largely influenced by successive EU enlargements.[50] Consequently, employees from low-wage Member States were drawn away from their home countries by the allure of higher wages and the provision of covered expenses for travel and accommodation.[51] Labour cost disparities, alongside demand and supply dynamics in the labour market, served as still serve as significant factors prompting the posting of workers. Companies based in regions with lower wage levels and social security contributions enjoy a competitive advantage over those situated in areas with higher wage levels and greater social protections. This phenomenon, commonly referred to as a 'competition posting',[52] predominates in sectors with low-value chains, notably construction, transportation, and agriculture, often sparking political contention. As a result, intra-EU migrant workers from newer Member States frequently find themselves in precarious and marginalised employment situations, with posted workers experiencing particularly adverse working conditions.[53] Concerns among Western European Member States about the influx of inexpensive labour potentially undermining social standards and fostering unfair competition contrast with objections from many Eastern European entities, which view such apprehension as

---

[48] Ostaijen and Scholten (2018), pp. 3, 67.

[49] De Wispelaere and Pacolet (2020), p. 34.

[50] De Wispelaere and Pacolet (2016), p. 13.

[51] Caro et al. (2015), p. 1606.

[52] Lens et al. (2022), pp. 34–37.

[53] Arnholtz and Lillie (2020), pp. 8–9.

protectionist measures.[54] The perpetuation of low wage levels in Eastern European countries is often viewed as conferring, on one side, an unfair competitive advantage, and a legitimate comparative advantage, on the other.[55] Consequently, the geographical discrepancies in wage costs present a systemic challenge within all major markets. However, the significant wage differentials stemming from the EU's enlargements have rendered internal market postings reminiscent of those between developing and developed nations. Once hailed as a paragon of regional economic integration, the EU now serves as a crucible for globalisation, offering valuable insights for international negotiations.[56] Therefore, should be highlighted that posting represents a complex issue involving numerous stakeholders, including trade unions, employer associations, EU institutions, and national governments. Employers typically advocate for minimal regulation to maintain low wages, whereas trade unions strive to safeguard established industrial relations framework. Low-wage Eastern European Member States often advocate for deregulation to bolster the competitiveness of their firms and benefit their workers, while high-wage Western European Member States aim to preserve their social models. Furthermore, these divergent interests have intersected in various ways, particularly during the revisions of EU legislation following the enlargement, a topic that will be further explored in subsequent sections.[57]

As a result, the Posting of Workers legislation in effect since 1996 was deemed inadequate due to the rising influx of posted workers, particularly from CEE countries, and the instances of fraud observed by several Member States.[58] This inadequacy sparked a significant backlash in 2004 surrounding a proposal by Internal Market Commissioner Fritz Bolkenstein. The proposal aimed to streamline the free movement of service providers by allowing them to operate temporarily under the regulatory framework of their home country, known as the general rule Lex Loci Domicilii. This led to protests against EU-led economic liberalisation in multiple countries, notably France, where concerns about 'Polish plumbers'[59] working under Polish labour law contributed to the rejection of the Constitutional Treaty in the May 29, 2005 referendum.[60] The aforementioned draft proposal faced criticism for encouraging social duping through its overly liberal approach.[61] It sought to denationalise the regulatory authority over services but met opposition in France and

[54] Kyriazi (2023), pp. 223–224.

[55] Lalanne (2011), p. 220.

[56] Ibid., p. 230.

[57] Kyriazi (2023), p. 224.

[58] Richard (2014), p. 1.

[59] The image of the 'Polish plumber' came as an emblematic figure that signifies the era of extensive liberalisation and the influx of labour characterised by individuals enduring low wages and arduous hours, striving to earn a modest income. See more in: Gnes (2010), p. 54.; Böröcz and Sarkar (2017), pp. 309–311.

[60] Kyriazi (2023), pp. 227–228.

[61] Lalanne (2011), p. 222.

the Netherlands, where it was viewed as a threat to the established social model.[62] In response, the French Government implemented tighter rules on posting on August 2, 2005, while Dutch authorities sought to control the influx of posted workers from CEE countries by maintaining the requirement for work permits. However, the Commission demanded the discontinuation of this practice, citing it as inconsistent with the freedom to provide services. Despite socio-economic concerns, the Commission remained committed to liberalising trade in services within the EU.[63] Therefore, the resistance against the proposal, symbolised by the 'Polish plumber', played a significant role in delaying the transformation of Western Europe post-nation-state.[64] Additionally, the Bolkenstein directive proposal underwent significant modifications, replacing the principle of the country of origin with the broader and less effective 'freedom to provide services' established by Directive 2006/123/EC of December 12, 2006, on services in the internal market.[65]

Subsequently, in a sequence of rulings handed down by the CJEU between 2007 and 2008 (Laval,[66] Viking,[67] Rüffert[68] and Commission v. Luxembourg[69]) the court consistently upheld EU market freedoms over national social policy.[70] Within this series of decisions regarding the posting of workers, the CJEU notably interpreted the PWD not as a 'floor' of rights, but as a 'ceiling'.[71] In response to mounting calls for the revision of existing EU law, the second Barroso Commission endeavoured to reconcile the conflicting priorities of free competition and worker protection, albeit with limited success. An initiative concerning the right to collective action in the context of free movement provisions, known as the Monti II regulation, was proposed but ultimately withdrawn.[72] Concurrently, the issue of posted workers sparked intense debate in the European Parliament, resulting in the adoption of several resolutions, notably the resolution of October 22, 2008, emphasising the necessity for the correct implementation, application and enforcement of the Directive. Against

[62] Böröcz and Sarkar (2017), p. 309.

[63] Lalanne (2011), p. 221.

[64] Böröcz and Sarkar (2017), p. 309.

[65] Gnes (2010), p. 54.

[66] Judgment of the Court (Grand Chamber) of 18 December 2007. Laval un Partneri Ltd v Svenska Byggnadsarbetareförbundet, Svenska Byggnadsarbetareförbundets avdelning 1, Byggettan and Svenska Elektrikerförbundet. Case C-341/05. ECLI identifier: ECLI:EU:C:2007:809.

[67] Judgment of the Court (Grand Chamber) of 11 December 2007. International Transport Workers' Federation and Finnish Seamen's Union v Viking Line ABP and OÜ Viking Line Eesti. Case C-438/05. ECLI identifier: ECLI:EU:C:2007:772.

[68] Judgment of the Court (Second Chamber) of 3 April 2008. Dirk Rüffert v Land Niedersachsen. Case C-346/06. ECLI identifier: ECLI:EU:C:2008:189.

[69] Judgment of the Court (Grand Chamber) of 24 May 2011. European Commission v Grand Duchy of Luxemburg. Case C-51/08. ECLI identifier: ECLI:EU:C:2011:336.

[70] See more: Davies (2008), pp. 126–148.; Barnard (2008), pp. 463–492.; Ashiagbor (2013), pp. 303–324.; Dorte Sindbjerg Martinsen (2015).

[71] Rocca (2020), p. 168.; Van Nuffel and Afanasjeva (2020), pp. 281–282.

[72] Kyriazi (2023), pp. 227–228.

this backdrop, the European Commission initiated a pilot project titled 'working and living conditions of posted workers'.[73]

Moreover, the Commission successfully introduced the 2014 Enforcement Directive,[74] aimed at addressing fraudulent activities and regulatory avoidance associated with worker posting.[75] This Directive established criteria to distinguish genuine postings, mitigate abuse, and prevent circumvention. It also outlined provisions regarding information accessibility, administrative cooperation, compliance monitoring, and specialised enforcement measures. However, despite the enactment of the Enforcement Directive, the Posting of Workers Directive faced criticism on several fronts. Chief among the concerns was its provision for only the minimum wage of the host country and the absence of a specific time limit for postings.[76] In contrast, the proposed amending Directive in 2016 introduced significant alternations that curbed employers' competitive advantage based on wage and social security disparities across the EU.[77] Hence, the Services Directive, the Laval Quartet, the Enforcement Directive and the revision of the PWD stand out as pivotal moments in a protracted narrative of intense politicisation. Posting of workers has evolved into a prominent European policy domain, drawing active engagement from politicians, legal experts, social stakeholders, and academics. This discourse transcends mere regulatory matters to encompass broader discussions on EU-focused policies.[78] Furthermore, the posting of workers has increasingly become a contentious and widely publicised issue, often cited as emblematic of unfair competition or 'social dumping'. This issue holds particular sensitivity in Member States where labour costs are high and face stiff competition from cheaper posted labour. There exists a prevailing sentiment that the deepening of the single market over recent decades has facilitated firms' ability to freely post workers, potentially exploiting social legislation to their advantage at the expense of more generous welfare systems. Such practices gained traction following successive waves of EU enlargement, which extended into progressively less affluent welfare states and lower-cost labour destinations, first moving southward and then eastward.[79]

---

[73] van Hoek and Houwerzijl (2012), p. 420.

[74] Directive 2014/67/EU of the European Parliament and of the Council of 15 May 2014 on the enforcement of Directive 96/71/EC concerning the posting of workers in the framework of the provision of services and amending Regulation (EU) No 1024/2012 on administrative cooperation through the Internal Market Information System, Official Journal L 159/11.

[75] Kyriazi (2023), pp. 227–228.

[76] Verschueren (2021), pp. 557–558.

[77] Kyriazi (2023), pp. 227–228.

[78] Arnholtz and Lillie (2020), p. 17.

[79] Maslauskaite (2014), p. 3.

3 PWD Revision Debate and the CEE Countries' Attempted Influence

In the context of European integration, prioritising market development has been a longstanding focus. However, since the latter half of the 2010s, there has been observative momentum towards advancing the concept of a 'Social Europe'.[80] Despite this, garnering widespread support for social initiatives within the EU has proven to be a challenging endeavour, and a specific instance exemplifying this challenge was the reform of regulations governing the posting of workers within the EU. This reform was initiated by the Juncker Commission in March 2016 and finalised in June 2018. This particular episode serves as an entry point for exploring the broader issue of decision-making within the EU's multilevel governance framework. It sheds light on the strategies employed by political leaders to navigate contentious policy areas and enact meaningful reforms.[81] The reform aimed to bring about a significant shift in approach by addressing concerns related to wages and working conditions for legally posted workers in other Member States. By aligning these conditions more closely with those of local workers, the reform sought to mitigate the risks associated with regulatory loopholes and, alternatively, the risk of social dumping through legal means.[82]

Following a period where it was considered unattainable during the Barroso II Commission era, the reform of the PWD regained prominence under the political directives set forth by Junckers' Commission.[83] He demonstrated particular receptiveness to the concerns raised by Member States primarily affected by labour mobility issues, where the posting issue held significant political weight. Moreover, there was a growing perception that unresolved issues persisted within the realm of posting despite the enactment of the Enforcement Directive. Simultaneously, the number of posted workers was on the rise, exacerbating discrepancies between the wages of local workers and those posted from abroad.[84] At that juncture, Juncker pledged to undertake a focused review of the PWD to ensure equitable remuneration for equivalent work performed in the same location within the Union.[85]

The European Commission subsequently presented its proposal for revising the PWD on March 8, 2016. Aligned with a political commitment, the proposal aimed to better synchronise the working conditions of posted workers with those of locally employed individuals engaged in similar activities.[86] This directive introduced new provisions in three key areas: (1) terms and conditions of employment applicable to

[80] See more: Zeitlin and Vanhercke (2018), pp. 149–174.; Klosse and Bekker (2013), pp. 103–120.

[81] Kyriazi (2023), p. 221.

[82] Bernaciak (2015), p. 230.

[83] Rocca (2020), p. 167.

[84] Kyriazi (2023), pp. 228–229.

[85] Van Nuffel and Afanasjeva (2020), pp. 271–272.

[86] Rocca (2020), p. 167.

posted workers, (2) temporary agency posting, and (3) long-term posting.[87] However, the revision of the PWD faced significant hurdles due to criticism from various stakeholders. Social partners, in particular, expressed hostility, feeling aggrieved for not being consulted despite the requirement outlined in Protocol 2 of the European Treaties, according to which the Commission may only waive consultations due to 'exceptional urgency', which must be explained in the proposal for new legislation.[88] However, the 2016 proposal lacked such justification. Consequently, BUSINESSEUROPE and ETUC jointly addressed a letter to the Commission, despite their differing reactions to the 2016 proposal. BUSINESSEUROPE opposed any intervention in the posting framework, asserting that the reform could impede the development of the single market and potentially reduce the share of cross-border services in the EU GDP. Conversely, ETUC welcomed the initiative but criticised the proposed reform for failing to address key elements to prevent worker exploitation, including full respect for the fundamental right to collective bargaining and action in the host Member State.[89,90] The 2016 proposal also elicited a mixed response from EU Committees and divergent opinions among Member States, culminating in a 'yellow card procedure' that underscored the divide between Eastern and Western states, to be further examined below.

4 'Yellow Card' Procedure as Failed CEE's Ambition

The reform of the PWD came to fruition just ahead of the tenth anniversary of the influential Laval decision, which, as articulated in the Monti Report, reignited the debate between proponents of increased market integration and those who perceive calls for economic liberalisation and regulatory dismantling as encroachments on nationally safeguarded social rights.[91,92] Commissioner for Employment, Social Affairs, Skills, and Labour Mobility, Marianne Thyssen, spearheaded the revision process[93] and has already garnered input from Member States during the obligatory consultation phase.[94] The initial correspondences were from labour ministers representing high-wage countries (Austria, Belgium, France, Germany, Luxembourg, the Netherlands, and Sweden), advocating for a substantial overhaul of the PWD centred on the principle of 'equal pay for equal work at the same location'. They emphasised the need for a more equitable balance between economic imperatives

[87] De Wispelaere et al. (2022), p. 29.; Furåker and Larsson (2020), pp. 109–139.

[88] See more in: Veneziani (2012), pp. 123–162.

[89] ETUC (2016), p. 1.

[90] Lasek-Markey (2023), p. 72.

[91] Monti (2010), p. 68.

[92] Rocca (2020), p. 168.

[93] Van Nuffel and Afanasjeva (2020), p. 287.

[94] Voss et al. (2016), p. 51.

and social standards to prevent instances of social exploitation. Conversely, ministers responsible for labour and social affairs from low-wage countries (Bulgaria, Czech Republic, Estonia, Hungary, Latvia, Lithuania, Poland, Romania, and Slovakia) conveyed divergent perspectives in their letter. They argued against an immediate revision of the PWD, advocating instead for a comprehensive assessment of the European Directive's impact and expressing concerns about potential adverse effects on the freedom to provide services.[95]

The landscape of both support and opposition was firmly established when the Commission unveiled its proposal in March 2016.[96] Almost immediately, Polish and Hungarian government officials articulated their dissent towards the proposal. By May 10, 2016, 14 parliamentary chambers from 11 Member States had formally notified the Commission of their objections to the proposals, citing the principle of subsidiarity.[97] This action initiated a 'yellow card procedure',[98] as outlined in Protocol No. 2 of the Lisbon Treaty.[99,100] The Communication issued by the Commission in 2016 elaborates on Protocol No. 2, which concerns the application of the subsidiarity and proportionality principles, allowing national parliaments to submit reasoned opinions if they perceive a legislative proposal as contravening the subsidiarity principle. If these reasoned opinions, accounting for at least one-third of all allocated votes, are submitted, the Commission is obligated to reevaluate the proposal. Subsequently, the Commission may opt to maintain, amend, or withdraw the proposal, providing a rationale for its decision.[101]

---

[95] Furåker and Larsson (2020), p. 127.; Fromage and Kreilinger (2017), p. 147.

[96] Proposal for a Directive of the European Parliament and of the Council amending Directive 96/71/EC of The European Parliament and of the Council of 16 December 1996 concerning the posting of workers in the framework of the provision of services, COM(2016) 128 final, 2016/0070(COD), 08/03/2016.

[97] Kyriazi (2023), pp. 228–230.

[98] So far, the 'yellow card' mechanism has been activated on three occasions, while the 'orange card' mechanism has never been utilised. The first one occurred in May 2012 when a 'yellow card' was raised concerning a Commission proposal related to the right to engage in collective action within the framework of freedom of establishment and freedom to provide services, known as 'Monti II'. In October 2013, 14 chambers from 11 Member States issued another 'yellow card' in response to a proposal for establishing the European Public Prosecutor's Office. Subsequently, in May 2016, a third 'yellow card was raised opposing a proposal to amend the directive on the posting of workers, about which there is more in this paper. See more: Pavy (2023).

[99] Protocol (No 2) on the application of the principles of subsidiarity and proportionality of the Consolidated version of the Treaty on the Functioning of the European Union, Official Journal C 115, 09/05/2008.

[100] Rocca (2020), p. 167.

[101] Communication from the Commission to the European Parliament, the Council and the National Parliaments on the proposal for a Directive amending the Posting of Workers Directive, with regard to the principle of subsidiarity, in accordance with Protocol No 2, COM(2016) 505 final, 20/07/2016, p. 2.

During the aforementioned procedure, the parliaments of all CEE Member States, excluding Slovenia,[102] were actively involved. Additionally, the Danish parliament, while expressing concerns regarding subsidiarity, took a different stance compared to the rest, marking it as the sole non-CEE participant within this cohort.[103] In opposition, six dissenting opinions[104] were forwarded to the Commission, asserting the absence of any breach of subsidiarity.[105] A significant opponent was the French government, largely influenced by its domestic political landscape. The then Prime Minister, Manuel Valls, notably threatened to cease the application of existing legal frameworks, specifically regarding EU law on posted workers, if swift modifications were not made by the Commission.[106] Within the European Parliament (hereinafter: EP), a noteworthy phenomenon emerged where territorial rather than ideological divisions shaped the parliamentary discourse. This division notably split the EPP and ALDE party groups, both of which had initially supported the Commission's proposal. Throughout the process, numerous CEE members of the EP expressed criticism at various stages, with a substantial number ultimately rebelling during the final roll call vote. Moreover, the consent of CEE S&D delegations was not assumed but was instead achieved through a series of debates and meetings within the party group.[107]

However, on this occasion, the initiation of a 'yellow card' procedure did not impede the progression of the reform of the PWD, but, instead, in response to widespread criticism, the European Commission released a Communication[108] countering the allegations made by national parliaments and announcing the continuation of the legislative process.[109] Significantly, the activation of the 'yellow card' procedure led to the suspension of the activities of the rotating Council presidency, then held by the Netherlands. The process resumed under the presidency of Slovakia, whose government had openly expressed criticism of the proposed amendment. While the Slovak presidency was perceived by participants as an 'honest broker', the process encountered delays nonetheless.[110] In early 2017, Malta assumed the EU Council presidency from Slovakia and proposed a compromise, which appeared to

[102] The CEE countries involved in the 'yellow card procedure' were: Bulgaria, Croatia, Czech Republic, Estonia, Hungary, Latvia, Lithuania, Poland, Romania and Slovakia.

[103] Fromage and Kreilinger (2017), p. 148.

[104] French, Italian, Portuguese, Spanish and UK have issued their opinions. However, it was surprising that Germany did not react since they are one of the most affected countries, in terms of both hosting and posting workers.

[105] Fromage and Kreilinger (2017), p. 147.

[106] Arnholtz and Lillie (2020), p. 19.

[107] Kyriazi (2023), pp. 229–230.

[108] Communication from the Commission to the European Parliament, the Council and the National Parliaments on the proposal for a Directive amending the Posting of Workers Directive, with regard to the principle of subsidiarity, in accordance with Protocol No 2, COM(2016) 505 final, 20/07/2016.

[109] Lasek-Markey (2023), p. 73.

[110] Kyriazi (2023), p. 229.; See more: Corti (2022), pp. 78–115.

advance discussions on the reform of the PWD. Momentum for the revision increased following Emanuel Macron's election as President of France in May 2017. The issue of posted workers and the concept of 'social dumping' had already emerged during the presidential campaign, during which Macron contested against Marine Le Pen, the leader of the far-right Front National.[111] Evidence of this can be found in French President Macron's utilisation of the posting of workers as a prominent aspect of his campaign during the 2017 presidential elections. Alongside other Western European Member States, France has been grappling with wage competition from workers posted from the CEE Member States, where wage levels are lower. This dynamics has contributed to the perception of posting of workers as a divisive issue, pitting CEE and Western interests against each other within the EU.[112] Following this election victory, Macron made addressing the posting of workers a focal point of his policy agenda. However, the Visegrád Group (V4) alliance comprising the Czech Republic, Hungary, Poland, and Slovakia, opposed an EU amendment, issuing a joint statement in May 2017. Despite Macron's efforts in June, positions remained unchanged. Poland successfully rallied Spain to join forces against the amendment. In August 2017, Macron embarked on a tour of CEE countries in a bid to garner support, excluding Poland and Hungary from his itinerary. During his visits, he held discussions with leaders from Austria, Slovakia, Czech Republic, Romania and Bulgaria. While Austria offered support to Macron, Slovak and Czech leaders engaged in dialogue despite their earlier opposition. Romania and Bulgaria began to show increasing support for Macron's stance. Tensions escalated between Macron and Poland, resulting in public disputes. Nevertheless, efforts to revitalise the V4 alliance persisted. In September, Juncker announced plans for a European Labour Authority (ELA)[113] and endorsed the amendment. By October, Macron's meeting with Spain'ss Rajoy indicated Spain's support for the posting proposal.[114]

Macron's diplomatic efforts in CEE yielded results, as by October 2017, the EU Council reached a compromise on the matter. Notably, the final wording of the compromise significantly deviated from the original draft. Not only did the EU legislator incorporate some of the amendments proposed by social partners and EU Committees, but it also introduced more substantial changes to the original Directive, which may have initially seemed too ambitious during the legislative process.[115] In May 2018, the EP passed the amending PWD with a considerable majority (70% in

[111] Lasek-Markey (2023), p. 73.

[112] Van Nuffel and Afanasjeva (2020), p. 272.

[113] European Labour Authority was one of the initiatives connected to the European Pillar of Social Rights, just as with the posting of workers. Its aim was to contribute to a more fair, effective and coordinated labour mobility within the EU. It should help the Member States and the Commission in their application and enforcement of the labour mobility EU law, just as in the cooperation in the social security systems. See more: Houwerzijl and Verschueren (2024), p. 245.; European Labour Authority [Online: https://www.ela.europa.eu/en], Accessed on: 27/03/2024.

[114] Kyriazi (2023), pp. 231–232.

[115] Lasek-Markey (2023), pp. 73–74.

favour, 23% against, and 8% abstaining). Although a notable portion of predominantly CEE MEPs from the EPP and ALDE factions rebelled against the reform, resulting in its rejection, the S&D faction remained united in its support. Formal approval from the EPSCO Council came in June 2018, with 22 Member States voting in favour and only two, Hungary and Poland, voting against. Croatia, Latvia, Lithuania, and the UK abstained from voting.[116] Hungary and Poland stood out as the only two Member States persistently opposing Directive 2018/957, voting against its adoption. Consequently, following their defeat in the 'yellow card' procedure and the subsequent Council vote, Hungary and Poland initiated legal action to challenge Directive 2018/957 before the CJEU, a matter that will be further elaborated on below.[117] However, Hungary and Poland's efforts to annul the Revised PWD, arguing that the protection afforded to workers exceeds what is permissible under the Treaty provisions on the free movement of services, did not halt the application of the PWD. It was scheduled to be enforced starting from July 30, 2020.[118]

5 One Last Chance: Hungary and Poland v European Parliament and Council of the EU Before the CJEU

The ongoing debate between proponents of free and equitable labour mobility persisted, as Hungary and Poland contested the revised PWD before the CJEU. They argued that certain aspects of the PWD imposed unjustified and disproportionate limitations on the freedom to provide services.[119]

Hungary put forth five legal arguments in support of its challenge: firstly, the contention that an incorrect legal basis was chosen for the adoption of the disputed Directive; secondly, the alleged disregard of Article 153(5) of the TFEU and misuse of powers; thirdly, a claimed infringement of Article 56 of the TFEU; fourthly, an additional alleged violation of Article 56 of the TFEU, asserting that the Directive hindered the effective implementation of the freedom to provide services; and fifthly, purported disregard of the 'Rome I' Regulation and the principles of legal certainty and legislative clarity.[120] Similarly, Poland relied on three legal arguments: firstly, the assertion that an incorrect legal basis was chosen for the adoption of the disputed Directive; secondly, an alleged infringement of Article 56 of the TFEU by Article 1(2)(a) and (b) of the disputed Directive; and thirdly, the purported improper

[116] Kyriazi (2023), pp. 232–233.

[117] Lasek-Markey (2023), pp. 73–74.

[118] Van Nuffel and Afanasjeva (2020), p. 288.

[119] De Wispelaere et al. (2022), p. 29.

[120] Judgment of the Court (Grand Chamber) of 8 December 2020, Hungary v European Parliament and Council of the European Union. Case C-620/18. ECLI:EU:C:2020:1001, par. 27.

inclusion of the road transport sector within the scope of the disputed Directive.[121] In the ensuing discussion, only the selected CEE countries' arguments (Hungary and Poland) will be examined and analysed from the perspective of their legitimisation, with additional attention given only to certain arguments presented by the CJEU in the relevant case.

As mentioned, Hungary and Poland's initial argument centred on the choice of legal basis. Their proposition of Article 153 of the TFEU as the legal basis was a deliberate ploy, as its provisions do not encompass wage regulations, while the PWD, both before and after the 2018 amendment, does indeed address the remuneration of posted workers.[122] However, the CJEU with the assistance of Advocate General Campos Sánchez-Bodona, determined that neither the PWD nor its revisions fall under the scope of Article 153 TFEU. The Advocate General concurred with Hungary's assertion that Directive 2018/957 primarily aims to safeguard the rights of posted workers. Nonetheless, he argued that this does not automatically necessitate the Directive to be grounded in Article 153 TFEU. He pointed out that Directive 20187957 introduced a significant yet confined modification to Directive 96/71. As per established court precedent, an amending act generally shares the same legal basis as the earlier act it modified,[123] which, in his view, was logical. Therefore, he argued that Articles 53(1) and 62 of the TFEU could serve as the appropriate legal basis for Directive 2018/957, as they did for the predecessor, Directive 96/71.[124]

From a formal standpoint, the argument holds merit; however, it fails to address how the freedom to provide services aligns with a reform primarily focused on enhancing the protection of posted workers. In response to this concern, the CJEU asserted that legislation enacted under Articles 53(1) and 62 of the TFEU must not only aim to facilitate the exercise of the freedom to provide services but also to ensure, when necessary, the protection of other fundamental interests that may be impacted by that freedom. In considering the dual objective of the PWD, the CJEU underscored that the pursuit of the free movement of services should not be absolute but rather conducted on a 'fair basis'.[125,126] By elucidating the concept of 'fair competition' in the realm of posted work, the CJEU emphasised that enterprises can compete on alternative grounds, such as workers' productivity and efficiency. This

---

[121] Judgment of the Court (Grand Chamber) of 8 December 2020, Republic of Poland v European Parliament and Council of the European Union. Case C-626/18. ECLI:EU:C:2020:1000.

[122] See more: Lasek-Markey (2022), pp. 194–218.

[123] Judgment of the Court (Grand Chamber) of 3 December 2019, Czech Republic v European Parliament and Council of the European Union. Case C-482/17. ECLI:EU:C:2019:1035, par. 42.

[124] Opinion of Advocate General Campos Sánchez-Bordona delivered on 28 May 2020, Case C-620/18, Hungary v European Parliament, Council of the European Union, par. 74–75.

[125] Judgment of the Court (Grand Chamber) of 8 December 2020, Republic of Poland v European Parliament and Council of the European Union. Case C-626/18. ECLI:EU:C:2020:1000, par. 56.; Judgment of the Court (Grand Chamber) of 8 December 2020, Hungary v European Parliament and Council of the European Union. Case C-620/18. ECLI:EU:C:2020:1001, par. 51.

[126] Lasek-Markey (2023), pp. 74–75.

perspective implies that while the climate of competition may be free, it is also equitable. This marks a departure from the stance adopted in the 'Laval quartet', indicating an evolution in the CJEU's position.[127] While the terminology of 'social dumping' is carefully sidestepped in both rulings dismissing Hungary and Poland's applications, it is evident that as the EU pursued the European Pillar of Social Rights, the CJEU has undertaken to restore the harmony between economic freedoms and social rights disrupted by the Laval case. Consequently, the CJEU maintains that the contested Directive establishes a new equilibrium among the factors that govern competition among enterprises established in different Member States.[128]

Both Hungary and Poland have underscored the violation of Article 56 of the TFEU. Hungary contended that PWD 96 adequately safeguarded posted workers by mandating payment of the minimum wage of the host Member State concerning remuneration.[129] Hungary asserted that the amendment was not conducive to the freedom to provide services; rather, it represented a direct intervention in economic relationships, undermining the legitimate competitive advantage of certain identifiable Member States where pay levels were/are lower. Consequently, the EU legislature has introduced a measure that distorts competition.[130] Also, Hungary and Poland argued that the provision outlined in point (c) of the first subparagraph of Article 3(1) of the amended PWD 96, which substituted the concept of 'remuneration' for that of minimum rates of pay, contravened the objective of ensuring equal treatment for workers of the host Member State and posted workers. They contend that it constituted a discriminatory restriction on the freedom to provide services, as it mandated undertakings established in one Member State to remunerate employees posted to another Member State according to the latter's practices, which are not obligatory for the former undertakings. This requirement placed an additional financial and administrative burden on service providers employing posted workers, as they were generally bound only by the obligation to pay the minimum wage. Consequently, while the minimum rates of pay in the host Member State were deemed adequate for its workers, they were deemed insufficient for posted workers.[131]

Hungary contended that the disputed PWD was unsuitable for achieving its stated objective, which was to foster a fairer competitive environment for service providers across different Member States. Specifically, Hungary raised objections to the wording of Recital 16 of the Directive, which suggests that undertakings

[127] Lasek-Markey (2023), p. 75.

[128] Verschueren (2021), p. 75.

[129] Judgment of the Court (Grand Chamber) of 8 December 2020, Hungary v European Parliament and Council of the European Union. Case C-620/18. ECLI:EU:C:2020:1001, par. 88.

[130] Judgment of the Court (Grand Chamber) of 8 December 2020, Hungary v European Parliament and Council of the European Union. Case C-620/18. ECLI:EU:C:2020:1001, par. 89.

[131] Judgment of the Court (Grand Chamber) of 8 December 2020, Hungary v European Parliament and Council of the European Union. Case C-620/18. ECLI:EU:C:2020:1001, par. 92.; Judgment of the Court (Grand Chamber) of 8 December 2020, Republic of Poland v European Parliament and Council of the European Union. Case C-626/18. ECLI:EU:C:2020:1000, par. 73.

compete based on factors beyond costs, implying that the price of the service would not influence consumer choice. Additionally, Poland argued that the EU legislature now considers the competitive advantage resulting from lower labour costs as inherently unfair competition, despite not previously characterising it as such.[132] Hungary and Poland also argued that, considering the temporary nature of service provision under the framework of posting of workers, the provisions of the contested Directive exceeded what was necessary to protect posted workers. Hungary proposed distinguishing between workers exercising their freedom of movement and those temporarily providing services within the posting framework. According to Hungary, the former works under the control of an employer from the host Member State, while the latter is not fully integrated into the society of the labour market of the host Member State. Consequently, the remuneration for workers from the host State should be sufficient to cover their living costs in that country.[133] Similarly, Poland contended that Article 3(1a) of the amended PWD, which introduced enhanced protection for workers posted to the host Member State for over 12 months, imposed an unjustified and disproportionate restriction on the freedom to provide services. Poland argued that while the principle of equal treatment applies to individuals exercising freedom of movement, meaning those permanently employed in the host Member State, it cannot be applied in the same manner to workers posted for periods exceeding 12 months, since posted workers are not fully integrated into the labour market of the host Member State.[134]

6 Conclusion: CEE Posted Workers as Collateral Victims of the Advantage Competition?

Following the above, and despite the CJEU's rejection of all the aforementioned pleas, the authors would like to additionally critically analyse the argumentation of Hungary and Poland from the perspective of the position of posted workers. Firstly, while Hungary and Poland may have been technically correct in their proposition of the legal basis, including Article 153 of the TFEU, their emphasis on this point seemed more strategic than substantive. The core issue lies not in the legal

[132] Judgment of the Court (Grand Chamber) of 8 December 2020, Hungary v European Parliament and Council of the European Union. Case C-620/18. ECLI:EU:C:2020:1001, par. 93, 95., Judgment of the Court (Grand Chamber) of 8 December 2020, Republic of Poland v European Parliament and Council of the European Union. Case C-626/18. ECLI:EU:C:2020:1000, par. 78.

[133] Judgment of the Court (Grand Chamber) of 8 December 2020, Hungary v European Parliament and Council of the European Union. Case C-620/18. ECLI:EU:C:2020:1001, par. 97.; Judgment of the Court (Grand Chamber) of 8 December 2020, Republic of Poland v European Parliament and Council of the European Union. Case C-626/18. ECLI:EU:C:2020:1000, par. 76.

[134] Judgment of the Court (Grand Chamber) of 8 December 2020, Republic of Poland v European Parliament and Council of the European Union. Case C-626/18. ECLI:EU:C:2020:1000, par. 80, 82.

framework but in the broader intent of the Directive to ensure fair competition and protect posted workers' rights, which CJEU recognised, yet it does not explain how the freedom to provide services fits in with a reform aimed primarily at improving the protection of posted workers. The focus of the clarification by the CJEU that Directive 96/71 had the same legal basis seems not clarified enough.

Furthermore, Hungary and Poland's concern about the potential distortion of competition and the unequal treatment of posted workers highlights their underlying aim to maintain a competitive advantage based on lower labour costs. While economic competition is a legitimate concern, especially for the economically more disadvantaged countries, involving the CEE countries, it should not come at the expense of posted workers' rights or lead to social dumping. The CJEU's approach, emphasising fair competition and the protection of workers' rights, strikes a balance that Hungary and Poland's argumentation seem to indirectly overlook. Also, when it comes to both countries' initiation of differentiation of rules for workers who temporarily provide services and those who are permanently employed, it should be noted that that distinction is valid due to the diversified positions of those categories of workers and the different TFEU bases for those categories, as the result of the previous CJEU decisions. However, it can be criticised the PWD 96 separation of the regime for posted workers due to its result of disabling the usage of the broader scope of protection given by Article 45 of the TFEU, including the prohibition of discrimination based on nationality, but one can question if, with the new amendment, these differences are still substantial, due to the extension of the main employment elements from the host country to the posted workers. The main problem with Hungary and Poland's distinction between those two regimes was that both countries appeared to be more of a way to justify lower wages and fewer protections for posted workers. While the temporary nature of postings may justify some flexibility, it should not be used as a pretext to undermine posted workers' rights or perpetuate social dumping. Even though the posted workers do not permanently stay connected to the labour market of the host Member State, it does not mean that they should be paid less for equal work. Frequently, CEE citizens utilise posting assignments as a means to enhance their standards of living in their respective home countries. Consequently, the higher wages received by posted workers not only elevate the standards of labour but also have the potential to enhance the overall standard of living within the sending country. This is attributed to the proficiency and contributions[135] of posted workers, coupled with their enduring ties to their country of origin. The authors would like to underscore that despite the amendments made to the Directive, there remains a deficiency in establishing a suitable basis for comparing the remuneration of posted workers with that of domestic ones. This disparity exacerbates the challenges associated with adhering to the newly introduced principle of equal pay. Similarly, the implementation of provisions concerning allowances for work-related expenses appears to be restricted to jurisdictions already possessing

[135] It should be noted, however, that there is no unified taxation regime for posted workers and no harmonisation of personal income tax on EU level. See more in: Lasek-Markey (2023), p. 125.

statutory regulations for their reimbursement, thereby presenting a parallel challenge.

Additionally, although Hungary and Poland did not explicitly use the term 'social dumping', their arguments indirectly raised concerns about the potential for it by emphasising the competitive advantage gained from lower labour costs in one country to undercut wages and working conditions in another. Both countries' arguments, particularly their focus on maintaining competitive advantage based on lower labour costs, could indirectly encourage such practices. Therefore, while Hungary and Poland's arguments against the revised PWD were presented from the perspective of protecting their competitive advantage on the EU labour market and by protecting the position of the service providers which post workers, which are now undoubtedly in a more disadvantaged position than before the amendment of the Directive, the question arises if the CEE countries indirectly prioritise the social dumping over the protection of workers' rights. Even though the arguments from Hungary and Poland are understandable and reasonable from the financial and competitive perspective, still the posted workers shouldn't be the collateral victims of the undertakings and countries' competition on the market. However, we should note that the amended PWD by its more restrictive provisions did potentially cause practical problems for service providers who post workers and potentially decreased the number of postings from the CEE countries due to more burden, which should be examined from a statistical point of view.

Finally, even though Hungary and Poland's action before the CJEU was dismissed and they transposed the amended Directive into their national legislation due to the deadline for transposition being on 30/07/2020, it should be noted that the CJEU's judgements in those cases were crucial as they provided fresh interpretations of numerous provisions within the PWD. Many of these had either not been addressed by the CJEU since the 'Laval quartet' or had never been interpreted at all before. It gave the CJEU the chance to show that the social objectives of the EU apply to the internal market and service provisions too, and that the market competition shouldn't be just free, but also fair. This approach can be seen as a step forward from the Laval case that caused so many controversies over the years. Therefore, notwithstanding the contentious nature of Hungary and Poland's action before the Court, we should appreciate that these events have ultimately provided clarity on the CJEU's stance regarding the treatment of posted workers on the EU labour market.

Legislation and CJEU Case-Law

Communication from the Commission to the European Parliament, the Council and the National Parliaments on the proposal for a Directive amending the Posting of Workers Directive, with regard to the principle of subsidiarity, in accordance with Protocol No 2, COM(2016) 505 final, 20/07/2016.

Consolidated version of the Treaty on the Functioning of the European Union (TFEU), Official Journal of the EU, C 326, 26 October 2012.

Convention on the Law Applicable to Contractual Obligations (Rome Convention) 80/934/EEC, Official Journal L 226, 9 October 1980.
Directive 2014/67/EU of the European Parliament and of the Council of 15 May 2014 on the enforcement of Directive 96/71/EC concerning the posting of workers in the framework of the provision of services and amending Regulation (EU) No 1024/2012 on administrative cooperation through the Internal Market Information System, Official Journal L 159, 28/05/2014.
Directive 96/71/EC of the European Parliament and of the Council of 16 December 1996 concerning the posting of workers in the framework of the provision of services, Official Journal L 18, 21 January 1997.
Judgment of the Court (Grand Chamber) of 11 December 2007. International Transport Workers' Federation and Finnish Seamen's Union v Viking Line ABP and OÜ Viking Line Eesti. Case C-438/05. ECLI identifier: ECLI:EU:C:2007:772.
Judgment of the Court (Grand Chamber) of 18 December 2007. Laval un Partneri Ltd v Svenska Byggnadsarbetareförbundet, Svenska Byggnadsarbetareförbundets avdelning 1, Byggettan and Svenska Elektrikerförbundet. Case C-341/05. ECLI identifier: ECLI:EU:C:2007:809.
Judgment of the Court (Grand Chamber) of 24 May 2011. European Commission v Grand Duchy of Luxemburg. Case C-51/08. ECLI identifier: ECLI:EU:C:2011:336.
Judgment of the Court (Grand Chamber) of 3 December 2019, Czech Republic v European Parliament and Council of the European Union. Case C-482/17. ECLI:EU:C:2019:1035.
Judgment of the Court (Grand Chamber) of 8 December 2020, Hungary v European Parliament and Council of the European Union. Case C-620/18. ECLI:EU:C:2020:1001.
Judgment of the Court (Grand Chamber) of 8 December 2020, Republic of Poland v European Parliament and Council of the European Union. Case C-626/18. ECLI:EU:C:2020:1000.
Judgment of the Court (Second Chamber) of 3 April 2008. Dirk Rüffert v Land Niedersachsen. Case C-346/06. ECLI identifier: ECLI:EU:C:2008:189.
Judgment of the Court (Sixth Chamber) of 27 March 1990, Rush Portuguesa Ldª v Office national d'immigration, Case C-113/89, ECLI identifier: ECLI:EU:C:1990:142.
Judgment of the Court of 17 December 1981, Criminal proceedings against Alfred John Webb, Case 279/80, ECLI identifier: ECLI:EU:C:1981:314.
Judgment of the Court of 3 February 1982, Société anonyme de droit français Seco and Société anonyme de droit français Desquenne & Giral v Etablissement d'assurance contre la vieillesse et l'invalidité, Joined cases 62 and 63/81, ECLI identifier: ECLI:EU:C:1982:34.
Opinion of Advocate General Campos Sánchez-Bordona delivered on 28 May 2020, Case C-620/18, Hungary v European Parliament, Council of the European Union.
Proposal for a Directive of the European Parliament and of the Council amending Directive 96/71/EC of The European Parliament and of the Council of 16

December 1996 concerning the posting of workers in the framework of the provision of services, COM(2016) 128 final, 2016/0070(COD), 08/03/2016.
Protocol (No 2) on the application of the principles of subsidiarity and proportionality of the Consolidated version of the Treaty on the Functioning of the European Union, Official Journal C 115, 09/05/2008.
Treaty of Accession of Spain and Portugal, Official Journal, L 302, 15 November 1985.
Treaty of Accession of the Czech Republic, Estonia, Cyprus, Latvia, Lithuania, Hungary, Malta, Poland, Slovenia and Slovakia, Official Journal of the EU, L 236, 23 September 2003.
Treaty of Accession of the Republic of Bulgaria and Romania, Official Journal of the EU, L 157, 21 June 2005.
Treaty of Accession of the Republic of Croatia, Official Journal of the EU, L 112, 24 April 2012.

References

Books and Publications

Alsos K, Eldring L (2008) Labour mobility and wage dumping: the case of Norway. Eur J Ind Relat 14(4):441–459
Alsos K, Mette Ødegård A (2020) Shifting employer strategies in light of institutional change. In: Arnholtz J, Lillie N (eds) Posted workers in the European Union: the political economy of free movement. Routledge, New York, pp 50–69
Arnholtz J, Lillie N (2020) European integration and the reconfiguration of national industrial relations: posted work as a driver of institutional change. In: Arnholtz J, Lillie N (eds) Posted workers in the European Union: the political economy of free movement. Routledge, New York, pp 1–30
Ashiagbor D (2013) Unravelling the embedded liberal bargain: labour and social welfare law in the context of EU market integration. Eur Law J 19(3):303–324
Barnard C (2008) Viking and laval: an introduction. Cambridge Yearb Eur Legal Stud 10:463–492
Barnard C (2012) EU employment law, 4th edn. Oxford European Union Law Library, Oxford
Bernaciak M (2015) Conclusion. In: Bernaciak M (ed) Market expansion and social dumping in Europe. Routledge, London, pp 226–234
Böröcz J, Sarkar M (2017) The unbearable whiteness of the polish plumber and the hungarian peacock dance around "Race". Slavic Rev 76(2):307–314
Bottero M (2021) Posting of workers in EU law: challenges of equality, solidarity and fair competition. Wolters Kluwer, Alphen aan den Rijn
Caro E, Berntsen L, Lillie N, Wagner I (2015) Posted migration and segregation in the European construction sector. J Ethnic Migr Stud 41(10):1600–1620
Corti F (2022) The politicisation of social Europe: conflict dynamics and welfare integration. Edward Elgar Publishing, Cheltenham
Davies A (2008) One step forward, two steps back? The viking and laval cases in the ECJ. Ind Law J 37(2):126–148
Dølvik JE, Eldring L (eds) (2015) Labour mobility in the enlarged single European market, vol 32. Emerald Group Publishing Limited, Bingley

Eichhorst W (1998) European social policy between national and supranational regulation: Posted workers in the framework of liberalized services provision, MPIfG Discussion Paper, No. 98/6, Max-Planck-Institut für Gesellschaftsforschung, Köln.
ETUC (2016) ETUC revision of the posting of workers directive: ETUC assessment for further consultation – orientation paper. European Trade Union Institute, Brussels
European Commission (2006) Report on the functioning of the transitional arrangements set out in the 2003 accession treaty (period 1 May 2004–30 April 2006). COM, Brussels
Fromage D, Kreilinger V (2017) National parliaments' third yellow card and the struggle over the revision of the Posted Workers Directive. Eur J Leg Stud 10(1):125–160
Furåker B, Larsson B (2020) Revision of the EU posting of workers directive, social dumping and trade unions' position. In: Furåker B, Larsson B (eds) Trade Union Cooperation in Europe. Cham, Palgrave Pivot, pp 109–139
Galgóczi B, Leschke J (2012) Intra-EU labour migration after Eastern enlargement and during the crisis. Working Paper 2012.13. ETUI, Brussels
Gnes M. (2010) European legal integration? New possibilities for EU and Non-EU citizens?. In: Matei L (ed) Normativity, fundamental rights, and legal order in the EU. Bucharest, "The Dialogues of EPLO at NSPSPA" Series, No.1/2010, pp 29–56
Hassan E, Siöland L, Akbaba B, Cinova D, Gasperini M, Geraci M (2023) Annual Report on Intra-EU labour mobility 2022. Publications Office of the European Union, Luxembourg
Houwerzijl M, Berntsen L (2020) Posting of workers from a blurred notion associated with 'Cheap Labour' to a tool for 'Fair Labour Mobility'? In: Arnholtz J, Lillie N (eds) Posted workers in the European Union: the political economy of free movement. Routledge, New York
Houwerzijl M, Verschueren H (2024) Free movement of (posted) workers and applicable labour and social security law. In: Jaspers T, Pennings F, Peters S (eds) European labour law, 2nd edn. Intersentia, Cambridge, pp 163–252
Kahanec M (2012) Labour mobility in an enlarged European Union. IZA Discussion Paper, No. 6485. Institute for the Study of Labor, Bonn
Klosse S, Bekker S (2013) EU governance of economic and social policies: chances and challenges for social Europe. Eur J Soc Law 2:103–121
Konjević T (2023) Free movement of workers within the EU: western solidarity or dystopian challenges for Central-East European Workers? Ljubljana Law Rev 83:119–144
Kyriazi A (2023) Making and breaking coalitions for a more 'Social Europe': the path towards the revision of the posted workers directive. Eur J Ind Relat 29(3):221–241
Lalanne S (2011) Posting of workers, EU enlargement and the globalization of trade in services. Int Lab Rev 150(3–4):211–234
Lasek-Markey M (2022) No turning back from social Europe: a new interpretation of the refurbished posted workers directive in Hungary and Poland. Ind Law J 51(1):194–218
Lasek-Markey M (2023) Law, precarious labour, and posted workers. A sociolegal study on posted work in the EU. Routledge, New York
Lens D, Mussche N, Marx I (2022) The different faces of international posting: why do companies use posting of workers? Eur J Ind Relat 28(1):27–45
Maslauskaite K (2014) Posted workers in the EU: state of play and regulatory evolution. Notre Europe - Jacques Delors Institute, Paris
Monti M (2010) A new strategy for the single market – at the service of Europe's economy and society. Report to the President of the European Commission José Manuel Barroso. Ref. Ares, 841541(2016)
Nuffel PV, Afanasjeva S (2020) The revised posting of workers directive: curbing or ensuring free movement? In: Cambien N, Kochenov D, Muir E (eds) European citizenship under stress: social justice, brexit and other challenges. Brill-Nijhoff, Leiden, pp 271–302
Nuti A (2018) Temporary labor migration within the EU as structural injustice. Ethics Int Aff 32(2):203–225
O'Leary S, Iglesias SS (2021) Free movement of persons and services. In: Craig P, De Búrca G (eds) The evolution of EU law, 3rd edn. Oxford University Press, Oxford, pp 506–545

Ostaijen MV, Scholten P (eds) (2018) Between mobility and migration. The multi-level governance of intra-European movement. Springer, Cham
Pacolet J, Wispelaere FD (2015) Posting of workers: Report on A1 portable documents issued in 2014, Network Statistics FMSSFE, European Commission
Richard S (2014) The management of posted workers in the European Union. The Robert Schuman Foundation, European Issues n. 300
Rocca M (2020) Stepping stones over troubled waters. Recent legal evolutions and the reform of the posting of workers directive. In: Arnholtz J, Lillie N (eds) Posted workers in the European Union: the political economy of free movement. Routledge, New York, pp 167–184
Sindbjerg Martinsen D (2015) An ever more powerful court? The political constraints of legal integration in the European Union. Oxford University Press, Oxford
Van Hoek A, Houwerzijl M (2012) 'Posting' and 'Posted Workers': the need for clear definitions of two key concepts of the posting of workers directive. Cambridge Yearb Eur Legal Stud 14:419–451
Veneziani B (2012) The role of the social partners in the lisbon treaty. In: Bruun N, Lörcher K, Schömann I (eds) The lisbon treaty and social Europe. Hart Publishing, Oxford and Portland, pp 123–162
Verschueren H (2021) The CJEU endorses the revision of the posting of workers directive. ERA Forum 22:557–567
Voss E, Faioli M, Lhernould J-P, Iudicone F (2016) Posting of workers directive - current situation and challenges. European Parliament's Committee on Employment and Social Affairs, Brussels
Wagner B, Hassel A (2016) Move to work, move to stay? Mapping atypical labour migration into Germany. In: Dølvik JE, Eldring L (eds) Labour mobility in the enlarged single European market, vol 32. Bingley, Emerald Group Publishing Limited, pp 125–158
Wispelaere FD, Pacolet J (2016) An Ad hoc statistical analysis on short term mobility – economic value of posting of workers. The Impact of Intra-EU Cross-border Services, with Special Attention to the Construction Sector. KU Leuven, HIVA Research Institute for Work and Society, Leuven
Wispelaere FD, Pacolet J (2020) The benefits of posting: facts and figures on the use and impact of intra-EU posting. In: Arnholtz J, Lillie N (eds) Posted workers in the European Union: the political economy of free movement. Routledge, New York, pp 31–49
Wispelaere FD, Smedt LD, Pacolet J (2022) Posted Workers in the European Union. Facts and Figures. Leuven, Posting.Stat Project VS/2020/0499
Zeitlin J, Vanhercke B (2018) Socializing the European Semester: EU social and economic policy co-ordination in crisis and beyond. J Eur Public Policy 25(2):149–174

Web Sources

European Labour Authority [Online: https://www.ela.europa.eu/en], Accessed 27 Mar 2024
Pavy E (2023) The principle of subsidiarity [Online: https://www.europarl.europa.eu/factsheets/en/sheet/7/the-principle-of-subsidiarity#_ftn2]. Accessed: 25 Mar 2024

The Challenges of the Implementation of EU Labour Law in CEE-Countries, with Specific Regard to Enforcement: The Case of Hungary

Attila Kun

1 Introduction: EU Labour Law and Its Central and Eastern European and Hungarian Perception

The adoption of European labour law norms in Hungary's labour law legislation began well before Hungary's integration into the EU. In regulating a number of legal institutions created in the nineties (e.g. collective redundancy or transfer of undertakings), the legislator paid due regard to the relevant European labour law solutions. The approximation of laws intensified during the period of Hungary's accession to the European Community and continues also at present. § 299 of the Labour Code (Act I of 2012 on the Labour Code, hereinafter: Hungarian Labour Code, HLC) lists the directives with which the HLC is designed to comply. Nineteen such areas of regulation are currently listed in § 299.

As a starting point it is worth noting that there seems to be several fundamental differences between the overall approach of labour law policy of the European Union and that of most Central and Eastern European (hereinafter: CEE) Member States in general and Hungary, more specifically. As an introduction and illustration, only two such fundamental differences are underlined here.

A. Kun (✉)
Faculty of Law, Department of Labour Law and Social Security, Károli Gáspár University of the Reformed Church in Hungary, Budapest, Hungary

Faculty of Public Governance and International Studies, Department of Human Resources, Ludovika University of Public Service, Budapest, Hungary
e-mail: kun.attila.sandor@kre.hu

K. Koldinská et al. (eds.), *Labour Law and Social Security Law in Central and Eastern Europe*, European Union and its Neighbours in a Globalized World 26,
https://doi.org/10.1007/978-3-032-04496-9_17

First, while the EU's labour law policy has a very strong social dimension[1] (see especially the narrative of the European Social Model[2] and the European Pillar of Social Rights (hereinafter: EPSR)[3]), in many CEE-countries, and especially in Hungary, labour law is rather conceptualised along the lines of the flexibility[4] side of the "flexicurity"[5] narrative. Furthermore, in Hungary, mostly the civil, private law origins and embeddedness of labour law is emphasized and not its social law aspects.

Second, while social partnership and collective labour law[6] values are inherent in the making and content of European labour law, in Hungary the entire collective bargaining[7] system seems to fade away and struggle with fundamental structural problems.[8] Autonomous self-regulation of the labour market via collective bargaining is limited. More generally, according to some opinions, postsocialist societies are—by default, as an overturn of the past—often "very individualistic, highly segmented and lack a strong grassroots institutional network",[9] which is not a good foundation for sound and democratic labour relations and social partnership. The current dysfunctionality of collective labour relations in general can also be, to a large extent, traced back to the deviant socialist traditions. In sum, the strength and autonomy of social partners—the basic precondition of sound industrial relations—suffers from structural problems in most of the postsocialist countries.[10] For example, Article 153(3) TFEU gives Member States the possibility to entrust the implementation of directives to the social partners, i.e. to agreements between the representative organisations of employers and workers. Hungary does not apply this

[1] Gyulavári (2009).

[2] In EU jargon, labour law is seen as part of social policy, the basis for which is laid down in the Treaty on the Functioning of the European Union (TFEU) (Articles 151 et seq.).

[3] The European Parliament, the Council and the Commission launched the European Pillar of Social Rights at the Gothenburg Summit in 2017. The Pillar sets out 20 principles to guide the way towards a strong, fair, inclusive and empowered social Europe for the 21st century. The Pillar is accompanied by an Action Plan setting out concrete initiatives to put the Pillar into practice. To this end, it proposes priority objectives for the EU to achieve by 2030. See for further details: https://ec.europa.eu/info/strategy/priorities-2019-2024/economy-works-people/jobs-growth-and-investment/european-pillar-social-rights_hu (downloaded 02.12.2024).

[4] Gyulavári and Hős (2012), pp. 252–269; Gyulavári and Kártyás (2015).

[5] Flexicurity is an integrated strategy for enhancing, at the same time, flexibility and security in the labour market. It attempts to reconcile employers' need for a flexible workforce with workers' need for security. Communication from the Commission to the European Parliament, the Council, the European Economic and Social Committee and the Committee of the Regions - Towards Common Principles of Flexicurity: More and better jobs through flexibility and security {SEC(2007) 861} {SEC(2007) 862}, COM/2007/0359 final.

[6] Kun and Ter Haar (2021).

[7] See for further details: Kun (2019), pp. 333–356; Gyulavári (2020).

[8] Gyulavári and Kártyás (2022), pp. 99–116, 114.

[9] Tóth András and Hosszú (2012), pp. 137–154, 152. (the conclusion is about Hungary but seems to be apt for extrapolation for the region).

[10] Casale (1997), p. 33.

option (presumably because of the general underdevelopment of industrial relations[11]).

In sum, while the impact of social partnership and collective labour law in general seems to be marginal in Hungary, in the EU it appears to emerge a new trend, a value-oriented paradigm shift in this respect, insofar as the fundamental rights/social/democratic/'human-centred'[12]/'human-faced'[13] narratives seem to be increasingly coming to the fore. Although the EU lacks clear competences in collective labour law, and EU collective labour law is very "patchy" and over-politicised,[14] it seems that this area has recently been more in the spotlight than before. Among others, the following documents exemplify this trend: the declaration on "A new start for social dialogue" (2015)[15]; the EPSR (2017),[16] 'Report on Strengthening EU Social Dialogue' ('Nahles Report', 2021)[17]; the European Parliament's report on democracy at work[18] etc. The question is, of course, to what extent the paradigm-shift described above will ultimately lead to substantive legal reforms and results in the (near) future (also with tangible effects in the CEE Member States), or to what extent it is merely rhetorical (political) in its nature.

---

[11] Furthermore, pursuant to Article 154 TFEU social partners at EU-level may negotiate among themselves in order to reach an agreement. For example, social partners may conclude an agreement and implement it in accordance with their own specific procedures and practices or those of the Member States ('voluntary' or, later, 'autonomous' agreements). The 2002 agreement on telework was the first to be implemented as an "autonomous agreement". This was followed by other autonomous agreements, such as on work-related stress and the European licence for train drivers providing interoperable cross-border services (2004), on harassment and violence at work (2007), on inclusive labour markets (2010), on active ageing and solidarity between generations (2017) and on digitalisation (2020). It is remarkable that these autonomous agreements (except for the one on telework) have had very little resonance in Hungary, even though they are also a—specific—source of EU labour law.

[12] *Cf.* "human-centred approach to the future of work"—ILO: Centenary Declaration for the Future of Work (2019). https://www.ilo.org/wcmsp5/groups/public/@ed_norm/@relconf/documents/meetingdocument/wcms_711674.pdf (downloaded 28.07.2024); Work for a brighter future - Global Commission on the Future of Work, International Labour Office, Geneva: ILO, 2019.

[13] *See:* Novitz (2021), pp. 445–459.

[14] More information: Kun and Ter Haar (2021).

[15] "A New Start for Social Dialogue" https://op.europa.eu/en/publication-detail/-/publication/eb9d76b4-9a82-11e6-9bca-01aa75ed71a1/language-en (downloaded 02.12.2024). Among other things, it affirmed that there is no social market economy without social dialogue.

[16] Principle 8. Social dialogue and involvement of workers.

[17] "Report on Strengthening EU Social Dialogue" Written by Ms Andrea Nahles, Special Advisor on Social Dialogue to Nicolas Schmit, Commissioner for Jobs and Social Rights, February 2021, https://ec.europa.eu/social/main.jsp?langId=en&catId=85&newsId=9916&furtherNews=yes (downloaded: 10.12. 2024).

[18] European Parliament (2021): Report on democracy at work: a European framework for employee participation in company affairs and the revision of the European Works Council Directive, (2021/2005(INI)), Committee on Employment and Social Affairs, Rapporteur: Gabriele Bischoff, 29.11.2021, A9-0331/2021.

2 The General Attitude of Hungarian Labour Law Towards EU Labour Law

The "official", fundamental "philosophy" and attitude of Hungarian labour law towards EU labour law can be clearly spelled out from the text of HLC and even more clearly from the explanatory memorandum (official ministerial reasoning) of the Act (and its Proposal).

Among the so-called "principles of interpretation", the Labour Code (§ 5(1)) states that "the provisions of this Act shall be interpreted in accordance with the legislation of Hungary and the European Union." One can have the impression that this provision has hardly any substantive legal content, it can be considered rather a program-like, purely declarative norm, a symbolic goal-setting, or more critically: a "showcase" rule. There are basically three main reasons for this.

Firstly, it is obvious that the Labour Code should be interpreted in accordance with the legal order of Hungary and the European Union, even if the law itself does not specifically state this. This follows from the structure of the legal system, from the Fundamental Law (i.e. the constitution), and it is in fact self-evident that legislation cannot be applied and interpreted in isolation from the rest of the legal system.

Secondly, it is worth noting—as some commentaries also point out[19]—, that it is hardly possible to create an artificial, 'a priori' hierarchy among the general principles of legal interpretation, since only the combined application of all methods of interpretation can lead to the correct interpretation of a given piece of legislation (for example, the reference to taxonomical interpretation cannot be used to dismiss logical, grammatical, purposive[20] etc. methods of interpretation, since this can easily lead to contra legem outcomes, i.e. to a result that is obviously contrary to the legal rule).

Thirdly, the legislator may have assumed that the declaration of the obligation to interpret the Labour Code in accordance with the European Union legal order[21] would give greater prominence to the use of Community law in judicial case-law than before. However, this objective does not seem to have been achieved. Egon Budai Mihály, in an empirical-statistical research,[22] has examined the role of the Curia (Hungarian Supreme Court) in the enforcement of EU labour law rules. For this purpose, he examined the decisions of the Curia in individual cases, taken between 1 January 2013 and 31 December 2017, on the basis of how references to the 'acquis' in the broad sense appear in their reasoning. Out of the 1,533 judgments analysed using the text mining method, only 60 judgments in which some reference

---

[19] Kártyás Gábor, Petrovics Zoltán, Takács Gábor: *Commentary on Act I of 2012 on the Labour Code* [electronic document], Wolters Kluwer CompLex Legal Library, HLC § 5.

[20] *Cf.*: Davidov (2016).

[21] *I.e.* the primary and secondary law of the European Union, the case law of the Court of Justice of the European Union and the general principles of law it has developed, but certainly also soft law "products".

[22] Budai (2019), pp. 29–38.

to EU law appeared in the research. The research also finds that the EU law argument often appears only as a secondary reference as connected to Hungarian law. Naturally, this kind of research has several methodological limitations,[23] but it still illustratively confirms the general experience and hypothesis that in Hungarian labour law in general, and especially in case-law, there is not a significant number and tradition of references to international or EU labour law.

The above-described limited relevance and narrow scope of the "principle of EU-conform interpretation" (§ 5(1)) can also be observed in case-law. For instance, in December 2023, the Curia ruled on the classification of platform work relations between a food delivery platform and a delivery driver.[24] This is the first platform work ruling in Hungary, and also in the CEE region.[25] In sum, the Curia stated that the platform worker is self-employed. It must be mentioned that at the time of the case and the judgement, the Proposal[26] for a Directive[27] on improving working conditions in platform work in the EU and its 'philosophy" was already public and well-known, but the Curia didn't pay any attention to it.

The (general) explanatory memorandum (official reasoning) of the HLC contains a very remarkable statement regarding the relationship of Hungarian labour law to EU labour law: "The Proposal attempted to make good use of the opportunities afforded by these in the course of the adoption of European labour law rules and to implement flexible regulations adjusted to the needs of the local labour market."[28] It is worth 'underlining' two points from this quote: 'to take advantage of' and 'flexible'. All this therefore predestines the Hungarian legislator to regard the EU labour law directives not only as a minimum—in line with their original purpose—but also as a maximum, and to "go to the wall" in implementing these rules as flexibly as possible. A further consequence of this attitude (as the current paper will attempt to illustrate this with examples below) is that legal harmonisation is therefore often superficial, formal, creative (in possibly both good and bad senses) and often 'dances' on the edge of EU compliance.[29]

Another frequent "trick" of the Hungarian legislator in course of transposing EU labour law directives is to slightly adapt the terminology. As the courts noted, where

[23] For example, it only formally examines the decisions of the Curia, and it is possible that the Curia applies EU law through the transposing provisions of the Labour Code (i.e. it does not have to cite the source directly). Therefore, the small number of cases that invoke EU law does not automatically imply any deficit in the EU-law basis of the case law.

[24] Curia, published decision: BH 1993/775.

[25] See for more details in English: https://global-workplace-law-and-policy.kluwerlawonline.com/2024/05/28/the-first-hungarian-platform-work-judgmentself-employment/ (downloaded 12.12.2024).

[26] Proposal for a DIRECTIVE OF THE EUROPEAN PARLIAMENT AND OF THE COUNCIL on improving working conditions in platform work, COM/2021/762 final.

[27] Directive (EU) 2024/2831 of the European Parliament and of the Council of 23 October 2024 on improving working conditions in platform work.

[28] General justification 16.

[29] Kun (2020), pp. 235–251.

a Member State transposes a Directive into its own legal order by applying concepts other than those used in the EU Directive, it may, by that technique, "completely disconnect the rules of the transposed law from EU law and the Directive which it was designed to transpose."[30] Accordingly, to put it simple, the risk of misinterpretation is high concerning this tactic of "word magic" and it is easy to "lost in translation". There are several such examples in Hungarian labour law. For example, while EU-law uses the notion of "consultation" in several directives (e.g. Directive 2002/14/EC), the HLC, at times, replaces this with other—often confusing—terms (e.g. "asking for the opinion" of employee representatives[31]). Whereas the Working Time Directive (see below, hereinafter: WTD) uses the concept of "reference periods", Hungarian labour law applies various similar, but often complicating terminology: working time frame / banking ("munkaidőkeret" in Hungarian), payroll period ("elszámolási időszak" in Hungarian). Similarly, the WTD's definition of shiftwork[32] is totally different from the HLC's concept of shiftwork.[33] Likewise, the WTD's concept of "autonomous" workers (as part of derogations[34]) and the HLC's respective perception of "flexible working arrangement"[35] are slightly different (triggering legal uncertainties in practice). In sum, several Hungarian legal definitions are not in sync with their EU-law based counterparts.

The above-described general attitude of 'formal' (or 'ticking the box'-type) and creative compliance is also recognized in the literature. For example, a recent ETUI-study paints a depressing but realistic picture of the regional (i.e. CEE) and national, Hungarian situation of labour law compliance: from a strictly formal point of view, employment regulation in CEE countries[36] including Hungary (with a fundamentally statist tradition of regulation) provides an acceptable level of protection for employees. "However, workers' formal rights are being violated and circumvented on a massive scale. Because the oversight system is non-effective, employees lack sufficient access to justice; furthermore, the courts and administrative bodies approach regulation in a highly formalised way so that the violations and

[30] Mfv.II.10.025/2024/6.

[31] § 264 HLC.

[32] § 2.5: "shift work" means any method of organising work in shifts whereby workers succeed each other at the same work stations according to a certain pattern, including a rotating pattern, and which may be continuous or discontinuous, entailing the need for workers to work at different times over a given period of days or weeks.

[33] § 90 HLC. The method of organizing the employer's work is: shiftwork, if its duration reaches eighty hours in a week.

[34] § 17(1)(a). The Directive allows derogations 'when, on account of the specific characteristics of the activity concerned, the duration of the working time is not measured and/or predetermined or can be determined by the workers themselves'.

[35] § 96(2) HLC: "The employer may permit - in writing - the employee to schedule his working time in the interest of autonomous work organization (flexible working arrangement). Where the employee is permitted to perform certain functions of the job at a specific time or period in light of their unique characteristics, this shall have no bearing on his flexible working arrangement."

[36] See for more details: Kun (2024b), pp. 89–100; Bronstein (2006), pp. 191–224; Shvelidze (2021).

circumventions become 'normalised' over time, rendering formal regulation ineffective."[37] The paper adds that post-socialist CEE countries are still characterised by a dominantly "statist system of the regulation of employment standards", as a pivotal legacy of the past and legal interpretation holds a basically "highly formalised and hierarchical approach."[38] Several important conclusions can be drawn from this finding. Most importantly, as the author points out, it is futile to ensure an acceptable level of formal regulation (including EU-compliance) if the dynamic operation of the law is problematic, ultimately not guaranteeing structural enforcement. The research also highlights the case of Hungary, where it finds that approach to legal interpretation is (hyper-)positivist and workers' access to justice is 'notoriously' limited.[39]

It is worth mentioning that it was a recent blatant symbol of the generally modest commitment of Hungarian labour law to EU labour law that the Hungarian Government challenged the amendment to the so-called Posting of Workers Directive[40] published on 9 July 2018 by filing an action for annulment with the Court of Justice of the European Union. This appears to be a very rare and tough step in the realm of EU (labour) law. There is neither the space nor the need here to go into the legal institution (posting) and the related discourse in detail, but it is clear that the debate on the revision of the Posting Directive has been structured along two distinct perspectives among EU Member States. In brief: the 'old', 'western' Member States that initiated the amendment, argued in favour of the principle of equal pay for equal work in the same place, while the 'new', 'eastern' Member States objected the reform and argued that it would reduce the competitive advantage of 'eastern' service-providers due to lower wages and would also reduce the competitiveness of the EU itself. In very simple terms, this means that while the 'old', 'western' Member States have tended to argue in favour of worker-protection and social concerns in this debate (and of course also along clearly protectionist lines of thinking), the 'eastern' Member States have tended to take a position driven by market fundamentalism and economic considerations. Hungary has become a quasi "spokesman" for this second position, an attitude—which, in view of what has been explained above—, also very vividly symbolises and summarises the general perception of EU labour law in Hungary. In support of its stance,[41] the Hungarian Government has invoked a number of legal arguments which summarise the official attitude to the issue. These legal arguments included, for example, the lack of an adequate legal basis, misuse of powers, infringement of the freedom to provide

[37] Muszyński (2020), 4., 23.

[38] Muszyński (2020), p. 6.

[39] Ibid. 17, 19.

[40] Directive (EU) 2018/957 of the European Parliament and of the Council of 28 June 2018 amending Directive 96/71/EC concerning the posting of workers in the framework of the provision of services. Originally: Directive 96/71/EC of the European Parliament and of the Council of 16 December 1996 concerning the posting of workers in the framework of the provision of services.

[41] Court of Justice of the European Union - Case C-620/18 Hungary v European Parliament, Council of the European Union, action brought on 2 October 2018.

services, infringement of the principle of clarity of the rules and thus of legal certainty. In the case, the Government thus essentially accused the European legislator of 'overprotecting' workers, exceeding its powers, disproportionate restrictions on economic freedoms (in this case, the freedom to provide services), excessive 'internationalisation' of collective labour law values and creating legal uncertainty. It cannot be alleged, of course, that Hungarian labour law is so markedly distanced from the EU labour law philosophy in all EU labour law-related issues (since the issue of posting has undoubtedly received a specific political context and spotlight throughout Europe), but it can be stated that this attitude can be identified in the EU labour law approach of Hungarian labour law in general, either directly or indirectly, with varying degrees of intensity.

3 Deficits of Compliance with EU Labour Law in Hungarian Labour Law: Illustrative Examples

The aim of this chapter is to—clearly without claiming completeness—illustrate the general EU labour law attitude of Hungarian labour law outlined above in a thematic, problem-focused way, by means of some illustrative, revealing, controversial, principled regulatory examples, in a snapshot manner. In doing so, the chapter discusses regulatory examples in respect of which—according to the prevailing, dominant streams of interpretation—at least the concern of non-compliance with EU law can be raised, i.e. full compliance is open to debate. For reasons of space, the present study is not suitable for an in-depth examination of the Hungarian legal harmonisation in relation to all EU labour law topics.[42]

The examples provided below essentially have three basic common denominators. On the one hand, they are illustrative indicators of what is apparent to be a general EU labour law attitude in Hungarian labour law (see above: minimum compliance, "going to the wall", a kind of detachment). On the other hand, they are typically aimed at weakening the level of protection of workers' rights and/or collective rights—simply put—in relation to EU-law-inclined ambitions. Nevertheless, it must be admitted, they are sufficiently 'intelligent', creative in a sense that they seek to ensure compliance with the directives in a textual (ostensible, superficial) way (sometimes 'dancing on the edge', creating considerable ambiguity of interpretation), while clearly doing little to fully embrace the substance, values and real purpose of the directives in question. The present paper does not claim that there is a clear violation of EU law in all the cases raised below (since directives as a "genre" in general, and the rather "open" wording of certain labour law directives in particular, always leave a great deal of room for manoeuvre for the transposing national law). However, it does claim that the Hungarian legislator's main aim is to achieve

[42] See for a similar study in Hungarian: Kun (2024a), pp. 3–23.

minimum, formal compliance by "ticking the box" of transposition, which attitude inevitably results in regulatory solutions that often 'dance on the edge' of compliance.

3.1 Collective Redundancies

As regards collective redundancies, Hungarian labour law ensures compliance with the provisions of Council Directive 98/59/EC of 20 July 1998 on the approximation of the laws of the Member States relating to collective redundancies. It is important to stress, however, that the Directive does not seek to fully harmonise Member States' rules in this area either but merely imposes certain targeted information and consultation obligations on Member States in relation to collective redundancies in order to further the protection of workers. The legislation is therefore primarily procedural in nature, with the obligation to inform and consult being at the heart of the procedure. It is for this reason that it seems particularly worrying that Hungarian labour law is in fact 'watering down' this essence of the Directive.

According to the Labour Code, the employer, if planning to carry out collective redundancies, shall initiate consultations with the works council (§ 72(1)). The current legislation breaks with the previous Hungarian regulatory solution, according to which in the absence of a works council, the employer had to initiate consultations with the trade unions and/or other employee representatives represented at the employer, and to continue such consultations until a decision was made or an agreement was concluded. According to currently effective HLC, consultations are obligatory only with the works council. Although the explanatory memorandum (official reasoning) to the law states that the law thus complies with the Directive, this cannot be taken for granted. According to the Directive (§ 2(1)), where an employer is contemplating collective redundancies, he shall begin consultations with the workers' representatives in good time with a view to reaching an agreement. Although the Directive states that 'workers' representatives' means the workers' representatives provided for by the laws or practices of the Member States (§ 1(1)(b)), it is a mistake to refer only to the works council in this setting in the context of Hungarian labour law and industrial relations. Recital 6 of the Preamble of the Directive refers to the fact that information, consultation and participation for workers must be developed along appropriate lines, taking account of the practices in force in the various Member States. In Hungarian practice, however, the current solution does not represent "development" but a step backwards, and it seems to neglect the normal, customary practical roles and functions of trade unions.

In this context, it can be concluded from the European Court of Justice's judgement that national legislation must provide for the possibility of negotiation even where an employer otherwise lacks formalised employee representation at the workplace level (Case C-383/92, Commission of the European Communities v United Kingdom of Great Britain and Northern Ireland).[43]

Thus, the solution of the HLC appears to be technically sound, seemingly in line with the Directive (since the works council undoubtedly represents the employees), but it does not even come close to achieving the very aim of the Directive, since in the absence of a works council the employer is not obliged to comply with the obligation for consultation set forth in the Labour Code. Some authors therefore correctly suggest that it is desirable to maintain the former practice, according to which, in the absence of a works council, the employer negotiates with the other employees' representatives, especially the trade union.[44] In fact, the issue should perhaps be settled by amending the legislation to ensure full compliance with the spirit of the Directive.

3.2 Atypical Employment Relationship: Fixed-Term Employment Contracts

The prevention of abuse arising from the use of successive fixed-term employment contracts or relationships is one of the main objectives of Council Directive 1999/70/EC of 28 June 1999 concerning the framework agreement on fixed-term work concluded by ETUC, UNICE and CEEP. Measures to prevent abuse (Section 5) contains the following: to prevent abuse arising from the use of successive fixed-term employment contracts or relationships, Member States, after consultation with social partners in accordance with national law, collective agreements or practice, and/or the social partners, shall, where there are no equivalent legal measures to prevent abuse, introduce in a manner which takes account of the needs of specific sectors and/or categories of workers, one or more of the following measures: (a) objective reasons justifying the renewal of such contracts or relationships; (b) the maximum total duration of successive fixed-term employment contracts or relationships; (c) the number of renewals of such contracts or relationships.

Hungarian labour law makes some use of two of the three options, but in both cases with very generous, soft solutions. Pro forma, therefore, it would be difficult to question the fulfilment of harmonisation here, but the merits and practical effectiveness of the 'measures to prevent abuse' are debatable.

Thus, § 192 of the HLC imposes two barriers "against" chains of fixed-term employment contracts of short duration.

On the one hand, the duration of a fixed-term employment relationship may not exceed five years, including the duration of an extended relationship and that of

[43] Court of Justice of the European Union - Judgment of the Court: C-383/92 Commission of the European Communities v United Kingdom of Great Britain and Northern Ireland., ECLI:EU:C:1994:234.

[44] Bankó et al. (2019), § 71.

another fixed-term employment relationship concluded within six months of the termination of the previous fixed-term employment relationship (§ 192(2)). The matter of the "maximum total duration" required by the Directive is therefore regulated by Hungarian labour law. However, five years can be considered a very broad maximum.

On the other hand, a fixed-term employment relationship may be extended, or another fixed-term employment relationship may be concluded within six months from the time of termination of the previous one upon the employer's legitimate interests. The agreement may not infringe upon the employee's legitimate interest (§ 192(4)). Thus, on the one hand, this procedure (prolongation, reestablishment) is only possible if there is a legitimate interest on the part of the employer and, on the other hand, it must not be aimed at diminishing the legitimate interest of the employee. There is therefore no specific limit on the number of times the employment relationship can be extended or the number of times a fixed term can be repeated. The legality of this can always be judged in the light of all the circumstances of the case, on the basis of the very open rule described above. It is doubtful to what extent the use of the very vague category of 'legitimate interest' corresponds to the concept of 'objective reasons' for renewal required by the Directive.

3.3 Atypical Employment Relationships: Temporary Agency Work and School Cooperatives

Pursuant to § 3(1)(e) of Directive 2008/104/EC of the European Parliament and of the Council of 19 November 2008 on temporary agency work (hereinafter: TAW), 'assignment' means the period during which the temporary agency worker is placed at the user undertaking to work temporarily under its supervision and direction. The purpose of limiting the period of TAW is to ensure that it cannot replace or substitute standard employment relationships. Although 'temporary nature' as a legal requirement is open to a very wide range of interpretations, it is doubtful whether the relevant provision of the HLC is in line with the Directive. According to the HLC (§ 214(2)), the duration of assignment may not exceed five years (including any period of extended assignment and re-assignment within a period of six months from the time of termination of his/her previous employment, irrespective of whether the assignment was made by the same or by a different temporary-work agency). This provision can be considered extremely flexible. In fact, it represents only a linguistic, formal correspondence with the Directive's provision, but not a substantive limit, as five years is an extremely long period both in international comparison and in terms of its practicality (the latter is supported by statistics: the average duration of the assignment is around three to four months, for example in

2009 the average length was 52 days[45]). Since long-term agency work, which is incompatible with the purpose of the Directive (and the idea of TAW itself), should be discouraged by law, the present regulatory solution seems to be completely inappropriate.

Besides the questionable domestic rule on the 'temporary nature' of TAW, the literature also reveals several other issues where the TAW-related provisions of the HLC are of concern in light of the TAW-Directive. István Horváth[46] points out, for example, that the HLC makes use of the possibility of derogation from the requirement of equal treatment in three areas,[47] and it applies derogation without the Directive's mandate in respect of two provisions in a controversial manner, but definitely in respect of one provision. It is not possible to elaborate on these here, but the statement must be agreed. Equally worrying is the exclusion of the application of the statutory rules on collective redundancies[48] regarding TAW in general, even though this does not comply with the provision establishing the scope of Directive on collective redundancies (98/59/EC). Furthermore, it is also rather indicative that the HLC, in contrast with the Directive, does not contain explicit rules on the collective rights of temporary agency workers.[49]

Another concern is that the employment of cooperative members (see: school cooperatives, general interest pensioners' cooperatives) is essentially regulated by the logic and construction of temporary agency work in the Act on Cooperatives,[50] but without the guarantees included in Directive 2008/104/EC and the HLC in relation to TAW. The employment of cooperative members is a unique non-standard form of employment in Hungary. In two of the forms of cooperatives referred to in the Act—school cooperatives and general interest pensioners' cooperatives—the legislator provides for the possibility of a specific triangular employment arrangement similar to that of TAW, which is a hybrid, sui generis legal relationship that

---

[45] Development of temporary work in Hungary between 2005 and 2009 (Source: Foglalkoztatási és Szociális Hivatal 2006–2010). Cited in Kártyás (2011), pp. 166, 212..

[46] Horváth (2019): Rugalmasabb biztonság. A munkaerő-kölcsönzés hazai szabályai – elsődleges figyelemmel az Európai Unió meghatározó jogközelítési normáira, *Munkajog*, HVG-ORAC 2019/3, 9-15.

[47] See § 219 of the HLC: Principle of equal treatment. Accordingly, the basic working and employment conditions of temporary agency workers shall be, for the duration of their assignment, those available to the employees employed by the user enterprise under employment relationship. As regards the amount of wages and other benefits, the provisions on equal treatment shall apply as of the one hundred and eighty-fourth day of employment at the user enterprise with respect to any employee:

(a) who is engaged with a temporary-work agency in an employment relationship established for an indefinite duration, and who is receiving pay in the absence of any assignment to a user enterprise; (b) who is recognized as a long-term absentee from the labour market as defined in Point 1 of Subsection (2) of Section 1 of Act CXXIII of 2004; (c) who is working within the framework of temporary agency work at a business association under the majority control of a municipal government or public benefit organization, or a registered public benefit organization.

[48] HLC § 222(4).

[49] See for more details: Kártyás (2016).

[50] Act X of 2006 on Cooperatives.

entails a lower level of labour law protection than provided for by the rules of the Labour Code. The legislator has artificially "outsourced" these forms of employment from the scope of labour law (and thus the Directive), although—as Sipka and Zaccaria points out—the phenomenon of employment as a member of these cooperatives fits exactly the definition of TAW in line with Directive 2008/104/EC.[51] Work performed in a cooperative relationship—where the member may fulfil the requirement of personal involvement also within the framework of the provision of services by the cooperative to a third party ("external service")—does not differ in content, only in name, from the legal concept of TAW.[52] In the light of the above, there is good reason to have reservations about the Hungarian legal solution regarding cooperative employment in the light of the Directive.[53]

3.4 Employee Participation: Information and Consultation

Directive 2002/14/EC of the European Parliament and of the Council of 11 March 2002 establishes a general framework for informing and consulting employees in the European Community (hereinafter: information and consultation framework directive, ICFDR).[54] Article 8 of the ICFDR (the so-called "Framework Directive") lays down strict requirements for the protection of rights. Member States shall provide for appropriate measures in the event of non-compliance with the Directive by the employer or the employees' representatives. In particular, they shall ensure that adequate administrative or judicial procedures are available to enable the obligations deriving from this Directive to be enforced. Member States shall provide for adequate sanctions to be applicable in the event of infringement of the Directive by the employer or the employees' representatives. These sanctions must be effective, proportionate and dissuasive.

The Hungarian legislation is particularly problematic in this respect. § 289 of the HLC states that the employer, the works council or the trade union may bring an action within five days in the event of any violation of the provisions on information or consultation. The court shall hear such cases in non-contentious civil action. This provision in fact institutionalises a so-called "lex imperfecta" rule, since although a breach of the information and consultation norms leads to an unlawful situation, which can be established by the court, the norm cannot in fact be enforced by the courts (in the absence of sanctions). Case-law has also confirmed that, in the case of a breach of the rule on consultation, a finding of illegality may be made in non-litigation proceedings, but that consultation cannot be enforced.[55] It is worth noting

[51] Sipka and Zaccaria (2017), pp. 23-30, 27.

[52] Ibid.

[53] See also: Kiss (2017) p. 499, Vol. 14 August 2017 No. 8; Kun (2016), pp. 71–91.

[54] On the importance of participation in general, see: Hungler (2020).

[55] Curia, EBH 2014.M.24.

that, although employee participation is undoubtedly a complex, ongoing learning process, the effectiveness of which certainly does not (only) depend on legal sanctions, the absolute unenforceability of participation rights in this way grossly and dysfunctionally—and contrary to the cited article of the ICFDR—undervalues the legal institution information and consultation.

Opinions are divided on the matter, what type (i.e. criminal, civil, administrative etc.) and how big sanctions could really fit to the requirement of "effectiveness, dissuasiveness and proportionality". On the one hand, probably the most suitable sanction would be a possibility to nullify measures executed by management without respecting the procedures of information and consultation. However, such a sanction striking the validity of the measure in such a context may not always pass the proportionality test. Sanctions of other kinds, including fines, seem to be more common and more appropriate in this regard.[56] However, Hungarian law contains no sanction at all in this regard. It must be mentioned at this point that it seems to be a general feature of the Hungarian approach to transposition of EU labour law directives to neglect the enforcement-side of EU labour law rules, and to disregard the obligation (contained in most of the directives) to provide for sanctions that are effective, proportionate and dissuasive.

It is also worth mentioning that § 7 of the ICFDR provides for the protection of workers' representatives, according to which Member States shall ensure that employees' representatives, when carrying out their functions, enjoy adequate protection and guarantees to enable them to perform properly the duties which have been assigned to them. It is questionable whether the fact that the HLC provides for such labour law-protection for the chairman of the works council (shop steward) only (not for the members of the works council) is "satisfactory" in this respect. Indeed, according to the case law of the CJEU, any measure transposing the Directive must ensure the minimum level of protection laid down in the said § 7.[57]

3.5 *Working Time (Examples)*

Directive 2003/88/EC of the European Parliament and of the Council of 4 November 2003 deals with certain aspects of the organisation of working time (hereinafter: WTD). There are several Hungarian working time rules whose full conformity with EU law is highly disputed in the legal literature. For example, Gábor Fodor T.'s comprehensive study on the subject[58] also lists a number of Hungarian legal institutions (e.g. the concept of working time, the calculation of annual leave in hours, the

[56] See for a general discussion of this matter: Jagodzinski (2015), pp. 172–174.

[57] *Cf.*: Court of Justice of the European Union - Judgment of the Court of Justice C-405/08 Ingeniørforeningen i Danmark v Dansk Arbejdsgiverforening, ECLI:EU:C:2010:69 (the so-called Holst case).

[58] Fodor T (2016), pp. 21–36.

concept of 'stand-by job'[59] as an opt-out, the concept of multi-shift work, payroll period, overtime work ordered for rest days etc.) most of which raise thought-provoking reservations regarding their EU-conformity. It is not possible to analyse all of them in detail here for reasons of space, but it must be underlined that all these issues are worthy of deeper discussion. Some examples are briefly presented below.

According to the WTD (§ 2.1.), "working time" means any period during which the worker is working, at the employer's disposal and carrying out his activity or duties, in accordance with national laws and/or practice. In contrast, the HLC (§ 86(1)) defines 'working time' as the duration from the commencement until the end of the period prescribed for working, covering also any preparatory and finishing activities related to working. Apparently, the two definitions are not in full consistency (especially the "period prescribed for working" wording of the HLC differs from the notion of being at the "employer's disposal" according to the WTD, because the HLC's definition seems to be narrower and relies more on the employer's discretion, prerogative, while the WTD rather builds on the sole fact of working).

The HLC expressly stipulates that working time shall not cover "travel time" from the employee's home or place of residence to the place where work is in fact carried out and from the place of work to the employee's home or place of residence (§ 86(3)(b)). However, in EU-law, the Court has held that travel time could, in certain cases, also count as 'working time', since the working time of workers could not be restricted to the time spent on the premises of their employer or the customers such as in that of workers without fixed places of work in the Tyco case.[60] The Court has ruled in this case on whether the time spent travelling to the first and from the last customer by workers without a fixed place of work qualifies as 'working time'. Accordingly, the HLC and the trends of EU labour law are not in full conformity regarding the calculation of travel time (which in certain cases can be classified as working time).

The HLC contains a unique legal category (§ 98), the so-called "payroll period" ("elszámolási idő"),[61] which, according to T. Fodor (and many other Hungarian labour lawyers) is a legal concept that is utterly "incomprehensible" under the WTD.[62]

Also generating EU-compliance-related debates is the issue of the "three-year working time frame/banking",[63] which highlights the friction between the

---

[59] § 91 HLC.

[60] Judgment in case C-266/14, Federación de Servicios Privados del sindicato Comisiones obreras ("Tyco").

[61] "Apart from working time banking, work may also be scheduled in such a way whereby the employee completes the weekly working time scheduled based on the daily working time and the standard work pattern over a longer period that the employer has determined, beginning on the given week."

[62] F (2016), p. 36.

[63] § 94(3): Where justified by objective or technical reasons or reasons related to work organization, the maximum duration of working time banking fixed in the collective agreement is thirty-six months. See also: § 99(7).

EU-concept of the "reference period" (WTD) and the domestic terminology (working time frame/banking). The WTD does not recognise—in fact does not allow—two types of "reference period" (averaging rule), although the Hungarian rule in question actually introduces two types of "reference period" (one for normal working time, called a working time frame, up to 36 months; one for scheduled weekly working time, up to 12 months). Experts observe that the three-year working time frame is not in line with EU law. Szabó and T. Fodor states that the "authors of the legislative proposal are operating with a logic that appears to be cunning but is in fact flawed".[64]

Another noteworthy dilemma is that in Hungarian labour law it is possible to order overtime work for rest days[65] (under certain circumstances), while in EU labour law, in terms of the wording of the Directive, "rest period" means any period which is not working time,[66] and the Court has also ruled that in the logic of the Directive, working time is 'placed in opposition to rest periods, the two being mutually exclusive'.[67]

It must also be noted that many EU labour law directives (including the WTD) use the requirement of 'appropriate collective agreements', but this matter is typically not addressed by the Hungarian legislator.

At this point it is worth mentioning that the WTD itself can be considered outdated, incomplete and imprecise on several points. In 2004, the Commission presented a proposal for a revision of the WTD. After the Parliament, the Commission and the Council failed to reach an agreement in 2009, another negotiation process between the European social partners stalled in December 2012 due to disagreements over the treatment of on-call time. The Commission relaunched the review and impact assessment process in 2013, conducted a public consultation in 2015 and issued an implementation report and an interpretative communication in 2017. Some aspects relevant to working time have since been included in other legal acts, such as the work-life balance (WLB)[68] and transparent and predictable working conditions (TPWC)[69] directives and the revised regulation on driving time. At the same time, the stagnation of the comprehensive review and update of the WTD also highlights the problems of EU labour law in general (such as the difficulty of

[64] Szabó and Fodor T (2018).

[65] § 143(4) HLC.

[66] § 2.2.

[67] Judgment in case C-303/98, Simap, para. 47; Judgment in case C-151/02, Jaeger, para. 48, Order in case C-437/05, Vorel, para. 24; Judgment in case C-14/04, Dellas and Others, para. 42; Judgment in case C-266/14, Federación de Servicios Privados del sindicato Comisiones obreras, para. 25; Judgment in case C-518/15, Matzak, para. 55; Judgment in case C-344/19, Radiotelevizija Slovenija, para. 29; Judgment in case C-580/19, Offenbach am Main, para. 30; Judgment in case C-107/19, Dopravní podnik hl. m. Prahy, para. 28.

[68] Directive (EU) 2019/1158 of the European Parliament and of the Council of 20 June 2019 on work-life balance for parents and carers and repealing Council Directive 2010/18/EU.

[69] Directive (EU) 2019/1152 of the European Parliament and of the Council of 20 June 2019 on transparent and predictable working conditions in the European Union.

finding compromises and the sometimes vague solutions due to the many compromises).

3.6 Rest Periods (Examples)

Recently, the MÁV-Start case[70] drew attention to the fact that the Hungarian labour law and the WTD's rules on rest periods are not necessarily in sync in all respects.[71] The case is rather symbolic, and it has raised extensive debates in Hungary and beyond.

In this important decision, the CJEU interpreted the WTD. The dispute originated from Hungary and focused on the relationship between daily and weekly rest periods. A train driver contested his employer, MÁV-START, the Hungarian state railway company, for not granting him a daily rest period of at least 11 h preceding or following a weekly rest period. The employer claimed that since Hungarian law stipulates a minimum weekly rest period well above that required by the WTD, its employee was not in an unfavourable position. To fully understand the decision, it is important to consider the legal context. The WTD requires 11 h of daily rest and 24 h of weekly rest, stressing that the daily rest is in addition to the weekly rest. On the other hand, in brief, Hungarian law provides 11 h of daily rest and a more generous 48-hour weekly rest. The Court established that the daily and weekly rest rights are autonomous and should be guaranteed separately, because the Directive provides these rights in two different provisions which pursue different social-policy objectives.

The Court stressed that if a country decides to give more than 24 h weekly rest period, it cannot use that to justify taking away other rights (namely, the daily rest period) the that employees are granted under the Directive. The daily rest period is not part of the weekly rest period. Even if a national regulation provides a weekly rest period of more than 35 consecutive hours (=11 + 24), the employee must be granted the daily rest period of 11 hours in addition to this weekly rest period. The employee is entitled to the daily rest period that precedes the weekly rest period. The CJEU added that, after work, the employees must immediately benefit from a daily rest period, and the weekly rest period can only start once the worker has benefited from the daily rest period. In sum, while Hungary would comply with the WTD by providing the minimum rest periods (to put it simple, 35 hours altogether), the current Hungarian rule, offering 48 hours of weekly rest without the mandatory 11-hour daily rest, falls short of the requirements of the WTD.

---

[70] Case C-477/21 IH v MÁV-START Vasúti Személyszállító Zrt. [ECLI:EU:C:2023:140].

[71] For more information see the thematic collection of articles published in the "Munkajog" labour law journal (ORAC) 2023/2.

The decision has far-reaching "everyday" implications and necessitates elementary reconsideration of working-time patterns on the labour market.[72] The Curia stated[73] that Hungarian courts should follow the judgment of the CJEU which provided a clear answer and it "does not give any further leeway to the Hungarian courts". The CJEU held that the definition of daily and weekly rest periods are autonomous concepts of EU law. It must be noted that even before the decision of the CJEU, the Hungarian legislator sought to resolve the problem by amending the HLC in line with a Constitutional court-decision on the topic.[74] The amendment (§ 104(5), effective as of 01 Jan 2023) states that "no daily rest period shall be scheduled if no working time is scheduled for the day immediately after the conclusion of work, or if no overtime work is ordered." However, in light of the CJEU's decision this legislative solution also creates legal uncertainty. Consequently, the legislator will need to act, but is rather emblematic—and confirms the arguments presented above regarding the generally hesitant, formalistic etc. Hungarian labour law-policy attitude towards EU labour law—that nothing has happened since the CJEU's decision (apart from the fact a big number of cases are pending at courts on this matter, and even more are expected). It seems to be essential to adapt the HLC on daily and weekly rest periods in order to be in full compliance with the WTD.

3.7 *Telework, as an Atypical Employment Relationship*

The case of telework is also a prime example of the phenomenon that the Hungarian legislator at times transposes EU labour law half-heartedly, or even by way of misinterpretation (which often causes serious real-life difficulties). The transposition of the European Framework Agreement on Telework agreed by ETUC, UNICE/UEAPME and CEEP on the 16th of July 2002 took place by a clear-cut legislative solution[75] in Hungary. It is to be noted that one can find relatively few examples in the EU for "transplanting" the Framework Agreement in such great detail into the national legislation, which primarily reflects the weak power of national social dialogue (structures and practices). Another possible explanation for this rather quick and "mechanical" transposition of the Framework Agreement into the Labour Code

[72] ECJ decision on working time in Hungarian case, Schönherr Rechtsanwälte, 13 December 2023, Newsletter, https://www.schoenherr.eu/content/ecj-decision-on-working-time-in-hungarian-case (downloaded 22.12.2024).

[73] Curia: Kúria Mfv.II.10.025/2024/6.

[74] In Judgment No 12 of 22 June 2020 of the Constitutional Court of Hungary, the court held that the interpretation of the Curia (Supreme Court, Hungary), according to which the daily rest and weekly rest period may be granted in a single period, was not compatible with Article XVII(4) of the Fundamental Law of Hungary, which guarantees the right of every worker to daily and weekly rest periods, on the ground that those rights are to be regarded as autonomous since they have different purposes. The interpretation of the Constitutional Court concerned a case relating to health workers.

[75] Act XXVIII of 2004.

might be the timing: Hungary joined the EU in 2004, so showing the image of a "good-performer" in terms of legal harmonization was certainly a policy priority at that time.

In brief, it can be presumed that the apparent, long-lasting conceptual confusion within Hungarian labour law as regards telework and/or so-called "home office"[76] (especially during the Covid-pandemic) can be ¾ to some extent ¾ traced back to the imprecise, short-sighted, rather mechanical implementation of the Framework Agreement. First, the HLC requires a sui generis ¾ "atypical" ¾ employment contract for telework. To be precise, in the employment contract the parties shall agree on the employee's employment by means of telework.[77] These rigid regulatory solutions seem to over-formalize telework, while the Framework Agreement only prescribes the "voluntary character" of telework (an aspect not emphasized expressly by the HLC) and perceives telework more like a form of "organising and/or performing work" (not necessarily as a separate, atypical employment status/contract). The correct, sensible transposition of the Framework Agreement could have saved the Hungarian labour market (and the labour law scholarship) from a bunch of unnecessary, formalistic debates.

4 Some Specificities of EU Labour Law That Make "Full-Hearted" Compliance Challenging

It must be noted that there are a number of inherent features and partly new trends in EU labour law that are contradictory to some extent, and may give rise to confusion, make it difficult to "associate" with, or in some respects undermine its prestige and authority. The aim in this chapter is neither to provide a comprehensive analysis nor a sharp, in-depth critique of EU labour law trends and processes, but to identify some notable and worrying features and trends that are likely to affect its reputation and effectiveness. In addition to the obvious outdated nature of several EU labour law norms (the WTD has already been referred to above in this respect, but one could also mention the 2002 Framework Agreement on telework, etc.), other specific, worrying features can be noticed. Some of these are mentioned below (with examples), for illustrative purposes: the very frequent contradictory messages, the increasing politicisation, the existence of a number of impractical rules, the phenomenon of 'softening up' and weak enforcement.

First of all, it is worth pointing out that the "big" goals of EU labour law policy can change and fluctuate very quickly and radically (even within a relatively short time span), sometimes propelling contradictory messages, creating uncertainties and even questioning the credibility, consistency and "honesty" of the policies in place. Two examples are given here. In the wake of the 2008 economic and financial

[76] Kun et al. (2023), pp. 81–234.

[77] § 196(2) HLC.

crisis, social dialogue and collective bargaining have come under increasing pressure from the European Commission (or the troika, i.e. the triumvirate of the Commission, the European Central Bank and the International Monetary Fund), resulting in increased decentralisation of collective bargaining in many countries,[78] a reduction in the proportion of workers covered by collective agreements and a weakening of state intervention in wage policy.[79] By contrast, after more than ten years, a whole new 'wind has been blowing': promotion of collective bargaining for wage setting is one of the main objectives of the Adequate Minimum Wages Directive[80] (and obliges Member States with less than 80% collective bargaining coverage to adopt action plans to promote collective bargaining). Another example of the phenomenon of 'conflicting messages' relates to the issue of working time. The Directive on transparent and predictable working conditions[81] sends the message that an employer should neither prohibit a worker from taking up employment with other employers, outside the work schedule established with that employer, nor subject a worker to adverse treatment for doing so.[82] In contrast, the interpretative communication on the WTD[83] states that in the case of so-called "concurrent contracts" (parallel employment), "the Commission considers that, in the light of the Directive's objective to improve the health and safety of workers, the limits on average weekly working time and daily and weekly rest should as far as possible, apply per worker." The two stipulations are rather contradictory. While the TPWC seems to incentivise parallel employment, the WTD (and its interpretation) aspires to limit it. Such messages can create considerable uncertainty for policymakers on national level.

Secondly, it is easy to detect signs of intense politicisation (and the resulting eventualities) in EU labour law policy. One example—at systemic level—is given below. The European Semester, as a framework for the coordination of economic, budgetary, employment and social policies within the EU, and the related country-specific recommendations (CSRs) quite often contain strong employment and social policy-related expectations.[84] In fact, beyond traditional legal harmonisation, these

[78] For example, in Romania, under pressure from the Troika and the Commission, a law radically weakening collective labour law was adopted in 2011 (Law No 62/2011), and then, also under pressure from the Commission, a completely different concept of legislation to strengthen collective bargaining and social dialogue was enacted in 2022, some ten years later (Law No 367/2022). Trif and Stochita (2024), pp. 73–77.

[79] For more information see Bruun et al. (2014).

[80] Directive (EU) 2022/2041 of the European Parliament and of the Council of 19 October 2022 on adequate minimum wages in the European Union.

[81] Directive (EU) 2019/1152 of the European Parliament and of the Council of 20 June 2019 on transparent and predictable working conditions in the European Union.

[82] Preamble (29) and Article 9 on parallel employment.

[83] Interpretative Communication on Directive 2003/88/EC of the European Parliament and of the Council concerning certain aspects of the organisation of working time, (2023/C 109/01).

[84] The new Romanian collective labour law (Law No 367/2022) mentioned above, for example, was clearly the result of such pressure. Trif and Stochita (2024). Interestingly and surprisingly, for example, Hungary has not been under such strong pressure for the same reason.

instruments of economic governance, which are political by nature, have a significant impact on national policies, including labour law. However, it seems somewhat arbitrary (even over-politicised) when, for which country and with what intensity the EU would use this instrument. No surprise that, for example, Schmitt and Rocca—undoubtedly somewhat cynically—label country-specific recommendations as new 'sources' of EU labour law.[85]

Thirdly, it is not uncommon in EU labour law for rules to be vague or, in some cases, utterly impractical. For instance, the derogation opportunity applicable in the WTD for so-called 'autonomous workers' requires, according to the overriding interpretation, that the working time of the workers concerned must be, "as a whole", not measured and/or predetermined or can be determined by the workers themselves.[86] This means that the derogation is not applicable to workers whose working time is only partially not measured or predetermined or can only partially be determined by the workers themselves. It is not difficult to realize that on this point the EU interpretation imposes an almost unachievable, highly unrealistic requirement. It would apparently be difficult to find workers (perhaps even at the highest levels of management) who have absolutely no employer-influence over their autonomy in relation to working hours.[87]

Fourthly, there is a trend towards the "softening" of EU labour law. This means, on the one hand, a frequent laxation ("inflation", in fact) of the binding force and normative clarity of traditional sources of law (hard laws), especially directives, and, on the other hand, the proliferation of various forms of non-traditional regulatory instruments, soft laws. A key example of the first phenomenon is the above-mentioned directive on adequate minimum wages itself, described by the literature as more like a collection of soft proposals in the form of a directive (i.e. legislation), because of its "very light approach" to the issues at stake.[88] According to other authors, this directive[89] serves more as a kind of specific guide for Member States than as a set of concrete obligations.[90] As an example of the second phenomenon mentioned above (the proliferation of various forms of soft law), the EU's labour law and social policy has recently placed a number of important issues on the agenda and thematised them in documents and instruments of various formats (but not legally binding). Some examples (besides the well-known, often used

[85] Schmitt and Rocca (2022), pp. 214–224; Bekker (2021), pp. 123–124.

[86] Article 17 of the WTD; Interpretative Communication (see above) IX A.

[87] It seems that the respective Hungarian concept of "flexible working arrangement" is much more realistic and pragmatic (even though, in a strict sense, it does not comply with the EU-interpretation): "The employer may permit - in writing - the employee to schedule his working time in the interest of autonomous work organization. Where the employee is permitted to perform certain functions of the job at a specific time or period in light of their unique characteristics, this shall have no bearing on his flexible working arrangement." § 96(2) HLC.

[88] Menegatti (2021), pp. 21–32.

[89] See also Kun and Szabó (2023), pp. 216–223.

[90] Sipka and Zaccaria (2022), pp. 1–8.

"communications"[91] etc. etc.): "Interpretative Communication" on certain aspects of the organisation of working time (see above), "Action Plan" to promote collective bargaining (see: Minimum Wage Directive), "Report" on social dialogue (Nahles report, see above), Council "Recommendation" on strengthening social dialogue in the EU,[92] Commission "Guidelines" on the application of EU competition law to collective agreements on working conditions for self-employed individuals,[93] proposal for a Council "Recommendation"[94] on individual learning accounts, etc.

Fifthly, it is worth referring to the fact that EU labour law has often been—and still is—subject to the reasonable criticism[95] (partly in connection with the abovementioned "soft law" trend) that while it places significant emphasis on the declaration of "big" goals and principles, it provides fewer tools for enforcement.[96] The earlier generations of directives were generally limited in this regard to declare—without any further specifics—that "sanctions must be effective, proportionate and dissuasive" (a common provision in directives, usually disregarded by the Hungarian legislator when transposing the directives). In recent times, there are some signs of a positive change in this respect, but modest for the time being. One such sign is that the newer generation of directives[97] contain somewhat more specific implementing rules, for example even under the heading of separate "horizontal provisions". Another such sign is the adoption of a directive on posting with a specific enforcement purpose,[98] or the establishment of the European Labour Authority.[99] At the same time, the need for effective enforcement is even more pronounced in the profession and in the literature. The most tangible sign of this is the proposal for a new labour law directive on effective enforcement, which has been put forward in a major 2022 volume by prominent authors Zane, Rasnača; Koukiadaki, Aristea; Bruun, Niklas and Lörcher, Klaus ('Proposal for a Directive on Effective

[91] COM. etc.

[92] Proposal for a COUNCIL RECOMMENDATION on strengthening social dialogue in the EU, COM/2023/38 final.

[93] Communication from the Commission, Guidelines (2022/C 374/02).

[94] European Commission: Proposal for a Council Recommendation on Individual Learning Accounts COM(2021) 773 final, Brussels, 10.12.2021, 2021/0405(NLE) {SEC(2021) 417 final} -{SWD(2021) 368 final} -{SWD(2021) 369 final} -{SWD(2021) 370 final}.

[95] See for more information Zane et al. (2022b).

[96] See also on the topic in general: Kun (2023), pp. 394–405.

[97] See for example the already cited 2019 directive on transparent and predictable working conditions, or the 2019 directive on work-life balance.

[98] Directive 2014/67/EU of the European Parliament and of the Council of 15 May 2014 on the enforcement of Directive 96/71/EC concerning the posting of workers in the framework of the provision of services and amending Regulation (EU) No 1024/2012 on administrative cooperation through the Internal Market Information System ('the IMI Regulation').

[99] Regulation (EU) 2019/1149 of the European Parliament and of the Council of 20 June 2019 establishing a European Labour Authority.

Enforcement').[100] This proposal has started to be discussed and taken up by both policymakers and academics.[101]

5 Concluding Remarks

In conclusion, it can be stated that the primary aim of the transposition of European labour law directives into Hungarian labour law is—generally and systemically—rather formal compliance ("ticking the box"-type of transposition) than substantive, purposeful internalisation of the regulatory, social-policy aims of the directives. While one of the basic—in general rather limited—harmonisation objectives of EU labour law rules is to balance and neutralise competition, it seems that the Hungarian legislator—for the time being—mostly prioritises competitiveness-related concerns and aims to moderate the intensity of the social policy rationales.

Truly 'internalising' and implementing the EU's Social Pillar and the spirit of the labour law directives would require not only formal legal harmonisation, but, as the Inter-institutional Declaration on the proclamation of the EPSR[102] clearly stated, *"a shared political commitment and responsibility"* (or 'policy delivery'[103]). It goes on to declare that the Pillar of Social Rights should be implemented at both Union level and Member State level within their respective competences, taking due account of different socioeconomic environments and the diversity of national systems, including the role of social partners, and in accordance with the principles of subsidiarity and proportionality.[104] This "policy delivery" therefore requires not only formal legislative solutions but also a deep commitment to certain principles. The general legitimacy of this approach is of course open to debate from the point of perspective of EU-policy, political science, etc., but it is hardly a fact that can be neglected and circumvented at present. As this paper has shown, Hungarian lawmakers and policymakers are a long way from such policy delivery, although it should be recognised that the EU itself does not always facilitate clear, committed identification (see for example the circumstances discussed in Subsection 4 of this Chapter).

---

[100] Zane et al. (2022a), pp. 503–520.

[101] See: European Centre of Expertise (ECE) in the field of Labour Law, Annual Conference: Enforcing EU labour rights, 28 May 2024, Brussels.

[102] Interinstitutional Declaration on the proclamation of the European Pillar of Social Rights, 2017/C 428/09, 13.12.2017, Preamble (17).

[103] Countouris (2024), pp.4, 9.

[104] Interinstitutional Declaration on the proclamation of the European Pillar of Social Rights, 2017/C 428/09, 13.12.2017, Preamble (17).

References

Bankó Z, Berke G, Kiss G, Szőke Gergely L (2019) Nagykommentár a munka törvénykönyvéről szóló 2012. évi I. törvényhez (Commentary to Act I of 2012 on the Labour Code), Jogtár, Wolters Kluwer, Budapest

Bekker S (2021) Hardening and softening of country-specific recommendations in the European Semester. West Eur Polit 44(1):123–124

Bronstein A (2006) Trends and challenges of labour law in Central Europe. In: Craig JDR, Lynk SM (eds) Globalization and the future of labour law. Cambridge University Press, Cambridge, pp 191–224

Bruun N, Lörcher K, Schömann I (2014) Economic and financial crisis and collective labour law in Europe. Hart Publishing House, London

Budai EM (2019) A Kúria szerepe az európai uniós munkajog érvényesülésében (The role of the Curia in the enforcement of EU labour law). In: Marianna N (ed) Válogatott tanulmányok az ELTE Állam- és Jogtudományi Kar tudományos diákköreinek a XXXIV. OTDK-ra nevezett dolgozataiból. ELTE Eötvös Kiadó, Budapest, pp 29–38

Casale G (1997) Collective bargaining and the law in Central and Eastern Europe: some comparative issues (ILO-CEET Working Paper, Budapest, No. 20. 1997)

Countouris N (2024) Enforcing EU labour rights- A look into the future of law enforcement: options and possibilities for action, A Thematic Working Paper for the Annual Conference of the European Centre of Expertise (ECE) in the field of labour law, EC Directorate General for Employment, Social Affairs and Inclusion, May 2024

Davidov G (2016) A purposive approach to labour law. Oxford University Press, Oxford

Fodor TG (2016) A Munka Törvénykönyve munka- és pihenőidő szabályozásának uniós jogi megfelelőségéről. Magyar Munkajog E-folyóirat (Hungarian Labour Law E-Journal, 2016/2, 21–36

Gyulavári T (2009) Az Európai Unió szociális dimenziója. OFA Kht, Budapest

Gyulavári T (2020) The Hungarian experiment to promote collective bargaining: farewell to 'principle of favour'. In: Gyulavári T, Menegatti E (eds) The sources of labour law. Kluwer Law International BV, The Netherlands

Gyulavári T, Hős N (2012) The road to flexibility? Lessons from the New Hungarian Labour Code. Eur Labour Law J 3(4):252–269

Gyulavári T, Kártyás G (2015) The Hungarian flexicurity pathway? New labour code after twenty years in the market economy. Pázmány Press, Budapest

Gyulavári T, Kártyás G (2022) Why collective bargaining is a 'Must' for platform workers and how to achieve it. In: Boto JMM, Brameshuber E (eds) Collective Bargaining and the Gig Economy. Hart Publishing, Oxford, pp 99–116

Horváth I (2019) Rugalmasabb biztonság. A munkaerő-kölcsönzés hazai szabályai – elsődleges figyelemmel az Európai Unió meghatározó jogközelítési normáira, Munkajog, HVG-ORAC 2019/3, 9-15

Hungler S (2020) The dual nature of employee involvement. L'Harmattan, Budapest

Jagodzinski R (ed) (2015) Variations on a theme? The implementation of the EWC Recast Directive. ETUI, Brussels

Kártyás G (2011) Munkaerő-kölcsönzés Magyarországon és az Európai Unióban (Temporary Work in Hungary and the European Union), Doctoral Thesis, ELTE, Budapest

Kártyás G (2016) Munkaerő-kölcsönzés Magyarországon és az Európai Unióban (Temporary agency work in Hungary and the European Union), Budapest, Wolters Kluwer Kft

Kártyás G, Petrovics Z, Takács G. Commentary on Act I of 2012 on the Labour Code [electronic document]. Wolters Kluwer CompLex Legal Library

Kiss G (2017) Employment relationship between school cooperatives and their member: the step-child of employment. US-China Law Rev 14:499, August 2017 No. 8

Kun A (2016) School cooperatives.: a 'Hungaricum' in labour law in the field of youth employment. In: Fernández Fernández R, Álvarez Cuesta H (eds) Empleo juvenil: Un reto para

Europa (Youth employment: A challenge for Europe). Sociedad Aranzadi, Cizur Menor, Spain, pp 71–91
Kun A (2019) Hungary: collective bargaining in labour law regimes. In: Liukkunen U (ed) Collective bargaining in labour law regimes. Springer International Publishing, Cham, pp 333–356
Kun A (2020) A munkajogi jogharmonizáció folyamatának eredményei és kérdőjelei. In: Bodnár Péter M (ed) Az Európai Unióhoz történő csatlakozásunkat követő hazai és európai jogfejlődés. Wolters Kluwer Hungary, Budapest, pp 235–251
Kun A (2023) Érvényesülési és kikényszerítési deficitek a magyar munkajogban: problématérkép és egyes megoldási alternatívák, In: Auer Ádám; Bankó Zoltán; Békési Gábor; Berke Gyula; Hazafi Zoltán; Ludányi Dávid (eds.): Ünnepi tanulmányok Kiss György 70. születésnapjára: Clara pacta, boni amici. Wolters Kluwer Hungary, Budapest, pp 394–405
Kun A (2024a) Az uniós munkajog hatása a magyar munkajogi jogalkotásra és joggyakorlatra, In: Pál Lajos; Petrovics Zoltán (eds) Visegrád 21.0 - A XXI. Magyar Munkajogi Konferencia szerkesztett előadásai. Wolters Kluwer Hungary, Budapest, pp 3–23
Kun A (2024b) The law of work in post-socialist European countries. In: Davidov G, Langille B, Lester G (eds) The Oxford handbook of the law of work. Oxford University Press, Oxford, pp 89–100
Kun A, Szabó SzI (2023) The impact of the "Minimum Wage Directive" - Directive (EU) 2022/2041 - in Hungary. REVUE DE DROIT DU TRAVAIL 2023/3 216–223
Kun A, Ter Haar B (eds) (2021) EU collective labour law. Edward Elgar Publishing, Cheltenham
Kun A, Szabó IS, Rácz-Antal I (2023) Hungary. In: Rymkevich O, Senatori I (eds) Digital employment and industrial relations in Europe. Fondazione Marco Biagi, Giappichelli Editore, pp 81–234
Menegatti E (2021) Much ado about little: The Commission proposal for a Directive on adequate wages. Ital Lab Law E-J 14(1):21–32
Muszyński K (2020) Reform and oversight mechanisms are not enough - access to justice for workers and employment standards in Central Eastern European countries, ETUI, Working Paper 2020.09
Novitz T (2021) Re-introducing a human face - the future of EU collective labour law? In: Attila K, Ter Haar B (eds) EU collective labour law. Edward Elgar Publishing, Cheltenham, pp 445–459
Schmitt M, Rocca M (2022) A new source for (EU) labour law? Eur Lab Law J 13(2):214–224
Shvelidze Z (2021) Chapter 12: European social dialogue and associated countries. In: Attila K, Ter Haar B (eds) EU collective labour law. Edward Elgar Publishing, Cheltenham, pp 194-207.
Sipka P, Zaccaria ML (2017) A szövetkezeti tagi munkaviszony jogi kockázatai, különös tekintettel az alapvető munkavállalói jogokra (Legal risks of the employment relationship of cooperative members, with special regard to the fundamental rights of employees). Munkajog, HVG-ORAC, 2017/1, 23–30
Sipka P, Zaccaria ML (2022) Tisztességes munkáért méltányos bérezés kontra versenyképesség – az európai minimálbér-irányelv jelentősége és várható hatásai, Munkajog. ORAC, 2022/4. 1–8
Szabó SzI, Fodor TG (2018) Soha nem elég? Avagy meddig rontható a munkajogi szabályozás? 2018. november 25., Mérce, https://merce.hu/2018/11/25/soha-nem-eleg-avagy-meddig-ronthato-a-munkajogi-szabalyozas/ (downloaded 02.12.2024).
Tóth András NL, Hosszú H (2012) Hungary's full-blown malaise. In: Lehndorff S (ed) A triumph of failed ideas. European models of capitalism in the crisis. ETUI, Brussels, pp 137–154
Trif A, Stochita R (2024) Romania In: De Spiegelaere S (ed) Time for action! How policy can strengthen (multi-employer) collective bargaining in Europa. UNI Europa – The European Services Workers Union, 73–77
Work for a brighter future - Global Commission on the Future of Work, International Labour Office. ILO, Geneva, 2019.
Zane R, Koukiadaki A, Bruun N, Lörcher K (2022a) Proposal for a directive on effective enforcement. In: Zane R, Koukiadaki A, Bruun N, Lörcher K (eds) Effective Enforcement of EU Labour Law. Hart Publishing, Bloomsbury Collections, Oxford, pp 503–520
Zane R, Koukiadaki A, Bruun N, Lörcher K (eds) (2022b) Effective enforcement of EU labour law. Hart Publishing, Bloomsbury Collections, Oxford

Balancing Legislation and Moral Capitalism: Enhancing Employee Access to Decision-Making

Dana Volosevici

1 Introduction

Given the growing recognition of employee involvement as a key element of organizational democracy and sustainable corporate governance, this chapter examines two approaches to promoting employee involvement within organizations. The first approach focuses on the sustained and comprehensive legislative efforts by European Union institutions to strengthen social dialogue and to create an effective framework that ensures employees are informed about, consulted on, and, in some cases, involved in making key corporate decisions. We will demonstrate that legislative progress has been rather slow, hindered primarily by differences among Member States regarding how employee participation in employers' decision-making processes is regulated. These national differences were influenced by varying approaches to the concept of the enterprise and, consequently, of the relationship between employer and employee. In essence, this involved a balance extending beyond the strict framework of labour relations, reflecting broader social values and shaping the very concept of work as a societal value.

A relevant example in this context is Germany, where its codetermination system exemplifies complex employee involvement in decision-making. The system arose initially from collective agreements, known as "codetermination bargains," which were only later codified into law.[1] This demonstrates the presence, within German society as a whole, of a unique understanding of the concept of work, developed

[1] See Bundesverfassungsgericht (1979); Wiedemann (1980).

D. Volosevici (✉)
Petroleum-Gas University of Ploiesti, Ploiesti, Romania
e-mail: dana.volosevici@vplaw.ro

K. Koldinská et al. (eds.), *Labour Law and Social Security Law in Central and Eastern Europe*, European Union and its Neighbours in a Globalized World 26,
https://doi.org/10.1007/978-3-032-04496-9_18

over centuries from the values of mutuality and solidarity promoted by guilds and unions since their foundation in the Middle Ages.[2] Moreover, the very conception of a corporation as *Unternehmen an sich*—a "thing in itself," rather than merely the product of shareholders' investments—enabled this approach to internal relations. This notion of *Unternehmen an sich* was adopted by the German Federal Constitutional Court (Bundesverfassungsgericht) when it upheld the constitutionality of the Codetermination Act of 1976.[3]

Another example of the importance of social perception of work and enterprise can be found in the experience of socialist states in Eastern Europe. At the same time that the German Federal Constitutional Court upheld the Codetermination Act, Eastern European states adopted, at least in theory, an ideological stance that equated the role of employees with that of owners. In Romania, for instance, the Constitution regulated the socialist ownership of the means of production, which was either state property, encompassing goods deemed the "property of the entire people" or cooperative property, covering goods owned by each cooperative organization.[4] The management of state socialist enterprises was carried out based on the principle of collective leadership, with the „direct involvement of the working people" in discussing and resolving the economic and social issues of the enterprise.[5] Although these legal provisions remained in force for several decades, until 1990, they were not assimilated within society as representing a social value. Consequently, immediately after the changes of 1989 and the reestablishment of private property, a polarized approach reemerged between the interests of owners and employees. Furthermore, since the early 1990s, Romanian unions have faced significant challenges, struggling for both survival and legitimacy.[6] Employee involvement in corporate decision-making was restructured through the transposition of the European *acquis* rather than by integrating values that had seemingly belonged to socialist society into the legislation.

The axiological weight of the employment relationship, and the connection between the concept of work and social values, allows us to propose a second approach—a moral perspective on the regulation of internal corporate relations. We have used the phrase *moral capitalism*, as it appears in some works, although we might just as easily have referred to *ethical capitalism* or, perhaps more in line with recent language, *sustainable capitalism*, while recognizing that these terms are not interchangeable. In recent years, the influence of private entities in the global marketplace has escalated significantly, creating a parallel power structure that rivals that of nation-states. For instance, in 2023, Walmart's sales soared to a remarkable

[2] See Teuteberg (1961), pp. 118–119.

[3] See Bundesverfassungsgericht (1979).

[4] Article 6 Constitution of Romania (1965).

[5] Great National Assembly (1971), article 42 of the Law 11/1971, on the organization and management of state socialist units, published in *Collection of Laws, Decisions, Instructions*, issued by the Great National Assembly of the Socialist Republic of Romania.

[6] See e.g. Trif & Paolucci (2019), Volosevici (2012).

606 billion USD,[7] a figure that eclipses the GDP of most countries within the Eurozone.[8] This illustrates not just the scale of such corporations but also their immense economic impact compared to traditional state economies. We are at a point where these economic conglomerates recognize the impact they have on society, often on a global scale, and take responsibility for mitigating the negative consequences of their activities and for addressing social inequalities arising from geopolitical or historical realities.

Among the ethical actions of corporations, we have chosen to analyse transnational company agreements as instruments of soft law that not only establish rights for employees but also standardize the regime applied to employees across countries with varying legal systems and traditions of social dialogue. We believe that these agreements could serve as a critical bridge, providing a unified approach to employee rights and engagement across multinational organizations, despite diverse local regulations.

This dual approach highlights the value and impact of integrating legislative measures with contractual tools to strengthen employee involvement. Through legislation on social dialogue and consultation, the EU helps to embed these practices within corporate governance, making them a standardized requirement rather than an optional practice. Conversely, transnational company agreements provide flexibility and adaptability, enabling corporations to craft tailored solutions that accommodate and incorporate the diverse legal frameworks and cultural contexts of their global operations. Each of these two approaches has emerged from the maturation of society and labour relations, with each influencing the other, as we will discuss in the following sections.

2 The Complex (Ongoing) Journey to a European Legal Framework for Employee Involvement

Workers' right to information and consultation constitutes a fundamental right established by the Charter of Fundamental Rights of the EU (Article 27). This is complemented by the right of workers and employers, or their respective organizations, to negotiate and conclude collective agreements and, in cases of conflicts of interest, to undertake collective action to defend their interests, including strike action (Article 28). In accordance with Article 153 TFEU the Union shall support and complement the activities of the Member States and may adopt directives in the fields of the information and consultation of workers. Although the Union has competence in the area of representation and collective defence of the interests of workers and employers, including co-determination, the provisions of Article 153 TFEU

[7] See Statista, (2024).

[8] Eurostat, nama_10_gdp.

do not apply to pay, the right of association, the right to strike, or the right to impose lock-outs.

Based on these competences, over the years, European legislation has established a framework for worker participation in the workplace, grounded in the laws and practices of the Member States and the fundamental freedoms of the EU, as will be further detailed in the legislative overview presented in the following sections. As noted above, however, there are significant differences between the laws and practices of the Member States, which generate tensions in negotiations, decision-making delays, and often compromises that have reduced the effectiveness and scope of measures for integrating employees into the decision-making process. Despite these obstacles, there has been, and continues to be, a strong interest and continuous effort at the EU level to create a comprehensive framework that ensures decision-making transparency within corporations and promotes employee involvement, particularly in decision-making processes that may impact the employment relationship.

A significant reason behind this European choice appears to be more related to the advantages of increased labour productivity and job satisfaction,[9] rather than the interest of lawmakers and employers in providing employee training in industrial or management fields or ensuring their meaningful integration in the decision-making process. Another frequently cited reason in European documents is the need to maintain a "balance between corporate flexibility and workers' security",[10] an approach intended to create a compromise between two elements often perceived as autonomous and antagonistic, with distinct interests and values. At the same time, however, as actions related to corporate social responsibility (CSR) have evolved and the European Commission has become more active in promoting CSR, the importance of social dialogue in advancing CSR initiatives has been emphasized, as well as the constructive role that European works councils have played in developing best practices related to CSR.[11]

Thus, an axiological redefinition of the employer-employee relationship has occurred, seeking common values by expanding corporate objectives beyond mere profit-making and adopting responsibility towards a range of stakeholders, including employees. Finally, a new phase of evolution involves the integration of sustainability into public policy objectives and even the establishment of a legal framework that mandates sustainability reporting obligations for a broad spectrum of enterprises. In fact, the EU's legislative actions, along with the voluntary commitments of businesses and academic debates around reevaluating the role of enterprises in society, have promoted the concept of workplace democracy.[12] European action, though relatively consistent, nonetheless has its own limitations. For instance, Principle 8 of the European Pillar of Social Rights, concerning Social Dialogue and

[9] See e.g. Locke & Schweiger (1979), Miller & Monge (1986).

[10] High Level Group on Economic and Social Implications of Industrial Change (1998).

[11] Howitt Report (2007), p. 12.

[12] See e.g. De Spiegelaere et al. (2019), Frega et al. (2019), Ferreras et al. (2020).

Involvement of Workers, is grounded in existing provisions without opening new pathways for social dialogue and worker involvement or setting priorities among existing ones, even at a guidance level.

2.1 *The General Framework for Employee Information and Consultation: A 20-Year Struggle to Achieve a Directive*

Analysing the long historical trajectory of creating a general framework for employee information and consultation highlights the importance that enterprises in most European states place on retaining control over both business decisions and the data preceding these decisions. In fact, beyond the employment relationship, this reflects a desire to maintain a distinction in status between investors, entrepreneurs, and their direct representatives—senior management—on the one hand, and workers, on the other, who are perceived primarily as labour whose rights should be limited to mainly financial entitlements arising from work performed. A striking example is the history of regulating the general framework for employee information and consultation, which was only established through Directive 2002/14, even though the first attempts to introduce employee involvement rights occurred as early as 1980 with the draft Vredeling Directive.[13] Through this draft directive, two rights were granted, *inter alia*, to employees of large undertakings or groups of undertakings within a single state: the right to periodic information and the right to prior consultation in cases of economic decisions impacting employees. The proposal, which underwent numerous amendments and multiple versions, was consistently blocked, with criticisms ranging from claims that it proposed an overly complex system to concerns that it infringed on voluntary systems of industrial relations.[14] The opposition from employer representatives, particularly the Union of Industrial and Employers' Confederations of Europe (UNICE), was so strong that even the attempt to regulate this issue through the negotiation of a European-level collective agreement on national-level information and consultation was blocked. UNICE's arguments ranged from the existence of already relevant legal frameworks at the national level to the view that the management of labour relations should fall exclusively within the purview of a company's internal organizational framework. Political agreement on the content of a directive establishing a general framework for employee information and consultation was only reached in 2002, following events such as the closure of the Renault plant in Vilvoorde, Belgium, in 1997,[15] without prior information and consultation of the employees, which demonstrated the inadequacy of national laws and the complex interplay of the Collective

[13] European Commission. COM(80) 423 final (1980).

[14] See e.g. Pipkorn (1983)

[15] See e.g. Dorssemont (2006).

Redundancy Directive (98/50) and the European Works Council Directive (94/45) in cases of cross-border restructuring.

Article 1(3) of Directive 2002/14 sets out, in language reflecting a shift in the relationship between employer and employees, the guidelines for defining or implementing practical arrangements for information and consultation. Thus, the employer and the employees' representatives "shall work in a spirit of cooperation," respecting their reciprocal rights and obligations and considering "the interests both of the undertaking or establishment and of the employees." Therefore, regardless of the national laws and industrial relations practices that may have existed in individual Member States concerning employee integration in decision-making, a minimum European framework has been established that is both legal and axiological. Employees' rights are not granted in opposition to the employer's interests; rather, the aim is to foster the idea of convergent interests between the two parties. Under the Article 4(2) of the Directive, employees have gained access to information on three main areas: the economic situation and strategic development decisions (a); employment situation, trends, and strategic measures (b); and significant decisions concerning work organization or contractual relations (c). While the first area only confers a right to information, the latter two provide for both information and consultation rights. Additionally, when information and consultation involve decisions likely to lead to substantial changes in work organization or contractual relations, the consultation must occur "with a view to reaching an agreement." Directive 2002/14 is without prejudice to the specific information and consultation procedures established in previous European directives and to any other rights to information, consultation, and participation under national law. In fact, this includes the Collective Redundancies Directive 98/59/EC, the Transfer of Undertakings Directive 2001/23/EC—evidence of the gradual evolution in creating the legal framework surrounding employees' rights to information and consultation[16]—and the European Works Council Directive 94/45/EC.

2.2 *Giving Employees a Transnational Voice: Challenges in Regulating the European Works Council*

The European Works Council Directive 94/45/EC is further evidence of the delicate balance between the interest of enterprises in protecting their decision-making authority and the broadening of their purpose beyond mere profit generation.[17] At a time when the regulation of the general framework for employee information and consultation at the national level had stagnated, the European Community took action to regulate the transnational aspects of employee participation in decision-making. The factors that supported this approach were based on both economic

[16] See e.g. Ales (2009).

[17] See Danis & Hoffmann (1995).

considerations and best practices already established by certain multinational companies, which, out of social responsibility, had voluntarily integrated employees into the decision-making process. Thus, in the 1980s, amidst growing competition, an increasing number of companies were expanding their operations across Europe and globally. As a result, decision-making within these companies was becoming more centralized, concentrating authority at higher management levels and reducing the autonomy of local or national managers to make independent decisions. This trend reflected a shift in corporate governance toward a more unified approach to managing operations, potentially impacting employees' rights in various subsidiaries to information and consultation. A number of multinationals, primarily from France and Germany, had previously voluntarily acted against this risk by establishing various types of jointly agreed European-level arrangements concerning employees' rights to information and consultation.[18] Against this backdrop, the Commission proposed the regulation of European Works Councils. Despite the existence of practices within multinational enterprises and the fact that regulation would remain at the transnational level, accommodating national practices regarding employee representation, the Commission's proposal had to be reformulated multiple times and even based on different provisions in order to be adopted.[19]

Council Directive 94/45/EC, as revised by Directive 2009/38/EC on the introduction of European Works Councils (EWCs) has general applicability in multinational companies with at least 1000 workers in the EU/EEA and at least 150 staff in two or more Member States, while two other directives target specific corporate operations: Directive 2004/25/EC on takeover bids and Directive (EU) 2017/1132 on certain aspects of company law, amended by Directive (EU) 2019 /2121 as regards cross-border conversions, mergers and divisions.

In this category too, the legislative framework is in a state of ongoing evolution, with proposals to revise the EWC Directive and to evaluate Directive (EU) 2019/2121 concerning cross-border conversions, mergers, and divisions. Specifically, by February 1, 2027, the European Commission is required to evaluate how effectively the safeguards protect employee participation rights during cross-border operations.

2.3 *Societas Europaea and Employee Involvement: Three Decades of Debate*

Another relevant example illustrating the importance of employee involvement in decision-making is the creation, in 2001, of the *Societas Europaea* (SE), a European public limited-liability company that can be established independently of the national laws of the Member States. In the context of enhancing the competitiveness

[18] See Hall (1992).

[19] See e.g. Gold and Hall (1994).

of the internal market and the need to position European companies to compete effectively with counterparts in Japan and the United States, the European Commission advocated for the introduction of such a legal structure over a period of 30 years—from the first draft proposal in 1970 until the adoption of Directive 2001/86/EC.[20] The main obstacle in creating the SE was the regulation of worker participation, especially as the Commission's proposal differed significantly from existing national systems. Over the years, proposals for worker participation ranged from a strict and protective system, which included a mandatory two-tier board where employees were members of the supervisory body, to a more flexible regulation as adopted in Council Directive 2001/86/EC. In fact, the primary aim of the Directive is to preserve the employee participation rights that already existed in the companies involved in establishing the SE, unless the parties decide otherwise.[21] Similarly, Member States are expressly called upon, through Article 11 of the Directive, to take appropriate measures in conformity with Community law to prevent the misuse of an SE for the purpose of depriving employees of their rights to involvement or withholding such rights.

2.4 *Sustainability: A Possible Axis for Enhancing Employee Involvement?*

These examples illustrate that, throughout the development of the European integration process, the shift from merely fostering a competitive internal market to establishing a responsible and competitive internal market has required a redefinition of the concepts and values attributed to the actors within this market. This progression has advanced further with the EU's adoption of sustainability-promoting policies, including the New Circular Economy Action Plan for a Cleaner and More Competitive Europe. Under these policies, new mechanisms have been established to ensure employees' access to information, granting them the right to be consulted on companies' strategic decisions. While these regulations primarily target sustainability goals, they have also significantly broadened employees' rights to information and consultation. This expansion reflects a progressive shift toward more inclusive workplace practices, ensuring employees are not only informed about but also actively involved in their organizations' sustainability efforts. In response to growing social and environmental challenges, the Non-Financial Reporting (NFR) Directive was enacted in 2014, setting minimum legal standards and promotes harmonization of non-financial reporting across EU Member States.[22] Building on this, the Corporate Sustainability Reporting Directive (Directive (EU) 2022/2464, or CSRD) marks a substantial advancement by mandating that companies disclose

[20] For a complete analyse, see Kenner (2005).

[21] See Edwards (2003), p. 459.

[22] European Commission (2014), Johansen (2016), La Torre et al. (2018), Samani et al. (2023).

information on environmental, social, and governance (ESG) topics in their annual management reports. The CSRD requires large companies to report on their progress in meeting the EU's five main environmental objectives: climate change mitigation, climate change adaptation, sustainable use and protection of water and marine resources, transition to a circular economy, pollution prevention and control, and the protection and restoration of biodiversity. Additionally, companies must report on business strategy, due diligence practices, value chain management, human rights policies, working conditions, social dialogue, fair wages, health and safety standards, social protection, and other social concerns.

To understand the scope of the directive, including the rights granted to employees, it should be noted that by 2025, the CSRD will apply to all large limited liability companies based in Europe, including subsidiaries of non-EU companies. In the following years, reporting requirements will be extended to listed small and medium-sized enterprises (SMEs) and to non-EU companies with significant business operations within the EU. Voluntary standards will also be developed for non-listed SMEs. Furthermore, the CSRD enhances the scope of information and consultation rights for employees, granting them access to relevant information and the means of obtaining and verifying sustainability information. This includes the right to form opinions that must be relayed to the company's board. The rationale behind this policy is supported by research[23] showing that sustainable companies incorporate worker feedback into strategic decision-making processes that affect the workforce as well as broader communities and regions. These rights aim to deeply involve workers' representatives in reporting activities. However, for these rights to be effectively exercised, it is crucial to either train employee representatives in the relevant reporting fields or establish collaborative mechanisms with experts swiftly.

Unlike other legal frameworks addressing employee involvement in decision-making, the CSRD includes provisions that broaden the company's focus and core values to cover social and environmental concerns as well. This is because the concept of sustainability itself goes beyond mere environmental impact; it requires attention to a wider set of values that influence not only the company but also its workforce, stakeholders, and the surrounding community. Thus, under the CSRD, companies are encouraged to view sustainability as an integrated business objective, shaping corporate strategies and actions with a balanced view of profit, people, and the planet. This approach reflects a shift towards a more comprehensive understanding of corporate responsibility that aligns with the evolving expectations of stakeholders and society at large.

It is yet to be determined how sustainability reporting will influence the extent to which employees are integrated into decision-making processes and whether it will result in more effective implementation of previously adopted legal provisions.

The legislative process for creating a robust and effective system for employee integration is still ongoing, primarily due to the lack of uniformity in national

[23] See Rapp et al. (2019), Ernst and Young (2020).

regulations. In the area of employee information and consultation, European action has been able to generate a relatively homogeneous level of national regulation, although the implementation of these provisions remains influenced by local industrial traditions. The transposition at national level of the directives regulating the information and consultation of employees have prompted considerable voluntary activity in terms of reviewing, modifying and introducing information and consultation arrangements even if this has been largely employer-led.[24]

In the area of participation in decision-making, national legislation is notably fragmented, with significant differences in the solutions chosen by lawmakers, especially under the influence of employers. In countries like Austria, Slovakia, Germany, Denmark, Hungary, Finland, France, Czechia, Luxembourg, and Sweden, mandatory board-level codetermination in the private sector is in place. Conversely, such mechanisms are missing in countries like Bulgaria, Portugal, Romania, Belgium, Cyprus, Ireland, Poland, Italy, Spain, the Netherlands, Malta, and Liechtenstein.[25] Nevertheless, in no fewer than 18 European countries, employees are legally entitled to some form of board-level representation, and the issue of employee codetermination is also under discussion in several countries that lack such legal provisions.[26]

The European Parliament[27] highlighted concerns about a fragmented regulatory landscape that could lead to uncertainty regarding the applicable rules and rights for both employers and employees. As a result, it was deemed essential to bolster the Union's capabilities in these areas through the adoption of a comprehensive framework directive. This directive would aim to consolidate and simplify current legislation while enhancing workers' rights, particularly in the areas of information, consultation, and participation.

One useful tool for identifying differences in legal regimes is the European Participation Index (EPI), developed at the ETUI.[28] The EPI is a country-level measure of worker participation rights, assessing key mechanisms of employee involvement: trade union representation in collective bargaining, workplace representation, and board-level employee representation (BLER). Analysis of this data reveals that many workers in the EU lack adequate representation across various facets of the mechanisms examined, particularly in terms of trade union membership and collective bargaining. This situation underscores the necessity for legislative alignment at the European level or for other actions, possibly by enterprises themselves, to voluntarily implement participation mechanisms.

---

[24] See e.g. Hall (2010).

[25] See e.g. Piasna & Theodoropoulou (2024).

[26] See e.g. Conchon et al. (2015).

[27] European Parliament (2021).

[28] See De Spiegelaere & Vitols (2020).

3 Corporate Voluntary Actions and Employee Involvement: Fostering Engagement Beyond Regulation

For over a decade, multinational corporations have exerted control over two-thirds of all international trade, with half of this comprising transactions within the same corporate group, underscoring the extent of their integrated global operations.[29] Furthermore, the strategic importance and economic leverage of major financial centres have reached such heights that their potential failure poses systemic risks.[30] These centres' financial difficulties could destabilize national economies, compelling governments to step in with rescue packages, despite facing strained public finances themselves. This dynamic underscores the shifting balance of power in the global economy, where private corporations play roles traditionally reserved for sovereign states. Against this backdrop of acquiring financial power and influence—economically, socially, and politically—companies have increasingly assumed an active role in society, committing to social responsibility and sustainable development within the communities where they operate. This shift reflects a broader acknowledgment of their significant impact on global economic and environmental systems.[31] With respect to their relationships with employees, corporate actions that focus on creating workplaces that uphold human rights, ensure decent working conditions, and support the overall well-being of employees are increasingly integral to a sustainable business model. In addition to companies' approach to social responsibility, there has evolved a focus on sustainability, and the publication of sustainability reports, as outlined above, has even become a legal obligation.

The redefinition of corporate objectives creates the conditions for companies that assume a role of social responsibility and sustainable development to go beyond mere legal compliance and establish their own mechanisms to ensure the effective integration of employees into the decision-making process, as well as to set up efficient mechanisms for informing and consulting them. This strategic and value-driven choice is all the more judicious as mechanisms that support democratic practices in the workplace have been shown to enhance the resilience and economic performance of companies and to allow for greater adaptability and flexibility at the workplace level, crucial for navigating structural changes.[32] Additionally, these practices improve the ability of companies to provide stable and quality employment. Therefore, the European Commission stated that the concept of democracy at work should extend universally, encompassing all workers and job types, and should be applicable across all work environments, including the private, public, and social sectors, irrespective of a company's size, industry, or organizational structure.[33] It is

[29] See e.g. Bilir et al. (2019).

[30] See Van Tulder & Roman (2019); Van Tulder et al. (2021).

[31] See e.g. Salmon (2007), Boltanski & Chiapello (2011).

[32] See Kluge & Vitols (2020)

[33] See European Parliament (2021).

relevant to recall that the foundation of legislative initiatives establishing the framework for employee involvement, both in terms of information and consultation, as well as decision-making participation, has been negotiated agreements, such as those in Germany, which underpin the codetermination system or those agreements through which employee information mechanisms were implemented prior to the entry into force of Directive 2002/14.

3.1 Transnational Collective Agreements: Embracing Voluntary Dialogue and Commitment

Within this framework of redefining corporate relationships—both externally with various stakeholders and internally with employees—we aim to analyse whether transnational company agreements (TCAs) could play a role in strengthening employee participation, promoting workplace democracy, and providing broader protection for employees beyond that guaranteed by national legislation. TCA is defined[34] as "an agreement comprising reciprocal commitments the scope of which extends to the territory of several States and which has been concluded by one or more representatives of a company or a group of companies on the one hand, and one or more workers' organisations on the other hand, and which covers working and employment conditions and/or relations between employers and workers or their representatives".

TCAs are therefore distinctive because they are voluntarily and innovatively agreed upon by the parties involved. They are formed outside of a legal framework which typically governs the representativeness of parties, negotiation procedures, or the mechanisms through which their effects are realized. This lack of formal regulation allows TCAs to more readily be classified as instruments of soft law rather than as binding legal outcomes of collective bargaining. Efforts have been undertaken to assess the feasibility of establishing binding regulations for the negotiation and implementation of TCAs; however, these proposals were ultimately rejected, primarily due to concerns about the administrative burdens they would impose on Member States and the potential infringement on the autonomy of social partners, especially employers.[35]

TCAs tackle priority issues and challenges encountered by both employers and workers at global or European levels,[36] allowing the parties to address specific concerns directly impacting the employment relationship. Key issues covered may include business growth and transformation, workforce renewal, vocational training, health and safety, financial participation by employees, equality and fundamen-

---

[34] See European Commission (2012).

[35] See ETUC Final Report (2016).

[36] See ETUC and Business Europe Report (2018).

tal labour rights. Recently, TCAs have increasingly taken on the role of regulating significant societal shifts in a sustainable way, addressing emerging issues such as digital transformation.[37]

Moreover, employee rights are addressed through a transnational lens, with TCAs functioning as a formal mechanism to provide employees across different countries with a unified minimum legal framework on pertinent aspects of their employment relationships, as well as a platform for expressing concerns and participating in decision-making processes. The unifying role of TCAs is both recognized and validated by trade unions and civil society, which actively pressure multinational corporations to adopt these agreements, primarily to ensure that fundamental worker rights are upheld throughout their operations, particularly within supply chains.[38] Indeed, the very fact that TCAs have proven effective in addressing sensitive issues such as the sustainable governance of global supply chains and in contributing to EU policy objectives has brought them into the spotlight at both the international and European levels in recent years.[39]

Throughout the 2000s, there were various efforts to establish a legal structure for TCAs, yet none solidified into a definitive framework. As a result, today, transnational negotiation remains predominantly unregulated, resting solely within the corporate domain, untouched by concrete legal obligations. This lack of formal regulation is compounded by the absence of industry-wide best practices or standard models for TCAs that could guide negotiations or implementation. Interestingly, while there exists a Database on transnational company agreements—developed through collaboration between the International Labour Organization and the European Commission—this resource falls short of being comprehensive or regularly updated, which diminishes its utility for informing or guiding corporate negotiations. The European Commission itself seems to maintain a hands-off approach regarding the promotion of TCAs. In its 2023 communication,[40] the Commission makes no mention of new initiatives to facilitate or promote this type of negotiation. This situation underscores a broader challenge within the field of international labour relations, where significant reliance on corporate goodwill and mutual interests continues to be the primary driver behind the adoption and execution of TCAs, without substantial external legislative or regulatory impetus.

---

[37] See ENGIE (2021).

[38] See International Labour Organization (2018).

[39] See Wieczorek and Pisarczyk (2021).

[40] See European Commission (2023).

3.2 *Voluntary Recognition of Representativity and Trust-Building Between Parties*

The structure of transnational companies can vary depending on legal, financial, and tax considerations. However, most often, transnational companies consist of a parent holding company and a network of subsidiaries, each legally recognized as a separate entity under different national jurisdictions. As business activities expand and become more complex, the number of subsidiaries tends to increase, which may lead to companies structuring themselves across multiple hubs, divisions, or tiers.[41] In the process of negotiating TCAs, although the parent holding company plays the primary role, it is necessary to ensure that each subsidiary of the transnational company provides valid consent in accordance with the applicable national regulations governing it. This aspect becomes even more critical in situations where TCAs establish rights with financial implications for the employees of the subsidiary in question.

In the context of worker representation, it is essential that their collective bodies are granted the authority—either directly or through a formal mandate—to advocate on behalf of employees at each subsidiary where the TCA's provisions are in effect. Workers can be represented through various structures[42] such as trade unions, corporate headquarters work councils, European Works Councils, or a global social dialogue body.

For example, the Global Framework Agreement on Social Responsibility and Sustainable Development, signed between Solvay and IndustriALL let to the establishment of the Solvay Global Forum (SGF)—a global body for employee representation, acting in parallel with the European Works Council. Under the Solvay Global Forum Agreement,[43] the forum, although "*not regulated by any international or local law*", has the authority, granted by the parties, to negotiate and enter into transnational agreements that impact all employees globally through collective contracts with Solvay. Based on this voluntarily recognized representativity, the parties entered into a Global Performance Sharing Agreement—an employee incentive program linked to the group's overall performance. The foundation of this agreement was the two-way dialogue, providing top management with an opportunity to directly assess the social climate and to communicate the Group's strategy directly to employee representatives.

In the example above, as well as in others, these transnational agreements are concluded by parties lacking the legal capacity to enter into collective agreements. Given the transnational nature of the agreements and the complexity of corporate structures, it would be challenging to establish a representational framework that could meet the validation requirements of multiple national legislations. Moreover,

[41] See e.g. Skinner (2020).

[42] See Surdykowska (2021).

[43] Concluded between Solvay SA and the SGF.

the relationships between the parties are built more on moral considerations than on the fulfilment of legally established conditions.

Therefore, it has been noted[44] that one of the primary outcomes of this type of negotiation is the establishment of a trust-based relationship between two partners who were traditionally perceived as having opposing interests. Trust forms the foundation of the negotiation process, beginning with the voluntary recognition of each party's representativeness and continuing with the identification of the issues to be addressed. The parties establish channels for information, consultation, and negotiation, enabling them to identify their specific needs, agree on their strategic importance, prioritize them, identify common needs and areas for compromise, and ultimately formalize these in the signed agreement. Given its transnational nature, the process is particularly challenging to manage, and the commitment of the parties to such a process underscores the importance placed on establishing a relationship founded on good faith.

It should also be noted that each party enters the negotiation process with the confidence that the other will honour the agreement reached, even in the absence of a legally binding obligation and despite the fact that resorting to the state's coercive power would involve cumbersome procedures with limited prospects for success. Such trust is crucial, as it ensures the effective implementation of the agreements across different national contexts and legal environments.

3.3 *TCAs: A Model for Enhancing (Traditional) Social Dialogue*

The moral redefinition of the relationship between employer and employees could serve as a model of best practices for social dialogue. On one hand, TCAs demonstrate a genuine willingness on the part of certain employers to enable employee involvement beyond legal requirements. At the same time, employees from countries with diverse legal regimes and negotiation traditions take on the responsibility of participating in an often-complex process to create a regulatory framework for labour relations. This situation should serve as an important motivational factor for legally recognized and regulated national structures, particularly for trade unions. Their situation in Europe is concerning, as over the last 20 years, trade union density has generally decreased across all Member States. Additionally, the proportion of workers covered by collective bargaining agreements declined from an estimated EU average of approximately 66% in 2000 to around 56% in 2019, with particularly significant drops in Central and Eastern Europe.[45]

Local trade unions, even if they do not participate directly in the negotiation of TCAs, are informed about the existence of global information and consultation

---

[44] See ETUC and Business Europe Final Report (2018).

[45] See European Commission (2023).

structures, the status and progress of negotiations, as well as their outcomes. Furthermore, these local entities may be indirectly involved in the negotiation process when assigned the tasks of identifying local issues, reporting on them, or assessing the presence or absence of certain practices or the implementation of specific legal mechanisms at the employer level.

Local bodies can serve as information hubs at each subsidiary level, thus enabling global structures to have a more structured position in the TCA negotiation process. The more employee representatives' positions within global forums are grounded in real issues, the more likely it is to drive the evolution of topics regulated by TCAs. Therefore, it is essential that social dialogue structures regulated by national law also assume an active role in the negotiation of TCAs, even if this role is mediated by global bodies, thereby ensuring that the concerns of the workforce are addressed comprehensively.

Another opportunity for trade unions arising from TCAs is the fact that the parties frequently rely on local social dialogue bodies to implement the agreements.[46] In some cases, the TCA explicitly states that, by assigning responsibilities for the agreement's implementation to social dialogue structures regulated by national law, the parties aim to strengthen social dialogue at the local level. As an example, Engie's Global Framework Agreement established the World Forum,[47] with responsibilities related to global social dialogue. The members of this body include Engie employees with union responsibilities within the Group, representatives of Engie management, and representatives of global union federations. The World Forum is intended as a platform for discussion and exchange on the Group's strategy, as well as for sharing information, particularly regarding the implementation, review, and compliance monitoring of the global agreements concluded by the parties. The existence of the World Forum does not, however, prejudice national legal provisions regarding social dialogue and trade union activities, nor does it replace the information and consultation procedures conducted within each subsidiary.

In another example, at Enel,[48] a Global Works Council (GWC) was established, serving as an informational body at the group level. Its role includes overseeing the implementation of the agreement with the company and initiating measures to strengthen and expand social dialogue within the company. The GWC is entitled to receive information on a wide range of topics, including economic and financial performance, investment programs and action plans, corporate restructuring and changes to business scope, employment policies, health and safety, environmental policies, vocational training, equal opportunities and non-discrimination, as well as sustainability plans and reports. Nonetheless, the information and consultation procedures with the GWC cannot be considered as fulfilling national legal obligations concerning employee involvement, leaving room for social dialogue structures at each subsidiary level to exercise their legally recognized competencies.

---

[46] See ETUC Business Europe Report (2018).

[47] ENGIE (2010).

[48] Enel Global Framework Agreement (2013).

On another level, TCAs facilitate a pervasive action of transmitting corporate values to the local subsidiaries. In some instances, this transmission occurs through the local implementation of a benefit or right that is not explicitly regulated by local legislation nor widespread in local HR practices. For example, the profit-sharing agreed upon in Solvay's Global Performance Sharing Agreement 2023 is an element that is not specific to all local legislations. Profit-sharing is important because it aligns employees' interests with the financial success of the organization, fostering a sense of ownership and motivating employees to contribute to the company's profitability.[49] It can enhance job satisfaction, reduce turnover, and improve productivity, as employees feel directly rewarded for the company's performance. However, it is not a benefit mandated by law in all national jurisdictions, nor is it a widely adopted HR practice. Therefore, its regulation through TCAs contributes both to expanding the rights granted to employees and to diversifying HR practices.[50]

Additionally, TCAs address issues related to the new realities of the employment relationship, such as the digitalization of work and the protection of employees against electronic surveillance, which can also serve as a source of inspiration for consultation and negotiation procedures at the national level.

TCAs can also ensure a more uniform approach to worker treatment and rights across diverse legal and cultural landscapes. This is particularly important in countries where employment standards are low or where work is perceived and valued differently from European Union standards. For instance, Engie's TCA stipulates, in Article 9, point 48, that when existing provisions are non-existent or inadequate, Engie shall establish, in consultation with employee representatives, social protection schemes that allow for an adequate level of social protection for all of its employees worldwide. Moreover, the TCA stipulates minimum benefits related to social aspects that reflect values upheld by the employer: parenthood (14 weeks of fully paid maternity leave and 4 weeks of fully paid paternity leave); incapacity benefit (minimum coverage equivalent to 12 months); health benefit (coverage of hospital costs up to a minimum of 75%); and death benefit (death cover for all employees, including the payment of a minimum capital equivalent to 12 months of gross salary).

Moreover, through Transnational Company Agreements (TCAs), procedures that contribute to combating corruption and other serious violations related to health and safety, environmental issues, human rights, labour and trade union rights, respect for people, privacy are expanded by implementing systems such as whistleblowing. Such systems are made available to employees and stakeholders of the group, allowing them to report any actions, events, or behaviour that could compromise the integrity and/or rights of individuals, affect group's operations, or result in serious liability consequences. This facilitates a culture of transparency and accountability within the organization.

---

[49] See e.g. Bah et al. (2024).

[50] See Demetriades & Biletta (2016).

4 Concluding Insights

Over the past two decades, both the world and the realities of the workplace have transformed. We are at a critical juncture where society is undergoing profound transformation: we are scrutinizing our relationship with artificial intelligence and its impact on the workplace (and humanity); tackling issues related to employee surveillance and standardization; and extending employment relations to encompass telework and platform-based work. Today, the concept of work has evolved significantly from the Fordist system's assembly line model, which primarily focused on securing basic rights and protecting employees through strikes and other confrontational methods. Workers not only have rights but also a context that allows them to move beyond traditional roles of control and subordination by employers. This very context is shaped by the new realities, where actions derived from state power are complemented by a new type of action in which private actors assume a regulatory role. These private actors are multinational corporations which, through their economic power, are able to significantly influence political power. At the same time, they serve as a model for other private economic actors and, through their societal actions and interactions with their own employees, can help disseminate good practices that may lead to widespread change.

As discussed in this chapter, transforming the traditional role of the employee into that of a dialog and decision partner of the employer has not been without obstacles, nor is it complete, despite good intentions declared for over 40 years. Additionally, it has been shown that most often, the action of legal regulation has been hindered by employer organisations who have sought to maintain a monopoly over decision-making within companies, or at the very least, to limit the influence of 'extrinsic' elements, as employees are often perceived. At the same time, however, actions by certain corporations that have voluntarily implemented mechanisms to involve employees in decision-making, as well as in information and consultation processes, have helped revive the European legislative process at a time when it had stalled. Thus, employee involvement is a multi-variable equation: it includes various national regulations as well as different approaches by companies, which depend on their size, values, and even their employer branding strategy.

Within this diverse framework, employees bear the responsibility of balancing legally granted rights with the voluntary commitments that companies undertake (or may be encouraged to undertake). Although the regulatory framework, shaped by legislation and voluntary corporate actions, is not without its flaws, it nonetheless equips employees with the tools to assert themselves as partners to their employers. Just as democracy at the state level requires not only a legal framework but also responsible citizens, workplace democracy demands that employees become engaged and informed participants, capable of giving substance and meaning to the rights they have gained.

References

Ales E (2009) Information and consultation within the undertaking: employees' right or employer's duty? In: Blanke T, Rose E, Voogsgeerd H, Zondag M (eds) Recasting worker involvement? Kluwer, Deventer, pp 7–21

Bah MOP, Sun Z, Hange U, Edjoukou AJR (2024) Effectiveness of organizational change through employee involvement: evidence from telecommunications and refinery companies. Sustainability 16(6):2524. https://doi.org/10.3390/su16062524

Bilir LK, Chor D, Manova K (2019) Host-country financial development and multinational activity. Eur Econ Rev 115:192–220. https://doi.org/10.1016/j.euroecorev.2019.02.008

Boltanski L, Chiapello E (2011) Le nouvel esprit du capitalisme. Gallimard

Bundesverfassungsgericht (1979, March 1) BVerfGE 50, 290, 315-6

Conchon A, Klugen N, Stollt M (2015) Table: worker board-level participation in the 31 European economic area countries. European Trade Union Institute

Danis J-J, Hoffmann R (1995) From the Vredeling Directive to the European Works Council Directive – some historical remarks. Transfer 1(2):180–187

De Spiegelaere S, Vitols S (2020) A better world with more democracy at work. europeanparticipationindex.eu, European Trade Union Institute (ETUI). http://www.europeanparticipationindex.eu/betterworldmoredemocracyatwork

De Spiegelaere S, Hoffmann A, Jagodziński R, Lafuente Hernández S, Rasnača Z, Vitols S (2019) Democracy at work, in ETUI and ETUC, Benchmarking Working Europe 2019. ETUI, pp 67–89

Demetriades S, Biletta I (2016) Win–win arrangements: innovative measures through social dialogue at company level. Eurofound, Luxembourg. https://www.eurofound.europa.eu/pl/publications/report/2016/industrial-relations/win-win-arrangements-innovative-measures-through-social-dialogue-at-company-level. Accessed 20 Apr 2024

Dorssemont F (2006) The Renault saga (revisited). Eur Co Law 3(1):5–10. https://doi.org/10.54648/eucl2006002

Edwards V (2003) The European company essential tool or eviscerated dream? Common Mark Law Rev 40(2):443–464. https://doi.org/10.54648/cola2003018

Enel S.p.A., IndustriALL Global Union, Public Services International, Filctem CGIL, Flaei CISL, Uiltec UIL (2013) Global Framework Agreement on Social Dialogue Guidelines. Signed in Rome, 14 June 2013. Available at: https://www.epsu.org/sites/default/files/article/files/19_-Enel_Global_Framework_Agreement-_inglese_14_giu_2013.pdf. Accessed 25 Apr 2024

ENGIE (2010) Global Framework Agreement on Fundamental Rights and Corporate Social Responsibility. Signed in Brussels, 10 November 2010. Available at: https://www.engie.com/sites/default/files/assets/documents/2020-10/engie-global-agreement-2010-en.pdf. Accessed 25 Apr 2024

ENGIE (2021) Global framework agreement on fundamental rights and ENGIE's social responsibility. Available at: https://www.engie.com/sites/default/files/assets/documents/2023-06/EN---ACI-ENGIE-vdef-122021.pdf. Accessed: 10 May 2024

Ernst and Young (2020, July) Study on directors' duties and sustainable corporate governance

ETUC and BusinessEurope (2018) Building on experiences. A win-win approach to transnational industrial relations in multinational companies. Final report

ETUC Final Report of 2016 - Roadmap on Transnational Company agreements: Progressing towards an Optional Legal Framework

European Commission (1980) Proposal for a Council Directive on procedures for informing and consulting the employees of undertakings with complex structures, in particular transnational undertakings, COM(80) 423 final, OJ C 297, 15 November 1980, pp 3–8

European Commission. (2014) Directive 2014/95/EU of the European Parliament and of the Council of 22 October 2014 amending Directive 2013/34/EU as regards disclosure of non-financial and diversity information by certain large undertakings and groups

European Commission (2023) Strengthening social dialogue in the European Union: harnessing its full potential for managing fair transitions, Brussels, 25.1.2023 COM(2023) 40 final
European Commission Staff Working Document (2012) Transnational company agreements: realising the potential of social dialogue. Brussels, 10.9.2012 SWD(2012) 264 final
European Parliament (2021), European Parliament resolution of 16 December 2021 on democracy at work: a European framework for employees' participation rights and the revision of the European Works Council Directive (2021/2005(INI))
Ferreras I, Battilana J, Méda D (eds) (2020) Le manifeste travail: démocratiser, démarchandiser, dépolluer. Le Seuil
Frega R, Herzog L, Neuhäuser C (2019) Workplace democracy- the recent debate. Philos Compass 14(4):e12574
Gold M, Hall M (1994) Statutory European Works Councils: the final countdown? Ind Relat J 25:177–186. https://doi.org/10.1111/j.1468-2338.1994.tb00703.x
Hall M (1992) Behind the European Works Councils Directive: the European Commission's legislative strategy. Br J Ind Relat 30(4):547–566
Hall M (2010) EU regulation and the UK employee consultation framework. Econ Ind Democr 31:55–69. https://doi.org/10.1177/0143831X10375631
High Level Group on Economic and Social Implications of Industrial Change (1998) Final report of the High Level Group on economic and social implications of industrial change (November, p 9)
Howitt R (2007) Corporate social responsibility: Implementing the partnership for growth and jobs. Report on behalf of the European Parliament, 2006/2133(INI). European Parliament. Available at: https://www.europarl.europa.eu/doceo/document/A-6-2006-0471_EN.html. Accessed: 14 May 2024
ILO (2018) Transnational company agreements: issues, approaches and practices a guide for employers' organisations and companies
Johansen TR (2016) EU regulation of corporate social and environmental reporting. Soc Environ Acc J 36(1):1–9. https://doi.org/10.1080/0969160X.2016.1148948
Kenner J (2005) Worker involvement in the *Societas Europaea*: integrating company and labour law in the European Union? Yearb Eur Law 24(1):223–259. https://doi.org/10.1093/yel/24.1.223
Kluge N, Vitols S (2020) Codetermination for the sustainable company I.M.U. Policy Brief 4. (PDF) Seiten
La Torre M, Sabelfeld S, Blomkvist M, Tarquinio L, Dumay J (2018) Harmonising non-financial reporting regulation in Europe. Meditari Acc Res 26(4):598–621. https://doi.org/10.1108/MEDAR-02-2018-0290
Locke EA, Schweiger DM (1979) Participation in decision-making: one more look. Res Organ Behav 1:265–339
Miller KI, Monge PR (1986) Participation, satisfaction, and productivity: a meta-analytic review. Acad Manag J 29(4):727–753
Piasna A, Theodoropoulou S (eds) (2024) Benchmarking working Europe 2024. ETUI and ETUC
Pipkorn J (1983) The draft directive on procedures for informing and consulting employees. Common Mark Law Rev 20(4):725–755
Rapp MS, Wolff M, Udoieva I, Hennig JC (2019) Mitbestimmung im Aufsichtsrat und ihre Wirkung auf die Unternehmensführung. Hans-Böckler-Stiftung No 424
Salmon A (2007) La tentation éthique du capitalisme. La Découverte
Samani N, Overland C, Sabelfeld S (2023) The role of the EU non-financial reporting directive and employee representation in employee-related disclosures. Account Forum 47(2):278–306. https://doi.org/10.1080/01559982.2022.2158773
Skinner GL, Chambers R, McGrath S (2020) Growth and structure of TNCs. In: Transnational corporations and human rights: overcoming barriers to judicial remedy. Cambridge University Press, Cambridge, pp 9–13

Statista, Walmart's net sales worldwide from fiscal year 2006 to 2024. Available at https://www.statista.com/statistics/183399/walmarts-net-sales-worldwide-since-2006/. Accessed 20 Mar 2024
Surdykowska B (2021) Transnational framework agreements and their environment – basic information. In: Pisarczyk Ł (ed) TCA or about David's negotiation with Goliath. Gdańsk
Teuteberg HJ (1961) Geschichte der industriellen Mitbestimmung in Deutschland. Ursprung und Entwicklung ihrer Vorläufer im Denken und in der Wirklichkeit des 19. Jahrhunderts. Siebeck Mohr (Paul Siebeck), Tübingen
The Grand National Assembly (1971) Law No. 11 of 1971 on the organization and management of state socialist units. Collection of Laws, Decisions, Instructions. Effective January 1, 1971
Trif A, Paolucci V (2019) Romania: from legal support to frontal assault. In: Müller T, Vandaele K, Waddington J (eds) Collective bargaining in Europe: towards and endgame, vol III. ETUI, Brussels, pp 505–523
Van Tulder R, Roman M (2019) Re-assessing risk: the increasing relevance of sustainability risk. In: Leonidou LC, Katsikeas CS, Samiee S, Leonidou CN (eds) Socially-responsible international business: critical issues and the way forward. Edward Elgar, Cheltenham, pp 158–183
Van Tulder R, Rodrigues SB, Mirza H, Sexsmith K (2021) The UN's sustainable development goals: can multinational enterprises lead the Decade of Action? J Int Bus Policy 4(1):1–21. https://doi.org/10.1057/s42214-020-00095-1
Volosevici D (2012) Analyse multi-facettes de l'intégration des salariés dans les sociétés commerciales, en France et en Roumanie. PhD thesis, Université de Bretagne Sud, Lorient
Wieczorek K, Pisarczyk Ł (2021) Transnational framework agreements: In search of a European legal framework. Stud Iurid 89:409-432. https://doi.org/10.31338/2544-3135.si.2022-89.21
Wiedemann H (1980) Codetermination by workers in German enterprises. Am J Comp Law 28(1):79–92. https://doi.org/10.2307/839736

From Decentralizing to Promoting Collective Bargaining: The Development of Industrial Relations in Poland

Błażej Mądrzycki and Łukasz Pisarczyk

1 Opening Remarks

In recent years, the European social policy has shifted from decentralizing collective bargaining, justified by the economic crisis and the need to support entrepreneurs (e.g. Laulom 2018), to supporting and promoting social dialogue: the European Pillar of Social Rights, the Directive on Adequate Minimum Wages (Brameshuber et al. 2024). The Directive on Adequate Minimum Wages ('the Directive') not only obliges the Member States to promote collective bargaining in wages (Article 4.1) but also provides for the obligation to adopt a unique action plan if the coverage of collective bargaining in a given MS is below 80 per cent (Article 4.2). It means a fundamental change in the approach towards industrial relations, particularly collective bargaining at a multi-company level, which is crucial for extending the collective bargaining coverage. Although the EU legislator has been accused of going beyond the treaties, and the future of the directive, following Denmark's claim and the opinion of the Advocate General, is uncertain, the promotion of collective bargaining is an element of the new social agenda. It can be assumed that the Union will use various legal instruments to increase the collective bargaining coverage: just as it acted for decentralization during the global economic

This chapter is a result of Project No. 2019/33/B/HS5/02067 financed by the National Science Centre in Poland.

B. Mądrzycki · Ł. Pisarczyk (✉)
University of Silesia, Katowice, Poland
e-mail: blazej.madrzycki@us.edu.pl; lukasz.pisarczyk@us.edu.pl

K. Koldinská et al. (eds.), *Labour Law and Social Security Law in Central and Eastern Europe*, European Union and its Neighbours in a Globalized World 26,
https://doi.org/10.1007/978-3-032-04496-9_19

crisis (Laulom 2025). Therefore, some of the considerations will remain relevant even if the directive is challenged by the Court of Justice of the EU. In the case of Poland, the promotion of collective bargaining was an element of the national reconstruction plan. Taking action in this area is a formal condition for the launch of financial assistance for Poland. Moreover, some Member States have already adopted appropriate measures to implement the Directive. This means that the mechanisms provided for in it, at least in some MSs, have led to specific legal changes. The idea of the Directive, the adopted goals and the actions taken to implement them will constitute a reference point for the development of a legal framework for collective bargaining even if the Court finds the directive invalid.

The article analyses the potential impact of the new European strategy on the development of industrial relations in Poland. Central and Eastern European countries ('CEECs') are among the MSs with the lowest coverage. Poland is the region's largest economy, and in 2023, it was reported to have the lowest coverage in the entire EU. As a result, the Polish case can be instructive regarding increasing the coverage. The authors consider what legal and organizational instruments can be used to improve the coverage. They confront the draft law on collective agreements submitted by the government with social partners' opinions and strategies to answer whether the new law can actually change the situation of collective bargaining or is it just a façade solution to avoid accusations of failure to implement the Directive. Finally, the authors also ask about alternative methods to improve the position of collective bargaining by referring to transnational industrial relations with the involvement of multinational companies (MNCs).

2 The Development of Collective Bargaining: Poland in the Background of Central and Eastern Europe

The current position of collective bargaining must be seen in a broader political and socio-economic development perspective. Poland is one of the CEECs that belonged to the Soviet bloc (1944–1989), has undergone a political transformation (after 1989), and has joined the European Union (2004). Although CEECs successfully transformed their political and economic systems, some significant differences between the West (the 'Old' MSs) and the East (the 'New' MSs) remain. One of the most noticeable is the differentiation in the collective bargaining coverage. In some 'Old' MSs, collective bargaining exceeds 80 per cent and covers almost the entire workforce. In others, it varies from 50/60 to 80 per cent, playing an essential role in setting up working standards.[1] The Member States with high coverage build a coordinated and coherent system of working conditions, including wages. In such a model, the position of both employers and workers is unified while the competition in labour costs is limited. The coordination and high coverage constitute an

[1] https://web-archive.oecd.org/temp/2023-10-03/577157-ictwss-database.htm

important element of the socio-economic system. They may be achieved thanks to the active approach of the social partners (Italy, Nordic countries), state intervention or a combination of both (Austria, Belgium, France) (see e.g. Liukkunen 2019; Gyulavári and Menegatti 2019).[2] Sectoral collective bargaining plays a crucial role in building wide coverage. In the majority of CEECs, the situation is radically different. In 2022 when the Directive was adopted, the collective bargaining coverage does not exceed 30/35 per cent.[3] The only exceptions were Croatia and Slovenia, with developed sectoral negotiations (see e.g. Stanojević and Poje 2019) and a relatively high coverage.[4] The position of collective bargaining in CEECs has been affected by several interrelated phenomena: the existence of the communist regime, the adoption of the neo-liberal agenda in the 1990s as well as the crisis of social partnership. All these phenomena are characteristic of the development of collective bargaining in Poland.

The communist period, which disrupted the proper development of industrial relations, is crucial for understanding the current situation. Despite its glorious "Solidarność" period, Poland began political transformation without real collective bargaining. On the one hand, Poland ratified ILO conventions Nos. 87 and 98 formally recognized freedom of association and the right to collective bargaining. On the other hand, the communist regime could not leave any space for voluntary and free collective bargaining. Voluntary collective bargaining is a democratic mechanism based on the freedom and autonomy of the social partners. The 'socialist democracy' was only a façade which hid the authoritarian regime. Moreover, the communist state was the primary owner and the organizer of socio-economic life. The economy was centrally planned. Trade unions were organized in one structure dependent on the state and communist party. Although after 1956 (the end of the Stalinist period), the system of sectoral collective agreements was established, it constituted a part of the central economic plan. It was carried out under the control of the authorities. As a result, parties negotiated collective agreements and could be treated as social partners in a strict sense while their freedom in setting up working conditions was strictly limited (Seweryński 1999).

The situation started changing in the 1970s due to economic difficulties. In December 1970, mass workers' protests against price increases were brutally suppressed by the police and army. After a short period of economic recovery (1971–1975), the Polish economy collapsed. It entailed a new wave of worker protests (1976). In 1980, strikes that broke out in various factories and shipyards entailed the appearance of an independent worker movement. Under the social pressure, the communist regime concluded a series of collective agreements with

---

[2] https://www.oecd.org/en/data/datasets/oecdaias-ictwss-database.html

[3] https://www.oecd.org/en/data/datasets/oecdaias-ictwss-database.html

[4] According to OCED-AIAS ICTWSS database collective-bargaining coverage in 2019–2021 amounted to: 13% in Poland; 15% in Romania; 19.1% in Estonia; 21.8% in Hungary; 24.4% in Slovakia; 26.6% in Lithuania; 27.1% in Latvia; 28% in Bulgaria; 34.7% in Czechia, 53%, 78.6% in Slovenia (https://www.oecd-ilibrary.org/employment/data/trade-unions/collective-bargaining-coverage_923f26fe-en; Müller and Schulten 2024).

striking workers. The most important result was the recognition of independent trade unions. On 10 November 1980, 'Solidarność' was formally registered. In 1981, when the social protests reached their peak, 'Solidarność' had ten million members. As the only truly democratic organization, 'Solidarność' became not only a trade union but also a *sui generis* political party. The agreements between 'Solidarność' and the communist authorities resulted from a genuine social dialogue. However, the period of freedom ended on 13 December 1981 when martial law was imposed. Free trade unions were suspended and then liquidated. In 1982, a new law on trade unions was adopted (Seweryński 1999). New trade unions began to be established under state control. The authorities feared the re-development of an authentic, universal worker movement. As a result, the basic structure of trade unions was company trade union organizations. The next wave of democratization began in 1988. As a result of social protests, the authorities allowed free trade unions to continue. In 1989, the political transformation was initiated. In 1991, the Parliament adopted new laws on trade unions and employer organizations and resolved collective disputes. In 1994, the legal framework of collective bargaining (Chapter XI of the Labour Code) was adjusted to a democratic and market environment. In 2000, the next amendment to the Labour Code extended the subjective scope of collective agreements to all labour law issues. Conditions for voluntary and autonomous social dialogues were restored (Gardawski 2015). However, the law maintained company-level structures of trade unions and did not promote collective bargaining.

The Law on Trade Unions adopted in 1991 recognized the central role of company trade union organizations. The maintenance of company-level union organizations was necessary for trade unions themselves. Representatives of company-level organizations are protected against dismissal (compare Rączka 2015) and enjoy the right to time off paid by the employer. Moreover, the employer must provide company trade union organizations with the technical means necessary to perform union activity. Trade unions did want to waive these rights. Concentrating on a company-level limit, however, the potential of trade unions. Sectoral structures weakened significantly. Consequently, company-level collective bargaining started prevailing over sectoral ones. At the same time, the state did not promote collective bargaining, particularly multi-company one. During the transition period, CEECs positioned themselves as cheap labour markets to attract foreign investments. Poland chose the path of radical (or even shocking) reforms in the neo-liberal spirit, the so-called Balcerowicz Plan (Kozłowski 2019). The neo-liberal agenda involved liberalization and decentralization of working conditions. Collective bargaining leading to increased working standards could have been an obstacle in implementing the transformation in a neo-liberal version (see e.g. Berend 2007; Orenstein and Bugarič 2022). In Romania, a relatively developed collective bargaining system was deconstructed as a response to the world economic crisis (Rosioru 2018).

Despite the abstemious approach of the state, the social partners still had a formal possibility to develop collective bargaining at various levels. In reality, however, the opportunity could not be used. Trade unions were in crisis. The number of members began to fall. There were no adequately strong and prepared sectoral structures. To achieve their goals, unions often chose the political and legislative path. In 1997, Akcja Wyborcza 'Solidarność' won the parliamentary election and formed the government. One of the key obstacles to developing collective bargaining in CEECs is the lack of a broad representation of employers (e.g. Gyulavári 2018). Only a limited number of organizations with a wide membership base have been established.[5] Moreover, the internal structure of companies is different in Poland than in Western Europe. Small and medium enterprises dominate (see e.g. Matveev and Atanasov 2010). As a rule, employers avoid collective standards, which would lead to a unification and increase of working standards. Western companies investing in Poland do decrease labour costs. Polish employers, mainly small and medium enterprises, expected working conditions enabling them to survive in the market. Employer organizations, which did not exist until 1989, were only just being formed, and their potential was limited. Moreover, employers raised that the negotiating room left to the social partners is too narrow since the law did not accept collective agreements modify the law in a way less favourable for employees Article 9 § 2 of the Labour Code). Consequently, collective agreements may only increase the obligations of employers. As a result, there were no forces interested in insisting on sectoral negotiations (compare Gardawski 2015). Despite the formal possibility provided by the Law amending the Labour Code in 1994, representative trade unions and employer organizations did not enter into the parties' rights to existing sectoral collective agreements. New agreements were not negotiated. Employers still covered by sectoral agreements sought ways to terminate or withdraw from these agreements. The last multi-employer collective agreement (in the public sector) was concluded in 2014. Company-level collective bargaining was carried out in special types of companies (state-owned enterprises) and some branches of the economy. However, even the number and coverage of company-level collective agreements systematically decreased (Mądrzycki and Pisarczyk 2022).

The legal framework of collective bargaining formed during the transition period is neutral and non-supportive for the social partners. Collective agreements are generally binding regarding workers but are limited to employers affiliated with organizations that are parties to collective agreements. Although formally possible, the extension of multi-company collective agreements has not been used in practice. Collective agreements are binding only on employers that either have concluded company-level agreements or are members of employer organizations. The parties to an inter-company agreement may even exclude member companies from its application scope. As a result, the *erga omnes* principle on the workers' side does not change the situation significantly. Moreover, some statutory solutions could be perceived as direct obstacles to developing collective bargaining. The procedure of negotiating collective agreements, including the registration requirement, was perceived as rigid. Social partners were not sure whether the registrar would accept a collective agreement they negotiated. The law also limited the personal scope of

[5] 'Lewiatan' the largest Polish employer organization declares to unite employers who employ around one million workers, https://lewiatan.org/

collective bargaining. First of all, it was a result of restricting freedom of association to employees only. The law also limited the personal scope of collective bargaining. First of all, it was a result of restricting freedom of association to employees only. The Article 2.1 of the Law on Trade Unions in the wording which remained in force till the end of 2018 provided that only employees (employed within the employment relationship) members of agricultural production cooperatives and those performing work on the basis of an agency contract, if they did not employ other persons had the rights to form and join trade unions. Collective rights of other civil law contractors and self-employed were not recognized. According to the law they could not form and join trade unions, even if they were in a situation similar to that of employees (compare Florek 2015, Hajn 2015). Theoretically, non-employees could be covered by provisions of collective agreements concluded for employees. However, the law did not regulate the influence of collective agreements on civil law contracts. As a result, the collective agreement was to act as a contract and not a source of law. Consequently, non-employees could waive their rights arising from collective agreements. In practice, they hardly fell into the scope of collective agreements. The limitations were found inconsistent with international standards (see e.g. Hajn 2015; Pisarczyk 2023b) and the Polish constitution: the judgment of the Constitutional Court of 2 June 2015[6] (Latos-Miłkowska 2023). Next, the law significantly limited the right to collective bargaining in the public sector. Article 239 § 3 LC provides that collective agreements cannot be concluded for all the civil servants in the governmental administration as well as for civil servant employed in public (e.g. municipal) administration whose employment contract is based on nomination. All civil servants in the governmental administration could not reach collective agreements. Although accepted by the Constitutional Court in the judgment of 17 November 2015,[7] the scope of the exclusion was also controversial from the perspective of international and constitutional standards. Last but not least, the right to conclude multi-company collective agreements in the private sector was limited to employer organizations (while a small part of employers are united in organizations).

In recent years, the region, in particular Poland, enjoyed significant economic development (e.g. Polster 2021). However, it has not entailed an increase in collective bargaining (Kahancová et al. 2024, p. 3). The improvement of workers' positions has usually been caused either by the market situation (general income growth, shortage of workers) or by state intervention (e.g. increasing the statutory minimum wage). Moreover, in some cases, the state may not be interested in sharing power with the social partners. Moreover, improving working standards, e.g. increasing statutory minimum wage, could be used as a political argument, which is particularly important due to growing populism (compare Gyulavári and Pisarczyk 2023; Becker 2024).

[6] K 1/13.

[7] K 5/15.

The current situation of collective bargaining, including the approach of the social partners, was analysed as a part of the National Recovery Plan (Mądrzycki and Pisarczyk 2022). The diagnosis confirmed the total breakdown of multi-employer collective bargaining and dispersion of company-level negotiations, which covers specific types of companies/specific sectors and a relatively narrow group of workers. Interviews with the social partners revealed the main obstacles in developing industrial relations, particularly sectoral or branch collective bargaining. According to employers, they need a greater flexibility in working conditions to compete with Western companies, which dominate as regards financial and technological resources. As a result, SMEs are not interested in unifying working conditions. Large companies, which theoretically could benefit from this process, did not want to intensify the social dialogue as a potential source of further obligations and burdens. As a result, employers and employer organizations are reluctant, or in the best possible scenario neutral, to implement multi-employer collective bargaining.

3 Increasing Collective Bargaining Coverage: New Social Policy of the EU

In the recent years, the policy of the EU towards collective bargaining has significantly evolved. To respond to the world economic crisis and increase the European economy's competitiveness, the EU supported decentralizing collective bargaining and flexibilizing working standards. Acting with international institutions the EU encouraged the MSs deeply affected by the crisis to reconstruct the legal framework of industrial relations. Sectoral collective bargaining was the primary 'victim' of the anti-crisis measures. In some MSs, the role of sectoral negotiations was significantly limited (Greece, Ireland, Portugal, Romania). It led to a significant decrease in the coverage by collective bargaining (Laulom 2018). After the recovery, some of these MSs were able to rebuild sectoral negotiations and increase coverage (Portugal) (Coelho Moreira 2018).

A turning point in the European policy towards collective bargaining was the adoption of the European Pillar of Social Rights (2017). The new approach was highlighted by principle 8 (Social dialogue and involvement of workers), which provides, inter alia, that the social partners shall be encouraged to negotiate and conclude collective agreements in matters relevant to them while respecting their autonomy and the right to collective action. Since adopting the Pillar, the EU implemented the policy of promoting collective bargaining, in particular, multi-employer (sectoral) negotiations. This was reflected in the national recovery plans adopted after the pandemic. Poland was obliged to diagnose the situation of collective bargaining and undertake appropriate legislative actions to increase the coverage by collective agreements. The Directive, which aims at improving the collective bargaining coverage in the MSs and facilitating the exercise of the right to collective bargaining on wage-setting, was adopted in 2022 (more about the Directive, see Brameshuber et al. 2024).

Article 4.1 of the Directive obliges the MSs to promote collective bargaining on wages. To this end, Member States, with the involvement of the social partners, in accordance with national law and practice, should: (a) promote the building and strengthening of the capacity of the social partners to engage in collective bargaining on wage-setting, in particular at sector or cross-industry level; (b) encourage constructive, meaningful and informed negotiations on wages between the social partners, on an equal footing, where both parties have access to appropriate information in order to carry out their functions in respect of collective bargaining on wage-setting; (c) take measures, as appropriate, to protect the exercise of the right to collective bargaining on wage-setting and to protect workers and trade union representatives from acts that discriminate against them in respect of their employment on the grounds that they participate or wish to participate in collective bargaining on wage-setting; (d) for the purpose of promoting collective bargaining on wage-setting, take measures, as appropriate, to protect trade unions and employers' organizations participating or wishing to participate in collective bargaining against any acts of interference by each other or each other's agents or members in their establishment, functioning or administration. The obligation to promote collective bargaining is addressed to all MSs, irrespective of the current coverage. However, if an MS finds the existing solutions satisfactory, it is not obliged to amend its national legal framework. Moreover, the collective autonomy of the social partners should be fully respected (e.g. Report 2023). A qualified obligation has been imposed on those MSs where the coverage by collective bargaining is below the adopted threshold (80 per cent). Such an MS is obliged to: (a) provide for a framework of enabling conditions for collective bargaining, either by law after consulting the social partners or by agreement with them; (b) establish an action plan to promote collective bargaining.[8] The action plan should set out a clear timeline and concrete measures to progressively increase the collective bargaining coverage rate, in full respect for the autonomy of the social partners. The Member State should review its action plan regularly and update it if needed.[9] In any event, such an action plan should be reviewed at least every 5 years. The action plan and any update thereof should be made public and notified to the Commission.

The obligations arising from the Directive cannot be treated as binding in terms of results (Report 2023). The MSs are obliged to strive to increase the level of coverage, at least by adopting measures provided for by EU law. However, EU law forces MSs to undertake comprehensive actions to increase coverage by collective bargaining. Although the Directive refers to bargaining on wage-setting, its

[8] The Member State are obliged to develop such an action plan after consulting the social partners or by agreement with the social partners, or, following a joint request by the social partners, as agreed between the social partners.

[9] Where a Member State updates its action plan, it is obliged to do so after consulting the social partners or by agreement with them, or, following a joint request by the social partners, as agreed between the social partners.

potential influence (due to the role of wages) is much broader, affecting the whole industrial relations system in MSs (compare Report 2023). The obligation to increase collective bargaining coverage must also be seen in a broader perspective. By increasing collective bargaining coverage, the EU will affect not only industrial relations systems but, in principle, entire socio-economic systems of the MSs, in particular CEECs which avoided a far-going unification of working standards. The EU strategy may be perceived as an attempt to restore the European social model (Vaughan-Whitehead 2015, p. 9) based on sectoral (trans-sectoral) negotiations covering large groups of workers (Laulom 2025). Increasing coverage means unifying and improving working standards and, as a result, changing the rules of distributing national income to make it more equal. Consequently, it will cause the next step in reconstructing the employment relationship and the parties' position thereto.

For the future of collective bargaining, the ruling in the case will be important:[10] Kingdom of Denmark v European Parliament and Council of the European Union (Case C-19/23) (2023/C 104/22). The Kingdom of Denmark is seeking the annulment of the Directive in its entirety. The primary argument for the request is a violation of Article 153(5) TFEU. The complainants point out that the contested directive interferes directly with the determination of the level of pay in the MSs and concerns the right of association, which is excluded from the competence of the EU legislature pursuant to Article 153(5) TFEU. To a large extent, the applicants' position was confirmed by the Court's Advocate General.[11] In his opinion, he pointed out that "In my view, those considerations should lead the Court to conclude that the AMW Directive must be annulled in full (...)" (Opinion of Advocate General). The ETUC takes a different view from the Advocate General. In their opinion[12] the ETUC invites the Court of Justice to: "Dismiss in its entirety (i.e. both the principle and alternative head of claim) the action for annulment brought by the Kingdom of Denmark, supported by the Kingdom of Sweden, and Uphold Directive (EU) 2022/2041 on Adequate Minimum Wages in the European Union in its entirety. (ETUC Counter-Opinion)". The final determination of the case rests with the Court of Justice. It should also be noted that one of the conditions for Poland to receive funds from the National Recovery Plan is the stimulation of collective labour bargaining. A possible annulment of the Directive by the Court of Justice should not affect the Polish regulations.

[10] Action brought on 18 January 2023—Kingdom of Denmark v European Parliament and Council of the European Union (Case C-19/23). Available at: https://eur-lex.europa.eu/legal-content/EN/TXT/?uri=oj:JOC_2023_104_R_0022

[11] Opinion of Advocate General Emiliou delivered on 14 January 2025, Available at: https://eur-lex.europa.eu/legal-content/EN/TXT/?uri=celex:62023CC0019

[12] The ETUC Counter-Opinion to legally dismiss the arguments brought by Advocate General Emiliou, ETUCE counter-opinion is available at: https://www.etuc.org/en/pressrelease/etuc-launches-counter-opinion-minimum-wage-directive-case

4 How Can We Increase Collective Bargaining Coverage?

To stimulate collective bargaining, the legal framework must be adjusted to the current position and possibilities of the social partners (see e.g. Kahn-Freund 1983). The MSs may resort to soft methods as well as put a pressure on social partners. The state may also play an active role as a direct or indirect employer (public administration, state-owned companies). Some initiatives can be undertaken within existing legal framework while others need legislative initiatives (point-specific amendments, a complex reconstruction of the legal framework).

Public administration or tripartite bodies may issue soft laws, e.g. guidelines, which encourage commencing collective bargaining and highlight its advantages. They may also provide social partners with professional (e.g. legal) and technical support. Social partners may be encouraged to bargain collectively based on tax or public procurement preferences. The state may establish bodies or institutions specialized in collective bargaining and providing the social partners with the necessary support. Collective bargaining may also be facilitated by mediation and arbitration mechanisms (see, e.g. Berthier and Leclerc 2025). However, such mechanisms may be insufficient in countries with low (very low) coverage. In this field, the legal framework's role may also be significant. A neutral legal framework will not stimulate social dialogue in countries like Poland, where trade unions and employers (employers' organizations) have remained passive or even reluctant to commence negotiations (compare Pisarczyk 2023a).[13] In such a situation, a state willing to effectively increase collective bargaining coverage should adopt a more active policy.

The state may go a step further by pushing the social partners to more active commitment. In some MSs (France, Romania), the law obliges social partners, at specific levels and in specific matters, to commence collective bargaining regularly. However, the law cannot oblige the social partners to conclude a collective agreement (Gernigon et al. 2000, p. 41). This solution entails the risk that the negotiations undertaken to fulfil the statutory obligation will be of a façade nature. Some employers may start a dialogue to avoid negative legal consequences, but without the intention of reaching an agreement. Quantity will not translate into quality. Nonetheless, the fact that trade unions and employers are involved in negotiations increases significantly the chance to work on consensual solutions. Mandatory collective bargaining does not, however, solve the problem of insufficient representation of employers and workers. There is also a threat that, due to the lack of sufficient sanctions, the obligation to negotiate will be ignored by the social partners (Constantin 2023). The solution which may reverse negative tendencies immediately is to recognize the generally binding force of collective agreements. Due to the weakness of trade unions and employers' organizations, a *de facto* binding force (like in the Nordic countries or Italy) is impossible to achieve. The extension must be attained by means of legal instruments. First, in can be a consequence of mandatory

[13] Such an approach of the state can be called 'hostile neutrality'.

membership of employers in chambers negotiating collective agreements (the Austrian model) (see, e.g. Brameshuber 2018). Second, the law may provide for or enable the extended application of collective agreements concluded by trade unions and employers' organizations. The *erga omnes* effect may be introduced either *ex lege* or as a result of public authorities (Müller et al. 2019). In Poland, 'Solidarność' proposed to recognize the *erga omnes* effect of collective agreements concluded by representative national employer's organizations.[14]

CEECs adopted various strategies in implementing Article 4 of the Directive: from passivity (Hungary) via direct involvement in collective bargaining (Lithuania) to a complex reconstruction of the legal framework (Romania[15]). Hungary found existing legal framework sufficient to restore collective bargaining. An increase in the coverage which has been reported in Lithuania resulted from concluding a number of sectoral agreements in the public sector (Blaziene and Jasiuniene 2023, p. 9). The Romanian law provides, *inter alia*, the obligation of employers to initiate collective bargaining as well as changes the criteria of representativeness (Constantin 2023; De Spiegelaere 2023). The Romanian case is somehow special since they tend to restore a system of collective bargaining deconstructed during the world economic crisis.

5 A Polish Way to Increase Collective Bargaining: The Draft Law on Collective Agreements

Given the weakness of the social partners, the state, in order to stimulate collective bargaining, had to adopt a more active attitude. This applies to both the reconstruction of the legal framework and direct participation in industrial relations. The reconstruction of the legal framework took place gradually.

The first step was to lift restrictions perceived as infringements on freedom of association. In 2018, the law recognized the freedom of association of workers (no-employees) performing paid work in trade unions (for more see Latos-Miłkowska 2023). Consequently, they also became beneficiaries of collective bargaining. However, the impact of collective agreements on civil law contracts has not been resolved. Unfortunately, the abolition of formal restrictions, caused by the amendment of the Law on Trade Unions which came into force on 1 January 2019 and recognized collective rights of workers who performed paid work outside the employment relationship did not change a real position of collective bargaining for non-employees. First of all, they do not join trade unions. As a result, no collective agreement covering this group only has been concluded while collective agreements

[14] https://www.tysol.pl/a37998-Nasz-wywiad-Piotr-Duda-W-przyszlej-kadencji-sejmu-emerytura-stazowa-i-uklady-zbiorowe

[15] The law on Social dialogue (367/2022).

covering both: employees as well as non-employees have been very rare. Collective actions to the benefit of platform workers (e.g. Glovo, pyszne.pl) took place outside the legal framework of collective bargaining (Pisarczyk 2023b).

In 2022, as a part of the National Recovery Plan, the government started analysing the collective bargaining situation and searched for legal solutions to increase coverage. As a result of this process, the government submitted in 2023 the first draft of a law reforming collective bargaining. One of the key proposals was the annual obligation for employers to commence collective bargaining with at least 50 workers not covered by collective agreements. Another revolutionary proposal was to allow the negotiation of company-level collective agreements with trade union delegates if a company trade union organization had not been established. The social partners welcomed the idea of reconstructing the legal framework of collective bargaining. However, they raised numerous comments and suggestions. As a result, new draft laws on collective agreements were adopted in 2024. The government proposes, inter alia: (1) to limit the duration of collective agreements to a maximum of 5 years (to assure employers that collective agreements are not "eternal" and may be changed); (2) to extend negotiations matters (however, without changing the employee privilege principle between the law and collective agreements); (3) to replace the registration procedure that was considered by the social partners as an obstacle in applying collective agreements (Mądrzycki and Pisarczyk 2022) by a much simpler notification; (4) to introduce the flexible possibility for employers to renounce a collective agreement concluded at a multi-company level; (5) to offer easier access to mediation; (6) to introduce new and more open principles of extending collective agreements concluded at a multi-company level.[16] After the next round of consultations, the government withdrew the most controversial proposals, which were challenged either by trade unions (temporary nature of collective agreements) or employers (trade union delegates, penal sanctions for employers who do not commence mandatory collective bargaining).

The final version of the draft law[17] provides concluding collective agreements for either definite or indefinite periods, depending on the parties' will. It maintained obligatory company-level collective bargaining for employers not covered by any collective agreement. The obligation will be imposed on employers employing at least 50 persons performing paid work on condition that there is a trade union organization in the company. Every 2 years, the employer will have to initiate negotiations with a view to concluding a company collective agreement. If the employer fails to fulfil the obligation, a company trade union organization may initiate a collective agreement. The employer cannot refuse to be involved in negotiating the agreement. The government withdrew, however, penal sanctions for employers who do not abide by the obligation. Company trade union organizations will conclude company-level collective agreements, not trade union delegates. At the same time,

[16] https://www.gov.pl/web/premier/projekt-ustawy-o-ukladach-zbiorowych-pracy-i-porozumieniach-zbiorowych

[17] https://www.gov.pl/web/premier/projekt-ustawy-o-ukladach-zbiorowych-pracy-i-porozumieniach-zbiorowych

multi-company collective agreements could be concluded by employer organizations and groups of employers organized ad hoc (on the condition that they are not members of any employer organization). Registration will be replaced by notification,[18] which will be effective *ex-lege*. As a result, registrars will not challenge collective agreements. The draft law unifies principles of concluding and applying collective agreements to employees and non-employees who perform paid work. It also lifted restrictions on concluding collective agreements for civil servants in governmental administration. However, restrictions have been introduced for uniformed services.[19] The draft law was intended to facilitate the extension of multi-employer collective agreements. The Minister could extend an agreement for Labour to an employer not covered by any multi-company collective agreement. A request from an employer organization, at least two employers or trade union organizations which have concluded a multi-company collective agreement will be required. Before extending an agreement, the Minister will have to consult the employer covered by the agreement or an employer organization that the employer has indicated. The extension is individual and is not the same as a generalization, which may lead to creating sectoral collective agreements. The construction justifies doubts about whether it will be used in practice and whether it may contribute to increasing collective bargaining coverage. Considering previous experience (the existing extension procedure has never been used in practice), one could not expect public authorities to extend collective agreements to a greater extent. Moreover, employers in economic difficulties will be entitled to withdraw from multi-company collective agreements.

An action plan to increase coverage is another vital element of the future law. The national social partners and the Minister of Labour will participate in preparing the plan. The plan may be adopted at the joint request of the social partners by agreeing or after consultation with the national social partners. The action plan is to set out a clear timetable and concrete measures to progressively increase the collective bargaining coverage while fully respecting the autonomy of the social partners. It should cover, in particular, measures: (a) building and strengthening the social capacity to engage in collective bargaining to set wages, particularly at the supra-company level; (b) encouraging constructive collective bargaining on wages, whereby the parties have access to relevant data; (c) protecting the exercise of the right to collective bargaining to determine wages and the protection of workers and trade union representatives from discrimination; (d) protecting trade union organizations, employers and employers' organizations participating or wishing to participate in collective bargaining from any interference or interference by their

[18] Notification to the Collective Bargaining Agreement shall consist in entering data through the form of the Collective Bargaining Agreement teleinformatic system made available on the website of the office serving the minister responsible for labour, as well as enclosing a digital reproduction of the content of the collective agreement, collective agreement or additional protocol.

[19] See more: https://www.gazetaprawna.pl/praca/artykuly/9756315,uklady-zbiorowe-pracy-nadal-wiele-zastrzezen-do-projektu.html

representatives or members in their establishment, operation or management. The Social Dialogue Council will review the action plan every 5 years.

The draft law misses, however, some instruments that can be used to support industrial relations. The government has not decided to allow in peius modifications. No financial incentives or technical and organizational support have been provided. Employers covered by collective agreements will not enjoy preferences in public procurement procedures and while using public funds. No institution has been established to support social partners (e.g., by legal assistance). Other soft law instruments have also been neglected. At the same time, the provisions concerning the action plan are not precise enough to be an actual trigger in developing industrial relations.

To summarize, the draft law modifies or abolishes provisions that could impede the development of collective bargaining. The proposed solutions may alleviate some concerns (especially of employers) and stimulate collective bargaining. However, conditions of low unionization and low activity of the social partners will not lead to a breakthrough. In particular, it is unlikely that multi-employer bargaining will develop.

6 The State as an Employer

To a certain extent, public authorities may stimulate collective bargaining without fundamental legislative changes. It is possible because the state remains the key employer—direct or at least indirect (with a real power to influence the decisions of formal employers). There are two areas where public authorities may effectively influence collective bargaining: public administration and state-owned companies. Public administration is a traditional interaction between various authorities (central or local) and workers' representatives. The state may be open to a dialogue with workers or limit (legally) collective bargaining. Similarly, the process of re-nationalization of the economy has occurred in some CEECs (Åslund 2021, pp. 20–22). Consequently, the states may control employers active in the banking, petrol or manufacturing sectors. As a result of political decisions, employers may be encouraged to join employers' organizations and be involved in collective bargaining. The last multi-company collective agreements were concluded in the mid-2010s by municipal authorities for employees of public schools. The number and coverage of such agreements remained, however, limited. The state's potential for influence can also be seen in company-level negotiations. A large part of company-level agreements have been concluded by state-owned companies (Mądrzycki and Pisarczyk 2022). An example was the initiation of collective bargaining in the most prominent Polish group of companies—Orlen. The effect was the conclusion of several collective agreements for various entities from the group and an increase in the scope of coverage to around 70 per cent.[20] However, the state's potential as an employer and owner has been used only to a limited extent.

7 Transnational Collective Agreements as a Trigger in the Development of Collective Bargaining?

Transnational collective bargaining, with the involvement of international companies, playing a key role in the global economy, has developed since the 1980s (see, e.g. Schömann 2012, ter Haar 2021). Due to the position of ICs, the agreements could be seen as a chance to protect and promote workers' rights. It was valid, especially for those countries where collective bargaining had broken down or not developed (e.g. in CEECs). The emergence of a new significant level of collective bargaining was expected. The idea of transnational social dialogue was promoted by regional trade unions, e.g. by the Polish Solidarność (Surdykowska 2021). However, the concept of collective bargaining in ICs stagnated. This is partially due to the ambiguous legal nature of TCAs and the lack of enforcement procedures, which discourage the social partners from commencing negotiations. The weakening of cross-border negotiations is also part of a broader crisis of social dialogue, which manifests in searching for alternative ways to regulate working standards (particularly employing legislation).

The potential of TCAs could be partially utilized by creating an appropriate legal framework. The EU is the only institution with the legal power to achieve this goal (e.g. Pisarczyk and Boguska 2023). Moreover, the question should be raised whether transnational agreements could be considered regarding the coverage of collective agreements set up by the Directive. Promoting TCAs could be a chance for trade unions in CEECs. However, the task has become more challenging due to the abandonment of work at the European level and the reluctance of employers and Western unions, which are afraid of losing their power due to the appearance of a new layer of collective bargaining. It will be difficult to overcome the impasse due to a general crisis that affects industrial relations in Europe. Nonetheless, trade unions, especially in CEECs, should be interested in striving for dialogue with essential actors in the contemporary economy, such as ICs. Nevertheless, TCAs could not be perceived as an alternative or even a trigger in the development of collective bargaining in the MSs, which, like Poland, face the challenge of increasing the collective bargaining coverage.

[20] https://raportzintegrowany2019.orlen.pl/nasza-odpowiedzialnosc/pracownicy-i-podwykonawcy/odpowiedzialny-pracodawca/

8 Conclusions

Increasing collective bargaining in Poland is going to be a particularly challenging task. There is no real social pressure or expectation to create a system based on collaboration between employers and workers (directly or within tripartite institutions). No international actors are willing to establish negotiations covering Eastern European subsidiaries, either. At the same time, the MSs will have to adopt measures satisfying requirements arising from the Minimum Wage Directive. Poland has attempted a comprehensive reconstruction of the legal framework for industrial relations. The aim is to eliminate restrictions on collective bargaining and to influence social partners to increase their activity. The government wants to facilitate collective bargaining for non-employees. It also lifted restrictions on concluding collective agreements for civil servants in the governmental administration. A meaningful change is the obligation for employers not covered by collective agreements to negotiate every 2 years in order to conclude a company agreement. However, the government has not decided on fundamental reforms to increase collective bargaining coverage. There are no effective incentives to stimulate multi-company collective bargaining. In particular, no mechanism has been created to generalise multi-employer agreements. It is a response to the needs of employers who are not ready to standardize wages and other working standards. Due to employers' opposition, company-level collective agreements will not be negotiated with trade union delegates if there is no company trade union organization. As a result, in many companies, even company-level collective agreements will not be negotiated. To summarize, despite fulfilling the formal criterion of supporting collective bargaining, the state will not change the position of industrial relations in the socio-economic model. Therefore, we should expect not profound changes but rather corrections that will not result in a fundamental strengthening of the collective bargaining system in Poland. It reveals that the collective bargaining model must result from a natural evolution and the needs of both employers and workers. While trying to implement external solutions, the implementation may be of a façade nature without touching the core idea of autonomous working conditions. Poland seems not ready to reconstruct its socio-economic system by increasing the role of industrial relations. At the same time the proposed legal framework does not close the way to autonomous actions of social partners. On the contrary, it facilitates collective bargaining. A lot will depend on the social partners themselves. In particular, a more active approach of trade unions may increase coverage by collective bargaining. Due to the weakness of transnational industrial relations, the state will have to solve the problem of increasing collective bargaining with the participation of national social partners.

References

Åslund A (2021) The biggest problem in post-communist transition: the privatization of large enterprises. CASE Working Papers 16(140) https://www.case-research.eu/files/?id_plik=6857
Becker J (2024) Governing neo-nationalism, trade unions and industrial relations: the cases of Hungary and Poland. Transfer 1:51–65
Berend IT (2007) Social shock in transforming Central and Eastern Europe. Communis Post-Commun 40(3):269–280
Berthier P-E, Leclerc O (2025) Incentivising collective bargaining. In: Laulom S (ed) Collective bargaining developments in times of crisis, 2nd edn. Wolters Kluwer
Blaziene I, Jasiuniene J (2023) Collective bargaining and inequality in Lithuania (Deliverable 3.1 National report for Lithuania). BFORE project VS/2021/0209, Leuven
Brameshuber E (2018) The importance of sectoral collective bargaining in Austria w: collective bargaining developments in times of crisis. In: Laulom S (ed) Collective bargaining developments in times of crisis. Bulletin of Comparative Labour Relations No. 99
Brameshuber E et al (eds) (2024) The EU directive on adequate minimum wages. Context, commentary and trajectories. Hart Publishing
Coelho Moreira T (2018) The revival of sectoral collective bargaining: the Portuguese experience. In: Laulom S (ed) Collective bargaining developments in times of crisis. Bulletin of Comparative Labour Relations No. 99
Constantin S (2023) Collective Bargaining in Romania: an obligation many employers neglects. https://accace.com/collective-bargaining-in-romania/
De Spiegelaere S (2023) Back on track: are we seeing a renaissance of collective bargaining in Romania? HESAMAG 27:8. https://www.etui.org/sites/default/files/2023-06/HM27_Back%20on%20track%20are%20we%20seeing%20a%20renaissance%20of%20collective%20bargaining%20in%20Romania_2023.pdf
Florek L (2015) The notion and scope of trade union freedom. Stud Iurid 60:41
Gardawski J (2015) 20 years of social dialogue in Poland. Stud Iurid 60:53
Gernigon B, Odero A, Guido H (2000) ILO principles concerning collective bargaining. Int Labour Rev 139(1):33
Gyulavári T (2018) Chasing the Holy Grail? Stumbling collective bargaining in Eastern Europe and the Hungarian experiment. In: Laulom S (ed) Collective bargaining developments in times of crisis. Bulletin of Comparative Labour Relations No. 99
Gyulavári T, Menegatti E (eds) (2019) The sources of labour law. Wolters Kluwer
Gyulavári T, Pisarczyk Ł (2023) Populist reforms in Hungary and Poland: same song, different melodies. Int J Comp Lab Law Ind Relat 39(1):49–70
Hajn Z (2015) The right of association in trade unions – the right of employees, or the right of the working people? Stud Iurid 60:107
Kahancová M, Mrozowicki A, Šćepanović V (2024) 20 years after: perspectives on industrial relations in Central and Eastern Europe since EU enlargement. Transfer 30(1):3–14
Kahn-Freund O (1983) In: Davies P, Freedland M (eds) Kahn-Freund's labour and the law. Stevens
Kozłowski T (2019) Was there an alternative to the Balcerowicz plan? Shaping the economic policy of solidarity camp in 1989. Stud Polit 47(4):97–115
Latos-Miłkowska M (2023) The right to unionise in Poland after the amendment of the law on trade unions. Eur Lab Law J 14(1):108–113
Laulom S (2018) From decentralization of collective bargaining to de-collectivization of industrial relations systems? In: Laulom S (ed) Collective bargaining developments in times of crisis. Bulletin of Comparative Labour Relations No. 99
Laulom S (2025) From decentralisation of collective bargaining to re-centralisation of industrial relations systems? In: Laulom S (ed) Collective bargaining developments in times of crisis. 2nd ed., Wolters Kluwer

Liukkunen U (2019) The role of collective bargaining in labour law regimes: a global approach. In: Liukkunen U (ed) The role of collective bargaining in labour law regimes. A global perspective. Springer

Mądrzycki B, Pisarczyk Ł (2022) Ekspertyza układy zbiorowe [Expert opinion on collective agreements]. Available at: https://www.gov.pl/web/dialog/krajowy-plan-odbudowy

Matveev M, Atanasov Y (2010) Determinants of small and medium sized fast growing enterprises in central and eastern Europe: a panel data analysis. Financ Theory Pract 34(3):269–295

Müller T, Schulten T (2024) Not done yet – applying the minimum-wages directive. Social Europe. https://www.socialeurope.eu/not-done-yet-applying-the-minimum-wages-directive

Müller T, Vandaele K, Waddington J (2019) Extension mechanisms in Europe. In: Collective bargaining in Europe, Brussels

Orenstein MA, Bugarič B (2022) Work, family, Fatherland: the political economy of populism in Central and Eastern Europe. J Eur Publ Policy 29(2):176–195

Pisarczyk Ł (2023a) Towards rebuilding collective bargaining? Poland in the face of contemporary challenges and changing European Social Policy. Ind Relat J 54:186

Pisarczyk Ł (2023b) Uphill struggle: collective bargaining for the self-employed in Poland. Transfer Eur Rev Lab Res 29(4):475–479

Pisarczyk Ł, Boguska A (2023) European framework agreements in multinational companies. What role for European Labour Law? Int J Comp Lab Law Ind Relat 39(2):247–264

Rączka K (2015) Special protection of employment stability of trade union officials. Stud Iurid 60:175

Report (2023) Report Expert Group Transposition of Directive (EU) 2022/2041 on adequate minimum wages in the European Union. https://ec.europa.eu/social/main.jsp?catId=1539

Rosioru F (2018) Collective bargaining in Romania: the aftermath of an earthquake. In: Laulom S (ed) Collective bargaining developments in times of crisis. Bulletin of Comparative Labour Relations No. 99

Schömann I (2012) Transnational company agreements: towards an internationalisation of industrial relations. In: Transnational collective bargaining at company level. European Trade Union Confederation, Brussels, pp 197–217

Seweryński M (1999) Polish labour law from communism to democracy. Dom Wydawniczy ABC

Stanojević M, Poje A (2019) Slovenia: organised decentralisation in the private sector and centralisation in the public sector. In: Müller T, Vandaele K, Waddington J (eds) Collecive bargaining in Europe. Brussels 2019

Surdykowska B (2021) Transnational framework agreements and their environment - basic information. In: Pisarczyk Ł (ed) TCA or David's negotiations with Goliath. Komisja Krajowa NSZZ "Solidarność", Gdańsk, pp 19–40

Ter Haar B (2021) The EU and transnational company agreements. In: ter Haar B, Kun A (eds) EU collective labour law. Edward Elgar

Vaughan-Whitehead D (2015) The European Social Model in times of crisis: an overview. In: Vaughan-Whitehead D (ed) The European social model in crisis. Is Europe losing its soul? International Labour Organization, Edward Elgar Publishing

Selected Issues Challenging the National Legislators in Light of EP and Council Directive (EU) 2023/970

Paulina Matyjas-Łysakowska

1 Introduction

Currently, there are no provisions in the Polish Labour Code[1] establishing the principle of salary transparency,[2] despite the explicit principle of equal pay (Article 18[3c] of the Polish Labour Code). In some European countries, there are tools to examine the level of salaries in terms of compliance with the principle of equal treatment in employment.[3]

The amount of a employee's salary is a personal interest of the employee, and disclosure of the amount by the employer without the employee's consent may constitute a violation of the employee's personal interest.[4] Therefore, in Poland, reinforcing the principle of equal treatment in employment by introducing the principle of wage transparency, allowing employees' work to be compared, will be a major challenge.[5]

For employees in public office, the situation is different.[6] The administrative judiciary says that the information on the salary of these persons is public informa-

---

[1] Act of 26 June 1974 Labour Code, consolidated text Polish Journal of Laws of 2023, item 1465; hereinafter: LC.

[2] Bentyn and Sobótka-Bentyn (2021), p. 29; Torbus (2022), p. 7.

[3] Veldman (2017), Duddington (2003).

[4] Resolution of the Supreme Court(7) of 16.07.1993, I PZP 28/93, OSNC 1994, no. 1, item 2; Szewczyk (2001), Wujczyk (2012).

[5] Walczak (2004).

[6] Piskorz-Ryń (1997).

P. Matyjas-Łysakowska (✉)
Jan Kochanowski University, Kielce, Poland
e-mail: pmatyjas@ujk.edu.pl

K. Koldinská et al. (eds.), *Labour Law and Social Security Law in Central and Eastern Europe*, European Union and its Neighbours in a Globalized World 26,
https://doi.org/10.1007/978-3-032-04496-9_20

tion. Issues relating to the conflict between the right to public information and the protection of the right to privacy were considered by the Constitutional Tribunal in its judgment of 20 March 2006.[7] The Tribunal held that the privacy of public office-holders, while being protected by Convention guarantees (in particular Article 8 of the Convention for the Protection of Human Rights and Fundamental Freedoms[8]), may be subject to limitations that may be justified by the transparency and accessibility of information about the functioning of public institutions in a democratic state. Persons performing such functions, from the moment they undertake them, have to accept a broader intrusion into their sphere of privacy than in the case of other persons. Thus, the disclosure of salaries of public office holders is real, compared to the disclosure of salaries of other employees.

The changes heralded by this directive aim to introduce the principle of salary transparency for all workers, with the aim of eliminating the pay gap between men and women for the same work or work of equal value.[9] The aim of the directive is not to introduce universal salary transparency.[10] Employees may disclose their pay for the purpose of enforcing the principle of equal pay (Article 7(5) of the Directive). Workers who have received information on the pay of others may not use it for any other purpose than to exercise their right to equal pay (Article 7(6) of the Directive).

The principle of equal pay finds its basis in Article 157 of TFEU[11] as well as in Article 4 of Directive 2006/54/EC[12]. Directive 2023/970 of 10 May 2023 is designed to strengthen the application of the principle of equal pay for men and women for equal work or work of equal value through pay transparency mechanisms and strengthened enforcement mechanisms. The directive entered into force on 6 June 2023 and Member States are required to implement its provisions by 7 June 2026.[13] The Directive contains a number of solutions to increase transparency in pay setting and pay increase policies through access to information (Articles 5–7 of the Directive), the imposition of reporting obligations on employers on the pay gap (Article 9 of the Directive), strengthening the legal protection of workers (Articles 14–23 of the Directive). The detailed solutions that the Directive proposes for the implementation of the principle of equal pay are not the subject of this paper. My

[7] Judgment of the Constitutional Tribunal of 20.03.2006, K 17/05, OTK-A 2006, No 3, item 30.

[8] Convention for the Protection of Human Rights and Fundamental Freedoms, drafted in Rome on 4 November 1950, as subsequently amended by Protocols No. 3, 5 and 8 and supplemented by Protocol No. 2, Journal of Laws of 1993, No. 61, item 284, as amended.

[9] Scott et al. (2023); Conley and Torbus (2019), pp. 145 et seq.

[10] Cullen (2024); Schnaufer et al. (2021); Tse (2023), Vol. 37(5).

[11] Official Journal Laws of 2004. No. 90, item 864/2 as amended.

[12] Directive 2006/54/EC of the European Parliament and of the Council of 5 July 2006 on the implementation of the principle of equal opportunities and equal treatment of men and women in matters of employment and occupation, Official Journal of the European Union L. of 2006. No. 204, p. 23.

[13] Subject to Article 9 of the Directive, which requires employers with 150 or more employees to submit wage gap information for the previous calendar year by 7 June 2027. This means that this group of employers should adjust their pay policies to the requirements of the Directive by the end of 2025.

focus is on the personal aspect of the Directive and the criteria that provide a platform for upholding the principle of equal pay.

2 Personal Scope of the Directive

Directive 2023/970 applies to all employers in the public and private sectors (Article 2(1) of the Directive). In the absence of a definition of employer in EU legislation, reference must be made to the concept of employer established in national legislation.

Directive 2023/970, according to Article 2(2), covers all workers with a contract of employment or an employment relationship as defined by the law, collective agreements or practice in force in each Member State, taking into account the case law of the Court of Justice. The scope of the concept of workers in EU law is not clear. It varies depending on the field in which it is to be applied. A distinction can be made between a general definition emerging from the Treaty on the Functioning of the European Union[14] and definitions emerging from secondary Union law.[15] The personal scope of directives is often defined by reference to the national law of the Member State, understood as acts, but also collective agreements and the practice of the Member States, taking into account the case law of the Court of Justice.[16]

Directive 2023/970 does not provide for personal exemptions for certain groups of workers. Member States may not decide not to apply the provisions of the Directive to any group of workers.

The Directive, for the purposes of Article 5, also applies to persons seeking employment. Applicants for employment have the right to information on their starting pay or pay range and the right to protection of information on their pay in their current position and previous employment relationships.

On the personal side, the Directive distinguishes between workers with an employment contract, among them various types of atypical employment and

[14] Judgment of the Court of Justice of 3.07.1986, 66/85, DEBORAH LAWRIE-BLUM v. LAND BADEN-WÜRTTEMBERG, ECR 1986, no. 7, item 2121; Judgment of the Court of Justice of 12.05.1998, C-85/96, MARÍA MARTÍNEZ SALA v. FREISTAAT BAYERN, LEX no. 111678.

[15] Directive (EU) 2019/1152 of the European Parliament and of the Council of 20 June 2019 on transparent and predictable working conditions in the European Union, Official Journal of the European Union L. of 2019. No. 186, p. 105; Directive (EU) 2019/1152 of the European Parliament and of the Council of 20 June 2019 on transparent and predictable working conditions in the European Union, Official Journal of the European Union L. of 2019. No. 186, p. 105; but also Council Directive 99/70/EC of 28 June 1999 concerning the framework agreement on fixed-term work concluded by ETUC, UNICE and CEEP (Official Journal of the European Union L. of 1999, No. 175, p. 43); Directive 2008/104/EC of the European Parliament and of the Council of 19 November 2008 on temporary agency work (Official Journal of the European Union L. of 2008. No. 327, p. 9).

[16] Pawłucki and Nowak (2021), p. 25 et seq.; Ludera-Ruszel (2020), p. 172; Matyjas-Łysakowska and Maroń (2023), pp. 86 et seq.

workers with an employment relationship defined by law, collective agreements or practice in force in each Member State, taking into account the case law of the Court of Justice.

One group of recipients of Directive 2023/970 are *"persons with a contract of employment"*. Probationary, fixed-term, indefinite-term contracts of employment determine the status of the worker. It is worth noting motif 18 of the preamble to the directive, where atypical forms of employment are mentioned explicitly and in detail. Among them: part-time employment, employment under fixed-term contracts and employment by a temporary employment agency, as well as employment in management positions.[17] There is no doubt that those atypical forms of employment should be included in the scope of the Directive.

The Directive also refers to *"workers who have an employment contract or employment relationship as defined by law, collective agreements and/or practice in force in each Member State, taking into account the case-law of the Court of Justice"*. The term *"employment relationship as defined by law"* should indicate persons who provide work within the framework of an employment relationship but on a non-contractual basis of employment, e.g. appointment, nomination, election. These employment bases occur in the public employment area. The legal status of these persons is governed by the so-called worker pragmatics (special acts), which contain pay regulations. Special acts take precedence over the general laws, i.e. the Labour Code. The Labour Code applies to matters not regulated by special acts. Of particular interest are those *"in an employment relationship as defined by collective agreements and/or practice in force in each Member State, taking into account the case-law of the Court of Justice"*. This includes workers working in the mandate system, e.g. domestic workers, on-demand workers, intermittent workers, service voucher workers, those working via online platforms (mainly self-employed), sheltered workers, trainees, apprentices. These groups of persons fall within the scope of the Directive, provided they meet the relevant criteria. The criteria in question are the principles for determining the status of a worker as shaped by the case law of the Court of Justice: the performance of work over a certain period of time; the performance of work in accordance with the instructions and under the supervision of the employer, who determines the tasks of the worker, issues work orders; the performance of work for remuneration.[18]

In order to have the status of a worker in the light of the case law of the Court of Justice, the basis of employment is irrelevant, what is relevant is the way in which the work is performed. It is accepted in CJEU case-law that *"the status of 'worker' within the meaning of EU law is not affected by the fact that a person has been hired as a self-employed person under national law, for tax, administrative or organisational reasons, as long as that persons acts under the direction of his employer as regards, in particular, his freedom to choose the time, place and content of his work,*

[17] Węgrzyn (2013), p. 3.

[18] for example, judgment of the Court of Justice of 9.07.2015, C-229/14, ENDER BALKAYA v. KIESEL ABBRUCH- UND RECYCLING TECHNIK GMBH, ZOTSiS 2015, no. 7, item I-455, thesis 37–38.

does not share in the employer's commercial risks, and, for the duration of that relationship, forms an integral part of that employer's undertaking, so forming an economic unit with that undertaking"[19] *A service provider person may lose its character of a self-employed person if it is completely dependent on their principal. If the service provider bears no financial or economic risk arising from the principal's activities and acts as an ancillary entity integrated into the principal's undertaking.*[20]

This means that even if there is no formal contract of employment between the parties, a person has same rights in terms of equal pay for equal work or work of equal value as a worker. The most important is whether a person performs work over a certain period of time, for and under the direction of another person, for which they receive remuneration in return.[21] The nature of the legal bond between one party and the other is not decisive.[22] It follows from the Court of Justice's judgments that it is the facts demonstrating the actual performance of work that must be taken into account, not the way in which the parties describe the employment relationship between them.[23]

A detailed analysis of the Court of Justice's judgments under the various directives shows that even in the light of the Court of Justice's case law, the definition of a worker is not uniform. I have indicated here the most characteristic features of a worker in the light of the Court of Justice's case-law, but it should be borne in mind that the concept of worker should be interpreted taking into account the objective criteria that characterize an employment relationship on the basis of a person's rights and obligations.[24]

---

[19] Judgment of the Court of Justice of 4.12.2014, C-413/13, FNV KUNSTEN INFORMATIE EN MEDIA v. STAAT DER NEDERLANDEN, ZOTSiS 2014, no. 12, item I-2411; Judgment of the Court of Justice of 4.06.2009, C-22/08, ATHANASIOS VATSOURAS I JOSIF KOUPATANTZE v. ARBEITSGEMEINSCHAFT (ARGE) NÜRNBERG 900, ZOTSiS 2009, no. 6A, item I-4585.

[20] Judgment of the Court of Justice of 4.12.2014, C-413/13, FNV KUNSTEN INFORMATIE EN MEDIA v. STAAT DER NEDERLANDEN, ZOTSiS 2014, no. 12, item I-2411; Derlacz-Wawrowska (2015), p. 23.

[21] Świątkowski (2014), p. 571; Kohutek (2015); Risak and Dullinger (2018), p. 23

[22] Skibińska (2016), p. 123 et seq.

[23] For more on the criteria for determining the status of a worker, see Judgment of the Court of Justice of 8.06.1999, C-337/97, C.P.M. MEEUSEN v. HOOFDDIRECTIE VAN DE INFORMATIE BEHEER GROEP, ECR 1999, no. 6, item I-3289; Judgment of the Court of Justice of 7.09.2004, C-456/02, MICHEL TROJANI v. CENTRE PUBLIC D'AIDE SOCIALE DE BRUXELLES (CPAS), ZOTSiS 2004, no. 8-9A, item I-7573; Judgment of the Court of Justice of 14.10.2010, C-428/09, UNION SYNDICALE SOLIDAIRES ISERE v. PREMIER MINISTRE AND OTHERS, ZOTSiS 2010, no. 10B, item I-9961; Judgment of the Court of Justice of 3.05.2012, C-337/10, GEORG NEIDEL v. STADT FRANKFURT AM MAIN, ZOTSiS 2012, no. 5, item I-263; Judgment of the Court of Justice of 26.03.2015, C-316/13, GÉRARD FENOLL v. CENTRE D'AIDE PAR LE TRAVAIL "LA JOUVENE" AND ASSOCIATION DE PARENTS ET D'AMIS DE PERSONNES HANDICAPÉES MENTALES (APEI) D'AVIGNON, ZOTSiS 2015, no. 3, item I-200; Judgment of the Court of Justice of 17.11.2016, C-216/15, BETRIEBSRAT DER RUHRLANDKLINIK GGMBH v. RUHRLANDKLINIK GGMBH, ZOTSiS 2016, no. 11, item I-883.

[24] Szewczyk (2021).

Establishing the existence of an employment relationship is very difficult, because in Poland, the doctrine and case law allow for a certain scope of subordination in non-employment legal relationships. If the content of the legal relationship between the parties (assessed not only by the content of the contract, but primarily by the manner of its performance) is dominated by features characteristic of an employment relationship (performance of work of a specified type for the employer and under his management for remuneration and at a place and time designated by the employer), then we are dealing with employment on the basis of an employment relationship, regardless of the name of the contract concluded by the parties.[25] Conversely, if the content of the legal relationship is not dominated by features characteristic of an employment relationship, it cannot be assumed that such a legal relationship exists between the parties.

The qualification of the legal relationship as an employment relationship based on the basis for the performance of work does not exhaust the subject. There are situations where a person, formally employed, pretends to have an employment relationship in order, for example, to obtain social security benefits.

The proper implementation of the Directive should take into account the Court of Justice's case law on the concept of "worker'". This is the only way of fulfilling the purpose of the directive and strengthening the application of the principle of equal treatment as regards pay. Otherwise, a certain category of workers may be left outside the protection guaranteed by Directive 2023/970, and this is only due to a different understanding of the term "worker". It may therefore be necessary not only to amend the Labour Code, but also to create universal guarantee regulations.

This conclusion leads to a more general question, about the concept of the worker in the modern world. It leads to the question of how to achieve effective protection for people providing work personally (not only employees). People who often do not have a strong position in the labour market and have to accept non-employment form of work, and are excluded from the group of recipients of the protective qualities of labour law.

3 Equal Work and Work of Equal Value

The principle of equal pay for equal work or work of equal value is set out in Article 157 of the Treaty on the Functioning of the European Union.[26] According to this provision, each Member State ensures the application of the principle of equal pay for male and female workers for equal work or work of equal value. Equal pay without gender discrimination means that the pay awarded for the same work is

[25] Judgment of the Supreme Court of 25 November 2004, I PK 42/04, OSNP 2005 No. 14, item 209 and the rulings cited therein.

[26] Official Journal Laws of 2004. No. 90, item 864/2 as amended.

determined on the basis of the same unit of measurement and that the pay for time work is the same for the same position.

Also in Directive 2006/54/EC of the European Parliament and of the Council of 5 July 2006 on the implementation of the principle of equal opportunities and equal treatment of men and women in matters of employment and occupation,[27] it is stressed that in order to assess whether workers can be considered to be in a comparable situation and whether they perform the same work or work of equal value, a number of factors should be taken into account, including the nature of the work and training and working conditions.

In order to remove the obstacles faced by victims of gender-based wage discrimination in exercising their right to equal pay, Directive 2023/970 clarifies in Article 3(1)(g) that work of equal value means work that is of equal value according to non-discriminatory and objective, gender-neutral criteria. Under Article 4(1) of the Directive, Member States undertake to take measures to ensure that employers have in place pay structures that provide for equal pay for equal work or work of equal value. Pay structures must make it possible to assess whether workers are in a comparable situation with regard to the value of their work on the basis of objective, gender-neutral criteria. These criteria include skills, effort, responsibilities and working conditions, and, where relevant, any other factors that are relevant to the place of work or position. It should be possible to compare the situation of workers with a hypothetical comparator (e.g. a worker who has previously worked in that position), it should be possible to compare salaries at different employers if the working conditions come from a single source (e.g. an act or a inter-company collective agreement).

The second challenge for the Polish national legislator will be the need to revise the concept of "equal work or work of equal value" in relation to the national legal solutions (Art. 18(3c) Polish Labour Code). The terms "equal work" and "work of equal value" have different meanings. Equal work is the same work in terms of the type of work performed in the first place. Equal jobs are identical jobs[28] (Rączka 2008). In the case of equal work, the criterion of comparison generally relates to the position, but it is not an exclusive criterion. Equal work does not necessarily refer to positions but, for example, to the duties performed by workersk.[29] If the positions differ in terms of scope and discharge of duties, they are then not equal.[30] The quantity and quality of work provided are the basic criteria for evaluating work for the purpose of determining remuneration (cf. Article 78(1) of the Polish Labour Code in conjunction with Article 18(3c) of the Polish Labour Code). The assessment of whether workers perform equal work should be made by taking into account the

[27] Official Journal of the European Union L. of 2006. No. 204, p. 23.

[28] Rączka (2008), p. 72.

[29] Judgment of the Supreme Court of 12 January 2010, I PK 138/09, LEX No 1324251.

[30] Judgment of the Supreme Court of 7 March 2012, II PK 161/2011, OSNP 2013 no 3–4 item 33, decision of the Supreme Court of 27 January 2022, II PSK 199/21, Lex 3340985.

quality and results of the work provided and not by simply comparing the type of work provided for in the contract.[31]

Work of equal value is work that is not identical, but comparable in terms of professional qualifications as evidenced by documents provided for in separate regulations or practice and professional experience, as well as comparable responsibility and effort (Article 18^{3c} § 3 of the Labour Code). It is a breach of the principle of equal treatment in employment if there is unequal treatment in terms of pay between workers performing the same work but also performing comparable, albeit not necessarily identical, work.[32] This means that it is possible to compare the salaries of workers working in different positions, provided that their work requires comparable professional qualifications confirmed theoretically or practically, and is work of comparable responsibility and effort.[33] The criteria on which comparisons are now made as to whether the work performed by workers is work of equal value are: comparable qualifications, comparable responsibility and effort.

The Directive indicates that the objective criteria to be used in applying the concept of work of equal value are skills, effort, responsibility and working conditions (recital 26 of the Directive and Article 4(4) of the Directive). The employer should balance each of these criteria according to which is relevant to the specific workplace or position. They may also include additional criteria if they are relevant and justified. Criteria must be applied in an objective, gender-neutral manner.

From the point of view of assessing whether work can be considered to be work of equal value, it is important to identify the applicable comparator who is doing the equal work or work of equal value. A hypothetical comparator is permissible under the provisions of the Directive. Thus, even in the absence of an actual comparator, a worker can show that they were not treated in the same way as a hypothetical worker of the other gender would have been treated.

The implementation of the Directives should take into account that the comparison of workers should not be limited to situations where women and men work for the same employer, as long as the terms and conditions of pay are determined on the basis of a single source and where these terms and conditions are equal and comparable (recital 29).[34] The comparison is not limited to workers employed at the same time.[35]

[31] Mitrus (2011), p. 39.

[32] Judgment of the Supreme Court of 22 February 2007, I PK 242/06, OSNP 2008 No 7–8, item 98.

[33] Judgment of the Supreme Court of 21 April 2021, II PSKP 28/21, Lex 3,229,405.

[34] Judgment of the Court of Justice of 17.09.2002, C-320/00, A. G. LAWRENCE AND OTHERS v. REGENT OFFICE CARE LTD AND OTHERS, ECR 2002, no. 8-9A, item I-7325; Judgment of the Court of Justice of 3.06.2021, C-624/19, K E.A. AND OTHERS v. TESCO STORES LTD, LEX No 3181795.

[35] Judgment of the Court of Justice of 27.03.1980, C-129/79, MACARTHYS LTD, ECLI:EU:C:1980:103.

4 Conclusion

Over the past 20 years, Poland has introduced a number of legal solutions to implement the principle of equal treatment of workers, in particular women and men, one element of which is precisely pay transparency.[36] However, as the experience of everyday life shows, there is still much to be done. There is a lot of work ahead of the Polish legislator, above all in terms of introducing pay transparency and expanding the right to information, introducing reporting obligations for employers and disclosing pay levels.

Firstly, the existence of subordination is essential and it is this feature that indicates work within the framework of an employment relationship.

Secondly, a solution should be found so that people performing work outside the employment relationship are also covered by protection. Currently, the protective function of labour law is not implemented in relation to people performing work outside the employment relationship. The protective function of labour law focuses on the employee. This trend is harmful. The measure of the development and quality of labour law should be axiological coherence in all legal relations based on work performed personally, and not the understanding of labour law as a privilege for one group—distinguished by a specific contract—the employment contract. Providing one group with numerous rights brings us closer to the limit of privileges of employees in relation to other people performing work.

This is particularly important as we face the challenge of strengthening the principle of pay transparency.

References

Bentyn B, Sobótka-Bentyn E (2021) Czy jawność wynagrodzeń zmniejszy lukę płacową? Monitor Prawa Pracy 3:29–34

Conley H, Torbus U (2019) Transparency and the gender gap. In: Conley DGH (ed) The gender pay gap and social partnership in Europe: Findings from "close the deal, fill the gap". Routledge, Abingdon, pp 145–166

Cullen Z (2024) Is pay transparency good? J Econ Perspect 38:153

Derlacz-Wawrowska M (2015) Koncepcja pracownika w rozumieniu art. 45 TFUE – prawo polskie a prawo unijne. Zeszyty Naukowe Zakładu Zabezpieczenia Społecznego Instytut Pracy i Spraw Socjalnych UW 4(4):22

Duddington J (2003) Employment Law. Pearson Education, Harlow

Kohutek K (2015) Glosa do wyroku TS z dnia 4 grudnia 2014 r., C-413/13. *Lex*, el

Ludera-Ruszel A (2020) The concept of "worker" under the principle of free movement of workers and its implications for the protection of workers in the European Union. Studia z Zakresu Prawa Pracy i Polityki Społecznej 27(3):167

DelPo Kulow M (2021) Beyond the paycheck fairness act. Mandatory wage disclosure laws – a necessary tool for closing the residual gender wage gap. Harv J Legis 50(2):385

[36] DelPo Kulow (2021), p. 428.

Matyjas-Łysakowska P, Maroń A (2023) Stosowanie umowy o pracę na okres próbny w świetle przepisów unijnych i krajowych. In: Duraj T (ed) Stosowanie nietypowych form zatrudnienia z naruszeniem prawa pracy i prawa ubezpieczeń społecznych - diagnoza oraz perspektywa na przyszłość. Wydawnictwo Uniwersytetu Łódzkiego, Łódź

Mitrus L (2011) Zasada równego traktowania w zatrudnieniu – "jednakowa praca" a "praca o jednakowej wartości". Glosa do wyroku SN z dnia 18 września 2008 r, II PK 27/08 Orzecznictwo Sądów Polskich (4)

Pawłucki M, Nowak P (2021) Koncepcja pracownika w dyrektywie PE i Rady (UE) 2019/1152 w sprawie przejrzystych i przewidywalnych warunków pacy w Unii Europejskiej a pojęcie pracownika w polskim prawie pracy. Praca i Zabezpieczenie Społeczne 3:24

Piskorz-Ryń A (1997) Jawność wynagrodzeń osób pełniących najwyższe funkcje w organach samorządu terytorialnego a prawo do prywatności. Samorząd Terytorialny (12)

Rączka K (2008) Komentarz do art. 18(3c) Kodeks pracy. In: Gersdorf KRM (ed) Kodeks pracy. Komentarz, Warszawa

Risak M, Dullinger T (2018) The concept of "worker" in EU law. Status quo and potential for change. Report 140. European Trade Union Institute, Brussels

Schnaufer K, Christandl F, Berger S, Meynhardt T (2021) The shift to pay transparency. Undermet pay standing expectations and consequences. J Organ Behav 11:69

Scott D, Karaeminogullari A, Tenhiala A, Varma A (2023) The employee perspective on pay transparency. J Total Rewards 32(3):1

Skibińska E (2016) Kwalifikacja prawna członka zarządu spółki kapitałowej jako pracownika w rozumieniu prawa unijnego. Monitor Prawa Pracy (3)

Szewczyk H (2001) Prawo do prywatności a ujawnienie danych o wynagrodzeniu pracownika. Monitor Pracowniczy (6)

Szewczyk H (2021) Jawność wynagrodzeń za pracę a unijna zasada "przejrzystości wynagrodzeń". Uwagi de lege lata i de lege ferenda. Praca i Zabezpieczenie Społeczne (11)

Świątkowski A (2014) Autonomiczne definicja pracownika [Autonomous definition of a worker]. Monitor Prawa Pracy (11)

Torbus U (2022) Przejrzystoś wynagrodzeń – uwagi na tle propozycji dyrektywy UE z 2021 r. Z problematyki Prawa Pracy i Polityki Socjalnej 3(20)

Tse FY (2023) Learning about pay at work. A labour process approach to pay transparency. Work Employ Soc 37(5)

Veldman A (2017) Pay transparency in the EU. A legal analysis of the situation in EU Member States, Iceland, Liechtenstein and Norway. Publications Office of the European Union, Luxemburg

Walczak K (2004) Wartościowanie stanowisk pracy ustawowym obowiązkiem pracodawcy? Monitor Prawa Pracy (9)

Węgrzyn G (2013) Formy zatrudnienia pracowników w Unii Europejskiej – aktualne tendencje. Prace naukowe Uniwersytetu Ekonomicznego we Wrocławiu (3)

Wujczyk, M. (2012). Prawo pracownika do ochrony prywatności. Warszawa

Concluding Remarks and Prospects: What Next in Social Law in the EU?

Kristina Koldinská

Membership in the European Union has profoundly influenced the development of labour and social security laws in the countries that joined the EU in 2004. EU integration has substantially standardized and improved labour and social welfare laws in Central and Eastern European countries, enhancing worker protections, improving working conditions, and promoting equality and social justice. However, several challenges persist. Not all EU standards have been fully implemented into national laws, and those that have been adopted often lack effective enforcement mechanisms.

The labour and social security laws of the countries that joined the European Union in 2004 have undergone significant transformation. As part of the European integration process, these member states were required to align their national legislation with EU directives and regulations.

Key areas such as anti-discrimination law, working time regulations, rules on posting workers, and work-life balance have undergone significant transformations. EU accession has also reshaped the functioning of social security regulations. Fundamental aspects of employee-employer relations, including collective bargaining and occupational health and safety, have seen notable changes as well.

Two decades after the accession of Central and Eastern European countries to the European Union, the transformative journey of labour and social security law in the region reveals both significant legal alignment and persistent structural tensions. While EU membership required the rapid adoption of the acquis, including complex frameworks governing labour rights and social dialogue, the process unfolded in a context marked by institutional fragility and ongoing socio-economic transition.

K. Koldinská (✉)
Faculty of Law, Department of Labour Law and Social Security Law, Charles University, Prague, Czech Republic
e-mail: koldinsk@prf.cuni.cz

K. Koldinská et al. (eds.), *Labour Law and Social Security Law in Central and Eastern Europe*, European Union and its Neighbours in a Globalized World 26,
https://doi.org/10.1007/978-3-032-04496-9_21

This book—remarkable both in its structure and in the diverse backgrounds of its authors—offers a compelling analysis of 20 years of social law development in the enlarged European Union. By examining various areas of social law across the Member States that joined in 2004, the monograph demonstrates not only how EU law has shaped national social legislation, but also how the Member States have, in turn, influenced and reshaped EU law in times of huge societal and structural changes.

As Cristina Mihes illustrates, reforms often weakened rather than strengthened collective bargaining, leading to increased decentralization and fragmentation. Company-level agreements, frequently negotiated without the robust involvement of trade unions, have displaced sectoral frameworks, eroding both legal certainty and the normative force of collective labour relations. The introduction of atypical agreements and restrictive criteria for representativeness have contributed to declining coverage, particularly for workers in small enterprises. At the same time, the absence of a coherent European framework for collective bargaining and the inconsistent definition of core legal concepts such as "worker" and "employment relationship" continue to generate uncertainty. These developments point to a deeper structural imbalance between the EU's economic integration goals and its social objectives—an imbalance that must be addressed if the promise of inclusive, decent work is to be realized across the continent.

The second part of this volume offers a multidimensional perspective on the evolving landscape of non-discrimination and equal treatment in employment and social rights within the EU legal framework, with a particular emphasis on Central and Eastern European countries. The analyses provided by the contributing authors reveal a complex interplay between EU legal standards and national practices, exposing both the transformative potential of EU anti-discrimination law and the persistent implementation gaps in Member States.

Dagmara Skupień, in her examination of the CJEU's rulings in Polish cases, underscores the expansive and progressive interpretation adopted by the Court of Justice in the domain of workplace discrimination. Her analysis highlights how the CJEU has not only dismantled legislative provisions in Poland that discriminated against fixed-term workers and women in the judiciary but has also curtailed the use of civil law contracts as a shield for discriminatory employer practices. The chapter makes a compelling case for the CJEU as a driver of social change, demonstrating how its rulings reinforce EU anti-discrimination directives and bridge national legal deficiencies, particularly in contexts where domestic implementation is incomplete or inconsistent.

Complementing this jurisprudential analysis, Marcin Wujczyk provides a broader labour law perspective on the evolution of Polish anti-discrimination laws. He situates these developments within the overarching influence of EU legal instruments, especially the increasing significance of directives such as the recently adopted Directive (EU) 2023/970 on equal pay. Wujczyk's discussion illustrates how EU law continues to push national systems toward greater transparency and enforcement in the realm of equality. EU law functions as a catalyst for more effective and structured responses to discrimination, particularly in areas where traditional mechanisms have failed to yield practical outcomes. This chapter reinforces the notion that the EU's normative pressure remains essential to counter the inertia or fragmentation of national legal systems.

A shift in focus to work-life balance and gender equality is offered in the contributions by Lucie Matějka Řehořová and Aleksandar Ristovski. Matějka Řehořová draws attention to the persistent barriers in the Czech Republic to achieving true reconciliation between professional and family life. Despite EU-driven improvements and formal compliance with key directives, the Czech legal and social system still struggles with entrenched gender roles and insufficient structural support—especially in relation to the duration of parental leave and limited flexibility in employment. Her conclusion is cautiously optimistic, recognizing the EU's positive influence but calling for sustained national reform, particularly in childcare infrastructure and employer practices.

Aleksandar Ristovski deepens this discussion by framing work-life balance as a core element of substantive gender equality, rather than merely a matter of flexible employment policy. His critical analysis of the Work-Life Balance Directive (2019/1158) reveals both the Directive's paradigm-shifting potential and its current limitations. Ristovski underscores the tension between the Directive's aspirations—such as promoting equal sharing of parental responsibilities—and the enduring reality of women as primary caregivers, both legally and culturally. He also scrutinizes the status of carers' leave and the non-absolute nature of flexible working rights, questioning whether these measures are sufficient to bring about systemic gender equality. Importantly, he broadens the discussion beyond the EU to consider how EU-level developments can inspire reform in candidate countries like North Macedonia, suggesting a ripple effect of EU legal norms even outside the Union's borders.

The theme of discrimination is further developed in the contribution by Henriett Rab and Márton Leó Zaccaria, who examine the social rights of older persons in light of Hungarian law, EU policies, and market dynamics. Their nuanced analysis reveals the ambivalence of anti-discrimination norms in the context of age: while EU and international standards promote active ageing and the protection of older workers, labour markets often favour efficiency and youth, leading to subtle or even justified distinctions based on age. The authors identify a growing need to reconcile market rationality with human rights principles, especially in light of technological transformations and demographic shifts. Their chapter calls for a more robust legal framework to ensure that age-related distinctions do not become an accepted form of discrimination under the guise of economic logic.

Finally, Jakub Tomšej offers a sobering case study of educational segregation of Roma children in the Czech Republic and other Eastern European countries. His chapter connects persistent ethnic discrimination to broader failures of EU anti-discrimination policy and enforcement. Despite the landmark judgment in *D.H. and Others v. Czech Republic* and subsequent national action plans, Tomšej argues that domestic responses remain insufficient, largely due to the weak enforcement mechanisms of the Race Equality Directive and the political fragility of national commitments. His call for a dedicated EU regulation specifically targeting educational segregation—complete with binding obligations, concrete implementation plans, and robust monitoring mechanisms—marks a clear demand for the EU to move beyond soft law and into the realm of enforceable social rights. His contribution broadens the concept of workplace equality to the foundational right to non-discriminatory education, thereby linking early systemic disadvantage to future labour market inequalities.

Taken together, the chapters in this section reveal that while the EU has developed a sophisticated framework for combating discrimination, the effectiveness of this framework often hinges on national willingness and capacity to implement it meaningfully. They show that EU law has indeed empowered courts, legislators, and civil society actors to challenge structural inequalities in employment and education. At the same time, however, they illustrate that legal transposition does not guarantee social transformation. Across the domains of gender, age, disability, ethnicity, and employment status, the need for more coherent, enforceable, and context-sensitive EU action is apparent. Whether through judicial interpretation, legislative innovation, or institutional reform, the EU must continue to refine its tools to uphold its core values of equality and human dignity in order to really influence societal development in own Member States. As the EU moves forward in an increasingly complex social and political landscape, it will need to balance subsidiarity with solidarity, harmonization with local responsiveness, and legal certainty with transformative ambition. The insights offered here are a valuable contribution to that ongoing endeavour.

Over the course of the last decades, the free movement of persons and coordination of social security within the European Union has been both a cornerstone and a battleground in the shaping of "Social Europe." That is why, the third part of this edited volume has sought to explore the shifting legal, political, and societal landscapes of social security coordination, particularly in the context of new regulatory challenges, ongoing tensions between national sovereignty and EU-level harmonisation, and the emergence of new forms of work, care, and mobility.

What emerges clearly is the complexity and dynamism of the EU's social security coordination system, which no longer revolves solely around the traditional logic of facilitating the mobility of workers. Instead, it must now grapple with broader social developments such as demographic change, digitalisation, remote work, increasing economic inequalities between Member States, and the transformation of welfare states under internal and external pressures.

One key theme running through the chapters is the evolving interplay between national systems and EU-level regulations, particularly how national practices both shape and are shaped by European law. Grega Strban's discussion of cross-border healthcare illustrates this point poignantly: while the EU has opened up new avenues for patients to seek medical treatment beyond their borders, these rights exist within a fragmented and legally complex framework. Cross-border healthcare, while representing a success story of European integration, still poses critical questions about accessibility, equity, and social solidarity. In theory, the internal market facilitates freedom of movement in healthcare; in practice, however, those who are more mobile, more informed, and wealthier are better positioned to benefit, raising questions about distributive justice and the role of public healthcare systems in the EU.

Jozsef Hajdu, in his analysis of the Hungarian health care system within the Digital Europe Programme, further complicates the picture. While digitalisation holds great promise for improving efficiency, transparency, and service delivery in healthcare, it also brings new challenges—particularly around data protection, patient autonomy, and the risk of depersonalisation of care. The Hungarian case shows that EU-driven digital transformation must be coupled with strong safeguards for individual rights, something that cannot be overlooked in a time when healthcare is becoming increasingly data-driven.

This asymmetry in benefits is echoed in the discussion by Martin Štefko on the legal regime of social security certificates (PD A1). His chapter highlights how EU law has created strong protections for the freedom of movement of services and workers through instruments like PD A1, but also how these protections can be exploited through regulatory arbitrage, misrepresentation, and even fraud. While the CJEU has gradually developed exceptions (such as the "criminal exception" in *Altun*), the enforcement of these rules remains decentralized and often inadequate. This raises serious concerns about the integrity of the system and the balance between market freedoms and the protection of social rights.

Luka Mišič takes this argument even further by analysing the tensions between EU social policy and free movement rights. The social security coordination system, he argues, is under increasing strain not only because of legal loopholes and changing labour patterns, but because of fundamental political and economic asymmetries within the Union. Whether it's remote work, strategic posting of workers, or the manipulation of competence rules, Mišič shows how Member States and economic actors have adapted creatively—sometimes cynically—to exploit the gaps in EU law. His analysis suggests that unless the EU finds new ways to adapt its legal framework—perhaps through genuine legislative reform—it risks perpetuating a form of regulatory competition that undermines both solidarity and the social rights of workers.

Together, these contributions suggest that social security coordination in the EU stands at a crossroads. On the one hand, the system has proven itself remarkably resilient. It has evolved from a technical instrument of labour mobility into a complex and multifaceted framework addressing a range of social risks and life situations. On the other hand, this resilience should not be confused with sufficiency. Social security coordination is not just a technical field—it is a fundamental expression of what kind of Europe we want to build. As such, it must remain at the heart of any future discussion about the shape and soul of the European Union.

As economic, political, and demographic pressures intensify, the current model may no longer be fit for purpose. If the EU is to sustain its social model and avoid deepening the divide between "centre" and "periphery," between mobile and immobile, or between insiders and outsiders, it must find ways to strengthen social rights across borders. This will require not only better laws and enforcement mechanisms but also a recalibration of values: from market efficiency to social justice; from competition to cooperation; from fragmentation to integration.

The above mentioned concerns are particularly evident in the case of long-term care (LTC), as described by Kristina Koldinská. While LTC has long been treated as a national policy domain, the aging of the European population has turned it into a continent-wide issue. Her chapter makes clear that while insurance-based solutions are helpful, they are insufficient in isolation. A comprehensive LTC strategy requires integrated care systems, better protections for informal and domestic carers, and a genuine commitment to social rehabilitation and dignity in aging. The EU, she argues, is well-positioned to lead this transformation—but only if it acts decisively and inclusively.

Alla Fedorova insightfully highlights, the activation of the EU Temporary Protection Directive in response to the war in Ukraine has revitalized the concept of temporary protection at the international level, yet it has also brought long-standing challenges into sharp focus—particularly the vague and inconsistent approach to the social rights of temporarily protected persons (TPPs). Despite the Directive's promise of minimum guarantees, the absence of clearly defined social obligations and the wide margin of discretion left to member states have led to disparities in support, leaving many TPPs in precarious conditions. Fedorova emphasizes the need for a clearer interpretation of these minimum guarantees under the Directive and advocates for their alignment with broader international human rights obligations to prevent poverty, homelessness, and social exclusion among displaced populations.

Parallelly, Yana Simutina and Olena Rym, in their analysis of Ukraine's employment framework for persons with disabilities, underscore the importance of aligning national legislation with European equality standards as part of Ukraine's broader Euro-Atlantic integration. They argue that recent legislative efforts reflect a paradigm shift toward inclusivity and greater social responsibility in employment practices.

Taken together, these chapters reflect the broader imperative for European states and candidate countries to prioritize the development of inclusive, rights-based social protections that respond effectively to both crisis-induced displacement and systemic inequality.

Last part of this volume is dedicated to several aspect of labour law. The transformation of labour regulation in Central and Eastern European (CEE) countries over the past two decades has occurred under the dual pressure of economic integration and the social policy objectives of the European Union.

In this context, the analysis by Mario Vinković and Tena Konjević offers a nuanced exploration of the evolving legal and political landscape surrounding the Posted Workers Directive (PWD*)* and the judicial responses by Hungary and Poland to its revised version. Their critique reveals an underlying tension between market-based competitiveness and the EU's social agenda. They dissect the legal arguments made by Hungary and Poland before the Court of Justice of the EU (CJEU) regarding the amended PWD, highlighting that while the countries were technically correct in contesting the legal basis, their actual goal appeared to be the preservation of a competitive edge through lower labour costs. The chapter underscores that this stance indirectly supports social dumping, even if such terminology is not explicitly used. By seeking to differentiate the legal regime of posted versus domestic workers, the two governments effectively questioned the applicability of equal pay principles. This reflects a broader struggle in the EU: how to reconcile freedom to provide services with equal treatment and protection of all workers. The authors argue convincingly that although temporary postings justify certain flexibilities, this cannot be used to justify undermining workers' rights. Notably, they critique the insufficiency of the current legal basis to ensure proper wage comparisons, and the limited scope of expense allowances under the new regime. These regulatory shortcomings disproportionately affect workers from CEE countries, who often rely on posting arrangements to improve their living standards back home. Thus, the chapter advocates for a more robust and fair application of EU social law principles, extending the social dimension of the internal market.

Attila Kun's contribution complements this analysis by turning the lens inward, focusing on Hungary's domestic implementation of EU labour law. Kun highlights that Hungary's transposition practices are largely formalistic—marked by minimal engagement with the social policy rationale of EU directives. This "tick-the-box" approach shows that while legal harmonisation has occurred, it has not been underpinned by meaningful political will or institutional capacity to effectuate substantive change. For instance, while Hungary has technically complied with transposition deadlines, the internalisation of the European Pillar of Social Rights remains superficial. Kun's chapter deepens the critique initiated by Konjević and Vinković by showing that not only do Hungary and Poland resist EU-level advances in labour protection when it threatens national cost advantages, but they also fail to deliver on the promises of those same laws once incorporated domestically. He rightly stresses that full implementation requires a cultural and political shift—what he terms "policy delivery"—which involves proactive commitment by policymakers and stakeholders, not mere legal transcriptions.

Both chapters converge on the insight that social Europe remains fragile in the CEE context, largely due to the mismatch between EU-level ambitions and national-level execution. While the EU Court has taken important steps to align market freedoms with social rights (as seen in the nuanced interpretation of the revised PWD), these efforts are undermined if Member States selectively engage with these norms based on short-term economic interests. Moreover, the absence of robust enforcement mechanisms and limited capacity for social dialogue—a theme common to both chapters—amplifies the risk of symbolic compliance.

In conclusion, these contributions underline a critical point: the success of EU labour law in CEE countries cannot be measured solely by legal transposition. Rather, it must be assessed by the degree to which these laws reshape institutional practices, empower workers, and foster inclusive socio-economic development. The Court's evolving jurisprudence and the EU's social policy instruments offer a path forward—but only if Member States, particularly in the CEE region, move beyond formalism and embrace the normative core of European social rights.

The past two decades have brought significant changes to the nature of work and labour law across Europe. Dana Volosevici explores how new workplace realities—ranging from AI and telework to increased corporate influence—are reshaping the employee-employer relationship. The chapter highlights the gradual, often obstructed, transition from employees as subordinates to decision-making partners. While legal regulation has faced resistance, especially from employer organizations, voluntary corporate practices have begun to revive legislative momentum. Still, meaningful employee involvement depends not only on laws but also on engaged workers willing to exercise their rights in an evolving corporate landscape.

Błażej Mądrzycki and Łukasz Pisarczyk analyze the stagnation of collective bargaining in Poland. Despite legislative reforms aimed at enhancing industrial relations—such as extending bargaining rights to non-employees and civil servants—the fundamental barriers remain. There is little societal or employer-driven support for expanding collective bargaining, and mechanisms to incentivize or generalize multi-employer agreements are lacking. As a result, while formal frameworks may exist, practical engagement remains limited. The future of collective bargaining in Poland thus relies heavily on the initiative of social partners, particularly trade unions.

Finally, Paulina Matyjas-Łysakowska's chapter examines Poland's readiness to implement Directive (EU) 2023/970 on pay transparency. While legal steps have been taken to promote equal treatment, especially regarding gender pay equality, significant gaps persist. The current labour law primarily protects those in formal employment relationships, leaving out many workers in non-standard arrangements. True progress in pay equity will require a shift toward inclusivity, ensuring that all individuals performing personal work—regardless of contract type—benefit from transparency and protection under the law.

The three chapters collectively underscore the evolving landscape of labour law in the European Union, shaped by a dynamic interaction between legal frameworks, societal expectations, and corporate practices. As work environments transform—through technological change, shifting employment models, and growing demands for equity—traditional regulatory approaches alone are no longer sufficient. Instead, meaningful progress depends on a dual approach: thoughtful legislative reform that responds to new challenges, and active engagement from employers, employees, and social partners alike. This balance is crucial to building a more inclusive, transparent, and participatory world of work across the EU.

After two decades of EU membership, the countries of Central and Eastern Europe stand at a pivotal point in the evolution of their labour and social security systems. This volume has traced the complex and often uneven journey of legal harmonization, institutional adaptation, and cultural transformation. From enhanced employee participation and the struggle for meaningful collective bargaining to the challenge of implementing pay transparency and expanding social protections, the region's experience reveals both the opportunities and tensions that arise when integrating national systems into a broader supranational legal order. The European Union has acted as both a source of legal standards and a catalyst for reform, yet it is equally clear that Member States have shaped EU developments in return—through local experimentation, resistance, and innovation.

The future of labour and social security law in Central and Eastern Europe will depend not only on continued legal alignment with EU directives but also on the capacity of national actors—governments, employers, trade unions, and civil society—to engage in constructive, forward-looking dialogue. As this book has shown, real progress emerges where law, policy, and practice meet, where rights are not only granted but meaningfully exercised, and where the evolving nature of work is matched by adaptive and inclusive legal frameworks. In that spirit, the region's next phase should not be seen merely as a process of compliance, but as a shared opportunity to redefine social justice, economic resilience, and democratic participation in the workplace.